Psychology of Religion
Religion in Individual Lives

Mary Jo Meadow
MANKATO STATE UNIVERSITY

Richard D. Kahoe
CHRISTIAN HAVEN HOMES

HARPER & ROW, PUBLISHERS, New York
Cambridge, Philadelphia, San Francisco,
London, Mexico City, São Paulo, Sydney
1817

Sponsoring Editor: Susan Mackey
Project Editor: Cynthia L. Indriso
Production Manager: Willie Lane
Compositor: Com Com Division of Haddon Craftsmen, Inc.
Printer and Binder: R.R. Donnelley & Sons Company
Art Studio: Fine Line, Inc.
Cover Design: Caliber Design Planning, Inc.

PSYCHOLOGY OF RELIGION: Religion in Individual Lives

Library of Congress Cataloging in Publication Data

Meadow, Mary Jo, Date–
    A psychology of religion.

    Bibliography: p.
    Includes index.
    1. Psychology, Religious. I. Kahoe, Richard D.,
1935–   . II. Title.
BL53.M438 1984   200'.1'9   83-18337
ISBN 0-06-044411-8

DEDICATION

Dedicated to the memories of William James and Gordon Allport—pioneer trailblazers and authors of classics in the psychology of religion.

Contents

Unit Three: Some Psychological Variables in Religious Perspective

List of Illustrations

Foreword

During the past several decades I have counted the psychology of religion to be one of the most audacious interdisciplinary fields of inquiry to be found in academia. Indeed, there have been many occasions in my 30 years in higher education when, if it had not been for the psychology of religion, I surely would have suffocated under the press of academic snobbism and intellectual stuffiness. Thus it is that the publication of *Psychology of Religion: Religion in Individual Lives* brings with it a breath of fresh air and more than a little enthusiasm.

With this volume Meadow and Kahoe have once again countered the cynical commentators who for over a half century have claimed the psychology of religion to be an abortive venture. Indeed, perhaps one of the field's most fascinating characteristics has been its survival propensities despite massive resistance from mainstream psychological studies and from mainstream religious studies. Much of this resistance, I suspect, has been confronted and at times partially overcome by two abiding factors: (1) the absolutely tantalizing and challenging factors implicit in attempting to interface two such interesting and complex fields as psychology and religion; and (2) the fact that a prestigious cadre of researchers-scholars-writers-teachers has managed to appear whenever the project has given signs of moving toward emaciation or calcification.

With the publication of *Psychology of Religion: Religion in Individual Lives,* Mary Jo Meadow and Richard D. Kahoe now join that cadre. And what is particularly pleasurable about this is that they do so within a Jamesian-Allportian spirit where there has never been room for an illiberal notion of the field. Allport's often quoted dictum, "A narrowly conceived science can never do business with a narrowly conceived religion," provides a didactic and a guiding theme for this volume; such is consistently manifested in both the book's comprehensiveness and in its authors' full appreciation of what Allport once called "sweet eclecticism."

I can only envy this new generation of students in psychological studies and in religious studies that now, thanks to *Psychology of Religion: Religion in Individual Lives,* has available a comprehensive text that is both substantially academic and at the same time thoroughly open to the realities of a lived world.

Orlo Strunk, Jr., Ph.D.
Professor of Psychology of Religion

Graduate School of Arts and Sciences
Boston University

Preface

"... The prejudice-complex, the religious sentiment, the phenomenological ego, and one's philosophy of life are important subterritories to explore in individual lives" (Allport, 1967, p. 21). This sentence from Gordon Allport's autobiography, discovered after the present volume was written and titled, gives rationale for the presentation of our view of the psychology of religion—with its focus on "individual lives." We offer this as an introduction to an old field, newly growing. We are indebted to early pioneers such as G. Stanley Hall and William James, new pioneers such as Gordon Allport, and the creative minds and plodding researchers who have come between and followed these leaders.

APOLOGIA

We write this book as psychologists. This means that we look at religion, and try to explain it, as scientists. Because the presuppositions that underlie psychology and religion are radically different, some people fear that such an endeavor reduces religion to less than it really is. This is not our intent. We believe it possible to examine our subject matter from a psychological perspective without saying that is all there is to religion. Whether religion goes beyond psychological explanation cannot be answered by psychology. Questions about the truth or reality of religion are outside the limits of our science. We can only describe and try to understand the experiences of people as they deal with religion in their lives. We cite examples from many of the world's faiths; however, since our readers are most likely to be familiar with Western Christianity, most of our references are to that tradition.

We have chosen to let major theorists about religion speak for themselves. Rather than try to produce an artifical consensus opinion about many debated issues, we prefer to let the reader realize the diversity of opinion that exists. Each reader is challenged to weigh evidence and come to his or her own conclusions. We have, however, shared our own opinions about the origins and development of religiousness in the individual's life. These are summarized in Chapter 22.

OVERVIEW

Theoretical integration continues to be sparse in our field of study, but empirically based developmental stage theories seem to hold the greatest promise for a broad understanding of religion in individuals. In this book, we make a special effort to integrate the psychometric approach of the recent period with the developmental theories. Because our topical approach may obscure the history of the psychology of religion for the new student in the field, Chapter 1 contains a brief historical overview.

The distinctive plan of this book includes five units of six chapters each. The first four chapters in each unit are basic content material; the fifth chapter focuses in some detail on major research in the unit's subject matter; and the sixth chapter applies some basic ideas of the unit.

Unit One emphasizes the development and functions of religion in humankind and in individuals. The second unit treats several significant religious phenomena that psychologists have studied: conversion, prayer, faith healing, ecstatic religious experiences, and mysticism. The next unit addresses some major psychological topics that are relevant to the religious life: faith and belief; conscience, shame, and guilt; will and self-management; and altruism or love.

Unit Four summarizes research and theories that emphasize psychometric dimensions of religiousness—the most fruitful research approach in the current psychology of religion. The last unit concludes our study with a critical evaluation of religiousness in terms of psychopathology and mental health.

PERSONAL FAITH

Although we write primarily as scientists, our personal religious orientations should be made explicit. In an area of study as value laden as religion, readers deserve to know the perspectives that have informed the material they read.

The first author was reared in a conservative Roman Catholic family. From early life, interior prayer and meditation were important to her, although in adolescence she rebelled against what she considered excessive dogmatism and legalism in her parents' faith. Several years later religious hungers led her back to an intensified practice of the Catholic faith and a strong focus on the interior prayer tradition. She returned to graduate studies, after eight years as wife and mother, explicitly to study religion as a psychologist. Exposure to different traditions led her to recognize their common understandings of the mystical (interior prayer) religious life. She came to realize that her commitment was more to this kind of God-search than to formal institutional religion. She agreed with William James that dogma and religious rules do not represent the essentials of religious life. Her practice of meditation deepened under yogic instruction, and she was initiated into an established yogic tradition. She worshiped with many groups, and then—after completion of this book—returned to the practice of her Roman Catholic tradition. Her Christianity is still permeated with Eastern religious understandings, and she might be considered heretical on many counts by those who make such judgments.

The second author came under the influence of a fundamentalist Protestant church when his parents were not active religiously. After he had a conversion experience at the age of twelve, the church became one of the most influential forces in his life. He attended a church-related college as a ministerial student. Fundamentalist dogmas were relinquished slowly and painfully, mostly as they threatened to disrupt relationships with close friends who were religiously less conservative. During college a growing interest in psychology and related human services led him away from a commitment to the pastoral ministry, but he has continued to be active in conservative denominations and churches. His professional career has been invested in teaching and administration at Baptist colleges and in psychological practice at an interdenominational, evangelical Protestant social service agency. Research, writing, and/or teaching in the psychology of religion have spanned almost all of his professional years. These combined religious, professional, and academic commitments reflect Allport's dictum, "A narrowly conceived science can never do business with a narrowly conceived religion" (1950/1960, p. x).

While writing this book, the authors' continual dialogue has brought the work to a position that avoids the more extreme expressions of any religious stance. We hope that these confessions will assist your own understanding of our book.

AUDIENCE

We have not tried to write a comprehensive tome to please other scholars. We hope to spark in students the fascination we find in a broad view that combines religious insight and psychological discipline. This book is aimed at a large population, with the college sophomore (who generally will have taken an introductory psychology course) as the major reader. Any intelligent lay reader should be able to understand almost all of the concepts we introduce. We should also attract many religious professionals who can appreciate a simple but scholarly view of religion as contemporary psychologists study it. Students in junior colleges and Bible schools should find the subject matter, reading level, and interest level appealing. Liberal arts and graduate students should be challenged by the balanced view and by the research chapters, while Bible school and seminary students should find the applications chapters helpful. Our objective approach should satisfy secular university audiences, but our sympathy for the religious quest should be appreciated in sectarian schools. The student or teacher who hopes to use this book either to bludgeon religion to death or to support his or her own religious preconceptions will, however, probably be disappointed.

APPRECIATION

Many authors have said that no book is written without the help of many people. We want especially to express our appreciation to those other people most intimately connected with the publication of this book. We thank first our publisher, Harper & Row, and several of their editors: George Middendorf, who helped us give birth to the work; Susan Mackey, sponsoring editor; and Cindy Indriso, project editor.

We thank also those colleagues who read, and in some cases reread, the text and made helpful suggestions: Orlo Strunk, Boston University; Sister Eileen A. Gavin, The College of St. Catherine; Virginia Staudt Sexton, St. John's University; Elaine Donelson, Michigan State University; and David Bakan, York University. Many students of the senior author offered thoughtful suggestions. We followed some of the advice offered, and regretfully decided against other.

Needless to say, we stand solely responsible ourselves for the final version of the text. We hope that our work might inform and broaden your own appreciation of religion in your own and other individual lives.

MJM & RDK

To the Instructor

James Dittes ("Psychology of Religion," *Handbook of Social Psychology,* 1969) outlined four positions from which psychology may view religion. In the most parsimonious (or reductionistic) view, psychological variables operate in religion exactly as they operate elsewhere. The second position holds that certain psychological relationships can be seen especially well in religious behaviors; thus religion provides a most appropriate setting for studying these relationships. Third, psychological variables may interact in unique ways within religion, producing psychological phenomena that are observable nowhere else. The final view considers the psychological variables in religion to be unique to that realm. The first and last positions virtually preclude a psychology *of* religion. The first allows nothing distinctively religious in psychology, permitting only basic psychology; the last does not allow psychology into religion, holding the latter aloof from mainstream psychological understandings.

Beyond our format outlined in the Preface, two additional structures underlie this text. The first is based on Dittes's typology. The studies and analyses in our Unit Two follow his third position. Basically religious phenomena are viewed within the context of general psychological principles. Thus topics such as conversion, prayer, faith healing, and mysticism are seen as expressions, at least in part, of basic psychological tenets. Unit Three is based on Dittes's second posture. The general psychological variables studied—belief, conscience, will, altruism—involve relationships that may be seen especially keenly within religious experiences.

   Another, even more basic, structure runs through our study. Unit Four climaxes a four-fold analysis of religiousness that begins in the very first chapters. The four reactions to "Human Limitedness" in Chapter 1 depict increasing levels of religious maturity: denying, hiding from, accepting, and living with limitedness. Chapter 2 classifies functions of religion into egocentric, social, growth, and individualizing modes. Chapter 22 weaves these categories (along with other concepts introduced along the way) into a coherent model, including a developmental sequence that personal religiousness seems to follow. Our two-dimensional model contrasts intrinsic and extrinsic religion on one bipolar dimension, with observance (institutional) and autonomy (individualistic) religion on another bipolar dimension, orthogonal with the first. Robust, dynamic, developing personal religiousness typically originates in egocentric, extrinsic forms, then develops in the direction of observance, or conformity to institutional norms. In some cases it progresses into intrinsic or self-giving religion; finally, and less frequently, it evolves into an autonomous or more individualistic form.

   Given the distinctive unit structure of this book (noted in the Preface overview), the implicit positions of Units Two and Three outlined above, and the quadriplex view of religion climaxed in Unit Four, the book's design is obviously not random. However, we have not strenuously limited our coverage to topics that fit a preconceived outline, nor forced material into inappropriate molds. While we have tried to present mainstream psychology of religion in a relatively comprehensive fashion, practical realities have mandated selectiveness. If we have omitted one or more of your favored topics, approaches, concepts, or studies, we should be glad to have your suggestions to consider for future revisions.

MJM & RDK

one

ORIGINS AND FUNCTIONS OF RELIGIOUSNESS

chapter *1*

Origins of Religion

Religion appears to be a universal human experience. Although not all people admit to being religious, some form of religion has existed in all cultures. We begin our study of religion in individual lives by trying to understand the origins of religion in humankind. Although "Why religion?" is mainly a psychological question, most early scientists who tried to answer it were anthropologists. Leuba, a pioneer psychologist of religion, said anthropologists and historians must discover what actually happened. Psychologists should point out "the several possible origins of the god-ideas, the characteristics of each, and the nature of the general causes which determine the dominance of particular gods" (Leuba, 1912, p. 90). Some early anthropological theories help answer our questions, and more recent approaches add to understanding religion's origins.

THE NATURE OF RELIGIOUSNESS

Existential Anxiety

Royce (1973, p. 19) argued for beginning the study of religion with existential anxiety, the uneasiness or apprehension that comes simply from being human and dealing with life's issues. Religions say that human life is full of problems and sorrows. The Buddhist tradition teaches that meditation—which should eventually lead a person to enlightenment—begins with experiencing grief. The Christian doctrine of original sin states that human beings are in a "fallen" condition in which they cannot, by themselves, behave as they ought. Hindu sages say that we all live in ignorance of the truth. All these traditions agree that something is basically wrong or incomplete about us.

Whether or not we have thought much about such ideas, we know that we are unable to manage some situations important to us. Sometimes unwanted feelings—depression, fear, loneliness, tension, jealousy—bother us. Events such as war, death, failure, hunger, and illness remind us that often we can do little about major threats to our life and satisfaction. Some people are disturbed by their inability to find any meaning in life or to see purpose in things that happen. Others worry about their own undesirable conduct or their inability to control the behavior of others.

The saying "There are no atheists in foxholes" recognizes a human tendency to turn to religion when faced with limits. The need to understand or control events, ourselves, and other people often leads to religious solutions. In *The Courage To Be,* Paul Tillich (1952a) summarized the major existential anxieties that religions describe and people experience: anxiety over inability to avoid death, fear of meaninglessness and purposelessness, and concern about the consequences of our own conduct. Elsewhere he said, "It is the finitude of being which drives us to the question of God" (Tillich, 1952b, p. 166).

Looking at how religion functions in people's lives, psychologist Paul Pruyser said: "Religion is, psychologically, something like a rescue operation. . . . It is born from situations in which someone cries, 'Help!' " (Pruyser, 1971, p. 80). Religious teachings agree. Theistic religions (those with an idea of God) usually say that people need God in their lives. Some other religions teach that people must come to deeper understandings than they have, or must be led to liberation or enlightenment. All agree that people need help.

Components of Religious Behavior

Scholars usually say that religion has three major parts. First, creeds are beliefs about how things are; they answer questions about the *why* of things—questions that science and technology cannot handle. The great sociologist Max Weber (1922) said that religion is concerned with the irrational aspects of life that defy scientific understanding.

Cultus, the second component of religion, refers to rituals and ceremonies. These give us symbolic ways to express religious feelings. Ritual also may give people a feeling of control in their relationship with God or Ultimate Reality. Ceremonies often mark such major life experiences as birth, puberty, death, marriage, and illness. Many traditions have special practices to celebrate these experiences.

Code—the third aspect of religion—consists of religious requirements about behavior, telling us what we should and should not do. These guide our own conduct, and help us feel life is safer and more orderly when other people also follow them.

We can think of these components of religion in terms of three major aspects of psychological functioning: thinking, feeling, and striving. Creed deals with cognitive functioning, cultus with affective (emotional) reactions, and code with conative (action-tendency) impulses. These components also relate to Tillich's three existential anxieties. Creeds provide meaning in life; rituals offer emotional solace in life-threatening and other disturbing experiences; and codes give us guidelines to follow so we can feel comfortable about the rightness of our conduct. Box 1.1 summarizes this.

Box 1.1   HUMAN FUNCTIONS, RELIGION, AND EXISTENTIAL ANXIETY

Human Function	Religion	Existential Anxiety
Cognition (thinking)	Creed	Meaninglessness
Affect (feeling)	Cultus	Death
Conation (striving)	Code	Behavior/guilt

Source: Compiled from Tillich (1952a) and multiple psychology and religious studies resources.

THEORIES OF RELIGION'S ORIGINS

Anthropologists' theories about religion's origins see human limitedness as the basis for religion. We shall look at several theories that match the psychological divisions made above: cognitive, emotional, and conative theories. We shall also note some other theories that view religion as innate to human existence. These theories also acknowledge human finitude, and see religion as a response to environmental events "wired in" over eons of human evolution.

Cognitive Theories

Cognitive origin theories are of two major kinds. One says religion began when people, thinking about experiences that were hard to understand, constructed explanations that led to religious beliefs. The second kind is more complicated. Some theorists thought that very simple and confused thinking in early human beings led to religious interpretations.

Explanations of Experience   Spencer believed that early humans were basically rational but thought of dreams as real experiences. They came to see themselves as having a dual nature: bodily existence and also a "shadow-self." Dreams of the dead led to beliefs that the shadow-self continued to live in a different state after death (Evans-Pritchard, 1965).

Tylor (1903) agreed that when early people thought about death, disease, and dreams, they concluded that some immaterial entity (soul) could account for them. Soul was seen as detachable from and superior to the body. The soul could transcend many human limitations and exist independently of the body. Dream experiences—the soul's wanderings when free of the body—proved this. People concluded that all material objects have personal souls, a belief called animism. This led to belief that gods inhabit such natural phenomena as trees and rocks, and finally evolved into belief in one Ultimate Reality or God.

Other scholars disagreed about how people got the idea of soul. Some said it came from the ability to visualize a person or thing when it was not actually present. This idea of ghost or soul led to the notion of God as a composite of the souls of prominent individuals. Rituals and taboos developed to handle fears associated with such beliefs (Evans-Pritchard, 1965).

Primitive Thinking   Lévy-Bruhl (1923) argued that early humans were not logical and could accept contradictions that rational thinking does not allow. These people felt subject to unknown powers that seemed to behave in unsystematic and incoherent ways. They considered these occult powers to be real and constantly acting in their lives. (Some contemporary cross-cultural scholars see differences in thought patterns of people in industrialized and nonindustrialized societies.) Although Lévy-Bruhl later abandoned his distinctions between alogical and logical thought, popular opinion considered primitives to be irrational. Some believe religion to be both primitive and irrational, also.

Lévi-Strauss (1958, 1962) thought that early humans had trouble thinking about abstract ideas and relationships. They translated them into concrete experiences of everyday life: trees, caves, animals, etc. (You do this when you dream; concrete objects stand for your ideas.) People built myths and rituals around these objects, and these symbol systems allowed them to manipulate the ideas for which the objects stood. Relationships between objects were used as models to explain other relationships. For example, the relationship between rain and the earth described that between a man and a woman. Because they explained things well, the chosen objects came to be considered sacred.

Emotional Theories

Emotional theories about religion's origins also fall into two main categories. Some theorists thought religion developed from unconscious fears and needs. Other theories say that religion came from the conscious experience of overpowering emotions.

Fears and Needs   According to psychologist Freud (1927), religion comes from reluctance to accept adulthood's harsh realities. When difficulties occur, people prefer to believe in an omnipotent "father" who controls harmful forces and assures them that everything will come out all right. Freud's origin story in *Totem and Taboo* (1913) says that in prehistory powerful men governed hordes of people. They kept the other men (their sons) under their power, and all the women for themselves. Resentfully, the brothers banded together and slew their father. Although they first enjoyed their freedom, they later began to miss the security and control provided by the now-dead father. So they deified (considered as a god) an animal—called a totem—and worshiped it as their dead father. The totem was held to impose the same moral restrictions the father had: avoidance of promiscuous sexual activity and serious strife within the group. In a later book, *Moses and Monotheism,* Freud (1939) extended his version of religious development into the Jewish and Christian traditions.

    Malinowski (1925) gave a psychologically similar explanation of religion's origins. He said that when people experience fear in life crises, religious ritual develops as a way to discharge feelings and manage anxiety. Another aspect of Freud's theory is found in Schleiermacher's (1893) opinion that religion comes from a sense of absolute dependence.

Overpowering Emotions   Marett (1914) noted that awe-inspiring experiences produce strong emotional reactions, often accompanied by vivid spontaneous actions or gestures. In such situations, people may treat inanimate objects as if they had life. (You may kick a chair—as if it were to blame—when you accidentally stumble on it.) People's experience of powerful forces led to physical actions that developed into dance and ritual, according to Marett. These rituals led to the idea that one was responding to some kind of life or spirit behind the awesome experience. Marett claimed that animatism (treating objects as if they were living) came before animism (belief in spirits).

    For Max Müller (1893) religion arises from awe and fear when facing nature. Awe leads to worship, and fear to propitiation. Natural objects produce a sense of the infinite and serve as symbols for it. Personification of symbols and development of religious mythology often follow. In all this, religion's "seed is the perception of the infinite" (Müller, 1878/1968, p. 48). Otto (1926) said similarly that the direct experience of the "Wholly Other," which produces fear, dread, fascination, and attraction, is religion's basis. Such experience, which Otto called "the numinous," will be discussed further in Chapter 10.

Conative Theories

A third group of theories focuses on human attempts to gain power and control things. This may refer to natural processes (trying to change things or events) or social control (managing people and society). Much contemporary interest in parapsychology and the occult has similar motivation.

Control of Natural Processes Frazer (1925) spoke of three stages of intellectual development: magic, religion, and science. People originally tried to control nature with magic. Magical, superstitious behaviors may become habitual when accidentally associated with good outcomes. (The anecdote is told of a man who carefully sprinkled some powder on his doorstep in the middle of a large city. When a friend asked, "Why are you doing that?" the man explained, "To keep the tigers away." His friend protested that there were no tigers anywhere near there. The man simply smiled and said, "Yes, it works wonderfully, doesn't it?") Superstitious practices can easily become rituals that give one a feeling of control.

When magic did not always work, people decided that events must be controlled by gods that could and would help them if properly approached. So they developed prayers, offerings, and rituals to entice the gods into aiding them. Frazer said that as science develops, people turn increasingly to it for controlling nature, and should eventually "outgrow" religion.

Anthropologist Marvin Harris (1974) suggests that practices necessary for human survival tend to develop according to need in a particular environment. Abstinence from pork, adaptive in desert lands, is reflected in Jewish and Islamic taboos. Killing cattle would be very dysfunctional in famine-prone India, and so must be forbidden. Such taboos are so crucial to a society's survival that the absolute authority of the prevailing religious tradition reinforces them. This theory, like many others, sees religion developing for the functions it serves—in this case, disease and famine control.

Social Control Durkheim (1915) said that primitive people realized that they could survive in a group, but not alone. Since it was difficult to conceive of society abstractly, a symbolic object—a totem—was chosen to stand for it. Collective rituals involving the totem evoked a deep sense of moral identity among the people. Religion thus developed from the need to celebrate and uphold society.

Radin (1937) argued from a Marxist perspective that powerful elements in a society create religion to keep weaker ones under control. Freud (1927) emphasized society's need to pacify the average person, and make up for the sufferings and privations that living in society imposes. He said that religion produces social control by supplying people with restrictive codes and promising eventual heavenly reward for acting in accord with them.

Human Nature Theories

We next consider theories that hold religion to be either an instinctive human response or a product of evolution of the species. The more sophisticated theories integrate biological, anthropological, sociological, and psychological data in the context of evolutionary theory.

Instinct Theories   Jastrow argued for "certainty that the religious instinct is . . . innate" (1902, pp. 100–101). Others said religion might stem from a strong, instinctive will to live, aroused by our need to save ourselves from fear of fate. "Religion is a reaction to our finite situation . . . as instinctive as a start or a shudder" (Hocking, 1922, p. 50).

Carl Jung (1959) also claimed that the structures for religious experience are deeply rooted in the human psyche. Archetypes (universal symbol patterns) in each person's mind contain the residue of all human experience, and help one manage incompletely understood experiences. Archetypal symbols typically have religious connotations. (See Chapter 2 for more about archetypes.)

Neo-evolutionary Theories   In his American Psychological Association presidential address, Donald Campbell (1975) said that human biological evolution has long since reached a practical limit. If we are to continue to advance, it must be through social evolution. Selfish biological tendencies that served an adaptive function in evolutionary history are detrimental to present human progress. Traditional morality and religion preach extreme moral demands to counteract selfish biology. Pulled in one direction by biological urges, and in the other by religious and moral demands, people come closer to a socially optimal level of cooperation. Campbell depicted these relationships in a mechanical model somewhat like Figure 1.1.

Drawing on genetic and neurophysiological explanations, Burhoe (1975) speculated on the origins of religious ritual and belief. He argues that the nature of the human brain and complex reality demand religion. Religious practices and beliefs begin and change in stress situations to serve as guides to efficient action. Ritual behavior springs from deep, primitive levels of the brain that are closely linked with emotional reactions. (Note the similarity to Marett's and Müller's

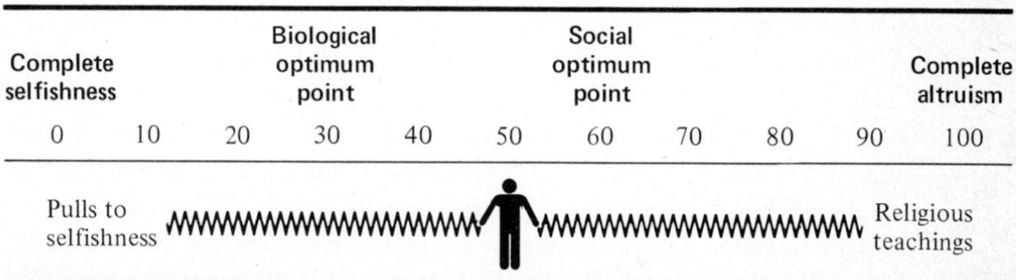

Complete selfishness		Biological optimum point			Social optimum point				Complete altruism
0	10	20	30	40	50	60	70	80	90	100

Pulls to selfishness 〰〰〰〰〰〰〰〰〰〰〰〰 Religious teachings

Figure 1.1   Selfishness-altruism continuum. (*Source:* Donald T. Campbell, On the conflicts between biological and social evolution and between psychology and moral tradition. *American Psychologist,* 1975, **30,** 1103–1126. Copyright 1975 by the American Psychological Association. Adapted by permission of the author.)

ideas.) Religious myths and beliefs, which are developed by more recently evolved parts of the human brain, provide rational explanations for ritual. As people accumulate knowledge, they use logic to turn these ideas into theology.

When language developed in the human species, the two halves of the brain became specialized. The left brain dominates in language, logic, rationality, and analysis. The right brain specializes in synthesizing and intuitive ways of grasping reality. Thus, half the brain is "rational" and half is not (Ornstein, 1977). The effects of religious ritual, symbols, myths, and prayers may be largely mediated by the right hemisphere of the brain. Theology and codified religion are functions of the left hemisphere. For Burhoe, religion is part of the innate given of human nature, and cannot be entirely rational since its practice serves to integrate both halves of the brain. These ideas are discussed more in Chapters 10 and 12.

EARLY PSYCHOLOGICAL STUDIES

With few exceptions, the scholars discussed so far have not been psychologists. At the time that anthropologists and other scholars were studying the origins of religion, psychology of religion was also developing. Mainstream psychology of religion has roots and branches primarily in the European and American traditions, though in some Eastern cultures psychology, theology, philosophy, and religion are not separate, but inherently related, subjects. Since our study is primarily influenced by American psychology of religion, we now look briefly at the development of the study in the New World.

The First Studies

Psychology of religion is almost as old as psychology itself in the United States. Less than 3 years after he earned America's first Ph.D. in psychology, G. Stanley Hall gave a popular series of Saturday morning lectures at Harvard University. On February 5, 1881, in the second lecture, Hall asserted that adolescence was the prime age of religious influence and conversion. This claim, more than any other, provided an impetus and core subject matter for the classical religious psychology that flourished for four decades thereafter. Hall founded *The Journal of Religious Psychology* and launched many psychology of religion students, notably E. D. Starbuck and James Leuba. Ages of conversion (usually averaging around puberty), types and variables affecting conversion, children's religious knowledge, factors in worship and prayer, and myriad other facts were gathered—almost entirely by questionnaire methods. Except for the relation of conversion and puberty, little theory was advanced in the classic period.

William James's *The Varieties of Religious Experience* (1902) reflected many of the interests of his day, though with more wide-ranging methods of investigation and explanation. More than any other, this book deserves classic status in psychology of religion. It emphasizes religious experience—notably conversion and mysticism. In other writings, James analyzed belief processes and other psychological factors in religion.

Later Viewpoints

In 1907 Sigmund Freud published a paper associating religious rituals with neurotic obsessive behaviors; a series of subsequent books by Freud established the psychoanalytic tradition in the psychology of religion. This tradition primarily seeks unconscious motives and bases for religious behavior, generally reducing religion to irrational or nonrational practices. Despite this reductionistic tendency, the popularity of psychoanalysis itself attracted many students to this new view of religion—including some who had personal religious commitments.

By the early 1920s the classical religious psychology began to flounder in America. James Leuba had maintained a consistent naturalistic position that devalued personal religious faith, much as the psychoanalytic approach did. Behaviorism struck roots and flourished, stifling serious interest in such subjective experiences as religion. Nobody assumed the mantle of Hall (who died in 1924 after publishing his major work on religion in 1917), Starbuck, or the other pioneers. Apart from psychoanalytic study (which continued on a separate track, apart from mainstream psychology), psychology of religion in America survived almost solely within the pastoral psychology movement. Seward Hiltner was a leader in that field; Rollo May left his influence before moving into secular and humanistic psychology traditions. In 1945 pastoral psychologist Paul Johnson wrote the only new psychology of religion text between the 1920s and 1950.

The Modern Period

Two 1950 milestones marked a renaissance for the psychology of religion in America. Gordon Allport published *The Individual and His Religion,* an elaboration of his personality theory in the specific area of religion. Quite different in scope, method, and subject was *The Authoritarian Personality* (Adorno, Frenkel-Brunswik, Levinson, & Sanford, 1950), a study of fascist conservatism and racial prejudice. One incidental finding was the tendency of church people to be more prejudiced than the nonreligious—a paradox in the light of religious teachings about universal love. Previously Allport (Allport & Kramer, 1946) had reported such a finding, and pursued the matter further in *The Nature of Prejudice* (1954).

As the association of adolescence with religious conversion had been a keystone of the classic school, no other problem fueled psychology of religion's renewal in the 1950s and subsequent decades so much as the problem of religion and prejudice. Gordon Allport contributed the greatest volume and quality of insight to that study. Old problems also received new attention, and novel phenomena, such as speaking in tongues (or glossolalia), provided new areas of study.

As questionnaires were the main methodology of the classic study, and literary speculation and case studies the major approach of the psychoanalysts, so formal personality and attitude measures have dominated empirical research in contemporary psychology of religion. In our continuing study throughout this book, you will meet again James, Freud, and Allport many times, as well as those more recent scholars who continue to inform our psychological understanding of religion.

REACTIONS TO HUMAN FINITUDE

Although most psychologists of religion have not been concerned with the origins of religion in humankind as a whole, many have studied those areas of life where human limits are reached. From the problem solving involved in conversion, through personal psychopathology and such social pathologies as prejudice and fascism, to questions about maximizing human potential, psychologists of religion have also concerned themselves with anxiety and finitude.

As do origins studies, much psychology of religion thus points to some lack, limitation, or insufficiency in human nature that religion tries, in one way or another, to overcome. Few people would deny that finitude is one aspect of being human. Religion easily taps into our finitude, and without any experience of personal limitation, we would not be likely to develop religion. An unlimited or infinite being has no need for religion; such a one would be God as most people define God. Winston King pointed out: "Experience of the 'Other Power' . . . makes one keenly aware of the tenuous and precarious nature of one's life as does nothing else" (1968, p. 12).

Although human limitation seems necessary for religion to occur, it does not automatically result in religiousness. People respond differently to finitude. Freud said:

> Critics persist in describing as "deeply religious" anyone who admits to a sense of . . . insignificance or impotence in the face of the universe, although what constitutes the essence of the religious response is not this feeling but only the next step after it. . . . The [one] who . . . humbly acquiesces . . . is . . . irreligious in the truest sense of the word [1927/1961, p. 52].

We now look at some different ways of reacting to finitude. Three basic choices exist: deny limitation, hide from limitation, or accept limitation. Each choice may take religious or nonreligious forms.

Denying Limitation

A person who openly denies limitation may be considered delusional (believing in a "crazy" way things that are not true). People who believe that their own wishes or thoughts have all-powerful effects have delusions of influence. Those who believe they are an infinite or very important person (e.g., Jesus or Napoleon) suffer delusions of grandeur. However, there are more subtle ways to deny limitation than these obvious distortions of reality.

Freud illustrates one subtle form of denial. While claiming to accept human limitation fully, he had such a strong confidence in science that he expected it to be the means of human salvation. He believed it could eventually abolish limitations. Freud was especially confident of his psychoanalytic techniques. He called himself the new Moses, and claimed that his therapy would free people from the guilt the teachings of Moses had given them.

A strong belief in the eventual accomplishments of science is only one way to deny human limitedness. For other people love, money, or special talents may give the feeling of being unlimited. Some forms of humanism—those that consider people to have godlike powers—also seem to deny limitation.

Some denial of limitation appears as religion. Here we tread the shaky ground between magic and religion (Frazer, 1925). Sometimes it is hard to distinguish between a trusting faith and a superstitious or magical use of religion. Some people believe that certain words, actions, or rituals will manipulate their God to conform to their desires. At least some of the time, many people use sacramental celebrations and petitionary prayer in ways that make them feel they can control the infinite. We often consider such behavior self-centered and self-serving, but we are still likely to call it religious.

Hiding from Limitation

Several decades ago were referred to as the Age of Anxiety. More recently, the times are described as an era of meaninglessness or valuelessness. Social critics say the present state results from people's refusal to face the realities of existence. Chronic boredom, purposelessness, and underlying fear of death and fate are called philosophical neurosis. People with such feelings have avoided making some basic decisions about life, and remain unanchored and unfocused.

Freud held that many people avoid personal neurosis by allying themselves with religion, which he considered the "universal neurosis" (Freud, 1927/1961, p. 72). Maslow (1954) noted that people may use a religious frame of reference to satisfy security needs. Church membership gives many people a sense of security, meaning, and community that allows them to defer developing their personal faith. They may go through the motions of conversion, confirmation, bar or bat mitzvah, or whatever rituals are common to their religious community—sometimes with strong sentimental emotionality, but without deep commitment. Such people are religious by habit only, and conform to and observe the religion into which they were born without examining it. Sometimes they may change to another denomination—rarely another religion—in the same essentially unengaged way.

Accepting Limitation

It is terrifying to face resolutely and acknowledge one's own finitude; this is probably why many people use an inherited religion to avoid doing so. If you saw only human limitation, and had no beliefs that offered hope of getting beyond it, you would probably despair. One hope of getting beyond human limitation rests on finding meaningfulness in one's limited condition. Some humanistic and existential thinkers say that individuals must find or create for themselves meaning for their own lives. Some do this simply by accepting their finitude.

People who say that meaning already exists—rather than believe that they must create it—usually hold that a power/purpose/intelligence greater than the merely human exists. This infinite process or being is sometimes seen as God, and sometimes not. In nontheistic (without God) beliefs, the greater-than-human may be the state, the human community, art, or any other thing large and important enough for people to devote themselves to and serve.

Pantheistic beliefs (holding that every existing thing carries divinity in it) fall between theistic and nontheistic positions. Some evolutionary theories—however scientific they may be—have strongly pantheistic overtones. They imply that some intelligence—greater than any single person's—develops and increases over time. They do not say that some intelligence "out there" (God) makes this happen, but simply that this greater-than-human intelligence exists and grows. Teilhard de Chardin (1959), a twentieth-century scientist and Christian, elaborated such views.

When someone accepts both personal limitation and a meaningfulness greater than the individual, that person usually tries to conform to the greater meaning. A willing subordination of oneself to a nontheistic purpose, such as the state, is religious in a broad sense. Such self-surrender to God defines religion in a stricter or narrower sense. Religious people consider this self-giving stance a more genuine religiousness than the magical or habitual religion already discussed. Such self-giving is called intrinsic religion—religion for the sake of religious value alone, without ulterior motives.

Living with Limitation

An intrinsically religious person believes in meaningfulness, but at times such vision may grow dim. Faith, or believing, cannot really be the same as seeing or knowing. It takes strength to admit that comforting religious beliefs might not be true. Such trials are common in the lives of many religious geniuses. Most highly developed religious people say that they had to stay faithful to a commitment even when they could not justify this by reason. Often they needed to understand their faith in a deeper and different way when their beliefs looked doubtful or untrue.

In times of emptiness and darkness, it is easy to retreat to the security of self-serving or social religiousness. This may be the wisest thing for some people to do, since paying the costs of highly developed religiousness is not easy. However, the person who wants to penetrate into the deeper mysteries of religion cannot run away. Buddhists say one must realize that there is absolutely nothing to which one can cling—and then must let go. Many traditions say that letting go —giving up religious comfort, security, and certainty—is an important step toward becoming a mystic. (See Chapter 10.) Religious mystics claim to have directly "experienced" God or Ultimate Reality, and thus to have received fuller understanding of the problems of faith and finitude.

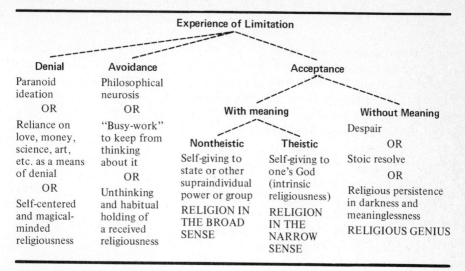

Figure 1.2 Reactions to finitude.

SUMMARY

Figure 1.2 summarizes possible responses to human limitation. It shows that religion can stem from all possible responses to finitude. Attempts to deny or distort the perception of limitation lead to self-serving, magical-minded religion. Avoiding recognition of limitation can be accomplished by hiding in an inherited religious tradition. Intrinsic (noninstrumental) religion requires acceptance of finitude as a precondition to offering oneself to a larger purpose or meaning. Finally, for religiousness to develop to fullest expression, times of loss of meaning must be accepted and faced without denial or escape.

Although we have suggested some reasons why people may develop particular approaches to religion, we have not explained why some people are religious and some are not. This problem will be considered later after we examine more closely some functions religion fills in individual lives.

REVIEW OF KEY CONCEPTS

The Nature of Religiousness
existential anxiety
the finitude of being
religion as a rescue operation
creed, cultus, and code
cognitive, affective, and conative functioning

Theories of Religion's Origins
"shadow-self" and dream experience
animism
concrete representation of ideas

chapter *2*

Functions of Religion

Most social scientists who study religion focus on its functions; this approach will be at least implied through this book. Psychologists, per se, are not in a position to argue the truth or falsity of any religious belief or behavior, but we can understand religion better by studying how it functions in individual lives. This chapter surveys the kinds of functions that religion serves for men and women. Little we say will strike you as novel or original. Our purpose will be served if you can see the great variety of ways religion works in people, and become sensitive to this wide range of religious experience.

A PROBLEM OF DEFINITION

We attempted no formal definition of *religion* in Chapter 1, though we noted various aspects of religion that different theorists emphasized. Nor are we now going to limit ourselves to any single definition of religion. As we review the functions of religion, somebody will be sure to object to some of them and say, "But that's not *real* religion!" Some will discount any religious approach that does not acknowledge a personal God. Others may say something is "not religion" because it is not related to an institutional church; some will reject other behavior because it is "merely a reflection of an institutional church."

William James gave this working definition of religion: "the feelings, acts, and experiences of individual[s] in their solitude, so far as they apprehend themselves to stand in relation to whatever they consider the divine" (1902/1961, p. 42). Broad as that definition is, we find it too limiting. Significant religious experiences occur in company as well as in solitude. James's definition minimizes or eliminates social religious activities such as corporate worship and culturally defined religious characteristics such as myth and theology. We exclude none of these from our psychology of religion.

Most psychological definitions of religion have adopted James's focus on individual perception of what is the divine or ultimate. We include in our understanding of religion those human activities that are concerned with ultimate meanings yet are related to no organized group. Some scholars speak of "invisible" religions (Machalek & Martin, 1976), which are individuals' own unique efforts to deal with ultimate problems—apart from traditional religious solutions. These ultimate problems have been identified with "the human condition"—our sense of finiteness before the whole universe, our being "a part of" nature yet "apart from" it, and our knowledge that some day our lives as we know them on earth will cease (Tremmel, 1976).

Our review of the origins of religion overlaps this chapter, but we now focus on the functions that religion serves in the present, not in the past. Some functions are relevant to both; others were added to religion later—not crucial in the origins of religion but acquired after religion became institutionalized. These added-on functions of religion may not be at the core of what we would define as religious, but they are a substantial part of what we actually find in religion as it now operates in the world. We classify the various functions into the broad kinds of human needs that they meet: egocentric, growth, cognitive, and social. These functions introduce a number of topics to be covered later in this book, and the classification scheme anticipates Unit Four, where we shall pursue a more formal, empirical understanding of religion.

EGOCENTRIC FUNCTIONS OF RELIGION

Religion functions, in part, to meet self-centered needs of the individual. These egocentric needs include bodily or physical drives, needs that are psychological in their origins, and needs that are produced by the social systems the person is in. In *Future of an Illusion* Freud cited three functions of the gods: "They must exorcize the terrors of nature, they must reconcile one to the cruelty of fate, particularly as shown in death, and they must make amends for the sufferings and privations that the communal life of culture has imposed" (1927/1961, p. 24). These can all be considered basically egocentric needs, reflecting Freud's limited view of religion.

Bodily Needs

We do not usually think of physical drives in relation to religion, but Gordon Allport (1950/1960, p. 10), talking about the role of organic desire in religion, quoted Dunlap: "There seem to be no desires that are not, or have not at some time been items in religions. Prayer certainly is an expression of desire, and there is nothing which [one] could desire that some[one] does not or has not prayed for" (1946, p. 126).

Food Food is a basic physical need, and anthropologists give many accounts of "primitive" religious rituals that surround the acts of planting, harvesting, and hunting. Although technology and a complex division of labor have replaced early peoples' direct dependence on the uncertainties of nature for food, millions of people still recite from Jesus' prayer, "Give us this day our daily bread."

Sex Kindled by Freud's view of religion as related to sexual repression, a number of theorists have emphasized religion as a function of sexual desires. They see sex symbols in religious myths and rituals, and sexual overtones are often only thinly veiled in many religious frenzies and mystical fantasies (Allport, 1950). The sexual functions of earlier fertility cults and ritual prostitution are even more conspicuous than these. We should not think, however, that those religious practices, primitive as they seem to us, gave only sexual expression. Sexual needs are an integral part of life, and a comprehensive religion cannot ignore them. Although we are most accustomed to religion's dealing with sex by way of taboos and prohibitions, religious traditions also provide for sexual expression and fulfillment in sanctioned relationships. Tantric yoga employs some rituals involving sexual expression, with the intention of teaching an understanding of sexuality and overcoming dependence on sex.

Fear of Injury   Fears of bodily injury and death figured prominently in two of the functions Freud cited—to exorcize the terrors of nature and to reconcile one to the fate of death. These functions are still served by religion; the term *foxhole religion* indicates religion that is primarily motivated by such fears. Studies of the high-risk occupation of open-sea fishing off New England show that quasi-religious rituals and taboos are related to the degree of risk (Poggie & Gersuny, 1972; Poggie, Pollnac, & Gersuny, 1976). Malinowski (1948) made similar observations among fishermen of the Trobriand Islands.

But do religious rituals actually help people deal with such fears? About 75% of combat soldiers said that praying helped them, and this was especially true of those who were exposed to the most stress and felt the greatest anxiety. Historical evidence among Jewish and Christian communities shows a shift toward greater use of ritual during periods of external stress and threat (Argyle, 1964).

Death Anxiety   Death, as an inherent part of the human condition, has received considerable attention as a function of religion. British medical students, who are in frequent contact with death and dying patients, become more religious while in college (Poppleton & Pilkington, 1963), although most college students decline in religiousness. Older people, among whom death is more of a present reality, seem generally to be more religious than younger people (Rogers, 1976). At least in Christian cultures, older people believe more strongly in immortality and life after death. We shall return to the subject of religion and the fear of death, especially in Chapter 23.

Psychogenic Needs

While death is the ultimate threat to a person's physical well-being, it is more than a physical problem. Because we are able to think, to reflect on our predicaments and destinies, much of the insecurity of human life originates in the mind, the psyche of the person. Thus security and a number of other human needs are considered psychological in origin, or *psychogenic.*

Security   We can feel insecure for a variety of reasons: the fundamental facts of the human condition, threats against our physical integrity (injury or death), individual losses or threat of loss of possessions or personal relationships. What can religion do about such insecurities or anxieties? From the psychological perspective it may not make much difference whether the actual, objective facts of the situation can be changed. It may be enough that *something* is prescribed for those anxious times. Studies of military personnel in combat indicate that *any* activity or duty can help people control their anxiety, even though it does nothing to reduce the actual danger (Shaffer, 1947).

Different religions provide different solutions. Religion typically gives assurance that "life and organization will win, that death and disorganization will lose" (Burhoe, 1975, p. 7). Christianity and Islam promise an afterlife of perfect bliss, and some native American religions gave assurance of a "happy hunting ground." Personal immortality, with or without bodily resurrection, is not so important to some other religions. The Buddhist seeks to transcend desire, which is seen as the root of all suffering. Similarly the Turkish *kismet* emphasizes a devout resignation to one's fate as "God's will." To the Hebrews the important thing was the promise that God would preserve the "Chosen People" as a group if they obeyed the Law. The Hindu goal is for the soul to attain "sufficient moral and spiritual purity to make possible its escape from the Wheel of Rebirth, and its return and reunion with . . . Brahman" or ultimate reality (Tremmel, 1976, p. 190). All of these different religious answers assure the believer that *something* can be done to resolve the human and individual plights that threaten our security.

Relationship   Some insecurities are based on deficiencies in relationship—our divorce from nature and our estrangement from other people. Religions typically offer relationships that help compensate for those anxieties. The major Western religions—Judaism, Islam, Christianity—offer a relationship with a personal God. Some major religions of the East—for example, Buddhism and Taoism—and many early religions tend more to encourage relatedness to nature. Tremmel characterized attitudes of the Taoists: "Flow with nature. . . . Feel the wind and go with it. See the sunset and be enchanted by it, merge into it. Taste the honey and be delighted. Do not try to create order; surrender to it as it moves Yang/Yin in all natural things and events" (1976, p. 194). The proffered relationships—to a personal God or to an all-encompassing Brahman—can allay some of the insecurity that comes from the uncertain relationships that threaten us.

Adventure   In writing about psychogenic motives for religious behavior, Allport noted, "There are hungers for self-expression, for adventure, for power, which, I believe, are properly classed as psychogenic, but these are readily recognized as being relatively self-centered and not so widely removed from the viscerogenic drives in which they originated" (1950/1960, p. 15).* Of these self-centered, or egocentric, psychogenic drives, we shall touch briefly on adventure and power.

Can religion provide adventure? At a weekend "humanistic psychology" conference, six morning meditations were scheduled—two in hatha yoga, two in t'ai-chi ch'üan, and one each in raja yoga and zazen (the sitting meditation of Zen Buddhism). The conference had nine other sessions with religious content; seven of those were similarly concerned with Eastern religions. In that Midwestern U.S. city, with at least 95% of the registrants being Americans of European extraction, we were overwhelmingly impressed that those religious experiences

---

*All 1950/1960 selections reprinted with permission of Macmillan Publishing Co., Inc. from *The Individual and His Religion* by Gordon W. Allport. Copyright 1950 by Macmillan Publishing Co., Inc., renewed 1978 by Robert B. Allport.

were merely new adventures—alternating with fads like encounter groups, Gestalt therapy, bioenergetics, and primal therapy.

Accounts of life in an earlier, more rural America suggest that sometimes a local revival meeting was the most exciting happening in the community and attracted adventure-seeking young people as do today's discotheque or drive-in movie or stock car races. Some contemporary religious movements seem to capitalize on the appeal of excitement or adventure. The emotional fervor of old-time revivalism appears in the charismatic movement, with its promotion of glossolalia (speaking in tongues) and faith healing in mainline Christian denominations. And whatever other functions they serve, handling snakes, drinking poisons, and taking psychedelic drugs add excitement to their religious contexts. Yes, religion can provide adventure.

Power and Status   Most people feel some degree of powerlessness when they consider their position in relation to the universe, or in relation to complex social systems. Religion compensates for this felt powerlessness. It assures the believer, "You are on the right side; keep the faith and you will win in the end."

Some accrued, added-on, functions of institutional religion provide other forms of power (and status, which is a symbol of power). One kind is perhaps mere symbol; we might call it empty status. You will recognize this type from television drama: the little insignificant guy who is forever aspiring to be the Grand Poo-Bah of the Raccoon Lodge, or the High-Exalted Mystic Ruler of some other secret organization. Several years ago in a Southern city a local character dubbed himself "Bishop Saint Psalm" and achieved some notoriety in a series of one-man demonstrations (during the civil rights movement).

In a less idiosyncratic form an unskilled laborer might become a deacon, elder, or other titled person in the church and thereby gain some feeling of power. Similarly, knowing that your pies are always the highlight of the church socials or that your organizational skills make the church bazaar a success may richly satisfy power and status needs. The pastor of a large church or leader in a complex religious bureaucracy or ecclesiastical hierarchy may achieve status and power of a very real nature—in terms of making things happen, spending money, moving other people, and enhancing one's own place in the sun.

Social Conditions

Some needs that religion serves spring neither from organic twitches nor psychic itches, but rather from social and cultural restrictions. The very fact that individuals, with their different needs and desires, live together in cooperating groups means that some personal impulses will be frustrated. And in almost every society some people are deprived more than others.

Social Deprivation   In American society women and blacks are seen to be deprived of opportunity relative to men and whites; they also tend to be more religious. Certain sects appeal to working class people, and their beliefs and practices seem to provide symbolic or substitute gratifications for the socially deprived state of the believers. Belief in a speedy end to the present world and a more blessed afterlife looks like symbolic compensation for social privation. In some of these churches in the Western hemisphere and especially in some African countries, the prolonged emotional, ecstatic services seem to provide even more direct relief of the tensions associated with social deprivation (Argyle, 1964).

Cargo Cults   Religion as a reaction to social conditions is also illustrated by the "cargo cults" of the South Pacific and Southeast Asia (e.g., Harris, 1974; Lanternari, 1963). After technologically advanced explorers and colonizers appeared among these people, they began to puzzle over the source of fabrics, metal tools, canned goods, and other cargo brought by the newcomers. They lacked the background to understand the production systems of modern civilization; and the missionaries' prescription of hard work, as the royal road to affluence, left them still impoverished by the modern standards.

From this situation emerged a long series of religious systems—mixtures of very transparent wish fulfillment, their own traditional religious myths, and misinterpretations of the missionaries' Christian teachings. Typically, dead ancestors were expected to make their appearance piloting a big canoe loaded with their own, the natives', share of cargo that had been withheld by the wealthy whites. As time passed the expectations of cargo cults kept pace with modernization, and they came to look for sailing ships, then steamships, World War II U.S. Navy LSTs, and airplanes. Whatever the exact form of the belief, though, the essential element was a wish fulfilling equalization of social privilege—inspired by the great discrepancies between their own poverty and the affluence of the exploiting colonizers (Harris, 1974).

GROWTH AND VALUE FUNCTIONS OF RELIGION

Despite our lengthy discussion of the egocentric functions of religion, not all human motives, nor all religious motives, are of that nature. People invest a great deal of effort in meeting physical and psychological needs. They also have potential to rise above self—to grow and press toward ideals or values.

Esteem Needs

Abraham Maslow's (1954) hierarchy of needs places esteem needs next after the basic physical, safety, and social needs. Esteem forms a kind of bridge to even higher needs. Allport (1950) considered the growth and value drives to grow out of lower-level needs. He used self-consciousness as an illustration. When a child becomes aware of itself, it craves self-expression, power, and pride, in an egocentric way. Ideally, though, the value the child invests in its own self becomes generalized to others. It is as if the child asks, "If I am so aware of myself, and value myself so highly, don't other people probably feel the same about themselves?" And so, in Allport's words,

> Abstracting from my physical individuality the general concept of selfhood, I
> gradually come to value whatever makes for the conservation of personal integ-
> rity anywhere. The [Human] Natural Rights, the Golden Rule, the Second Com-
> mandment of Christ, are varied statements of the value that I affirm
> [1950/1960, p. 16].

Maslow said that esteem needs may partially be met by recognition or praise
from others, but they are best satisfied when a person behaves in a way that she
or he approves of. This requires the person to shift focus from self to external
ideals. Self-esteem is developed by directing oneself in accordance with ideals or
values outside of oneself.

Self-actualizing Needs

Originally Maslow placed self-actualizing needs at the top of his hierarchy. After
physical, social, and esteem needs are satisfied, he said, a person is still not complete: "A new discontent and restlessness will soon develop, unless the individual
is doing what [she or] he is fitted for. . . . What [one] *can* do, [one] *must* do.
This need we may call self-actualization" (Maslow, 1954, p. 91). The specific form
taken by the need for self-actualization depends on the person's unique pattern
of talents and innate capacities.

An individual obviously may become self-actualized apart from any religious considerations, yet many religious people see their talents and capabilities
as a kind of stewardship for which they are accountable. While religions frequently encourage some renunciation and discipline of lower-level needs, they
seldom approve the deliberate neglect of talents or abilities. Maslow considered
self-actualization a biologically based need that should emerge in the course of
normal development when lower-level, egocentric needs have been sufficiently
gratified. However, higher needs do not necessarily arise automatically whenever
lower-level needs are satisfied; special encouragement may be required before they
emerge.

Self-transcendence Needs

Later Maslow suggested a need beyond and above self-actualization. He identified
what he called "metaneeds," which involve rising above or transcending self. In
Maslow's words,

> Transcendence refers to the very highest and most inclusive or holistic levels
> of human consciousness, behaving and relating, as ends rather than as means,
> to oneself, to significant others, to human beings in general, to other species,
> to nature, and to the cosmos [1971a, p. 275].

He considered the transcendent metaneeds instinctive and necessary for full positive mental health.

Maslow characterized lower-level, egocentric needs as based on deficiencies in the human state and called them "deficiency needs" or "D-needs." Metaneeds were called "being needs" or "B-needs." Many human activities can operate on either the D-need or the B-need level. People who "have to" love because of their deficiencies, from D-needs, are seeking to satisfy their own social needs; people who love out of B-needs come closer to the ideal of love taught by all religions. Metaneeds generally are concerned with the higher, self-transcendent values that are promoted by the world's major religions. Some of the values, which Maslow called the "Values of Being," or B-values, are used to describe God in many traditions, e.g.: Truth, Beauty, Goodness, Holiness, Love, Compassion, Justice, Surrender, Responsibility, Unity, Order, Perfection, and Completeness.

All religions suggest that to rise above a self-serving animal level, human beings must recognize and work toward higher, self-transcending values. Maslow's theory represents one conception of how self-transcendence might develop. Allport also cited Harald Höffding as saying that all religion is "motivated by the individual's desire to conserve value" (Allport, 1950/1960, p. 17).

COGNITIVE AND INDIVIDUALIZING FUNCTIONS OF RELIGION

The egocentric functions of religion, and to a lesser extent the growth and value functions, relate to feelings: insecurity, desires for adventure and power, and (more subtly) some positively held values. In terms of the classic psychological dichotomy, we now turn from feeling to thinking, from affect to cognition. Yet this shift is far from absolute. Feeling and thinking are intimately interrelated. Our feelings affect the way we think, and the things we think about affect how we feel. Milton Rokeach's work on belief systems illustrates the interrelatedness of feeling and thinking: "All belief-disbelief systems serve two powerful and conflicting sets of motives at the same time: the need for a cognitive framework to know and to understand and the need to ward off threatening aspects of reality" (1960, p. 67). In this section we shall focus on those cognitive frameworks, though Rokeach emphasized the defensive functions of beliefs.

The Need for Cognitive Structure

Our complex and competent brains have needs of their own—to process information, to know and to understand. The world of experience is complicated and ever-changing, and given a complex brain, there exists the need to comprehend, to give structure and meaning—almost like the mountain that must be climbed, just because it is there. Some of the early anthropological theories of the origins of religion stressed such attempts to give meaning to the world. You will recall Tylor's theory that spirits were conceived to explain phenomena such as dreams and death, and Frazer's theory that human needs to understand relationships between events led to magic, as a sort of primitive religion.

Even those who acknowledge religion as an attempt to understand may say that science now provides a more reliable understanding of nature. Of course that is true within limits. Scientific accounts of the nature and causes of earthquakes, tornadoes, volcanic eruptions, and floods are superior to earlier explanations of those events. But science does not provide all of the answers. It might tell, in general, how a tornado is formed, but it would not presume to tell *why* a particular tornado struck a particular place at a particular time and killed or maimed a particular person.

Scientific truths are necessarily tentative, partial, incomplete, and fragmented:

> The universe is simply incomprehensible. Fragments of it may be fairly well understood, but not the interrelation of these fragments, and certainly not the design of the whole. Every[one] wonders at times about the void which gave way to creation, and about the successive links that connect this original void to [one's] own momentary state of wonder. To many . . . religion is primarily a search for complete knowledge, for unfissioned truth [Allport, 1950/1960, pp. 19–20].

Despite present and future advances of science and technology, many meaningful questions await religious insights. The giving of meaning to life is a primary function of religion.

The Need to Explain Ourselves

Several theorists have suggested that religious feelings and behaviors precede religious thoughts. Sometimes religious thinking serves to explain to people the meaning of their feelings or acts. Tremmel has spun a little fantasy that illustrates this function of religious thought. He portrays a primeval man, at the dawning of religious awareness:

> One day with his trusty club in hand, our man went forth to bash a bear for dinner. He guessed that the bear might be in the rocks beyond the swamp. He did not like the swamp. It was full of powers. Not things like bears or wolves, but things you could not really see. Things weird, demonic, unseen. As he hesitated, he observed that he had come to the edge of the swamp at a point he had never been before, at a place where there was a most fantastic tree, very gnarled and wind-bent, but very strong, full of mightiness. He sensed that it was a *special tree.* A tree stronger than the swamp things. He did not think such things exactly; he felt them along his spine. Coming closer to the tree he saw a place on the trunk where the bark had been rubbed smooth by passing animals. He touched the smooth place. It was good to touch, to slide his hand over. Somehow it made him feel strong. After a short time he continued his journey through the swamp to the other side, without mishap. And on the other side he had good luck. He did not even have to fight a bear. He found and bashed a ram instead. After that he crossed the swamp many times, but always first he went to the place of The Tree and touched the smooth spot. Later, maybe, he started to think about it, but only after The Tree had, in fact, become a thing of "religion," and his performance a "religious act" [Tremmel, 1976, pp. 13–14, minor deletions not indicated].

The cognitive creations that give structure to the world and explain our own religious feelings and rituals take two overlapping forms—myth and theology. Myth does not mean a falsehood; rather a myth is a story, typically a story of the origin of the ritual that the myth explains. Theologies are more abstract than myths, though theology is quite apparent in some stories, and story may play an important role in theology. These relations among feeling, ritual, myth, and theology seem to make theology "derived"—after the fact of the important religious experiences. However, some scholars think that early people might have been more "thinking animals" than we have given them credit for being. Paul Tillich is quoted as saying that "theology is as old as religion" (Tremmel, 1976, p. 118). Myth and theology are significant human expressions that deserve more empirical psychological study than they have received.

The Need to Deal with Universal Experiences

One of the most significant yet controversial contributions of the Swiss psychiatrist Carl Jung was the notion of the "collective unconscious"—a storehouse of subconscious memories from the whole history and prehistory of the human race. This is a difficult notion to communicate in a short space, but in general it holds that certain experiences of human beings are so nearly universal that they form a potential part of the mind of every person born. Hall and Lindzey put it this way:

> Racial memories or representations are not inherited as such; rather we inherit the *possibility* of reviving experiences of past generations. They are predispositions which set us to react to the world in a selective fashion. These predispositions are projected on the world. For example, since human beings have always had mothers, every infant is born with the predisposition to perceive and react to a mother [1970, p. 83].

What does this idea of a collective unconscious have to do with religion? An important aspect of it is what Jung (1959) called "archetypes," which are universal ideas that typically have a large emotional component. The above quotation implies the archetype mother. Jung posited other archetypes with religious connotations: hero, demon, virgin god or goddess, wise old man, divine child, and others. They are typically represented in symbols that have a heavy emotional impact. Whether or not this type of symbol springs from a collective unconscious, religions possess and transmit them in rituals and mythologies.

Jung pointed out, for example, that we all must deal with what he called the "shadow" side of our personalities—all of those things in us that we reject for moral or aesthetic reasons. Almost all religions offer the symbol of an evil spirit or devil to stand for those aspects of our personalities that we reject. We also have countersexual aspects of our personalities and sexual impulses to manage; religions offer virgin gods and goddesses to stand for the "perfect" member of the opposite sex—an archetypal image that reflects aspects of one's own hidden personality. We need, also, to be nurtured and loved; mother goddesses stand for the source of unconditional love. Jung noted that these symbols occur not only in religion but also in folklore, fairy tales, dreams, and literature.

Often it is painful to recognize the conflict-laden experiences, which surround these symbols, as part of our own psychological functioning. So we may "project" these psychological experiences onto some symbol or person outside of ourselves. This process is analogous to the projection of movies or slides. The picture is actually in the projector, but its image is thrown out away from the projector so that it is seen on a screen at a distance. Similarly, when we project our own feelings or experiences, we think that our experience is really "out there" and do not see it as part of ourselves. It is easier to say, "The devil tempts me to anger" than to admit, "I am a hostile person and lose my temper."

Sometimes instead of projection we identify ourselves with one aspect of our own psychological life and think it is the whole of us. Charles Manson, for example, became the "wise old man" to his followers and encouraged them to call him Jesus Christ. Sometimes we neither identify with nor project conflicts; to recognize them and deal with them directly is the healthier approach. Often, however, we just refuse to acknowledge their existence and let them grow outside of awareness until they begin to run us, beyond our control—as some people come to feel possessed by the devil or by their "shadow" tendencies.

The usefulness of religion in helping people deal with universal human conflicts should be obvious. Although it is best to know your own psyche and deal directly with conflict, the next best thing probably is to project it onto some safe religious symbol. To wrestle with the devil is better than to risk being possessed by the devil.

The Need to Be Oneself

In serving cognitive needs, each religion provides a more-or-less coherent answer to the fundamental puzzles of the human condition. Allport said, "All the great religions of the world supply, for those who can subscribe to their arguments and affirmations, a world-conception that has logical simplicity and serene majesty" (1950/1960, p. 19).

Some may not be able to accept an established theology. Allport noted, "Most individuals, however, are not sufficiently contemplative nor sufficiently imitative to adopt in toto the explanation offered by any one master theologian" (1950/1960, p. 19). People vary in the degree to which they need to remake a given religion to suit their individual molds.

Religious beliefs may be individualized in two contrasting ways. Some people hold a religion (beliefs, practices, ethics—the whole lot) quite casually. They are inclined to accept just the parts of their religious systems that are convenient and helpful at the moment; this is a relatively egocentric use of religion. On the other hand, some people have temperaments or experiences that make significant portions of their given religious package unacceptable. Yet they labor to develop their own most consistent, well-integrated, and intellectually defensible religious solutions. The development of their religion is obviously a self-actualizing process. People can handle their religious cognitions, then, in either egocentric or growth ways.

SOCIAL FUNCTIONS OF RELIGION

The sociologist Durkheim emphasized the function religion plays in forging and preserving a social order. Religion functions variously in the social and cultural areas of human life.

Promoting the Integrity of Society

Freud's point about religion compensating for the privations of society has relevance here in another way. Insofar as people are kept from being too dissatisfied, the whole society is rendered stable.

Ethics and Morality   Virtually all religious systems promote an orderly society by declaring and enforcing certain moral codes, which include rules for interpersonal conduct. From Freud's primordial trio of taboos (incest, cannibalism, and murder), to the *yamas* of hatha yoga (five restraints that regulate relations with others), the Hebrew Ten Commandments, and Christ's law of love and the "second mile" (Matthew 5 : 41), all religious codes help maintain a stable social order—insofar as the codes are internalized and followed.

Even secular-minded political authorities may encourage churches and Sunday schools in lower socioeconomic areas as a measure to reduce crime. Some people may be skeptical about the effectiveness of religion in reducing socially disruptive behavior, because we see so many cases where the ethical teachings don't take. Empirical studies of sexual promiscuity, drug abuse, and the like do show, though, that religion is the best predictor of not engaging in socially disapproved behaviors (Gorsuch, 1976).

Civil Religion   Sociologist Robert Bellah (1968) and others have identified a slice of American culture that they call "civil religion." They observe that, somewhat apart from the traditional religious systems in the United States, there is a common "religion" that undergirds and supports the "American way of life." This civil religion, which serves a primarily social or cultural function, embodies "certain ultimate American values such as belief in progress, the dignity of the individual, social justice, political democracy, religious tolerance, restraint in outward conduct, and thrift" (Tanenbaum, 1975, p. 469). While few doubt this set of ideals, the ultimate value of such a civil religion has been hotly debated (e.g., Neal, 1976). The ambivalence of religious persons about civil religion is reflected in this joint Jewish-Catholic-Protestant statement, summarizing a 1972 colloquium:

> We affirm a common fund of such shared values as equality, individual liberty, religious and cultural pluralism, and civic responsibility for social justice. At the same time we are very much concerned about the exploitation and abuse of

the symbols and values of the civil religion by those who would manipulate it for the purpose of serving their own private and national interests. In this sense the civil religion must be subjected to continuous judgment and critique in order to prevent its being transformed into idolatrous and demonic cultural religion [Tanenbaum, 1975, p. 472].

Conformity

Complementary to the previously noted need for people to individualize their religion, people vary in the tendency to conform to their culture. The psychological tendency to conform serves the interests of religion, but religion also functions to feed conformity. The urge to conform is so strong among preadolescents that Waddington (1960) saw it as biologically determined. Conformity helps to bind members of a society together in a common identity.

Religion provides standardized rituals to which children can conform. Following these practices helps children identify themselves as Buddhists or Jews or Catholics or Pentecostals. When they become old enough to ask, for example, "Why do we eat this unleavened bread," then myth and theology become related:

> We were slaves unto Pharaoh in Egypt. And the Lord, our God, took us out from there with a strong hand and an outstretched arm. . . . Therefore, it is our duty to thank, praise, laud, glorify, uplift, extol, bless, exalt and adore Him who did all of these miracles for our fathers and for ourselves [The Haggadah of Passover].

Then, "when the myth is learned it too is at first accepted without question for the same reason the ritual is adopted. The in-group is safe and familiar and therefore whatever it does and says is good and right" (Allport, 1950/1960, p. 26). So religion provides materials for people's conformity needs, and the conformity welds the identification of the group and helps keep it intact.

Affiliation

A final social function that religion serves is *affiliation*—gregariousness, the herd instinct, just wanting to be with other people. Religion offers many people an opportunity for sheer social contact, quite apart from the inherently religious purposes of church. Religions differ widely in the degree to which they offer social interaction. In many low-church Protestant congregations, visiting among worshipers before and after services, and other specifically social activities, are inseparable parts of the religious life. Although some, such as Muslims, tend to divorce social intercourse from religious worship and ritual, people always feel some interpersonal communion with other worshipers.

How much is social contact a legitimate part of religion? It certainly is not a basic reason for religious activity. In a Baptist church meeting a recently divorced mother testified, "We were here without a family. We were looking for a family, and this church has become one for us." That implies more than just affiliation, of course, but social contact was a part of ministry to that family in their time of need. On the other hand, going for the "social kicks" can be a purely egocentric use of religion.

In an airport we picked up a brochure titled, "Need a Friend?" It was a promotional piece for a group of churches in the metropolitan area. The first of three statements on "Friendship," observed that "people need friends." The message quickly moved to the idea of giving oneself to "the greatest Friend a person can have, Jesus Christ." While it started with an egocentric motive, the tract soon turned to value and actualizing terms that were considered the heart of religion. So the social functions of religion can also overlap the egocentric and growth functions. These interrelations will be reconsidered in Chapter 22 more systematically.

SUMMARY

We have surveyed most of the functions of religion that social scientists have suggested. A further understanding of the functions and the ways in which they work in individual human lives will be developed in the rest of this book. A more immediate question is how some of these religious attitudes and behaviors arise, grow, and are nurtured in the developing human being. The next four chapters will be devoted to that question.

REVIEW OF KEY CONCEPTS

A Problem of Definition
    James's definition of religion
    "invisible" religion

Egocentric Functions of Religion
    Freud's "functions of the gods"
    religion and bodily needs—food, sex, fear of injury, death anxiety
    ways religion relates to psychogenic needs: security, relationship, adventure,
        power, and status
    religion and social deprivation—cargo cults

Growth and Value Functions of Religion
    Maslow's hierarchy of needs: esteem and self-actualizing needs
    self-transcendence needs—metaneeds
    D-needs, B-needs, and B-values

Cognitive and Individualizing Functions of Religion
    Rokeach's functions of belief-disbelief systems
    religion and needs for cognitive structure
    religion and the need to explain ourselves—myth and theology
    dealing with universal experiences
    collective unconscious and archetypes—the shadow
    projection and identification
    the need to be ourselves

Social Functions of Religion
    ethics and morality
    civil religion
    conformity needs and religion
    affiliation needs and religion
    promotion of religion through people's needs

chapter 3

Development of Religiousness in Individuals

INTRODUCTION

Religion grows and develops in individual lives. It is not born full grown, nor is it static. Whenever a religious impulse begins to grow within a person, it has at least the potential to mature into a more complex, integrated, and adaptive system.

Some religious growth parallels the development of the child into adulthood. A child is not mature religiously any more than it is mature intellectually or emotionally. Even an adult does not come immediately to a mature faith. The Christian apostle Paul made this point: "I fed you with milk, and did not give you solid food because you were not ready for it. You are not ready for it even now" (1 Corinthians 3 : 2). The milk/food metaphor is also used in Hebrews 5 : 12–14 and followed immediately by the charge, "Let us, then, go beyond the initial teaching about Christ and advance to maturity."

Virtually all higher religions urge development in religious practice, faith, and belief. Some of those who advance the farthest are identified as masters, gurus, prophets, or other religious leaders. Among the others, though, there are differences in religious maturity. Some members of any religious community remain religious "babies." This is regrettable, just as childish behavior is inappropriate for adults in any area of development.

Growth Versus Stability

Sometimes a religious sentiment fails to develop because of opposing tendencies. All living systems tend toward growth and also toward stability—toward maintaining constancy or balance. These two opposing but complementary forces are found in physical and other psychological systems as well as in those that we call religious. The forces determine and inhibit religious development. This chapter will examine the sources of growth and the tendencies that limit and direct religious growth. Later we shall focus on other issues of religious development.

SOURCES OF GROWTH

Many psychological processes contribute to religious growth. None of these processes is unique to religion; psychologists as far back as William James (1902) have noted that there is no religious instinct per se. Almost any psychic activity can be directed toward religion.

Experience

A basic source of all development, religious or otherwise, is experience—anything the person encounters or lives through. Some experiences are mediated by the sensory and perceptual systems. Others are not so clearly from outside sources. Awareness of an experience may be on an unconscious or emotional level rather than on the level of verbal consciousness. The following examples illustrate the variety of experiences that may contribute to religious growth. They are by no means exhaustive.

Parental Care A parent tenderly expresses love by regular, rhythmic feeding and changing of the infant. Such mundane care may be instinctive, is often well done, and is crucial to the development of what Erikson (1959) called "basic trust." Without such experiences the child will scarcely be able to feel or understand the love of God or come to trust and have religious faith. In Chapter 6 we shall examine ways in which experiences with parents influence the way children conceive of God.

Stories and Tales The stories and myths a child is told or read lead to particular ways of construing reality. They make it easier or harder for children to understand spiritual truth, God's nature, and other religious teachings they are later exposed to.

Religious Images How many years was our concept of God molded and limited by that stereotype: a well-meaning picture of God in a movie or children's Bible story book, a benevolent grandfather with white curls and long flowing beard, hovering up there in the clouds somewhere?

Interfaith Contact How do you handle meeting someone of another religious faith, who believes just as strongly and devoutly as you do —and who appears to be sane and intelligent? Meeting such a person can challenge our development.

Interpersonal Judgment Many students have found themselves challenged spiritually by what they see as hypocrisy in another person's faith and life. Faced with someone else's inconsistency, they themselves are pressed to make their own religion more than an innocuous social facade.

Personal Crisis A conservative Christian, who knew that such things happen only to other people, finds herself involved in a divorce. What reevaluation of moral absolutes will she make? What, if anything, will she discover about grace, forgiveness, and second chances? Many have made such personal traumas into avenues of religious growth (Smoke, 1976).

Existential Crisis A person, by reason, may become aware of the human condition. In an existential crisis an individual may encounter that despair which Kierkegaard called "sickness unto death":

> The torment of the despair is precisely this: not to be able to die. . . . So to be sick *unto* death is . . . that even the last hope, death, is not available. When death is the greatest danger, one hopes for life; but when one becomes ac-

quainted with an even more dreadful danger, one hopes for death [Kierkegaard, in Bretall, 1946, pp. 341–342].

Out of such states of despair, Kierkegaard said, religious growth is most likely to occur.

Mystical Experience   Finally a person might have a profound experience like that of the Quaker mystic Rufus Jones:

> I was walking alone in the forest, trying to map out my plan of life, confronted with issues which seemed too complex and difficult for my mind to solve. Suddenly I felt the walls between the visible and invisible grow thin . . . I felt as though I was face to face with a higher order of reality than that of the trees or mountains. I went down on my knees there in the woods with that same feeling of awe which compelled [people] in earlier times to take off their shoes from their feet. A sense of mission broke in on me and I felt that I was being called to a well-defined task of life to which I then and there dedicated myself [Jones, 1932].

Some growth may come thus. Chapter 10 deals in detail with such mystical experiences.

Needs

Needs in the psychological sense sometimes result in drives that move and direct the person. This movement and direction lead to more and varied experiences—which of course are basic to growth. Chapter 2 identified some of the needs that religion serves. Needs as basic as food and sex may engage one in a religious quest. For example, a farmer may pray for rain for his crops, which represent food for him and his family. If rain comes, he will be more likely to pray for rain and other things that he needs, for needs not only lead us into experiences. If they are fulfilled, the behavior that leads to fulfillment will be stamped in or reinforced.

Walters and Bradley (1971) identified a long list of motivations that, at least sometimes, relate to religion: anger, hatred, and aggression; love; vocation, achievement, and work; conformity, dependency, acquiescence, and relation to authority; guilt, fear, morality, and ethics; self-concept, self-esteem, religious identity, and perception of death. More could surely be added. The need for social contact can lead a person into a church or religious group. An adolescent or college student, permissively reared, and deprived of the security of clearly defined limits and discipline, may need a high level of authoritarian structure. She or he may be a prime target for a rigid, fundamentalistic religious cult.

Most of the needs we have talked about are "deficits" that lead to religious growth indirectly. Some other human drives promote growth more immediately. Many of the higher animals share with humans the exploratory and curiosity drives. These drives can lead to innumerable experiences with religious implications: visiting worship services and reading literature of different faiths, practicing meditation or taking hallucinatory drugs that may produce mystical states, or sampling forbidden sins to see if the consequences are really as dire as the preacher warns.

Other psychologists have proposed drives toward self-actualization (Maslow, 1954) and "effectance" (White, 1959). These point to human tendencies to be the best we can. To actualize oneself, one may find it necessary to press beyond the current, immature level of one's faith, and sometimes to reject religious teachings that are inconsistent with personal experience. The drive for effectance might push a young woman more fully to master the interior prayer life prescribed by her religious order, or to improve the discipline of meditation in which her guru has instructed her.

Social Relationships

Religion can be practiced in solitude, but it does not develop without the stimulation of other people. It may be true that we love because God first loved us (1 John 4 : 19), but it is primarily through others that we experience such love.

The family is principal among the social relationships that contribute to religious growth. The major religions in the last 10,000–15,000 years—from Confucianism, Hinduism, and Zoroastrianism; to Judaism, Christianity, and Islam; to the Aztec, Maya, and Inca—all have had "a very rigid and almost identical family system." Without exception those religious systems have been concerned with the sanctity of family relations more *"than any other mundane subject"* (Zimmerman, 1974, pp. 2, 6).

The crucially important parent-child relations involve greater intimacy, more time, and consequently stronger emotional bonds (positive or negative) than any other relationships. There are good psychological, social, and even biological reasons for the traditional family, and Zimmerman (1974) predicts a return to that pattern—with less public involvement in providing child-related services. The importance of the family for religious development should be apparent throughout this book. You will find a hint of it in David Elkind's observation that "it is an idle and unfounded fantasy to believe that religious emotions will be built within a child who is sent to religious school while [her or] his parents avoid Church attendance" (1964a, p. 646).

In a study of religion among 451 Catholic, Baptist, and Methodist high school sophomores, the factor that primarily influenced church attendance was the parents' own attendance of church services. However, other social relationships may also influence religious growth. In the same study, peer pressures and influences of church leaders were the important factors in instilling religious attitudes and participation (Hoge & Petrillo, 1978). Friends may rouse religious interests in a child from a nonreligious family. A roommate or spouse may challenge one's religious orthodoxy. A chance encounter with a charismatic religious leader may redirect the course of one's life. Possibilities are endless.

Emotions

The strong emotions roused by close interpersonal relationships partially account for their influence on religious development. Emotions in themselves are a crucial part of religion and contribute to the totality of personal faith. Almost any emotion, like any need, can be associated with religion, but some are specially salient. Trust, hope, love, friendship, compassion, ecstasy, bliss, and awe (the Hebrew "fear of the Lord") are among the higher emotions in many religions. Religion has sometimes valued the emotion of zeal, directed either to evangelism or persecution of "infidels."

Emotions may be the first psychological processes that contribute to individual religiousness. Elkind observed that *"the child can experience religious emotions before [it] can entertain religious thoughts"* (1964a, p. 646). Consequently the very earliest religious training might be focused on emotional development. As noted earlier, basic trust, established in infancy, is a basis for religious feelings (Erikson, 1959).

Learning

Strictly speaking, any change in behavior or knowledge due to experience is learning. We shall deal here only with more specific skills, behaviors, associations, and knowledge that are considered to be taught and/or learned. Walter Clark referred to these behaviors when he said, "A great deal of what passes for religion among children is simply the repeating of phrases by rote or the performance of religious motions" (1958, p. 101). For either adult or child, a frequent initial step in acquiring religious identity is to practice some ritual, even without knowing what it means. Religious beliefs (and to some extent emotions) tend to follow from ritual behaviors that a person has been taught to perform.

Other learned elements of religiousness are not so deliberately taught. Tremmel tells that after being reared in the Roman Catholic Church, the Protestant worship services never "felt religious." After several years he thought to ask himself why the Catholic cathedral he was entering gave such an immediate sense of holiness:

> Immediately I knew why. It was the smell: the lingering odor of incense and burning candles. It smelled right! The thing wrong with a Methodist Church was that it did not smell religious [1976, p. 218].

Earlier psychological accounts of learning tended to be mechanistic, implying a passive learner. Habits or facts were added, like bricks in a building—except in cases in which one directly interfered with another. Most contemporary views of learning depict a more active and dynamic organism than did the classic associationism just described. Learning is a process of organization and reorganization of mental or cognitive units. Learning must have a neurophysiological basis (i.e., it involves changes in the nervous system circuits activated). The important thing to note is that any learning, unlike a simple reflexive response, is expressed through performance of an incredibly complex array of neural activities. Not even "simple learning" is really simple. Furthermore, each item of learning affects and is affected by other psychological processes—perception, emotions, drives, attitudes, etc.

Physical and Psychological Maturation

Religious development is not independent of physical and psychological maturing. The latter by no means guarantee the former, but religious growth must await some degree of maturity in the physical or psychological realm. Maturation depends in part on the advance of years, growth of nervous system tissues, and activation of certain endocrine glands and their hormones. To some extent, though, it requires appropriate experience, stimulation, and/or practice. A child cannot pray until it learns to speak; it cannot speak until it has had the stimulation of a language community (even if limited to parents and siblings); but that stimulation is effective only when certain neural connections are made in the brain and to the muscles involved in speech.

Freud stressed the role of one particular "psychosexual" stage in the development of morality. In the "phallic stage" between ages 4 and 6 children were said to form the Oedipus complex. They are attracted to the parent of the opposite sex and feel hostility or envy toward the like-sexed parent. For the young boy this is a particularly acute conflict, since he feels powerless before the strong father figure who is the object of his antipathy. The conflict is finally resolved by the boy identifying with his father and internalizing the father's prohibitions and values. Thus is born the "superego"—what Freud considered to be a reservoir of the conscience and the ego ideal or model self. Psychoanalysts do not all accept this exact pattern, but they do agree on some kind of identification with parents and adoption of their values. As Hoffman asked,

> Why should a person criticize and blame [one]self for not behaving in accord with the standards of another person even in that person's absence, unless [one] has somehow come to view [one's] own behavior from that person's perspective rather than its relevance to [one's] own impulse gratification? [1971, p. 217].

Another maturational stage crucial to religious faith is adolescence. The newly activated sexual hormones, changes in primary and secondary sexual characteristics, search for self-identity, rebellion against parental restrictions, and changing expectations from society (Knox, 1975) often lead to turmoil, from which a radically transformed religious faith or lack of faith may emerge. Chapter 7, on conversion, will discuss the importance of adolescence for religious wakening.

New Developmental Levels

The cliché that nothing succeeds like success is conspicuously true for religious and psychological development. At least according to a number of stage theorists of development (see Chapter 4), psychological growth occurs in a stepwise manner. Each successive stage is in effect a stepping stone to the next higher level. A new stage represents a new way of thinking and perceiving, and opens the door to new needs.

One implication of this perspective is that religious growth is neither willy-nilly nor haphazard, but progresses in a predictable direction. An experiment by Turiel (1966) illustrates this process. He had an adult attempt to persuade children to make moral judgments that had previously been identified as either more mature or less mature than the children's judgments. The children were more easily convinced of the more mature moral position, indicating a tendency to advance in moral thinking.

No existing theory of religious development integrates all of the above sources of growth. Any given theory draws from two or more of them, as Freud's idea about the formation of the superego combined psychophysiological stages explicitly with interpersonal relationships and at least implicitly with needs and emotions. We now turn to some of the principles by which these elements are typically combined in the process of religious growth and development.

PRINCIPLES OF GROWTH AND DEVELOPMENT

According to Jean Piaget's theory of cognitive development, persons faced with new experiences can do one of two things. First, they may apply an old mental or behavioral pattern (schema) to the new situation; Piaget called this process "assimilation." On the other hand, an old schema may be changed to deal with the new experience better; he called this process "accommodation." The most effective or adaptive cognitive development comes from a harmonious combination of assimilation and accommodation.

Piaget's two processes are akin to the earlier-cited tendencies toward stability and growth, respectively. We may conceive of all of the sources of growth discussed earlier as being reflected in cognitive patterns. There is a certain amount of security in maintaining the status quo, using *assimilation,* seeking stable states. Insofar as we find such security, we tend not to change, grow, or develop. Fortunately there are also impulses toward growth. Failure to deal with reality is itself a source of insecurity, and tends to force *accommodation,* change, and growth. We can scarcely avoid bumping into new experiences that our old schemata (plural of *schema*) just will not assimilate. It becomes as difficult to resist growth as to grow.

Growth As Integration

When we conceive of growth as accommodation or change in cognitive structures, it may be easier to see that it involves complex transformations—integration of new with the old. Religious growth is not like a tree laying down a new growth ring each year, or a nautilus adding successive chambers to its shell. It is more like the metamorphosis from a caterpillar to a butterfly, or like the change in the pattern of iron filings in a magnetic field when a new magnet is introduced into the field.

In order to maintain some equilibrium—to integrate new experiences or growth elements with the old schemata—a person may use any of a number of tactics. Some of these are efforts to avoid the effects of new experiences; others show more openness to change. The various processes outlined below, suggested by a variety of psychologies, include ego theory and attitude change theories.

These theories share the premise that people are motivated to be or to appear consistent. Wrightsman (1968, p. 193) said that these are "rational" motives; he implied that when people tolerate a sense of inconsistency, they are somehow accepting irrationality. On the other hand, Aronson (1972, p. 94) sees the tendency to maintain merely *apparent* consistency as irrational. Such consistency often can be achieved only by falsifying reality.

No matter how we view the processes that inhibit and promote change, religious development—indeed all psychological development—often follows a tortuous path. These processes may be used whenever a person is confronted with any source of potential religious growth.

Selective Inattention   People may deal with experiences that do not readily fit their existing schemata by simply not paying attention to them. The greater the conflict (incongruity) with what they already know or how they already operate, the more they tune it out. Morlan (1950) read sermons to classes of college students with typically "inquiring minds." A selection from *Great Sermons of the World* was characterized as "pious, but very nice humbug." Another was from John Stuart Mill's relatively shocking *The Idea of God in Nature.* Predictably, the students remembered much more of Mills. Further, when the "humbug" was read first in order, it turned the students off to the whole experience, so they remembered little of any of the readings.

Misperception and Distortion   The tendency toward assimilation and maintaining the status quo may also lead to distortion of the new material—being either perceived incorrectly or changed in memory. One study presented a number of logical and illogical syllogisms to college students, to be rated as right or wrong. Students who had been identified as proreligious made more mistakes in the direction favorable to religion than unfavorable. And the stronger their proreligious attitudes, the more proreligious and the fewer antireligious errors they made (Feather, 1964).

Devaluation and Rejection   Without actually distorting the content of an experience, there are myriad ways one can effectively exclude it from accommodation, integration, and internalization. Susan may reject an interpersonal relationship, perhaps questioning the other person's motives, rather than try a new path of spiritual exercise that might be shown her. Gary may discredit what another person would consider a profoundly religious mystical experience, attributing it instead to a "bad trip" from some impure drugs. Or Bonnie, an early adolescent, may deny her new sexual urges—because her religious teachings prohibit their expression—rather than work to discover their proper place in a spiritual life. As with the other processes that have been reviewed, rejection severely limits growth and development, and does so at some expense to the person's accepting and coping with reality.

Compartmentalization   The person who compartmentalizes accepts the new source of potential growth, but fails to integrate it with prior schemata. Suppose Bonnie were unable to suppress her sexual needs. She might have declared her religious faith off limits to her sex life. She would be able to experience sex, but by psychologically segregating or compartmentalizing it from her religion, she limits the possibility of development in both areas. The familiar stereotype of a Sunday morning Christian is a more pervasive example of this psychological process.

Bridging Cognitions   When two cognitions or beliefs are inconsistent, one way to reconcile them is to produce a new cognition that bridges the two, making them more compatible. Consider one of our students, Debbie, a bright college student and a committed Baptist. Most Baptist churches had clear teachings that women should be submissive to men and not try to assume traditional male roles. Religiously committed women of Debbie's background, then, tended strongly to reject principles of the women's liberation movement. Debbie, however, had inspected feminist ideals and found them desirable—yet without rejecting her Baptist faith. How did she reconcile the teachings of her church and her liberal attitudes toward women's roles? Probably by bridging them with a third cognition. Perhaps she told herself, "The Baptist faith also says that I have the privilege of interpreting the Bible for myself; I do not find it inconsistent with the liberation of modern women." Or maybe she reasoned, "The church is always twenty years behind any social movement; I'm just ahead of my times." Then she might have appropriated a saying like, "A foolish consistency is the hobgoblin of little minds," and thus agreed to live with the inconsistency.

   This last resolution has a more general application; some people are able to tolerate more inconsistency than others. This capacity may stem from their holding such general bridging cognitions as:

> I am a fallible human being.
> I don't have to be perfect or always consistent.
> Sometimes I fail to live up to my values or principles.
> I can make mistakes and be forgiven.
> I can continue testing what I should believe and do, to try my best to discover what is right or true—without having to rush into any premature decision.
> I can tolerate some ambiguity (inconsistency, uncertainty) [Aronson, 1972, pp. 138–139].

   Cognitions or schemata of this kind tend to promote optimum growth and adaptation—maintaining a balance between Piaget's assimilation and accommodation. Feather (1964) found that religious students who were high in tolerance for ambiguity made fewer errors in judging the logic of proreligious and antireligious syllogisms.

Reevaluating Old Systems   When a new experience conflicts with old systems, an integration can come partly through reexamination and reevaluation of the old systems. A youth who has been taught to accept the Genesis creation story as literally true will surely experience conflict when faced with the doctrine of evolution in biology classes. The scriptural account may be faced with some searching questions, for example: Who wrote the story? How did they know? What was their evidence? What was the purpose for writing the Book of Genesis? What was the world view of the people for whom the account was written? The religious account will not necessarily be rejected on the basis of such an examination, but it will probably be seen in a different and more mature light.

Seeking Confirming Experiences   Finally, persons faced with new sources of religious growth may seek new experiences that are likely to confirm the new direction, and convince them that they are right to abandon a previous way. New converts typically engage in a multitude of activities to confirm their decision—joining church groups, engaging in Bible studies, practicing meditation rituals, chanting, proselytizing, or whatever is expected by the new faith. This process surely leads to growth in the new religion. However, it may reflect a failure to evaluate the system objectively.

These processes of stability and growth are not necessarily exhaustive, just exhausting! Perhaps they adequately convey the complexities and roadblocks in the way of religious development.

Congruence Among Systems

Consistency tends to be maintained not only within a person's religious system. Other psychological and cognitive systems tend also to be consistent with one's religious faith and development. Persons who are self-centered in their relations with other people tend to have a self-serving religion. Those who have very conservative religious opinions tend to be political conservatives also (Kahoe, 1977b).

Religion and science have engaged in a long warfare. Some have seen the successive waves of Copernicus, Darwin, and Freud as gradually but irrevocably reducing the scope and influence of religion. Obviously no world view from any classical religion corresponds in detail to Isaac Asimov's (1972) latest "guide to science." Yet many scientists (albeit a minority) continue to hold to one or another religious faith. How are the scientific and religious systems made compatible?

Almost 40 years ago the well-known learning psychologist Ernest R. Hilgard (1944) gave a remarkably thorough answer to this question. We do not have space for his complete discussion, but we note the solution he considered the most promising. When religion and science deal with the same subject matter, Hilgard said, they select or abstract their data differently. Just as a human being can provide data for the studies of physics, physiology, biochemistry, psychology, sociology, and economics, so psychology and religion can say different things about a person, without reflecting on the validity of either. For example, social psychology attempts to form generalizations about human conduct that will assist in its understanding, prediction, and control. Religion attempts to understand the person "to regulate . . . conduct according to a theory of value sanctioned through a conception of the relation of the individual to the universe" (Hilgard, 1944, p. 291).

Hilgard's solution compartmentalizes religion and science somewhat, though by methodology and intent rather than by content. However, the process is rational and consistent with the logic of science. Still, some may object to even that degree of isolation of systems, either from a theological or a psychological viewpoint.

David Bakan (1966) poses a different solution. He sees both religion and science as attempts to search out the nature of humankind and the world in which we live. The *search,* rather than the answer, is most significant. Both religion and science become "idolatrous" when they exalt either their methods or their conclusions above the quest and its focus on the still unknown—the "unmanifest" (pp. 6–9). Both assume that "the fundamental reality is that which is beyond the manifest" (p. 9), and apart from idolatrous shortsightedness, they have no quarrel.

The Will to Grow

Some theories of development view growth as a relatively passive process—something that will come about with the passage of time and a minimum of attention. Against that implication the existentialist Kierkegaard asserted a more radical, transforming process of development in which "a person, through faith, encounters God and thereby is enabled to take the leap from one stage to another through an activated decision to grow. . . . [One] decides upon faith whether or not it is better . . . to grow or remain as [one] is!" (Oates, 1973, p. 86). Such a purposive view of people is not typical of contemporary psychology, but it does have articulate exponents (e.g., Rychlak, 1977).

Kierkegaard and other theologically oriented writers assert that religious growth is not solely a human function. It also involves the intentions and interventions of the deity. Such a proposition is beyond the scope of psychology as a science, and from that perspective can be neither denied nor affirmed.

As you reflect on the principles of integration illustrated above, you should realize that they are essentially ways in which persons can resist growth, accommodate growth, or encourage growth in their religious systems.

AN EXAMPLE: PIAGET'S MORAL JUDGMENTS OF CHILDREN

Some of the principles of religious development may be illustrated by Jean Piaget's theory of moral judgment (Flavell, 1963). Piaget's theory competes only with psychoanalytic theory as the most influential perspective on the development of morality in children. It has stimulated more detailed research and theories that will be reviewed in Chapter 4.

After developing his theory of mental development in children, Piaget extended his methods to the realm of moral reasoning. In a series of studies he interviewed children, as much in their natural environments as possible. He asked questions about the rules of the games of marbles they played—where the rules came from, if they could be changed, etc. He told stories that posed moral dilemmas, and asked what the main character should do, and why. He asked questions of culpability, for example, whether a child was "naughtier" who broke 15 cups by accident, or who broke one cup while engaged in misbehavior. Similar problems and questions about punishment and justice were posed.

In general Piaget found greater individual differences and more age overlap in the area of moral judgments than in cognitive abilities. Yet he cautiously suggested at least two stages of morality.

Initially children show a "morality of constraint"—operating in the setting of a dominant adult and an inferior child. Children take the adult rules, prohibitions, punishments, and rewards as moral absolutes, accepting the letter rather than the spirit of the law. Acts are seen in terms of their consequences rather than their motivations; that is, the child who accidentally broke the 15 cups was worse than the offender who broke one. The schemata in this stage are imposed by adults onto children, who seem to accept them but flagrantly simplify and distort them.

Later, having advanced to higher levels of cognitive skill, children develop a "morality of cooperation." This morality develops not from unilateral relations with adults but from mutual relationships with peers—in the give and take of play, sharing, and discussion. It emphasizes the motives of one's own and others' behavior, and the social implications of misbehavior. Moral behavior is preferred because of its positive effects on the social unit, rather than because of personal reward or punishment.

From his theories Piaget arrived at the opinion that children should not primarily be taught in an adult-to-child fashion. Rather, group projects should focus on intellectual or moral tasks that require peer interaction, exchange of ideas, and dealing with problems relevant to their normal environment. Further implications of Piaget's theory and other perspectives on religious training will be drawn in Chapter 6. Ideally a theory-based religious education would provide continuous feedback and improve our understanding of the principles of religious growth.

REVIEW OF KEY CONCEPTS

Introduction
 tendencies toward growth and stability

Sources of Growth
 growth impelled by experiences—parental care, stories, images, interpersonal contacts, crises, mystical experiences
 drives toward growth—deficit needs, curiosity drives, self-actualization, "effectance"
 role of social relationships—family and other—in growth
 emotions and growth—early influences
 basic trust

elementary processes of learning
dynamic nature of learning
Freud's theory of moral development by identification
psychological and physical maturation
directionality to growth

Principles of Growth and Development
assimilation and accommodation
Piaget's schemata
motivation to appear consistent—rational or irrational
selective inattention and misperception
compartmentalization and devaluation
bridging cognitions
toleration of ambiguity
reevaluation and confirmation of cognitions
congruence of science and religion: Bakan's and Hilgard's solutions
Kierkegaard's notion of the will to grow

An Example: Piaget's Moral Judgments of Children
methods: moral dilemmas and culpability
morality of constraint versus morality of cooperation
Piaget's prescription for moral education

chapter 4

Stage Models of Development

Across the life span development occurs: physical, emotional, cognitive, and spiritual. Some theorists, seeing common patterns in human growth, have composed models to describe developmental sequences. This chapter presents some developmental models relevant to religion and also some others specifically concerned with aspects of religious development.

MAJOR TYPES OF STAGE DEVELOPMENTAL MODELS

Psychological developmental models fall into two basic types with different assumptions: developmental crises models and structural developmental models.

Developmental Crises Models

Developmental crises models are simpler than structural models. In a crises model, stages are defined by events related to the person's chronological age and social environment. As a person matures, changes that take place in the body—such as puberty—require adaptation. People also are socialized as they develop. A child must learn when and where to relieve certain bodily tensions—as in toilet training—and how to express certain feelings and motives—learning "manners." At times, the culture places certain expectations or tasks upon the individual. Children must acquire an education; later, people are expected to mate, have children, and engage in productive work.

In developmental crises models, all these events push one through the stages and require different kinds of adjustment. Regardless of how a particular stage is or is not handled, changing circumstances will force one into the next stage. Individuals thus have differing readiness to manage each stage as they enter it.

Structural Developmental Models

Assumptions The structural developmental models, while more complex, are still age-related, but assume a much less direct relationship between age and developmental stage. Stages are defined by the appearance of particular psychological characteristics that describe each stage. A person cannot move to a higher stage until the preceding one has been satisfactorily managed. Each stage builds on the preceding stages, and lays the foundations for later stages. Thus the stages must occur in a fixed order. No stages can be skipped, although some may be passed through more quickly than others. Everyone follows the same sequence of development, but different people develop at different rates of speed.

As the stages imply a change in the psychological structures that underlie behavior, they are qualitatively—rather than quantitatively—different. Some traits—such as uncontrolled impulsivity—disappear as one develops, and others—such as cognitive complexity—appear. One may not have more or less of such characteristics as intelligence at different stages, but will show it in different ways with different strategies. The overall result is that qualitatively different functioning occurs in the different stages. Not all people reach the higher stages. Since each stage will be the last that some people attain, people can be typed according to the level they have achieved.

Piaget's Model of Cognitive Development Piaget's (1929) model of cognitive development illustrates the structural stage model. Since organizing thinking is a major human behavior, many theorists consider cognitive development very important for other kinds of development. Piaget defines four major stages based on the processes that underlie cognition. It is important to understand that he is not talking about the content of cognition—what one is thinking about—but rather the way one goes about thinking. Of course, certain kinds of cognitive content are impossible without certain capabilities.

The first stage—*sensorimotor*—roughly spans birth to 2 years of age, and begins with mere reflex activities. It develops into trial-and-error behavior for problem solving, and some thinking that leads the infant to conclude that certain results follow certain actions. The *preoperational* stage begins as early as 18 months and lasts until about 7 years of age. The child has acquired language, but magical and egocentric thinking still occur. For example, a child may conclude that it is night because she or he is sent to bed. Thinking and problem solving are not yet logical.

From about 7 to 11 years of age children are in the *concrete operational* stage. Logical problem solving occurs; the child analyzes relationships and tries to understand events. Abstract verbal concepts are not comprehended, but the child can manipulate concrete verbal symbols and classify objects by similarities of function and appearance. The capacity for *formal operations* develops from about age 11 to 15. One learns to view issues from different vantage points, and to solve problems by mental manipulations. Facts and events are mentally organized to produce logical solutions to complex problems.

PSYCHOLOGICAL GROWTH MODELS RELEVANT TO RELIGION

Some developmental models are highly relevant to religious growth. We shall consider one crises and one structural model in this context.

Erikson's Psychosocial Stages Model

In his developmental crises model, Erikson (1963, 1968) identified stages of psychosocial development that cover the entire life span. The stages are organized around different interests or concerns that maturation or social pressures arouse in the individual. Each stage has its own "task" that requires new ways of interacting with others and managing new motives and drives.

Each new capability prompts a crisis to be resolved. Different abilities dominate different periods of life, and each has a critical period when its failure to develop most harms the personality. However, since each succeeding stage sums up in some way the previous ones, earlier problems may return and be resolved. Issues for later stages can also be anticipated. Box 4.1 lists Erikson's stages with their related maturation periods, conflicts/problems to be solved, social organization principles, and strengths (virtues) to be developed. We also include the ways Aden (1976) relates each stage to religious faith. We shall discuss some implications of each stage for religious development.

Trust or Mistrust An intense emotional conditioning toward life occurs when irrational feelings dominate the infant. If the outer world shows sufficient predictability and concern for the infant's well-being, a basic trust in life is established. The amount of trust acquired depends on the quality of care given—not the quantity. Satisfactory care allows the baby to trust its own feelings and to see the universe as kind. Problems that occur here lay the basis for severe emotional disturbances later in life.

Erikson considered basic trust necessary for the religious ethos. Trust makes possible surrender to Providence and the experience of reverence. Religion is a sign of trustworthiness in the community that enables one to develop hope and drive. Even with the best of infant care, however, some feelings of abandonment or "paradise lost" are likely to occur. Religious rituals deal with separation and abandonment concerns (Erikson, 1977), and sometimes they degenerate into

Box 4.1 ERIKSON'S PSYCHOSOCIAL STAGES

Stage	Maturation level	Task or conflict	Social principle	Strength or virtue	Faith (Aden)
Trust or mistrust	Oral-sensory	Trust own perceptions and others' goodness	Religious ethos	Hope and drive	Trust
Autonomy or shame/doubt	Anal-muscular	Gain impulse control	Law and order	Willpower, control	Courage
Initiative or guilt	Genital-motor	Self-guidance and self-punishment	Economic ethos	Purpose, direction	Obedience
Industry or inferiority	Latency	Acquire rudiments of technology	Technological ethos	Skill, method	Assent
Identity or role confusion	Adolescence, youth	Integrate all one's personal identifications into one	Ideology	Devotion, fidelity	Identity
Intimacy or isolation	Young adulthood	Make commitments, accept obligations	Ethical sense	Love and bonding	Self-surrender
Generativity or stagnation	Middle adulthood	Become teacher and guide of next generation	Arts and sciences	Care and production	Unconditional caring
Integrity or despair	Late adulthood	Acquire post-narcissistic love of the human ego	Leadership integration	Wisdom and renunciation	Unconditional acceptance

Source: Compiled from Aden (1976); Erikson (1963, 1968, 1977).

magical attempts to manipulate the object of devotion. Freud said that communion services in which one "swallows" one's God are attempts to feel united with a source of security.

Autonomy or Shame and Doubt   As muscular capacities develop, a child becomes active in the world and encounters environmental demands. One of the earliest is toilet training. So the child can learn self-control without losing self-esteem, autonomy must grow at a rate with which the child can cope. Self-control problems that are too difficult cause shame and doubt. Shaming makes a child feel small, completely exposed, and looked at; this leads to self-consciousness. Doubt occurs when the child is unsure of his or her ability to handle self and feels that things are out of control.

An appreciation of law and order, rights and obligations, privileges and limitations must be established in this stage. Some religious rituals deal with issues of approval and disapproval. Although practices such as religious confession can be helpful, they may also be wrongly used to seek continual approval and assurance of being "in grace."

Initiative or Guilt   With children's increasing locomotor skills, competition and rivalry begin. Others interpret their behavior in terms of personal responsibility. Self-punishment, self-guidance, guilt, and conscience become possible. Children at this stage may resent their parents' allowing themselves behavior about which they have taught the child to feel guilty.

Sometimes behaviors that show enjoyment of new motor and mental powers are interpreted to children as bad conduct. This may crush initiative and leave a child feeling that all enjoyment of oneself is evil. When children are overcontrolled, too many activities become guilt-tinged—yet children must learn that some behavior is not permitted. Religious rituals may shape a child's self-image and suggest behaviors to imitate (Erikson, 1977).

Industry or Inferiority   All societies demand education in the culture's technology. Young people learn to win recognition by producing things. An active adjustment to the laws of impersonal things—to the life of tools and work—must be made. If one's own skills seem inadequate, feelings of inadequacy or inferiority may lead to discouragement about developing skills and to becoming a dropout from society.

Religious ideas of stewardship and the accomplishment of God's will are relevant to the tasks of this stage. So are notions of differing religious gifts and tasks. One might view oneself as a "tool" to accomplish particular goals of God. Ritual related to this stage involves cooperation in producing the ritual forms (Erikson, 1977).

Identity or Role Confusion   The period of identity or role confusion, roughly spanning puberty until the end of formal education, begins with one's sense of sameness challenged by changes in one's body. Typically adolescents become very sensitive to how they are seen by others and gather in groups of similar people who can define themselves by each other. By seeing oneself reflected in another, self-concept is clarified. Having others react to one in a consistent way helps one establish a solid sense of who one is. Some people make a premature commitment to a friend, leader, sexual partner, or career in order to solve identity problems.

Young people who are unsure of themselves may be very susceptible to simple—even cruel—totalitarian doctrines. Some use intense commitment to poorly understood religious ideas to solve identity problems. Many cults encourage childlike and unthinking devotion to strong authorities to give one identity. The practice in established religions of initiating young people into religious adulthood (baptism, confirmation, bat or bar mitzvah) at puberty is questionable on developmental grounds. One cannot make a solid commitment of oneself until identity is firmly established. Such practices might abort development of identity as any other premature commitment would.

Intimacy or Isolation Young adulthood is the time to make commitments. Undoubtedly many people enter this time of life poorly equipped for it. There is risk in trying to bind one's identity to a commitment before one is sure of it. Estrangement or inadequate relationships are dangers during this stage. Making commitments to other persons, ideologies, vocations, and ways of life requires that one "develop the ethical strength to abide by such commitments, even though they may call for significant sacrifices and compromises" (Erikson, 1963, p. 263). In "faith as self-surrender . . . the individual . . . turns toward and becomes committed to God as the final source of life and meaning" (Aden, 1976, p. 227).

Generativity or Stagnation Erikson (1974) distinguished this stage from the preceding two:

> In youth you find out what you *care to do* and who you *care to be*—even in changing roles. In young adulthood you learn whom you *care to be with*—at work and in private life, not only exchanging intimacies, but sharing intimacy. In adulthood, however, you learn to know what and whom you can *take care of* [p. 124]. [Emphasis in the original.]

One's commitments typically bear fruit: children, products, artistic or scholarly work. In generativity one becomes a "founder" who guides and establishes those fruits. An individual who does not acquire this attitude will regress into excessive self-preoccupation and self-indulgence.

Generative behavior sounds like what many religions encourage people to develop over the entire life span. Sometimes a zeal for overcoming self-centeredness may be instilled before one has established an appreciation of his or her individuality and personal worth. Trying to love one's neighbor without loving oneself is a very difficult undertaking!

Integrity or Despair As one ages, personal integrity should become the mainstay of life and provide a serene confidence in life's basic goodness and meaning. Erikson (1963) said that you can recognize integrated people; their children are not afraid to live because they are not afraid to die. This entire stage appears to be a religious task. Indeed, religion usually advocates the pursuit of integrity throughout all of life. Religion may protect people from denial, despair, or psychosis by helping them live with an integrity that sustains trust. Those who do not achieve integrity despair as they sense time running out—loathing life, fearing death, and lamenting things both done and not done. The integrated person completes the trust task begun in infancy.

Loevinger's Model of Ego Development

Loevinger (1976) describes four distinct areas of human development: physical, intellectual, psychosexual or psychosocial, and ego. We have looked at Piaget's ideas about intellectual development and Erikson's psychosocial stages. Loevinger's (1966, 1976) ego model is a structural developmental one. Although ego development is related to age, individuals develop at different rates and reach different levels. Loevinger believes that for most people one of the middle stages in her model will be their highest. Occasionally growth begins again—even late in life—and an individual may progress further.

Ego development includes four major components: impulse control or moral style, interpersonal style, conscious preoccupations, and cognitive style. Most religions consider impulse control an integral part of their code and also urge the development of principled interpersonal relations. People's conscious preoccupations indicate what is of deepest importance to them. Regarding cognitive style, Eastern religions—more than Western ones—value ambiguity, a sense of paradox, and cognitive uncertainty. Box 4.2 highlights the model's major features at different levels of ego development.

Impulsive Stage   At the impulsive stage, one affirms one's existence by exercising self-will. Rules are not accepted; an action is considered bad only if it is punished. Temper tantrums indicate the exploitive nature of interpersonal relationships. Other people are seen as sources of supply, and judged according to how much they give. Such behavior, expected in a young child, is immature in an older child or adult. Adults fixated at this level may use "running away" to solve problems. They consider trouble to be in places rather than situations. For example, one might say, "I don't have a drinking problem; the problem is that I have to pass a bar on the way home." Impulsive people see responsibilities as burdens and make many self-centered demands.

Self-protective Stage   People at the self-protective stage have an expedient morality and observe rules only to gain advantage. The chief rule is: "Don't get caught." A simple hedonism governs their lives: Avoid work, look for fun, get plenty of nice things like money. Life is a zero-sum game: Whatever you win, I lose. Such people inadequately understand life's complexities and see themselves as pawns of fate. They try hard to deny vulnerability, but want to retaliate for hurts suffered. They divide the world into "people you control" and "those who control you." Humor is often hostile, and gross prejudices and stereotyped pic-

Box 4.2 LOEVINGER'S EGO DEVELOPMENT STAGES

Stage	Impulse control, "moral" style	Interpersonal style	Conscious preoccupations	Cognitive style
Symbiotic		Symbiotic	Self versus nonself	
Impulsive	Fear of punishment, impulsive	Exploitive, dependent, receiving	Bodily feelings, sex, aggression	Conceptual confusion, stereotypes
Self-protective	Externalizing blame, opportunistic	Manipulative, wary	Advantage, wishes, things, self-protection	Same as Impulsive
Conformist	Shame, guilt, obedience	Belonging, superficial niceness	Appearances, social acceptability	Conceptual simplicity, clichés
Self-aware	Realizing contingencies and different standards	Being helpful, importance of relationships	Self as separate, psychological causation	Awareness of individual differences
Conscientious	Self-evaluated standards, self-criticism	Intensive, responsible, mutual	Self-respect, achievement, motives, traits	Conceptual complexity, patterning
Individualistic	Coping with inner conflict	Cherishing of interpersonal relationships	Communicating, process and change	Toleration for paradox and contradiction
Autonomous	Coping with conflicting needs/duties	(Above)[a] and respect for autonomy	Self-fulfillment, role conception	Objectivity, toleration for ambiguity
Integrated	Reconciling inner conflict, renouncing the unattainable	(Above)[a] and cherishing individuality	(Above)[a] and identity	(Above)[a]

[a](above) means those characteristics listed in the immediately preceding stage.
Source: Adapted from Loevinger (1976, pp. 24–25). Used with permission.

tures of others are held. Naturally, religions disapprove of both this and the preceding impulsive adjustment.

Conformist Stage   Conformists identify with authority and obey the rules simply because they are the rules. They value "niceness," and disapproval is a potent sanction with them. Adults at this stage—appropriate for a school-age child—are conceptually simple. They are moralistic and have very simplistic formulas for what should and should not be—with no exceptions. They judge behavior by rigidly absolute standards of right and wrong, and strongly disapprove of deviance from conventional gender and social roles. They deny inner conflicts and frown on in-group hostility. Conformists often greatly sentimentalize people, relationships, and things. Many people stop development at this level (Loevinger, 1976).
    Conventional religion may foster conformist adjustment. Its emphasis on love of others and its discouragement of recognizing negative feelings mask discordant aspects of oneself. Rule morality and intolerance of religious doubt reinforce conformity, and may lead to hostility toward "heretics" or those with differing moral opinions. Conformity, however, *is* an accomplishment and requires the ability to identify personal welfare with that of a group.

Self-aware Level   Loevinger (1976) considers the self-aware level a transition time common to high school or college students moving out of conformity. It is the most common terminal level of development. Forced recognition that one does not always meet stereotyped social norms encourages self-awareness. With such heightened self-consciousness, the group's absolute guidelines for conduct and self-definition cease to work. One becomes aware of multiple possibilities in situations, recognizes exceptions to rules, and starts to evaluate conduct according to context. Capacity for self-criticism and understanding of psychological causation develop. Encounter or sensitivity groups, which encourage expressing feelings and trying out nonconformist behaviors, attract self-aware people. Highly conservative religions may see such development as a threat.

Conscientious Stage   In those who develop this far, early adulthood is the modal age for becoming conscientious. Very few people reach it earlier. Its internalized morality is defined more by motives and consequences than by rules. One feels real guilt over failure to keep self-chosen and personally defined ideals. Interpersonal relationships are understood in terms of feelings rather than actions; friendship is based on shared values rather than shared social activities. Conscientious people are highly critical of themselves, and may also try to impose their ideals on others—not for the sake of conformity, but because they see true value in them.

Individualistic Level   This transition period is marked by a greater awareness of individuality and concerns about dependence. Tolerance for both oneself and others increases. As conscientious striving for achievement and excessive "moralistic" responsibility for others lessen, interpersonal relationships become more intensive. Awareness of inner conflict increases. Preoccupations include personal development (as opposed to simple achievement) and social problems. Individualistic people think naturally in terms of psychological causation, and distinguish between processes and outcomes.

Autonomous Stage   At the autonomous stage impulse control ceases to be a problem, and moral concern focuses on priorities and appropriateness. One acknowledges and copes well with inner conflict. The autonomous person sees reality as a complex whole and holds broad, abstract social ideals. A greatly increased respect for individuality and a high degree of tolerance for others develop. Freedom from excessive conscience demands makes it easier to allow others to choose their own paths and make their own mistakes. The autonomous person cherishes personal ties and tries to understand self in the social context. The autonomous can unite and integrate apparently incompatible ideas and alternatives.

Integrated Stage   The integrated stage represents the crown of Loevinger's (1976) developmental process. Such development—which goes beyond coping to a full maturity—is extremely rare. Loevinger sees similarities between this stage and Erikson's idea of integrity.

MODELS OF ASPECTS OF RELIGIOUS DEVELOPMENT

Some models of development are more clearly related to religious concerns. Four are presented here.

Hindu Life Stages

A very simple life stage model, similar to Erikson's, comes from the Hindu Code of Manu (VI. 87–8). The ideal life has four stages: student, householder, forest-dweller, and renunciate.

Student   The student's time is spent developing skills needed for one's later life work. Emotional and spiritual disciplines build character and mature personality.

Householder   In this active participation in life, one marries, raises children, and serves the community as a responsible citizen. Disciplined enjoyment of pleasures is allowed.

Forest-Dweller   When children are old enough to take over family responsibilities, one gradually retires from such affairs. Life is increasingly given over to religious practices and spiritual development.

Renunciate   Entry into the renunciate stage is often marked by a funeral-like ritual. One becomes dead to all obligations and relationships to pursue spiritual truths without distraction.

Kohlberg and Moral Development

Morality is an integral part of most religions. Kohlberg (1969, 1976) described six stages (three levels of two stages each) of moral development in a structural developmental model based on Piaget (1932, 1970). "Stages, as cognitive, are largely defined by competence, not by performance. A capacity for judging in terms of moral principles is not always translated into morally principled behavior" (Kohlberg, 1977, p. 189). Kohlberg's stages are determined by the *process* by which one arrives at moral solutions—not by the *content* of that solution. It is *how*—not *what*—one decides that determines the level of moral judgment. We shall illustrate the stages with the moral dilemma of a woman deciding about abortion.

Premoral (Preconventional) Level   Initially ideas of good and bad behavior are developed according to the consequences one incurs, rather than by standards. This agrees with Loevinger's (1976) understanding.

In the *punishment-and-obedience* orientation, avoiding bad outcomes is the major motivator. One obeys rules or a superior power to keep out of trouble. A woman at this level may choose abortion to keep from angering her husband by the pregnancy, or to avoid the discomfort of bearing a child. She may choose against abortion for fear of "burning in hell" or of rejection by others who disapprove of abortion.

At the second stage—*instrumental-relativist*—one defines right action as that which satisfies one's own needs and those of others who might reciprocate. Choices are pragmatic. Our woman might choose abortion to get a favor from her husband or to free herself for more enjoyable activities. She may choose against abortion because she expects God or her husband to reward her for bearing a child.

Conventional Level   At the conventional level one seeks to maintain the expectations of others or society regardless of the consequences. Here people typically follow traditional moral imperatives defined by religion or society.

Persons in the *good boy/nice girl* orientation seek to please or to be approved of by others. They may conform to stereotyped ideas of what is good or right, or to what someone else wants; the behavior of many in the Watergate scandal reflects Stage 3 reasoning. Our woman might choose abortion because it is "expected" in her circumstances or simply to please her husband. Her decision against it would similarly be based on external considerations—such as "pleasing" God by being a "good girl."

Maintaining social order is important to one in the *law-and-order* orientation. Right behavior requires respect for the rules and for duly constituted authority such as church or state—the mentality of Nazis or others who surrender personal moral responsibility to authority. It is unlikely that a woman at this level would choose abortion, but she may do so because her husband commands it and she accepts his authority. The woman might reject abortion because it is against the moral guidelines of her church.

Principled (Postconventional) Level The principled person goes beyond simplistic application of an authority's guidelines. Personally derived and/or chosen principles govern choices.

The *social contract* orientation emphasizes mutually agreed upon obligations and privileges. These may be implicit or explicit contracts between individual and society, or agreements between persons—so long as they do not violate others' rights. One recognizes that personal values are relative. Decisions regarding abortion could become very complex. The woman might choose abortion because a baby would make it difficult to fill prior commitments to her husband and children. She may reject abortion because she holds that, by engaging in intercourse, she makes an implicit contract with any consequent conception that she will nurture its growth into human life.

Kohlberg's *universal ethical principles* orientation is highly controversial. Its principles are very abstract, and data on it come almost exclusively from people with considerable training in moral philosophy. None of Kohlberg's (1977) longitudinally studied subjects reached this stage. (See also Chapter 5.) This stage consists of adopting abstract principles—*not rules,* as in previous stages—that one believes are highly consistent and universal. They usually reflect justice, equality, and respect for individual persons.

An Additional Consideration Kohlberg (1973) hypothesized that a seventh stage might exist, although he has not developed this idea. He says that persons "from Socrates to Martin Luther King, who lived and died for their ethical principles, have something like a strong Stage 7 orientation" (Kohlberg, 1973, p. 204). This hypothetical stage—concerned with answering the question "Why live?" and with seeing oneself as part of a cosmic process—is likely to have a religious base. However, Stage 7 must transcend the conventional morality of most religious people and be clearly postconventional. Conventionally religious people might easily but incorrectly see their (likely) Stage 4 reasoning as representing Stage 7.

Fowler's Structural Developmental Model of Faith

Fowler's (1975, 1976, 1977, 1981; Fowler & Keen, 1978) six-stage model of faith development incorporates features of Piaget's, Erikson's, and Kohlberg's thought. Some major aspects of the model are outlined in Box 4.3. This model is not concerned with the *content* of faith or *what* one believes. Its focus is on processes and structures, "a person's way of seeing him- or herself in relation to others against a background of shared meaning and purpose" (Fowler, 1981, p. 4). Thus the *how*—not the *what*—of faith is important. People's commitments to a particular faith or world view may be held in very different ways.

Intuitive-Projective Faith The stage of intuitive-projective faith—appropriate to the preschool child—is a fantasy-filled time for imitation of others. The religious feelings and practices of significant adults can permanently and powerfully influence the child. Thinking is egocentric, and fact and fantasy are poorly distinguished.

Box 4.3 FOWLER'S STRUCTURAL DEVELOPMENTAL FAITH STAGES

Stage	Perspective taking	Locus of authority	Social awareness	Role of symbols
Intuitive-projective	Rudimentary empathy	External power and visible authority	Family, primal others	Magical-numinous
Mythic-literal	Simple perspective taking	Authority roles and trusted persons	"Those like us" in many ways	One-dimensional and literal
Synthetic-conventional	Mutual role taking, third-person view	Tradition, valued group and persons	Conformity to class norms	Multidimensional and conventional
Individuative-reflexive	Mutual with self-selected others	Group or leaders of chosen commitment	Self-aware adherence to chosen ideas	Critical translation into ideation
Paradoxical-consolidative	Mutual with others outside of chosen group	Dialectic of chosen norms with others	Transcendence of class interests	Postcritical rejoining of symbol and idea
Universalizing	Mutual, with commonwealth of Being	Purified judgment, attentive to Being	Identification with the species	Unification of reality mediated by symbols

Source: Adapted from Fowler (1981, pp. 244-245); Fowler & Keen (1978).

Mythic-Literal Faith Children usually reach the mythic-literal level by 7 or 8 years of age. One starts to differentiate religious claims from fantasy, and adopts the stories, beliefs, and observances of one's religious community. Beliefs and moral rules are held literally and concretely. Authorities are asked for answers to any conflicts. Deity images are anthropomorphic. Some adults remain at this stage.

Synthetic-Conventional Faith By age 12 or 13 one's experience of the world commonly has been greatly extended. Faith must meaningfully and coherently integrate all one's involvements. One accomplishes this by accepting the consensus of "meaningful others" in one's environment, by choosing authorities. Typically, differing opinions are resolved by establishing a hierarchy of such authorities; for example, believe first the church, then teachers, then parents, etc. This is the faith mode of many people who adhere to institutional authority.

Individuating-Reflexive Faith Capacity for the individuating-reflexive faith style ideally emerges at college age or young adulthood, though upheaval in later life may also result in it. It brings assumption of responsibility for managing one's own choices and commitments. The breakdown of the previous stage often pushes people to ideas outside their understanding of conventional religion. An inspiring leader or an appealing idea may bring conversion to a chosen faith. Certain universal tensions that synthetic-conventional faith can avoid arise: subjectivity versus objectivity, feeling versus thinking, autonomy versus heteronomy, particular versus universal, individual versus community, self-fulfillment versus service to others, and the relative versus the absolute. People often resolve such tension by choosing one value wholeheartedly and excluding the other; for example, giving oneself over completely to service of others and neglecting the demands of self-fulfillment.

Paradoxical-Consolidative Faith One is unlikely to reach the complex stance of paradoxical-consolidative faith before midlife. At this stage, people acknowledge validity and truth in faiths other than their own—maintaining their own commitments while recognizing their relativity. This often involves reviving the tensions settled in the previous stage, and learning how to live with them. Such people are fully aware of and willing to pay the cost of identifying themselves beyond the narrow limits of their own community. However, the discomfort of living "between an untransformed world and a transforming vision" (Fowler, 1981, p. 198) may paralyze a person's action or lead to cynical withdrawal.

Universalizing Faith The very rare universalizing faith stage implies well-developed religious genius. Universalizers "may offend our parochial perceptions. . . . They threaten our measured standards of righteousness and goodness and prudence. . . . [They] frequently become martyrs for the visions they incarnate. . . . They have become . . . actualizers of the spirit of an inclusive and fulfilled human community" (Fowler, 1981, p. 200).

Yogic Chakra Psychology

The word *chakra* means wheel, and the chakras are spinning centers of spiritual energy. These are constructs (explanatory ideas) rather than actual material entities, of course. However, there is a striking correspondence between physical chakra points defined by yogis thousands of years ago and some major nerve plexes identified by contemporary physiology (Brena, 1973). One can define an individual's level of spiritual development by the chakra where his or her spiritual energy is concentrated. Progress through the chakras occurs as in structural models from Western psychology. Box 4.4 shows some major features of each chakra.

Root Chakra *(Mūlādhāra)*   The root chakra is at the base of the spine. It is related to the struggle for survival—with its associated fears, paranoia, concerns for health and the body, and preoccupation with safety (Goleman, 1977). A materialistic world view governs, and an inclination to guard and hoard discourages growth and enthusiasm (Campbell, 1974). Energy is unconscious and under the control of primitive instincts (Rama, Ballentine, & Ajaya, 1976). With mastery of this energy, one attains freedom from sin by learning to avoid intentional repetition of known mistakes (Radha, 1978).

Genital Chakra *(Svādhisthāna)*   This center, located opposite the root of the genitals, embodies sexuality and sensuality (Goleman, 1977). The pleasure principle governs life at this level, which is symbolically associated with orgies and fertility rites (Campbell, 1974). Its tasks involve controlling sensual urges (Chaudhuri, 1975) and dealing with the instinct to pleasure. Mastery of this chakra's energies leads to freedom from enemies—that is, from one's passions (Woodroffe, 1973).

Navel Chakra *(Manipūra)*   The navel chakra, associated with the adrenal glands, which produce emotional arousal, is located at the solar plexus (navel), center of digestion (Rama et al., 1976). (In spite of lore to the contrary, yogis do not actually gaze at their navels. They may meditate on this chakra for control of its energies, but *only* under a teacher's direction.) Energy focuses on turning the world to one's own aims, and is associated with such symbols as holy wars and human sacrifice (Campbell, 1974). Foremost is the urge to be powerful and influence others, using persuasion and manipulation for one's own interests (Goleman, 1977). Competition, money, mastery, prestige, and the outward signs of success are important goals. One may become enchanted with power and grandeur (Chaudhuri, 1975). Those controlling this energy are promised the highest wealth: recognition that worldly attainment does not bring real happiness (Gnaneswarananda, 1975). One learns to create happiness by rejecting strivings that destroy harmonious relationships (Radha, 1978).

Heart Chakra *(Anāhata)*   The heart chakra, located near the cardiac nerve plexus, is below the breast bone where the ribs meet. It bridges the three lower (ani-

Box 4.4 CHARACTERISTICS OF YOGIC CHAKRAS

Chakra	Element	Symbol	Active power	Cognitive sense	Gland	Offering on alter
Root	Earth	Square	Locomotion	Smell		Fruit
Genital	Water	Crescent	Prehension	Taste	Gonads	Water
Navel	Fire	Triangle	Elimination	Sight	Adrenals	Flame
Heart	Air	Hexagon	Procreation	Touch	Thymus	Incense
Throat	"Space"	Circle	Speech	Hearing	Thyroid	Flower
Eyebrow	Mind	Point			Pituitary	Mind
Crown						God

Source: Compiled from multiple yogic resources.

mal) and three upper (divine) chakras. One learns to acquire selfless love and caring for others that combine clear-sighted detachment with compassion (Goleman, 1977). Powers resulting from mastering this chakra must be understood symbolically. The ability to enter another's body at will can be seen as capacity for deep understanding and empathy. The ability to protect and destroy worlds refers to transcending the past, transforming the present, and creating with generative love the world of the future (Radha, 1978). To render oneself invisible can mean overcoming self-seeking in one's activities.

Throat Chakra *(Visúddha)*   The throat chakra, in the notch in the collarbone, is located where nurturance is taken in, and has to do with being receptive and acquiring trust (Rama et al., 1976). Yoga thus considers learning to receive love properly more advanced than giving love. Tasks include realizing one's own unique intrinsic value (Chaudhuri, 1975) and the clearing of consciousness of secondary things, to experience divinity fully (Campbell, 1974). The rewards of mastery include final freedom from worldly desires. One now is able to destroy dangers "by increased awareness, greater discrimination, and more care in all actions and reactions, no longer mechanically responding to events" (Radha, 1978, pp. 312–3). Knowledge of the past, present, and future implies an understanding of how one should behave, and attainment of knowledge brings one closer to a life that reflects goodness, beauty, and truth.

Eyebrow Chakra *(Ājnā)*   The eyebrow chakra, located between the eyes, is the "third eye" of cosmic consciousness. If offers perfect control over the personality (Chaudhuri, 1975). Intuition begins operating and is "a stable, reliable function of the higher levels of consciousness and awareness from which a wider range of information is accessible. . . . Intellect and emotion flow together and become integrated, permitting a new kind of knowing" (Rama et al., 1976, p. 265). With this, one achieves union with the divine and operates free of all selfish desires (Radha, 1978).

Crown Chakra *(Sahasrāra)*   The crown chakra, located at the "soft spot" on an infant's head, stands for identification with the divine. Even Western religious practices seem to take this concept seriously. Tonsuring (making a bald spot) Christian monks, the Jewish skullcap, and religious art showing a halo or a burst of light from this area all indicate its respect in diverse religious traditions.

SOME FINAL CONSIDERATIONS

Interpretative Cautions

Validity   Most of these models were developed as tools for understanding observed behavior. They differ in the amount of scientific validating research done on them. Research is especially needed on structural models, which posit real—and potentially verifiable— changes in psychological processes underlying observable behavior.

Box 4.5 TABLE OF MODEL CORRESPONDENCES

Erikson	Loevinger	Kohlberg	Fowler	Yogic chakra	Hindu life stage
Trust or mistrust	Symbiotic		Undifferentiated		
Autonomy or shame/doubt	Impulsive	Punishment and obedience	Intuitive-projective	Root	
Initiative or guilt	Self-protective	Instrumental-relativist	Mythic-literal	Genital	Student
Industry or inferiority	Conformist	"Good boy"/"nice girl"	Synthetic-conventional	Navel	
Identity or role confusion	Self-aware	Law and order			
Intimacy or isolation	Conscientious	Social contract	Individuating-reflexive	Heart	Householder
Generativity or stagnation	Individualistic			Throat	
	Autonomous	Universal principles	Paradoxical-consolidative	Eyebrow	Forest-dweller
Integrity or despair	Integrated	Loyalty to Being	Universalizing	Crown	Renunciate

Source: Compiled from Erikson (1963); Loevinger (1976); Kohlberg (1969, 1973, 1976); Fowler (1981); Hindu Code of Manu; and multiple yogic resources.

Evaluating Levels   Most of these theorists emphasize that individuals can commonly understand levels more advanced than their own and find them appealing. In evaluating oneself and others, it is easy to mistake an understanding of higher-level functioning as an indication that one has actually reached it. Since most of these models define an obviously conformist or conventional position, we must realize that nonconformist behavior may indicate failure to attain conformity as well as growth beyond it. Such behavior is not easy, on the surface, to evaluate. For example, social protesters fall on both sides of conformity. If they loot, burn, destroy, and ignore the rights of other people, the odds are greater that they have never achieved a capacity to conform than that they have outgrown it.

Relations with Behavior   Relationships between thinking and behavior are not clear in these models. Ideas are different from overt behavior related to them. Kohlberg (1977) said that statements of Richard Nixon's sometimes were as high as Stage 4 reasoning, but that much of his behavior reflected only Stage 2.

Moral development offers a good example. The moral principles that one claims are likely to be higher than those actually used in solving a moral dilemma. The guidelines we use for making moral decisions, however, are also likely to be at a higher level than our behavior consistently shows. This supports the position that people are likely to overestimate their own actual functioning considerably.

Similarities Among the Models

You have probably discerned very similar ideas in many of these models. Different scholars see different correspondences between them, depending upon which aspects of each theory they emphasize. Box 4.5 offers one such comparison. Erikson and Hindu life stages—not structural models—are included to indicate the "appropriate" time of life for emergence of the developmental levels posited by the other theories.

REVIEW OF KEY CONCEPTS

Major Types of Stage Developmental Models
    developmental crises models
    structural developmental models
    process versus content in structural models
    qualitative versus quantitative differences in behavior
    Piaget's sensorimotor, preoperational, concrete operations, and formal
        operations stages

Psychological Growth Models Relevant to Religion
    Erikson's psychosocial stages
    effect of child rearing on religious feelings
    relationships between identity and commitment

Research in the Development of Religiousness

We shall take various approaches in the research chapter for each unit, to illustrate the varieties of research efforts in the psychology of religion. We may describe research projects in sufficient detail to be used as models for students' own studies. Sometimes we integrate a number of studies in a narrow area of psychology of religion, both to show major trends of research findings and to illustrate the complexities of research. In the present chapter we describe and illustrate three research models in the development of religiousness (or psychological development in general). We then summarize several studies in the religion of old age.

MODELS OF DEVELOPMENTAL RESEARCH

Longitudinal Method

The longitudinal method is an ideal standard, seldom accomplished in developmental psychology. For a number of people, the researcher observes, measures, and records one or more psychological variables (any observable characteristic that varies or differs among people or over time). At one or more later times the *same* people are again measured on the same variables. Systematic changes over time are often attributed to the process of "development."

Bender (1958) reported a longitudinal study of religious (and other) values among the 1940 class of Dartmouth College. Of six values, religion showed the greatest change—a highly significant increase between 1940 and 1955. This was a minimal longitudinal study, with measures at only two points. Several problems of longitudinal research are shown in this simple study. Six of the original 124 Dartmouth seniors had died. Six others never returned the follow-up questionnaire. Still, the response (112 of 118) was a "95 per cent triumph" (Bender, 1958, p. 41)—truly an extraordinary response for such research. However, 29% did not repeat the psychological test, and 49% were not interviewed. We cannot be sure that the latter made the same changes as the respondents.

Bender had the insight to make another comparison, to verify the apparent developmental increase in the religious value. In 1955 he also gave the values scale to 66 current Dartmouth undergraduates. Behold, their average religious value score was almost identical with that of the 1940 graduates in 1955! The increase in religiousness was apparently a function of changing times (over World War II), not a standard feature of growing older in the 15 years after college graduation. So the results of a longitudinal study, however useful, may not necessarily stand on face value.

Cross-sectional Method

Bender's little "tag-on" study illustrates the cross-sectional method—the most commonly used type of developmental research. At a given time, two or more groups of people, similar in all important respects other than age, are observed/measured/recorded. Any differences among the age groups are attributed to developmental changes.

The cross-sectional method has problems, just as the longitudinal does. Persons of different ages may differ on psychological or other variables for reasons other than developmental. Seventy-year-old Americans are, on the average, less well educated than 30-year-olds. If they differ in religiousness it may not result from 40 years of aging. Instead, differences may result from the fact that the older ones received less education and experienced two world wars and a major depression that the younger ones can only read about. The variety of contaminating variables is almost endless and cannot be fully controlled in a simple cross-sectional study.

Table 5.1   PERCENTAGES OF "VERY IMPORTANT"
            RELIGIOUS BELIEFS

Age group	5 years ago %	Present %
18–24	29	38
25–29	39	51
30–49	45	55
50 and older	66	71

Source: Princeton Religion Research Center (1979).

Retrospective Method

A third method attempts to make observations for the present and for one or more times in the past. A Gallup Poll (Princeton Religion Research Center, 1979) asked a large sample of Americans, "How important to you are your religious beliefs?" and also how important they were "five years ago." Since the sample was divided into five age groups, the answers also constituted a cross-sectional study. For the age groups and two points in time, the percentages who considered religious beliefs "very important" are given in Table 5.1. Both the cross-sectional data and the retrospective data indicate increases in the importance of religious beliefs as Americans grow older.

SOME RESEARCH EXAMPLES

A Longitudinal Study

Perhaps the most important longitudinal study in the psychology of religion is Kohlberg's (1963, 1968, 1969) work on stages of moral development (see Chapter 4). Kohlberg studied 75 boys at approximately 3-year intervals, from preadolescence into adulthood. He adopted Piaget's method of posing moral dilemmas, which were explored in structured interviews. This is his most famous dilemma:

> In Europe, a woman was near death from a special kind of cancer. There was one drug that the doctors thought might save her. It was a form of radium that a druggist in the same town had recently discovered. The drug was expensive to make, but the druggist was charging ten times what the drug cost him to make. . . . The sick woman's husband, Heinz, went to everyone he knew to borrow money, but he could only get together about . . . half of what it cost. He told the druggist that his wife was dying, and asked him to sell it cheaper or let him pay later. But the druggist said, "No, I discovered the drug and I'm going to make money from it." So Heinz got desperate and broke into the man's store to steal the drug for his wife [Kohlberg, 1963, 1969].

The interviewer asked if Heinz should have stolen the drug, and if it was right or wrong, and why. Would it have been all right if he had stolen for a good friend, for someone who was not a friend, for himself, etc.? And, should a judge send Heinz to jail for stealing?

From responses to a series of such moral problems, given to the same boys at intervals over a 12-year period, Kohlberg found that development of moral reasoning followed a predictable order—always in one direction and skipping no steps (except that some at Stage 6 may not have gone through Stage 5). At any one time a person was likely to be in the same stage on half of the 25 aspects of moral thinking that Kohlberg worked with.

One aspect studied was the value of human life. Its six stages, in brief, were: (1) The value of human life is confused with the value of physical objects or attributes associated with a person, (2) human life is valued insofar as it satisfies needs of oneself or other persons, (3) the value of human life is based on other people's affection for the person, (4) life is seen as sacred in terms of moral or religious rights and duties, (5) life is valued in terms of both community welfare and a universal human right, and (6) the sacredness of life is a universal human value.

As boys grew older they moved from one step to another. Tommy at 10 said it was better to save the life of a lot of unimportant people than of one important person because, "a whole bunch of people have an awful lot of furniture and some of those poor people might have a lot of money and it doesn't look it" (Stage 1). At 13 he was Stage 2, and at 16 in Stage 3 he said of "mercy killing," "It might be best for her, but her husband—it's a human life—not like an animal; it just doesn't have the same relationship that a human being does to a family."

Richard was more advanced at 16 and gave a Stage 4 answer to the same dilemma: "It's not a right or privilege of man to decide who shall live and who should die. God put life into everybody on earth and you're taking away something from that person that came directly from God." He was at Stage 5 at age 20, and at 24 he said, "A human life has inherent value whether or not it is valued by a particular individual" (Stage 6).

Figure 5.1 shows the shift in stages of moral reasoning from age 10 to 13 to 16, for middle-class urban boys in the United States.

A Retrospective Study

One of our own studies (Kahoe, 1977b) shows the usefulness and potential validity of the retrospective method. A personality inventory had been given to 518 freshmen in a denominational college. Seven years later we mailed a questionnaire to about two hundred of the more religiously oriented former students, primarily to measure their degree of religious conservatism or liberalism. Twenty questions determined their conservatism at the time of the study. The 142 respondents answered the same set of questions in terms of their attitudes "at the time you were first starting to college." The latter was the crucial retrospective measure, and depended on their accurately and honestly recalling what their attitudes and beliefs had been at that time. Tying the measure to a distinctive period of their lives should have made the task easier. That time also coincided with the personality measures they had taken earlier. Table 5.2 suggests that the retrospective measures of conservatism actually did tap the students' beliefs at the time they were freshmen. The figures in the table are correlation coefficients (measures of "association" between the respective pairs of variables). "Prior" measures, taken from the freshman personality inventory, had

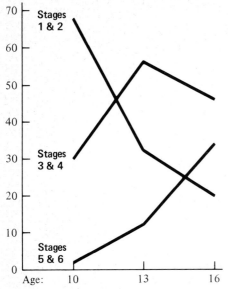

Figure 5.1 Moral judgments by stages, at three ages. (*Source:* Kohlberg, 1968. Reprinted from *Psychology Today Magazine.* Copyright © 1968 Ziff-Davis Publishing Company.)

higher associations with the retrospective measure of religious conservatism than with present conservatism. Concurrent measures, which were also taken from the mail questionnaire, were more strongly associated with present levels of conservatism. However, the retrospective measures were also found to be less reliable or stable than the current ones. That is, trying to think back and judge your attitudes 7 years earlier is not as accurate as reporting what you feel and believe now.

In the 7 years after they started to college, about three-fifths of the students became more liberal in their attitudes; about one-fifth became more conservative; one-fifth were unchanged. As is commonly found in such studies, conservatism was generally related to lower levels of education (at the time of the study). However, the retrospective measure of religious conservatism was

Table 5.2 CORRELATIONS WITH CONSERVATISM FOR TWO TIME PERIODS

Criteria	Retrospective religious conservatism		Present religious conservatism
	Prior measures		
Extrinsic religion	−.17	>	−.08
Responsibility	.18	>	.06
	Concurrent measures		
Dogmatism	−.01	<	.17
Intrinsic religion	.29	<	.43

Source: Kahoe (1977b).

uniquely associated with a *higher* level of *subsequent* education. Conservative religiosity seemed to promote educational pursuit in this particular group.

The advantage of the retrospective method was that we did not have to wait 7 years to identify the factors related to change in religious conservatism. By hitching onto the earlier personality test measures, we were able to test the retrospective measures and also to study the importance of more personality factors in the development of religious attitudes.

A Cross-sectional Study

Elkind (1964b), like Kohlberg, adopted aspects of Piaget's methodology in his study of the development of religious identity—a good example of the cross-sectional method. At each of seven age levels (generally 6–12) Elkind interviewed at least 30 children from Jewish, Protestant, and Catholic groups—more than 700 in all.

The interviews posed six novel questions about each child's religious group: for example, (1) Is your family Jewish? Are you Jewish? Are all boys and girls in the world Jewish?; (2) Can a dog or cat be Jewish?; (3) How do you become a Jew?; (4) What is a Jew?; (5) How can you tell a person is Jewish?; (6) Can you be Jewish and American at the same time? Analysis of the children's responses identified three well-marked stages in the development of religious identity.

The first stage (usually ages 5–7) revealed a global concept of denomination, as a proper name that was often confused with other group terms. For example, from a 6-year-old: What is a Jew? "A person." How is a Jewish person different from a Catholic? "Cause some people have black hair and some people have blond."

At the second stage (usually 7–9) children had a differentiated but concrete conception of their group. An 8-year-old answered: What is a Catholic? "He goes to mass every Sunday and goes to Catholic School." To the question of being an American and of the denomination at the same time, children at this stage might concretely answer, "I'm an American and I'm a Protestant."

The third-stage children (10 and older) held appropriately abstract concepts of their faith. A 12-year-old said to: What is a Catholic? "A person who believes in the truths of the Roman Catholic Church." Can a dog or cat be a Catholic? "No, because they don't have a brain or intellect."

By using the cross-sectional method Elkind did not have to wait for the children to grow older to reach his conclusions. However, he compensated for the individual differences by using a sample almost ten times as large as Kohlberg's. Since Elkind's subjects were from a limited age range, there is little chance that the basic results were affected by changes in the society or culture.

THE DEVELOPMENTAL RELIGIOUS PSYCHOLOGY OF AGING

Starbuck (1911) thought that religious faith increased in importance as people aged. Despite his skimpy evidence, this view became "part of the folklore of the psychology of religion" (Maves, 1960, pp. 698–749). To the contrary, Orbach (1961) argued that religion primarily serves needs of the youth in our society, and he noted that religious activity decreases in old age. Considerable research has focused on the religion of later life, and there have been several reviews of this research (e.g., Bahr, 1970; Heenam, 1972; Moberg, 1965). Unfortunately, the research and the reviews often reach conflicting conclusions.

The results are clearer if we do not consider religion as a whole but instead examine different aspects or "dimensions" (Moberg, 1965; Stark, 1968). We shall look at three of the more important categories of religiousness that relate to the developmental psychology of aging.

Subjective Religious Experience

A longitudinal study of gifted persons found that when the group averaged age 56 they had greater interest in religion than they had expressed 10 and 20 years earlier. Similarly, a number of retrospective studies reflect gains in the importance of religion. For example, among 140 retired blacks in South Carolina, 57% said religion held more meaning than before retirement, and only 2% said it had less (Lloyd, 1955). Similarly, of 243 older rural New York state residents, 62 said the church and clergy were more important than formerly, and 17 reported they were less important (Warren, 1952). Moberg (1965) reports other such studies, in which the respondents may interpret the general term *religion* in whatever way they consider important. The studies may be biased by the common social expectation that people look to religion in any time of trouble.

Stark's (1968) cross-sectional study of over 2850 Californians identified more specific religious experiences: sense of being saved, of the presence of God, and of being punished by God for wrongdoing. This measure of religious experience was consistently related with age only for conservative Protestants (not for liberal or moderate Protestants or for Catholics). Among conservative Protestants the percentage scoring "high" increased from 79% for those under 20, to 96% for ages 60–69, and 100% for those 70 and over. Probably the effect held only for that group because the experiences specified in the research are more emphasized among them than in the other religious communities.

Religious Beliefs

Stark (1968) also related religious orthodoxy to age in his California study. Orthodoxy was measured by belief in a personal God, divine Jesus, biblical miracles, and the devil. This measure of belief was not regularly related to aging. However, Protestants who had been 26 and younger at the outbreak of World War II tended to be less orthodox. Stark attributed the liberalizing change to a shift of Protestants to the cities; the liberalizing, urbanizing, effect did not occur with Catholics, who as a group tended already to be urban.

Stark included another question about belief in life after death. Among Protestants this belief steadily increased until after age 70 it was held to be "completely true" by 70% of liberal, 87% of moderate, and 100% of conservative Protestants. Similarly a study of almost 500 residents of New York City (mostly Jews) found that belief in life after death increased from 30% at ages 30–35, to 40% at 60–65 (Barron, 1961). Immortality seems, indeed, to be the only religious belief that substantially rises with aging. Even William James, who never considered himself religious, said in 1904 in response to a question from James B. Pratt, Do you believe in personal immortality?: "Never keenly; but more strongly as I grow older." If so, why?: "Because I am just getting fit to live" (James, 1926/1973, p. 125).

Stark (1968) cited opinion that most other beliefs in the supernatural declined with age. A *Catholic Digest* survey (Our Father in Heaven, 1953) found that 80% of those 18–34, 76% of those 45–54, and 81% of those 65 and older believed in "God as a loving father." Whatever shifts occur may be slight.

Religious Behavior

Orbach (1961) emphasized the decline in church attendance with age. The one major exception to this trend (in his cross-sectional study of over 6900 adults in the Detroit area) was Jews, whose synagogue attendance steadily increased with age. This exception reflects an inherent defect in the cross-sectional method. Since America has seen a historical decline in Jewish orthodoxy, the older Jews had more orthodox training and continued to attend more than did younger age groups.

Many other studies and reviews show that church attendance declines with age, typically after 60. Morgan (1937) found that among 381 pensioners in New York state, 93% formerly attended church, but only 43% continued to do so. Of those who no longer went, 53% cited physical inability and 39% indicated a loss of interest or belief. Physical incapacities of age are usually blamed for the decline in attendance of the elderly. Morgan's last group (loss of interest/belief) may reflect Orbach's observation that "casual" churchgoers, with advancing years, become either regular attenders or nonattenders. The 39% probably had been among the merely casual churchgoers.

Many studies have found, though, that along with less public worship, the elderly engage more in private prayers, devotional activities, and Bible reading, and in listening to and watching religious radio and television programs. This finding comes from cross-sectional studies, and no known longitudinal or retrospective study verifies an actual increase as individuals grow older.

Conclusion

The relationship of religiosity to later life aging seems to depend largely on what questions one asks, or what aspect of religion is studied. To some extent it is affected by the research methodology, though consistent results are usual when any given aspect of religion is studied by the different methods. The importance of looking at different aspects or dimensions of religion will receive special attention in Unit Four.

REVIEW OF KEY CONCEPTS

Models of Developmental Research
    description of longitudinal method and example
    methods in cross-sectional method
    how the retrospective method works

Some Research Examples
    Kohlberg's moral dilemmas
    development of "value of human life"
    shifts in moral reasoning from age 10 to 16 for U.S. boys
    Kahoe's conservatism measures
    validity and reliability of retrospective measures
    liberal shift
    effect of early religious conservatism
    Elkind's interviews
    the three stages of religious identity—ages and general concepts
    significance of number of subjects in Elkind's study

The Developmental Religious Psychology of Aging
    general trends of aging for subjective religious experience
    possible bias in retrospective studies
    Stark's study: findings and reasons for limitations
    Stark's orthodoxy measure and its relation to aging
    trend for belief in life after death
    religious participation in later life: church attendance and other activities
    limitations of the findings

chapter 6

Applications: Education in the Religious Life

As a distinct and rather well developed discipline, religious education draws on theology, philosophy, education, sociology, and psychology for many of its concepts and techniques. This chapter briefly considers religious education issues that relate to developmental religious psychology.

CONTENT VERSUS ADJUSTMENT

Religious educators long debated whether curricula should focus on the cognitive content of a faith or on behavior and psychological adjustment. Should learners be indoctrinated in the history, creeds, and mythology of the particular faith tradition? Or should they be taught and nurtured toward moral behavior and integration? The latter position prevails and is exemplified by a proposed "psychotherapeutic model" for religious education. Brink reasoned that religion, like psychotherapy, is aimed at the total person ("feeling, willing, and acting as well as thinking," 1977, p. 409) and is tested by how well one functions in actual life situations.

The Case for Content

The true believer of any religious faith is likely to plead that the best way to achieve personal balance, maturity, and constructive behavior is to produce the "good Muslim," or Hindu, or Jew, or Christian, or Presbyterian—one who believes and behaves in accordance with the particular tradition. As we suggested in Chapter 1, each religious faith incorporates a system of living that is adaptive for at least some times and settings. However, no system possesses all the answers for every situation. There are times when straightforward indoctrination in a faith fails to achieve interpersonal and intrapersonal harmony.

The Case for Adjustment

Our religious concepts rest more on what we experience than on what we are told. Aristotle's *Politics* held that beliefs in God related to an individual's relationship with the family. Freud considered God to be merely a projection of one's human father. This basic idea has spawned many and varied studies on sources of individuals' God concepts.

   Contrary to Freud's theory, in the earliest objective, statistical study of the relationship of God concepts to parental images, concepts of God were closer to mother than to father images (Nelson & Jones, 1957). A more recent clinical study, *The Birth of the Living God* (Rizzuto, 1979), found evidence to support Freud's general theory that God concepts arise from children's interactions with their parents, especially in the resolution of the oedipal conflict. However, the maternal image contributed as much as the paternal image to the concept of divinity.

   A variety of statistical methods have been used to relate God concepts to parental concepts, and the conclusions have not always been consistent. One study compared four methods with both psychiatric patient and nonpatient samples. The most appropriate method showed the God concept to be significantly more similar to the mother image than to the father image; this was especially true for patients, suggesting that "unresolved attachments with mother" (Nicholson & Edwards, 1979, p. 15) play a role in the development of pathology. Adlerian theory suggests that the *preferred* parent's image would have more effect on the God image, regardless of gender. The same study found this to be true, but only for nonpatients.

Another study compared the Freudian and Adlerian theories with a social learning theory (God concept should be similar to the image of the same-sex parent) and self-esteem position (God image should resemble the self-image). Like many other studies, it found a great deal in common among all of these images—that is, one's concept of God tends to resemble images of both parents and of oneself. However, the Adlerian and self-esteem positions received the strongest support (Spilka, Addison, & Rosensohn, 1975). The close relationship of God concept with self-concept brings the religious education task close to the general task of child-rearing. Sound child-rearing and the development of self-esteem in children (e.g., Segal & Yahraes, 1978) lay the foundation for religious education—indeed for all religious faith. Religious education begins in the cradle, if not—as Hindus say—in the womb.

The Case for Balance

As with most debates, the content/adjustment controversy is best resolved by a balance between the two extremes. Elkins (1976) called for such a balance within the conservative Jewish tradition, while pointing out dismal failures of traditional content-centered approaches. As children's mental capacities develop, the religious education task typically shifts from a nearly pure adjustment emphasis toward more of the content of their faith.

SHAPING VERSUS NURTURING

A second distinction is almost a nonissue, because it has been rather decisively resolved in one way. Oates notes the contrasting views:

> We see younger persons as lumps of damp but quickly drying clay that must be molded to fit our desire before it is too late. . . . They are not cups to be filled, clay to be molded, or mirrors for our vanity. They are persons in their own right. They are emerging selves in the making through the power of faith [1969, p. 22].

Most other religious educators agree that when children are properly nurtured, they spontaneously grow, blossom, and flourish.

Shaping Behavior

The notion of shaping behavior, even positively valued moral and religious behavior, is distasteful to most religious educators. It seems to violate common religious values of human dignity and free choice, and is identified with widespread biases against "manipulative behaviorism." Religious education has largely ignored or rejected behavioral approaches to child training (Elias, 1974). However, common notions of the uses and potentials of behaviorism are simplistic and counter to modern views of behavioristic psychology.

A primarily behavioral approach can help religious educators focus on behavioral goals. Virtually any religious system includes ideas about what the ideal person should be or do. Without goals, the desired behavior, attitudes, or characteristics may not be achieved. Children differ in basic temperamental patterns, and must be treated differently to encourage any given outcome (Segal & Yahraes, 1978, Chapter 4; Thomas, Chess, & Birch, 1968). So it is impossible to achieve any religious ideal consistently, without adopting certain clear goals—behavioral or otherwise.

If, for example, kindness is identified as a desirable religious behavior, different children will require different combinations of modeling, reinforcement, verbal instruction, and other methods to shape their behavior toward interpersonal kindness. A behavioral approach would clearly define "kind" behavior and use whatever techniques were required to get that behavior with some consistency.

Nurturing Behavior

Cognitive developmental theorists such as Piaget and Kohlberg assume that the potential for growth is inherent in every child. The individual needs only some minimum of environmental materials to work with, to realize that potential. Distorted versions of this theory have led some parents to provide no religious nurture. They assume that the "right" religious ideals will spontaneously develop as the child matures. This error is as naive as not speaking to a child for fear of unduly affecting its language preferences.

Actually, most sensitive proponents of the "nurturing" position balance the child's innate potential with a recognition of the need to provide certain kinds of moral and religious "nutrients." For example, while emphasizing that "children are not plastic clay," Ligon said,

> The best way to describe the ideal role of the teacher and parent in the process is that of creating a "favorable climate" in which the child can learn. A favorable climate may involve making the child's way easy or making it difficult. It may mean direct challenge or indirect motivation. It may involve being very permissive in some things and using strict discipline in others. But the fact remains that the main job—namely, learning—is done by the growing child, not by the teacher [1956, p. 51].

Similarly, a study in religious education titled *Love or Constraint?* advocated a balance between shaping (constraint) and nurturing (love). "A father who dares not assume his responsibilities or give orders because of . . . an excessive humility is just as baneful an influence on the child as the father who wishes his authority to be considered as absolute" (Oraison, 1961, p. 95).

READINESS

The concept of *readiness* has had more impact on religious education than any other contribution of developmental psychology. The optimum periods for certain educational tasks are called *teachable moments*.

> When the body is ripe, and society requires, and the self is ready to achieve a certain task, the teachable moment has come. Efforts at teaching which would have been largely wasted if they had come earlier give gratifying results when they come at the *teachable moment,* when the task should be learned [Havighurst, 1952, p. 5].

Almost exactly the same principle was discovered in the Character Research Project of Union College, Schenectady, New York—a 50-year endeavor without equal in religious education. They refer to the "optimum age levels," at which any particular attitude or character trait may be communicated (Ligon, 1956, pp. 63–64).

Developmental Tasks

Religious education has responded to the concept of readiness by recognizing what Havighurst (1952) called "developmental tasks." At any age one should master certain physical, mental, personality, moral, or other psychological tasks. Investigators with the Character Research Project had parents rate their children on hundreds of attitudes relevant to character development. Each attitude tended to form in most children at some particular age. The resulting "age-level calibration" is essentially a statement of appropriate developmental tasks for each age (Ligon, 1956, p. 63).

In *On Becoming Children of God* Oates (1969) used concepts of several developmental and personality theories to examine the religious education implications of developmental tasks from infancy through high school. Religious tasks have also been related to Erikson's eight stages (Aden, 1976).

However the developmental tasks are identified, religious educators seek to determine how the religious system can contribute to mastery of each task. How can the myths, stories, doctrines, creeds, moral codes, etc., promote this particular aspect of personality development? Posing the problem this way helps resolve the content versus adjustment issue discussed earlier.

Cognitive Levels

As early as 1903 John Dewey observed that for a long time the child was treated like "an abbreviated adult, a little man or a little woman" (1903/1974, p. 6). The concept of readiness emphasizes the opposite. Children do not think or learn like adults. Nonetheless many children's sermons, Sunday school lessons, and other religious instructions still discuss sin, the Eucharist, forgiveness, grace, and other theological concepts—all on an adult level obviously over the children's heads.

Dewey noted that the differences between children and adults were "those of mental and emotional *standpoint,* and *outlook,* rather than of degree" (1903/1974, p. 6, emphases added). As we noted in earlier chapters, Piaget, Kohlberg, and others have specified just what these differences in children's perspectives are.

Dewey further warned that if children are confronted with religious ideas before they are able to understand them, the ideas may be distorted or rejected. Before children's own experiences naturally rouse religious questions, they cannot appreciate the answers, and may treat them with contempt, irreverence, skepticism, or distaste.

More recently Ronald Goldman studied the required English school religious education curriculum. He found that the children had learned very little content, and the levels of the curriculum materials differed greatly from appropriate cognitive developmental levels identified by Piaget. Goldman (1964a, 1964b, 1965) echoed Dewey's concerns, provoking considerable controversy within religious education.

CHILDREN AND RELIGION: TO TEACH OR NOT TO TEACH

Not to Teach

Goldman and some other Piagetian theorists have argued that young children simply should not be taught religion.

Pre-formal Religious Education   This does not mean that children should receive no moral or character education before adolescence. Batson recommended "pre-formal religious education," to prepare children to handle later "religious existential conflicts and crises" (1974, p. 311). Such training should take place, Batson said, in the supportive context of the religious institution. The content of this early education comes from the current conflicts and needs of the learner. The Union College Character Research Project identified developmental cycles that span infancy through senior high school. These cycles provide typical conflicts that pre-formal and later religious education can address, as children establish new outlooks on life. Although early cycles do not deal with strictly religious existential crises, they involve emotional, cognitive, and coping processes that prepare one for later religious crises (Koppe, 1965).

One sensitive Sunday school teacher effectively faced a 3-year-old's life crisis. Overhearing Jane tell a friend, "My mommy went away last night and I cried," she stopped short and listened. "The lady staying with me said if I didn't stop, my mommy wouldn't come back." The teacher put her arm around Jane and said, "Did you tell your mommy what the babysitter said? I think she would like to know. Because mommies do come back, even if you cry. And I bet when your mommy comes home she tiptoes into your room to kiss you good-night." Other children listened, sat down on the floor, and talked about times their mothers had gone away. Though the Bible readings and story, prayers, and other class plans were neglected, "it's possible that more Christian education occurred on *that* morning than on other mornings when more traditional things had been done" (Westerhoff, 1970, p. 48).

Religious Content   Still, in the model Batson proposed, there is "no mention of God, Jesus, various 'children's' Bible stories or of worship" (1974, p. 315). Instead the religious educator merely provides the context in which children can grow in desirable ways, without teaching them the content of any particular faith tradition. Batson suggested that children might be taught certain religious symbols—to have that language available for later religious conflicts. But he argued against the idea. Children would understand the symbols in concrete ways that create difficulty in distinguishing between symbol and reality. He said a child can more readily distinguish "make-believe" and "real" in other stories and pictures than in a system "which adults take as seriously as they do religious language" (Batson, 1974, p. 315).

To Teach

Batson criticized Goldman's assumption that "the primary character of religion is understanding or interpretation of life's experiences" (1974, p. 305). He observed that religious stories probably aim more to convey an *experience,* a feeling or emotion, of divine love, justice, etc., rather than a mental *understanding* of such concepts. Many religious educators consider Goldman and even Batson too conservative. Elkind (1964a), as cited in Chapter 3, said that religious education feeds the emotions more than the mind. Particularly in young children, the emotions are more ready for religious training and more like those of adults than are the conceptual or cognitive systems. The 4-year-old who says a table grace has not yet learned much about God or prayer, but is developing feelings of gratitude and thankfulness, which will become part of subsequent religious values. The understanding of the act will develop with further cognitive maturity.

RELIGIOUS EDUCATION FOR CHILDREN

Vehicles for Teaching

Stories   Stories and parables constitute a universal language that figures in almost all religions. In the Sufi Muslim and Hasidic Jewish traditions, for example, stories are a major means of communicating the faith. Such religious tales communicate on many levels, making them especially useful in the religious education of children at different stages of cognitive development.

Contrary to Goldman's critique, Berryman (1979) advocates the use of parables with young children—but without offering adultlike cognitive interpretations. With structured, Montessori-type materials, the children can act out and visualize the parable of the Good Shepherd, for example—experiencing it in whatever ways their minds are prepared, and being enriched by the novel story and the emotions it produces. Denis (1974) similarly reports use of parables among North American Indians—they are not explained, but the listeners are allowed to process them intuitively. Such stories are a partial solution to the problem of "talking and hearing across stage differences" (Berryman, 1979, p. 282).

Religious History, Myth, and Symbol   Many other religious stories have a different status from parables. They are considered true on one level or another; they are not just told for the sake of an implied truth or moral. Most Bible stories—Adam and Eve in the garden, Moses on Mount Sinai, Jesus' miracles—have this status. Almost all children and many adult believers accept their literal truth; other adults may give them symbolic meaning. Problems may arise in cross-stage communications, when adults attempt to force symbolic interpretations on children who still function at literal and concrete levels. At other times adults may respond to children's or adolescents' doubts with dogmatic assertions that the stories are "really true," curbing the natural development of abstract, formal mental operations.

Few adults can effectively communicate across cognitive levels. Many would unnecessarily feel hypocritical if they taught children on the latter's natural, concrete levels, while they as adults held beliefs on another level. When Pope John Paul II visited Mexico in 1979, some observers criticized the fact that he frequently referred to the Virgin Mary in his addresses to the masses, and focused on Jesus and the scriptures when speaking to church officials. An American archbishop, John R. Quinn, defended the "seeming duplicity":

> The common people are not able to deal with complex issues, so the Pope speaks to them of Mary. However, he can speak of Christ and the Scriptures to the bishops. After all, the Lord used parables with the common people, and spoke differently to his disciples [Conrad, 1979, p. 624].

Moral Laws   Cross-stage differences in moral judgment—such as those elaborated in Kohlberg's and Loevinger's models in Chapter 4—pose a similar problem. Most parents and religious educators are at more advanced stages than the children they teach. Unless adults understand the early levels of children's morality, they are not likely to teach at an optimum level. They may, for example, reject the preadolescent's compulsive need for rigid, conventional moral codes. Or they may teach nothing at all, sensing that their own more mature ideas are not appropriate to the children.

Toward Cross-stage Religious Education

Resolution of the dilemmas of cross-stage communication is probably the most pressing research need in the psychology of religious education. Stages in religious thinking are well established, but how can the teaching of a religious faith relate to them? Piaget's idea of mature moral judgment has been seen as consistent with the teachings of Jesus (Clouse, 1978) and the traditional ethics of Judaism (Rosenzweig, 1977). However, others see the Orthodox Jewish emphasis on the law as contrary to Piaget's and Kohlberg's highest stages, and provide evidence that Jewish education can produce reversals in Kohlberg stages (Selig & Teller, 1975). Many Protestant fundamentalists similarly emphasize legalism more than abstract higher principles.

Elkind and others reject Goldman's aversion to religious education of the very young and his fear that it leads to concrete thinking that hinders religious growth. Elkind cites Piaget's own research to suggest that children naturally go through the successive cognitive stages with little or no systematic teaching. "The child's erroneous ideas about religious matters . . . are spontaneously given up as the child's thought becomes more socialized and objective" (1964a, p. 646).

If children are to receive religious education on a level appropriate to their development, how can this best be done? How can suitable emotions, patterns of thought, and abilities to deal with social and existential crises be developed—without the child's being fixated at an immature level of thinking? We have already suggested the use of parables and stories, with a minimum of adult-style interpretation. Children probably should be allowed to forge ideas suitable to their cognitive needs, and be nudged toward immediately higher levels, but neither forced toward distant more mature levels nor influenced to retain concrete ideation that they tend to outgrow.

Adults may use questions, dialogue, and peer interaction to encourage the development of religious ideas, while honoring the child's level of thinking—rather than declaring traditional, authoritarian dogmas. Just as children readily give up ideas of the tooth fairy and Santa Claus, when they begin to question them and receive sensitive answers, so primitive religious ideas can give way to increasingly mature concepts. Exactly how to handle these issues, for optimum religious growth, is an empirical question that should challenge decades of research in religious education and psychology.

REVIEW OF KEY CONCEPTS

Content Versus Adjustment
　　for and against focus on content of a religious faith
　　evidence for focus on adjustment in religious education
　　nature of a balance between content and adjustment

Shaping Versus Nurturing
　　need for shaping in religious education
　　the responsible pattern for nurturing in religious education

Readiness
　　definitions: *readiness, teachable moments,* and *developmental tasks*
　　the significance of cognitive levels
　　Dewey's and Goldman's cases for not teaching religion to young children
　　Batson's notion of "pre-formal religious education"
　　why Batson urges omitting religious content in early religious education
　　basis for Elkind's endorsement of early religious education

Children and Religion: To Teach or Not to Teach
　　how parables are used in early religious education
　　the major issue with regard to most "Bible stories"
　　pitfalls to avoid with regard to such stories and symbols
　　problems in teaching moral "laws"

Religious Education for Children
　　resolution to problems of cross-stage religious communication

two

SOME RELIGIOUS EXPERIENCES IN PSYCHOLOGICAL PERSPECTIVE

Conversion

INTRODUCTION

Convicted with Charles Manson on seven counts of first-degree murder, Susan Atkins grappled with her soul on California's death row:

> The thoughts tumbled over and over in my mind. Can society forgive me for such acts against humanity? Can it take this guilt off my shoulders? Can serving the rest of my life in prison undo what's been done? Can anything be done?
>
> I looked at my future, my alternatives: Stay in prison. Escape. Commit suicide. As I looked, the wall in my mind was blank. But somehow I knew there was another alternative. I could choose the road many people had been pressing on me. I could follow Jesus. As plainly as daylight came the words, "You have to decide. Behold I stand at the door, and knock." Did I hear someone say that? I assume I spoke in my thoughts, but I'm not certain, "What door?"
>
> "You know what door and where it is, Susan. Just turn around and open it, and I will come in." Suddenly, as though on a movie screen, there in my thoughts was a door. It had a handle. I took hold of it, and pulled. It opened. The whitest, most brilliant light I had ever seen poured over me. In the center of the flood of brightness was an even brighter light. Vaguely, there was the form of a man. I knew it was Jesus. He spoke to me—literally, plainly, matter-of-factly spoke to me in my nine-by-eleven prison cell: "Susan, I am really here. I'm really coming into your heart to stay." I was distinctly aware that I inhaled deeply and then, just as fully, exhaled. There was no more guilt! It was gone. Completely gone! The bitterness, too. Instantly gone! How could this be? For the first time in my memory I felt clean, fully clean, inside and out. In twenty-six years I had never been so happy [Atkins, 1977, pp. 228–230, minor deletions not indicated].

Susan Atkins experienced conversion, which William James called "the process, gradual or sudden, by which a self hitherto divided, and consciously wrong inferior and unhappy, becomes unified and consciously right superior and happy, by consequence of its firmer hold upon religious realities" (1902/1961, p. 160).

Conversion continues to be one of the most fascinating and widely studied topics in the psychology of religion. In the first two-thirds of this century there were more than 500 publications on the subject (Scroggs & Douglas, 1967).

Sometimes *conversion* is used to refer to mere change from one religious tradition to another—when, for example, a person changes to a spouse's church "for the sake of the children." Unless there is the unifying quality specified in James's definition, though, we prefer to refer to it as a change in religious affiliation. Using James as a reference point, we generally see conversion as representing a significant turning point from one state of mind to a superior and more integrative state.

TYPES OF CONVERSION

Numerous types or classifications of conversions have been suggested. While we cannot be exhaustive of these typologies, we shall discuss the more significant variations.

Crisis Conversion

The prototype or "model" conversion is relatively sudden and dramatic, involving an abrupt resolution of a personal conflict that may or may not have been conscious. Susan Atkins's conversion represents this type, which James (1902) called "self-surrender." Such striking experiences were expected by the churches of the Great Awakening of the eighteenth and nineteenth centuries—notably the Presbyterians, Baptists, and Methodists—and now particularly among Baptists, Pentecostals, and other "evangelicals."

Pioneer students of the psychology of conversion focused on the crisis type. George Coe (1900) found that 31% of a group of 77 converts experienced "striking transformation"; others had more gradual conversions. Later Elmer Clark (1929) found crisis conversions in only 6.7% of 2174 cases. Among students in theological schools the incidence of sudden conversions has ranged from zero in an Anglo-Catholic school (Scobie, 1973) to 45–56% in evangelical seminaries (Drakeford, 1964; Ferm, 1959; Scobie, 1973). In a 1978 survey of over 1000 American teenagers, 33% reported having had a conversion experience; of these 18% had "sudden" experiences—including 20% of Protestant youth and those from the South, and 14% of young Catholics (Princeton Religion Research Center, 1979). These figures cannot be directly compared, since the definitions of crisis or sudden conversions vary from study to study. It is apparent, though, that the rate depends largely on the theological expectations of the generation or the religious tradition.

Crisis conversions have identifiable stages, varying somewhat by who describes them. First comes a period of confusion, unrest, or conflict—partly conscious but sometimes largely unconscious. The person may be depressed or guilt-stricken over real or imagined sins; feel divided and torn, empty or incomplete; or feel that life has lost all sense of meaning. This torment was seen early in Susan Atkins's conversion.

The second stage of crisis conversion involves a sudden sense of illumination or insight, often with very strong emotions. Frequently the stage features a climactic self-surrender. In a radical shift of life pattern, the center of the person's universe shifts from self to the deity or the demands of the new religious faith. Susan's illumination began with an apparent auditory hallucination, "You have to decide," and continued with the ensuing dialogue. John Wesley's classic conversion showed a similar sudden resolution of a conflict that was apparently unconscious:

> I went very unwilling to a society in Aldersgate Street where one was reading Luther's preface to the *Epistle to the Romans.* About a quarter before nine,

while he was describing the change which God works in the heart through faith in Christ, I felt my heart strangely warmed. I felt I did trust Christ, Christ alone for my salvation; and an assurance was given me that He had taken away *my* sins; even *mine,* and saved *me* from the law of sin and death [Wesley, 1938, pp. 475–476].

The third stage brings a sense of unity, peace, calm, and relief. Susan Atkins reported an unprecedented happiness, John Wesley a new sense of assurance.

Gradual Conversion

Other conversion experiences may show a distinct turn to a new life and faith, without the sudden crisis of our first type. Some of the same elements and stages may be observed, but on a conscious level. James followed Starbuck (1903) in calling this the "volitional" type of conversion, implying that the person's will is more actively and consciously involved than in "self-surrender."

Early pioneers of the psychology of religion and many contemporary students find the crisis style of conversion more interesting than the gradual kind. Most theologians, particularly of liberal faiths, encourage the more insightful and voluntary, less emotional form of conversion—which is illustrated by the following case.

Sheldon (Van) Vanauken, a literary scholar from America, went with his wife Davy to study at Oxford. Avowed atheists (though Davy's father had been a Methodist minister), they found their new friends to be witty, intelligent, deeply committed Christians. Their stereotype of Christians as stuffy, hidebound, and stupid was deeply shaken. Vanauken soon followed up a long-term "resolve some day to have another look at the case for Christianity" (Vanauken, 1977, p. 82). Bringing home an armload of books on Christianity, Van warned his wife:

"But listen, Davy. We're just having a look, you know. Let's keep our heads. There are enormous arguments against Christianity."

"Oh, I know!" she said. "I don't see how it could be true. But—well, how would you feel if we decided that it *was* true?"

"Um," I said. "I'm not sure. One would know the meaning of things. That would be good. But we'd have to go to church, and all that. And, well, pray. Still, it would be great to know meanings and, you know, the purpose of everything. But, dammit! It *couldn't* be true! How could Earth's religion—*one* of Earth's religions—be true for the whole galaxy—millions of planets, maybe? [1977, p. 83].

Although Van's doubts and uncertainties were more intellectual, less emotional, than for a typical crisis conversion, the unrest was there. Months later, after many discussions between themselves and with friends, and exchange of some letters with the fellow Oxford scholar and Christian apologist C. S. Lewis, Davy recorded in her diary: "Today, crossing from one side of the room to the other, I lumped together all I am, all I fear, hate, love, hope; and, Well, DID it. I committed my ways to God in Christ" (Vanauken, 1977, pp. 95–96). Two months later, after what he called a "second intellectual breakthrough," Van was in his room pondering one of his exchanges with C. S. Lewis. Davy was there, and:

> She had heard me mutter, "My God!" And then, as she looked up, I'd said, rather tensely, "Wait." A couple of minutes went by. Then I said: "Davy? . . . dearling . . . I have chosen—the Christ! I *choose* to believe." She looked at me with joy [1977, p. 99].

Van's conversion was not without emotion, but note the word (in his italics) that describes his resolution: *choose.*

It is difficult to say what percentage of religious persons experience a gradual conversion, for studies differ widely in their definitions and classification schemes. Drakeford's (1964) and Roberts' (1965) studies of theological students found 44% and 40%, respectively, of the gradual type, contrasted with sudden conversion. The 1978 survey of American teenagers found that of those reporting a definite turning point, 82% were gradual (Princeton Religion Research Center, 1979). Scobie (1973) classified the experiences of 170 British seminarians into three styles; about half of the students in each of the five schools claimed a gradual conversion.

Unconscious Conversion

James (1902) concluded that some people were not able to experience religious conversion. He regretfully included himself among those. Some, he thought, may be intellectually too pessimistic or materialistic to "imagine the invisible." Others may be too temperamentally insensitive and barren to experience the "enthusiasm and peace" of religious faith.

Here we focus on those persons who are manifestly religious but have not experienced conversion. They may have grown gradually into religion without having ever felt a turning point in their faith. Starbuck found this type in his study. Their religious growth was relatively uneventful. As Starbuck put it, "Frequently all that can be said is that they *grew* out of a religion of childish simplicity, and have now put away childish things" (1903, p. 298).

Starbuck identified four conditions that permit such a gradual development: (1) religious surroundings in childhood, (2) reasonable freedom from rigid dogmas, (3) needs of the child being carefully met at every point in its development, and (4) a certain stable mixture of faith and the freedom to doubt. One of his cases illustrates. A young woman reported:

> Mother was patient and gentle with me. I had church and Sunday school associations of the pleasantest kind; I was not taught anything about hell and Satan. I have not changed my childhood phrase, "Our Father in Heaven," except to widen the term [1903, p. 299].

For his survey of conversion experiences among British seminarians, Scobie (1973) adopted Brandon's (1960) terminology and called this kind of development "unconscious conversion." Overall 30% of his respondents claimed this conversion type, but there was a range from 9% to 45% among schools of varying theological traditions.

Many religious educators prefer the steady, orderly development of religious faith to relatively convulsive conversions. However, there may be reservations about that approach also. Starbuck concluded:

> A few persons seem to have an uneventful development because they do not leave the religion of childhood, perhaps never wake up to an immediate realisation of religion. They raise the question whether it would not have been conducive to growth even to have suffered a little on the rack of doubt and storm and stress [1903, p. 310].

Reintegration

We usually think of conversion as a transition from irreligiousness to religiousness, or from one faith tradition to another. The term is also used in another sense: from a state of spiritual "disintegration to one of positive integration and effectiveness of life along the lines of whatever faith commitment one has already accepted" (W. H. Clark, 1973, pp. 24–25).

When former president Jimmy Carter characterized himself as a "born-again Christian," he was not referring to his commitment to the Baptist faith as a youth. Instead his critical turning point came after he was already an active deacon in the Plains Baptist Church. After losing his first election for the governorship of Georgia, his health, economic condition, and of course political standing had suffered. He ached within:

> I began to realize that when I had successes I had no sense of gratification or enjoyment; when I had failures it was a deep personal bitterness and sometimes confusion and despair. And there was just something missing in my life—a sense of peace, a sense of higher purpose [Norton & Slosser, 1976, pp. 32–33].

As he walked in a Georgia pine woods with his sister Ruth, she counseled him: "You've got to look beyond yourself for God's purpose. You've got to be less self-centered in all of your life. . . . Jimmy, you've got to recognize that your mind can't achieve the change you're looking for" (Norton & Slosser, 1976, p. 36). As they knelt and prayed there in the pine forest, Carter made a commitment that led to what he calls "a sense of complete dependence on the Holy Spirit."

Coe (1900) found 202 experiences of religious awakening among 99 men, suggesting that multiple conversion experiences are not uncommon. One of Baer's (1978) subjects had been reared as a Greek Orthodox, become a "Billy Graham type of Christian" as a teenager, and later was baptized into fundamentalistic Protestant and Mormon churches, before finally converting to a Mormon schism, the Aaronic Order. (There was no indication of how thoroughly integrative each of these serial conversions was.)

Conversion is not necessarily a once-and-for-all thing. There may be several spiritual crises in a person's development, and any one (or more than one) may be considered decisive.

Programmed Conversion

Oates (1973) coined the term *programmed conversion* to refer to the institutionalization of conversion in the Protestant churches that drew their major strength from the Great Awakening. In those denominations conversion has become a major entrance requirement into the faith. It is expected of youth in the church after they reach the "age of accountability," and is frequently associated with "revival meetings."

Conversion becomes virtually a ritual, a personal response to the "ritual of the invitation," which is usually the final part of a revival or other preaching service. The public response may be a sudden resolution of a spiritual conflict, as in crisis conversion. It might reflect a volitional conversion, a gradual religious growth, or a reintegration—seen either as a new or "real" conversion or a recommitment.

Conversion or Confirmation   The conversion decision may be made easier for a child by preparatory or "seekers" classes. Such practices resemble confirmation in more sacramental churches and bar mitzvah (for boys) or bat mitzvah (for girls) in Hebrew congregations. Increasingly the latter are not automatic rituals when children reach a given age, but imply a willing choice by the child to "confirm," as personal, the faith that hitherto had been transmitted by the parents. In either conversion or confirmation the crucial thing from a psychological perspective is whether children make the faith their own, whether it becomes an integrating force in the fabric of their lives. Some programmed conversions in evangelical churches are so socially influenced by peers or adults that they are as mindless as the most routine and automatic confirmation in a liturgical church.

Revival Conversions   Revival meetings typically have as their main purpose the stimulation of public conversions, with the music, sermons, and related publicity and personal "witnessing" all directed toward that end. Camps, retreats, "cursillos," and some other mass meetings have the same intent—particularly if we include recommitments of believers. Although the revival meetings of the Great Awakening are considered the prototypes of contemporary revivals, precedents are considerably more ancient. The preaching of the Hebrew prophet Jonah to the city of Nineveh, and the Christian apostles at Pentecost (Acts, Chapter 2) are in the spirit of the most spiritual contemporary revivals.

Surely some revivals are tawdry, and some are economically motivated. It is impossible to depict a typical revival meeting or response to it, but the following may be representative. Peter Jenkins, author of the best-selling *A Walk Across America* (1979), had come to Mobile, Alabama, in his cross-country hike. On his way to a party,

I glanced up and saw this big billboard: "Come to the revival." I really didn't know what a revival was. I had preconceptions of these real poor country people screaming and falling in the sawdust, you know, things I'd seen in the movies.

The idea just occurred to me: "Listen, Peter, you've been to a lot of boring parties. You know exactly what's going to be the outcome. You're going to have a hangover." I decided that instead of going to the party that I'd go to the revival, just because I'm a curious person. I went thinking that it would be in a tent, which it wasn't (it was in the Mobile municipal auditorium), and thinking there would be maybe 100 people. But there were about 10,000 people there.

Robison is an outstanding, dramatic, powerful evangelist. He's the most powerful preacher I've ever heard. He makes excellent points in logical sequence. He loosened his tie, and he was really screaming at the top of his lungs. Every time he'd point, he'd just inadvertently point right at me. I knew that what he was saying was the truth. So after he preached an excellent sermon, I realized in a very rational way that this is what I needed. I needed to forsake my ways and come to the Lord. I purposed that I was going to be a Christian for the rest of my life. So I stood and accepted the Lord. From then on I was sold out to God [Lee, 1979, pp. 55, 58, minor deletions not indicated].

Other faith traditions have other programmatic approaches to repentance, conversion, and recommitment. The Jewish Yom Kippur is an annual day of repentance. Hindu, Buddhist, and Muslim feasts and pilgrimages are frequently times of fervent recommitment. In terms of organization and efficiency, an old-time Methodist might envy the evangelistic efforts of Rev. Sun Myung Moon's Unification church. An initial street corner or campus contact leads to an invitation to the church center.

At this meeting, and at subsequent meetings and dinners at the center, the potential convert is surrounded by the warmth and friendship of the Family. Soon, he or she is invited to participate in a weekend workshop.

These highly structured workshops include long hours of theological discussion based on Moon's teachings. There is little time for sleep, and no time for private reflection. In small groups, potential converts are encouraged to bare their souls and are presented with testimonials about the joy, peace, purpose, and love to be found in the Family. Before the weekend ends, commitment to a week-long workshop is sought. About one-fourth of the weekend participants agree. At the week-long workshop, the tempo escalates: training becomes more rigorous and "hard sell," regimentation more severe. Bombarded, allowed little sleep, and cut off from family and former friends, the week culminates in pressure for commitment to full-time membership [Batson, 1976a, p. 1].

Secular Conversion

The two-edged sword of conversion can cut both sacred and secular. Not all conversionlike experiences are religious in content. Oates (1973, pp. 107–108) observes that what Abraham Maslow called "peak experiences" very much resemble conversion in their dynamics and effects. A chapter of Starbuck's pioneering study of religious conversion described "Conversion as a Normal Human Experience." He collected considerable questionnaire data to demonstrate that sudden, crisis resolutions and changes may be observed in ordinary life. One woman reported:

> I once had a teacher whom I simply detested. I disliked her so much that I thought of her constantly. One day I happened to pass her in the hall. I do not know what she did. In fact, I think she did nothing, but just as quickly as she passed me my hatred turned to love. I know it sounds foolish to speak of loving anyone like that, but I positively adored her [Starbuck, 1903, p. 141].

Other cases are as simple as abrupt changes of food tastes.

Counterconversion A special form of secular conversion has been called counterconversion. Basically it represents a conversion from religiousness to irreligion. James (1902/1961, pp. 150–153) offers several such cases of counterconversion. Pratt told of the Italian priest Robert Ardigo. Having defended his faith against scientific positivism for years, he suddenly realized that he had become a positivist:

> The new system I found, to my very great amazement, almost complete, and unshakably settled in my mind. . . . My last reflections had snapped the last thread that still held me bound to belief. Now it suddenly came to me, as though I had never in my life believed, and had never done otherwise than study, to develop the purely scientific tendency in myself [Pratt, 1920, pp. 120–127].

Conversion is not exclusively a religious experience. Its potential resides in the human psyche and may be shown in many ways. Psychologically conversion has variously been likened to breaking of habits, one-trial learning, acceleration of growth, psychotherapy, regression in the service of the ego, intellectual insight, sudden reorientation, hypnosis, brainwashing, an acute confusional state, and an acute hallucinatory reaction.

These psychological models and analogies to conversion, separately or together, do not fully explain conversion. They make it more accountable, more intelligible, but they do not answer ultimate questions about religious experience. They do not eliminate the possibility of divine intervention, which is outside the realm of psychological study. Nonetheless, we may conclude with Starbuck that *"however inexplicable, the facts of conversion are manifestations of natural processes"* (1903, p. 143). We now turn to some of the major social and psychological factors involved in religious conversion.

FACTORS IN CONVERSION

Conflict and Neurosis

Psychological studies of conversion have, from the beginning, often implied that the phenomenon involved pathological or neurotic elements. Emotional temperament, guilt, and conflict have been strongly associated with crisis conversions in particular.

Freud's only writing specifically on conversion employed concepts and language of pathology. A young physician was converted soon after he saw an old woman on a dissecting table. Freud said the situation stimulated oedipal jealousy and anger, which were directed at the father figure (God) for the sadistic, sexualized degradation of the mother (represented by the old woman). The rebellions against father and God were entwined, resulting immediately in feelings of religious disbelief. However, the need to resolve the oedipal conflict supposedly forced the physician to convert to his childhood faith (Freud, 1928).

Some conversion studies have looked exclusively at psychotherapy clients. Probably if we studied love or sex, leadership or politics, among such a population, we would find sick love, pathological leadership, and so on. Even so, most of these studies conclude that the resolution of conflicts in conversion may be either regressive and pathological *or* integrative of personality and maturing.

Among 43 theological students Roberts (1965) found that crisis converts had experienced guilt no more often than gradual converts, prior to their conversions. His study also showed that those who converted to a faith other than that of their upbringing were no more likely to become neurotic or psychotic—contrary to earlier findings (e.g., Salzman, 1953). Of course seminarians are a biased sample also.

With regard to pathology in conversion, we can best follow James's rejection of the "genetic fallacy." That is, we evaluate religion not on the basis of its origins, but on its results. "By their fruits ye shall know them, not by their roots" (James, 1902/1961, p. 34).

Abnormal and Paranormal Signs

Christensen (1963) emphasized the role of auditory and visual hallucinations in religious conversion. (Psychologists understand hallucinations as "sensory" experiences of one's own mental processes, perceived as if they originated outside of oneself.) When respondents are not restricted to psychiatric patients, hallucinations are rare. Moreover, when they occur in a religious conversion, they are usually separate from the psychoses and other extreme pathological states (where hallucinations are best known in clinical psychology and psychiatry). In Susan Atkins's conversion at the start of this chapter, you noted both auditory and visual hallucinations, but Susan was in no sense psychotic. The experiences were more like a classic religious vision or revelation. They might, therefore, better be classed as paranormal rather than abnormal.

A striking case of the paranormal is reported in the conversion of Dr. Richard Alpert. Fired from the Harvard University psychology department after LSD experiments in association with Timothy Leary, Alpert went to India to search for "the keys to the knowledge of enlightenment," particularly among Buddhist monks. He drove one day to a remote Himalayan mountain with a young American, who wanted to visit his Hindu guru. The night before their arrival Alpert had been under the stars, thinking of his mother, who had died 6 months earlier following an operation on her spleen.

After they reached their destination, the American's guru called Alpert, and said:

"Come, sit down here." So I sit down. He looks at me and he says: "You were out under the stars last night. You were thinking about your mother." I said, "Yes." He said to me, "She died last year." "Yeah." He closed his eyes. "She got very big in the belly before she died." This is all in Hindi, and he closed his eyes and he suddenly looked me directly in the eye and he said in English, "Spleen." What happened, in effect, was that my mind went fast—first I got totally paranoid. I mean, I assumed suddenly that I was in a science fiction scene, and this was the head of the world interpol or something, this was a huge plot to take me over. But the plot was too absurd; my mind couldn't handle that. Finally my mind went until it just sort of—gave up. You know, the red light goes on and it says, "Tilt," or "Reject," or "This program is not compatible with the data you are feeding in."

At that point there was a simultaneous experience which was incredible of a very violent, very painful wrenching in my chest which was like a door long closed being opened—one of those squeaking heavy doors being scrunched open—and I started to cry and the crying was neither sad nor happy. The closest I could feel was, "I'm home." [Dass, 1974, p. 109, minor deletions not indicated].

The guru renamed Alpert "Ram Dass," and he has become a full-time yoga disciple and teacher.

Striking as such reports are, psychology is not able to do much with them, other than observe them. Some students—particularly the theologically oriented—insist on maintaining room for divine intervention in conversion experiences. Perhaps these paranormal experiences can best serve to keep our science humble.

Deprivation and Overstimulation

The class of factors we call deprivation and overstimulation is a mixed bag, containing as it does opposite influences, and somewhat different uses of deprivation. Baer's (1978) study of converts to the Aaronic Order found that most conversions were related to economic or psychological deprivation. Some converts had experienced reversals of health, finances, or social status within 1 or 2 years of their investigating the Order. Others had had a lifetime of deprivations that predisposed them to conversion to a minority religious group. Similarly O'Dea (1966, pp. 59–65) noted the conversion to new religious movements in times of social disruption—particularly Puerto Rican immigrants converting to Pentecostal groups in New York City.

Sales (1972) did a systematic study of conversions to eight American denominations during the years 1920–1939. Additions to the "authoritarian" denominations tended to be associated with years of economic depression, while conversions to "nonauthoritarian" churches peaked in years of economic growth.

Deprivation, then, is associated with a particular kind of religious faith—one that offers security through a relatively rigid structure and dogma. More specifically, for example, the Presbyterian church in the United States attracted 30% fewer converts during the 6 "bad" years than during the 7 "good" years. Inversely, the Seventh-Day Adventist church attracted 68% *more* converts in the bad than in the good years. Sales similarly identified 4 good and 4 bad economic years in the Seattle, Washington, area between 1961 and 1970. The United Presbyterian church (nonauthoritarian) attracted more converts during the good years; the Roman Catholic church (authoritarian) drew more during the bad years.

Sensory Deprivation and Stimulation   Sargant (1957, 1969) emphasizes two contrasting ways that one may be "opened" to a conversion experience. One is by "sensory deprivation," best illustrated by methods of contemplation and meditation. The contrast is overstimulation of the nervous system, for example "by means of drumming, dancing and music of various kinds, by the rhythmic repetition of stimuli and by the imposing of emotionally charged mental conflicts needing urgent resolution" (1969, p. 510). Some revivalistic methods provide such a high degree of stimulation. Recall Peter Jenkins's report of the evangelist's "screaming" and pointing. Think, too, of the Unification church's bombardment of potential converts during their workshops, at the same time they are cut off from normal social stimuli and opportunities to reflect alone. Surely sensory deprivation and overstimulation may affect some religious conversion experiences.

Social Influence and Suggestibility

Social influence and suggestibility have been studied in relation to conversion from the earliest investigations. An early study contrasted persons who expected climactic conversion experiences but either did or did not experience such. Of those who experienced conversion, 13 of 14 were readily hypnotized, thus proving to be suggestible. Of those who failed to experience crisis conversion (though expecting it), 9 of 12 were clearly resistant to hypnosis, and 2 seemed to be so (Coe, 1900, pp. 128–133).

Recently college students were given a test of hypnotic suggestibility. Those who were extremely high (14%) and extremely low (12%) were compared. The "low suggestibles" were more likely to be unconverted. Of those who were converted, *all* of the "high suggestibles" reported crisis-type experiences; the converted "low suggestibles" tended to report more intellectual or situational factors in their conversions (Gibbons & DeJanrette, 1972).

Hypnotic aspects of revival meetings have been pointed out (Matheson, 1979), along with other efforts at social influence. A study of conversions to the Unification church identified seven factors in conversion, three of which were social in nature: (1) friendship bonds with members of the church, (2) few attachments to nonmembers, and (3) intensive interaction with the church group (Lofland, 1966, p. 7). These factors have not been found in every study of conversion (e.g., Seggar & Kunz, 1972), but among nine males who had been converted to a fundamentalistic commune, the third factor (above) was the single consistent influence (Austin, 1977). Of 35 cases of conversion to the Mormon Aaronic Order, 32 involved relatives, spouses, or friends who were influential in the decision to convert (Baer, 1978).

Social influence and the individual's susceptibility to such influence both appear to play significant roles in the likelihood of converting and in the kind of conversion experience. When social factors are the primary ones involved in conversion, though, one might question the durability and further development of the religious commitment.

Religious and Theological Background

Family background is as important for conversion as for general religious development. Clark (1958, p. 204) said that not a single member of the Oxford Group (an evangelistic society prominent in New England) was brought up in an irreligious family. This is not an invariable fact, of course. Of the conversions reported in this chapter, Sheldon Vanauken and Richard Alpert came from families that did not go to church, temple, or synagogue. Susan Atkins, Peter Jenkins, and Davy Vanauken were reared in at least nominally religious families. A study of 347 Australian seminarians found that students from the less religious families were more likely to report vivid or crisis-type conversions. Presumably those from more religious homes were equally religious, since they were studying for the ministry, but had a more gradual religious development (Stanley, 1965).

Many observations confirm that persons are more likely to report a definite conversion experience if they were reared in a religious tradition that expects one. You recall the differences among religious schools in Scobie's (1973) percentages of sudden conversion and unconscious conversion. Similarly the 1978 survey of over 1000 American teenagers found that 46% of Protestants and only 22% of Catholics reported a "born again" experience. Also 46% of those from the Bible Belt South reported conversion, compared to 23% in the East and 25% in the West (Princeton Religion Research Center, 1979).

Dissonance and Attributions

Social psychologists have developed several related cognitive theories (understandings of mental processes) that are relevant to the psychology of religion. These will be discussed in more detail in Chapter 13 (Belief), but we introduce them briefly here to relate them to conversion.

Cognitive dissonance exists whenever there are inconsistencies within a person's beliefs or attitudes. This state of uneasiness motivates the person to make changes in the cognitive system—to resolve the inconsistencies or to account for the feelings, thoughts, and behaviors. Attribution theories focus on ways people explain the causes of their own feelings and behavior.

One conversion that can readily be interpreted in terms of cognitive dissonance involved the son of a London Baptist minister, who came to Philadelphia in 1688. Though not a professed Christian himself, Elias Keach accepted an invitation to preach in a Baptist church.

> Doubtless familiar with his father's sermons, he launched boldly into his message. While addressing the congregation, the enormity of his offense dawned upon him. He fell on his knees and confessed his hoax to the church. They led him to Christ, and he became the first pastor of the Pennepak church [Drakeford, 1964, p. 259].

The dissonance between the young man's disbelief and his brazen behavior was so great that he quickly resolved it by becoming a believer.

An experiment with non-Catholic Yale students required them to write an essay entitled "Why I Would Like to Become a Catholic"—a position contrary to their true feelings and beliefs. There was either strong or weak pressure to produce the essay. The weak-pressure condition produced stronger dissonance, since the students could not justify their act by the pressure applied. As predicted, the low-pressure (high-dissonance) condition produced more attitude change favorable toward Catholicism. The theory implies that conversion is more likely to be sincere and committed if it occurs with high dissonance, that is, where there is relatively little pressure or other external justification for making such a religious change (Brock, 1962).

So it may be with conversions to the Buddhist sect, Nichiren Shoshu, which has spread to America. Observations of a New York City Nichiren group identified the central activity of private and public worship to be chanting the title of the "Lotus Sutra," which is the specific object of the faith. The chant—*Nam myoho renge kyo*—has little meaning in Japanese and even less in English. Potential converts are told, in effect, to try chanting the words 1 hour each morning and evening for 100 days, and see what it will do for their lives. When people make such a commitment—reorganize their lives to accommodate the ritual—on such an unsubstantial basis, the dissonance is likely to be high. They are likely to attribute any good events in their lives to their chanting, and to convert to the Nichiren Shoshu faith to make their behavior and their beliefs consistent (Proudfoot & Shaver, 1975).

Nobody claims that dissonance and attribution account fully for any religious conversion. Nonetheless many observations of conversion are consistent with the theories.

Age

Age has been more widely studied than any other factor in conversion, perhaps because it seems relatively simple and objective. However, many issues of conversion age have not been resolved.

Adolescence   Early students of the psychology of conversion declared it a phenomenon of puberty. They readily noted, however, that some conversions occurred several years before adolescence, and some many years after. Two indices of age were used in the early research—the arithmetic average and the peak age of conversions (the mode). Both appeared in the adolescent years. Three studies around 1900 found average ages of 16.6, 16.4, and 16.6 (Johnson, 1956, p. 127). Starbuck (1903, p. 204) reported two studies that found averages of 13.7 and 14.8 for females, 16.3 and 16.4 for males—corresponding to earlier puberty for girls. In one group of 272, the peak was at 16; in a sample of 235 men and 254 women, the men peaked at age 16, but the women had almost identical modes at ages 13 and 16 (Coe, 1900). The modes of conversion are not reliable in many of these studies because of the small number of cases.

Conversion was sometimes identified with periods of greatest bodily growth, sometimes with the psychological stress and storms of adolescence. Starbuck devoted six chapters (82 pages) of his *Psychology of Religion* (1903) to adolescence, emphasizing not only the "storm and stress" and "doubt" of the period, but also higher drives: expanding social consciousness, intellectual integrity, search for identity. He considered even turmoil to be constructive: "the instability and anxiety and uncertainty, and even the extreme pain, is one of nature's ways of producing a full-fledged, self-poised human being with a high degree of self-reliance and spiritual insight" (Starbuck, 1903, p. 263).

Preadolescence By the 1920s a shift in the age of conversions was apparent. A 1922 study found the average age of conversion to be 14.6, and in 1929 it was 12.7 (Johnson, 1956, p. 127). In 1964 Drakeford observed that Southern Baptist leaders thought most conversions occurred in the 10–11 age range. A 1962 study within that denomination (Sunday School Board of the Southern Baptist Convention, 1965) included the following percentages of total conversions* that occurred at each age through adolescence (see Table 7.1).

The most common ages of conversions among Southern Baptists, in 1962 at least, were 9 and 10. There was no indication of peaking in adolescence, nor of girls converting earlier than boys. However, in terms of averages, the *median* was at the upper end of the thirteenth year. That is, 49.7% of the male and 50.8% of the female conversions occurred before the thirteenth birthday. This figure is close to E. T. Clark's 12.7 average in 1929.

What seems to have happened here is the effect of programmed conversions. As conversion became institutionalized and expected, children developed the expectation of being converted, and gradually were prepared for that time when they would make their professions of faith. Although the public conversion occurs at one point in time, it has usually been a gradually developing process. We previously noted the time of preadolescence as one of social conformity. The apparent surge of conversions among 9- and 10-year-olds, regardless of gender, strongly suggests that the effect of conformity has replaced the earlier effects of puberty as a major factor in at least programmed conversions.

---

*Data for this study were based on "baptisms," the ritual by which a person becomes a member of the Baptist faith. Baptism follows one's initial "profession of faith," usually quite shortly. Typically individuals are also baptized when they are converted from another faith (including most other Protestant denominations). We cannot estimate how many of the latter would qualify as true conversion experiences, and how many were changes of convenience. The study included baptism of 4087 males and 4521 females.

Table 7.1 PERCENTAGES OF SOUTHERN BAPTIST BAPTISMS FOR YEARS 6–19

Gender	Ages at baptism (conversion)													
	6	7	8	9	10	11	12	13	14	15	16	17	18	19
Female	0.5	2.5	6.8	11.3	12.7	8.6	8.3	5.2	4.7	3.4	2.6	1.9	1.5	1.6
Male	0.7	2.3	5.4	12.3	12.3	8.5	8.0	5.3	4.4	3.4	2.5	1.8	1.5	1.7

Source: Sunday School Board of the Southern Baptist Convention (1965), Appendix D.

Postadolescence   While some scholars saw the age of conversion falling, others thought the typical age had been underestimated by earlier studies. The early work had used mostly college students, seldom older than young adults, and so excluded older conversions—which would have increased the average age.

One proponent of an older conversion age surveyed three churches and found the average conversion ages to be 43, 46, and 41, respectively (Ferm, 1959). Among 77 persons, aged 15 and older (but obviously including a number of older adults) the median age was 20 for both crisis and gradual conversions (Jones, 1937). Almost 30% of the 1962 Southern Baptist conversions (baptisms) came at or after age 20 (Sunday School Board, 1965). Age distributions for these adult data are shown in Table 7.2.

Jung emphasized the mid-30s as a period of moving to a more internal orientation that is conducive to religious integration. Hiltner considered conversion most likely and "cultivatable" in the 30s. And Erikson's analysis of adult developmental stages suggests the mid-life "integrity crisis" as a prime time for conversion. None of these expectations is confirmed by the Southern Baptist data.

For persons who are disposed to join a church in childhood, mid-life crises probably take the form of reintegration, such as Jimmy Carter's. These would seldom be reflected in baptisms in the Southern Baptist data. Such reintegration of the spiritual life may be a most crucial turning point, and such persons are therefore likely to cite it as their "born-again" or "conversion" experience. Earlier they probably would have reported the time they joined the church or made a youthful decision. These second or third experiences likely raised average conversion ages above the adolescent years in some studies.

EFFECTS OF CONVERSION

Positive Benefits

Almost by definition, conversion (particularly crisis conversion) is followed immediately by positive emotions. A partial report of reactions from three studies is given in Table 7.3. Note that questions and methods of collecting these reactions varied from study to study and cannot be directly compared.

Most of a sample of 63 converts reported changes in certain kinds of behavior. All 30 (47%) who had either engaged in sex outside of marriage or drunk alcoholic beverage said they stopped that behavior. Similarly 67% reduced profanity, 87% gossiping, 78% criticism, and 41% aggression. There were also increased abilities to communicate with groups (90%) and with individuals (57%), and increased generosity of time with family (83%), help to friends (90%), to charities (81%), and to church (89%) (W. P. Wilson, 1972). Jones (1937, pp. 366–369) summarized the beneficent moral and prosocial results of "pagan" Greek initiations, Buddhist and Hindu revivals, and Moslem Sufi conversions, as well as Christian conversion.

Paloutzian (1976) studied effects of a university campus revival "characterized as rational and logical in tone." New converts showed the highest "purpose

Table 7.2 PERCENTAGES OF SOUTHERN BAPTIST BAPTISMS FOR 5-YEAR ADULT PERIODS

Gender	Age periods for baptism (conversion)					
	20–24	25–29	30–34	35–39	40–44	45–54[a]	55–65[a]
Women	7.3	5.2	4.4	3.4	2.6	1.5	0.7
Men	7.0	5.0	4.7	4.2	3.1	1.4	0.9

[a]Frequencies in these 10-year periods have been halved to be equivalent to 5-year periods.
Source: Sunday School Board of the Southern Baptist Convention (1965), Appendix D.

Table 7.3   IMMEDIATE REACTIONS TO CONVERSION

Feelings at conversion	Starbuck %	Drakeford %	Ferm %
Happiness	31	90	
Peace	37	82	
Calmness	7	52	
Relief, release	16	67	90
Joy	44		90
Oneness with God	33		
Sense of responsibility	10		
Partial disappointment	18		

Source: Starbuck (1903); Drakeford (1964); Ferm (1959).

in life" of all groups. Converts of 1 month previous had a temporary "relapse," which was mostly restored by 6 months after conversion.

Relapse and Struggles

Relapses and doubts are by no means rare following conversion. Some postconversion struggles noted by Starbuck are summarized in Table 7.4. He specifically noted, though, that compared to those with gradual religious growth, the conversion group had less "alienation from conventional standards," while they had more religious difficulties such as noted in Table 7.4 (1903, p. 357). Argyle (1958), however, found sudden converts the least likely to remain believers.

Revival Conversions

A number of scattered studies have attempted to follow up the effects of conversions at revivals. Among 73 converts at Boston revivals between 1948 and 1950, changes were reportedly no more profound than church attendance and Bible reading (W. H. Clark, 1958, p. 204). In the 1954–1955 Billy Graham revival in England, about 2.5% of those attending made public "decisions," 75% of these being new converts without prior church affiliations. About 64% of those were

Table 7.4   CASES REPORTING POSTCONVERSION STRUGGLES

Type of struggle	Females %	Males %
Complete relapses	5	7
Periods of inactivity and indifference	65	30
Struggles with old habits	26	32
Struggles to attain an ideal	33	15
Storm and stress	38	35
Doubts	38	57
At least one of the above	93	77

Source: Starbuck (1903).

still attending church 8 months after their conversions (Argyle & Beit-Hallahmi, 1975).

Even less positive were results of "Here's Life, America" crusades in two American cities in 1977: only 3% of those who made decisions bothered even to join a church (Power to the Laity, 1978). Liston Mills (1963) did a 1-year follow-up of a spontaneous 3-week revival in an Indiana church. Of the 125 who made decisions during the revival, at least 37 could not even be located a year later. Only 12% of those contacted had assumed responsibilities in their churches; 41% attended less than once a month. Only 34% of those under 16 who made "professions of faith" followed up by joining a church (Oates, 1973, p. 105).

None of these studies is likely to bring joy to the heart of a professional evangelist! But neither did any include a comparison or control group—for example, persons who attended but did not make public decisions, those who converted in regular church services, unconsciously converted believers. There may also be differences between revivals conducted as part of the program of a local church and those orchestrated by itinerant evangelists. The Southern Baptist study (Sunday School Board, 1965) indicated that about 30% of the additions to the churches were made during revivals or other special efforts; an estimated 33% of the conversions of children and youth aged 6–16 were made during the revivals. Revivals, then, are neither inconsequential nor absolutely crucial.

Postconversion Growth

William James was skeptical of the long-term effects of conversion per se. "Converted [people]" he said, "as a class are indistinguishable from natural [ones]; some natural [ones] even excel some converted [ones] in their fruits" (1902/1961, p. 195). He went on: "If we roughly arrange human beings in classes, each class standing for a grade of spiritual excellence, I believe we shall find natural [people] and converts both sudden and gradual in all the classes" (1902/1961, p. 196).

We might view conversion as one event in religious development. What follows it is more important than the conversion experience itself. Conversion is sometimes an acceleration of religious growth, but maturation is a continuing process. Religious geniuses have always recognized this. The striking success of the preaching of John Wesley lay more in the methodological follow-up, cultivation, and development of the converts than in the conversions as such.

Some of the success of a healthy versus an unhealthy, regressive conversion experience may lie in the quality of later contacts with adherents of the new faith. Especially studying conversions from one faith to another, one author noted that besides emotional ties to the former faith, one-third of the converts had to give up their professional work or had trouble keeping up with their work. Nearly all had suffered loss of most of their closest social contacts. He warned:

> Responsible propagandists must be highly sensitive to the possible harm that may be done to a potential convert. Having interfered with the patterns of [one's] social, mental, and emotional life, they have a responsibility to look out for his [or her] future well-being [Harms, 1962, p. 126].

Conversion Shock

Subsequent need for religious nurture and growth notwithstanding, there is evidence that a crisis conversion experience may produce a deep and lasting commitment to a faith. Such can be expected on theoretical grounds. In pointing out the similarities of conversion to brainwashing and hypnosis, Sargant (1969) noted the strength of learning acquired under conditions of emotional stress. He recalled that some of Ivan Pavlov's dogs (of classical conditioning fame) were trapped in their laboratory cages during the 1924 Leningrad flood. Rescued just before they would have drowned, they were thereafter highly sensitized to even a trickle of water under the door of their room. Further, some of the dogs, in the excitement and exhaustion, lapsed into a state of stupor and emotional collapse. Their previously conditioned reflexes were completely wiped out, and new ones were readily conditioned. So might a lifetime of bad habits be obliterated in an emotional conversion crisis, to be replaced with a new faith.

W. H. Clark (1958), who coined the term *conversion shock* to identify this process, observed that most outstanding religious leaders have experienced such crisis—for example, Isaiah, Paul, St. Augustine, Socrates, Mohammed, the Buddha, Luther, and Tolstoy. Whereas only 6.7% of E. T. Clark's cases had experienced crisis conversion, there was a much higher rate among his preachers and missionaries (W. H. Clark, 1958, p. 214). More recent figures are 18% for American teenagers, 7.6% for college students, and 23% for adults, compared to 56%, 56%, 55%, and 20% in various studies of seminary students.

A recent study involving separate samples of 84 college students and 177 adults found that in both groups, those with sudden conversions were significantly stronger in an internalized, committed faith (Paloutzian, Jackson, & Crandall, 1978). Commenting on religious educators' and liberal theologians' preferences for gradual conversions and religious development, Clark remarked, "If gradual awakening is in every respect to be desired, it is a little hard to explain this seemingly high incidence of crisis among the spiritual *elite*" (W. H. Clark, 1958, p. 214).

SUMMARY

Conversion is not a singular kind of experience. There are different kinds, and different factors operating in different conversion experiences. There are also diverse effects of religious conversions.

One may be tempted to thread lines through the sections and subsections of this chapter, like a children's puzzle, and reach some coherences. For example, "crisis conversions are effected by emotional conflicts and tend to persist," or "programmed revival conversions are effected by social influences and tend to result in mere church attendance—and often not that." Such generalizations, however, would be too glib to match the facts. There are too many exceptions. Some crisis conversions fall by the wayside (many, according to some students), and some produce nominal followers. Some conversions that start in revival meetings produce robustly committed religious leaders, as do some unconscious conversions (slow unfolding of faith).

Conversion *is* a frequently observed step in religious development. Often it is a most crucial step. Almost never does it in itself produce a fully integrated religious individual. In a phrase, it is neither necessary nor sufficient for a mature faith. To study and understand religious conversion in its varieties, though, should enhance our conceptions of individual religious development, which we began in the previous unit.

REVIEW OF KEY CONCEPTS

Introduction
    James's definition of conversion

Types of Conversion
    three stages of crisis conversion
    nature of gradual or volitional conversion
    prerequisite conditions for unconscious conversion
    nature of reintegration
    programmed conversion compared with confirmation
    background and characteristics of revival conversions
    illustrations of secular conversion
    counterconversion
    some psychological models of conversion

Factors in Conversion
    evidence for and against conflict and neurosis explanations
    abnormal and paranormal signs in conversion
    relation of social deprivation to authoritarian and nonauthoritarian conversions
    effects of sensory deprivation and stimulation
    suggestibility and hypnotic aspects of conversion
    three social factors in Unification Church conversions
    effects of family backgrounds on conversions
    theological and geographic factors in kind of conversion
    implications of cognitive dissonance theory for conversion
    relevance of attributions to conversion
    classic relevance of puberty and adolescence to conversion
    contemporary evidence on preadolescence and conversion
    programmed conversion and conformity
    critique of classical studies
    contemporary evidence on postadolescent conversions
    major conclusions on factors in conversion

Effects of Conversion
    positive emotional benefits—"purpose in life"
    moral and prosocial behaviors related to conversion
    relapse—its incidence and struggles, storms and stress

Prayer and Faith Healing

When U.S. Secretary of State Henry Kissinger prayed at the Wailing Wall in Jerusalem, Israeli Premier Golda Meir reportedly said, "Look at that schmuck—talking to himself beside a pile of stones" (Valeriani, 1979).

THE NATURE OF PRAYER

Nothing distinguishes the religious from the nonreligious more than prayer. Friedrich Heiler called prayer "the most spontaneous and the most personal expression of religion" (1932, p. 119). William James called it "the very soul and essence of religion" and went on to say, "Prayer is religion in act; that is, prayer is real religion" (1902/1961, p. 361).

Premier Meir's agnostic assumption also raises a crucial issue with regard to prayer. Is the person really talking to self or to a Divine Other? Is prayer merely auto-suggestion, verbal self-stimulation, or does it make contact with a Power beyond oneself? From a strictly scientific perspective we cannot give firm answers to these questions, but they raise important psychological issues that we cannot ignore.

Prayer As Communication

We define prayer as communication with a (presumed) Divine Other. Communication may be one-way, but two-way communication is more complete, of course. In prayer, then, there should be an expectation that God will respond in some way that can be understood by the pray-er.

Like other communication, prayer may be nonverbal as well as verbal. It may be an attitude of attentiveness toward Divine Reality, without words either uttered or unuttered. Corporate or private rituals, with or without accompanying spoken or chanted address to the Deity, may be the equivalent of prayer. A liturgical dance in a contemporary church ("Praise [God] with timbrel and dance," Psalm 150 : 4) or a rain dance among preliterate peoples may function like prayer. Sacraments may be prayer equivalents. Simpler private rituals such as genuflecting before an altar or making the sign of the cross may be motions of prayer. Within Latin American folk Catholicism mere physical contact with the effigy of a saint may be considered an effective act of propitiation or a protection from danger (McEwen & Aseltine, 1979); a soldier may finger a crucifix or religious medal when under bombardment.

Of course these behaviors may be as mindless and naive as throwing spilt salt over one's shoulder; they may degenerate into magical spells or charms—superstition rather than prayer. However, this danger exists also for verbal prayers. Some petitions so naively attempt to manipulate the Deity that they are more superstitious than religious acts. Of course a thoroughgoing atheist may consider all prayer superstitious, and few psychologists would attempt to make an absolute distinction between prayer and superstition. We assume there is a difference of degree, that the one shades into the other; the zone of demarcation should be apparent before this chapter is done.

The Scope of Prayer

Prayer, like religion, appears to be virtually universal. Even among people who say they have no need for religion, some still pray on occasion. Various surveys have found that as many as 87% of youth pray (Princeton Religion Research Center, 1979). One study found that more than half of the psychologically healthiest persons, and 64% of the most disturbed, prayed in circumstances of "catastrophe"—such as loss of a spouse by death or divorce, serious injury, or detention in jail. Marriage and legal troubles were occasions for prayer among 10% and 11% (respectively) of the healthiest, and 50% and 63% of the most troubled (Lindenthal, Myers, Pepper, & Stern, 1970).

Prayer is found in all cultures and may mark any significant human event. Prayers are often ritually prescribed for births, baptisms, puberty, weddings, and funerals. Liturgical Christian churches call for special prayers for each season, indeed each week of the Christian calendar. The Jewish Talmud ordains prayers for private and public, for morning and afternoon, for entering and leaving the house of worship, for going to bed and for rising, and for going to the bathhouse and to the privy (Rosner, 1975).

TYPES OF PRAYER

Prayer, like religion itself, is rooted in human needs and emotions. In a study of 630 Swedish children Klingberg (1959) found that of all religious experiences, prayer involved the deepest emotional reactions. Among almost 3700 students the most common reasons given for praying were (in order of frequency): to ask for personal benefits, to give thanks, to talk to God, to ask for guidance, to comply with habit, to seek comfort, to ask help for others, and to ask forgiveness (Pixley & Beekman, 1949). Prayers are as different as the desires and feelings that incite them.

Petitionary Prayer

Deficits are both the most primitive and the most common motives to prayer. Heiler (1932) identified the cry for help as the original form of prayer. More expansively, a poster in a friend's office recommended:

A prayer
to be said
when the world
has gotten you down,
and you feel rotten,
and you're too doggone tired
to pray,
and you're in a big hurry
and beside you're mad
at everybody.—

help!

Fear may motivate prayers of petition. Allport commented (on the report of a serviceman who had flown 30 missions over Germany in World War II), "Prayer is continuous with hope, as hope is continuous with fear" (1950/1960, p. 56). Illness also incites prayer: "Wishing is praying, and who, if sick, does not wish with all the intensity of his [or her] soul for recovery?" (Spivak, 1917). Other more crass desires may lead to prayer, as the report (Yancey, 1979) of a man who prayed for a brown Winnebago—and got exactly that!

Petitionary prayers are the most problematic type, partly because they can be so self-serving, as the immediate example shows. Most of the study and research on prayer concerns petitionary prayer, and we defer a fuller discussion until later in the chapter.

Intercessory Prayer

A special class of petitions is prayer for the needs of another person—an interceding or intercession on behalf of the other. Because of the human capacity for empathy, the needs of another person, particularly someone we care for, may be as sorely felt as our own. To illustrate prayer, Jesus told of a man who was visited by a hungry friend in the middle of the night. The host went to a neighbor and asked for food to give to the friend—something the man obviously would not have done for his own needs (Luke 11 : 5–8). Intercessory prayers may be for another's spiritual, psychological, or material benefit, but perhaps most common are prayers for health or healing. Faith healing, a result of such religious exercises, will be examined later in this chapter.

Thanksgiving

Sir Francis Galton (1883) noted that people share with other animals the impulse to pour out their feelings in sound. The expression of our emotions and aspirations is a powerful and pervasive root of prayer. Perhaps the feeling of thanksgiving or gratitude finds the most common expression in prayers. When we feel that the necessities and joys of our lives are abundantly provided, we may be moved to express gratitude to the divine source of such bounty.

Thanksgiving is usually the first kind of prayer that parents teach children. "Wait a minute," you say, "do we give thanks because we feel the need or because we have been taught to do so?" Surely this illustrates the unity of human functioning. Not only do we act out our feelings, but also our actions influence our feelings. As we—children or adults—develop the habit of giving thanks, we are more likely to feel gratitude for our gifts. The same holds true of other expressive prayers; each mode of prayer both expresses and cultivates the respective religious emotion.

Adoration and Praise

As thanksgiving may spring from perceived answers to petitionary and intercessory prayers, and other blessings, so thanksgiving may generalize to prayers of adoration and praise. Thanksgiving focuses on what an individual has received, but when individuals perceive the divine source of creation, order, and beauty, they may be impressed with awe and wonder. God or the Divine is seen as one to be praised, adored, worshiped.

Confession, Dedication, and Communion

The desire for relationship and communion with Deity motivates other kinds of prayers. When people see themselves as estranged from God by their own shortcomings and wrongdoings (sin), they may seek to repair the rupture by repenting, confessing the sin, and asking forgiveness. The form of such prayers will vary with each person's theology or tradition. Ritual cleansing or baptism may be an acted-out form of confession or repentance prayer.

With or without confession, a believer may feel strongly the need to commit self to the Deity. Prayer of dedication is illustrated by Isaiah's response, "Here am I; send me" (Isaiah 6 : 8).

One of the higher forms of prayer is the prayer of communion. Here one desires only to experience a relationship with God, to know and to be known, to be present to Deity. The prayer does indeed seek something for the pray-er, but the motive is purely spiritual.

Meditation

Meditative prayer can be considered a systematically developed form of the prayer of communion. It typically involves a technique, which may vary rather widely among religious traditions. Just as petitionary prayer may become a superstitious charm, so meditation shades from the devoutest prayer to a mere technology to produce emotional control and mental sensitivity. (Chapter 10 discusses meditation further.)

Meditation is most prominent among Eastern religions, particularly in Hindu yoga and Zen Buddhism. These disciplines typically call for relaxation of physical tensions with focused concentration on some sensory or verbal event, for example, the breath in one's nostrils, the flame of a candle, a geometric design (mandala), or a repeatedly uttered or thought word or phrase with religious significance (a mantra). Meditation is represented in Judaism (particularly the Hasidic tradition) and Islam (e.g., Sufism). It is a major ingredient in the Catholic mystical tradition and is more generally identified with the discipline of interior prayer among the religious of virtually all Catholic orders and among devout lay persons.

Although structured meditation has been relatively rare in Protestant Christianity, it has recently surged—perhaps partly in response to the popularity of Eastern meditation among youth. Priscilla Brandt's book *Two-Way Prayer* (1979) represents an assimilation of Eastern patterns into Western spirituality. In brief, the four steps of "two-way prayer" involve (1) quiet relaxation, (2) confession and repentance, (3) focusing on God's works, and (4) listening, to insure a dialogue, not a monologue or sheer self-manipulation.

Objective and Subjective Prayer

James B. Pratt (1920), a pioneer in the psychology of religion, distinguished between objective and subjective prayer. Objective prayer focuses on the object of one's religious devotion: the Divine Other. Subjective prayer primarily points back to the pray-er. Self-centered, or at least person-centered, needs inspire subjective prayer, of which the petitionary and intercessory forms are typical.

We can also distinguish between prayers of thanksgiving (in which the immediate attention is on the benefits received by the pray-er) and adoration (which is directed to the Giver of those benefits). Some of the other forms of prayer may be primarily objective or subjective, depending on the precise motives and attention of the person. A prayer of communion might serve primarily to relieve the subject's loneliness and insecurity, or it may reflect one's pure, heartfelt desire to experience a relationship with the Deity.

Pratt and subsequent writers have emphasized that self-centered, subjective prayer is self-limiting and self-defeating. Spiritual and personal growth more reliably follow a turning outward from self, as one focuses on the Ultimate in objective prayer. This perspective leads us to some of the issues and research with regard to petitionary prayer.

PROBLEMS OF PETITIONARY PRAYER

On the surface at least, petitionary prayers implore divine powers to supply believers with benefits, tangible or intangible. Theological and empirical questions abound. Is this a proper use of religion or Deity? How does it differ from magic? What is the efficacy of such petitions; that is, do they work? If so, in what areas and situations are they effective? If not, why do people continue them? Answers to these questions touch theological and devotional bases, but we shall attempt as objective an analysis as we can in a rather short space.

Prayer, Superstition and Magic

Human beings are superstitious insofar as they (1) perceive causal connections among events that merely occur together, (2) perceive relationships where none exist, and (3) think they can control events that are really beyond their control (Myers, 1978, p. 174). Magic is guided by the third element of superstition. No religion, however advanced, is completely without elements of superstition and magic. These traits have been called "archaic" (Godin, 1971, p. 130), implying their origins in primitive religions. Perhaps more pervasively, they arise spontaneously in the thinking of children, and frequently persist when a believer otherwise thinks and behaves in an adult fashion.

Godin says that, if a prayer or prayerlike ritual is used in a magical way, that is, to manipulate or put pressure on God to act in a certain manner, "its worth as a religious expression is reduced and even compromised" (1971, p. 130). Similarly Rosner asserts that "the idea that God *must* answer a prayer is presumptuous and represents a transgression in Judaism" (1975, p. 297)—as in almost all higher religions. He continues, "Prayer in Judaism is thought to be efficacious if offered by the right person at the proper time with the proper intent under the proper circumstances" (1975, p. 298). William James's (1902/1961, pp. 364–369) discussion of styles of prayer life may clarify the potential of prayer for both magical abuse and spiritual attainment.

Styles of Prayer Life

The Favored Life   James told about George Müller of nineteenth-century Bristol, England, who equipped hundreds of missionaries, built and ran five large orphanages, educated over 100,000 students, and distributed over 100 million copies of religious literature—on hardly more than prayer and faith. Müller let people know only of his general needs, but repeatedly found the specific needs of his work met. For example, all the food might be gone after a meal, but by the next mealtime more would have been provided, yet without his ever borrowing a pence.

Many Christians still exemplify this style of prayer. Ben Kinchlow, of a popular religious television program, tells when he was a drug counselor at Christian Farms in Texas:

> Our very first night on the farm, a young junkie came in. He was high as could be. As he began to come down, he was panicky because he knew what was ahead when his body began to crave the dope again. We prayed and asked for God's help and all the symptoms disappeared. Since then, I don't have trouble praying for people with "hopeless" problems. Right from the start of my Christian life I was taught to think that all Christians should pray and expect God to answer [Hazard, 1979, p. 70].

Persons who seem to lead such favored lives typically have a narrow and primitive religious perspective. As James said of George Müller, he conceived of God very concretely as his "business partner," hardly more than a "supernatural clergy [person] interested in the congregation of tradesmen and others in Bristol who were . . . saints, and in the orphanages and other enterprises (1902/1961, p. 366). However, the cases cited suggest a self-dedication to the Divine or the

Ultimate that rescues them from the crass, manipulative, magical use of petitions that characterizes the man who prayed for the brown Winnebago.

The Led Life   James characterized the led life as a less "beggarlike fashion" of relying on the Almighty for support. Still, persons so led may experience abundant, though more subtle, proofs of the active influence of God in their lives. Within this guided life one feels that:

> books and words (and sometimes people) come to one's cognizance just at the very moment one needs them; one glides over great dangers as if with shut eyes; great obstacles are suddenly removed; when the time has come for something, one discovers thoughts, talents, and even pieces of knowledge and insight, in one's self, of which it is impossible to say whence they came; persons help us as if they had to do so against their will. The highest resources of worldly wisdom are unable to attain that which, under divine leading, comes to us of its own accord [James, 1902/1961, pp. 367–368, quoting from C. Hilty, 1900, minor deletions not indicated].

The Harmonized Life   The harmonized style of prayer life is characterized by prayers of dedication and communion. Real, though subjective, changes are wrought by it. According to James, this style is based on the belief that:

> by cultivating the continuous sense of our connection with the power that makes things as they are, we are tempered more towardly for their reception. The outward face of nature need not alter, but the expressions of meaning in it alter. So when one's affections keep in touch with divinity, fear and egotism fall away; in the equanimity that follows, one finds a series of purely benignant opportunities. We meet a new world when we meet the old world in the spirit which this kind of prayer infuses [1902/1961, p. 368, minor deletions not indicated].

Such an attitude of harmony is perhaps most characteristic of such Eastern faiths as Taoism and Buddhism. Submissiveness to the flow of the natural order has some element of petitionary wishfulness, though at the polar extreme from George Müller's prayer habits.

Development of Prayer Styles

These varieties of petitionary prayers generally parallel a developmental progression. Goldman (1964a) found that up to 9 years of age children view the effectiveness of prayer magically. From 9 to 12 they think prayer works by other people bringing about beneficial material changes. After 12 or 13 children increasingly consider psychological and spiritual changes to be the primary effects of prayer.

With age children's belief in the efficacy of petitionary prayers gradually decreases. Nonetheless, there is no such decline in their judgments of the appropriateness of such praying in a particular situation (see Chapter 11) (Brown,

1966a). This paradox indicates that the function of petitionary prayer changes as one matures in the religious life.

The Efficacy of Petitionary Prayer

Testing Prayer   Claims for the effectiveness of prayer almost irresistibly invite empirical test. If prayer really works, it should be simple enough to design experiments to prove it. In the 1870s Sir Francis Galton proposed that prayers be made for rain over half of England, and for fair weather over the other half. A simple comparison of rainfall differences would tell the story. Since such blatant testing of God was not acceptable, Galton revealed that he had collected data on the number of stillbirths to praying and nonpraying parents, and the longevity of public figures who would be the natural subjects of intercessory prayers: kings, clergy, and missionaries. There were no differences in stillbirths; kings were the shortest lived; and clergy tended to die younger than either lawyers or physicians (Galton, 1883).

Myers (1978, pp. 182–183) expresses a number of scientific and theological objections to such tests of prayer. There are also good psychological reasons to challenge such undertakings, obvious as they may seem. Consider the consequences of highly positive results of the studies. For at least some people prayer would no longer be a matter of religious faith and self-examination; it would be a tool, a technique. Like throwing a light switch or feeding instructions into a computer, it would be a self-serving device to get something done for us. As C. S. Lewis wrote, "[One] who knew empirically that an event has been caused by . . . prayer would feel like a magician. [One's] head would turn and [one's] heart would be corrupted" (1947, p. 214). Similarly Father John Dunne of Notre Dame University notes, "The quest for certainty is self-defeating, whether it is about God, about someone we love, or about the significance of our selves" (Woodward, Manning, Whitmore, Copeland, & Mark, 1979, p. 47).

If a deity can meaningfully answer a believer's prayer, and if prayer is to remain a spiritual rather than a magical exercise, then surely that same deity would make sure that all empirical studies of the efficacy of prayer will turn out inconclusive! The evidence for the effectiveness of prayers, as they touch events in the material world, remains outside of the domain of science. The faithful who want to believe can believe, and the skeptic who chooses not to believe could not be convinced.

Psychological Effects   Even Galton noted that prayer may produce significant psychological results, and most believers would agree. What are the evidence for and the consequences of prayer's psychological effects? Johnson (1956) cited ten psychological effects of prayer, which are summarized in Box 8.1. There are few hard empirical data supporting such results, but a substantial body of testimony and considerable theological and psychological theorizing maintain them. Gay (1978) cites a number of ways in which prayers and religious rituals serve the same functions as psychotherapy. However, the religious practices operate in dis-

---

Box 8.1   PSYCHOLOGICAL EFFECTS OF PRAYER

1. Makes us aware of our needs and of realities, as we face the One who knows all, and as we examine ourselves

2. Allows confession and a sense of forgiveness as we see ourselves, not so much as weak, but as inadequate, since self-sufficiency is self-deception

3. Engenders faith and hope that relaxes tensions, worries, and fears, and brings confidence and peace of mind

4. Puts our lives in perspective as our meditations solve problems and produce practical plans of action

5. Clarifies goals to which we can dedicate ourselves, focus our lives, and unleash latent powers to achieve

6. Renews emotional energy, through the euphoria of communication with the Divine

7. Makes us responsive to needs of other persons and channels our social and altruistic motives

8. Affirms our values and prepares us to accept with joy whatever happens

9. Fosters our loyalty to the Ultimate and perseverance in devotion

10. Integrates our personalities through focusing upon a supreme loyalty

Source: Johnson (1956, pp. 132, 143–144).

---

tinctive and not inferior ways. The section on faith healing indicates more psychological benefits of prayer.

The Necessity of Belief   There is another problem. As Pratt (1920, p. 336) noted, the psychological values of prayer are primarily due to the belief that prayer has effects that go beyond the psychological—that it changes material events, health, feelings, and behaviors of other people, etc. Persons who believe that prayer has *only* psychological results are not likely to pray at all, especially to petition God for specific benefits. They may pray for their own anxieties and cares to be relieved—or for their minds to be tuned to optimum effectiveness—as an exercise in auto-suggestion or self-deception.

However, it is not easy to dispel real dangers—the hazards of serious illness, the risk of an accident, an approaching hurricane. Most believers consider these appropriate occasions for prayer, even if they doubt its efficacy (Brown, 1966a). No sheer self-manipulation can be so effective in those times as devout prayer. But for the prayer to avail, even psychologically, there must be either belief that there is a Divinity that cares and will protect the faithful, or such faith in the rightness of the natural order that one can fully accept any event that might occur ("as Allah wills" in the Islamic faith).

Prayer must falter and fail as a magical act apart from personal faith. Writing as a psychologist and a believer, Myers concluded,

> In the last analysis, our prayer is not prompted by any rationally defensible theory . . . but by a mysterious faith that craves dialogue and personal relationship

with its source. . . . I continue petitionary prayer partly because this is so natural a way of sharing concerns with my creator [1978, pp. 191, 193].

FAITH HEALING

Prayers for restoration of health are among the most common petitionary and intercessory prayers. Likewise, prayer is the most frequently employed ritual in faith healing. When we have asked classes of students, even in a denominational college, how many believed in faith healing, only about 5% would admit such belief. Nonetheless, faith healing (given an appropriate definition) must stand as well established as any phenomenon of science.

Variations of Faith Healing

Faith healing occurs in innumerable contexts. The following cases are illustrative, not exhaustive.

Group Healing Ceremony   Frank (1961) summarized one case of primitive healing. Four days before the ceremony, a shaman held a diagnostic session with the patient (who suffered from "soul loss," which we would call an agitated depression), her husband, and a friend. She was encouraged to release her pent-up frustrations and to recall the event that precipitated the current attack. She also was to arrange a feast, medications, and a suitable supportive group to assist with the ceremony—which lasted from 4 P.M. until 5 A.M. After the feast, the healer performed a long series of rituals with wax dolls, offered gifts to evil spirits, and massaged the patient—first with whole, unbroken eggs, and then with his own sandals. About 2 A.M. the patient, naked save for a loincloth, was sprayed with an alcoholic "magic fluid" that gave her a severe chill. Finally the shaman broke the eggs (used in the massage) into water, and read in them the proofs that the disease had been cured. After a few days of fever the patient recovered, and a month later seemed to have developed a new personality, with all emotional and social symptoms gone (pp. 46–49, summarized from Gillin, 1948).

A Western Shrine   A retired French accountant, paralyzed on one side of his body and nearly blind, experienced a strange sensation while visiting the Catholic shrine in Lourdes in 1970. He regained his sight within hours and could walk without crutches. When doctors could find no sign of his former disabilities, the Roman Catholic church formally proclaimed his cure a miracle—the sixty-fourth certification in the history of the shrine. Among the millions who visit Lourdes each year (over 30,000 of them sick), relatively few experience even uncertified cures, but most find great spiritual benefit. A shrine official says, "It is not an emphasis on curing the sick, but it aids the solitude of the sick and they come to understand that their suffering is worthwhile."

Those cures that do occur at Lourdes resemble normal healing. Restoration of tissue and regaining of weight take the usual time. Wounds or sores are filled

with scar tissue, not virgin skin, and no amputated limb has been miraculously
restored (Frank, 1961, pp. 53–59; Keerdoja & Sciolino, 1979).

Mass Media Healing   On a popular religious television show the director's wife
said she believed God did not want her to suffer the trauma of a scheduled hernia
surgery. One Sunday she felt moved to immerse a wart on her finger in the Communion glass. She reported "a sudden energy rushing through her, and discovered
the next day that her hernia had been healed" (Yancey, 1979, p. 32). Twenty
thousand viewers of the same program write each year to report healing as a result
of the show.

Medical Practice   When a patient is suffering from fatal illness, chronic pain,
guilt feelings, or depression from the loss of a loved one, one Midwestern physician asks if she or he would like to be prayed upon. If the patient agrees, he or
she is seated in a chair, with the physician and several others from the office or
hospital forming a circle. After a brief meditative silence, the physician, standing
behind with his hands on the patient's head, prays for healing love in the body,
mind, and spirit of the patient.

What do such diverse ceremonies have in common? A physical or mental
disability; a desire for healing; a belief system that lends credence to the procedures; and usually a supportive social group. The persons healed are, like those
at Lourdes, "almost invariably a simple people—the poor and the humble; people
who do not impose a strong intellect between themselves and the Higher Power"
(Cranston, 1957, p. 125, cited by Frank, 1961, p. 59).

How Faith Healing Works

Two Experiments   A physician asked a prominent faith healer to try to cure
three severely ill, bedridden women by absent treatment, without their knowledge. Nothing happened. Then he told the women about the healer, built up their
confidence in him, and assured them that at a certain time on a certain day he
would treat them. The healer actually was not working that day, but all three
of the women dramatically improved at the time of the supposed prayer. One
with a chronic gall bladder infection lost all her symptoms and went home and
had no recurrence for several years. One who had failed to recover from major
surgery, and was virtually a skeleton, was permanently cured. A woman dying
of widespread cancer lost a great deal of excess fluid, recovered from anemia,
and went home to resume her household duties almost symptom-free until her
death (Frank, 1961, pp. 60–61).

Forty-six ill persons were treated with "laying-on of hands." Blood samples
showed increased hemoglobin values, whereas there were no such changes in the
hemoglobin of 29 comparable control patients. The statistically significant finding
was similar to that of three other studies reported by the same researcher
(Krieger, 1975, 1976).

Both gross and refined measures indicate that something real can happen in faith healing. How can faith or prayer or other spiritual events affect one's physical condition?

Body-Mind-Spirit Unity   The separation of the human being into body, mind, soul, spirit, or such entities was foreign to the Hebrews and other Eastern peoples. The Greeks introduced it into common Western thought. Yoga is one Eastern tradition that has consistently maintained a unity of the person. That is why physical and breathing exercises, relaxation, and meditation are all part of the yoga spiritual system.

The scientific view sees what we call mind as a function of the brain, part of our body. The brain/mind controls virtually all bodily functions, while the body supplies the brain with nutrients, protection, etc., as part of itself. What we call soul or spirit cannot, scientifically speaking, be separated from other mental or psychological functions. Some contemporary thinkers postulate conscious, mental, spiritual entities separate from the brain/mind, but these have not gained credence in the scientific community. We believe the scientific facts and world view can account for most if not all of what we call faith healing. This is not, however, to deny possible divine activity.

The Nature of Disease   A physician, writing on faith healing, tells three ways disease can occur. (1) An imbalance may occur among parts of the body; (2) invasions by other living entities (bacteria, viruses) may cause the body to malfunction; (3) disruptions may be caused by failure of mental control of the nervous systems and the hormonal system. In all of these it is the functioning of the body and its components (including mind) that determines health or disease (Mes, 1975, pp. 18–20).

The brain/mind is or can be involved in virtually any disease. Of the patients in any general medical clinic, from 50 to 90% suffer from emotionally, mentally induced problems, rather than purely organic disorders. One set of problems, the psychophysiological disorders, are caused primarily by chronic nervous tension, overreaction to stress, or other psychological causes. Actual changes in bodily tissues or functions are produced in these disorders, illustrating the unity of body and mind.

The mind is involved in other diseases also—even those primarily caused by foreign invasions. Not everybody exposed to a common cold or influenza contracts the disease. The level of stress or mental stability is a major factor in susceptibility. Warts are known to be caused by a virus, but mental cures, including hypnosis, are the most effective known to science. If a physician authoritatively tells a person that dutiful applications of about anything (adhesive tape, tincture of Merthiolate, or a patent medicine) will rid him or her of the warts, they will typically disappear in 2–3 weeks. With regard to disease or health, a basic principle is, "If the mind is at peace, with itself and the world outside, the whole pattern will function as economically as possible" (Mes, 1975, p. 21).

Healing Through Faith   All healing takes place through the normal reactions of the body, under control of the brain/mind, regardless of the bedside manner of a family physician, a shaman's healing ceremony, or a Christian prayer meet-

ing. Only through the mind can the body's functioning be restored (though antibi-
otics and surgery may eliminate stressors that contribute to the disorder).

In most cases of illness the primary factor, or an important secondary one,
is the restoration of a balanced state of mind. That is what faith can do, and it
does not (scientifically speaking) matter whether the faith is placed in God, a shaman, a sugar pill, or tinged alcohol on a wart.

> Faith in something that is thought to be able to control the events in the often
> inimical world of reality, leads to a placing of one's fears and worries about the
> future in its care—with a consequent relaxation of the inner, personal tensions.
> . . . The inner person stops interfering with the functions of [the] body, stops
> pulling levers that should not be pulled and pushing buttons that set things in
> motion at the wrong time [Mes, 1975, p. 35].

As far as we can know scientifically, then, it is actually *not* faith that heals,
nor the thing in which we place faith. It is the *body* that heals itself. Faith just
stops the disruptions in the system that caused or prolonged the illness. If the
disease is such that the body cannot cure itself (or has progressed beyond the
point of cure), then neither can faith—short of a miracle. And by definition a
miracle involves a transgression of God's normal laws (Mes, 1975, p. 36).

Conclusion

Given our understanding of faith healing, we can scarcely doubt the psychological
effects when one prays "in faith believing" with "expectant trust" (Weatherhead,
1951, p. 26). If, however, one prays as a demand, pressure, or manipulation of
deity, prayer is used as a magical charm.

More than 25 years ago a surgeon discovered in the medical literature 90
cases of certain cancer that disappeared without medical treatment (Everson,
1958), and such remissions continue to occur within and without the context of
faith healing. Not just in health and illness, but in all aspects of the natural order,
the unknown is immense. We still have a most imperfect understanding of natural
law—which *can* be interpreted as simply the laws that God has written and follows. Even scientifically informed believers often pray for apparent miracles,
without presupposing the ways and the limits of what they consider the Almighty.
Some have suggested that prayer should not be made for physical cures or other
specific petitions, but for sufficient faith and trust to stop being afraid.

Perhaps our scientific, psychological views of prayer must forever fail to
say just *how* a believer might pray. But we think these are some important issues
that must be faced in a mature religious faith. *Certainty* must be forever banished; if
one is to be truly religious, trust, faith, and hope demark the arena of the exercise.

REVIEW OF KEY CONCEPTS

The Nature of Prayer
   Heiler and James on the crucial role of prayer in religion
   verbal and nonverbal communication in prayer

chapter 9

Trancelike Religious Experiences: The Lesser Ecstasies

Not as crucial as conversion, as basic as prayer, or as profound as mysticism, the religious experiences in this chapter will be discussed in broad strokes only. The title of the chapter attempts to characterize the varied experiences, without great precision. Some versions of each experience may be trancelike, while others may not. Some are felt as ecstatic, others not. We shall treat possession, glossolalia, various other "automatic" behaviors, and psychic experiences.

POSSESSION

Mary had been very close to her grandmother, who had given her a Bible with the instruction that she must believe everything in it or else go to hell. Mary began to withdraw socially when the grandmother died; 5 years later, at 17, she was admitted to a psychiatric hospital "possessed by the devil." Mary had begun to experience sexual feelings about the time she entered high school. Sexual experimentation led to overwhelming guilt and visions of Satan. Mary became increasingly fearful of death and reportedly told Satan he could have her soul, if only he would let her live. Since then she has been battling Satan for her "mind" (Schnaper & Schnaper, 1969).

Considering the Spirits

Cases of "possession" raise a number of psychological issues. Probably the most fundamental is the very idea of spirits. You will recall from Chapter 1 that primitive animism (belief in spirits as a major explanation of various events) was one hypothetical origin of religion. At least some branches of the major religions continue to use the concept of spirits as supernatural, disembodied beings. Many people base their very religious faith on a relatively concrete view of spirits. Others find no need to think in such specific terms. The word *spirit* is also used to refer to the abstract quality of the whole or a part of creation. Only a child is likely to think that Charles Lindbergh's plane, *The Spirit of St. Louis,* was named after a ghost! More sublimely, modern translations of Christian scripture have Jesus saying, not that God is *a* spirit, but that "God is spirit, and those who worship must worship in spirit and truth" (John 4 : 24).

The personified use of *spirit* is even more of a problem in science. Appeal to unobservable spirits produces only pseudoexplanations and untestable hypotheses. Science has been able to give materialistic explanations to many of the events that primitive spirits supposedly controlled. While glib scientific generalizations seem to dispel the mysteries of the world, they make it more difficult for us to identify with the unity of all creation. Paradoxically, many creative scientists are almost instinctively (if not conventionally) religious. Daily they ponder the vastness of puzzles that never end, but seem only to expand their boundaries with each new discovery of quasars or quarks. Many people, understanding science only superficially, rebel against materialism. So in recent years the public has been fascinated with the occult, astrology, and other nonmaterial explanations of reality.

We realize, then, that we violate trends in the popular culture when we analyze possession and similar phenomena within a scientific framework. Psychology seeks to understand the human brain/mind—an unbelievably complex puzzle that is capable of a spectacular number and variety of reactions that partake deeply of mystery. We see the mind as the primary source of the phenomena of this chapter. People who underestimate the vast potential of the brain/mind may be inclined to believe these mysteries come from elsewhere—from spirits, ethers, or psychic events.

Through this discussion of spirits, however, we do not intend to undermine religion or to deny any possibilities of spirits or psychic, nonmaterial energies. As we push back the veil of the mysteries, we try to depict the human mind as itself wondrous—but at least partially understandable and a fruitful object of further study. At the very least, we aim to maintain a healthy skepticism of "spirits," while admitting that we cannot dispel all mysteries. Even so, some psychologists would interpret the events in this chapter in quite different ways.

The Reality of Evil

Evil is a fact of human existence, though different people will interpret different facts as evil. Numerous tendencies within and pressures from without distort and divide human personalities and relationships. Only the most libertine of people would deny that some behaviors are wrong—and they would probably insist that taboos and prohibitions are themselves evil. Mary's supposed possession, at the beginning of this section, depicts the reality of the "demonic" in human lives. However, quite ordinary avenues of indoctrination, temptation, and guilt were involved in her gradually giving herself to "Satan," which personified evil for her.

Pempel (1977) looked for evidence of the demonic in records of altered states of consciousness. She identified numerous and varied forms of "demonic obstacles": enticing distractions that kept meditators from reaching the deeper levels of consciousness, visual experiences of horrible monsters like those from medieval texts, symbols of individuals' personal shortcomings, anxieties about death, and profound despair. Anything that interferes with personal growth, with relationships, with ultimate value, or with acceptance of reality, may be considered evil or demonic.

All of us possess tendencies toward disintegration and distortion of higher potential, as well as tendencies toward growth. Virkler and Virkler (1977) suggest a continuum of demonic involvement in temptations toward evil—from sinful human nature, to demonic temptation, to demonic oppression, to demonic possession. In general, what we call our tendencies depends on how willing we are to accept them as belonging to ourselves. When we recognize evil tendencies as part of our own nature, we speak of original sin, or the like. However, as the iniquity is increasingly disowned, and seen as coming from a personified, external symbol of evil, we blame the devil. From a psychological perspective the only difference is the individual's unwillingness to accept the demonic as part of one's own personality. Demonic possession represents the extreme to which one's mind may be divided; the "normal" self is submerged and the evil part is in control of much or all of one's actions. Some have suggested that Hitler must have been demon-possessed, for his behavior was so thoroughly evil.

Nor is all possession by demonic elements. Some religious experiences are seen as possession by the Christian Holy Spirit or by forces of good. In some primitive religions an invading spirit is sought and welcomed. Possession is characterized by some discrepancy between what the person does and what he or she consciously wills to do; the personality seems to be invaded and partly controlled by a new and alien power (Bourguignon, 1976, p. 6). Carl Jung (see Chapter 2) wrote of numerous alien mental forces, including the feminine side of man, masculine side of woman, and the "shadow" or demonic aspects of personality. Interestingly, two recent cases of supposed demonic possession were of transsexual men (Barlow, Abel, & Blanchard, 1977; Martin, 1976), which suggests that the feminine forces were seen as linked with the demonic.

Belief in Possession

The phenomenon of possession fundamentally depends on human belief. Erika Bourguignon's anthropological study *Possession* (1976) made the point:

> Where no belief exists in such spirit entities or in the ability of such entities to behave in such a way, "possession" as a concept will, of course, not exist either. Thus *possession* is a term which refers to *belief* of a group of people under study, or, perhaps, to the belief held by a given author [1976, p. 6].

She points out that the behaviors called possession by some peoples may occur in other groups, but they will receive different explanations.

Belief in spirits and possession has waxed and waned, flourishing in prehistory, early history, and the Middle Ages in the West; it diminished for a while in the Greek and Roman civilizations, and again in the last two centuries. In very recent years possession beliefs have increased, along with other signs of disenchantment with scientific materialism. Western religions are typically divided; more progressive or liberal groups deny possession and conservative elements defend the concept. Along with literal interpretations of scriptural texts, the following kind of reasoning characterizes many conservative Christian writers:

> It is unlikely that [Jesus] would have permitted . . . followers to believe in demons if the existence of such spirits was not real. If Jesus and his disciples were confused about this, we would have to conclude that [Jesus] was confused about other things reported in scripture, and the authoritative basis of the Bible disappears [Collins, 1969, p. 67].

Among different periods and peoples, numerous symptoms have been attributed to possession—apparent blindness, muteness, lameness, epilepsy, sleeping sickness, hysteria, multiple personality, disrespectful behavior, etc. (Bourguignon, 1976). When these disorders occur apart from belief in possession, they are not likely to respond to rites of exorcism. From a psychological perspective, then, exorcism is much like faith healing. It depends on the victim's belief in the method of cure. In Blatty's (1971) novel, *The Exorcist,* the psychiatrist recommended exorcism as a treatment precisely because it fit the victim's beliefs.

Some cases of exorcism are indistinguishable from faith healing. A man claiming to have "two devils in his head" came to a seventeenth-century English jurist, asking for exorcism. The judge reported:

> I perceiving what an opinion he had of me, and that 'twas only melancholy that troubled him . . . got a card, and lapt it handsomely up in a piece of taffata, and put strings to the taffata, and . . . gave it to him, to hang about his neck; withal charged him, that he should not disorder himself neither with eating or drinking, but eat very little of supper, and say his prayers daily when he went to bed, and I made no question but he would be well in three or four days [Montgomery, 1974, p. 1183].

The "exorcism" was a total success. In a recent case of a 21-year-old male transsexual, who had begun dressing as a woman when he was 5, and was scheduled for sex-change surgery, the cure was alternately called faith healing and exorcism. Two and a half years after the healing experience he showed "normal male identity" (Barlow, Abel, & Blanchard, 1977).

Distinguishing supposed cases of possession from recognized psychological disorders seems to follow social and theological trends, for example, Pope Paul VI's encouraging demonology as "a very important chapter of Catholic doctrine that ought to be studied again" (Alpert, 1973, p. 60). Within evangelical Christian circles the issue of differential diagnosis has raged without any resolution.

Martin's (1976) study of five exorcisms suggested some criteria from a Roman Catholic tradition; however, some of them are quite subjective. Occurrence of supposed psychic phenomena, as one criterion, merely substitutes one mystery for another (see later in this chapter). In the final analysis the only thing distinguishing cases of "possession" was that they eventually responded to rites of exorcism. Such responses can be understood psychologically as personality reorientation based on strong suggestion and the victim's acceptance of a belief system that includes the possibility of such effects. Changes of such magnitude occur in psychotherapy (though seldom with such suddenness), in religious conversion, and in faith healing, without the claiming of departure of any personalized spirits from the person.

Dynamics of Possession

The appearance of an apparent full-blown case of possession is such an extreme human behavior that it has attracted considerable popular and professional attention. (One bibliography on spirit mediumship and possession contained about 9600 references—Glazier, 1975.) As already observed, though, possession can be seen as one extreme of a behavioral continuum that includes quite commonplace events. In everyday experiences a degree of possession can be seen whenever our feelings and behaviors are shaped by external forces that we have not helped to develop, such as family or country (Swanson, 1978). One national survey asked, "How often have you felt as though you were very close to a powerful spiritual force that seemed to lift you out of yourself?" The question implies some degree of possession—being penetrated and overwhelmed by an outside force. Thirty-five percent of Americans surveyed reported one or two such experiences; 5% said "often" (Greeley, 1975).

Psychiatric Interpretations   When feelings or experiences of divided personality reach a psychopathological level, psychiatrists refer to them as dissociative reactions. Amnesia and multiple personality are the better known forms of dissociation (though much rarer than some popular literature would lead us to believe). Scientifically oriented mental health professionals would diagnose most so-called possession cases as multiple personality. We do not fully know why some people respond to internal conflicts by assuming alternative or dissociated personalities, but using the psychiatric instead of theological (possession) terminology does not merely trade one mystery for another. Studies of multiple personality from Morton Prince's *The Dissociation of a Personality* (1913), through Thigpen and Cleckley's *The Three Faces of Eve* (1957), to *Sybil* (Schreiber, 1973) tell us much about these disorders—without using utterly invisible, personified spirits for explanation.

Learning Interpretations   The development of alternative personality forces (whether called possession or multiple personality) may be learned. The third of Eve's "faces," and a later fourth personality, developed after her therapists began to explore (and perhaps encourage) the appearance of the alternating personalities. Many of Sybil's 16 personalities are similarly suspected of being, at least partially, products of therapeutic intervention. In her study of possession within Haitian folk religion, Bourguignon clearly identified the learning process:

> Children are taken to ceremonies in participating families from the earliest days of their lives; they hear stories about spirits as they hear anecdotes about people in their families and neighborhoods . . . so that by the time they experience an altered state they have learned the basic information relevant for appropriate behavior. What remains to be learned are the cues that will initiate the altered state and an explicit identification with a given spirit entity [1976, p. 17].

This is a situation in which temporary "possession" by spirits is invited and encouraged in a trance state, as part of a religious ceremony. We shall see similar patterns in some Christian experiences.

Motivational Interpretations   Several psychological and social factors may favor belief in and experiences of possession, for example, rigid social class and status differences, and compensation for humiliation. Jungian theory holds that consciously denied aspects of personality develop unconsciously and, when sufficiently strong, abruptly "possess" the conscious personality. Involuntary possession, then, may be a way for a person to express strongly felt but prohibited feelings, without being blamed—"the devil made me do it." In a Jewish case of possession the dybbuk (devil) announced during the exorcism that it had entered the victim because she had had illicit sexual relations. This "possession" can be seen as a self-imposed punishment for guilt, and the "exorcism" provided a public means of confession (Bourguignon, 1976, p. 54).

Wonderful are the ways of the human mind, and marvelously varied the ways in which it can be programmed to produce behavior. When people believe in demonic or other possession, they may act as if invaded and controlled by alien forces. They may respond to exorcism to repudiate the disapproved part of their personality. Few psychologists need recourse to discrete "spirits" to explain and understand such behavior. But since the spirits are by definition invisible, neither can we absolutely deny them.

GLOSSOLALIA

Few recent religious phenomena have received more comment and research than glossolalia, or speaking in tongues. In sounds that resemble a foreign language, believers speak (or pray—since the utterances are usually directed toward God) though without any known meaning. Many students of glossolalia and some of its practitioners interpret it as a form of possession. However, the invading spirit is taken to be the Holy Spirit and is welcomed or invited. Very often, though, believers interpret tongues as a gift of the Spirit—accepting the behavior as their own, but not as something they could produce by mere will.

Glossolalia is not a strictly Christian experience; May (1956) has reviewed its occurrence in a number of other religious traditions. Nor is it necessarily religious; psychotics may speak in a similar manner. Linguistic analyses of glossolalic speech fail to find grammatical or other criteria of a natural language (e.g., Samarin, 1968). The New Testament prototype of glossolalia (Acts 2 : 4–11) suggests that the speech is an actual language that the speaker has not learned by any natural means. Contemporary accounts of such accomplishments by Christian glossolalists have not been scientifically verified.

Spontaneous or Learned?

Like conversion and many other religious experiences, glossolalia occurs in both original and copied or "programmed" forms. There are undoubtedly cases in which a person spontaneously begins to speak meaningless words in a religious context; Samarin (1969) cites three such cases from his own research. Whether in Pentecostal denominations where tongues-speaking is a regular practice, or in the modern charismatic movement among Roman Catholic and mainstream Protestant groups, most glossolalists seek the experience.

Samarin (1969) has noted that one does not learn glossolalia as one would learn a natural language or dialect. His subjects did little proselytizing, and leaders did not teach precise sounds or words. Nonetheless, there was a kind of coaching that, given a believer who earnestly wants a new religious experience, promotes the initial tongues-speaking. In a large weekend charismatic conference Samarin (1969/1973, p. 381) observed this kind of guidance by the clergy in charge:

Come on now. Speak out. You cannot talk in tongues when you're talking in English. You're still begging. There you are. He's talking. Keep talking. Say it again. Come on. Hallelujah. He's praying a new language. You start off, and He gives the language as soon as you begin.

Given the influence of such leaders, many writers have suggested the similarity of glossolalia to hypnotically induced behavior. Kildahl (1972, pp. 44–45) found that a deep sense of trust in a glossolalic leader was necessary for one to start speaking in tongues. Although glossolalia can occur in private as readily as in the presence of respected leaders (at least once the behavior is acquired), in most cases it appears to involve some degree of modeling and the influence of another person. Kildahl (1972, p. 42) found tongues-speakers lower in psychological measures of autonomy, suggesting greater suggestibility and dependence on others. Vivier (1960), however, found glossolalists slightly lower than nonglossolalists in a measure of suggestibility.

The recurrence of glossolalia in various cultural and historical settings and the basic originality of every glossolalic act suggest that its potential lies deeply embedded in the human mind. Samarin (1972) thinks that any of us can produce glossolalic speech if we are willing to drop our inhibitions. He compares it to improvisational jazz, with syllables used as the musician uses notes. It seems likely that within the structure of the brain/mind there are "switches" of some sort that can relax the usual controls over our language functions, and spontaneously produce quasi-linguistic sounds—given the appropriate motivation, social influence, and psychological state.

Trance State

The kind of letting go just discussed tends to produce an altered state of consciousness or trance state. A number of writers have related this condition to "regression in the service of the ego." That is, the relaxation of inhibition returns one to a less mature, less rational state, but in the interest of restructuring or integrating portions of the personality. Such relaxation of controls requires a certain degree of trust or security. Persons who took part in one series of charismatic meetings but failed to speak in tongues were found to be higher in anxiety, depression, and hostility than those who experienced glossolalia during the seminars (Lovekin & Malony, 1977).

Psychopathology

Early critics of tongues-speaking tended to interpret it as neurotic or pathological (Cutten, 1927). As suggested above, though, numerous studies have found glossolalists to be as well adjusted as nontongues-speaking persons from similar backgrounds (Hine, 1969).

Others have found rather pervasive evidence that prior to their tongues-speaking, these persons came from more disturbed backgrounds than the average person who does not speak in tongues (Richardson, 1973). Kildahl found that 85% of his tongues-speakers "experienced a clearly defined anxiety crisis preceding their speaking in tongues" (1972, p. 57), compared to 30% of the control group. (See Chapter 11 for more details of this investigation.)

Many have interpreted these findings to support an integrative, growth-producing effect of glossolalia. The only known longitudinal study of tongues-speaking, in which psychological measures were made before and after the acquisition of glossolalia, failed to find such effects. Those who attended the charismatic seminars showed more interest in religion, fewer personal problems, less anxiety, and greater ego strength—both during the seminars and 3 months later. However, the effects occurred whether or not the participants succeeded in speaking in tongues. The benefits were from the seminar, not tongues-speaking per se (Lovekin & Malony, 1977).

Functions of Glossolalia

Different types of glossolalia may serve different functions. Pattison (1968) distinguished between "playful" glossolalia used for ego expansion and "serious" glossolalia used for ego compensation (reintegration of a disturbed personality). Possibly integrative changes occur in some contexts of tongues-speaking, even though Lovekin and Maloney failed to find any in their study.

Hine (1969) emphasized the use of glossolalia as an act of public commitment, to show clearly one's identification with and acceptance of a radical religious ideology and life-style. Speaking in tongues serves as a "bridge-burning" that irrevocably sets the individual apart:

> In a society where public display of intense emotion is reserved for spectator sports, and where the appropriate background for spontaneous and uninhibited self-expression is the cocktail party, the abandonment of one's self to a joyous flow of unintelligible vocalizations and possibly some non-consciously controlled physical behavior is considered indecent if not insane [1969, p. 224].

Similarly McGuire observed that the Catholic charismatic movement served to affirm "the relevance of Christian beliefs in today's world" (1975, p. 100). In the wake of Vatican II changes in the Roman church, believers could no longer maintain their certainty in traditional church beliefs and authorities. Charismatic gifts in general and glossolalia in particular gave reassurance of eternal truths and a religious world view.

These interpretations are consistent with Lovekin and Malony's findings that the charismatic seminars had general effects, rather than specific effects of tongues-speaking. Spiritual commitment is more important than any single ecstatic experience, which is but an affirmation of one's faith.

OTHER AUTOMATIC RELIGIOUS BEHAVIORS

Glossolalia is one of a class of intense religious experiences that James (1902) called "automatisms." These motor and sensory behaviors may occur in trancelike states and are experienced as control from without the person. Automatic writing, dancing, shouting, running, falling into a faint, hallucinations, and walking on or handling fire are among these experiences—not all of which we can discuss.

Like glossolalia, these experiences are sometimes interpreted as cases of benign (desirable) possession, and sometimes they are seen as gifts or blessings. Dancing and fainting in the United House of Prayer for All People (Alland, 1962) were seen as possession. Similar behavior in many other black and Pentecostal churches may be viewed as "blessings of the Lord," or simply reported as behavioral facts. Fire handlers of Southern Appalachia say that believers may handle fire if they have sufficient faith in God (nonpossession) or by special anointing of the "Holy Ghost" (a possession state) (Kane, 1978, p. 117).

Interpretations

Psychopathology   To an outside observer many automatisms look like symptoms of hysteria, schizophrenia, epilepsy, or other psychiatric disorders. Many researchers report predisposing factors of guilt, anxiety, and frustrations resulting from social deprivation. Such variables well may underlie these religious reactions, but careful studies seldom find any special incidence of disorder among believers who practice them. Gerrard and Gerrard (1966) compared Pentecostal snake handlers from West Virginia with members of a conventional Protestant church in the same area, using the Minnesota Multiphasic Personality Inventory. The *conventional* church members tended to be more defensive and higher in hysteria (and the older members more depressed). The snake handlers differed only in being "more exhibitionistic, excitable, and pleasure-oriented . . . and are less controlled by considerations of the general culture" (Gerrard & Gerrard, 1966, p. 56).

Trance   Deliberately sought trance states, rather than "ego-alien" disorders, characterize these intense religious experiences. Like possession in Haitian folk religions and glossolalia, these behaviors tend to be learned. The first trance is the most difficult, but once the breakthrough is made, further trances are virtually assured (Alland, 1962).

In the United House of Prayer for All People Alland identified a number of physical, psychological, and social factors that seemed to promote the trance states: a hot, stuffy room high in carbon dioxide; loud, rhythmic, repetitious music; fasting; high motivation to attain a trance; strong social models; and isolation from the rest of the community. Many consider the trances to be a form of hypnosis. Others have related the states to conditions of increased perceptiveness or temperaments of "exalted sensibility" (James, 1902/1961, p. 372).

A peculiar and specific altered state appears to occur among fire handlers of Appalachia. While fire walking does not necessarily require a trance (Christopher, 1970, pp. 236–250), an altered state may occur in some cases, as it seems to in Appalachia. These believers hold their hands in the flames of kerosene torches for up to 15 seconds and expose other bodily members to similar heat without burns or blisters. They may be burned by the flames if they do not feel the special "anointing," described by one practitioner as:

A shield comes down over me. I know when it's around me. It's cold inside. My hands get numb and cold. . . . When the shield comes, it's good for anything. . . . Nothing can harm me [Kane, 1978, p. 119].

In an intriguing summary, Kane cites over 50 years of hypnotic experiments in which no pain, burn, or blister occurred when subjects received the suggestion that a dangerously hot object, applied to their skins, was safe. On the other hand, subjects who were told that the experimenter's finger was a "red-hot iron" suffered blisters from its touch. When subjects were hypnotized to believe that one arm would be invulnerable to a hot object, they reported numb feelings strikingly similar to the fire handlers' "anointing." Apparently an altered state can induce partial insensitivity to heat among believers who subscribe to such a faith system and are motivated to receive that spiritual gift.

Functions of Intense Experiences

Many writers and much indirect evidence suggest that these intense religious experiences serve to integrate personalities that initially are fragile and disorganized. As for glossolalia, though, there is little or no proof of this function. The almost orgiastic pleasure and ecstasy of the experiences would seem to serve as compensation for the relatively deprived condition of the practitioners' lives. Alland (1962) noted that "dancing for God" substituted for social dancing that was forbidden by the church. Such religion has often been portrayed fictionally, as in Joyce Carol Oates's *Son of the Morning* (1978).

James emphasized that "beliefs are strengthened whenever automatisms corroborate them" (1902/1961, p. 272). This function reflects the commitment to a deviant belief system that Hine (1969) noted for glossolalia. We recently heard a charismatic Christian speaking of being "slain by the Spirit" (falling into a sudden faint). "When that happens," he said, "you know it has to be God." One's own behaviors and experiences that are unexplainable (to the believer) provide striking reassurance to the faithful; this may be the irreducible function of these experiences.

MEDIUMSHIP, ESP, AND THE PSYCHIC

In this section we include a variety of phenomena that have been called psychic. Mediumship (communication with the supposed spirits of the dead), ghosts, and poltergeists assume disembodied spirits. The whole range of extrasensory perception (telepathy, clairvoyance, precognition, and psychokinesis) involves apparent human powers that challenge the known laws of the physical universe. Out-of-the-body (OOB) and certain near-death experiences (NDE) may involve either or both kinds of belief. Volumes have been written on each of these phenomena, and we presume to lump them together in this limited space only with great hesitancy.

Perspectives

True Believers Persons who consider psychic phenomena real often employ practices that disturb careful scholars. For whatever reasons, they often discuss them along with subjects like hypnosis, biofeedback, and faith healing (e.g.,

Moore, 1977) that we have no trouble treating and explaining scientifically. They often use substandard logic. An "expert parapsychologist," for example, wrote:

> A hunch is a basically illogical feeling about a person or situation. . . . Following a hunch means to go against purely logical reasoning. If the hunch turns out to be correct, one has had a mild ESP experience. If the hunch turns out to be false, it may not have been a hunch at all but fear [Holzer, 1974, p. 15].

He was able to identify ESP only after the fact, which proves nothing.

In most of these areas considerable fraud has been exposed, from the viewpoints of science (e.g., Hansel, 1966) and of professional magic (e.g., Christopher, 1970). While not all cases are demonstrably fraudulent, many people are thus led to question the other cases. On the other hand, true believers tend to believe all cases that are not proven false. Finally, in the whole area of the psychic, many spectacular studies and reports are published, some with apparently rigorous scientific trappings. However, numerous failures to obtain similar results, when others repeat the experiments, seldom receive such attention (e.g., Bowles & Hynds, 1978, pp. 20, 102).

Magicians   Professional magicians are among the strongest critics of psychic pretensions. They assert that sleight of hand can reproduce most of the feats of "psychics," without recourse to paranormal powers or forces. However, students of magic recognize development of an unusual ability in mediums, public performers of apparent psychic feats, and stage magicians alike. That is the development of keen powers of observation, so far from our mundane capacities as to resemble an altered state of consciousness. For example, at least one professional magician routinely offers to waive his fee if he cannot find the check hidden somewhere in a vast auditorium (in a place known to the audience but not to him). In minutes he is able to go directly to the hiding place, guided by very subtle cues given by members of the audience—an astonishing feat of an astute brain/mind, but not psychic by any claim.

Scientists   Despite apparent technical controls and high levels of statistical significance, scientists usually reject apparent demonstrations of ESP and the psychic. Perhaps unfairly, they usually *assume* either coincidence, fraud, or poor controls. They are more likely to reject ESP than religious statements because ESP practitioners and researchers make different claims for their phenomena. ESP claims to be "really real," on the same order as material events, but not accountable for by known physical laws. Most scientists will continue to reject ESP claims until the phenomena can be integrated with established physical forces and principles. Meanwhile some reputable researchers continue carefully controlled studies of psychic phenomena, sometimes with reasonably consistent findings. If and when these data are thoroughly scrutinized by the scientific community, replicated, and reconciled with other theoretical and empirical systems, the psychic may then be embraced by science.

Psychologists   Students of human behavior tend to be skeptical of psychic claims because they realize the high probabilities of selective perception and selective memory involved in reports of such experiences. Many people want to believe in the psychic. Psychologists hired a magician to perform some mind reading and other psychic tricks before an introductory psychology class, forewarning the students that all they would see were tricks. After the performance, however, most of the students were convinced that the magician was indeed psychic. After all, they had seen it with their own eyes! (Benassi, Singer, & Reynolds, 1980).

On the other hand, as certain phenomena show sufficient regularity, psychologists may accept them as reliable accomplishments of the human brain/mind. Many can accept the reality of certain visions among a percentage of persons who narrowly escape death—given the relative consistency of reports by different investigators and from different time periods (e.g., Moody, 1975; Ring, 1979b). Psychologists will certainly differ about just which experiences prove acceptable and what explanations they receive, as honest differences of interpretation are inevitable in this area of investigation.

Theologians   The apparent evidence of psychic forces seems irresistible to many religionists. ESP and the like appear to give evidence for, and reinforce belief in, the nonmaterial. Yet at the same time they may approach the degree of technology and truth claimed by science itself. The motivation for such appeals to the psychic (in support of religious tenets) resembles the desire to prove the material efficacy of petitionary prayer (Chapter 8). The effort assumes that religious truth requires outside support. In this regard "the psychic" functions much like other phenomena in this chapter—belief in spirits and in possession, glossolalia, and other automatisms. They all may be used to support one's religious beliefs.

Religious appeals to the psychic have special hazards, though. The claims for the psychic being real render them subject to eventual disproof. Such a demonstration might unnecessarily undermine religious beliefs that come to depend on psychic evidences. More significantly, though, focus on the psychic courts triviality in religious faith. Even a believer in psychic phenomena concluded:

> The danger lies in the recipient's resting content with these trivialities and ceasing to seek a deeper and real communion with God. . . . It can lead to an abandonment of the search for truth by other more orthodox and more strenuous and more profitable means, calling for a measure of self-discipline [Moore, 1977, p. 116].

In Eastern meditative traditions, such as yoga and Buddhism, psychic occurrences are seen as natural by-products of meditation. Aspirants are cautioned against being lured by them, as they are not the ultimate goal of spiritual practice and can lead one astray.

Such warnings may be appropriate for any of the religious experiences discussed in this chapter. Next we turn to what many consider the core religious experience and a primary source of religious conviction through the ages—mysticism.

REVIEW OF KEY CONCEPTS

Possession
"spirits" in animism, religion, and science
brain/mind complexity
continuum of evil and demonic possession
psychological view of evil
historical trends in belief in possession and exorcism
relation of exorcism to faith healing
distinguishing possession from psychopathology
everyday experiences of possession
dissociative disorders
learning interpretations of possession
motivational factors in possession

Glossolalia
definition and nature of glossolalia
glossolalia as spontaneous or learned
relation of glossolalia to trance states
psychopathological interpretations of glossolalia
glossolalia as commitment and "bridge-burning"

Other Automatic Religious Behaviors
nature and variety of automatisms
interpretations of automatisms—example of fire handling
functions of automatic religious behaviors

Mediumship, ESP, and the Psychic
some examples of the psychic
true believers' logic and reactions to fraud and nonreplication
magicians' views of the psychic
psychic as heightened powers of observation
scientists' views of the psychic
selective perception and memory
effects of wanting to believe
limitations of psychologists' acceptance
theological implications of the psychic
hazards of preoccupation with psychic events

chapter 10

Mysticism, Spirituality, and Consciousness

I saw nothing but God alone, without myself and outside myself. The sight is so absorbing that nothing else can be seen or enjoyed or desired. The being both of body and soul remains as if dead, unable to act. . . . But how can I describe in words the immeasurable and the indescribable? . . . It is impossible to express it in words, or for anyone to understand it who had not experienced it. . . . All my faculties have lost their natural activity, and are altogether imprisoned and plunged into the furnace of divine love, with such profound, exceeding joy. . . . I see without eyes, I understand without mind, I feel without feeling, and I taste without taste. I have no shape nor size, so that without seeing I see such divine activity and energy that, beside it, all those words like perfection, fullness and purity and that I once used now seem to me all falsehoods and fables when compared with that Truth. . . . This sight, which is not seen, cannot be spoken of or thought of [Garvin, 1964, pp. 82–83].

Thus wrote Catherine of Genoa, a medieval Christian mystic. Similarly, Blaise Pascal wrote: "Fire! God of Abraham, God of Isaac, God of Jacob, not of the philosophers and the wise. Security, security. Feeling, joy, peace. Joy, joy, joy, tears of joy" (Pascal, 1670/1889, p. 2).

What is this captivating experience that so completely takes over an individual and makes other interests seem worthless by comparison? In this chapter we explain the characteristics of religious mysticism, compare it to other intense experiences, and explore ways of studying and evaluating it.

THE PHENOMENON OF MYSTICISM

What Mysticism Is Not

Many mystics, reporting their experiences, begin by saying what their experience is not. Since many experiences are incorrectly called mystical, we begin by saying what mysticism is not. "Mysticism is not to be associated with occultism or superstition, nor with psychical research, nor with an application of the fourth dimension to psychology, nor with a cult of vagueness, nor with a special love of the mysterious for its own sake" (Hocking, 1929, p. 255).

Ellwood (1980, p. 32) said we should also exclude such religious experiences as acceptance of salvation, enthusiasm for religious ideas, feelings of religious commitment, "warm feelings" in religious activity, and interpretation of events as God's intervention. The ecstatic experiences considered in the previous chapter are also not mysticism.

Mysticism thus excludes all vague, mysterious, or "spooky" experiences such as hunches, intuitions, insights, precognition, and ESP—all of which some people call mystical. Also excluded are religious experiences characterized primarily by heightened emotion or ecstasy, such as the joy of conversion, the intensity of glossolalia, the fervor of deep piety. However good or valuable such experiences may be to an individual, they are not mysticism.

Characteristics of Mysticism

Some scholars distinguish kinds of mysticism. Zaehner (1957) described two major types. *Sacred mysticism* has a distinctly religious character, while *profane mysticism* simply involves a unitive experience. Finer distinctions can be drawn. In theistic mysticism, one seeks unity—but not identity—with God. The goal of monistic mysticism is identity with some universal divine principle. Nonreligious mysticism seeks union with something or everything, including all of nature (Parrinder, 1976).

Many scholars of mysticism list characteristics common to all mysticism. Box 10.1 compares three opinions. The quotes beginning this chapter suggest the ineffability, passivity, sacredness, and deep joy of the experience—as well as mystics' conviction of the reality of their experiences. We now examine the more important characteristics in greater detail.

Sense of Unity   A prominent aspect of mysticism is a sense of the oneness of all things, in which awareness of oneself as a separate entity disappears. Meister Eckhart, a great Christian mystic, taught: "As long as [the soul] is aware and self-conscious, it will not see or be conscious of God. But when, for God's sake, it becomes unself-conscious and lets go of everything, it finds itself again in God" (Blakney, 1941, Sermon 6).

Ineffability   Mystics have great trouble trying to explain their experiences. It might be like trying to explain redness to a blind person, or the sound of a flute to one who is deaf. Mystics use figures of speech, poetry, and symbolic references—especially sexual and oral (eating) imagery. References to "a dazzling darkness," "the formless Form," or "the cloud of unknowing" "show the inadequacy of language to express the experience" (Johnson, 1953/1971, pp. 329–330).

Reality   Mystics insist strongly that their experiences are real. Pascal's conviction (above) is very common to mystics, who say they do not *believe,* but *know.* Their certainty that they have touched Ultimate Reality is unshakeable.

Transcendence of Time and Space   The great Spanish mystic John of the Cross wrote: "Many hours pass while [the soul] is in this state of forgetfulness; all seems

---

Box 10.1   CHARACTERISTICS OF MYSTICISM

Stace	James	Deikman
Unity		Unity
Transcendence of space and time		Transsensation
Objectivity and reality		Intense reality
Deep positive mood		
Sacredness		
Paradoxicality		
Ineffability	Ineffability	Ineffability
	Noetic quality	
	Transience	
	Passivity	
		Unusual sensations

Source: Deikman (1966, pp. 324–338); James (1902/1961, Lectures 16 & 17); Stace (1960a, Chapter 2).

but a moment when it again returns to itself" (Lewis, 1889, Vol. I, p. 127). Awareness of location in space similarly may disappear.

Noetic Quality   Mysticism gives one a sense of "infused" knowledge—knowing other than by the senses or thinking. Thomas Aquinas, medieval philosopher and theologian, declared that everything he had written—his entire life's work—was "straw" compared to what he saw in an intense mystical experience. Teresa of Avila, a sixteenth-century nun, said: "The understanding, if it understands, does not understand how it understands, or at least can comprehend nothing of what it understands" (Peers, 1960, p. 179).

Paradoxicality   John of the Cross captures the paradoxical quality of mysticism: "My spirit was endowed with understanding, understanding nought. . . . [One] who really ascends so high annihilates [oneself], and all . . . previous knowledge seems ever less and less; . . . knowledge so increases that [one] knoweth nothing" (Lewis, 1891, Vol. II, pp. 624–625).

STAGES OF MYSTICAL DEVELOPMENT

Most scholars describe three main stages of mystical life: purgative, illuminative, and unitive (Furse, 1977; Smith, 1977). Some sources—such as Underhill (1911) and classical mystical theology—add two others. After an initial awakening, the mystic goes through self-chosen purgation, a passive night of the sense, illumination, the dark night of the soul, and mystical union (Arintero, 1949–1951; Garrigou-LaGrange, 1947–1948).

The Purgative Life

After conversion to the committed spiritual life, potential mystics actively try to purge life of everything contrary to spiritual endeavor. Typically they combat personal faults, cultivate increased awareness, use some meditative techniques to focus awareness, and practice various other ritual, ascetic, and spiritual disciplines of a particular tradition. This initial stage is one of active striving, with some anguish over the costs but with feelings of accomplishment.

The Passive Purification of the Senses

The apparent mastery disappears. Potential mystics feel overwhelmed with personal failure and inadequacy, and may believe that God has withdrawn support from them. They are forced to recognize that, in their early enthusiasm, they overcontrolled themselves and underestimated the force of their established habits. They notice many subtle faults of which they were previously unaware. The strong sexual and aggressive urges that are often reported probably result from prior denial of such instincts. Spiritual guides warn people against mistaking this relatively mild trial for the much more severe dark night of the soul, which characterizes a more advanced state.

The Illuminative Way

The first stages of mystical experience are sometimes accompanied by visions, hallucinations, and other such phenomena that more advanced mystics attribute to personality weaknesses. The would-be mystic enjoys scattered episodes of peace, experiencing an "ultimate presence." Virtue becomes easier as outbreaks of anger, greed, gluttony, and other impulses diminish. One tries to give up even allowable pleasures that stand in the way of greater closeness to God.

The Dark Night of the Soul

The mystical path is then complicated by the apparent loss of religious meaning, the very basis of spiritual endeavor itself. The mystic feels completely abandoned by God, incapable of faith or hope, and heavily burdened by the demands of religious love and perseverance. Completely alone, without consolation, one continues on the path. A Hindu saying claims: "The sides of the mountain are strewn with the bones of those who fail to make it to the top."

Religious literature reflects the terrible anguish of this period. The Bengali poet Tagore (1913/1971, p. 37) grieved: "Ah, love, why dost thou let me wait outside at the door all alone? . . . If thou leavest me wholly aside, I know not how I am to pass these long, rainy hours. . . . My heart wanders wailing with the restless wind." Perseverance in an often very long period of distress is necessary for the crown of mystical attainment, the unitive life.

The Unitive Life

Mystics describe the highest stage of mystical life according to how they understand Ultimate Reality. Some report indestructible union with their God, others a state of pure consciousness, and yet others union with the totality of Being. Such differences likely reflect the predisposing effects of belief systems and particular practices. Bharati (1976, pp. 80–81) claims that essential mysticism is always a "zero experience" about which little can be said. What mystics talk about are those things in their awareness that they associate with the experience.

"The mystic is the man or woman who has fallen in love with God. Not just the lover of God but the happy victim of an experience that is at once total, shattering and transforming" (O'Donoghue, 1979, p. 148). Mystics' "entire life is an orison, and finally God descends and enfolds [them] . . . forever" (Schneiderman, 1967, p. 100).

BECOMING A MYSTIC

Most people recognize meditation as a common preparation for mysticism. However, "most techniques of meditation do not exist as solitary practices but are . . . understood . . . only as an integral part of a whole discipline" (Naranjo & Ornstein, 1971, p. 143). We now look at meditation and some disciplines surrounding it.

Spiritual Practices and Self-discipline

Moral Practices   Traditional teachers insist that mysticism rests on a firm moral base. Buddhists consider *sīla* (moral purity or virtue) prerequisite to meditation practice. Their first five precepts are "abstaining from killing, stealing, unlawful sexual intercourse, lying, and intoxicants" (Goleman, 1977, p. 3). For those seeking greater growth, other prohibitions are added. Great Christian mystics offer similar instruction. Teresa of Avila (Kavanaugh & Rodriguez, 1979) taught that seekers cannot enter the "interior castle" before overcoming important failings.

The first step of Hindu yoga—*yama* (restraint)—mirrors closely the Buddhist precepts: refraining from inflicting harm, lying, stealing, excessive sensual indulgence, and greed. The second yogic step—*niyama* (observance)—requires virtue: purity of body and mind, contentment, disciplinary asceticism, gaining of self-knowledge by the study of spiritual matters, and surrender to God.

Body Disciplines   Eastern religion—much more than Western religion—emphasizes body disciplines. Many popular Western practices for health, flexibility, and poise originally were body disciplines associated with Eastern spiritual traditions: t'ai-chi ch'üan, hatha yoga, and jujitsu (judo).

The third and fourth steps of yoga illustrate such disciplines. *Āsana* (posture) is of two kinds: sitting postures for meditation, and postures said to have therapeutic effects on bodily imbalances and disorders. *Prānāyāma* (breath control) is practiced to calm emotion, relax the body, and energize one for either action or meditation.

Religious Rituals   Many religious rituals produce a mood of reverent concentration that prepares one for meditation. Sacramental rituals, scripture reading, singing, and chanting are often used. Orange-robed devotees chanting "Hare Krishna; Hare Rāma" on street corners are practicing a time-honored preparation for meditation. Some Islamic Sufi orders have been called whirling dervishes because of their ritual dance—whirling around the still point in the center—to induce a meditative state. For twentieth-century mystic Simone Weil (1951), a deeply concentrated recitation of the Lord's Prayer commonly triggered mystical moments.

Renunciations   In most religions, people who want to cultivate the interior life can retreat to ashrams or monasteries. Solitude enhances involvement in spiritual matters. Vows—such as the Catholic monastic ones of poverty, chastity, and obedience—help one renounce material prosperity, dependence upon human relationships, and self-will. Many traditions require the aspirant to give up not only evil or harmful things, but also good things that may be distracting. The Buddhist *Visuddhi-magga* lists some possible sources of attachment: family, reputation, followers, projects, travel, and studies.

Meditation Preparation   Much that is currently called meditation is really exercise preparatory to meditation. The most common Christian preparation is discursive meditation, in which one thinks about religious stories or ideas. One might reflect on the sufferings of Jesus or on an idea such as resurrection. Such practice focuses thought on religious concerns, but does not still it as true meditation does.

Eastern traditions are more likely to prepare with centering exercises. Transcendental Meditation (TM) withdraws attention from various scattered awarenesses and directs it to an object of meditation. This practice—called *pratyāhara* (sense withdrawal)—is the fifth step of yoga. Losing awareness of a radio playing because you become deeply engrossed in something else is analogous to what *pratyāhara* tries to accomplish. Once attention has been successfully focused, the meditator is involved in *dhārana* (concentration), the sixth yogic step.

Methods of Meditation

True meditation—the absorbed and undistracted flow of conscious attention—is *dhyāna,* the seventh step of yoga. "Meditation emphasizes the cultivation of receptivity, of emptiness" (Naranjo & Ornstein, 1971, p. 36). "All meditation systems either aim for One or Zero—union with God or emptiness. The path to the One is through concentration on Him[/Her], to the Zero is insight into the voidness of one's mind" (Goleman, 1977, p. xix). Meditation thus leaves one open to experience mystical consciousness. Many books teach meditation techniques. LeShan's *How to Meditate* (1974) is good for beginners, though most traditions recommend having an experienced guide after the initial stages of practice.

The Way of Forms   The Way of Forms (Naranjo & Ornstein, 1971), or concentrative meditation, involves a focusing of awareness on some real or imagined visual, auditory, or kinesthetic pattern. A common Buddhist and yogic practice is the counting of one's breaths. Sometimes meditators use visual objects; some are external (e.g., a candle flame) and some internal (e.g., a mental image with high symbolic significance). Many systems give the disciple a *mantra*—or "sacred word"—upon which to concentrate. A Christian example is the "Jesus prayer" from Eastern Orthodoxy: "Lord Jesus Christ, have mercy on me a sinner." Focusing attention on such a prayer or mantra can lead to constant subliminal awareness of it—even when one must direct attention elsewhere.

In concentrative meditation, a mental one-pointedness is achieved when everything peripheral is eliminated from awareness. Dwelling upon one continuous stimulus breaks down established habits of perception. If you have never tried to make your awareness one-pointed, try to watch the second hand of a watch, keeping *only* the sweep of the hand in your mind. Without practice, few people can keep other thoughts from intruding for even 30 seconds.

Psychologically, the repetition of a constant stimulus is like the absence of any stimulus. Psychologists call this the *ganzfeld effect.* To experiment with this, cut a Ping-Pong ball in half and keep the halves over your eyes for 20–30 minutes. Observe what happens to your vision as you try to "see."

The Expressive Way   In a second type of meditation—the Expressive (or Inner) Way (Naranjo & Ornstein, 1971)—the meditator tries to observe images arising from his or her unconscious mental processes. These images—just like dreams—are believed to come from one's own needs and desires. Allowing oneself to experience them should satiate the desires that produce them. Organized religions tend to avoid this method, fearing many pitfalls—one of which is "possession" by the images produced.

Shamanism, a mysticism of possession, best illustrates this technique. The shaman has intense experiences that cause him or her to be considered a prophet, medium, healer, and source of direct contact to the spirit world. In Western cultures, most such people would be considered mentally ill, and their behavior called fits, hysterics, or schizophrenic breaks.

In some traditions, people deliberately alter bodily functioning to produce direct experience of unconscious symbols or images. In American Indian vision quests, aspirants often undertook exposure, prolonged fasts, isolation, and physical torture to bring the desired visions (Larsen, 1976). The intense ascetic practices of some Christian mystics parallel this. Psychedelics have been used for this purpose in Indian peyote cults (Harner, 1973) and the Eleusinian mysteries of classical times (Wasson, Hofmann, & Ruck, 1978). Most contemporary established traditions discourage deliberate alterations of consciousness.

The Negative Way   In the Negative (or Middle) Way (Naranjo & Ornstein, 1971), the meditator tries to delete both internal and external forms from awareness, to experience directly consciousness itself. Such detached awareness is most common in the Zen tradition. The Zen practitioner "just sitting" merely observes percepts and fragments of thoughts, not following after any of them, but calmly watching them go by. In such intense, objective attention to the here and now, one withdraws from interaction with the external and internal environment.

The practice is like diving through a school of fish to reach the ocean floor. By avoiding distraction by the many thoughts floating around in the mind, one can see what lies behind them. One is said to see the world "as it is," without imposing habitual or personal meanings on it. By removing oneself from ordinary perceptual frameworks, one views reality with an entirely fresh and expanded awareness. It keeps open all possible ways of understanding experience.

MYSTICISM IN A MAP OF CONSCIOUSNESS

"Our normal waking consciousness . . . is but one special type of consciousness, whilst all about it, parted from it by the filmiest of screens, there lie potential forms of consciousness entirely different" (James, 1902/1961, p. 305). Besides waking consciousness, the average person is aware only of dreaming and sleeping *(Māndūkya Upanishad)*. James (1910) explained mystical consciousness with the analogy of land at water's edge. The part above the water is conscious awareness and that below the water level is unconscious mentation. Mysticism occurs when the water level suddenly drops to reveal portions of land previously hidden.

Some scholars have tried to "map" consciousness. Others describe "layers" of the human being that correspond to levels of reality and consciousness. Box 10.2 compares several such ideas.

Box 10.2 LEVELS OF PERSON AND COSMOS

Reality level	Upanishadic sheath	Selfhood (Smith)	Consciousness (Bucke)
Material-physical	*Annamaya*—body of food	Body	
Vital-vegetative	*Prānamaya*—body of vital energy	[Life]	
Mental-animal	*Manomaya*—body of mind	Mind	Simple consciousness
Celestial-human	*Jnānamaya*—body of discernment	Soul	Self-consciousness
Causal	*Ānandamaya*—body of bliss		Mystical consciousness
Infinite	*Ātman/jīvātman*—divinity within	Spirit	

Source: Compiled from Bucke (1923); Smith (1977); *Taittirīya Upanishad.*

Many models view consciousness as "inner space." We offer a model that draws together work of several theorists: Fischer (1971, 1978), LeShan (1976), Ring (1974, 1976), and Wilber (1977, 1979, 1980; Wilber & Meadow, 1979). The model describes states of consciousness associated with increasing hyper-(over) arousal and hypo-(under) arousal (Fischer, 1971). Wakefulness, sleeping, and dreaming—states with which we are all familiar—as well as mysticism and other altered states are "located" in this composite model, which is summarized in Box 10.3. This model is presented to help understanding, and does not posit these states to be real in the way layers of rock deposit are real!

The Reality of the Material World

LeShan's (1976) "sensory reality" reflects the world of ordinary waking consciousness. It posits that events occur in space and time, with causes preceding them. Objects are separated by space and time, and can influence each other only when in direct contact. The past can only be remembered, and only the present can be observed. The future can sometimes be changed when appropriate action is taken. All information comes directly or indirectly from the senses. Science is based on such understandings. Many people so take for granted this way of seeing reality that they do not recognize its underlying assumptions.

Ordinary Waking Consciousness   This everyday consciousness has little to do with mysticism. In it, we are mildly hyperaroused when engaged in activities, and hypoaroused in relaxation (Fischer, 1971). Prior to Freud—who called it the mere above-water tip of a large "iceberg" of consciousness—many people considered this the entire domain of mind.

Preconsciousness   The part of the iceberg that rests at the waterline is preconsciousness. Its mental contents are not in full awareness, but we can easily retrieve them. If we ask you to think of your mother, she springs easily into mind even though you were not thinking about her before we asked. Such preconscious contents often surface in the hypoarousal of daydreaming or reverie. In hyperarousal, such contents may surface when an external stimulus—such as our request—draws out a memory.

The Reality of the Unconscious Mind

The reality of the unconscious mind is best understood by recalling what can happen in your dreams. There is no difference between a thing, its name, and symbols that stand for it. Once things have been connected, they can become identical or stand for each other. In this reality, you can affect things by manipulating symbols that stand for them. There exists an energy that can be harnessed and used for either good or bad. Nothing happens by accident; all events are intended in some way. Ordinary concepts of space, time, and causation, however, are meaningless (LeShan, 1976).

This consciousness underlies astrology, superstition, fairy tales, art, myth,

---

Box 10.3   A MODEL OF CONSCIOUSNESS

Hyper-(high) arousal	Hypo-(low) arousal
THE REALITY OF THE MATERIAL WORLD	
Ordinary waking consciousness	
Daily activities	Relaxation
Preconsciousness	
Retrieval with stimulus	Reverie, daydreaming
THE REALITY OF THE UNCONSCIOUS MIND	
Psychodynamic unconscious	
Creative insight, dreaming, anxious or neurotic thinking	Hypnogogic/hypnopompic imagery, *zazen* practice
Ontogenetic unconscious	
Some nightmares, hallucinations, visions	Nondream sleep images, *makyō* (see text)
THE REALITY OF UNEMBODIED CONSCIOUSNESS	
Transpersonal consciousness	
Preorgasm, visions and locutions, "possessions," religious ecstasy	Awed absorption, "interior" light and harmony, deep egoless sleep, Zen *satori*
Transcendent consciousness	
Catalepsy, ecstatic union	*Samādhi* with content
THE FARTHEST REALITY	
The ultimate	
Mystical rapture	*Samādhi* without content
The void	
Godhead, *nirodh*, Tao, Self	

Source: Compiled from Fischer (1971, 1978); LeShan (1976); Ring (1974, 1976); Wilber (1977, 1979, 1980; Wilber & Meadow, 1979).

---

dreams, voodoo, magic, and the occult. Although some religious people frown on its practices, many religious rituals also reflect its assumptions. It is manifested in the sacramental use of such materials as water, fire, and food, when these objects are taken to stand for or actually become other objects.

Psychodynamic Consciousness   Freud called the underwater body of the iceberg the unconscious. By definition, it refers to processes outside of normal waking awareness. When we are somewhat hyperaroused, we may get creative insights or hunches that can be considered eruptions of unconscious material—as can some anxiety-laden and "magical" neurotic thinking.

Hypoarousal produces such psychodynamic material as hypnogogic imagery, which occurs just before we fall asleep. In *zazen* (a Zen meditation practice) and some concentrative meditations, one often becomes aware of bits of forgotten memory coming to the surface of awareness. As we descend deeper in consciousness, we easily flip from underaroused to overaroused conditions, and vice versa (Fischer, 1978). Going between dreaming and dreamless sleep is an example of this.

Ontogenetic Consciousness   Areas close to the limits of personal consciousness have been called ontogenetic (Grof, 1972; Ring, 1974), and are concerned with human finitude, birth, death, suffering, and being a separate individual. We are at the underwater sides of the iceberg, where iceberg is melting and becoming ocean and ocean is freezing and becoming iceberg, and it is hard to know what is iceberg and what is ocean.

In some dreamless sleep, certain symbols and images are thought to arise from deeper than dreams. Common occult and archetypal (see Chapter 2) images abound in this realm. Yogis hold that occult powers may come to one who understands this consciousness. Buddhism recognizes a meditative state called *makyō*—"the world of the devil"—referring to the hallucinations that may arise as one goes deeper into meditation.

The overaroused person at this level may be highly anxious and hallucinate images of birth, death, and impending disaster. Some nightmares are seen as springing from this area. Therapies that ask people to experience their own birth or death claim to deal with ontogenetic material. Many religious scriptures claim that, in order to live fully, one must be willing to die. Such statements may imply that one must experience this painful region to pass to mystical consciousness.

The Reality of Unembodied Consciousness

Most religious cosmologies reflect a mode of thinking that considers all objects to be somehow united with the larger whole of reality. The Mystical Body of Christ is one such idea. In this reality, everything that one part does affects the entire whole, and tremendous cosmic forces may be brought to bear on one part (LeShan, 1976). ESP and psi phenomena can be explained as resulting from nonmaterial connections between parts of the greater reality.

Belief in the effects of petitionary prayer, the value of vicarious atonement, the cosmic effects of evil, and many other religious ideas show this mode of understanding. The "worlds" created by psychotics often make similar assumptions. When people translate the rules of this reality into everyday language, they are called religious or crazy depending on how many other people share their beliefs. Most religious people have not actually *experienced* this consciousness, but verbally assent to such ideas as a learned belief.

Transpersonal Consciousness   The realm of transpersonal consciousness lies just below the base of our metaphorical iceberg. Consciousness is now the sea in which individual consciousness (the iceberg) rests, but can still refer back to its own iceberg. Awareness of oneself as a separate entity is easily lost; time, space, and causality are meaningless. Experience of being part of or in touch with enormous "energy" is common. Mysticism can be said to begin here, but not all experiences here or beyond are mystical ones.

The hyperarousal just prior to sexual orgasm led Fischer to call it "a poor [person's] ecstasy" (1978, p. 36). Sexual imagery may be used to describe religious mysticism in this realm. Visions, locutions, and religious ecstasy are common in high arousal. So also are a variety of peak experiences (discussed later) and "possessions." Mental and perceptual processes are fragmented, as in schizophrenic episodes.

Hypoarousal may bring some peak experiences of stillness and awed absorption, nonphysical "interior" light, harmony, or soothing vibrations (Wilber & Meadow, 1979). Here also occurs Zen *satori,* or "awake" enlightenment (Fischer, 1978). One also enters this realm in deep, egoless sleep. The peace and serenity that follow a good night's sleep reflect the consolations of transpersonal consciousness.

Transcendent Consciousness   At the level of transcendent consciousness, our iceberg no longer exists. All is sea; self-awareness has disappeared. Except for split-second orgasmic experiences, people seldom reach these realms. Hyperaroused transcendent consciousness can produce catalepsy (muscular rigidity) and ecstatic union with a personalized image of deity. On the hypoaroused side, yogis call the experience "*samādhi* with seed" (with content). One's ego merges with the object of meditation, and only this exists in awareness. A yogic source says, "The drop of water that I am becomes the ocean that is Brahman."

The Farthest Reality

In the fully unitive world view of mystical consciousness, the entire universe is seen as one vast process or flow. All things make up the total fabric of being, and cannot be seen as having divisive boundaries. Space and time become unreal. The sense of separate selfhood does not exist, so one cannot have personal intentions for any self, including oneself. All is a complete oneness. It is nearly impossible to translate this reality into everyday language. People who try are variously considered saints or fools.

The Ultimate   At the ultimate level even "sea-ness" disappears. There is no content, but only God, existence, or consciousness itself. There is no external or self-awareness. If hyperaroused, the experience is of mystical rapture (Fischer, 1978). If hypoaroused, it is "seedless *samādhi*"—*samādhi* without content.

The Void   The void is the loss of experience itself that is the final reach of consciousness. Not all mystics acknowledge this state. One arrives at it from either mystical rapture or seedless *samādhi* (Fischer, 1978). In Chinese thought, the Tao is the originating void that underlies the phenomenal universe. Buddhists call this state *nirodh,* or "no prison." The Zen Buddhist *Heart Sutra* says:

> Form is emptiness, emptiness is form; emptiness does not differ from form, form does not differ from emptiness. . . . There is no decay and death, no extinction of decay and death. There is no suffering, no origination, no stopping, no path. There is no cognition, there is no attainment, and no non-attainment [Conze, 1958, pp. 81–82].

Christian mystic Meister Eckhart wrote about the Godhead that lies behind any image of God, and called it void, inert, and empty: "God acts. The Godhead does not. It has nothing to do, and there is nothing going on in it" (Stace, 1960b, pp. 142–157).

MYSTICISM AND OTHER ALTERED STATES OF CONSCIOUSNESS

Scholars do not agree upon any one classification of altered states of consciousness (ASC). Krippner (1972a) offered one of the most complete lists: dreaming, sleeping, hypnogogic, lethargic, rapture, hysteria, fragmentation, regression, meditation, trance, reverie, daydreaming, internal scanning, stupor, coma, stored memory, expanded consciousness, and normal waking state. Harvard psychiatrist Andrew Weil holds that "a desire to alter consciousness periodically is an innate, normal drive analogous to hunger or the sexual drive" (1972a, p. 66). We now compare mysticism with some other altered states.

Mysticism and Psychedelic Drugs

People commonly cannot distinguish between reports of spontaneous mystical experiences and psychedelic drug experiences. These states appear to be strongly related.

Some Drug-induced Experiences   Psychedelic-induced experiences often have religious implications and overtones (Krippner, 1970), and reach at least the ontogenetic level of our model (Clark, 1969, 1979a; Knight & Clark, 1975, 1976). Grof's (1972, 1973, 1976) extensive work with mind-altering drugs describes subjects' initial drug responses as typically aesthetic, followed by their working through personal, psychodynamic material. Next comes "the shattering encounter with . . . critical aspects of human existence and the deep realization of the frailty and impermanence of [the human] as a biological creature" (Grof, 1973, p. 25). Grof (1976) also describes visions, locutions, and psi phenomena that could be considered transpersonal.

   Lilly (1972) emphasized the religious and mystical import of his own psychedelic experiences. He used numbers to identify his states—some of the most important of which correspond to levels in our model. "Pure 48" is alert waking consciousness. In "+24" one's automatic (see Chapter 9) responses suggest unconsciously governed behavior. At "+12" Lilly experienced a combined "grief-joy" for all humans, suggestive of the ontogenetic. At "+6" all consciousness was reduced to a small point. Lilly reported meeting spirit guides here, and felt he could move around in his body and out into the cosmos (transpersonal realm). A transcendent experience of union with energy and matter was reported for "+3."

Set and Setting Effects   Psychedelic agents are commonly used in religious settings to trigger ASCs in shamanism and among some American Indian groups (Harner, 1973). In controlled settings where personal growth is a major motivation for taking the drug, experiences differ from those of ordinary "street" usage. American Indians avoid abuse problems by taking the agents in natural forms, in a ritual setting, with advice from elders who know the experience, and for religious ends rather than to escape boredom (Weil, 1972b).

Pahnke (Pahnke & Richards, 1966) studied "experimental mysticism" in a Good Friday service. Five groups, of four subjects each, participated in a double-blind study. (Neither the experimenter nor any subjects knew who got active drug and who got placebo.) Ninety minutes before the service, half the subjects in each group were given psilocybin (a psychedelic agent) while the other half were given a vitamin. After a 2 ½-hour religious service, individuals' reactions and group discussions were tape recorded. Within a week all subjects completed a questionnaire and were interviewed for 90 minutes. Nine of the ten psilocybin subjects reported "mystical consciousness" while only one vitamin subject did—and he to a minor degree. Six months later, the effects of the experience still distinguished the two groups at a high level of statistical significance.

Evaluation   Psychedelic drugs clearly produce progression into deeper altered states, although Clark (1968) found that strength of dose was not directly related to intensity of experience. He concluded that the drugs do not directly cause the experience, but simply release it in subjects with the capacity for it. Researchers have reported positive effects of religion-related LSD ingestion with terminal patients (Richards, 1978), nonproductive artists (Clark, 1977), prisoners (Leary & Clark, 1963), alcoholics, and psychiatric patients (Abramson, 1960, 1967).

Many experts recommend caution. "Drugs, which can be helpful when wisely used, become dangerous when foolishly used. The sudden insight becomes 'all' and the patient and disciplined 'working through' is postponed or devalued" (Maslow, 1970, p. 101). Another concern is that "drug experience strongly reinforces the illusion that highs come from external, material things rather than from one's own nervous system, and it is precisely this illusion that one strives to overcome by means of meditation" (Weil, 1972b, p. 90). Although many drug users turn to meditation, few people go in the opposite direction (Pelletier & Garfield, 1976). Some scholars hold that "the deepest and most personally significant spiritual encounters come to those who were prepared for them" (Havens, 1964, p. 224), and suggest that any lasting value in ASCs induced by drugs will come only with spiritual seeking and self-discipline. "If the aftereffect of the LSD works out in the subject's seeking of mystical enlightenment through sustained self-effort, then LSD deserves credit for promoting a true mystical mind expansion" (Gilbert, 1971, pp. 187–188).

Mysticism and Psychopathology

"In delusional insanity, paranoia, . . . we have a diabolical mysticism, a sort of religious mysticism turned upside down" (James, 1902/1961, p. 334). Some experiences show, at the same time, evidence of both mysticism and psychopathology (Goldstein, 1979). How do we determine if there are differences?

Some Case History Material   Daniel Schreber spent half his life in mental institutions. He saw himself as "locked into" a stressful relationship with God whose "miracles"—which included a sex change—were intended to destroy his reason (Schreber, 1955). Custance (1951) obsessed about a "positive" and "negative" dualism, which he paradoxically fused in such concepts as "religious lust" and "negative goddess of mercy." Hennell's (1967) thinking focused on cosmic destruction from which came an enigmatic visionary double of himself—a numinous and paradoxical "savior." Boisen (1936, 1960) reported complex revelations with heroic religious tasks given him. Since both mysticism and insanity may involve transpsychic experiences, distinguishing a mystic's world view from a psychotic delusion can be difficult (Bregman, 1977, 1979a, 1979b; Wilber & Meadow, 1979).

Regressive Interpretations of Mysticism   Mysticism has been seen as an attempt to return to infantile omnipotence (Freud, 1939) and as frustrated sexual drives (Leuba, 1925). Prince and Savage saw both mysticism and schizophrenia as regressive withdrawal, but said "a psychosis is a pressured withdrawal with . . . an incomplete return. A mystical state is a controlled withdrawal and return" (1972, p. 132). Wapnick argued that retreat from social realities characterizes both states, but that "differences in the preparation reflect the essential difference between the mystic and the schizophrenic" (1969, p. 65). A mystic's purpose is expansion of consciousness, while psychotics flee a world in which they cannot function. The ultimate regressive explanation claims that mysticism is the experiencing of the union of sperm and ovum (Maven, 1972).

Similarities and Distinctions   Zales (1978) believes that mystics and schizophrenics alike feel they are rejecting something bad, feel alienated, have been disappointed in interpersonal relationships, and have constructed for themselves a more gratifying reality. Mystics, however, engage in only a partial retreat that facilitates adjustment, and can share their world view with some others. Laing (1979) claims that schizophrenics battle images that religious people used to call demons, and that these experiences are like those from which religion originally developed. Greeley sees both experiences as altered states, but says that "to compare mysticism with schizophrenia is like comparing bread with steak because they are both foods" (1974, p. 40). The "schizophrenic patient is actually experiencing inadvertently that same beatific ocean deep which the yogi and saint are ever striving to enjoy; except that, whereas they are swimming in it, [she or] he is drowning" (Campbell, 1979, p. 200). Campbell (1972) also argues that preparedness makes a key difference.

Peak and Ecstasy Experiences

"Are we a nation of mystics?" asked Greeley and McCready (1975). They concluded that we are, on the basis of people's answers to the question: "Have you ever had the feeling of being very close to a powerful spiritual force that seemed to lift you out of yourself?" Hay and Morisy found that slightly more than one-third of Great Britainers reported "having been aware of or influenced by a presence or power, whether referred to as God or not, which was different from their everyday selves" (1978, p. 257). Researchers' findings that more than one-third of all people acknowledge such experiences clearly differs from the classical literature, which considers mysticism a relatively rare phenomenon. Are these people really reporting mystical experiences?

Peak Experiences   Popular interest in common mysticism began with Maslow's discussion of peak experiences. "The universal nucleus of every known high religion . . . has been the private, lonely, personal illumination, revelation, ecstasy of some acutely sensitive prophet or seer" (Maslow, 1964, p. 19). He believed that supernatural explanations of "peaks" reflect culture-boundness and that similar experiences, triggered by various circumstances, can be understood in secular terms. Peak and mystical experiences are a "passive, aesthetic sort, experiences that beat their way in upon the organism, flooding it as music does" (Maslow, 1954, p. 300). Maslow describes cognitive and emotional similarities between peaks and mysticism. "The person at the peak is godlike . . . in the complete, loving, uncondemning, compassionate and perhaps amused acceptance of the world and of the person," and peaks produce "a true integration of the person at all levels" (Maslow, 1968, pp. 92, 96).

The Triggers of Ecstasy   In her book *Ecstasy* Laski (1961) described many "triggers"—religion, art, nature, sex, creativity, understanding, etc.—that can precipitate ecstatic (peak) experiences. Students of Maslow (Allen, Haupt, & Jones, 1964) also reported various types of such triggers.

   Hay (1979) sorted some experiences reported as mystical into these categories: being controlled or guided by a power, awareness of presence of God, awareness of presence in nature, answered prayer, unity with nature, psi or parapsychological experiences, awareness of an evil power, and conversion. Using Greeley's (Greeley & McCready, 1975) question, Thomas and Cooper (1978) also found that about one-third of people claimed ecstatic experience. Analysis of their subjects' reports gave the following breakdown: no experience (66%), uncodable (8%), mystical (2%), psychic (12%), and religious consolation (12%). A similar analysis of other studies would likely yield far fewer mystics than the one-third rate typically reported. Most ecstatic experience is of a type traditionally not considered mystical.

Questionnaire Studies   Several researchers have attempted to quantify mystical experience in questionnaires. Hood's (1970) Religious Experience Episodes Measure asked people to compare the similarity of their own experiences to reports of mysticism. His later Mysticism Scale (Hood, 1975a) has been more highly researched. (See Chapter 11.) Since Hood's scale consistently classifies one-third of his subjects as mystics, it probably measures peak or ecstatic experiences rather than mystical ones.

Another research of ecstatic experience (Brown, Spilka, & Cassidy, 1978) also broke down into a variety of parapsychological, psychopathological, hallucinatory, and religious consolation experiences. Greeley questioned the quantitative study of mysticism: "Is it not ludicrous to think that questionnaires, IBM cards, and computer outputs can deal adequately with human experience of direct and immediate contact with the Really Real?" (1974, p. 89).

Some Other Altered States

Hypnosis   Although some do not consider hypnosis an ASC (Barber, 1969), it evidently does move a person toward hypoarousal. Sleeplike effects occur, and EEG records demonstrate a pain-dulling effect (Hilgard, 1969). Some researchers report individuals' reliving of early childhood experiences or even what they claim to be their own births and past lives (Wambach, 1979). If such claims are valid, hypnosis produces ontogenetic or even transpersonal consciousness. Yogis insist that, despite any similarities, meditation and hypnosis are different processes.

Near-Death Experiences   Reports (Moody, 1975; Ring, 1979b) of near-death out-of-body experiences describe feelings of separation from one's body; various psi experiences; perceptions of light, harmony, and peace; and apparent encounters with nonmaterial personalities. Such reports suggest the transpersonal level.

Evaluating Altered States Experiences

About religion, James insisted: "By their fruits ye shall know them, not by their roots" (1902/1961, p. 34). Stace (1960b) similarly held that the course or cause of mystical experience does not determine its genuineness. What, then, can one say of the altered states just discussed? Kellenberger (1978) suggested some criteria for three elements of mysticism: experience, awareness, and state of being.

Experience   Ellwood said that to consider an experience mystical, "first, the experience must have sufficient intensity. . . . Second, the experience must be in a context that makes the mystical interpretation the most available" (1980, p. 33). Mental set and preparedness strongly influence the interpretation one puts on altered states. Some lesser experiences probably are called mystical because of a religious context. Some other experiences get so labeled because of their intensity—though they lack any religious significance.

Clearly, both mystics and those experiencing other altered states travel some same areas on our map of consciousness. Few experiences other than mystical go past the transpersonal realm, and many fall short of it. Some produce only emotional reactions and/or the peace that comes with increased attunement to one's own inner processes. Would-be mystics work through experiences at levels that are terminal points for other altered states.

Pruyser cautioned that many people:

> have no inkling of the great demands it makes in self-discipline and assiduous training. . . . If mysticism is practiced as pill-induced instant mysticism without schooling, discipline, hard work, regular study, and self-abnegation, its benefits are of a very different order from those gained by the classical mystics [Pruyser, 1971, p. 85].

An intense ASC can be an invitation to mysticism; probably most who have drug, pathological, and peak highs do not accept the invitation.

Awareness   Mysticism is "a realization . . . that something is true. . . . It would come to religious knowledge and be what in various traditions is called wisdom" (Kellenberger, 1978, p. 179). This goes beyond simple perceptual experience and implies more lasting cognitive changes. Murshida (a Sufi teacher) Ivy Duce reflected on the temporary nature of many experiences:

> You can get a high but you come down with a thud. So why not work for . . . a permanent gain which you can count on? . . . They say it's mystical because they've encountered scenes that they were not aware of before. But that does not make them mystical [Kaplan, 1979, pp. 35–36].

Clark describes one expected change: "Mystical experience develops compassion and sympathy. . . . It breaks through the superficial levels of seeming and appearance to . . . where all people are one" (1965, p. 157). Those who value highs should recall that "repeatedly, the mystical literature stresses that sensate experiences are not the goal. . . . It is only when these are transcended that one attains . . . *direct* (intuitive) knowledge of fundamental reality" (Deikman, 1979, p. 191).

Such basic personality change is fundamental to mysticism, which requires that the person persevere in a mystical way of life. Visionaries who do not meet this demand are "aborted" mystics. "The unitive experience does not happen all at once; the mental training takes years" (Thayer, 1979, p. 238).

State of Being   The attitude necessary for mysticism "has variously been described as egolessness, overcoming pride, or dying to self. . . . It emphatically is not an experience of ecstasy" (Kellenberger, 1978, p. 179). In the "pseudonirvana" of attachment to one's own progress, one may cease working continually to overcome egoism and complacency (Goleman, 1977, p. 28). Mysticism is for the religiously serious-minded.

Underhill describes the mystical state of being:

1. It is an organic life-process, a something which the whole self does.
2. "Its aims are wholly transcendental and spiritual. . . . Heart is always set upon the changeless One,

3. a living and personal Object of Love; never an object of exploration.
4. Living union with this One . . . is obtained neither from an intellectual realization of its delights, nor from acute emotional longings. . . . It is arrived at by an arduous psychological and spiritual process [Underhill, 1911/1974, p. 81].

Experiences produced other than by deliberate cultivation of a mystical path rarely lead to this kind of stance. "The mystic gives [herself or] himself whole-heartedly to God because [she or] he wants from the Supreme Being much more than . . . a sense of communion. . . . The mystic wants nothing less than God" (Schneiderman, 1967, p. 93). Are we a nation of mystics? Not by these criteria!

EXPLANATIONS OF MYSTICAL EXPERIENCE

Since one cannot measure mysticism, psychology's understanding of it is highly speculative. Most explanations focus simply on the experiential aspects, and not on the way of life.

Specialization of Brain Functions

Some modes of consciousness are neurologically specific. The analytical left hemisphere of the brain is associated with logic and sequential thinking, and the intuitive right hemisphere is nonrational, artistic, and synthetic. Altered states are considered right-hemisphere functions (Ornstein, 1977). (See also Chapter 12.)

Jaynes (1976) speculated that reflective, verbal consciousness is fairly recent in human history. Earlier, the brain hemispheres acted independently (bicameral functioning). Problems that custom and habit (left-hemisphere functions) could not handle were deliberated unconsciously in the right hemisphere. Its solutions were then hallucinated (perceived as originating outside oneself), and considered the guiding voices of gods. This bicameral functioning has been suppressed in modern people to cope with increasingly complex civilization, leaving them feeling abandoned by the gods. Religion developed as "nostalgic anguish for the lost bicamerality" (Jaynes, 1976, p. 297). Jaynes considers religious frenzy, poetry, glossolalia, hypnotism, occult symbols, schizophrenia—altered states in general—throwbacks to bicameralism. Mysticism would be one such throwback.

Brain as Filter or Creator of Reality

Letting Reality Through   Although "thought is a function of the brain" (James, 1898, p. 10), it does not follow that spiritual realities exist only in the brain. Such a conclusion implies that the brain creates thought. James argues that the brain might have other functions, such as a releasing or a transmitting one.

If a universe of other genuine realities exists behind the material world, the brain could be the means by which these realities are released into the material world. The brain may be a "gap in the curtain" that keeps different dimensions of reality separate. The brain also could serve as a transmission station, letting loose in this world portions of another reality according to its capabilities. It imposes the limitations of its own capacity as a transmitter upon the realities it transmits. Mysticism would represent a widening of the gap in the curtain, or an increase in the brain's capacity to transmit another reality.

Structuring Material Reality Pribram (1971, 1976; Ferguson, 1978) suggests that the brain actually constructs the reality of the material world by interpreting information from other dimensions of reality that transcend the assumptions (space, time, causality) of the material world. One can extend this speculation to say that consciousness—rather than brain, which is itself a material entity—imposes order on successively grosser levels of reality. If each level is seen as providing a template to determine the nature and limits of grosser levels, this notion matches assumptions underlying much of Eastern mysticism.

Pribram proposes that mysticism involves direct access to an underlying ultimate realm—a view mystics have long held. He suggests that brain circuits on the amygdala (part of the brain stem) that have been linked to disturbances in perception may be involved in mysticism. Mysticism would thus be a purely natural phenomenon, but one reflecting a reality other than that with which we are most familiar.

Biochemistry and Altered States

Prior to the mid-1960s, when experimentation with psychedelic drugs became illegal, researchers studied biochemical reactions associated with drug-induced cognitive and perceptual changes. Some people appear to be biochemically more prone to such experiences (Clark, 1979b). Adoption of a mystical way of life may produce biochemical changes that, in turn, produce ecstatic experiences. As some drugs alter brain chemistry, so also fasting, asceticism, prolonged vigils, and other practices of mystics probably do.

Deautomatization of Experience

Attention is an important variable for an understanding of alterations of consciousness. Meditative practices are "a deliberate attempt to . . . 'turn off' the active mode of normal consciousness . . . to enter the complementary mode of 'darkness' and receptivity" (Ornstein, 1977, p. 159). In ordinary waking consciousness, many motor and perceptual behaviors are habitual or automatic; this is efficient for everyday life. Deautomatization (Deikman, 1963, 1966)—a breakdown in this process—makes us aware of stimuli we had not before noticed.

Meditation practices, some drugs, and acute psychoses produce deautomatization by breaking up ordinary perceptual and attentional processes. Deikman's (1971) research concluded that both mysticism and schizophrenia allow rediscovery of cognitive or sensory states and long-forgotten experiences that had been lost from awareness. The sudden, extreme change to a receptive mode of functioning uncovers things that were there to be seen all along, but which had been excluded from attention.

Predisposing Personality Characteristics

Are some people more disposed by personality toward mysticism than others? Intuitively, we want to say yes, even though the great mystics had very different styles and personal characteristics. While trying to develop a measure of hypnotic susceptibility, Tellegen (1979; Tellegen & Atkinson, 1974) found a consistent personality factor that he called "absorption."

Absorption is:

> a disposition for having episodes of "total" attention. . . . This kind of attentional functioning is believed to result in a heightened sense of the reality of the attentional object, imperviousness to distracting events and an altered sense of reality in general [Tellegen & Atkinson, 1974, p. 268].

This trait describes the ability to become absorbed in both fantasy and external reality—movies, nature, etc. It is the capacity to commit fully to an object all one's available resources for perception, attention, thinking, and imagination—clearly a capacity meditators try to develop. Absorption is consistently related to hypnotizability (Tellegen, 1978). The trait may measure one's general capacity for experiencing altered states of consciousness.

What Causes Mysticism?

Psychology cannot now delineate the causes of mysticism in any definitive way. It has suggested some possible predisposing factors, and described the effects that certain practices might have for mystical experience. Mysticism may not lend itself well to scientific investigation. If it pertains to an entirely different order of reality than that of science, whatever explanations science can offer will reduce mysticism by the limits of an inappropriate method. It is also beyond the scope of psychology to pronounce on the reality status of the perceptions of mystics.

REVIEW OF KEY CONCEPTS

The Phenomenon of Mysticism
  mysticism contrasted with occult, parapsychological, or devotional
    experience
  major characteristics of mysticism: unity, ineffability, reality, paradoxicality

Stages of Mystical Development
  purgative, illuminative, and unitive life
  passive purification of the senses and dark night of the soul
  "zero experience"

Becoming a Mystic
  śila, yama, and niyama
  body discipline
  discursive meditation and centering exercises
  dhārana and dhyāna
  Way of Forms, Expressive Way, and Negative Way

Mysticism in a Map of Consciousness
> consciousness as "inner space"
> hyperarousal and hypoarousal
> sensory reality
> *zazen*
> ontogenetic realm
> *makyō*
> transpersonal consciousness
> *satori*
> *nirodh*

Mysticism and Other Altered States of Consciousness
> Lilly's psychedelic experiment
> experimental mysticism
> paranoia and mysticism
> preparedness and mystical experience
> peak experience
> categories of ecstasy
> quantitative study of mysticism
> evaluation of experience
> Underhill's description of mysticism

Explanations of Mystical Experience
> bicameral functioning
> gap-in-the-curtain theory
> deautomatization of experience
> absorption
> the reality of mysticism

chapter 11

Selected Research in Religious Experiences

This chapter focuses on an assortment of significant research efforts in the psychology of religious experience. We shall sketch and briefly evaluate studies of conversion, prayer, faith healing, glossolalia, and ecstasy experiences.

CONVERSION AND PERSONALITY

Pioneer psychologists of religion considered persons of certain temperaments or personalities to be more susceptible to conversion, particularly to sudden or crisis conversions. Several studies have used standard personality measures to investigate both causes and effects of conversion. Personality tests may be used to compare persons who have experienced a religious conversion with those who have not been converted or who have experienced a different type of conversion. Such investigators usually assume that any differences identify conversion-prone persons—implying that personality is relatively unchangeable and that the preconversion personality pattern is still identifiable after the conversion.

Other studies also give personality tests to converted persons, hoping to discover *effects* of religious conversion. Those researchers assume that their tests can reflect the integrative effects of the religious experience. The particular personality measures usually can be defended to indicate appropriately either relatively permanent or relatively changeable aspects of personality. Still, the typical research design leaves much to be desired from the viewpoint of good psychological investigation.

A Longitudinal Study

A longitudinal design might best study the preconditions and effects of conversion as a religious developmental experience. Such a study is very difficult to accomplish; we know of only one longitudinal study of conversion—R. Ward Wilson's (1976a) doctoral dissertation. He tested 533 youth in the late fall and again in the early spring of the 1971–1972 school year; some were associated with an urban "soft-sell" Christian evangelistic group (Young Life), and the others attended a rural high school. Wilson found 11 who were converted between the two testing times, 9 of them coming from Young Life. The converts were compared with various groups of nonbelievers and previous converts from the total sample. Fifteen personality scales, 12 values scales, a dogmatism scale, and 10 scales measuring various attitudes toward Christianity were included in the study.

Convertible Personality   The literature repeatedly identified virtually no charac-teristic of a preconversion personality, other than suggestibility. Several modern and classical studies found converts to be more suggestible to hypnotic induction. Wilson, however, found no personality scale that identified potential converts. He attributed the contradiction to the fact that Young Life does not employ high-pressure tactics, and the other studies had identified sudden, crisis conver-sions.

Conversion Effects   Wilson's study found three personality variables on which the 11 converts changed—made "personality reorganizations" unlike those of other groups. In his terms, the converts changed "from high impulsivity to greater sobriety," increased on "practical dogmatism" and on "expansive believ-ing" (Wilson, 1976b, p. 10). The third change especially was seen as a shift from relative neuroticism to healthful adjustment. Stanley (1965) found lower neuroti-cism among theological students who had experienced crisis conversions. He con-sidered low neuroticism a factor predisposing one to sudden conversion. Perhaps, instead, it was an *effect* of the conversion experiences.

Evaluation

Research on conversion would benefit from more longitudinal studies, such as Wilson's, but with a greater variety and number of converts and kinds of conver-sion. His study, however, illustrates the potential insights of such research, as well as the great effort required to carry it out.

A CROSS-CULTURAL STUDY OF PETITIONARY PRAYER

The Study

In Chapter 8 we referred to L. B. Brown's (1966a) study of petitionary prayer. He gave questionnaires to 1101 boys and girls (ages 12–17) in the United States (Maine), New Zealand, and Australia. Seven situations that might involve prayer were posed: outcome of a football game, safety during battle, avoidance of detec-tion of a theft, receipt of payment of a loan, good weather for a church picnic, survival of a boy overboard at sea with a shark approaching, and health of a sick grandmother. Two most important questions asked for each circumstance were: "Is it right to pray in this situation?" and "Are the prayers likely to have any effect?"

   The full event and questions for the shark item are given here for illustration (Brown's article also gives the football game item):

> *Shark escape.* James fell into the sea from a yacht. He started to swim towards the boat that was coming to rescue him, but he saw the black fin of a shark between him and the boat. He prayed that he might escape the shark.

1. Was James right to pray for his escape?
2. What kind of a prayer might he have offered?
3. Would the fact that James prayed make it more likely he would escape?
4. If the man in the boat rescuing James prayed, too, would James be even more likely to escape? [Brown, 1966a, p. 209].

Results

The Situations   There were large differences among situations in the percentage of youth who gave an unqualified "yes" to the effectiveness of prayer: theft 5.7%, picnic 26.7%, football 34.2%, debt 41.0%, battle 44.8%, shark 48.3%, and grandmother 57.2% (if she knew she was being prayed for). Children from all three countries had similar views of the effectiveness of prayer in the different situations. There was less agreement among cultures as to the appropriateness of prayer, largely because the New Zealanders were less approving of prayer before battle. In general the appropriateness of prayer was related to views of its effectiveness (the correlation coefficient was $+.79$). Almost without exception, more children in each group thought prayer was appropriate than thought it would be effective. Overall appropriateness percentages were: theft 13.2%, football 56.2%, battle 58.5%, picnic 64.0%, debt 72.5%, shark 89.2%, and grandmother 90.2%.

Ages   With advancing age fewer children believed petitionary prayers to be effective. For example, among Australian girls ages 12–13, 47% thought prayers for the football game would be effective, compared to 33% for 14–15, and 23% for 16–17. Equivalent percentages for appropriateness of such prayers were 65%, 52%, and 55%. This reflects the general finding that age has little to do with beliefs about the appropriateness of the various prayers.

Cultures and Denominations   The views of effectiveness and appropriateness of prayer in the seven situations differed little among the three cultural groups, or among Protestant, Catholic, and unchurched youth. The denominational groups differed somewhat in the *form* or wording of prayers, as questioned in several of the situations. With regard to a question whether the respondents themselves had ever prayed for specific favors, the Americans were most likely to respond affirmatively (girls 91%, boys 80%), Australians next (80% and 67%), and New Zealanders least (74% and 67%). Girls in each group were more likely than boys to have offered such prayers.

Evaluation

Our space allows only some of the major findings and none of Brown's theoretical interpretations. He was able to draw conclusions from the variety of "dimensions" he examined in one study: three age groups, three cultures, seven situations, and two major and several minor questions about each situation. Probably no other religious experience has been analyzed in such scope within a single study.

FAITH HEALING AS A RITUAL

The Study

One of the most systematic studies of faith healing was done in the Seattle, Washington, area by two psychiatrists and a psychologist (Pattison, Lapins, & Doerr, 1973). Pastors of churches that practiced faith healing provided names of 43 church members who had experienced the ritual of faith healing. The investigators interviewed and tested these 19 men and 24 women, who ranged in age from 16 to 80.

Results

The Healing Experience   The 43 interviewees had experienced a total of 71 healings—an average of 15 years previously, some as recently as 2 weeks before the interview. Most had experienced one faith healing, but 18 of them had experienced from two to five healings. Table 11.1 summarizes characteristics of the healing experiences.

Psychological Characteristics   The psychological evaluations produced little admission of worries, anxieties, restlessness, depression, or anger among the healed subjects. However, interviewers observed all of those symptoms. A personality test, the Minnesota Multiphasic Personality Inventory, showed a rather consistent, essentially normal pattern, except for conspicuous denial of problems and "a tendency to report oneself in a *highly socially acceptable* manner" (Pattison et al., 1973, p. 401). Subjects' relatively high scores on Hysteria suggested a tendency to deny psychological or emotional complaints; such denial can lead to physical symptoms.

Interpretation of Faith Healing   The interviewers found that the respondents' perceptions of having been healed were related more to their participation in a healing ritual than to direct observation of changes in their physical symptoms. The research report, however, neither supported nor disclaimed the physical real-

Table 11.1   CHARACTERISTICS OF 71 FAITH HEALING EXPERIENCES

Severity of prior illness		Residual symptoms	
Life threatening	12	None	57
Moderate disability	38	Minor	6
Minimal complaints	21	Moderate	7
Medical treatment		Severe	1
None	40	**Participation in healing**	
Occasional	16	**rituals**	
Continuous	15	Private self-prayer	9
Remission of symptoms		One church ritual	45
Gradual	36	Two rituals	2
Instantaneous	35	Over two rituals	15

Source: Pattison, Lapins, and Doerr (1973, p. 399).

ity of the healing experiences. The researchers found no evidence that new physical symptoms replaced the ones that were eliminated by faith healing. The healing experiences made no notable changes in the life-styles of those healed—they were generally devout before and after healing. However, those who had been converted as adults did report that "life had become more peaceful and satisfying" (Pattison et al., 1973, p. 400) after conversion. The major religious change after healing was: "All reported that their *certainty* in their belief in God and in their religious convictions was *markedly increased* after their faith healing experience" (Pattison et al., 1973, p. 401). Their relatively deviant religious system, including the glossolalia most of them had experienced, was seen as a generally "adequate ego coping system" (Pattison et al., 1973, p. 406). Faith healing is but another ritual that helps some members of those churches practicing it to deal with psychological stresses.

Evaluation

The church healing ritual is just one of the many settings in which faith healing can and does occur. The researchers in this study may have done the best they could to get representative cases of faith healing. At least the research participants had much in common, and the study was able to give a remarkably thorough look at one type of faith healing. The psychological tests and interviews (including reports of the healing experiences and religious life before and after them) provided enough detail to draw balanced conclusions about the experience of faith healing in these individual lives.

GLOSSOLALIA AND PERSONALITY

The Study

Perhaps the best single book on glossolalia is John P. Kildahl's (1972) *The Psychology of Speaking in Tongues.* We can summarize only one small study from Kildahl's 10-year investigation of the subject. Twenty glossolalists were selected from mainline Protestant churches and carefully matched with 20 other "very religious" members from the same or similar churches. All 40 were interviewed in depth and given psychological tests—including the Thematic Apperception Test and the Minnesota Multiphasic Personality Inventory (MMPI).

Results

Personality In general the tongues-speakers were neither more nor less mentally healthy than the control group (nontongues-speakers). The glossolalists showed significantly less depression than the control group on the MMPI, and their low level was unchanged a year later. Kildahl observed that speaking in tongues is an understandable antidote to depression: "Glossolalist[s] believe that God Almighty, Creator of the ends of the universe, is with [them] and approves of [them] in [their] belief that [they are] all right" (1972, p. 46).

On the other hand, the tongues-speakers were significantly lower in need for personal autonomy, as revealed in their Thematic Apperception Test stories. Their reports of relationships with leaders in the tongues movement also showed their intense dependence on authority figures: "A profound sense of trust in a leader is necessary for beginning to speak in tongues. . . . But a persisting relationship appears to be equally vital if the practice is to continue to be an important part of one's life" (Kildahl, 1972, pp. 44–45).

Crises   Not long before they began to speak in tongues, 85% of the glossolalists had experienced anxiety crises—variously involving religious values, guilt, meaning of life, marital difficulties, financial concerns, ill health, and general depression. Only 30% of the nonspeakers reported such anxiety crises, leading Kildahl to believe that anxiety is a significant factor in developing tongue-speaking abilities (1972, pp. 57–58).

Evaluation

Although the design of Kildahl's study resembles that of the faith healing study, an important difference is the control group (nonglossolalists). Without such a comparison, it is impossible to know for sure whether the personality of a specialized group is related to the particular religious experience or is generally characteristic of religious persons or a subcultural group.

ECSTASY AS A NORMAL PERSONALITY VARIABLE

The M Scale

In Chapter 10 we introduced Hood's (1975a) work on measuring peak experiences (at least a mild form of mysticism, he thought) as rather common experiences. The *M* (for mysticism) *Scale* was carefully designed to measure eight of Stace's (1960a) criteria for mysticism; four items for each criterion produced a scale of 32 items. Samples for four of the categories are as follows:

> Ego quality: I have had an experience in which something greater than myself seemed to absorb me.
>
> Unifying quality: I have had an experience in which I realized the oneness of myself with all things.
>
> Noetic quality: I have had an experience in which ultimate reality was revealed to me.
>
> Religious quality: I have had an experience which I knew to be sacred [Hood, 1975a, pp. 31–32].

Instructions for the M Scale ask respondents to check on a five-point scale how much each phenomenon applies to their own experiences. The scale is objectively scored by counting the magnitude of responses to the 32 items. The M Scale is about as reliable as other personality or attitude scales of its kind.

Research with the M Scale

Hood and others have done considerable research with the M Scale as a measure of experiences that share common elements with classical mysticism.

Church Activity   One early study (Hood, 1975b) compared M Scale scores of students who varied in church attendance and affiliation. The highest M Scale scores were for those who *never* (average score of 131) or *frequently* (129) attended church, declining from both extremes to 105 for *rarely* and 111 for *moderately;* the middle category, *occasionally* attending, obtained the lowest average (102). The extremes with regard to church attendance reported the most ecstatic experiences.

In the same study those who planned to change their church membership had higher M Scale scores than those who were uncertain or planned not to change—suggesting that churches do not usually meet the spiritual needs of the mystic. However, when asked about quitting church altogether, those who said they would definitely quit had the lowest scores, and the highest were for those who probably would not quit.

Stress and Ecstasy   Hood (1977) used the M Scale to relate ecstatic experiences to expected and real stress. High school seniors participated in a week of "wilderness challenge" activities just before graduation. Hood measured the degree of stress they *expected* before doing several activities (raft trip, canoe trip, rock climb, and a 24-hour "solo"), and then the *actual* stress after the experiences. The M Scale was modified to measure students' reactions specifically to each activity. He found that neither anticipated stress nor actual stress was directly related to ecstatic experience. Rather, the conflict between expected and real stress tended to produce ecstasy. Table 11.2 summarizes the average M Scale scores. Since nobody anticipated or found the canoe trip stressful, there are no data for the high-anticipated/low-actual stress condition; the three other activities were highly stressful, with some students expecting high stress and some not. The next year Hood (1978) repeated the study with only the "solo." Actual stress was naturally varied by rain on 3 of the 5 solo days. He used a different but similar measure

Table 11.2   *M SCALE* SCORES RELATED TO ANTICIPATED AND ACTUAL STRESS

Actual stress level	Anticipated stress level	
	High	Low
High		
Raft trip	103	122
Rock climb	98	113
Solo	98	122
Low		
Canoe trip		97

Source: Hood (1977, p. 161).

and again found that the conflict between anticipated and real stress produced more ecstatic experience. High expected stress with low real stress (no rain) actually produced the highest average score (52.8), while low expected/high actual was similar (51.4). The low/low group had an average score of 42.1, and the high/high group had the lowest (32.4). (Perhaps they were too wet and upset to feel anything but misery!)

Evaluation

We have expressed reservations about how closely the M Scale comes to measuring anything like classical mystical experience. One can make the point that what it measures is at least a glimmer of the real thing. Certainly as rare as true mysticism is (existing among almost surely no more than 2% of the population), it is easier to do research with convenient tools and populations like the M Scale and students than with known mystics. What remains (and Hood is investigating this) is to explore the degree to which the research findings with "personality variable mysticism" coincide with the nature, circumstances, and effects of mysticism as classically defined and experienced.

REVIEW OF KEY CONCEPTS

Conversion and Personality
    significance of longitudinal versus cross-sectional studies of preconversion
        personality and conversion effects
    design of Wilson's study and relation to previous findings about
        conversion-prone personality
    relation of neuroticism to conversion

A Cross-cultural Study of Petitionary Prayer
    design of Brown's study
    perceived effectiveness and appropriateness of prayer in various situations
    age and views of effectiveness and appropriateness of prayer
    relationship of cultures and denominations to prayer
    evaluation of Brown's study

Faith Healing as a Ritual
    design of the study of healing rituals
    major trends for: number of healings and of rituals, severity of illness, medi-
        cal treatment, speed of symptom remission, residual and substitute
        symptoms
    psychological characteristics of the healed
    major religious significance of healing
    limitations and strengths of the study

Glossolalia and Personality
    design of Kildahl's study

chapter 12

Applied Psychology of Worship

Worship is derived from words for *worth* and *ship.* To worship is to grant a condition of worth to the Deity, the Infinite Mystery, the Ultimate Reality—however conceived by the individual. The various religious experiences examined in this unit may all, in one way or another, be forms of worship. While worship is common to all religious traditions, its forms vary widely. Acts of worship include possession–trance-inducing dances in Haitian *voodoo,* chanting of the *Lotus Sutra* in Nichiren Shoshu, handling of fire or snakes in an Appalachian Pentecostal church, the placing of a bowl of rice before a Shinto shrine, and the lighting of a lamp before a Hindu household altar. Even within Christianity worship ranges from a formal high church Catholic liturgy, to the spontaneous singing and preaching at an Old Regular Baptist foot-washing service, to a silent Quaker meeting in which literally not a word is spoken.

Fascinating as these varieties of worship may be, they are not, as such, our immediate interest. Nor shall we attempt an exhaustive theoretical understanding of the structure and functions of worship. As the applied focus for the present unit, this chapter simply considers some of the psychological dimensions and functions of worship, and then suggests general principles that may facilitate worship. Given the variability of worship in the human race, we could not possibly relate to all this variety in our limited space. Although our discussion attempts to transcend parochialism, it deals mostly with worship within the general Judeo-Christian tradition that is familiar to most readers. While we try to advance relatively objective psychological principles, certain suggestions may show unintended theological bias.

THE NATURE OF WORSHIP

Private Versus Public

Psychologically speaking, worship is a private experience, in which an individual feels an intimate personal relationship with the Divine. This focused attention and experience of direct communion with the Ultimate is akin to mysticism, which indeed might be considered an extreme form of worship (Clark, 1958, pp. 331ff; Tremmel, 1976, pp. 244–245).

Worship can occur in a solitary setting, but it is typically institutionalized in a worship service. Some services may foster true worship, while others may hinder it. From one perspective, worship is inherently more than a private affair. A Menninger psychiatric hospital chaplain defines it as:

> *any social ceremony, in a setting of solemnity, whereby experiences are celebrated as occasions of participation in widely valued processes.* The indispensable prerequisites of worship are: (a) a shared myth, (b) common values (or evils), and (c) the readiness to convert primarily human experiences into symbols and rituals. Worship, so conceived, can never be strictly a private matter [Klink, 1967, p. 17].

While we shall be concerned primarily with public worship, we observe that the goal should be for individuals to experience worship.

Objective Versus Subjective

The distinction made between objective and subjective prayer also holds with regard to worship. Objective worship is not only directed to, but is also intended only for, God. If no worshipers come to a scheduled Roman Catholic Mass, the priest conducts the service nonetheless. It is for the honor of God, and not primarily for the people (Pratt, 1920).

Subjective worship is superficially directed to God, but its emphasis is actually on the immediate needs, concerns, and interests of the congregation. Many

Protestant services are primarily directed toward the people, with a sermon (an exhortation to the congregation) the focus of the hour. Some Christian hymns are said to "encourage subjective wallowing in one's own emotions, while offering the worshipper little occasion for contemplating the objective mercies of God" (Porteous, 1966, p. 47). When rituals, sermons, and hymns encourage sentimentality, escapism, magical thinking, and preoccupation with one's own needs and feelings, little true worship will occur—whatever the psychological and social benefits might be.

Like objective prayer, objective worship turns the attention of the person away from personal concerns to ultimate mysteries and the cosmic design. Such an outward focus is, of course, necessary for optimum growth and development, so—paradoxically—objective worship is more self-enhancing than the self-directed variety of subjective worship.

Effects of Worship

Pruyser (1968, p. 182) suggests that worship redirects energies from defensive uses, so that the worshiper gains new zeal and realizes more latent powers. One study found religious devotionalism and worship to be a distinctive source of racial tolerance and other progressive social attitudes (Campbell & Fukuyama, 1970). There can be little doubt from biographical accounts of religious leaders that encounters with God—the Divine, however conceived—may be radically energizing.

The worshiper is inclined to attribute such new strength to divine infusions. From a psychological perspective, however, to attribute such energy to divine grace explains little:

A radical materialism which envisages waves of dynamic particles moving from one body to another calls for a strenuous fantasy. But the fact is that one does feel invigorated through some religious exercises, just as one feels physically more ebullient and buoyant when one falls in love. . . . This is supernaturalism only when one first affirms the notion of a disembodied, ghostly, immaterial god. It is magical thinking only when one's intention was to extort from one's deity a portion of . . . power for one's own use [Pruyser, 1968, p. 183].

Pruyser also likens the effects of worship to the aesthetic uplift one might receive from observing an artistic masterpiece. Such analogies enable the hard-headed scientist to accept the reality of worship's effects, but they are likely to strike the believer as woefully inadequate. Like the efficacy of prayer, the impact of a worship experience usually depends on a conviction that communication with the Divine actually occurs.

ON FOSTERING WORSHIP

Those who plan and conduct worship services ideally have a two-fold obligation: to worship and to create a situation in which others are optimally moved to worship. There are limits to which the structure of a service determines the inner experience that is the essence of religious life. Such personal encounter, however individualistic, should be recognized as the reason for any worship service. Bakan, following Tillich, defined idolatry as the confusion of means with ends. To make rituals, myths, or worship services themselves the objects of worship is idolatry—"the loss of the sense of the existence of the unmanifest, the loss of the sense of search, the loss of the continuous freshness of the encounter with the unmanifest" (1966, p. 6).

Religious traditions differ in how much worship forms may vary. Some dictate every motion, word, and intonation; others allow considerable spontaneity. The principles in this section necessarily apply more to the latter than to the former traditions, but they should generally be relevant to the fostering of worship in all faiths. Our considerations will center on several dichotomous processes or values that should be reconciled in worship experiences.

Left Brain Versus Right Brain

Religious worship, more than any other human experience, we believe, should involve the whole person. Modern neuropsychology has identified distinctive functions of the left and right hemispheres of the human brain. In almost all right-handed persons and many left-handed ones, the left, logical, "linear" hemisphere tends to control the religious activities of theology, sermonic and other discourse, hymns, and musical melodies. The intuitive, "wholistic," right (in most people) hemisphere is more involved in visual art, symbol, ritual, imagery, analogy, metaphor, drama, tonal qualities of music such as that of the Middle and Far East, and probably mysticism (Ornstein, 1977; Meyer, 1975).

Balance and Integration   Virtually all highly developed religions incorporate both left- and right-hemisphere elements, though the balance may incline one direction or the other. Much of Christianity would presumably be enhanced by more right-hemisphere elements in its worship. Some Eastern faiths have likely been overly intuitive and nonrational.

Radical changes in worship style should not necessarily be made on psychological grounds. But an apparent imbalance suggests need to reexamine the tradition and theology, to see if the wholism of the faith has inadvertently eroded. Every worship service need not be perfectly balanced by right and left elements. A service of dance or drama may have special impact on a congregation jaded with logical discourse—or vice versa. A religious tradition that allows and even encourages experimentation in worship forms offers more promise of well-integrated worship than one locked rigidly into a set style—unless the latter is exceptionally well balanced.

Spontaneity and Form   Clark addressed a paradox in religious forms. As a religious tradition matures, it typically evolves from relatively spontaneous worship to a fixed liturgical form. The looser style appears more subjective although it is associated with religious creativity. Clark wrote,

> While objective, liturgical worship would seem the type most psychologically justified, and while actually this kind of service does seem to yield the best results and to be preferred by the greater number of cultivated people; nonetheless the early, more effective stages in a religious movement tend to be those associated with non-liturgical worship [1958, p. 334].

Perhaps this paradox can be explained in terms of left- and right-hemisphere functions. The white-hot fervor of a new religious movement comes from the originator's immediate experience with God. The direct experience partakes of the mystical, and is primarily a function of the intuitive right hemisphere—perhaps the seat of original religiousness. This zeal is shared by the leader's direct followers, but in a generation or two the movement becomes rationalized, codified, and largely reduced to left-hemisphere theologies and dogmas. Lacking the right-hemisphere expressions of the original movement, leaders substitute other right-hemisphere elements to provide a degree of balance to religious services.

Commenting on this stage of development, as various liturgical and aesthetic features are added to the worship style, Clark said,

> A liturgical service nearly always has the recommendation of some measure of beauty. At its best this latter may serve as a poignant and appropriate symbol of a deep experience of worship, enhancing it and conveying to it religious accents echoing down the centuries. At its worst it may be merely a superficial bit of esthetic indulgence that hides from the pseudoworshiper the fact that spiritually speaking [she or] he is simply going through liturgical motions [1958, p. 335].

The potential bankruptcy of liturgical formalism is suggested by the charismatic movement of the 1960s and 1970s, which primarily affected liturgical churches—enlivening them with such nonrational expressions as glossolalia. Apparently aesthetics alone is not enough for many people; God must be experienced more directly.

Individual Needs People differ in the extent to which they seem to process events primarily through the right or left cerebral hemisphere. Research is needed on how such psychological differences relate to responsiveness to different modes of worship. The different forms of conversion that depend on hypnotic suggestibility, probably relate to differences in hemispheric preferences (Gibbons & DeJanrette, 1972; Meyer, 1975). It is fanciful to imagine whole congregations exclusively of right- or left-hemisphere responders. Worship services probably should be designed to provide spiritual grist for persons at both extremes—and different in other psychological traits. Research might clarify the degree to which this is possible, and what the ingredients in such worship services might be.

Mystery Versus Reality

Most definitions of public worship include the ideas of solemnity and celebration. Worship must have something that clearly distinguishes it from a meeting of the garden society or the Rotary Club. It needs to promote and impart a sense of awe and mystery—usually with an appropriate admixture of joy. Yet, for most people, faith and worship are deficient if totally apart from the cadences of everyday reality.

Reality Needs   Perhaps the Vatican II reforms within Roman Catholicism best illustrate this tension. The traditional, solemn rituals, performed to antique rhythms in an unknown (to most worshipers) tongue, alienated large numbers of the younger generations of Catholics. Even before the Vatican II Council, local experiments, such as jazz masses, rendered the traditional ritual in the musical vernacular. Vatican II reforms can generally be considered attempts to meet the needs of worshipers. As we pointed out in the previous section, though, the history of religious faiths tends to move toward more, rather than less, liturgical form.

Mystery Needs   No single pattern of worship fosters a personal sense of awe and communion with the Unmanifest. The splendor of solemn Mass in a Catholic cathedral may do so, but so may a "bare and stripped Quaker meeting," devoid of ritual, symbol, or set order of worship (Clark, 1958, p. 340). Even in very formal, liturgical, high-church worship, substantial parts of the service do not require active participation of the worshipers. So they can seek whatever inner light they choose to pursue.

Within many evangelical, low-church Protestant groups the sense of divine mystery might be more strenuously cultivated. Many Catholics may similarly criticize some post-Vatican II worship. A service in which every minute is programmed with activity and focus on the here and now is most unfavorable to personal engagement with the Divine Mystery. If the minister is not making announcements or preaching, the song leader is enjoining all the people to sing together. Worshipers have no time to seek God in the solitude of their own selves. Times of personal devotions are often encouraged, but too seldom realized, in such faiths. The public services of many Christian groups probably would be improved by more often incorporating periods of silent prayer, encouraging meditation during the offertory, making prayers "objective" times of praise and adoration, and selecting hymns that are directed to the glory of God—both in words and in manner of singing.

Of course changes in orders of worship are risky. The Catholics' or Episcopalians' formal liturgies are as heretical to many low-church people as the spontaneity (or "disorder") of a Pentecostal service would be to the former. As responsible as the Vatican II reforms were, they did not find favor with all Catholics. (Some observers suggest that a major dissatisfaction with the reforms was a dearth of "good" contemporary music to fill the new orders of worship; the spirit of change has to deal with established definitions of suitable elements of worship.)

Worship Versus Service

Just as prayer can be used in a narrow self-serving way, so also worship can be a retreat from the world of human needs. On the other extreme, the much maligned "social gospel" may so concentrate on salving human distress that the divine source of inspiration and power is slighted. We can hold to an ideal of objective worship, while still recognizing that an outcome of such experience is a personal growth that impels the worshiper to self-transcending service. This principle may seem foreign, though, to a faith that takes a relatively passive, pessimistic, or fatalistic position.

The Christian gospels present a drama of the worship-service conflict in the story of the transfiguration of Jesus. After Jesus took three of his disciples up a mountain, they experienced a resplendent religious vision. One disciple, Peter, impulsively proposed that they remain in that hallowed place, but Jesus responded by leading them back down to where the other disciples were trying to heal a convulsive boy. Jesus' cure of the boy suggests that worship is needed but does not replace the service of human needs—a stance shared by the major world religions.

WORSHIP AND BELIEF

Many minds boggle at accepting traditional theologies and ancient myths, at least in a literal, left-hemisphere sense. The rituals and symbols of worship, presumably processed by the right hemisphere, may mediate what Coleridge (1817, Chapter 14) called the "willing suspension of disbelief." A number of writers have attributed the contemporary sense of futility and rootlessness to our loss of traditional myths and symbols—with no new ones to replace them (Campbell, 1972; May, 1960). A seeker, confronted with the symbols and rituals of a celebration of the Eucharist or the Passover or a pilgrimage to Mecca, might spontaneously confess, "This is a myth grand enough to believe in."

Moberg (1971a, p. 572) noted the way symbols, songs, creeds, and rituals promote group cohesion and aid in strengthening the convictions of members of a faith. These functions have already been seen in such religious behaviors as glossolalia, exorcism, and fire handling. A study of institutionalized faith healing identified its main function as supporting a belief system (Pattison, Lapins, & Doerr, 1973). The inherent noetic quality of mysticism endues it with a certainty of the Beyond. Belief in the paranormal, answered prayer, and possession may similarly support religious beliefs.

Why do Christians continue to go to some "worship" services that focus almost entirely on converting the one or two "sinners" present? Wahking suggests that they have "created a liturgy which is a re-enactment of their own conversion experiences" (1966, p. 53), which assures them of their salvation.

Rituals may appeal to belief by acting out the myths or history of the faith. The Feasts of Lights and Tabernacles commemorate events in Jewish history, as Communion follows Jesus' command at the Last Supper, "Do this as a memorial of me" (Luke 22 : 19). Similarly the Muslim's profound bow in prayer expresses in action the key Islamic doctrine—submission to God. And Hindu cosmology (view of the universe) is summed up in the objects offered at the altar. Jung (1958, 1964) said that symbols reach far back in human memory, tapping into the "collective unconscious" formed in the earliest eons of humankind.

The sharing in public worship can assure people that their faith is not idiosyncratic or peculiar. A Christian who returned to church after divorce from an unbelieving husband testified, "Worshiping together again has reaffirmed my beliefs." Others were apparently engaged in the same affirmations. Established rituals, liturgies, and traditions lend further conviction, for generations of the faithful have done the same. Undoubtedly part of the appeal of the Latin Mass was the knowledge that Roman Catholics of a hundred cultures and dozens of generations had partaken of the identical rite.

The very act of worship must itself reinforce belief. This effect is even stronger when a public commitment is made—whether an offering of material goods, or an affirmation to do or not to do certain things. Like the Nichiren Shoshu believers' endless chanting of *"Nam myoho renge kyo,"* heavy commitments of time, means, and effort arouse cognitive dissonance. The dissonance may most readily be resolved by strengthening the belief system that asks such acts of devotion.

Public worship serves many positive functions, but its misuse, distortion, or imbalance may actually limit the religious life. Those who plan worship services should be responsible not to manipulate believers, but to provide experiences that maximize the opportunity to celebrate personally the awe and majesty of God, the Divine, the Infinite Mystery.

REVIEW OF KEY CONCEPTS

The Nature of Worship
    origin and meaning of the word
    varieties of worship
    private and/or public worship
    distinctions between objective and subjective worship
    effects of objective worship
    scientific versus religious explanations of the effects of worship

On Fostering Worship
    the aim of worship
    left-brain versus right-brain functions—balance and integration
    limitations of liturgical formalism and aesthetics
    individual differences in response to worship forms
    reality needs versus mystery needs
    Vatican II reforms in worship
    varieties of Christian worship
    results of changing the order of worship
    worship versus service—New Testament example

Worship and Belief
    right hemisphere in relation to rituals and symbols
    role of rituals in acting out myth, theology, and cosmology
    worship, cognitive dissonance, and belief

three

SOME PSYCHOLOGICAL VARIABLES IN RELIGIOUS PERSPECTIVE

Belief and Religious Faith

"There is no God but Allah; and Mohammed is the apostle of God" (Islamic affirmation). [Jesus the Christ said:] "I am the Way, the Truth, and the Life" (Christian New Testament). [The Lord Buddha said:] "Every disciple should discard conceptions of one's own selfhood and a Universal Selfhood" (Buddhist *Diamond Sutra*). "Hear O Israel: the Lord our God, the Lord is One" (Jewish prayer). [Lord Krishna said:] "I am the origin of all this world. There is nothing whatever that is higher than I" (Hindu *Bhagavad-Gītā*). "The Tao that can be named is not the eternal Tao" (Taoist *Tao Te Ching*). But they are all saying different things! Can they all be right? How do I decide who is right and who is wrong? Is there any way I can know for certain? Questions like these may plague religious persons.

Our entire lives are based on many beliefs that we seldom realize are beliefs, which we accept as true without logically convincing evidence.

> Most of these beliefs we state categorically. We say . . . "Greek temples are more beautiful than Egyptian temples," "I ought to work rather than play tennis today." . . . We might reasonably preface each of these propositions by the words, "I believe." . . . Every proposition becomes in fact a judgment. . . . We take our judgments seriously [Trueblood, 1942, p. 24].

NATURE OF BELIEF

Belief is viewed in many different ways. Each sheds a different perspective on the nature of belief.

Belief as Meaning

The idea of meaning colors Fromm's definition of religion: "any system of thought and action shared by a group which gives the individual a frame of orientation and an object of devotion" (1950/1967, p. 22). Beliefs satisfy "the need for a cognitive framework to know and understand" (Rokeach, 1960, p. 67). Although most people turn to religion or science for their answers, some turn to different sources to satisfy this need. Even "astrology may function as a surrogate for more conventional religious commitments" (Wuthnow, 1976, p. 157). What is the relationship between science and religion as sources of meaning? Some say that religion answers *why* questions, while science answers *what* and *how* ones.

Belief as Choice

Religions may consider belief a duty. Some Christian scriptures (see Hebrews 11 : 6) seem to require one to hold certain beliefs. This implies that we can choose what we will believe.

Beliefs are choices, but reality limits our freedom to choose, according to Pruyser (1974). However, reality does not reveal itself equally to all, and thus may be disputed. Each person is in touch with only part of it. Our own personal histories make "beliefs function as love and hate objects" (Pruyser, 1979, p. 11). We choose to believe that which most satisfies us.

Living and Dead Options   William James (1897c) said belief options have three important dimensions. First, they are living or dead according to our ability to believe them. Sometimes reason makes certain beliefs impossible; for example, I cannot believe that the $2.00 I just put in my pocket is $200. Many people who consider all religion a dead option are simply rejecting certain superstitions, against which their intelligence rebels.

Most dead belief options have become so because of our own life experiences and behavior. Our early education, our hopes and fears, our emotional conditioning, our prejudices, and our positive and negative life experiences all make some things easy—and others impossible—for us to believe. Few Western students would accept Islamic beliefs, even if someone fervently tried to convince them that such belief is necessary for their ultimate welfare. Most people reared as Muslims would have similar difficulty with ardent pleas for Christian belief.

Forced and Avoidable Options   Some options are forced and others avoidable. You can live your entire life without deciding what you believe about the latest research in biochemistry. But some situations—such as human relationships—demand belief choices. How we decide to act with a person helps produce the eventual truth of the relationship. If you decide not to risk a friendship with someone, you make such a friendship impossible. If you take the risk, your faith-in-advance in the friendship goes a long way towards establishing it. Religion works much the same way. One who refuses to have faith in God cannot experience God. In religion—as in human relationships—"a fact cannot come at all unless a preliminary faith exists in its coming. . . . Faith in a fact can help create the fact" (James, 1897c/1969, p. 209).

Momentous and Trivial Options   What you decide will taste good for dinner tonight is a trivial belief; it will have little importance in your life. However, what work you undertake, with whom you relate, and what choices you make about religious matters are momentous ones because they have great effects on your life. This is James's third distinction regarding belief options.

Choosing Religious Belief In religion, we cannot wait for conclusive evidence before deciding about belief. We cannot *know,* but only believe or disbelieve. Not to decide is to decide against, since beliefs guide our behavior. Skeptics prefer to lose the possible goods of religion rather than risk error regarding faith. This decision is based as much on emotions and desires as is the believer's. Skeptic and believer both risk being duped.

> In either case we *act,* taking our life in our hands. No one of us ought to issue vetoes to the other, nor should we bandy words of abuse. We ought . . . to respect one another's mental freedom. . . . We have the right to believe at our own risk any hypothesis that is live enough to tempt our will [James, 1897c/1969, pp. 212–213].

Belief as Character Trait

Trust Erikson considered basic trust necessary for religious growth. Without this capacity for receptivity and openness, belief is impossible. "Trust born of care is . . . the touchstone of a given religion . . . faith in the goodness of one's strivings and in the kindness of the powers of the universe." For the person of mature faith "death loses its sting" and one has "integrity enough not to fear death" (1963, pp. 250–251).

Dependency For Freud, religious belief is based on unresolved dependency needs. People do not wish to give up the security of having a father to take care of life's difficulties for them. One remembers the care of his or her father and "reserves to [oneself] the right to control the gods by influencing them in some way or other in the interests of [one's] wishes" (Freud, 1913/1946, p. 115). Religious beliefs have strong control over people because they are "fulfillments of the oldest, strongest and most urgent wishes of [hu]mankind. The secret of their strength lies in the strength of these wishes" (Freud, 1927/1961, p. 47).

Consistency "Rational faith is rooted in an independent conviction based upon one's productive observing and thinking" (Fromm, 1947, p. 205). Faith in oneself, others, or God is based on perception of an underlying consistency and value—and action on that basis. "Only the person who has faith in [one]self is able to be faithful to others" (Fromm, 1947, p. 206).

Belief as Process

Some view belief as a dynamic interplay between varying degrees of certainty. Allport described the process:

There is first a period of raw credulity, most clearly seen in the child who believes indiscriminately.... Some religious belief among adults is of this unquestioning variety—childish, authoritarian, and irrational. Normally, however . . . doubts . . . flood into one's life. They are an integral part of all intelligent thinking. . . . Mature belief, the third stage, grows painfully out of the alternating doubts and affirmations that characterize productive thinking [Allport, 1950/1960, p. 139].

For Rumke, unbelief is a stunting of personal development. Young children readily accept magical and fairy-tale explanations until about 7 years of age. If religious belief is still offered later in that form, confusion may follow. One must discard magical belief to develop mature belief. Religions often make the costly mistake of encouraging insincere, childish, or unquestioning belief. Mature faith cannot develop when one blocks openness to various spiritual experiences by repressing normal doubts and crises (Rumke, 1949).

STYLES OF BELIEF

Beliefs vary on many dimensions. Here we examine some of the most important ones.

Central and Peripheral Beliefs

Some of the major work of psychologist Milton Rokeach (1960, 1968) involves the study of belief. Figure 13.1 shows his ordering of important beliefs according to their centrality of personality.

Core Beliefs with Consensus Learned by personal experience, core beliefs with consensus are reinforced by other people's belief in them. Such taken-for-granted beliefs form the most inner core of one's belief system. They consist of one's understanding of nature, oneself, and social relationships. "This is my mother," "My name is Alice," and "That is a cat" are examples. Such beliefs are virtually indestructible.

Primitive Beliefs with No Consensus Primitive beliefs with no consensus are equally strong and undeniable to a person, but others do not support them. Since one feels that others are not in a position to "know," their disagreement does not matter. "Examples of such beliefs are those held on pure faith—phobias, delusions, hallucinations, and various ego-enhancing and ego-deflating beliefs arising from learned experience" (Rokeach, 1968, p. 9). One might believe, "People can't be trusted," "I have committed the unpardonable sin," or "The devil tempted me last night."

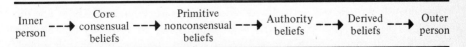

Figure 13.1 Continuum of belief centrality. (*Source:* Constructed from Rokeach, 1960, 1968.)

Authority Beliefs   As children develop they learn that others might not share many of their beliefs. For help in deciding what to believe, one relies on authorities—at first, one's parents. Later one accepts or rejects other authorities, such as teacher, church, or state. Authority beliefs are more changeable than primitive beliefs because one knows that some informed other people do not accept the authority. Some examples are: "The doctor knows best," "The Bible is God's word," or "_____ is the only true religion."

Derived Beliefs   One who accepts a certain authority believes what the authority says to believe. If you know a person's authorities, you know a lot about his or her other beliefs. If John is a Southern Baptist, you expect him to consider drinking sinful. If Sue is a Catholic, you expect her to oppose remarriage after divorce. These "second-hand" beliefs come from an authority, not from personal experience. They may change as one reevaluates one's understanding of authority or changes authorities.

Inconsequential Beliefs   Beliefs that are only matters of taste are not strongly connected with a person's other beliefs. Based on personal experience, they may be held strongly like primitive beliefs, but a change in them affects the belief system very little. Examples are preferring Bach over rock, trout over salmon, or orange over green.

Implications of Belief Centrality   The more central a belief, the more difficult it is to change it. Deeply ingrained primitive beliefs are extremely difficult to modify, but changes in these beliefs may greatly affect less central beliefs. However, changing more peripheral beliefs—such as authority choices—may leave central beliefs untouched.

Destroying consensual core beliefs could destroy a person's sanity. Psychotherapy often tries to change nonconsensual primitive beliefs that are harming the person. Consequent changes in self-concept or world view often affect authority beliefs. A change in authorities usually brings new derived beliefs.

Open and Closed Belief Systems

Open Systems   People with open belief systems generally view the world as a friendly place that can be trusted (Rokeach, 1960). They do not see authority as absolute, nor are others judged by their agreement or disagreement with one's own authorities. Beliefs derived from different authorities are in touch with and modify each other. Religious beliefs will be compatible with one's scientific beliefs, and beliefs about the state will be compatible with those about human relationships.

Closed Systems   People with closed belief systems are dogmatic. They view the world as threatening, and authority as absolute. Once an authority figure states a position, the person with a closed belief system considers the matter ended.

Other people are evaluated according to their agreement with one's chosen authorities. Peripheral beliefs are isolated from each other, so great incongruities may exist between beliefs derived from different authorities (Rokeach, 1960). One may reject contraception out of "reverence for life," yet accept killing civilians in warfare. Or hold that all people are equally important to God, yet believe that God has revealed necessary truths to only one group of people.

Generally, the more insecure people are, the more dogmatic they become. "Religious statements are held more strongly than the factual ones, perhaps to avoid the uncertainty which would necessarily follow from a weaker acceptance" (Brown, 1962/1973, p. 48). One preserves security by considering a very limited perspective on the world as absolute. "Dogmatic creedal formulations, legalistic codes . . . are some of the devices practiced in the name of religion to make the ambiguities of life seem less than they are" (Dittes, 1959/1973, p. 256). Dogmatic people quickly reject ideas outside their own belief system—usually with inadequate understanding of them; they are all simply considered "error." Belief that one has exclusive possession of the truth has adverse effects on religious development (Fromm, 1950). Box 13.1 compares open and closed systems with similar ideas.

Belief and Faith   Watts distinguished belief from faith; he considered them almost opposite states. A believer insists that reality be structured the way she or he says it is, while in faith one's mind fully opens to truth. "Belief clings, but faith lets go" (Watts, 1951/1968, p. 24). The believer does not follow the direction in which the thumb of religious belief points, but starts to suck the thumb itself for security. Believers hold the objects of faith (religious symbols and words) to be truth themselves, rather than signposts pointing to truth—an attitude Fromm (1950) called "idolatry."

To avoid self-deception, one must build religion on faith rather than belief (Watts, 1951). Having too many specific beliefs leaves little room for faith. Belief acts contrary to what the world's great religions prescribe; it tries to hold onto ideas to feel secure. However,

> if you try to capture running water in a bucket, it is clear that you do not understand it and that you will always be disappointed, for in the bucket the water does not run. To "have" running water you must let go of it and let it run. The same is true of life and of God [Watts, 1951/1968, p. 24].

Box 13.1 **OPEN AND CLOSED STYLES**		
Rokeach	**Watts**	**James**
Open	Faith	Empiricists
Closed	Belief	Absolutists

Source: Compiled from James (1897a), Rokeach (1960), Watts (1951).

Absolutists and Empiricists   Left to instinct, we all tend to be absolutists—a weakness of human nature (James, 1897a). Absolutists say that not only can we gain truth, but we can know for sure when we have it. However, certainty that one's own beliefs are more true than those of others is just one more belief!

> There is indeed nothing which someone has not thought absolutely true, while [a] neighbor deemed it absolutely false; and not an absolutist among them seems ever to have considered that . . . the intellect, even when truth is directly in its grasp, may have no infallible signal for knowing whether it be truth or no (James, 1897c/1969, p. 203).

Empiricists believe they can gain truth, but do not know for sure when they have it. They are open to new ideas and will revise their thinking.

James also defined two related ways of seeking truth. Tender-minded rationalists seek truth with the intellect. Emotionally, they want the comfort of believing that all good things are certain and all bad things impossible in the long run. Highly tender-minded people may use religion with the hope that just wishing will make beliefs true.

Tough-minded individuals consider facts only and hold that "seeing is believing." The radically tough-minded often reject religion altogether. A course between these two extremes submits beliefs to a practical test. Whatever proves helpful in living a better life deserves to be considered true; beliefs that fail this test should be discarded (James, 1892).

Literal and Symbolic Beliefs

Concretizing Symbols   Symbolic religious language becomes concrete in the minds of many religious people (Maslow, 1964). The larger a religious movement becomes, the more codified is the leader's message. Subtleties are overlooked, and the prophet's symbolic expressions are taken to be literally true. "Heaven" becomes a physical place rather than a state of being. "God" becomes a ruler on a throne in the sky. When a religious organization packages its message in creeds and dogmas, individuals often are not allowed to use alternative symbolic ways to express religious meaning.

Interpreting Religious Language   Probably no one would agree that the Hebrew Bible statement "All flesh is grass" means that human bodies are made up of grass; people interpret this symbolically to mean that human life is fleeting. One misunderstands religious faith when one believes it means only an understanding of religious language in a concrete or literal fashion. Some people "may, on the basis of a literal, naive, unexamined interpretation of religion, reject all religion," while many religiously committed people use "religious statements to seek their deeper symbolic meanings which lie beyond their literal wording" (Hunt, 1972, p. 43). Thus, some people accept literal understandings that others reject, and some interpret religious statements symbolically.

Hunt (1972) developed scales to measure literal, antiliteral (nonbelieving), and mythological (symbolic) stances regarding traditional Christian beliefs. A modified version of Hunt's scales produced high endorsement of the mythological position. The literal and mythological believers did not differ on "intelligence, authoritarianism, or racial prejudice. Religious Believers as a group were . . . significantly less intelligent and more authoritarian than . . . Skeptics" (Poythress, 1975, p. 271).

Certain and Uncertain Beliefs

Differences in the certainty with which beliefs are held have long been recognized. Aristotle listed four degrees of assurance about an opinion: certainty, belief, suspicion, and doubt (Lewinsohn, 1961).

Conviction Beliefs reinforced by sense perception, reason, and the beliefs of others are called knowledge. Beliefs that lack such supports, and are strongly believed by their holders, are called delusions. Faith is an in-between case; we seldom consider another's faith to be either sure knowledge or delusional. Faith rests on probabilities and is held with varying degrees of certainty. Even a low degree of faith can produce great energy if it is one's major hope (Allport, 1950).

Strength of belief is related both to one's expectancies for the future (Scheibe, 1970) and the amount of effort put into belief-related behavior. Walter Clark's four levels of belief show increased activity with increasing certainty: (1) stimulus-response verbalism—parroting of belief statements; (2) intellectual comprehension—logical examination and understanding of a belief; (3) behavioral demonstration—actual behavior flowing from conviction or habitual acceptance; and (4) comprehensive integration—the level found in the "wholesome" and "admirable goodness" of a saint (Clark, 1958, pp. 220–223).

Doubt Doubt is an unstable condition produced by the collision of a belief with a contradictory fact or other belief (Allport, 1950). People doubt in various ways. (1) Reactive doubting may be triggered by a traumatic event or by unconscious mental life—such as a negative attitude toward one's parents. Many reactive doubters have deep religious concern; a very negative reaction to religion betrays a great interest in it.

(2) Some doubt because of the presumably physical origins of religious interest. They do not want to be duped by their glands and vaguely understood urges. (3) The failures and hypocrisy of institutional religion lead others to doubt. (4) If one doubts or believes from self-interest, faith is given up when it ceases to serve personal need or advantage. (5) Other doubters are disturbed by changes in religious understandings over history. They cannot see such changes as human attempts to grasp the nature of the divine.

(6) Some doubting comes from scientific habits of thought that demand demonstration. One simply cannot test religious hypotheses as if they were scientific ones. (7) Referential doubting also comes from science, and refers to the continuing conflict between scientific evidence and the specific contents of religious teachings. Religious language necessarily uses images based on space and

time—the same language used by science; however, the significance of religious discourse cannot be determined by tests of literal meaning. "What religious language signifies primarily are aspirations, self-imposed ideals, approval of one way of life and disapproval of others . . . the hoped-for completion of knowledge and the intended perfection of one's own nature" (Allport, 1950/1960, p. 137). (Religious language is further discussed in Chapter 27.)

Agnosticism   Agnosticism is not the same as doubting; agnostics stand between the claims of believers and unbelievers in a quite different way (Pruyser, 1974). Some have never felt moved to be religious but, knowing that reliable others have, willingly say they do not know. Others who have had an intriguing but confused glimpse of religious reality add "could be" to their "I don't know," but are very unclear about it. A third group have had clearer vision, but are unable to decide exactly what they experienced.

Pruyser describes a fourth group of agnostics who may have done much thinking about their understandings, but do not want to make rash commitments. They consider the risk of error too great to foreclose judgment. A fifth group are rather "paradoxical. They may have had more than a glimpse at the door. . . . They come to an 'I don't know' which has the meaning of 'If I claimed I knew . . . my pretensions may obscure what is really there' " (Pruyser, 1974, pp. 155–156). Thus, agnostics acknowledge that they have not seen the whole of truth, and are wary of making any arrogant claims for their own understandings.

DEVELOPMENT AND MAINTENANCE OF BELIEFS

Beliefs are functional for believers. Religious belief "makes easy and felicitous what in any case is necessary" (James, 1902/1961, p. 57)—dealing with life's problems.

> Whether they are adaptive or defensive, corporate or idiosyncratic, realistic or fantastic, *beliefs are coping devices* enabling a person to make sense of . . . existence, improve one's lot, endure . . . fate, obtain an identity, and procure a modicum of happiness" [Pruyser, 1979, p. 14, emphasis in original].

How do we acquire and maintain our useful religious beliefs?

Learning

Indoctrination and Religious Education   Parents, teachers, and the social milieu transmit many beliefs. Freud objected strongly to such education of children:

> We introduce children to the doctrines of religion at an age when they are neither interested in them nor capable of grasping their imports. . . . Thus by the

time the child's intellect awakens, the doctrines of religion have already become unassailable [Freud, 1927/1961, p. 78].

(Chapter 6 discussed more current opinions about religious education.)

Conformity and Identification   People take on the positions of groups to which they belong—beginning with the family group—even without explicit education. One learns to say—and eventually believe—what nearby others say. Pressures to conformity are often subtle and strong.

People who do question common religious beliefs are often made to feel guilty, inferior, or deviant. Freud (1927) listed three responses likely to be given doubters: (1) They may be told that the teachings deserve belief because they were believed by one's ancestors; (2) they may be told that the religious authorities possess proofs of the beliefs, or be directed to scriptures—often the very thing under question!—as authority for the beliefs; or (3) they might be told that it is evil to question the authenticity of religious beliefs. Thus, some people learn to consider doubt disrespectful, erroneous, or sinful.

Attribution

People are meaning-makers. We try to label, interpret, and understand our experiences. Allport called this desire to make sense of things a "bias of intelligibility." Although religion often provides satisfying answers to vexing questions, "the bias of intelligibility is by no means peculiar to the religious outlook on life. It saturates mental processes of all types" (Allport, 1950/1960, p. 24).

The Attribution Process   Psychologists have recently drawn together ideas such as Allport's to produce attribution theory. Attributions are the causes one uses to understand one's experiences. Events are usually explained by referral either to personal characteristics—such as "my intelligence" or "her clumsiness"—or to the external situation. One might credit a success either to a drive for achievement or to a lucky break. "Among religious attributors, however, a third category of causal explanation based on supernatural influence is added. . . . In many instances it is also a preferred attribution" (Shaver, 1979, p. 2).

Many religious testimonies can be interpreted as attributions that help one to understand an experience. Cheryl Prewitt, crowned Miss America in 1979, reported:

Eleven years ago, she was in a car accident and her left leg was crushed. . . . Doctors told her she would never walk again. When she was 17, she attended a revival meeting and she says that she prayed, then watched her shortened leg grow back to normal "in a matter of seconds." . . . She also said her pageant victory was a miracle ["Thankful for miracle," 1979].

Religious Belief and Supernatural Attributions   Religious people thus may explain events as "the will of God" or describe atypical occurrences as "miracles."

When things do not conform to their wishes, they can say that God always answers prayer, but the answer may not be ours (Wuthnow & Glock, 1974). They can look for threads of meaning in life by seeing events as sent from God.

Ritzema studied attribution processes in evangelical Christian college students. He found that "the tendency to invoke such [supernatural] explanations was positively correlated with other measures of religious belief and practice" (1979, p. 286). Positive outcomes were more frequently attributed to God than negative ones. Like other attributions, "supernatural attributions can be in turn justified or unjustified, reality-based or wish-fulfilling, and rational or irrational" (Ritzema, 1979, p. 292).

Confirming Attributions   Once one has made an attribution, confirming evidence is easy to find. Early in life one develops a "guiding fiction" for understanding oneself, others, and life. Once formed, this guiding fiction is very resistant to change because one sees only confirming evidence and ignores disconfirming evidence (Adler, 1927). The guiding fiction would consist of attributions made early in life, and be like a primitive belief in Rokeach's system.

When alternate explanations of an event are possible, people choose one consistent with their guiding fiction. Proudfoot and Shaver reported that a young woman who had practiced religious chanting for 2 years developed a severe asthma. "She continued to chant and was fortunate enough to find a clinic in Manhattan where her asthma was cured. She was elated and attributed her good fortune to her continued chanting" (1975, p. 327). Various conversions, scriptural accounts, and other religious phenomena can be explained in terms of attribution theory.

Cognitive Dissonance

Although attributions tend to be confirmed by selective perception, one still encounters some disconfirming evidence. Cognitive dissonance theory helps explain what happens when important beliefs are threatened.

The Effects of Dissonance   People develop feelings of internal uneasiness or dissonance when their attitudes and behavior are inconsistent with each other (Festinger, 1957). Religious people might call some such cases bad conscience. Smokers must ignore or discount health warnings about smoking if they are to avoid painful dissonance.

Dissonance may also occur when one's experience disconfirms previous attitudes. Cognitive dissonance is very unpleasant and most people try to diminish it. Common ways to reduce dissonance include the "sour grapes" reaction—saying that you did not really want something that has proven unattainable—and the "sweet lemon" reaction—convincing yourself that you really like something you did not want to happen. (Chapter 7 reported a study by Brock on religious dissonance.)

Disconfirmation of Beliefs   Consider this problem:

> Suppose an individual believes something with his [or her] whole heart; sup-
> pose further that he [or she] has a commitment to this belief, . . . has taken
> irrevocable actions because of it; finally, suppose that [she or] he is presented
> with evidence, unequivocal and undeniable evidence, that [the] belief is wrong:
> what will happen? The individual will frequently emerge, not only unshaken, but
> even more convinced of the truth of [the] belief than ever before. Indeed, he
> [or she] may even show a new fervor about convincing and converting other
> people to [the] view [Festinger, Riecken, & Schachter, 1956, p. 3].

Festinger illustrated these processes with the belief of early Christians in the im-
minent return of the Christ. In addition to all the conditions described above
(strong belief, intense commitment, and the failure of the Christ to return), the
individuals involved had social support from other believers. As time went by,
belief was intensified and evangelization increased (Festinger et al., 1956).

The belief was so important to the believers, and the price paid for their
commitment to it was so great, that disconfirmation would produce very painful
dissonance. Discarding the belief would reduce dissonance but, when one has paid
high costs in behavioral commitment, almost anything else would feel preferable.
Dissonance could also be reduced by denying the disconfirmation, but one would
have to be grossly out of touch with reality to do so. One effective way to reduce
dissonance is to get more and more people to agree that the belief (perhaps in
modified form) is true—hence the proselytizing (Festinger et al., 1956).

Festinger's researchers studied a doomsday group that expected God to rescue them by spaceship shortly before a great disaster was to occur. Group members had completely disrupted their previous lives to prepare for this event, dis-
posing of possessions and employment. When the predicted date for the event
passed, believers intensified their belief, holding that the event would still occur
eventually, and increased their efforts to convince others of this expectation (Festinger et al., 1956). In a similar doomsday group increased belief, but no active
attempts to convert others, occurred after the group's prophecy failed (Hardyck
& Braden, 1962).

Batson (1975) got students in a church group to publicly declare themselves
believers in Christ's divinity. He then confronted them with compelling evidence
that the resurrection of Jesus was contrived and that their church leaders had
renounced their faith. Some students belittled the disconfirming evidence. Those
who believed it, however, intensified their belief in the divinity of the Christ. This
tendency was expressed elsewhere by a young woman who said, "I never defended
my religious beliefs more strongly than when I was least sure of them."

Summary

An interplay of learning, attribution, and cognitive dissonance produces and
maintains beliefs. James said that one who wishes to believe—but finds it difficult—can do much to bring it about. To believe:

> we need only in cold blood ACT as if the thing in question were real, and keep acting as if it were real and it will infallibly end by growing into such a connection with our life that it will become real (James, 1890/1952, p. 661).

Learning supplies content for the belief. Attributions, once begun, become easier as one selects interpretations that fit the chosen belief system. The dissonance aroused by disconfirming evidence will lead to strengthened belief to protect the investment already made in the belief.

In the next chapter, we consider the consequence of some very important beliefs. We examine shame, guilt, and conscience.

REVIEW OF KEY CONCEPTS

Nature of Belief
>   frame of orientation
>   options: living and dead, forced and avoidable, momentous and trivial
>   belief as forced, momentous option
>   religious belief and dependency
>   credulity, doubt, and mature faith
>   unbelief as developmental arrest

Styles of Belief
>   core and primitive beliefs
>   authority and derived beliefs
>   belief change and belief centrality
>   open belief systems
>   dogmatism
>   faith versus belief
>   tender-mindedness and tough-mindedness
>   concretizing religious symbols
>   certainty and behavior
>   bases of doubt
>   science and religious doubting
>   agnosticism in relation to doubt

Development and Maintenance of Beliefs
>   functional nature of belief
>   bias of intelligibility
>   the attribution process
>   supernatural attributions
>   guiding fiction and confirmation of attributions
>   cognitive dissonance
>   ways of resolving cognitive dissonance
>   effects of disconfirmation of important beliefs
>   interaction of learning, attribution, and cognitive dissonance in belief development and maintenance

chapter *14*

Guilt, Shame, and Conscience

Many people's strongest and deepest beliefs are concerned with the right way to behave. Very often these beliefs are connected with religious values, since religions commonly offer conduct guidelines. However, people can evaluate their conduct, and have strong ideas about right and wrong behavior, without their being connected to any religious idea. Many important thinkers, including the great psychologist William James (1897b), have seen no necessary connection between morality and religion.

All normal people have had times of feeling bad about their behavior. It may involve wanting to sink through the floor, become invisible, or simply disappear. Or just uncertainty about whether the right thing was said or done, or said and done in the right way. Or a nagging little feeling of worthlessness or sinfulness. Obviously, people prefer not to experience these unpleasant emotional states! In this chapter, we see how such feelings develop, distinguish them from each other, and discuss their relationships with conscience, morality, and religion.

THE EXPERIENCE OF ANXIETY

The word *anxiety* has different meanings for different people, though everyone agrees that it involves feelings of uneasiness, of things not being quite right, and general expectation of negative outcomes. Freud (1926), one of the first personality theorists to discuss anxiety, described three major kinds: reality anxiety (fear), social anxiety (shame), and moral anxiety (guilt).

Normal and Neurotic Anxiety

Is it normal to feel anxious? Freud considered anxiety in reaction to external danger to be normal; anxiety based on fear of unconscious impulses was considered neurotic. Many psychologists disagree with this view, since it suggests that shame and guilt are usually neurotic. Most psychologists consider any anxiety out of proportion to the existing threat maladaptive. However, knowing when anxiety gets out of proportion can be very difficult.

Janis (1962) called "reflective" any anxiety proportional to the objective situation. Reflective emotion thus appropriately reflects reality. It is influenced by thinking, changes in the environment, and new information. The emotional intensity mirrors the actual amount of real threat. Reflective emotional states are an important aspect of normal adjustment.

Rollo May (1977) similarly considered anxiety proportional to danger normal, while neurotic anxiety is out of proportion and cannot be relieved by removing the threat. Fear characterizes normal anxiety, and avoidance habits are seen in neurotic anxiety, according to Arnold (1960). Neurotic anxiety comes from habitually coping with negative feelings by withdrawing from challenges and distorting perception. People may experience fear, shame, or guilt either reflectively or in a maladaptive, overreacting way.

Reality Anxiety and Fear

Reality anxiety refers to real threats in the external environment. It is an uneasy feeling about potential personal dangers, usually physical ones. This is considered an objective anxiety, even when there is not much real danger, because it is concerned with the external, objective world. If you fear that a gang of thugs on the street is waiting for you, your feeling is reality anxiety, even if only a very slim chance exists that they are really after you. Your reality anxiety would be either neurotic or reflective depending on the degree of real danger. Reality anxiety is simple fear (Janis, 1962).

From a psychotheological perspective, Narramore (1974) discussed fear of punishment for bad behavior. When a person's "guilt" is concerned with such things as going to hell, being punished by God or religious authorities, or losing a chance for salvation, the experience is better called reality anxiety (fear of personal harm) than guilt.

Social Anxiety and Shame

One kind of social anxiety is fear that impulses of which you are unaware will lead you to act in ways that bring blame upon you. This is a global fear of disapproval or shame, of other people's negative reactions to you. One fears the environment, as in reality anxiety, but here it is the *social* environment, others' attitudes toward you. Social anxiety is what you feel when you fear your minister will learn that you have sexual fantasies. A "hot, flushed face is . . . characteristic of shame" (Izard, 1977, p. 424).

When you experience social anxiety, you often are not consciously aware of the feared impulses; you know only the terribly uneasy feeling of threat of trouble hanging over you. Such anxiety manifests in a dream so common that almost everyone has had it. Haven't you dreamed of running away from something fearsome—a monster, a big black bear—that is slowly gaining on you? The fearsome thing might stand for unrecognized impulses that, if you act upon them, will bring blame and disapproval on you.

Shame is concerned with how your actions or knowledge about you will affect others' opinions and actions toward you. Social disapproval or expectation of rejection because of planned behavior triggers it. When the threat is great enough, it can deter you from certain behaviors. Reflective shame becomes greater the more likely you are to be detected in a questionable behavior, the greater the possible humiliation in having something about you known, or the more likely you will be blamed or censured. Belief that "no one will ever know" is the most effective way of quieting anticipatory shame. If fear of being found out is the chief motivation keeping people from a certain action, you will likely get them to do it if you can convince them that no one will ever know (Janis, 1962).

The usual first response to shame is to keep questionable thoughts, plans, and actions secret. One may also seek reassurance of acceptability from others. Some ashamed individuals strongly want to escape from public view, and cut themselves off from others. The more one does this, the fewer opportunities one has for the desired reassurance. An extreme reaction to shame is suicide. In the culturally endorsed Japanese practice of *hara-kiri,* one "saves face" by self-destruction when in a shameful situation from which there seems to be no escape.

Some people are deeply ashamed to have even minor faults or personal weaknesses revealed to others. Appearing inadequate to the slightest extent distresses them. Such overreacting is a disturbed way of experiencing shame.

Arnold considers shame to be somewhat more internal than most other theorists. It refers specifically to a personal appraisal that one is blameworthy. Shame is rooted in our nature and concerned with loss of *self*-esteem rather than the esteem of others (Arnold, 1960). It can occur upon being caught in an unworthy act, but also on realizing one's capacity for such acts. For example, one might be ashamed of nudity because it brings into awareness lack of control over sexual impulses. This awareness of being less than ideal can make one too ashamed to engage in reprehensible conduct after becoming aware of the urge to do so.

The fear of being "found out" by others in a way that makes one lose face is embarrassment (Arnold, 1960). It has no necessary moral connotations, but it always has reference to one's relation to the group and to loss of others' esteem. For example, one may be embarrassed by tender feelings or by a lack of social grace, as well as immoral conduct. Both shame and embarrassment can occur when one is exposed to unfavorable judgments.

Moral Anxiety and Guilt

Freud's third type of anxiety—moral anxiety—is clearly related to guilt, having negative reactions to oneself. Blaming oneself, or feeling evil, bad, wrong, or dirty, sets the emotional tone of this "conscience anxiety." "In intense guilt, the person's face takes on a heavy look" (Izard, 1977, p. 424).

Reflective guilt follows awareness of an inclination to do something one considers morally or ethically wrong (Janis, 1962). The amount of guilt is in proportion to the inclination, with much less guilt for a passing thought than for an anticipated bad action. The greatest guilt comes with actual serious transgressions. Information about the consequences of one's actions will increase or decrease reflective guilt, depending on how this modifies the way one sees the situation.

Guilt inspires one to watch oneself carefully for wrong thoughts or behavior, and to attempt to renounce undesirable impulses. The guilty individual often seeks reassurance of personal value, sometimes by confession. Since forgiveness or acceptance from another person offers some assurance of one's worth, confession may reduce personal self-condemnation. Voluntarily embracing shame, by confession, helps dispel guilt.

Inflicting such shame on oneself can be a self-punishment. People who feel guilty may also punish themselves with deprivations or acts of expiation. Self-punishments must be carefully chosen, both for psychological meaningfulness and for their ability to prepare one to behave differently. Then they can leave one assured of real desire for a principled life, and can help uproot old habits and establish new ones. Unfortunately, many people who punish themselves do so in maladaptive ways. An extreme instance, often associated with very severe guilt, is suicide. Some people who commit suicide feel that someone as wicked as they should no longer pollute the earth.

Disturbed guilt reactions produce severe guilt for very minor offenses. Individuals who feel guilty, bad, or wrong much of the time probably have disturbed guilt reactions. Such neurotic guilt, produced by trivial actions or even mere fantasies, is not responsive to new information.

For Arnold (1960) guilt is a subjective judgment of culpability. In addition to shame, fear of loss of esteem, fear of punishment, and fear of being discovered, this judgment also brings feelings of remorse and repentance. Remorse makes one want to be rid of the guilt, and may lead to such unproductive reactions as merely wishing it away or blaming oneself. It can also produce reparation and desire for punishment. Punishment alone cannot reduce the negative feelings as well as the receiving and acceptance of forgiveness can (Arnold, 1960).

Beyond Shame and Guilt

Narramore (1974) contrasted psychological guilt and immature self-condemnation with constructive sorrow, which leads to productive changes in attitude and behavior. Arnold (1960) also says that repentance or contrition goes beyond regretting a wrongdoing to deciding to avoid future wrong. Both theorists suggest that beyond emotional guilt is an objective guilt state that can be judged independently of feelings. This "real" guilt must be dealt with before psychological guilt feelings can be treated (Arnold, 1960).

Yoga psychology agrees with the distinctions just made. The psychological experience of guilt is considered an unproductive by-product of spiritual disorder, and often bears little relationship to one's real guilt. This real guilt is prior to disturbed psychological functioning, and causes all the individual's physical and mental suffering. All human disorder has spiritual causes; the greater the spiritual disorder, the more pervasive will be the total disorder (Brena, 1972).

DEVELOPMENT OF SHAME AND GUILT

Shame is commonly considered more primitive than guilt. Capacity for guilt is related to increased feelings of personal responsibility for conduct.

A Depth Psychology Viewpoint

Shame   In Erikson's (1963) "autonomy versus shame and doubt" stage (see Chapter 4), the prototypic shame experience occurs. The child has soiled its pants and stands stripped, before a shaming parent, with the evidence of its shame still on its body. Psychologically, shame is a "visual" experience; the child is "exposed" and "looked at." Ashamed people want to disappear, to make it impossible for others to notice their exposure.

Dreams of being naked in front of others, or being "caught with one's pants down," symbolize the shame experience. Being shamed makes one feel small, and can lead to "small" behavior. Shaming beyond endurance leads to defiance and can make a person essentially "shameless." The excessively shamed person may determine to get away with as much as possible.

Doubt   Doubt, with roots in the same life stage, comes from having a "behind"—an area one cannot see, which can be controlled by forces outside oneself (Erikson, 1963). The prototypic doubt experience is being unable to control the anal sphincters. A doubting person fears what may have been "left behind"—feces in the prototypic experience—as evidence of personal failure or inadequacy. Others' negative reaction to what of one's speech, appearance, and other behaviors are left behind leads to doubt about one's personal worth and adequacy.

Guilt   Freud said that guilt occurs when one fails to distinguish between doing something bad and wishing to do so. Fear of being discovered is not important because one realizes that, whether anyone else knows or not, nothing can be hidden from one's own internal judgment. People who feel guilt torment themselves for bad behavior without needing external judgment. Freud noted that the more virtuous people are, the more they distrust their own behavior. Those least blameworthy reproach themselves the most severely for small failures.

In Erikson's (1963) "initiative versus guilt" stage, parents begin to interpret the child's initiating behavior in terms of guilt and responsibility. The guilt experience is "auditory"—the "small voice" accusing and scolding the "sinner." Individuals made to feel guilty over many things become angry. Resentment builds as they submerge many of their strongest desires. Such people tend to moralistic overseeing of others, and harshly condemn those who taste forbidden fruits. Sometimes they scapegoat other people in socially approved ways, mistreating them in the name of virtue or religion.

Classical Conditioning (Learning) Approach

Learning theory's classical conditioning (or simple learning) can help to account for some emotional states, such as guilt. This kind of learning occurs when some signal or cue in the environment repeatedly gets paired with another event that is emotion-laden. Think about the favorite song of lovers. Whenever that song—associated with their good times together—is played, it recalls happy feelings. If the couple breaks up, the song often causes great sadness.

Acquiring Guilt Responses   When one does something that draws a bad reaction from the environment, some signal or cue usually precedes the bad reaction. When a child breaks a vase, the mother looks angry before she punishes the child. When a certain look on the mother's face causes the child emotional distress because of its prior association with punishment, the child is experiencing reality anxiety. The child's anticipated fear of detection *before* the mother comes is probably shame, or fear of the mother's disapproval (the angry look).

The child's reaction might move back farther. Bad feelings may start even before the child does anything, just from *thinking* about doing something inappropriate. When the child's emotional reaction comes solely from its own behavior or thinking, the reaction is guilt. In this chain of events, control of the child's behavior moves from actual punishment, to the threat of punishment, through shame at anticipated disapproval, to the child's inhibition of contemplated bad conduct.

Criminal Behavior   Individuals—both animal and human—differ greatly in their responsiveness to classical conditioning. "Psychopathic" criminals (who show great insensitivity to people, and can "in cold blood" harm or cheat others) may lack a full capacity for learning guilt. On different classical conditioning tasks—eyeblink (Miller, 1964; Warren & Grant, 1955) and galvanic skin response (Hare, 1965; Lykken, 1955)—psychopaths performed poorly compared to others. Other studies (Schachter & Latane, 1964; Schoenherr, 1964; Schmauk, 1968) show them inferior in learning conditioned fear. Eysenck (1970, 1976) summarized many such studies, and suggested that criminal behavior rests on a strong biological basis.

UNDERSTANDING SHAME AND GUILT

Social Bases of Shame and Guilt

Historical Overview   Notions of guilt were rare in Western religion before A.D. 500. Earlier humankind, aware of powerlessness before many natural forces, had less basis for considering people to be in charge of their fates. Since concern with physical and ritual purity appears in some religions of the Hellenistic and Roman periods (Cumont, 1956), shame was probably present. Mystery cult religions emphasized ritual purity, and the individual's responsibility extended at least to preparing oneself for participation. Before tending to religious concerns, worshipers prepared themselves by ritually removing the inadequacies that cause one to avoid facing the deity. Other more fatalistic religious systems allowed more basis for disclaiming any individual responsibility.

From early history, religious prophets tried to move people from shame to guilt mentality. The Hebrew Bible prophets are probably most familiar to Western readers. Dodds (1957) traced similar developments in Greek history. As notions of ritual purity gradually yielded to ideas of moral purity, guilt and belief in personal responsibility increased. This trend continued until the Renaissance. With the emphasis of modern thought on scientific determinism, guilt concerns lessened (Tillich, 1952a). Avoiding "getting caught" is now the main controller of many people's behavior. Menninger (1973) deplored this cultural trend, and argued that our very survival might depend upon restoring a sense of personal responsibility.

Anthropological Understandings   Anthropologists distinguish "shame cultures" from "guilt cultures" (Benedict, 1946). They tend to consider shame an earlier response, seeing it as the major moral sanction in primitive cultures. Many also consider relatively pure guilt to be largely confined to the Judeo-Christian tradition. Thirty years ago, the United States was called a mixed shame and guilt culture in which people are especially sensitive to shame (Piers & Singer, 1953); since then, both seem to be decreasing.

In shame cultures moral sanction rests in the reactions of other people: criticism, ridicule, ostracism, and contempt. Guilt cultures rely on an internalized conscience and the feelings of sin and guilt that come from violating it. Shame cultures are concerned with saving face; people react to their own behavior with strong emotions, which range from pride to shame. Guilt cultures foster responsibility, and consider individuals' needs and desires less important. Guilty people are prone to depression and more willingly suffer persecution.

Mead (1950) criticized many anthropological interpretations as overly simplistic. Many variables must be considered in classification of a culture according to its behavior-controlling sanctions. One should distinguish whether positive or negative emotion is emphasized (e.g., pride versus shame, superiority versus guilt), and what reference group is used for the individual (parents, peers, the entire community, spirits, God, or oneself).

After examining many criteria anthropologists use to distinguish shame and guilt cultures, Ausubel (1955) argued that shame and guilt are not dichotomous and mutually exclusive processes. He outlined some ways in which they interact, including "moral shame," an intermediate position between shame and guilt.

Measuring Guilt Emotions

Researchers have developed few standardized measures of this "generalized expectancy for self-monitored punishment for violating or anticipating the violation of internalized standards of socially acceptable behavior" (Abramson, Mosher, Abramson, & Woychowski, 1977, p. 375). Mosher first measured guilt in sentence-completion form, and later developed both forced-choice and true-false guilt scales (Mosher, 1966). These scales measure three types of guilt: sex guilt, hostility guilt (guilt over assertiveness or antisocial behavior), and morality conscience guilt (guilt over failing to conform to conventional expectations).

Summary of Shame and Guilt Theories

The theorists reviewed are talking about essentially the same phenomena. With only slight differences, they trace a clear-cut developmental sequence in emotional reactions to one's own questionable conduct. They sometimes give these experiences different names, but outline three to five separate levels of development. Box 14.1 lists these stages with the names each theorist gives them. Some theorists studied earlier (Chapters 2 and 4) whose work is relevant are also included.

First is simple fear where one reacts to potential threats—such as punishment—in the physical environment. Next comes concern over social approval or disapproval, along with a need to "look good" (competent, correct, adequate, right) to others. Shame follows real or anticipated disapproval. Following this is concern over general acceptability as a person and member of one's group. Conformity to an established code ensures acceptance. Outcasts feel isolated and doubt their personal value. Many theorists see the next stage as the highest. Concern shifts to one's own evaluation of self; one seeks to maintain self-esteem without regard to other persons or a reference group. Guilt follows failure to maintain one's personal standards. Finally, several theorists suggest a possible objective evaluation of conduct that does not depend on experiencing negative emotion.

ORIGINS AND DEVELOPMENT OF CONSCIENCE

In Chapters 3 and 4, we studied some ideas about conscience development. We now look at some other psychologists' ideas about how conscience begins and develops.

Sigmund Freud

According to Freudian theory, the individual is born with one structure of personality—the id—that contains all one's instincts, urges, and impulses. From the id's interaction with environmental realities, the ego—the manager of personality—comes into being during infancy. The superego, which develops around 3–5 years of age, restrains and limits the ego—especially regarding satisfaction of id impulses (Freud, 1933). (Although we talk about the id or the ego "doing" things, remember that we are simply referring to psychological processes. People do not "have" ids or superegos in the same way they have brains and gall bladders, but these concepts are useful for discussing personality functioning.)

Freud argued that initially "bad conscience" is simple fear of losing love when one recognizes that parents react negatively to certain behaviors. In a young child conscience can never be more than this, and many adults also function this way. For them, the place of the parent is taken by the community as a whole or by a deity created in the image of the parent. According to Freud, such people will allow themselves to do anything so long as they cannot be "found out" or blamed.

Superego develops out of the child's intense fear of parental punishment. The child resolves conflicts between personal desire and parental authority by becoming a miniature of the parent. This "identification" involves seeing oneself in terms of another person or group and "choosing" to become like that outside influence. The personality takes in the standards and morals of society through parental instructions.

The id seeks pleasure, the ego adapts to reality, but the superego demands

Box 14.1. SHAME AND GUILT IN STAGES

	Concern over physical consequences of behavior	Concern over approval or disapproval of others	Concern over acceptability and group membership	Concern over personal self-esteem and self-reaction	Concern over objective evaluation of self and situation
Freud	Reality anxiety	Social anxiety	Social anxiety	Moral anxiety	
Janis	Fear	Shame	Shame	Guilt	
Arnold	Fear	Embarrassment	Shame	Remorse	Repentance
Narramore	Fear of punishment	Fear of rejection	Fear of isolation	Fear of losing self-esteem	Constructive sorrow
Erikson		Shame	Doubt	Guilt	
Ausubel		Shame culture	Moral shame	Guilt culture	
Maslow	Safety needs	Love needs	Esteem needs	Self-esteem needs	Self-actualization needs
Loevinger	Impulsive	Self-protective	Conformist	Conscientious	Autonomous
Kohlberg	Premoral	"Good boy"/"nice girl"	Social order	Social contract	Conscience principles

Source: Compiled from Arnold (1960), Ausubel (1955), Erikson (1963), Freud (1926), Janis (1962), Kohlberg (1963, 1980), Loevinger (1976), Maslow (1954), Narramore (1974).

perfection in meeting standards. The parent's attitudes, values, and morality determine what standard of perfection the child will seek as parental demands are internalized and become part of the child's own mental functioning. The parent no longer must say "no, no" when the child wants to do something questionable; the child will internally say "no, no."

Conscience is one part of superego functioning—the proscribing part that tells you what *not* to do. The prescribing part, which says what one must *do* to be worthwhile, is the ego ideal. Conscience says, "You must *not* steal cookies from the cookie jar," and "You must *not* hit the little girl next door." The ego ideal says, "You *must* love Mommy and Daddy," and "You *must* say your prayers before you go to bed." If you *do* what conscience says *not* to do, you feel bad about yourself; if you do *not* do what ego ideal says to *do,* you feel bad about yourself. Conscience contains all the "thou shalt nots," while ego ideal contains all the "thou shalts."

Sears, Maccoby, and Levin

In an extensive study of child-rearing patterns, Sears, Maccoby, and Levin (1957) identified three forms of control that should be very familiar to you by now: external control, self-control based on fear of punishment or hope of reward, and inner control (conscience) based on parental conduct standards. Conscience control develops by identification, and gradually over years. The content of the child's conscience depends heavily upon the perceived content of the parent's conscience. Conscience control is operating when a person: (1) resists temptation with no one else controlling; (2) instructs oneself to comply; and (3) feels guilty when temptation is not overcome.

One likely motive for identification is the child's desire to reproduce pleasant experiences; another may be worry about parental affection and approval. When children play-act at being the parent, they can reassure themselves of support and relive pleasant experiences. Such dependency motives help ensure identification. The parental behavior most effective for producing conscience involves controlling the child by threatening a usually warm and affectionate relationship by withdrawal of love. The parent who makes love contingent upon good behavior produces the child with the strongest conscience. Either too strong or too weak a conscience is a handicap. Social living demands some impulse control, but overcontrol makes an anxious and unhappy life.

Magda Arnold

Arnold (1960) considers Freud's treatment of conscience by identification highly inadequate. Children take their parents as models because they consider them admirable and as having qualities the child lacks. The child simply wants to be like the parents and imitates their behavior. The same process occurs whenever one finds a desirable value. One disciplines oneself to choose this value over lesser ones.

Religion strongly molds people's ego ideals. Belief in a loving God and Parent of all extends one's ideals beyond mere self-interest or social cooperation. It leads one to seek the highest possible ideals, as in St. Paul's "It is no longer I that live but Christ lives in me" (Galatians 2 : 20).

One should continually correct the self-ideal by reflection to mature it (Arnold, 1960). Faulty or mistaken ideals work against human nature and invite disharmony. Choosing an inadequate self-ideal—less than one's nature demands—leads to boredom and unhappiness. (Note the similarity to Maslow's ideas about self-actualization in Chapter 2.)

Gordon Allport

Capacity for conscience exists in almost everyone, but with great cultural relativity. However, many contents of conscience are strikingly similar across cultures (Allport, 1950). The actual prohibitions and requirements of an individual's conscience are determined largely by upbringing. A person reared as a Catholic may feel guilty for using contraceptives, considering it against natural law, while a Unitarian neighbor may feel guilty for failing to do so, considering that irresponsible.

Mature individuals review the original codes imposed upon them. As conscience matures, three broad changes occur. (1) External sanctions, based on coercion and fear of punishment, yield to the internal ones individuals supply themselves. (2) The "musts" of childhood, upheld by prohibitions and fear, are replaced by preferences and "oughts" necessary for self-respect. (3) Specific habits of obedience are discarded; self-guidance rests on a personal framework of values. Not all one's original "musts" become "oughts"; one's mature values provide guidelines for decision making.

It is clearly arrested development to refrain from certain behaviors for fear of God's punishment (Allport, 1950). Mature conscience operates more from love than from fear—from one's desire to express the commitment made to a particular way of life. Mature guilt does not reduce to fear, but to disgust at violation of a value. Mature conscience requires long-range goals and some understanding of what one wishes to become. One then commits oneself to behavior consistent with these goals. Many people lack commitment to values; even the best integrated must sometimes reconcile inconsistencies between value and behavior. Having conscience necessitates guilt, doubt, anxiety, and a continual battle between impulse and ideal.

Social Learning Theory

Most social learning theorists see little evidence for a single intrapsychic moral agency like conscience or superego (Mischel & Mischel, 1976). They believe that people's moral behavior usually varies with different times, places, and circumstances. Research indicates much specificity regarding moral behavior (Allinsmith, 1960; Burton, Maccoby, & Allinsmith, 1961).

Some social learning theorists study problems associated with conscience such as delay of gratification and resistance to temptation. Yet these theorists believe that temptation and guilt responses are not necessarily related to each other or to similar child-rearing practices (Bandura & Walters, 1963). Not only overt behaviors, but also attitudes and emotions, are learned independently by observing others. Behavior control is thus not best understood with such ideas as conscience or guilt. (Chapters 15 and 16 further discuss social learning ideas.)

TYPES OF CONSCIENCE

A crucial concern, well recognized by many theorists, regards the processes of conscience. This problem can be posed another way: What different kinds of conscience exist? Or on what different bases do questions of conscience rest? Some stage theorists (Chapter 4) have partially answered these questions, but more remains to be said.

Legalism

Theologian Joseph Fletcher (1966) described three major alternatives for moral decision making. The first, legalism, insists that existing rules and laws determine what is moral. The rules are authoritative directives, and not mere guidelines; one must follow the letter of the law. Every problem is forced to fit some existing law. The first of Kohlberg's (1976) four decisional strategies for conscience stresses this respect for the prescribed rules of the normative social or moral order.

One's "Freudian conscience" has a legalistic preoccupation with all the rules about right and wrong learned as a child (Maslow, 1971a). Such legalism is behind much intolerant smugness in religion, according to Goodenough (1965). Legalistic insistence upon unquestioning obedience can lead to such tragedies as "holy wars," aggressive proselytizing, and national disasters like Watergate or the Nazi treatment of the Jews.

Fromm (1950) dramatically described people with legalistic or "authoritarian" conscience. Their cardinal sin is disobedience, with obedience to designated authorities the cardinal virtue. Because they feel powerless and in need of external control, they may consider leaders of the most inhumane systems as deeply wise and good. When such people violate conscience, they are frightened by their disobedience to a powerful authority (parent, church, state, God). Such failures demand that violators throw themselves upon the authority's mercy. In authoritarian religions that offer ritual atonement, violators can alleviate guilt feelings by ritually affirming dependence upon those qualified to offer forgiveness; confession is one means of doing this. However, their self-contempt leaves them less able to love genuinely, and more likely to violate conscience again.

Other Structured Solutions

Welfare Considerations Kohlberg's (1976) second approach is based on "utilitarian welfare consequences" for oneself and others. This strategy emphasizes the decision's consequences—good or bad outcomes for self and others. Fletcher's

(1966) situation ethics is very similar. A commandment of love dictates choice. The most moral decision is the one most consistent with love, that which provides the greatest good and best serves the welfare of all concerned.

Justice   The decisional strategy with which Kohlberg (1976) is most in sympathy identifies morality with justice. It is oriented toward liberty, equality, reciprocity, and contracts between persons. Arnold (1960) considers moral laws universally valid and binding, and believes that they can be derived from understanding human nature (Arnold & Gasson, 1954). She describes these laws primarily in terms of ideals of justice.

Individualized Conscience

Antinomianism   One of Fletcher's (1966) strategies eschews external standards. *Antinomianism* literally means "against law," and in traditional Christian theology refers to belief that one saved by the Christ is above the law. One begins decision making with no preconceived principles or rules, and relies upon the situation itself to provide the answers. Abandoning all claims for generally valid norms, one makes moral decisions spontaneously. Arnold (1960) considers such self-expression dangerous. She thinks goals should point beyond the individual lest they degenerate into behavior based on simple likes or dislikes without any discipline.

Supralegalism   Supralegalism goes beyond the established rules for moral decision making by appealing to a higher law that takes precedence (Goodenough, 1965). Supralegalism can never play a large part in organized religions since they require conformity to agreed-upon standards. It can also easily turn into sublegalism, since people tend to justify their own questionable behavior. (Compare this with Loevinger's pre- and postconformist stages in Chapter 4.) (Goodenough's ideas are further discussed in Chapter 19.)

Humanistic Conscience   Fromm (1950) contrasted authoritarian conscience with humanistic conscience. In the latter, self-realization is the chief virtue; the cardinal sin is loss of personal integrity. The strengths of the human individual are emphasized, as is the need to develop and understand oneself. Conscience warns when one is in danger of losing oneself; it signals a violation of self. These failures draw kind concern, not scorn and self-contempt. Awareness of guilt is not an experience of powerlessness, but helps people recognize all their powers. Guilt produces a desire to do better in the future, not from fear but from desire for personal growth.

Intrinsic Conscience   Kohlberg (1976) considered an approach that identifies morality with an idealized moral self more mature than legalistic or welfare considerations. One independently follows one's own idea of what constitutes a good person. Maslow's (1971a) similar "intrinsic" conscience is based upon our understanding, both conscious and unconscious, of our own nature: capacities, limita-

Box 14.2 TYPES OF CONSCIENCE

Morality according to:	Established laws of existing authority	Demands of the situation itself	Internally developed/intuited standards	Interaction between situation and personal impulse
Fletcher	Legalism	Situationism		Antinomianism
Kohlberg	Prescribed rules	Welfare, justice	Idealized self	
Maslow	Freudian conscience		Intrinsic conscience	Intrinsic conscience (?)
Goodenough	Legalism	Supralegalism	Supralegalism	
Fromm	Authoritarian conscience		Humanistic conscience	Humanistic conscience (?)
Arnold	Laws of justice	Laws of justice		Undisciplined whim

Source: Compiled from Arnold (1960), Fletcher (1966), Fromm (1950), Goodenough (1965), Kohlberg (1976), Maslow (1971a).

tions, talents, destiny, and vocation in life. Intrinsic conscience records in the unconscious mind every falling away for which one is responsible, every crime committed against one's own true nature. If there are too many, this conscience may rightly lead one to despise oneself.

This exacting taskmaster insists that we refuse to deny our own nature for any weakness or advantage. Maslow believed people often deny this conscience to satisfy the Freudian one and spare themselves the pain of growth in conscience and moral understanding. People who choose against intrinsic conscience often punish themselves later in life with neurotic distress and the realization of having failed to live to the fullest. Sometimes such pain and conflict lead to renewed commitment and a return to the path of growth.

Synthesis of Types of Conscience

Some common threads—summarized in Box 14.2—run through these approaches. All see legalism as the most common way to resolve moral dilemmas. Established bureaucracies (church, state) find this most congenial, and it has definite advantages for the preservation of social order. It also has potential for serious abuse.

The remaining possibilities offer more opportunity for growth, but risk irresponsibility and potential social chaos. Religious leaders are challenged to provide ethical leadership that respects freedom of conscience and divergent opinion but also recognizes risk. To avoid rule- and obedience-oriented codes and promote individual growth and freedom, without encouraging opportunism and irresponsibility, is a delicate task.

SUMMARY

We have traced how negative emotional reactions to one's conduct develop, and also distinguished different types of these reactions and types of conscience. Since ethical considerations prohibit experimental research on such negative emotional states in humans, we rely mainly on spontaneous reports of such experiences.

We found striking congruences among the different theorists reviewed. Most consider conscience a unitary personality function—a view not all psychologists endorse. Most of their work has evaluative connotations with approval of guilt over shame responses, nonlegalistic over legalistic morality, and individuality over conformity. Some experimental research to help you personally evaluate such judgments was presented in Chapter 5. The following chapter continues these considerations with discussion of self-control and self-management, or implementation of one's behavior choices.

REVIEW OF KEY CONCEPTS

The Experience of Anxiety
    types of anxiety
    reflective emotion

reality anxiety versus guilt
triggers of shame
reactions to shame
reactions to guilt
disturbed guilt reactions
yogic ideas about guilt

Development of Shame and Guilt
shame as a visual experience
shame and shamelessness
doubt and self-worth
guilt and virtuous behavior
guilt as an auditory experience
classical conditioning and shame/guilt emotions
criminal behavior and conditioning

Understanding Shame and Guilt
ritual purity and shame
shame cultures versus guilt cultures
moral shame
Mosher guilt scales

Origins and Development of Conscience
superego and fear of loss of love
identification
differences between conscience and ego ideal
determining the operation of conscience
conscience strength and contingent love
Arnold's theory of conscience
cultural relativity of conscience
"musts" and "oughts"
mature guilt, according to Allport
specificity of moral behavior versus unitary conscience

Types of Conscience
legalism
authoritarian conscience
situation ethics and welfare considerations
antinomianism
supralegalism
humanistic conscience
intrinsic conscience
individual growth versus social order in conscience

chapter *15*

Volition and Religious Hope

Our society's emphasis on scientific determinism has led more and more people to view themselves as natural phenomena, subject to the same laws as the rest of nature. However, as the general public increasingly accepts determinism, some scientists question its generality. Debates about human "free will" have been resurrected, with discussion about the extent of, limits on, and experience of freedom.

PROACTIVITY AND REACTIVITY

Questions about free will and determinism can be cast in terms of *proactivity* and *reactivity*. Proactive people resist habit and custom, believe they make their own futures, and try to develop themselves according to their goals and values (Bonner, 1965, pp. 65–66). Reactive people behave in a more determined fashion, responding to, rather than initiating, events.

Arguments for Determinism

Psychoanalysis   Sigmund Freud made many people aware of unconscious determinants of behavior. Mowrer (1961) commented that Freudian psychology thus completed a picture of human functioning that began with deterministic Calvinist theology. This theology suggests that, since good comes only from God, people are not responsible for any good they do, although they may be held accountable for evil they produce. The Freudian discounting of all responsibility was a logical conclusion to this Calvinist opinion.

Behaviorism   Behaviorism, the predominant contemporary psychological model, views human responses—like those of the rat—as reactions to environmental stimuli. Reward, punishment, and nonreinforcement produce the likelihood of different responses in different situations. For example, when you see a police car on the freeway, you reduce your speed if you are going over the speed limit. Of course, most contingencies that control our behavior are not so conscious and obvious. We are moved by many very subtle environmental effects outside our awareness.

    B. F. Skinner, the foremost behaviorist, holds:

> We must assume that behavior is lawful and determined. We must expect to discover that what [one] does is the result of specifiable conditions, and that once these conditions have been discovered, we can anticipate and to some extent determine [one's] actions [Skinner, 1953, p. 26].

Skinner later said that we must move beyond fictitious concepts like "freedom and dignity" to engineer a satisfactory life for all people. We must abolish the idea of the "autonomous [person] (one who initiates action and so is responsible for it) [and] turn to the real causes of human behavior (the environment)" (Skinner, 1971, p. 191).

Science and Determinism   Freud and Skinner both describe "reactive" psychologies—crediting behavior to biologically based urges (Freud) or to environmental stimuli (Skinner). Science rests on such deterministic assumptions. Determinism proved a reasonable basis for natural science, and was adopted by the social sciences. However, there is little reason "to suppose that both atomic physics and human behavior must follow the same kind of laws" (Bolles, 1963, p. 183). An indeterministic or voluntaristic model might prove more useful for social scientific understanding.

Even the natural sciences are finding that strict determinism distorts their disciplines. The small indeterminacies that physicists have detected do not, however, affect their predictions of the movements of tangible, visible objects. Although such findings undermine the notion of a "clockwork" universe, they do not necessarily support free will. "Although free will may require at least a dash of indeterminacy, indeterminacy does not establish free will or moral responsibility" (Myers, 1978, p. 212).

Biological Bases of Choice

Patients who have suffered brain damage have lost "the capacity to deal with that which is not real—with the possible" (Goldstein, 1939, p. 30). Not only have these people lost certain skills, but they have also lost their capacity to analyze situations, determine the relevance of cues, and choose accordingly. The lost capacities are those that distinguish human beings from lower animals. This means loss of "the highest [human] capacity, the capacity for freedom" (Goldstein, 1940, p. 238). Capacity to choose requires a certain minimum intactness of brain functioning.

Appetites   Drives are strongly biological. Addictions and emotional reactions often compel attention and action. These experiences have an established biological basis, and restrict one's range of choice in obvious ways. Maslow's (1943, 1971a) "basic needs" also are held to have a biological basis—even the higher needs of esteem and self-actualization.

A study of prolonged semistarvation showed the effects of strong drive on self-management. The subjects, chosen because of their good mental health and demonstrated willpower, became increasingly irritable, inefficient, distractible, and obsessed with ideas of food as the study progressed. Table manners deteriorated, and they became addicted to many substitute pleasures. Their self-control was effectively undermined (Franklin, Schiele, Brozek, & Keys, 1948).

Habits   Habits may limit our seeing available behavior options. We respond to one particular stimulus to the exclusion of others. Ach tried to get subjects to dissociate learned nonsense syllables—a nonconflictual task that involved only attentional effort. Subjects experienced many bodily sensations, particularly of the skeletal musculature, as if their responses were biologically grounded (Lapsley, 1967b; Pruyser, 1967). Anyone who has tried to break a habit knows how strongly one's body resists such an effort!

The Value of Believing in Freedom

Maslow (1971a) disapproved of "control" as an aim of a science of human beings.

> I won't go so far as to say that the question of free will must necessarily be involved here in its old and classical philosophical form. . . . I can certainly say that descriptively healthy human beings do not like to be controlled. They prefer to feel free and to be free [Maslow, 1971a, p. 14].

The More Satisfying Option   For James (1897c) both free will and determinism were rationally defensible positions. However, a deterministic position on human conduct makes moral responsibility ridiculous; determinism outrages the moral sense. Since free will was a more satisfying belief, James decided: "My first act of free will shall be to believe in free will" (Perry, 1948, p. 121).

Better Functioning   Allport (1950, 1955) said that free will provides a sense of working with multiple possibilities in a framework of choice. It allows us to evaluate and rank-order the choices by which we live. Belief in free will includes the belief that effort counts, that one can reorient oneself and influence outcomes. Determinists believe they are controlled by impulse and situations, and their destinies are beyond their control. They feel bound by habits, and may explain their behavior by a variety of nonvolitional factors. Many psychologists agree with Allport that people function best when they believe themselves free.

The Reality of Freedom

Psychology cannot assess the reality of freedom. If the effort we spend binding ourselves to a particular choice is not simply a matter of circumstances, our wills are free. However, after we spend a certain amount of time doing so, we can never know if we could have spent more or less. The psychological experience of having alternatives may be a delusion (James, 1892, 1897c).

PSYCHOLOGICAL VIEWS OF VOLITION

Focus of Attention

James saw the problem of willpower as one of attention. Whatever captures attention determines action. Holding a certain content in your mind ends willing, and automatic processes then take over. Once you allow contrary thoughts to enter your mind, action is inhibited. Consider getting out of bed in the morning. If you start thinking about how nice it would feel to catch a few more winks, or how chilly the room will be, or how comfortable the bed is, the likelihood of getting up on time decreases. If you keep your thoughts solely on getting up, you quickly do so.

The "effort of attention is thus the essential phenomenon of will" (James, 1892/1961, p. 317). For this reason, most Eastern religions consider the control of mental content to be a central component of the spiritual life. Anyone who has tried to practice meditation knows how difficult such focusing of attention is. James held that choosing and believing are essentially the same psychological act: The mind looks at an object and decides whether or not to let it "be so."

Intense focus on what one wants *not* to do does not usually bring good results, however. Relaxation of such effort and a focus on higher-order motives can have a steering effect on lower motives (Allport, 1955). Thus, thinking of long-range goals and aspirations sometimes absorbs desire for incompatible behavior. Again, one acts on conscious mental contents.

Intentionality

Brentano, a contemporary of William James, developed the Aristotelian idea of intentionality. He saw all psychological activity as intending, or oriented toward some object or goal (Brentano, 1874). Intending thus is oriented toward the future and implies that one will find a means to accomplish one's goal. "Long range intentions . . . have the power to order habits, thoughts, traits, into a unity of function. . . . This term designates the presence of the rational and ideational component in all productive striving" (Allport, 1950/1960, pp. 148–149).

Rollo May, who most fully developed the idea of intentionality, sees our age as one of disordered will, ennui, and apathy. This despairing sense that nothing really matters negates commitment and the ability to will. We become free through being aware of our deep motivational forces, not by denying them or trying to force control of them by willpower.

> Freedom is the individual's capacity to know that [she or] he is the determined one, to pause between stimulus and response, and thus to throw . . . weight, however slight it may be, on the side of one particular response among several possible ones [May, 1969, p. 175].

Protest signifies half-developed will. Protesters know only what they are against—not what they are for. Since they do not *act,* but only *react* to what they oppose, they are not free. They also usually project blame for their dissatisfactions onto others—an inadequate solution that places power and responsibility outside themselves.

Intentionality, the key to will, is not simply the having of intentions, but is the underlying structure of meaning that makes one able to have intentions. This frame of orientation reflects how one understands the world and all of life. (Compare this with Fowler's understanding of faith in Chapter 4.) One cannot have intentionality without values and purpose in life, and one's capacity for commitment depends upon intentionality. Meaning and values produce intentionality, which makes choice and commitment possible. Born with the potential for freedom, we must grow into it (May, 1969).

Alternativism

Although people feel free, we must recognize limits to freedom. The more one understands oneself, the more she or he can recognize limits and weigh them against inclinations. People with more available options are also freer than those with limited possibilities. Skills, education, training, intelligence, and information all increase freedom (Allport, 1955).

Fromm (1964) says that one cannot speak of freedom in general, but only of freedom for a particular person at a particular time in a particular circumstance. Similarly, one cannot choose good or evil in the abstract; one chooses particular behaviors that prove to be means to either good or evil. The choice is always about a specific act. For example, one cannot choose whether or not to give up smoking; one can only choose whether or not to smoke this cigarette at this time—and can make that same choice over and over again.

Our choices are often between action dictated by irrational passion and that based on reason. Reasonable choices serve growth, while passions enslave people into acting against their own good. "Freedom is nothing other than the capacity to follow the voice of reason, of health, of well-being, of conscience, against the voices of irrational passions" (Fromm, 1964, p. 131). Choosing either growth or passion increases the likelihood that one will so choose the next time. Some people consistently make growth choices, and others lose this capacity. Most of us make both kinds of choices.

Freedom depends on the strength of these opposing forces and on awareness. Religion and psychotherapy agree that increasing one's awareness increases freedom. A central theme of many Eastern religions is that ignorance chains one to the wheel of determinism; awareness brings liberation.

Fromm lists some important awarenesses. (1) One knows from experience—not just from being told by others—that certain actions bring good outcomes and others bad ones. (2) One learns what one must do—and avoid—to accomplish chosen goals. (3) One understands some of the motives—perhaps unconscious—behind particular impulses or desires. (4) One recognizes the limits on one's possibilities. This includes knowing how much temptation one can take before giving in to it. (5) One observes the consequences of one's choices, and is able to learn from experience and mistakes.

Finally, one must will to act regardless of the cost; willing demands action, whereas wishing does not. Fromm agrees with many religious traditions that we ultimately choose between remaining greedy and continuing to suffer, or renouncing greed and ending suffering. One cannot expect God, someone else, or fate to force this decision. Religion makes one aware, but leaves the choice to the individual. Fromm concluded: "There is never indeterminism; there is sometimes determinism, and sometimes alternativism based on the uniquely human phenomenon: awareness. . . . Nothing is uncaused, but not everything is determined" (Fromm, 1964, p. 143).

Implicit Theory of Responsibility

Easterbrook (1978) recommended viewing volition on two orthogonal dimensions (see Figure 15.1). One dimension assesses the intendedness, planfulness, or purposefulness of an act. The other contrasts chosen with imposed actions. Sometimes we intentionally do things we would not choose, like paying a fine. Sometimes also we unintentionally choose things, such as many habits or neurotic symptoms. Since we usually consider only voluntary (chosen, intentional) actions as free ones, this model refines our understanding of volition. The theory recognizes that:

> some unsatisfactory effects of intentional acts may have been intended without proper understanding of all the consequences of the intended result. These are called mistakes. It also recognizes that some effects of intentional actions may be unintended: the accidental ones [Easterbrook, 1978, p. 20].

Developmental Perspectives on Volition

Several developmental models (Chapter 4) and perspectives on conscience (Chapter 14) help us understand volition. These opinions describe control of behavior as moving from external compulsion or threat to social control to more inner control. Each step is more free than the previous one. The most free person is one whose behavior is no longer controlled by emotion (beyond shame and guilt) and for whom impulse control has ceased to be a problem (Loevinger's autonomous stage).

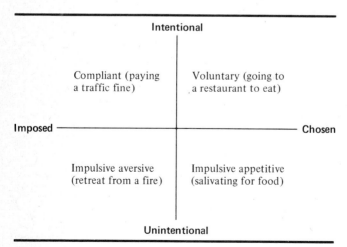

Figure 15.1   Easterbrook's model of volition. (*Source:* Easterbrook, 1978, p. 19. Used with permission.)

THE EXPERIENCE OF VOLITION

The Existential Experience of Will

Awareness of will occurs in three steps: (1) recognition that will exists, (2) realization of having a will, and (3) discovery of being a will. "After the conviction, the certainty, that will exists, and that one has a will, is acquired, comes the realization of the close, intimate connection between the will and the self" (Assagioli, 1973, p. 11).

Assagioli also described three characteristics of volitional functioning in a normal, healthy person. Strength of will—often the only aspect considered—is simply the will's energy or momentum for action. Will must also be skillful and good. Many religious rituals and practices try to help people make will good, and give them knowledge essential for skillfulness.

Some people have strong, unfilled needs for meaning, joy, and union with values that point beyond themselves. These needs are satisfied with the highest human aspiration: ultimate fusion with the "universal will." Religions often describe this as union of human will with God's will. "Essentially, it means tuning in and willingly participating in the rhythms of Universal Life" (Assagioli, 1973, p. 130).

Responsibility and Error

Fromm (1941) considered freedom to be terrifying for many people since it forces them to be responsible for life management. In an "orientation by proximity to the herd" (Fromm, 1950, p. 57), they try to transfer control and responsibility for themselves to a leader or group. Arieti (1972) agreed that "the will to be human" can be a burden. Some people choose lives—such as in a cult—where they do not have to make decisions. Because they fear making mistakes, they passively comply with an authoritarian system.

Human limitedness and the many possible choices one has make mistakes easily possible. Arieti (1972) identified five major volitional mistakes. (1) Sometimes one does not have enough information for an informed choice. (2) One might make errors of judgment in trying to understand the facts. (3) One might follow wishes or impulses instead of best judgment. (4) Even when people think they have made reasonable choices, motives outside of their awareness may be moving them. (5) Sometimes one makes a poor choice because of fear of others' reactions.

One great source of fear is "oughtness" (Arieti, 1972, p. 90). When other people's expectations or social pressures take on a sense of oughtness, seeing what is just and good becomes difficult. Many religious beliefs, dogmas, and myths become associated with distorted oughtness. Some of these led Christian Crusaders to slaughter Muslims, Catholics to massacre Huguenots on St. Bartholomew's Day, Turks to murder Christian Armenians during the First World War, and—more recently—clergy to encourage war in Southeast Asia, Irish Protestants and Catholics to kill each other, and Jews and Arabs to be locked in continuing struggle.

Types of Decisions

James (1890, Vol. II) distinguished five types of volitional decisions. (1) Sometimes, when all the arguments pro and con a course of action are considered, the balance seems easily to fall to one side. In two additional decision types, one wearies of the struggle before having all the facts and simply yields to an accidental circumstance leading in one direction. This impetus may come from the environment (2), or it may be an impulse within the person (3). (4) In other decisions, a change of mood or set—such as grief, fear, or conscience—may suddenly end deliberation. (5) Only in the fifth kind of decision does one feel effort in deciding. Here one must force oneself to select one course of action over another. Although such decisions occur very seldom, we remember making them. Most other decisions occur without effort, often without conscious reflection, and are not remembered as decisions.

Disorders of Will

James described two main disorders of will: explosive will and obstructed will. Explosive will has defective ability to inhibit responses; impulse immediately leads without reflection to action. Obstructed will has trouble initiating activity. The mind's focusing capacity cannot attend to anything leading to action. Tremendous effort seems needed to make any decision at all.

Arieti (1972) described similar volitional pathologies seen in psychiatric patients. (1) A psychopathic will cannot say "no" to itself, and has no capacity to delay gratification. More complex psychopaths may convince themselves that they have a mission in life that makes them more important than others; Hitlers and Neros thus justify their feeling that they deserve privileges and gratifications denied others. (2) Obsessive-compulsive wills are restrained by tyrannical internal laws that invariably submerge wishes. (3) Catatonic wills are in the worst shape; they are often incapable of any voluntary action. They cannot will or wish, but only fear. Since they attach tremendous responsibility to even the slightest manifestation of will, the implications of willing anything immobilize them.

BEHAVIORAL CONCEPTS RELEVANT TO VOLITION

Conformity

People often so readily adopt the behavior of others around them that no choosing seems to occur. Sociologist David Riesman (1961) described two conformist types: the other-directed draw direction from people around them, and the tradition-directed conform to the patterns of their social groups. Similarly, social psychologist Herbert Kelman (1961) described three processes of social influence. (1) One complies to get a favorable reaction from others. (2) In identification, the individual conforms to a group with whom she or he is associated. (3) Internalization occurs when a person adopts others' values because they are appealing values. (Note the similarity to the discussion of conscience development from Chapter 14.)

People seldom are willing to act directly contrary to their values if asked to do so. However, they will frequently join crowds engaging in forbidden actions (Zimbardo, 1969). When values are not involved, but only simple agreement with the judgment of others on trivial matters, a higher rate of conformity occurs (Asch, 1956). Fisher (1964) found a positive relationship between religiousness (Allport-Vernon-Lindzey religious scale) and social acquiescence; he concluded that religious people tend to conform more.

Modeling

People learn by watching others; this is called modeling or observational learning. Parental modeling appears much more important than specific training in formation of moral choices. Research (Bandura & Kupers, 1964; Bandura & Mischel, 1965) shows that children readily adopt many behaviors modeled for them. (These ideas are further discussed in Chapter 16.) The effect of television violence highlights the importance of modeling. Viewing aggressive models, even those not personally significant, increases aggressive behavior in children (Bandura & Huston, 1961; Feshbach, 1956; Mallick & McCandless, 1966).

Delay of Gratification

The ability to postpone gratification closely touches the willpower issue. *Time-binding* is a technical term for spanning the time between impulse and gratification (Jones & Gerard, 1967). Many people tolerate delays that others cannot—such as prolonged career preparation, postponement of eating and sexual pleasures, or even total renunciation of some gratifications for religious or moral reasons. Delay is accomplished most successfully when one can distract oneself from awareness of the frustration (Mischel & Ebbeson, 1970; Mischel, Ebbeson, & Zeiss, 1972). (Note the congruence with James's ideas about attention and will, discussed above.)

Older children and those from higher social classes have greater ability for such delays (Golden, Montare, & Bridger, 1977; Weisz, 1978). Modeling effects are potent for children's capacity for delay. If exposed to models delaying gratification for a longer or shorter time than their own original inclinations, children tend to change toward modeled periods of delay (Bandura & Mischel, 1965). Willingness to delay depends on the outcomes one expects (Mischel, 1966, 1968)—on trust that waited-for rewards will actually later be available. One must also be able to believe that she or he can meet any requirements for getting delayed rewards (Mischel & Staub, 1965). Thus, ideas about future-life heavenly rewards may help bind impulses toward more immediate gratifications if one believes that she or he will actually be able to get a greater benefit for doing so.

Self-efficacy

White postulated that a desire to be competent or effective, to master tasks for their own sake, may motivate behavior. Much self-direction is undertaken "because it satisfies an intrinsic need to deal with the environment" (White, 1959, p. 319). Other theorists use the idea of ego strength to convey the same idea.

Bandura demonstrated that a person's own successful action is more conducive to perceived self-efficacy than are emotional arousal, verbal persuasion of one's competence, and observations of others' abilities. In turn, "the strength of people's convictions in their own effectiveness is likely to affect whether they will even try to cope with given situations . . . how much effort people will expend and how long they will persist" (Bandura, 1977, pp. 193–194).

Perceived Locus of Control

Rotter (1966, 1971) measured people's beliefs about whether their rewards came from their own efforts or from external sources. On his forced-choice Internal-External Scale, subjects choose with which statement in each pair they more strongly agree. Each item offers a choice between belief that an outcome depends upon one's own efforts and belief that it is due to chance, fate, or other people.

Most locus of control research finds that "internals" (people who see themselves as responsible for their outcomes) more actively manipulate their surroundings and are superior to "externals" in coping with the environment. Generally, more intelligent, more highly educated, and higher-social-class people show a strong internal orientation (Rotter, 1971). Many less privileged people may simply have learned that they have little control over their lives. Between 1962 and 1971, however, college students became increasingly external (Rotter, 1971)—a trend that supports opinions that feelings of personal responsibility are decreasing.

Internals are more likely than externals to remember information (Seeman, 1963), seek new information relevant to problems (Davis & Phares, 1967), use available information in solving problems (Phares, 1968), and take overt action for social change (Gore & Rotter, 1963). Internals also can more successfully persuade others to change their minds, and quit smoking (men) or lose weight (women) (Rotter, 1971). Such studies suggest that people who show an internal locus of control more effectively engage in volitional behavior than do others. Some studies (Kahoe, 1974a; Strickland & Shaffer, 1971) have found intrinsic religiousness (see Chapters 1 and 20) positively related to internal locus of control.

Learned Helplessness

Lefcourt (1973) argued that perception of personal control aids health and survival. The positive effects of considering oneself in control have been demonstrated with surgery patients (Langer, Janis, & Wolfer, 1975) and with nursing home elderly (Langer & Rodin, 1976). (Recall Allport's belief that people function better when they perceive themselves as free.)

Observing animals exposed to inescapable stress, Seligman (1975) developed the concept of learned helplessness. Both animals and people, when their efforts have no effect on their outcomes, become passive, apathetic, and depressed.

People become most depressed and least capable of effective action when they see their helplessness as due to causes that are: (1) permanent, not temporary; (2) internal (personality) rather than environmental; and (3) generalized over much of their functioning rather than limited in scope (Abrahamson, Seligman, & Teasdale, 1978).

RELIGIOUS HOPE AND COPING

To take action, to cope with the demands of social and environmental challenges, requires a set of positive mood and belief. Religions have typically called this set *hope*. Although many religions contain elements of pessimism or even fatalism, most also profess a hope that may move the devout to cope more effectively with their world.

Hope as Shared Imaginative Vision

Lynch's (1965) early psychology of hope anticipated some of the above psychological theorizing and research. He said that mental illness comes from an inability to wish—without which one cannot hope. "An ideal human wish, a wish that is effectively human and humanly effective, is imaginative and accompanied by a correspondingly full act of the imagination in relation to what it wishes" (Lynch, 1965, pp. 148–149). Without such imaginative restructuring, one's hope for some outcomes causes despair regarding other outcomes that superficially might seem contradictory. For example, you might believe that you cannot have both your own will and the will of God, or both personal autonomy and close interpersonal relationships.

Hope must be realistic. A naive belief that *anything* can be hoped for may quickly lead to hopelessness. Such hopelessness often manifests itself as boredom—a self-centered hostile withdrawal—and apathy. (Recall May's opinions on will.) Unrealistic expectations of oneself and life underlie some hopelessness. Hope requires trust, mutuality, and the ability to wait (Lynch, 1965). Development of hope rests on basic trust (see Chapter 4) and the ability to reach out to the future in a responsible way without excessive dependency on others (Meissner, 1973). Negative views of oneself may cause one to avoid such responsibility and cease striving.

Both imaginative and communal aspects of hope are important in Meissner's understanding. "It is an act of shared imagination—of *imagining with*. The loss of hope lies in the loss of a capacity for shared imagination and its replacement by private imaginings" (Meissner, 1973, p. 17). Hope is thus an activity of sharing creative vision with other people—not of solitary daydreaming. Religious beliefs effectively help sustain hope when they ask the individual to look to the future and mobilize energy to will it (Meissner, 1973).

Some scholars emphasize more the communal or relational aspect of hope. "The language of hoping does not accentuate action verbs, but verbs of relationship. . . . One hopes with, through, and sometimes for someone else. Hoping is basically a shared experience" (Pruyser, 1963, p. 92). Also, "hope . . . is the *state of being* in which one exists in true relationship to others" (Mills, 1979, p. 51). Hoping places us both in and beyond our experience and gives a peace that transcends either magical thinking or stoic acceptance (Mills, 1979).

Hope and Social Action—Revolutionary Hope

Working with learning models, Mowrer (1960) defined hope as the experience that accompanies a signal that reward is available. (He also associated joy with the presence of a reward, fear with a signal for punishment, and sorrow with the presence of a punishment.) For human beings, such an "awareness of the possibility of free and constructive response to actual change" (Wentz, 1969, p. 27) has been called "revolutionary hope." Such vision opens people to their present while driving them toward unrealized future horizons. Some thinkers go so far as to say that "the key to human existence is . . . the hopes which [one] holds for the future state of humanity and the world" (Braaten, 1967, p. 213).

Hope underlies all people do to improve conditions. "All science is built on hope. . . . [One] can't help hoping, even if [one] is a scientist; [one] can only hope more accurately" (Fromm, 1947, p. 215). Some people, however, use the word hope as a cover for passivity and resignation—waiting for something to happen. Such inactivity is incompatible with our concept of hope which "is neither passive waiting nor is it unrealistic forcing of circumstances which cannot occur" (Fromm, 1970b, p. 9).

Hope implies a state of expectation gained through one's experience. Hope must have a basis of faith—not a certainty of particular external facts or events, but a sureness about one's own values—and, in turn, it sustains faith. Sometimes it requires great courage to resist temptations to compromise hope and faith. For Fromm (1970b), religious ideas like the resurrection and messianic hopes might better be applied to transformation of the here and now rather than to possible supernatural realities.

Such hope—coping with challenges of the material world—was noted in an effective Mexican Protestant mission. Conversion from their traditional folk religion required these Mexican Indians to show an unprecedented degree of decision and commitment. Further, the new religion

> made the bold claim that individuals . . . can take positive action to bring about change in this world. Protestantism probably appealed . . . because it offered them hope towards solving some of their most pressing socio-economic problems [Turner, 1979, p. 256].

Hope in Devotional Life—Hope for Things to Come

"If reality does not first give us reasons for despairing, it cannot give us grounds for hoping" (Pruyser, 1963, p. 92). Archeological findings from around 100,000 B.C. suggest that then religion was already providing "some plausible source of meaning and hope" (Burhoe, 1978, p. 40) in response to the human dilemma. Religious hope, however, ultimately has an element of uncertainty. "There can be no empirical verification of hope, for it is of the nature of hope to press towards that which cannot yet be seen" (Braaten, 1967, p. 217). Hope reduces one's sense of self-importance since "it means surrender, not only to reality-up-till-now, but also to reality-from-now-on, including unknown novelties" (Pruyser, 1963, p. 94).

Hope has been considered a right-brain function (see Chapters 10 and 12) operating by intuition, imagination, and inspiration. "Our problem in dealing with hope is that we persist in trying to . . . treat it as a linear, abstract, logical phenomenon that may be willed into being as a matter of individual achievement" (Carrigan, 1976, p. 47). Carrigan asks pastors to see hope as relational and to encourage contagious enthusiasm. They should apply creative imagination to issues, never glossing over tragic realities or making unreasonable promises, avoiding both shallow optimism and pessimistic despair. Recognizing hope as a right-brain function, religious leaders should not try to reach it through rational argument or set a timetable for its fruition (Carrigan, 1976).

The Christian Bible states: "There are three things that last forever: faith, hope, and love" (1 Corinthians 13 : 13). We have discussed the first two of these. Our next chapter turns to the third.

REVIEW OF KEY CONCEPTS

Proactivity and Reactivity
    distinguishing proactive and reactive behavior
    Freudian psychology and Calvinist theology
    behaviorism and "freedom and dignity"
    indeterminacy and free will
    brain damage and freedom
    effects of semistarvation on self-control
    James's "first act of free will"
    the reality of freedom

Psychological Views of Volition
    "the effort of attention"
    intentionality
    protest and will
    freedom, according to Fromm
    ignorance, awareness, and freedom
    Easterbrook's dimensions of volition
    mistakes and accidents in Easterbrook's theory

The Experience of Volition
    conviction of being a will
    orientation by proximity to the herd
    Arieti's volitional mistakes
    "oughtness," fear, and volition
    types of decisions, according to James
    explosive and obstructed will
    psychopathic, obsessive, and catatonic will

Behavioral Concepts Relevant to Volition
    other-directedness and tradition-directedness
    compliance, identification, and internalization
    time-binding
    effective facilitators of delay
    self-efficacy
    internal versus external locus of control
    effects of learned helplessness

Religious Hope and Coping
    role of imagination in hope
    realistic and unrealistic hoping
    hope, joy, fear, and sorrow (Mowrer)
    revolutionary hope
    hope as a right-brain function

chapter 16

Altruism and Religious Love

It has often been said that love is the most misunderstood word in the dictionary. Part of the problem is that this one word describes so many different experiences. Different styles and objects of love also abound to confuse the person who tries to understand it. Some consider love an emotion; others call it a choice, an art, a discipline, a gift, a commitment, or an unexplainable phenomenon. Although this chapter primarily focuses on love as related to religiousness, we first view it from a general psychological perspective.

SOME VIEWS OF LOVE

Love as Need

Psychologists commonly consider love a human need. James wrote: "No more fiendish punishment could be devised . . . than that one should . . . remain absolutely unnoticed. . . . A kind of rage and impotent despair would ere long well up in us" (James, 1890/1952, pp. 293–294). In urging the importance of loving others, religion implicitly recognizes this human need.

Some Theories   In his hierarchy of human needs, Maslow (1968, 1971a) said needs for love and belongingness develop once basic physiological (survival) and safety needs are met. Family and friendships satisfy some love needs, but in a mobile and rapidly changing society many people have trouble getting such needs met. Maslow believed that sensitivity groups and religious communes result—at least in part—from people's trying to satisfy love needs. One needs "unconditional positive regard" early in life to develop a healthy personality (Rogers, 1951). This need is so important that a young child's behavior comes to be guided "not by the degree to which an experience maintains or enhances the organism, but by the likelihood of receiving . . . love" (Rogers, 1959, p. 225).

    Many of Murray's (1938) human needs—including affiliation, deference, dominance, exhibitionism, nurturance, sex, and succorance—represent belongingness needs (Forgus & Shulman, 1979). Two needs that distinguish humans from animals are concerned with love. Needs for relatedness are best handled by caring relationships, while needs for rootedness require concerned participation in society (Fromm, 1955). Social learning (Rotter, Chance, & Phares, 1972) and cognitive behavioral theories (Forgus & Shulman, 1979) include love among the few needs they emphasize.

Supporting Research   Several classical studies in psychology (Goldfarb, 1943; Ribble, 1943; Spitz, 1946) described developmental retardation and severe health problems—sometimes leading to death—in human infants deprived of contact and handling. Goldfarb (1955) and Bowlby (1969) found institution-raised children handicapped in loving relations with others during adolescence. Harlow's (1974) experiments with infant monkeys related contact deprivation in infancy to later abnormal behaviors such as inability to mate normally, social withdrawal, compulsive habits (such as rocking back and forth), and—when forcibly mated—inability to mother infants. Extensive interactions with playful peers eventually overcame these difficulties in some monkeys. "Love therapy" healed the inadequate social behavior.

Love as Contract

Fromm (1956) deplored the "marketing orientation" in which people package themselves as "commodities" and hope to find a bargain for their own "exchange" value. However, Sullivan defined love as mutual satisfaction and security, one's "collaboration" with others in relationships that "pay off" (Sullivan, 1953, p. 246). (He elsewhere defined love as when another's needs and security become as important as one's own.)

Social psychologists Thibaut and Kelley (1959) view relationships as bargaining events. "Every individual voluntarily enters and stays in a relationship only as long as it is adequately satisfactory in terms of . . . rewards and costs" (1959, p. 37). Three key concepts summarize their social exchange model: (1) rewards and costs, (2) outcomes and profits (balance of costs and rewards), and (3) comparison level (evaluation against standards based on one's experiences and alternatives). Although such viewpoints seem antithetical to religious concerns, some people's "charity" may rest on hopes of eventual, greater heavenly rewards—an ultimate "payoff."

Love as Caring

Caring involves responsible concern for another (Rubin, 1973). May (1969) considers care the source of both love and will. "Love is the active concern for the life and growth of that which we love" (Fromm, 1956, p. 26). For Jourard, "a near synonym for loving is giving" (1974, p. 245). Giving is one major way religious people are urged to express their caring love. Allport (1950) considered giving love to be very therapeutic for the giver; the practice of caring for others helps resolve one's own suffering.

Love as Intimacy

Some theorists define intimacy as the exchange of vulnerabilities. "Vulnerability is always at the heart of love" (Buscaglia, 1972, p. 205). "Love is self-disclosure"

(Jourard, 1974, p. 260). For Rubin (1973), desire for close and confidential communication is the essence of intimacy. Social penetration theory (Altman & Taylor, 1973) says that trust begins with an act of self-disclosure. "Who can love me, if no one knows me? I must risk it, or live alone" (Kopp, 1975, p. 270). All these features are highlighted in Menninger's definition of love: "yearning for mutual identification and personality fusion" (1942, p. 72).

Intimacy exists on many levels: spiritual, intellectual, emotional, physical. Emotional intimacy is usually the most difficult to achieve. It requires mutual accessibility, expression of one's true feelings, nonpossessiveness, and an investment of time and energy (Dahms, 1980). Trying to force intimate knowledge of another through power never yields the knowledge that loving fusion with another does (Fromm, 1956). Allport (1961) considered warm personal relationships a criterion for intimacy. One facet of this is compassion, with which one empathically understands the difficulties of another's life.

Love as Creative Energy

Early philosophers—Aristotle, Hesiod, Parmenides, Empedocles—considered love the force that moves all things in the universe and makes them function together in harmony. Freud's late thought expanded the idea of libido from a narrowly sexual one to one of a life force pitted against destructive forces. This life instinct unites and integrates both the individual and the social organism (Freud, 1930). Memories of love maintained survivors of concentration camps; thus, human "salvation . . . is through love and in love" (Frankl, 1962a, p. 59).

Love as creative energy is closest to religious ideas of God's love for humankind and all creation. Teilhard de Chardin considered love a cosmic integrating force that produces successively higher levels of systems. Human life brought the possibility of voluntary participation in mutually beneficial cooperative relations. "Driven by the forces of love, the fragments of the world seek each other so that the world may come into being" (Teilhard de Chardin, 1959, p. 264). Love creates love. A Sufi text says: "When love of God waxes in thy heart, beyond any doubt God hath love for thee" (Rumi, Mathnavi III, in Nicholson, 1964, p. 122).

TYPES OF LOVE

Just as different scholars emphasize different features of love, various types of love are also described. These differ according to the features of love emphasized and the object of the love. Box 16.1 summarizes major characteristics of some loves.

The Natural Loves

Affection *(Storge)*   The Greek word *storge* (pronounced store-gay) translates "affection, especially of parents to offspring" (Lewis, 1960, p. 53). It refers to love one has for comfortably familiar people—both family and others in the near environment. Seldom can one mark the beginning of affection; one slowly realizes

Box 16.1 TYPES OF LOVE

The love	Common object	Goal of love	Dangers of love
Affection	Family	Support, nurture	"Incestuous" possession
Friendship	Peers	Shared vision and goals	Exclusiveness, paltry vision, "superiority"
Erotic love	Member of the other gender	Completion of oneself	"Idolatry," isolation from other people
Self-love	Oneself and one's life	Appreciation and fulfillment of oneself	Narcissism or self-absorption
Agape, or charity	Humankind as a whole	Unselfish service to any and all	Fostering dependence or rewarding poor coping
Love of God	Highest value one can conceive of	Gift of self to the highest value	Clinging to a poor understanding of God

that one has grown accustomed to another and finds that presence pleasurable. Psychologists studying mothers' attachment formation have concluded that physical proximity early in the infant's life greatly fosters it (e.g., Bowlby, 1969; Vietze, O'Connor, Falsey, & Altemeier, 1978), confirming the familiarity basis of affection.

Affection is the kind of love needed for survival, and gives one courage to confront life (Arieti & Arieti, 1977). Without this basis for trust (see Erikson, Chapter 4), the dis-eases (described above) that come from lack of love may occur. Affection needs both to give and to receive love. Sometimes the need to give love—need to be needed—makes one try to keep a loved one needy or conforming. Not only do parents thus try to "own" their children, but also children sometimes fear to leave the security of family affection. Fromm (1950, 1956) called such relationships "incestuously" ingrown.

Affection love can be insatiable. Demanding proofs of his daughters' affection led to the downfall of Shakespeare's King Lear. Religions recognize the growth-stunting potential of affection: "Anyone who puts . . . love for father or mother above . . . love for me does not deserve to be mine" (Matthew 10 : 34ff). Leaving the security of affection may require leaving cherished beliefs and practices of one's parents, as well as their protective care. Sometimes religion gives one a new family; "anyone who does the will of God is brother and sister and mother to me" (Mark 3 : 31ff).

Friendship *(Philia)*   "Birds of a feather flock together" refers to friendship; you can know a lot about a person by knowing that person's friends. Friendship is love between equals who share a similar vision. "All friendship implies a certain degree of communion; a certain likeness must exist between friends, a more or less essential community of interests" (Lepp, 1966, p. 26). This peer love, most common to same-gender relationships, has sometimes been erroneously associated with homosexuality. Reductions of sex-role stereotypes may make friendship between the genders more possible and common in the future than in the past.

Psychiatrist Sullivan (1953) believed a "chum" necessary for appropriate preadolescent development. Throughout life, people who develop deep friendships value them greatly. They may partially correct for lack of affection in early life (Harlow, 1974). Friendship most often is based on spiritual and intellectual intimacy, though emotional intimacy also occurs. Some people use the term *friend* loosely, to refer to mere acquaintances—not real friends (Lewis, 1960).

Of the natural loves, friendship is most comfortable to religion. Religious groups often consist of friends bonded together by shared ideals. Although seldom achieved in fact, religious fellowship ideally involves spiritual friendships. Judas's betrayal of Jesus describes the most painful possibility of friendship: betrayal by one who shared your vision.

Romance *(Eros)*   Heterosexual love is the most widely discussed love. (Erotic impulses draw some people to members of their own gender. Most psychologists believe this is not a matter of choice.) Typically, erotic love develops for another who matches closely one's personal image of ideal beauty (Lee, 1976); this is not limited, however, to physical beauty. Eros is a "craving for complete fusion, for union with one other person. It is by its very nature exclusive and not universal" (Fromm, 1956, pp. 52–53). Eros can "obliterate the distinction between giving and receiving" (Lewis, 1960, p. 137). One overcomes aloneness by surrender to values seen in the other.

Many myths present the idea that humans are split in two, and that union with another person reunites one with missing parts of oneself. Reducing this completion-seeking union to sexual interest alone is a mistake. May deplored our society's tendency to do so; "we fly to the sensation of sex . . . to avoid the passion of eros" (May, 1969, p. 65). Religions often fear eros because it can consume too much of one's interest, but even more they fear the separation of sex and eros. They commonly impose restrictions on sexual expression. In some temple prostitution, sexual release symbolizes one's gift of self to the deity. For some people, religious commitment is reflected in remaining celibate until marriage—or for one's entire life. Religions typically urge that one seek self-completion in union with God. Interestingly, religious mysticism (Chapter 10) is often described with erotic love imagery.

Love of Self Most psychologists believe self-love essential for ability to love others. "We are free to love others only as we become free to love ourselves" (Hodge, 1967, p. 221). "If I am unable to care for myself, I am unable to care for another person" (Mayeroff, 1971, p. 49). Religious people sometimes wrongly equate self-love with selfishness; however, such love is simply respect for one's own uniqueness and personhood. Maslow (1971a) called people's fear of accepting their own unique purpose and value "the Jonah complex." The story of Jonah (Hebrew Bible) describes this faulty choice. Jonah's "martyrdom" did not show appropriate love of self or others.

"Selfishness and self-love, far from being identical, are actually opposites" (Fromm, 1956, p. 60). People who properly love themselves avoid the self-preoccupation, unhappiness, and hostility that selfish people fall into. Self-depreciation and impatience with oneself are not religiously appropriate behaviors, but show instead a proud self-preoccupation. Many religious traditions urge us to "love our neighbor as ourself," but do not say to despise oneself in the attempt to love others. "To love ourselves, to find ourselves acceptable, is a call to discipline and achievement" (Fairchild, 1978, p. 213).

The Spiritual Loves

The loves just discussed bring human satisfactions that make them rewarding. Some other loves, typically considered religious, may require more than common human motivation.

Love of Humanity *(Agape)* The general love of humankind shows a "sense of responsibility, care, respect, and knowledge of any other human being, the wish to further [that] life" (Fromm, 1956, p. 47). It is characterized by nonexclusiveness, and assumes the basic equality and identity of all persons in spite of incidental differences in status, abilities, and personal development. It combines care and creativity, for by loving the unworthy, one sometimes stimulates them to become worthy (James, 1902).

This *agape* (pronounced ah-gah-pay) love, which religions promote, has various names: Christian charity, yogic *ahimsā* (pronounced uh-heem-sah), and social justice. Its nature is "esteem for the other, the concern for the other's welfare beyond any gain that one can get out of it" (May, 1969, p. 319). When this love is reduced to a bartering situation—for example, loving others to earn heaven—it loses its focal characteristic of nongain. Contemporary psychology has become increasingly interested in studying this love, under the name of altruism.

Love of God   Most people have experienced some "intense craving for what is not limited or relative. They seek what will substitute . . . certainty for mystery, perfection for imperfection, goodness for evil, justice for injustice, and love for hate" (Arieti & Arieti, 1977, p. 78). This love of God—or the Absolute or Ultimate Reality—yearns for the highest good, often considered as a personal God.

Love of God is similar both to eros—emphasizing love as intimacy—and creative energy, which helps explain their often intense rivalry. It also manifests as care (Chapter 8). Its many facets depend on the individual's culture, needs, and learning history (Fromm, 1956). It paradoxically has produced both tolerance and intolerance of others, charity and persecution, and maturity and gross immaturity.

Impersonal Loves

Some people love impersonal things. Love of animals usually is affection (Lewis, 1960). Love of nature, work, or one's country may mirror erotic or divine love. The Arietis (1977) described a general love of life—like Fromm's (1964, 1973) biophilia—which is similar to love of God. Religions typically disapprove of impersonal loves only if they distract people from love of God and humankind; then they are called idolatry.

THE PRACTICE OF LOVING

"Is love an art? Then it requires knowledge and effort." Thus Fromm began his classic *The Art of Loving* (1956). Love, he insisted, is a matter of loving rather than being loved, difficult rather than easy, and of learning how to love rather than finding the right object for love.

Barriers to Loving

Fear   Most psychologists consider fear the major barrier to loving. Some (Moustakas, 1961; Tanner, 1973) describe loneliness as a fear of love. Religions recognize fear as "love's great obstacle" (Arieti & Arieti, 1977, p. 12), and claim that love can heal fear. "Love contains no fear—indeed fully developed love expels every particle of fear" (1 John 4 : 14). Adverse circumstances can enhance bonding between people when one person supports the other and allays fear.

Fear of other people is usually fear that one will be found inadequate, inferior, or "less" in some way (Arieti & Arieti, 1977, p. 49). This uneasiness may make one withdraw before a feared rejection can occur. Some people are afraid they will "lose" themselves by being vulnerable to others, or be overwhelmed by involvement in another person (Lepp, 1963). Sometimes one fears being hurt from having come to expect the worst from others (Jourard, 1974, p. 257).

Other Barriers   People who feel unlovable believe that no one would want whatever they have to offer. They broadcast their own "unworthiness," and when others act on this message, their low self-esteem and inability to love are reinforced. People with a "marketing orientation" (Fromm, 1956) seek their best return for giving "love," and refuse to give without anticipating positive payoffs (Lepp, 1963).

Some people believe that love means controlling others or letting oneself be controlled. Some are unwilling to leave family security to love "strangers." Others remain selfish and self-centered because of immature needs or inadequate self-discipline. Some retain antagonisms that are barriers to love. Others feel awkward or embarrassed when trying to love. Finally, some people will not take the time to know others and their needs, or to minister to them.

Mature and Immature Love

Among the many things our society calls love, theorists distinguish between mature and immature loving.

Deficiency Love and Productive Love   Some people whose love needs are inadequately gratified love others from a deficiency stance. They are strongly dependent on a loved one, crave love excessively, and desperately fear losing love. Maslow (1968, 1971a) contrasts this with "Being-love," which enjoys giving as much as receiving, and cares for the freedom, growth, and satisfaction of another.

Fromm (1956) similarly distinguished love styles. "Immature love says: 'I love you because I need you.' Mature love says: 'I need you because I love you' " (Fromm, 1956, p. 41). Symbiotic loves are like Maslow's deficiency love. Productive love sees love not as a feeling, but as a difficult activity at which one works.

Needing/Giving/Appreciating   Although "Need-love" does not last any longer than the need, "another kind of love may be grafted on the Need-love" (Lewis, 1960, p. 30). Sometimes we can offer "Gift-love" which longs to serve. Either of these loves may become "Appreciative-love" which "gazes and holds its breath and is silent, rejoices that such a wonder should exist" (Lewis, 1960, p. 33). Appreciative-love for another person has erotic characteristics; directed toward God it is a love of adoration.

Characteristics of Mature Love

Prescott (1957) summed up some characteristics of mature love. (1) Empathic sharing of the other's experience helps one understand the other's needs and feelings. (2) Deep concern for the other's welfare makes possible (3) pleasure in giving to the other. Finally, (4) a mature lover respects the other's uniqueness, and non-possessively allows freedom for growth and change. Fromm's (1956) summary is similar. Responsibility—capacity to "respond" to the other—respects the other's individuality in care-giving. Knowing another makes this possible. This loving knowledge comes from fusing with the other and making the other's experience one's own. It is not a "head" knowledge achieved by analyzing or "dissecting" the other person.

Maturity involves receiving as well as giving love. Accepting love lets others be givers and helps one realize one's untapped potentials. (Recall that yoga psychology—Chapter 4—sees receiving love well as harder than giving it.) Giving or receiving, this discussion would be incomplete without reference to the well-known New Testament description of *agape* love. Some of its major characteristics are: patience, constructiveness, nonpossessiveness, lack of anxiety or need to impress others, good perspective on oneself, good manners, not pursuing selfish advantage, not gloating over others' wrongs, truth-loving, and with endurance, trust, and hope that can outlast anything. You can read it for yourself in 1 Corinthians 13.

ALTRUISM

In 1964 New Yorker Kitty Genovese returned home from work at 3 A.M. She was attacked by a man who stabbed her, drawing 38 neighbors to their windows by the noise. Although the assailant took over an hour to kill her, no one intervened—not even to call the police.

Defining Altruism

The Genovese case spurred great interest in studying prosocial behavior and the apparent indifference toward Kitty Genovese. Although the frequency of such events leads many to call human nature inherently hostile and aggressive, others believe "that *homo sapiens* is supremely a loving animal and a caring one" (Gaylin, 1976, p. 17). "Positive social (or prosocial) behavior is simply defined as behavior that benefits other people" (Staub, 1978, p. 2). Sharing, bonding, caring, helping, cooperation, altruism—even some aggression—can be prosocial.

Not all prosocial behavior is altruistic. In altruism there is no expectation of personal benefit. Leeds (1963) gave three criteria for defining an altruistic act: (1) the act is not for self-gain, but is an end in itself; (2) the act is performed voluntarily; and (3) the act results in some good. Schwartz (1977) described four steps of deciding whether or not to act altruistically: (1) perceiving the need and one's possible responsibility; (2) rousing feelings of moral obligation in line with norms and values; (3) defensively assessing costs, possibilities, and outcomes; and (4) acting or not acting.

Bases of Altruistic Behavior

Genetic Arguments   Animals of many species risk their own lives to defend their young or, sometimes, other kin. Sociobiologists (Wilson, 1975) argue that natural selection for altruism occurs. Since altruistic self-sacrifice increases the chance for survival of bearers of one's genes, the same altruistic genes that led one organism to sacrifice itself for the others are carried on by these others.

Other scholars (Gould, 1976) explain such behaviors in humans by learning. When an aged Eskimo volunteers to stay behind and starve so the younger family members can travel to survive, that family is more likely to survive than those who take aged members with them. However, that sacrifice would be celebrated in song and story, thus encouraging similar altruism in survivors; one need not appeal to genes to explain the behavior. Hamburgh (1980) claims that the Holocaust teaches us that genetically based altruism is not sufficient to deal with the complex ethical issues humans face. These require particular sensitivities to the specific and often unique needs of others.

Psychologists tend to agree that biological evolution cannot sufficiently account for complex human behaviors, and that social evolution must take over where biological evolution leaves off (Batson, 1978; Campbell, 1975). Many sociobiologists and other scholars accept this position (Burhoe, 1977, 1978; Dawkins, 1976). Although religion may be considered a societal mechanism for overcoming innate selfishness and encouraging altruism (Campbell, 1975; see also Chapter 1), "all religions are products of the same general process of selection that produced animal and plant life" (Burhoe, 1977, p. 14).

Biological Dispositions   Altruistic behavior cannot occur without some biological potential for it. Maslow (1954) posited a biological base for his need hierarchy, including needs to love and be loved. Bowlby (1969) argued that instinctive reciprocal mechanisms in an infant and its caretaker elicit a sequence of attachment responses.

James believed in "an organic affinity between joyousness and tenderness" (1902/1961, p. 226); when we are happy we want to treat others well. Further, associations with others that produce positive affect can lead to valuing them (Byrne, 1971, 1974). Thus, affectionate involvements with kin and other people may mediate altruism (Messick, 1976). The Arietis (1977) note that, since love is pleasurable, it must be connected with pleasure centers in the brain, which are probably in the limbic system. Emotion-arousing loves may involve limbic participation, while more cognitive loves—such as universal love of humankind—might be more neocortical.

Research supports an association between good feelings and altruism. People who have received unexpected gifts or pleasant surprises—such as cookies (Isen & Levin, 1972), a returned dime in a pay telephone (Levin & Isen, 1975), or a gift of stationery (Isen, Clark, & Schwartz, 1976)—were more helpful than control subjects when asked for a service. Similarly, happy people (Rosenhan & White, 1967; Isen, Shalker, Clark, & Karp, 1978) and people receiving good news (Hornstein, 1976) tend to be more cooperative and charitable. Success experiences make teachers (Isen, 1970), college students (Berkowitz & Connor, 1966), and children (Isen, Horn, & Rosenhan, 1971) more generous and helpful. Aversive environments reduce helping (Mathews & Canon, 1975). Findings on negative emotions are mixed (Cialdini & Kenrick, 1976). Either positive or negative emotion may produce more altruism than do neutral feelings.

Maturation   Sharing has been found in children as young as 2 years of age, with further increases from ages 4 to 13 years. These changes likely result from learning and specific developmental variables, since intelligence and general cognitive development show little relationship to altruism (Rushton & Wiener, 1975). Moral development level is significantly but not strongly related to altruism (Mussen & Eisenberg-Berg, 1977).

Personality Variables   Altruistic people generally have high ego strength. Prosocial young children are also outgoing, active, self-controlled, and emotionally open (Mussen & Eisenberg-Berg, 1977). Altruistic preadolescents show high ego strength, self-confidence, and satisfaction with peer relationships (Mussen, Rutherford, Harris, & Keasey, 1970). Adults who feel they can control situations (Gergen, Gergen, & Meter, 1972) and who have high ego strength and self-confidence (Staub, 1974; Trimakas & Nicolay, 1974) are more altruistic. Some people with relatively low self-worth may volunteer in public situations because of fear of rejection (Jarymowicz, 1977).

> People who tend to have positive moods, high self-esteem, and a positive sense of well-being may be less preoccupied with themselves, have a greater sense of potency or strength, and perhaps even feel more benevolence towards others than individuals characterized by more negative moods, low self-esteem, and a poor sense of well-being [Staub, 1978, p. 308].

Those who value social relationships are more altruistic than those who rate aesthetic or political values higher (Krebs, 1970). Valuing helpfulness and equality facilitates helping behavior, while valuing ambition reduces helping (Staub, 1974). Staub (1978) found a prosocial orientation associated with high ranking of prosocial values, feeling of responsibility for others' welfare, valuing of people, and nonmanipulativeness. In sum, the major personality characteristics associated with altruism are high ego strength and the holding of prosocial values.

These findings suggest that if religious people feel in a positive harmonious relationship with the Ultimate, think themselves blessed by their God, value helpfulness and other people, and believe that they as individuals have a unique value—ideas generally recommended by religions—they should consistently be more altruistic than people without such opinions. Religious people may not be noticeably more altruistic because so few deeply believe in these ideas.

Other Factors Affecting Altruism

Child-rearing Practices   Practically from birth children watch their parents. Such models communicate to children what behavior is appropriate and expected. Many studies conclude that observing prosocial models increases—at least temporarily—children's generosity and helping. Some results show that selfish models reduce a child's altruism (Mussen & Eisenberg-Berg, 1977). Rosenhan compared highly dedicated civil rights workers with people who took part in only one or two activities. Parents of the highly committed had actively worked for altruistic causes, while those of occasional participants were "at best, mere verbal supporters of prosocial morality and at worst, critical about those moralities. It was common . . . that their parents preached one thing and practiced another" (Rosenhan, 1972, p. 342).

Research on direct education to prosocial behavior—preaching—shows mixed findings. Preaching has some effect, but is greatly enhanced when congruent behavior is also modeled, and when prosocial demands are supported with arguments for altruistic behavior. Inductive techniques (explaining the consequences of selfish behavior) provide much more effective discipline regarding altruism than use of power (such as physical punishment) or withdrawal of love or privileges. Induction probably increases capacity for empathy, with resultant altruism (Eisenberg-Berg & Geisheker, 1979).

"Role-taking ability is a forceful antecedent of prosocial behavior" (Mussen & Eisenberg-Berg, 1977, p. 134). Actual practice of altruism subsequently increases it. Children trained in role playing prosocial behavior later tend to show altruistic behavior (Friedrich & Stein, 1975; White, 1972). For such reasons, some people advocate compulsory social service for all young people (Muller, 1978). In summary, while direct education to altruism may increase helpfulness, modeling has stronger effects. If children subsequently practice the altruistic behavior that is modeled, the effects will be even greater. "Assuming responsibility . . . has a positive effect on prosocial behavior" (Mussen & Eisenberg-Berg, 1977, p. 99).

Societal/Environmental Factors   Helping behavior is generally unrelated to social class, gender, and family size (Mussen & Eisenberg-Berg, 1977). Social institutions such as church and school can influence altruistic behavior through education, modeling, and practice. What they do is much more important than what they say. Religions work against prosocial ends when they encourage formation of groups that support their own interests against others (Batson, 1978).

The mass media—especially television—potently influence altruism and aggression. Exposure to prosocial television broadcasts increases such behavior in children. "In the past, children have seen and learned violence on TV's window and today they continue to do so. In the future they might, instead, learn constructive solutions to the problems they will face" (Liebert, Neale, & Davidson, 1973, p. 171).

Situational Determinants of Altruism   Situational factors have the greatest effect of all on altruistic behavior. An early study noted that the more observers there are to an emergency, the less likely anyone is to help. When responsibility does not focus on one person, the result may be that no one helps (Darley & Latane, 1968). Additional studies support this finding, although personality characteristics (such as high self-esteem) and other situational factors (such as assignment of responsibility) may moderate its impact (Byrne, 1974; Staub, 1978). Characteristics of the others who are present are also important. One helps more when others present are considered unable to help (Bickman, 1971). The presence of children inhibits helping, but not so much as does that of adults (Ross, 1971). Strangers inhibit helping more than friends (Latane & Rodin, 1969).

The more ambiguous a situation, the less likely it is that altruistic behavior will occur (Clark & Word, 1974). People may be confused about what to do in an uncertain situation and fear risking a mistake. In general, the more explicit one's responsibility to help another is, the more help will be given (Tilker, 1970); such responsibility greatly clarifies a situation, and alleviates fear of others' disapproval. Similarly, when people believe they have "permission" to get involved in a problem situation, they are more likely to do so (Staub, 1971). Familiarity with the environment in which help is needed also increases helping (Latane & Darley, 1970).

Characteristics of a person needing help are important. We help those we like and those who depend on us (Baron, 1971; Berkowitz & Daniels, 1964). People are more likely to help when others are judged not responsible for their problems. Dependent females receive much more help, and independent females much less help, than either dependent or independent males (Gruder & Cook, 1971). Thus, women are rewarded for conforming to sex-role stereotypes and punished for failing to do so. When someone strongly needs help, race does not affect bystanders' helping (Piliavin, Rodin, & Piliavin, 1969; Wispe & Freshley, 1971).

The Cost of Helping   The more clearly a serious need is seen, the more likely helping is (Latane, 1970; Yakimovich & Saltz, 1971). Exceptions to this occur when helping would cause one great discomfort or inconvenience (Staub, 1978). Fear of personal danger inhibits helping; rural people more readily let a needy stranger into their homes than do city people (Levine, Villena, Altman, & Nadien, 1976). People help less when it involves contradicting a person who threatens or humiliates them (Latane & Darley, 1970). In sum, the cost and consequences of helping are important determinants of altruism. People balance such factors as danger, effort, inconvenience, and possible embarrassment against self-esteem and the inner rewards of being altruistic. The greater the personal sacrifice, the less likely is helping (Midlarsky & Midlarsky, 1973).

A cost and reward model of helping behavior summarizes these conclusions. Others' needs create emotional states in observers. The greater and more uncomfortable the arousal, the more one will want to reduce it—and at as little cost as possible. This may involve either helping or not helping. One weighs the costs and rewards that will come from each possible action (Piliavin & Piliavin, 1972). Although by definition altruism does not involve personal benefit, such understandings suggest that internal consequences of one's action may govern prosocial behavior. The rewards are simply not externally observable, and may be as subtle as one's own sense of self-esteem or personal righteousness.

Some Summary Conclusions

People who do not help others in need may be more confused or afraid than indifferent or alienated. Byrne (1974) encourages a massive societal effort to educate people on how to respond effectively to others' need. Adults should model appropriate behaviors, and specific skills must be taught.

A proposed model for training altruistic behavior sounds like movement from extrinsic to intrinsic motivations (discussed further in Chapters 20
and 22). Kanfer (1979) says that altruistic behaviors may at first have to be
encouraged by social approval and reward, since egocentric behaviors are
more probable. Gradually, as such behavior is repeatedly associated with
positive experiences, it will come to be valued and rewarding in itself, and
eventually preferred.

REVIEW OF KEY CONCEPTS

Some Views of Love
    different understandings of love
    unconditional positive regard
    love deprivation and health
    Harlow's deprived monkeys
    the marketing orientation
    social exchange model
    intimacy, vulnerability, and self-disclosure
    love as cosmic integrating force

Types of Love
    familiarity basis of affection
    dangers of affection-love
    the basis for friendship
    friendship and religious fellowship
    personal image of ideal beauty
    eros and self-completion
    separation of sex and eros
    the Jonah complex
    selfishness and self-love
    agape, charity, and *ahimsā*
    agape and nongain
    idolatry and impersonal loves

The Practice of Loving
    love and fear
    "Being-love"
    deficiency love/"Need-love"
    immature versus mature love
    Appreciative love
    characteristics of mature love

Altruism
    prosocial behavior and altruism
    natural selection for altruism
    social versus biological evolution
    relationships between joy and altruism
    self-esteem and altruism

religiousness and altruism
effects of preaching on prosocial behavior
inductive techniques in training for altruism
effects of ambiguity on altruism
cost and reward model of helping behavior
Kanfer's method of training for altruistic behavior

chapter *17*

Research in Psychological/Religious Variables

This chapter briefly surveys some representative research in dogmatism, guilt and moral judgment, locus of control, and helping in emergency situations. Although the literature on these topics is large, we consider only studies with special relevance for religion.

RESEARCH IN DOGMATISM

Dogmatism and Religiousness

Denominational Differences   Rokeach (1960) developed scales to measure his concept of dogmatism (Chapter 13), and found Catholics generally more dogmatic than Jews or Protestants. Although some other studies (DiRenzo, 1967; Koepp, 1963) support this finding, geographical locale might be a more important variable. Kilpatrick, Sutker, and Sutker (1970) found Southern students who were nonbelievers or Catholics less dogmatic than were Protestants and Jews. The Catholic students were as dogmatic as Northern Catholic students, but Protestants and Jews were much more dogmatic than their Northern counterparts, leaving them more dogmatic than the Catholics in this region. Study of differences in dogmatism between religious groups may not be appropriate because of such possible confounding with other variables.

Religious Correlates of Dogmatism   Church attendance is related to dogmatism (Steininger, Durso, & Pasquariello, 1972), and religious people in general—especially those with fundamental beliefs—score high on dogmatism (Stanley, 1963). Nuns from conservative religious orders are significantly more dogmatic than those from liberal ones (Bohr, 1968). Swindell and L'Abate (1970) found college students' dogmatism significantly correlated with Glock and Stark's (1965a) Fundamentalist Attitudes Inventory ($r = .32$), measuring religious fundamentalism, and with Silverman's (1954) Religious Attitudes Questionnaire ($r = .26$), which assessed similarity of beliefs to those of theology students.

Gilmore (1969) found that even fundamentalists vary greatly in dogmatism scores. One can hold orthodox views, but in a nondogmatic fashion. One may, for example, believe in the authority of scriptures, but be open-minded toward others' views.

Dogmatism and Orthodoxy

Dogmatism Distinguished from Orthodoxy   The Rokeach Dogmatism Scale does not have religious content, and measures general dogmatism rather than specifically religious dogmatism. Meadow's (1977b) Belief Rigidity Scale contains items that are relatively free of content specific to any particular religion, but that reflect a rigid and authority-centered set toward religious beliefs. Religious orthodoxy, the holding of traditional religious beliefs, is still different. Box 17.1 contains sample items for dogmatism, religious dogmatism, and orthodoxy.

Orthodoxy and Religious Dogmatism   Many early measures of religiousness were simply measures of belief orthodoxy. One such measure—inappropriately called religious dogmatism—ranked, from highest to lowest scorers, these groups: fundamental Protestant, Baptist, Catholic, Presbyterian, Methodist, and Episcopal (Fagan & Breed, 1970). More regular church participators show greater religious orthodoxy (Gaede, 1977; Hadden, 1969). Orthodoxy is positively related to self-reported feelings of love and happiness, negatively related to hate feelings, and unrelated to sadness (Balswick & Balkwell, 1978).

Meadow's (1977b) religious dogmatism is related to orthodoxy, correlating .44 with a measure of the traditional Christian concept of God, and .63 with approval of the institutional church. It is negatively related ($-.25$) to liberalism of religious affiliation. This scale also correlates significantly (.41 and .35) with two measures of authoritarianism.

Francesco's (1962) short scale of religious dogmatism, which he called "conventionalism," includes such items as belief that everyone should practice a religion and that children should have religious education. This scale was related to general conservatism and orderliness; strong conscience; and lack of autonomy, dominance, and aggression.

Some Conclusions

Although distinguishable from each other, dogmatism, religious dogmatism, and fundamental orthodoxy are consistently related to each other. Since religious people are often taught to accept beliefs on scriptural or church authority, religiously orthodox people have a built-in bias toward dogmatism—at least as related to religious beliefs. However, individual differences exist, and not all people in conservative religious groups are dogmatic. Dogmatism scales may be as biased against religious people as authoritarianism measures are against political conservatives (Scobie, 1975).

GUILT AND MORAL JUDGMENT

What makes people feel guilty? Does religion make a difference? One interesting study (London, Schulman, & Black, 1964) assessed people's judgments of the morality of particular actions and the guilt or self-satisfaction associated with doing them.

Judging Behaviors' Morality

Procedure   College students were given a list of 33 behaviors and asked to respond to them on a seven-point scale under three different conditions. They first

Box 17.1 DISTINGUISHING DOGMATISM AND ORTHODOXY

Dogmatism (Rokeach)	Religious dogmatism (Meadow)	(Christian) belief orthodoxy (Brown)
It is better to be a dead hero than a live coward.	There is no doubt about the truth of my religious beliefs.	Jesus Christ was the son of God.
Most people just don't know what's good for them.	Other religions do not possess the truth as mine does.	The world was created by God.
There are two kinds of people in this world: those who are for the truth and those who are against the truth.	True faith leaves no room for doubts and questions.	The spirits of human beings continue to exist after the death of their bodies.

Source: Brown (1966b), Meadow (1977b), Rokeach (1960).

rated each item according to how they felt their religion would evaluate it on a continuum of sinfulness to virtue. Next they indicated how much guilt or self-satisfaction engaging in each behavior would produce in them. Finally, they gave their own personal opinions about whether the behaviors should be avoided or performed. Results were analyzed by major faith groups: Catholic, Jewish, and Protestant.

Results The largest difference among groups—17 statistically significant items—was obtained on the ratings of their religions' opinions. The groups differed on only six items in the guilt or satisfaction individuals felt for doing a behavior. Eight items were rated differently as behaviors to be sought or avoided. Table 17.1 summarizes the data. Condition I is ratings for the religions, II guilt or satisfaction experienced, and III personal ratings of correctness of the behavior. For the items showing statistical significance, the order in which the groups scored is given by the letters C (Catholic), J (Jewish), and P (Protestant). The group listed first gave the most negative, conservative, or avoiding reaction to the item; the last given has the most positive or permissive attitude toward the behavior.

Items that showed no differences among the groups included: admitting your faults to yourself, working for high grades in school, disagreeing with parents, falling in love with a married person, stealing, lying, feeling hostile toward a friend, cheating on exams, giving to charity to get others' approval, aggressively striving for success, and swearing.

Summary Group Findings

Overall, Catholics evaluated their church's beliefs the most stringently, and Jews the most liberally. Protestants reported the most guilt, and Jews were the most comfortable with themselves. Jews' personal evaluations of the behaviors were more permissive than those of either Catholics or Protestants.

Catholics were least concerned about stealing, and Jews about premarital intercourse. Protestants most strongly endorsed not fighting back. Catholics gave considerably more negative ratings to items concerning sexual behavior: masturbating, petting, contraception, and sexy thoughts. Protestants rated most severely giving money to charity to lower one's taxes, smoking, gambling, attacking an evil person, and social drinking; thus impulse and habit control seem their major concerns. Jews did not rate any items significantly more severely than the other groups.

Dimensions of Guilt and Ethics

Using the same items and several more, Black and London (1966) factor analyzed replies of other students. This procedure clusters together the items that vary most regularly with each other, and thus defines the general categories under which the students' ethical concerns cluster.

Several factors appeared across all three modes of response to the items.

Table 17.1   MORAL JUDGMENT AND GUILT RATINGS

Number	Item	I	II	III
2.	Flirting	CPJ		
3.	Donating to charity to lower one's taxes	PJC		PJC
5.	Showing anger in an argument	CPJ		
7.	Getting drunk	CPJ		
8.	Feeling respect for religious leader		CPJ	
9.	Praying			JCP
11.	Masturbating	CPJ		
14.	Competing with others for personal gain			CPJ
16.	Disobeying one's parents		JPC	
17.	Smoking	PCJ	PJC	
18.	Doubts about existence of God			CPJ
19.	Premarital intercourse	CPJ		
20.	Premarital intercourse with loved other	CPJ		
22.	Reporting another's cheating to teacher	JPC		
24.	Turning other cheek, not fighting back	JCP	CJP	JCP
26.	Gambling	PJC		PJC
27.	Attacking an evil person	PCJ	PCJ	
28.	Questioning validity of own religion	CPJ		
29.	Social drinking	PCJ		
30.	Petting	CPJ	CPJ	
31.	Contraception or birth control	CJP		CPJ
32.	Thinking sexy thoughts	CPJ		CPJ

Source: London, Perry; Schulman, R. E.; & Black, M. S. Religion, guilt, and ethical standards. *The Journal of Social Psychology,* 1964, **63**, 145–149. Copyright 1964 by the American Psychological Association. Adapted by permission of the author.

One cluster was concerned with religious skepticism; another described action-motive conflicts (doing desirable acts for the wrong reasons). Several other factors appeared only on the second (guilt) and third (personal ethic) response modes. One cluster grouped religious practices such as praying and seeking God's help. Others described righteous self-assertion (such as attacking an evil person), sex and asceticism, competitiveness, and aggression.

RELIGIOUSNESS AND LOCUS OF CONTROL

We now review representative studies relating Rotter's (1966) locus of control variable (Chapter 15) to religiousness.

Social-Psychological Variables

Religious Identification Studying 465 U.S. college students, Shrauger and Silverman (1971) found Protestants significantly more internal in locus of control than Jews. Catholics scored between these two groups. Khan and Hassan (1977) found 50 Hindu students significantly more internal than 50 Muslim students.

Another study (Javillonor, 1971) found no significant differences between Pentecostalists and people from other religious orientations; however, people who had been in the Pentecostal group less than 6 months were more external than were long-time (6–10 years) members. Coulson and Johnson (1977) found glosso-lalists (tongues-speakers) (Chapter 9) more internal than nonspeakers. Unfortunately, their nonspeakers came from a different denomination (Methodist) than their speakers (Pentecostal-Holiness), and this confounds the findings. The researchers believe that the differences may be accounted for by internals' more easily choosing membership in a nontraditional sect—an opinion not consistent with Javillonor's (1971) (above) findings.

Religious Participation One study (Benson & Spilka, 1973) found internal locus of control significantly related to frequency of religious discussion ($r = .18$), devotions ($r = .30$), and hours spent in church activities ($r = .19$) for Catholic high school boys. Among Shrauger and Silverman's (1971) college students (above), those who indicated regular participation were significantly more internal than those indicating occasional or rare participation. However, while Protestants and Jews tended to be more internal the greater their religious participation, this relationship did not hold for Catholics.

Locus of Control and Belief

Supernatural Beliefs Berman and Hays (1973) found no relationship between locus of control and belief in life after death. In Ghana, Africa, externality was found related to supernatural beliefs (Jahoda, 1970).

Scheidt (1973) repeated the Jahoda study with Western students. He administered the Locus of Control Scale to 1200 students, then solicited interviews by phone from 20 scoring strongly external and 23 strongly internal. The students, who believed they were being picked at random from university students, took a 32-item attitude questionnaire, indicating on a seven-point scale their agreement with each item. The scale assessed belief in astrology, witchcraft, phrenology, hauntings, sorcery, extrasensory perception, and fortune-telling. As a group, the external students showed significantly stronger belief in these items. The author concluded that the "over-all I-E difference may be mediated by a tendency for externals to respond more than internals to hearsay testimony as to the validity of supernormal phenomena" (Scheidt, 1973, p. 1161).

Beliefs About God In a group of 128 Catholic high school boys who considered religion important and had strong belief in God, no relationship was found between locus of control and the perception of God as controlling. Internal locus of control was related to seeing God as loving ($r = .28$); externals were significantly more likely to see God as vindictive ($r = .23$) or as "impersonal allness" ($r = .18$) (Benson & Spilka, 1973).

Silvestri (1979) asked Episcopalian adults to choose the opinion about their achievements that best described their own belief: That all credit belongs to God, that they contribute their share and God helps them, or that God leaves them free to do by themselves. Those who chose the first option (the "God-dependent") were significantly more internal than the others. Silvestri concluded that they felt free from the effects of chance, luck, or other people on their outcomes since they considered God in control of their lives.

General Conclusions

Although differences in locus of control have been found among religious groups, no firm agreement exists as to their cause. They may reflect either the socializing processes of the faith groups or, with self-chosen affiliations, a tendency for people to choose a denomination compatible with personality. Religious participation is generally positively related to internal locus of control.

People more external in locus of control are more accepting of a variety of unorthodox supernatural beliefs than are internals. Internals tend to have more positive images of God than do externals. Faith that God orders one's life may foster internal locus of control by helping one feel free from the effects of general external factors.

RELIGIOUSNESS AND EMERGENCY HELPING

Emergency Helping Behavior

Darley and Batson (1973) concluded that reading the parable of the Good Samaritan did not significantly affect the emergency helping behavior of seminary students. Greenwald (1975) reanalyzed their data and concluded that the reading increased helping by more than 50%. Among college students, Annis (1976) found no relationship between helping "a lady in distress" and several religion measures: literal scriptural belief, a religious values scale, and frequency of prayer and church attendance.

Nelson and Dynes (1976) found that frequency of personal prayer was related to ordinary helping behavior, but not to helping in disaster emergencies, such as a flood. The researchers believe that the social reinforcements one gets for helping in disasters probably control that helping, while helping in everyday situations is supported by religious reinforcements. Frequency of church attendance was related to helping in disaster, however. The researchers attribute this to the church's providing people with organizational means of such helping, that is, a knowledge of what is needed and how to do it.

Religious Orientation and Emergency Helping

Procedure   Batson (1976b) studied helping behavior in relation to three religious orientations: seeing religion as a means to other ends (extrinsic), seeing it as an end in itself (intrinsic), or seeing it as quest (search for answers to personal and social crises). (These religious orientations will be discussed further in Chapters 20 and 22.) He assessed 40 seminary students on these religious orientations and a measure of doctrinal orthodoxy. Subjects were later confronted with a shabbily dressed man slumped in a doorway near an alley through which they had to pass, alone and at different times.

Findings   Sixteen seminarians (40%) stopped to help; religious orientation was not related to whether or not one stopped. Some seminarians persisted in trying to help even when the man assured them he was okay and wished to be left alone; others offered more tentative help, and withdrew at the man's request. Tentative helpers scored significantly higher on the quest orientation and lower on doctrinal orthodoxy than persistent helpers. Persistent helpers tended to see religion as an end in itself.

Interpretation   The more tentative helpers—who scored high on religion as quest—were responsive to the "victim's" statements about his needs and wishes. Their helping thus seemed more appropriate to the situation. The persistent helpers—seeing religion as an end, and high in orthodoxy—seemed to decide that the man needed particular kinds of help they could offer, and would not abandon this opinion. Batson concluded that religiousness (as end) might not be helpful in situations where responsiveness to the particular quality of a situation is needed. It might encourage unsuitably zealous and determined behavior.

Summary

Reports of general relationships between emergency helping behavior and a variety of religious practices are conflicting; thus the relationships are likely to be complex. Religiousness may influence "private" kinds of emergency helping more than it does helping in public or large-scale emergencies. The style of one's religiousness appears to influence style of helping, though perhaps is not related to whether one helps or not. More orthodox and devotional believers are likely to be more indiscriminate and persistent in helping than are those who adopt a searching and questioning religious stance.

REVIEW OF KEY CONCEPTS

Research in Dogmatism
> confounding of denominational differences
> dogmatism and conservatism
> distinguishing dogmatism and orthodoxy
> relationship of dogmatism and orthodoxy

Guilt and Moral Judgment
> Catholics' evaluation of their church's opinion
> Protestants and guilt
> differences in evaluation of personal ethics
> Catholics and sex concerns

chapter *18*

Achieving Integrated Religiousness

We live in an existential vacuum when we lack personal purpose in life. "Human being fades away unless it commits itself to some freely chosen meaning" (Frankl, 1962b, p. 100). Frankl calls the resulting neurotic symptoms a "noogenic neurosis"—disturbance in a person's spiritual and aspirational characteristics. In this chapter we look at some ways to achieve integrated religiousness, a healthy foundation for purpose and commitment in one's life.

KEEPING A FAITH

One student burst into tears after a class in which faith was discussed. She explained that another professor had "accused" her of "needing" religious belief when she made some comment about religion several years before. Since that time, she had been trying to rid herself of this "unbecoming" need. She said that William James had made it "respectable" for her to believe again, and now she was going to return to her faith. While many people readily accept the reasonableness of other needs—sex, security, achievement, friendship—this story illustrates that religious or spiritual needs are often considered inappropriate for educated people.

Need for Meaning

Joseph Campbell defines myth as a story or "symbol that evokes and directs psychological energy" (Clarke, 1972, p. 50). Although a myth need not be historically factual to carry its meaning, it should not be considered a fantasy or an erroneous opinion. Our myths offer us an understanding of the world around us, provide rituals that support the social order, awaken our sense of awe and mystery, and guide us through the stages of life. "A great many Christian theologians make an effort to prove that religious faith itself is a 'rational act,' [though] nobody ever arrived at faith . . . from a process of reasoning" (Lepp, 1963, p. 2). The truth in myth stands outside historical fact, scientific demonstration, or logical deduction.

How can one find a myth that works? William James's solution (Chapter 13) was to acknowledge that prior wishes, hopes, learning history, behavior, culture, all influence one's ability to believe or disbelieve anything. His recommendation—to act as if one already believes what one wants to believe—sounds radical. Many people might object that they would simply be brainwashing themselves, or painting themselves into a corner. James would probably not argue strongly against this criticism. He would simply point out that it is going to happen anyway; whatever behavior you choose to follow will influence your later beliefs. In his way, you can consciously help determine what kind of beliefs you will adopt. You decide on a world view in which to invest, and it will become increasingly important to you. An individual's accepted beliefs provide working hypotheses for guiding life and a framework of meaning that helps shape daily decisions. The more one does this, the more "real" the guiding world view becomes.

Keeping Self-honesty

If we realize that we are programming ourselves into certain beliefs by the way we behave, how can we stay honest with ourselves in our beliefs? How can we determine whether or not we are believing something simply because we want to believe it, because it makes us feel good? We probably can never completely reassure ourselves about this, and perhaps we had best simply acknowledge that some of this satisfaction is probably involved in every choice or rejection of beliefs.

Yet honesty requires that one be willing to examine beliefs. Carl Jung (1965) repeatedly faced his doubts and insecurities about the religiousness his family taught him—often with great fear. He believed in letting symbols "speak" to him, and refused to "translate" them literally or in some preconceived fashion. In doing so, he discarded some particular beliefs, but his underlying faith deepened.

Allowing oneself to doubt has a creative role in religious life. It keeps us aware of our human limitedness. Challenging our assumptions helps beliefs stay alive and vital to us and keeps us from worshiping our religious symbols instead of what they stand for. People who avoid doubt limit their freedom by seeking a dehumanizing certainty. A deepening faith does not need to hold tightly to particular beliefs. "A particular belief serves as a vehicle for spiritual growth; when it ceases to stimulate growth, it needs to be released" (Kaplan, 1978, p. 38).

Living with Insecurity

For Alan Watts (1951), the answer lay in learning to live with insecurity. He claimed that the world's great religious leaders, such as the Christ (the "anointed one") and the Buddha (the "enlightened one"), lived in this way. Unfortunately, their followers often try to capture in creeds and codes those very truths that they taught could not be so captured. Watts pointed out that if you try to save or hold your breath, you lose it; trying to hold onto it securely brings about its loss. Or, "one who aims at life achieves death" (*Tao Te Ching*, 50). (See also Luke 9 : 23–24; John 12 : 24–26.) The search for security can lead to distortion of truth, and it makes impossible the deeper understandings of a tried and tested faith.

When we refuse to examine religious beliefs, we attempt to hold onto something that we think we already know, or try to confirm our own sense of certainty. Seeking God in this way is asking that our own preconceived ideas about the unknown be "certified" for us, that God be exactly as we insist God is. To learn anything new, to avoid the error of demanding that reality conform to our expectations, we must be willing to have particular beliefs disconfirmed. Since no one human being possesses the totality of truth, this is a reasonable humility. Understanding that faith is a choice and a risk can prepare us to "bet" an entire lifetime on the values we want actualized in our lives. Such a position can sustain us by the probability that faith can give birth to these values (Allport, 1950). To deepen faith, we must tolerate ambiguity and avoid magical thinking and security seeking (Oates, 1973).

MANAGING GUILT

Unresolved guilt has many negative effects on a person. Beyond its emotional discomfort, some psychologists believe it can lead to such psychiatric symptoms as depression and distortion of reality.

Developing a Mature Conscience

Some people have overly severe consciences, and feel great guilt for unimportant faults. Since these feelings come from one's understanding of the moral code taught one—however distorted it may be—revising judgment about conscience matters is often very difficult and painful. Accepting the opinions of well-informed clergy still may not resolve the emotional upheaval involved. Psychotherapy may enable some people to reduce excessive guilt.

Overly scrupulous people, with impossible moral expectations of themselves, are highly self-centered. They set themselves above the common run of people, trying to prove their own superiority—to themselves, others, or God. Often they have a deeper, more basic sense of guilt, which they suppress by concern with petty matters. Recognition of the real deeper guilt can alleviate the scrupulosity. Often this unrecognized guilt is concerned with the very pride that keeps them overly preoccupied with themselves.

Other people have underdeveloped consciences and allow themselves questionable behavior. The underlying guilt they are denying may lead to suffering from a poor self-concept, feelings of inadequacy or inferiority, or depression. Others convince themselves that they are unique people for whom ordinary rules do not apply. They are able to exempt themselves from any moral guideline that would curb their freedom.

People with conscience disorders can sometimes help themselves. It requires painful self-honesty and willingness to accept outside opinions from knowledgeable people. Sometimes also they must refuse to agree with others' narrow judgments. Counselors skilled in pastoral work can help them see where they are too severe or too lax in their opinions. Both religion and psychotherapy offer helpful tactics to manage guilt.

Confession and Guilt

Confession, a time-honored religious practice, is also an integral aspect of much psychotherapy. Secrets—especially those that leave one feeling guilty—work against personal integration. James's highly valued confession: "For [one] who confesses, shams are over and realities have begun; [one] has exteriorized [one's] rottenness. If [one] has not actually got rid of it, [one] at least no longer smears it over with a hypocritical show of virtue" (James, 1902/1961, p. 360).

Not all approaches to confession are equally helpful. Too often religious confession fails to be functional (Mowrer, 1961, 1964). The ritual is often an empty, quickly performed formality. It is done secretly to a confessor who will carefully guard the secret, rather than to significant other people—especially wronged others. Penances typically do not disrupt established bad habits or provide a basis for establishing new ones. They seldom provide for adequately repairing the harm done; instead, the practice of absolution may "remove" the individual's responsibility for correcting the effects of misdeeds. Jung (1933) similarly argued that confession in psychotherapy provides only temporary relief, unless it results in character transformation.

"Integrity therapy" (Drakeford, 1967), developed from Mowrer's ideas, defines a therapeutic confession as one that drops all sham and pretense, withholding nothing out of shame. Although confession may initially be made to only one person, one must become willing to acknowledge failings to the important other people in one's life. The focus must be on one's weaknesses rather than strengths, and one is not allowed to excuse oneself or blame others for the problems. One must be willing to listen to the judgment of others about oneself—including recommendations for reparation and behavior change.

Avoiding Unresolved Guilt

Mowrer (1961, 1964) described the steps by which a person acquires unresolved guilt. First, one behaves in some way that violates one's standards. If one openly acknowledges the wrong action and repents, no lasting problems result. However, most people react with hypocritical secrecy; they present a face to other people that they know is a sham. Finally, the burden of secret guilt becomes so unbearable that they develop symptoms that broadcast the problem to others. Neurotic symptoms are thus an involuntary confession of guilt. Mowrer feels that people who become neurotic from guilty secrets at least have enough moral character to punish themselves for unacknowledged guilt. Those who can live with secret guilt without emotional disturbances are morally less well developed.

Mowrer's prescription for guilt-free living reverses this process. We should promptly acknowledge faults, and try to make up for them. We also should keep secret some good things we do instead of making sure that everyone knows all about them. We shall then have good, not guilty, secrets. Since our secrets determine what we think about ourselves, this way of living gives us good self-esteem and freedom from guilt. Mowrer notes that this idea is reflected in Christian scripture (see Matthew 6).

Mowrer (1961, 1964) considers Alcoholics Anonymous (AA) the contemporary movement that most captures the spirit of early Christianity. In AA—and the other "Anonymous" programs—one openly acknowledges failures, confesses, and actively works to repair harm done. Members of AA commit themselves to an examined life, admit mistakes and need for help, and help others as they have been helped.

CONDUCTING LIFE

Several years ago, "The devil made me do it" blazed across the front of a popular T-shirt. When done seriously, this kind of blame projection reflects low-level ego development (Chapter 4). "Too often religion is used to dull consciousness and to displace responsibility, rather than as a life style which enables us to be fully human" (Woodruff, 1978, p. 32). An integrated religiousness requires one to take responsibility for oneself.

Self-responsibility

William Glasser, who has worked with delinquents, criminals, and the insane, developed "reality therapy." This approach requires individuals to take control of their lives and assume responsibility for their outcomes. One is not allowed to blame problems on heredity, illness, other people, or circumstances. All problems are interpreted as due to the person's own irresponsibility (Glasser, 1965). "The individual becomes more responsible by gaining an increased ability to acknowledge . . . faults, to exercise . . . freedom of choice, and to respond to [a] situation in a fitting way" (Aden, 1979, p. 164).

Self-discipline

Discipline is unappealing to many people, yet without it an integrated religiousness is impossible. William James said that the hell theologians talk about can be no worse than that which people fashion for themselves when they habitually develop their characters in the wrong way (Allen, 1967).

Discipline, however, can be misplaced or growth-inhibiting. It is not likely to be helpful if it is motivated mainly by fear, encourages denial of feelings, operates indiscriminately, is not associated with clear objectives, or leaves one feeling victimized. Feeling guilty or threatened when omitting a discipline also signifies inappropriate self-discipline. Adaptive discipline is not a means of avoiding psychological pain, but primarily reflects a desire to realize chosen values. It operates flexibly, though with sustained effort. Taylor (1962) discusses some dangers of discipline in a Christian perspective.

Some people have trouble effecting self-discipline. Three main obstacles to self-discipline are: parental spoiling, perfectionism, and feelings of inferiority (Hauck, 1976). Spoiled people have not learned to postpone gratifications. Others avoid self-discipline because they are strongly driven to meet perfectionistic standards in everything they do; they will not undertake anything until they consider complete success likely. Still others constantly judge themselves, focus on their faults, and consider themselves inferior, draining energy from more productive tasks. Hauck's *How To Do What You Want To Do* (1976) is an excellent manual of self-discipline.

Self-management

Many self-help books are devoted entirely to problems of self-management. (For example, see Martin & Poland, 1980; Rudestam, 1980; Watson & Tharp, 1977; or Williams & Long, 1979.) While all psychotherapies try to improve self-management, behaviorally oriented therapies especially emphasize it. We shall briefly review two such approaches.

Behavior Modification   Attempts at behavior modification typically follow definite patterns. They first define the goal sought. Then they specify the target behaviors necessary to reach the goal. Self-observation and self-monitoring record the frequency of both desired and incompatible behaviors. Next a particular plan to increase the frequency of target behaviors is worked out, based on sound psychological knowledge. This may involve self-punishment, self-reward, avoidance of particular situations, or the seeking of others' assistance. Both the antecedent conditions that draw one to particular behaviors and the consequences of one's acts are important. A program is often revised after it is evaluated for effectiveness. A serious student can make great progress by personal efforts and the help of a behavior modification book. Available books discuss a wide range of addictive and compulsive behaviors, including smoking, overeating, impulsive buying, poor studying, exercise, underassertiveness, and some sexual compulsions.

Mind Control   A second major approach involves controlling mental contents. (Recall William James on will in Chapter 15.) Available techniques include changing one's use of language, restructuring ways of understanding or interpreting life events, self-instruction techniques, thought stopping, altering expectancies, and engaging in positive self-talk. Propst (1980) developed a mind control technique using a person's religious imagery to make desired changes. Books are available to help individuals wanting to work by themselves. (See DiCaprio, 1976; Ellis & Harper, 1976; and Maltz, 1975.)

Some Life Conduct Guidelines

Many people asked Abraham Maslow how to actualize themselves. He always advised them that self-actualization is a by-product of living one's life appropriately; it cannot be achieved by working directly for it. He suggested several general guidelines. (1) Attend fully and selflessly to whatever you are doing at any time. (2) When in any doubt at all, be honest. (3) Recognize and acknowledge your feelings and impulses. (4) Know your own psychological defenses and strip yourself of them. (5) Make growth choices instead of fear-based ones. (6) Choose worthwhile activities and attempt to do them well. (7) Be open to and appreciate moments of ecstasy. (8) Do not "desacralize" (discount the value of what you cannot achieve); do not be ashamed to see things "under the aspect of eternity" (Maslow, 1971a, pp. 45–50). These rules for psychological development resemble various religious teachings.

A yogic source (Arya, 1976) offers guidelines for decision making in doubtful cases. (1) Consult the scriptures of your tradition, recognizing the dangerous possibility of interpreting them to say what you wish. (2) Consult with spokespersons of your tradition, realizing that you may be inclined to choose leaders who will say what you wish to hear. (3) Bearing in mind—but not slavishly accepting—what you learned in the first two steps, ask yourself if "down-deep" you truly feel right about the action. (4) If your answer is yes, then be certain you are willing to pay, *without resentment,* the cost of the action.

LEARNING TO LOVE

Without a doubt, love is the most commonly urged religious attitude. Many traditions summarize their entire teaching in statements about love. Unfortunately, some people have mistaken ideas about love, or lack necessary knowledge to be loving.

Misplaced Efforts to Love

Compulsive Do-Gooding   When people strongly wish to do good, they can easily lose sight of the unique needs of those they seek to serve. Remember the devout seminarians studied by Batson who were so involved in their efforts to meet another's presumed need that they could not recognize when their help was unwanted. The motives that underlie compulsive do-gooding are not appropriate to integrated religiousness. One's "compulsive desire to do good hides only superficially [a] need to be wanted, and [the] basically insensitive attitude and lack of acceptance of other people becomes apparent" (Hooker, 1977, p. 65).

Enabling   Another misplaced love is enabling. People frequently tolerate bad behavior from others without demanding change. Many alcoholics and brutal, insensitive, or ungrateful people are accepted with kindness and support by loved ones, who see such acceptance as their religious duty. This inadvertently reinforces bad behavior, since there are no consequences for it. Many enablers bolster their own self-esteem by being martyrs, justifying by religion this destructive choice. Therapists who work with alcoholics or abusers recommend to their families "tough love," which insists upon signs of behavior improvement for one's continuing in the relationship. This provides motivation for improvement, and releases the accepting person from the misguided martyr role.

Starting to Love

Overcoming Obstacles   Fear that prevents loving makes one expect hostility from others. It encourages self-protective defenses such as withdrawal, suspiciousness, or dishonesty. A fear-driven person is self-centered, and cannot see things from another's viewpoint. When people establish antagonistic relationships, they tend to avoid each other. This "autistic hostility" (Newcomb, 1947) restricts opportunities for communication and experiences that could resolve fear and hostility. Some scriptural passages (e.g., Matthew 5 : 25ff) apparently recognize this and urge people to take the first step in reconciling differences with others.

Inadequate gratification of other needs, low frustration tolerance, and lack of healthy self-love make one less able to love others (Jourard, 1974). Skill in expressing love is related to general competence, contact with reality, and degree of emancipation from parents. Without a healthy self-structure, reasonable ideals, and a high valuation of love, one cannot love effectively. Helpful books such as *How To Be Your Own Best Friend* (Newman & Berkowitz, 1971) are widely available. Although one can explore these issues by oneself, in some cases a therapist may help.

Prerequisite Attitudes   Fromm said love is an art that must be practiced. Any art requires certain prerequisite attitudes: self-discipline, concentration, patience, and a strong concern with mastery of the art. Fromm's *The Art of Loving* (1956) suggests ways to establish such attitudes and others more specific to loving itself. One must be humble enough to be objective about oneself. One must have faith in both the other person and oneself—a conviction of one's own and others' goodness. Faith in ourselves lets us trust that our love for others will endure. Faith in others is based on awareness of their potentials; it does not mean overlooking their faults. Loving requires the courage to risk, and to accept pain and disappointment. Acquisition of such attitudes does not come by wishing alone, but by sustained practice.

Some Tactics for Loving

Given appropriate attitudes and absence of serious obstacles, how does one begin to love effectively? Since fear puts distance between people, establishing trust is important. Be open in sharing yourself with others and allow them to talk openly about themselves without fear of your reaction. When you disapprove of others' behavior, be sure they realize that does not mean rejection of them as persons. Listen, and offer warmth and empathy; you don't have to solve problems. Finally, be consistent and make no promises you cannot keep.

Love and hate beget like attitudes in others. Sorokin (1971) found that between 65 and 80% of friendly or hostile approaches to others drew a similar response. He taught students with antagonisms toward others to practice doing good deeds for the others. Within 3 months, this practice had turned many hostile relationships into friendly ones. This is consistent with research in altruistic behavior (Staub, 1978), which shows both giving and receiving kindness can lead to liking.

RELIGIOUS PRACTICE AND PERSONAL INTEGRATION

Religious practices may be engaged in either productively or regressively. Some specific religious practices can be related to issues of personal integration.

Traditional Practices

Earlier chapters have shown how prayer can enhance serenity. Similarly, meditative practices—developing attitudes of self-emptying, receptive waiting, and patience—open one to whatever fruits of the religious search may come. Confession, properly used, can offer self-knowledge, relief from guilt, and the motivation for necessary life changes. However, engaging in religious practices with the goal of obtaining personal rewards greatly diminishes the positive effects. As means of giving oneself to religious value, however, they often produce remarkably integrating effects.

Rational Ritual

Religious ritual can be put to obsessive use (Freud, 1907). Although some people practice rituals out of fear and anxiety, rituals also can serve growth. The rational use of ritual "expresses strivings which are recognized as valuable by the individual" (Fromm, 1950/1967, p. 105). In group celebration of shared values, one expresses solidarity with others of like mind. This strengthens the community and offers support in living a religious life. Religious community points to "the possibility of a new age in which people discover themselves again as members of the human family, and . . . find healing and peace, as well as new incentives for living" (Meserve, 1977, p. 79).

Summary

Although all human institutions have flaws, religious teachings in many traditions also foster mental health. We have cited numerous Christian sources, likely to be familiar to most of our readers. Jewish teachings also encourage "open-mindedness and a search for knowledge, self-discipline and self-acceptance, and an appreciation of the value of life, social relationships, and virtues of all human beings" (Goodnick, 1977). Similar attitudes are found in all major religions.

    Ideally, religious works integrate the individual who engages in them. In the last analysis, the fruits produced by an individual's religion provide the bases for judging the religiousness. An integrated religiousness should produce serenity rather than worry, productive striving rather than guilt, a sustaining faith that offers meaning to one's life, and the capacity to love others and direct oneself according to chosen values.

REVIEW OF KEY CONCEPTS

Keeping a Faith
    noogenic neurosis
    functions of myth
    beliefs as working hypotheses
    the creative role of doubt
    the search for security in belief

Managing Guilt
    scrupulosity and self-centeredness
    underdeveloped conscience
    William James on confession
    nonfunctional confession
    integrity therapy
    neurotic symptoms as confession of guilt
    self-esteem and one's secrets

Conducting Life
    blame projection and ego development

reality therapy
adaptive self-discipline
the practice of behavior modification
mind control techniques
how to self-actualize
yogic directives for decision making

Learning to Love
motives behind compulsive do-gooding
"tough love" and enabling
autistic hostility
prerequisite attitudes for the art of loving
establishing trust in relationships
Sorokin's method of overcoming antagonisms

Religious Practice and Personal Integration
obsessive versus rational ritual
the fruits of integrated religiousness

four

CHARACTERISTICS AND MEASUREMENT OF RELIGIOUSNESS

Ways of Being Religious

What does it mean to be religious? Your answer is likely quite different from that given by the next person. We tend to think of religiousness as what we ourselves do when we are religious. Yet we recognize different religions, and admit that their members are also religious in some way. In this chapter, we study religious differences by considering basic religious attitudes, not by looking at socially defined groups such as particular faith traditions.

THE INDIVIDUAL AND THE INSTITUTION

A major distinction is between institutional and individual ways of being religious. For some people, religion means observing a community's rituals and dogmas, and for others it means following one's own unique path as one works it out. Box 19.1 summarizes some understandings of these opposing positions, which are discussed below.

Personal and Inherited Religion

Walter Clark (1958) described three types of religiousness according to the immediacy of the individual's religious experience. "Primary religious behavior" rests on one's inner experiences of the divine—akin to mysticism—combined with efforts to harmonize one's life with those experiences. Intense religious involvement characterizes this stance.

"Secondary religious behavior" approximates this fervor. Perhaps the individual at one time had an intense experience that led to new habits and the assumption of certain religious obligations that continue to modify how she or he

---

Box 19.1 INSTITUTIONAL AND INDIVIDUAL RELIGIOUS STANCES

Institutional stance	Theorist	Individual stance
Tertiary religiousness	Clark	Primary religiousness
Adhesion religion	Nock	Conversion religion
Priest/ecclesiastic	Maslow	Prophet-mystic-peaker
Observing a religion	Dewey	Being religious
Authoritarian religion	Fromm	Humanistic religion
"Secondary accretions"	James	Deep personal experience

Source: Clark (1958), Dewey (1934), Fromm (1950), James (1902), Maslow (1964), Nock (1961).

lives. However, secondary religiousness is somewhat routine and uninspired. "Tertiary religious behavior," the most common type, is accepted on somebody else's authority. The early religious behavior of children is tertiary, and for many adults it remains the only religiousness experienced. Tertiary religious observance is a rather mechanical product of imitation and conditioning.

Chosen and Habitual Religion

A distinction between conversion and adhesion religion makes similar points (Nock, 1961). "Adhesion religion" consists of communal practices endorsed by one's society. Such religion is part of the cultural context within which a person develops and is usually adopted without much reflection. Adhesion religion is static and fixed; usually it focuses on specific practices that mark life's progress. This religion of "public order" serves group needs and involves time-honored traditions that may be laden with high emotional value.

"Conversion religion" occurs when one stakes everything on a new life, inspired by a message that demands renunciation of previous ways. This chosen stance produces a dramatic reorientation of life. Based on awareness of deeply personal needs, this dynamic choice has a life-pervading ardor and commitment. Often the choice sets one at odds with established traditions.

Prophets and Priests

Abraham Maslow's (1964) prophet-mystic-peaker has had very intense first-hand religious experience. This individual is usually a solitary person who finds it hard to fit into the existing religious orthodoxies. Prophets and founders of new religions are of this type, and they often suffer persecution and misunderstanding at the hands of established traditions. Maslow believed that institutional religion often makes it difficult—if not impossible—to have such genuinely personal religious experience, although, left to themselves, most people would be capable of it.

The priest or ecclesiastic is the conservative element in religion "who is loyal to the structure of the organization which has been built up on . . . the prophet's original revelation . . . to make the revelation available to the masses" (Maslow, 1964, p. 21). These people cast the revelation into a form suitable for "mass consumption"—a program of "concretized symbols," often offered to followers with the advice that its acceptance is essential for spiritual well-being. Intensely loyal to the organization itself, true priests feel threatened when people have first-hand intense religious experiences that may wean them away from the institution.

Being Religious and Observing a Religion

According to Dewey (1934), truly religious people submit themselves to an ideal that comes from personal experience and pervades all of life. Their faith is in intelligence, truth, and human powers—rather than in the official representatives of a tradition. Religious people have deep, personal convictions of the values they espouse, and their faith involves moral consequences as well as intellectual assent.

They seek to unify themselves with values, reaching beyond the "actual" to attain a better "possible."

In contrast, those who simply observe a religion stress obedience and reverence, a fear-motivated morality, and servile dependence. Endorsing institutional practices relative to the conditions of society and culture, such people appear encumbered by history and tradition. Their institutions offer followers security and peace, exerting an emotional hold on them. Since they believe that their system has a monopoly on ideals, accommodating oneself to the system is very important. Such people adhere to the "actual" with no desire to reach out for more.

Authoritarian and Humanistic Religion

Fromm's (1950) distinction between authoritarian and humanistic religion (see Chapter 14) describes similar stances. Authoritarian religion is likely to develop when people are subjugated and accustomed to dependency. It is inevitable when religion allies with secular power. When individuals feel free and responsible, humanistic religion—with an emphasis on self-realization—may develop.

Experience and "Accretions"

James considered dogmas, creeds, and rituals "secondary accretions" to real religion, which is found in deep personal experience of the divine. Such experience, however, "spontaneously and inevitably engenders myths, superstitions, dogmas, and metaphysical theologies, and criticisms of one set of these by the adherents of another" (James, 1902/1961, p. 339). Such "accretions" often turn God into a "metaphysical monster which . . . is an absolutely worthless invention of the scholarly mind" (1902/1961, p. 349). James thus considered most institutional manifestations of religion an "absurd" distortion of this "most important" endeavor that religion is.

SOME RELIGIOUS AND SPIRITUAL PATHS

Some scholars offer more complex discussions of ways of being religious. Their typologies typically consider both individual and institutional spiritual paths, often related to the psychological functions of thinking, feeling, and choosing ways to behave.

Pictures on the Curtain

Erwin Goodenough (1965) outlined eight major ways to define the essence of religiousness. All but the last of these (mysticism) are "curtains" we use to shield ourselves from encountering Ultimate Reality. On the curtains we paint "pictures of divine or superhuman forces or beings that control the universe and us, as well as codes of ethics, behavior, and ritual" (Goodenough, 1965, p. 8). These pictures give us an illusion of control and security. No one picture exists in isolation, but each reflects what some people emphasize in religion.

Legalism Legalism tries to solve the problem of making decisions about behavior by specifying exactly what is expected of the individual. We need not make personal decisions when we have a code that dictates what to do in any situation. Legalism works best where there are few diverse elements in the population, and the good person simply obeys its laws. When everyone agrees with a code, considering it absolute is much easier. For instance, monasteries and ashrams sometimes provide small societies where one law of life is unanimously adopted.

Psychologically, legalism makes life more peaceful by resolving many uncertainties. People find great security in the comfort of knowing that they are right with God when they conform strictly to the code. All people have some tendency toward legalism; Judaism and Christianity contain especially strong currents of it. To many people, legalistic morality and religion mean the same thing. Legalists follow the letter of the law, since such codes represent the essence of religion for them. For other people, laws of conduct are only one important part of religion.

Supralegalism In supralegalism—going above or beyond legalism—"the demands of the codes of society are by no means totally flouted. But . . . a higher law with a greater power and dignity takes over on more important matters" (Goodenough, 1965, p. 104). This higher law sometimes makes demands that do not agree with established morality.

Goodenough considers Jesus a supralegalist, although most of his followers accept a legalistic code based on only some of his sayings. Most supralegalists' followers try to make legalisms of their teachings. When this happens, some teachings become laws while others are disregarded in an apparently arbitrary fashion. Most Christian churches take Jesus' teachings on divorce very seriously, but ignore those on pacifism and self-mutilation, which are just a few sentences away in the scriptures (Goodenough, 1965).

In the Sermon on the Mount, Jesus may have been trying to illustrate the utter impossibility of living legalistically; "the law, as law, is made so all-inclusive that we can never get any satisfaction from it, for we disobey it constantly" (Goodenough, 1965, p. 107). The "safe road is the road of legalism, but all moral progress has come from supralegalists" (1965, p. 118). However, since supralegalism works against the interests of organized religion—witness the difficulties Jesus had with the established tradition of his times!—it was inevitable that an institution founded on Jesus would establish legalistic codes.

Orthodoxy Orthodoxy is concerned with belief in the correct things. Most people get their beliefs from existing ones in their society. Some accept those closest at hand—what their parents taught them—while others search for an absolutely certain and indisputable body of belief. In orthodoxy, people find security in the conviction that their beliefs are the right ones, guaranteed to be Truth. "The common denominator among the orthodox of all kinds is not what they believe, but that they have accepted a pattern of thought as true" (Goodenough, 1965, p. 124).

Orthodox tendencies lie deep in human nature, since we need beliefs to give meaning to our lives. Living with uncertainty is very difficult. The savage treatment given heretics reflects the painful insecurity that the orthodox suffer when their beliefs are challenged. Many people center their entire concept of religion on orthodoxy, on holding "true" beliefs. The beliefs to which *they* subscribe constitute the essence of religion.

Supraorthodoxy Supraorthodoxy "usually begins with an emotional experience, but quickly comes to express itself as an idea" (Goodenough, 1965, p. 127). From the experience, one builds personal conceptions about the nature of reality and the meaning of life. Supraorthodoxy characterizes those persons who refuse to take orthodox religious explanations as a basis for their own understanding, and then create for themselves some other intellectual framework. The Buddha, Spinoza, and Kierkegaard are some prominent supraorthodox individuals. "Supraorthodoxy is religious security that arises . . . from one's own intellectual creativity in metaphysics or theology" (Goodenough, 1965, p. 135).

Aestheticism Aestheticism seeks to impose form on experience and promote security in a sense of beauty. Some people create artistic forms, while some appreciate others' creations. Aesthetic religiousness can use many forms including art, literature, the dance, ritual sex, and music. Responses range from frenzied involvement to quiet appreciation. Although seeing aestheticism as religion's essence is not common in Western culture—especially in its more intense manifestations—many people acknowledge its importance to them. In worship services, aesthetic elements play a large part in many organized religions. Fewer people take the more individualized approach of considering aesthetic experience the essence of religion.

Symbolism and Sacramentalism "Symbolism and sacrament may be discussed together because both find their goals through an object or act in the material world itself, though not by . . . aestheticism" (Goodenough, 1965, p. 143). The object or act represents more than what meets the eye; it is one's God at work in the world. To the outsider, someone eats a small wafer of bread; to the person eating that wafer, divinity is contained in it, and by the act of eating it, one becomes related to that divinity.

People to whom sacrament is foreign sometimes call it superstition or idolatry. Yet many people have some urge to make tangible the Divine or sacred. Sacrament is a more "contained" religious expression than direct aesthetic religiousness. Particularly in times of stress, many people find themselves drawn toward religious holy objects and symbolic activity. For some people, they represent the essence of religion.

The Church The church may be "taken as a corporate body, superior to the individual, itself the medium of revelation, in which the individual can find divine guidance, protection, and the means of grace" (Goodenough, 1965, p. 147). Affiliation with a church group and subordination of oneself to its hierarchy become, for some people, the core of religion—their way of establishing safe contact with the "Beyond." Many members of various religious or political groups hold that salvation comes from membership in and obedience to the one, true, and proper organization—their own. Viewing such an identification as the essence of religion is much more common to Western than Eastern religion.

Mysticism   Mysticism is an attempt to identify oneself directly with the Holy or Divine, rather than using behavior, beliefs, objects, actions, or membership to accomplish this. "Always the most devout people have gone beyond these patterns; they have identified themselves with the sources of the patterns and so have risen above the human path of conformity" (Goodenough, 1965, pp. 151–152). Mystics achieve their end when all religious formulations lose their value. In the complete loss of human categories, they find the "All and Only" of reality.

Four Paths of Yoga

Yoga describes four major paths of spiritual development, each of which is manifest in religions around the world (Johnson, 1953; Naranjo, 1972). Although an individual may specialize in a particular path as most suited to him or her, all paths contain elements of the others.

The Way of Action   Called *karma yoga* in the Hindu tradition, the way of action emphasizes "right conduct"—behavior in accord with one's *dharma* (literally, that which contains one's true being). All religious traditions require a certain basic morality as a necessary starting point for right conduct, though they emphasize different features of conduct and suggest different practices for those who want to do more than the minimum required.

Western religions urge development of traditional virtues and a more stringent observance of such moral precepts as the Ten Commandments. In monasteries and ashrams, members adopt a group's rule of life, which adds special precepts and practices to ordinary moral behavior. People who emphasize such right conduct as a spiritual path may attach undue importance to self-restraint and being "perfect." William James (1902) described the self-centeredness of would-be saints who keep detailed records of both their acts of virtue and their petty faults.

A second way of action, more common in Eastern religion, is "actionless action"—tending to the present moment only, with no concern for the results of one's labor. The Hindu classic, the *Bhagavad-Gītā,* enjoins: "Therefore do thy duty perfectly, without care for the results; for one who does duty disinterestedly attains the Supreme" (III, 19). Also: "In this world people are fettered by action, unless it is performed as a sacrifice. . . . Let thy acts be done without attachment, as sacrifice only" (III, 9).

In a third approach to right conduct, one listens to one's inner voice rather than traditional rules. The teaching "Do not follow in the footsteps of the ancients; seek what they sought" (Naranjo, 1972, p. 56) advises religious people to keep their eyes on their goal rather than on rules for getting there. Church leaders are not fond of such ideas, although many great mystics deviated from the common teachings of their religions when they felt strongly about an issue.

However, abandoning the ordinary path always leaves much room for self-deception. St. Augustine's "Love God and do what you will" assumes that one truly close to God will want to do only what is appropriate.

The Way of Emotion or Love   Western traditions typically encourage devotion to God, a practice called *bhakti yoga* in Hinduism. The *Bhagavad-Gita* quotes Krishna, the incarnate deity, as saying: "The one who sees Me in everything and everything in Me, that one shall I never forsake, nor shall that one lose Me" (VI, 30). The Christian gospel of John contains the same teaching. Such love of God must be shown as love of other people also, lest devout persons sentimentally project all their unfulfilled cravings onto God.

Although *bhakti* is highly respected in some Eastern traditions, another Eastern approach is to transcend emotional reactions. One refuses to allow emotions—particularly negative ones—to develop. One Eastern teacher (Krishnamurti, 1978) says one should simply observe the presence of an emotion ("anger is") instead of identifying with it ("I am angry").

A third approach encourages focus on internal states. One is told to ventilate feelings by such practices as confession of guilt or acknowledgment of fear and anger. Focusing awareness on feelings is supposed to produce liberating breakthroughs. Self-preoccupation and emotional binges are possible pitfalls of this approach.

The Way of Knowledge   The knowledge referred to in the way of knowledge is not "book" or conceptual knowledge, but the knowledge of ultimate mysteries. Western religions cultivate an attitude of faith. The believer adopts a particular religious mythology or set of symbols—assuming their truth—and uses it as a "road map." One follows the map to travel closer to spiritual realities. St. Augustine said, "Understanding is the reward of faith. . . . Unless you make an act of faith you will not understand" (Naranjo, 1972, p. 87). Dangers in this approach include blind belief and dogmatism.

A second knowledge approach, especially emphasized in Buddhism and some *jnāna yoga,* is to strip oneself of all road maps and register bare experience. The seeker tries to understand personal experience without any preconceptions or categories in which to place observations. The mental discipline necessary for this approach is very difficult to cultivate; few people can do it.

A final *jnāna* approach is to develop one's own set of symbols and meanings—creating one's own individual faith, questioning and possibly rejecting much of traditional faiths. The person following this approach runs the risk of being considered psychotic (crazy) in the West, since our society has low tolerance for views of reality out of the ordinary.

The Way of Awareness or Identification   The way of awareness is most common in mystical traditions, where awareness goes by many names. Christian monastics often call it recollection. Eastern traditions refer to mindfulness, remembering, or one-pointedness. This practice may involve maintaining constant awareness of oneself in relation to the divine or one's duty. One may regularly use a mantra or short prayer to encourage identification with Ultimate Reality, or may affiliate with like-minded people for mutual support and encouragement.

Another common Eastern approach is to maintain a "pure" awareness as much as possible, keeping the mind stilled and "contentless." A third way is to maintain full awareness of all ongoing external and internal events. All awareness practices are strongly akin to meditation and help keep one in a meditative frame of mind throughout the day. This is a cardinal point in *rāja yoga,* or the royal path to union with the divine.

Paths of Life

Charles Morris (1942) based his typology of religious approaches on the extent to which they emphasize doing, experiencing, and restraining. Each of the world's major religions—in its purest form—has its own unique specialization. However, not all members—and sometimes not most—of a particular group reflect its ideal characteristics. People typically do not change to a religious group reflecting their own personality type, but try to impose their own attitudes on the group to which they belong.

Buddhist Approach   People high in self-restraining and low in experiencing tendencies find the Buddhist approach appealing. This individualistic approach stresses self-sufficiency, solitude, and reason; one turns action tendencies back upon oneself to learn self-control and detachment from desire. Gautama (the Buddha) is the chief spokesperson for this typically Eastern type of religiousness. It is rarely found in the West except in some monastic traditions and in persons attracted to Eastern religious philosophies.

Dionysian Approach   The Dionysian person is dominated by experiencing tendencies, with low interests in doing. "When this passion to plunge with abandon into the waters of elemental life becomes a center of orientation, it takes on the form of a religion" (Morris, 1942/1973, p. 61) which encourages the explosive release of feelings in intense and dramatic festivals. In orgies, one loses self and merges with nature or other people. Such individualistic celebration with the god of wine and revel is not common in Western religion. Groups with highly emotion-laden services—such as snake handling or frenzied revivals—approach this orientation.

Promethean Approach   The Promethean is an action-oriented person with poorly developed restraining tendencies, "a maker, an inventor, an experimenter, engaged in the continual cooperative reconstruction of the world in which he [or she] operates" (Morris, 1942/1973, p. 102). This type is named for the mythological character who dared to steal fire from the gods for the betterment of humankind. The Promethean person, inherently restless and drawn to action and doing, cannot be committed to dogmas or institutions that stand in the way of accomplishment and development. Although not common in Western religion, Promethean elements dominate Western science and capitalism.

Apollonian Approach   The strongly action-oriented Apollonian minimizes experiencing tendencies. Rational moderation characterizes this approach, named for the god of cultural achievement. Apollonians strongly support existing social structures, are capable administrators, and operate best in a stable society. Morris considers both Chinese Confucianism and contemporary Christianity highly Apollonian in nature, although the latter was not so in its origins.

Christian Approach   Fundamentally and traditionally, the Christian approach emphasizes restraining tendencies, with action tendencies the weakest. Persons with this stance are dominated by a self-depreciating love of God. They subordinate themselves in adoration of God, and put their trust in the power of God's love.

> The individual does not merely follow certain courses of action approved by the society, but he [or she] deliberately and with devotion to others subordinates [her- or] himself, controls [her- or] himself, in order to advance the careers of others [Morris, 1942/1973, p. 131].

Mohammedan Approach   Strong experiencing and weak restraining tendencies mark the Mohammedan approach. Followers live outwardly, without being centered in themselves, and lose themselves in a group united under a strong leader. They consider the group a vehicle of cosmic destiny and pour tremendous energy into achieving its aims and supremacy. They are highly confident and often warlike. Morris considers this the approach taken by Christian Crusaders, early followers of Mohammed, and contemporary Fascists, Nazis, and Communists. "The words and the warriors are different; the patterns and the cycles are as of old" (Morris, 1942/1973, p. 146).

Maitreyan Approach   Morris's final type, named after the "ideal friend" whom the Buddha promised would come, is his notion of "good" religion. Such religiousness blends and balances action, experiencing, and restraining, as well as the social and individual components of religion. Morris considers Taoism to possess much of this attitude, while Hinduism has the tolerance and universalism that it requires. This approach recognizes differences in natural tendencies among people and attempts to balance them, but with great tolerance and acceptance of diversity. Such religiousness transcends the sectarian divisiveness of insistence on certain behaviors, beliefs, codes, rituals, and attitudes. For Morris, this ideal religiousness combines reasonable self-management and a spirit of growth and openness with the celebration of love and support for all people.

Four Spiritual Types

One of our (Meadow, 1978a) models describes a typology of religious styles based on personality characteristics. Two dimensions of personality were crossed with each other to form a model with four types (see Figure 19.1). (Creating such models is discussed and exemplified further in Chapter 22.) The first dimension, introversion-extraversion, describes whether one's attention is primarily oriented to

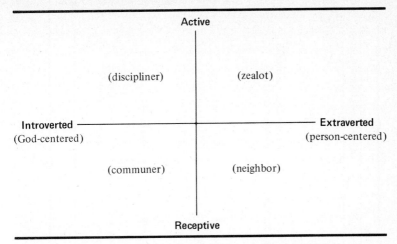

Figure 19.1   Meadow's four spiritual types. (*Source:* Meadow, 1978a.)

the world outside or to inner life—thoughts, feelings, imaginings, insights, etc. The other dimension is an activity-passivity one. Some people's religiousness emphasizes a more active, doing style while others stress more passive, accepting, or receptive virtues.

Active-extraverted "zealots" typically view the order of the world as their vocation. They are devoted to conforming themselves and others to these activist values. They are a variant of a *karma yoga* approach. The receptive-extraverted "neighbors" try to bear witness to religious love, and live a life of compassionate service. Their *bhakti yoga* emphasis is turned toward other people.

The receptive-introverted "communer" is of mystical temperament, likely to follow a *rāja yoga* path. Communers emphasize development of life with God, with preference for time spent alone in prayer or meditation. The active-introverted "discipliner" is highly introspective, tends to deny feelings, strongly develops "will," and prefers to avoid involvement in the world. Their discipline may be intellectual (akin to *jnāna yoga*) or moral.

CONCLUSIONS AND IMPLICATIONS

Contemporary Expressions of the Types

Echoes of the religious paths just outlined exist in many contemporary expressions of religion in America. Box 19.2 presents some in their relations to the four typologies presented.

Individual Paths   Contemporary Western society increasingly tolerates and encourages individual religious paths. Undoubtedly many people privately establish for themselves codes of conduct, ways of experiencing religious feelings, understandings of life, and development of inner life.

Some group trends in individualism can also be observed. Ethical societies—which eschew emotionalism or creedal statements in religion—develop non-

Box 19.2   RELIGIOUS AND SPIRITUAL PATHS

Source	Action	Feeling	Thought	Awareness/identification
			Psychological function	
		Institutional paths		
Goodenough	Legalism	Sacramentalism	Orthodoxy	The church
Morris	Mohammedan	Christian	Apollonian	
Contemporary expression	Messianic cults, People's Temple, Moral Majority	Pentecostal groups, "Hare Krishnas," Divine Light	Jesus People, Unification church	Communes, ashrams, utopian societies
		Mixed paths		
Yoga	Karma yoga	Bhakti yoga	Jnāna yoga	Rāja yoga
Meadow	Zealot	Neighbor	Discipliner	Communer
Morris				Maitreyan
		Individual paths		
Goodenough	Supralegalism	Aestheticism	Supraorthodoxy	Mysticism
Morris	Promethean	Dionysian	Buddhist	
Contemporary expression	Ethical societies, "Religion" of science	Peyote cults, snake handlers, Wicca	Astrological and occult systems, new cosmologies	Imported Eastern practices and meditation

Source: Goodenough (1965), Meadow (1978a), Morris (1942), and various yogic resources.

traditional guides to conduct appropriate to the current world situation. Wiccan (nature/witch religion) groups and peyote cults foster highly individualized and intense religious feelings. Still other people adopt astrological or occult world views as individual belief systems, and groups with unique cosmologies proliferate. People are also adopting and practicing many varieties of meditation and other Eastern religious practices.

Institutional Paths   New religious movements also illustrate institutional paths. Messianic cults focus on action, and see themselves as having an important task; the People's Temple of Jim Jones was essentially a visionary legalistic cult. The Moral Majority emphasizes strict moral controls as a major focus of religiousness.

Such groups as the "Hare Krishnas" and Divine Light Mission, with highly symbolic ritualized practices, cultivate religious feeling in an institutional context. So do many Pentecostal church groups. Some Jesus People groups exemplify neo-orthodoxy. The Unification church demands controlled rational thinking and allegiance to its new orthodoxy. Finally, some people flock to the new "churches" found in communes, ashrams, and other attempts at utopian society.

Evaluation of Religious Diversity

Some religions (such as Buddhism) more strongly emphasize individual elements in religion, while others (such as Judaism) emphasize communal ones. Most have incorporated both tendencies. Roman Empire religion showed an interesting balance between personal and communal emphases, which were maintained by different systems. The state religion was predominantly communal, with the priestly caste carrying out ceremonies on behalf of the populace. The mystery cults that came into Rome from the Orient exemplified a personalized religion, and attracted many citizens (Cumont, 1956).

Need for Diversity   Historically, religious diversity has been important. The great differences we see in religion—the many distinct creeds, rituals, codes, practices, and attitudes—suggests a human need for such. Early training experiences, culture, geography—a great variety of physical, biological, psychological, and social phenomena—shape a person's religious expression. Temperamental and personality differences make diversity necessary within any given religious tradition. Being a Christian or a Jew or a Buddhist does not mean the same thing for all who identify themselves with each group.

The factors that make for such differences within a tradition also make for communalities between traditions. Scholarly people—be they Hindu Brahmins or Roman Catholic Dominican monks—will approach religion in similar fashion. The ardent devotee in one faith will behave much like the ardent devotee in another; the particular form of ritual may be different, but the intense love and longing for one's God—be it Jesus or Krishna—is the same. Tolerance is fostered by recognition of differences existing within one's own tradition, as well as the common basic human tendencies it shares with other traditions.

Individual or Institutional Religion?   Persons who choose individual religion feel a religious obligation to become most fully what their personal vision entails. This demands independence of limiting cultural and social stereotypes and institutions—an approach favored by Maslow (1964), Fromm (1950), Dewey (1934), and James (1902). Some spiritual writers view the attainment of a highly personal religious expression as an indication of spiritual maturity. (This will be discussed further in Chapter 22.) On the other hand, history provides many examples of people whose strongly personal religion bore clear signs of mental and emotional disturbance, resistance to authority, and self-preoccupation.

Many people appreciate the values of institutional religion for the social order. The emphasis on culturally prescribed virtues and the performance of one's duty, as seen by the religious institution, promotes social cohesiveness. Institutions can play an important role in an individual's religious development. Ritual provides opportunity for expressing and strengthening the religious sentiment; shared beliefs and world view offer support. Yet deep involvement with institutional structures is sometimes related to problematic conservatism, fundamentalism, and dependency. A strong institutional orientation may indicate an unhealthy personal need for the security of tight structure, close controls on behavior, and other people to take responsibility for decision making.

Another Factor for Consideration   Motivations for holding either an individual or institutional approach to religion may vary. Some people adhere to institutional religion because they are not sufficiently sophisticated to go beyond it or mature enough to surrender its security. Still other mature and sophisticated individuals remain institutionally involved because they consider religion a communal matter. Some people rebel against institutional demands or are unwilling to acknowledge value outside themselves; others simply need more freedom for their development than institutions can allow, or feel called to a unique path.

In the next chapter, we look at motivations for religious behavior. This work introduces us to the psychometric (measurement-based) assessment of religious dimensions—the approach to studying religion that is the major focus of this unit.

REVIEW OF KEY CONCEPTS

The Individual and the Institution
    Clark's primary, secondary, and tertiary religiousness
    conversion religion and "public order"
    role and loyalties of the "priest" in religion
    contrast between being religious and observing a religion
    creeds and theologies, according to James

Some Religious and Spiritual Paths
    "pictures on the curtain"
    Jesus as supralegalist
    common denominator of orthodox religious people

chapter 20

Religious Motivations— The Intrinsic and Extrinsic Dimensions

INTRODUCTION

The intrinsic and extrinsic religious orientations have produced more research, debate, and controversy than any other dimensions in the psychology of religion. The light generated by the two dimensions has greatly illuminated recent psychological views of religion. We shall describe the intrinsic and extrinsic religious orientations and trace their development in the psychology of religion. Since the concepts are not unique to religion, a sketch of their equivalents in other areas of psychology will clarify the religious dimensions. Finally we shall review research that shows how much light the religious orientations have shed on the relationship of religion to other attitudes and behavior.

Nature of Intrinsic and Extrinsic Religion

The subjects of the present chapter are closely related to two of the basic religious functions we discussed in Chapter 2. The extrinsic religious orientation is concerned primarily with the egocentric functions of religion. The intrinsic relates principally to the value-centered or growth functions. You may have guessed also that objective and subjective forms of prayer and worship discussed in previous chapters are relevant here. Subjective prayer and worship, being centered on the person, reflect an extrinsic motivation for religion. Intrinsic motivations are more at work in objective prayer and worship—focusing as they do on the object of worship. Similarly Maslow's D-needs, which arise out of deficiencies in the person, speak to the extrinsic religious orientation. B (Being)-needs are intrinsic to the person's very being; the need to give love, for example, may exist for its own sake. These ties with needs and motivations indicate that the intrinsic and extrinsic orientations deal basically with the motives or driving forces in people's behavior—in this case their religious behavior.

GENERAL INTRINSIC AND EXTRINSIC MOTIVATIONS

Gordon Allport introduced the terms *intrinsic* and *extrinsic religious orientations* in 1959, but the concepts were foreshadowed in the psychological literature of the 1950s. The following notions all contrast two opposing concepts: one personal orientation toward serving the self or ego, and a contrasting tendency that has a reference outside of the experiencing person. In evaluative terms, psychologists have considered the self-orientation to reflect a degree of maladjustment, whereas the outward-looking orientations have been related to positive mental health.

Task Orientation and Ego Orientation

When some person has been fully engrossed in a job, you may have heard another remark, "Boy, is he (or she) ever ego-involved in golf (or learning Spanish or building sand castles)!" Most psychologists used to think that any extraordinary effort was motivated by a threat to the person's ego or at least by a need to enhance self-worth. Social psychologist Solomon Asch (1952) challenged this notion, distinguishing two kinds of motivation that he called "task-orientation" and "ego-orientation." Some behaviors obviously are oriented toward meeting the person's physical or psychological needs and are appropriately called ego-oriented or egocentric. On the other hand, people frequently approach a task in such a way that the task itself becomes the focus of the behavior; Asch called such behavior task-centered.

A 3-year-old child, for example, insists on doing certain things—opening doors, climbing steps, dressing—by herself or himself. The tasks do not just meet the child's specific needs but appear to be ends in themselves. Consider also children playing. Are they absorbed in the play itself (task-oriented), or are they primarily interested in whether Mother or some other adult is watching and giving praise for the activity (an ego orientation) (Asch, 1952, pp. 300–303)? Asch recognized that our physical and psychological needs demand periodic ego orientation, but he considered the task orientation superior for many occasions. He concluded:

> Task orientation frees one for seeking and understanding situations in their own terms. . . . An attitude of intrinsic interest may provide a more serene relation to the task. . . . In general we would expect a task-oriented person to be more steady and reliable [1952, pp. 311–312].

On the other hand,

> focusing on the self may interfere with giving oneself freely to the task. . . . self-centeredness may inhibit the formation of interest . . . and the ego may simply not be able to furnish the forces for dealing with certain situations [Asch, 1952, pp. 311–312].

Two-Factor Theory of Job Motivation

Similar concepts developed in industrial psychology. In the study of job satisfaction and dissatisfaction Frederick Herzberg (1966; Herzberg, Mausner, & Snyderman, 1959) and his colleagues found that such intrinsic factors as responsibility and professional growth were primarily related to positive job satisfaction. However, workers usually mentioned factors extrinsic to the work itself (security, safety, interpersonal relations, etc.) as most crucial when they were distinctly dissatisfied with their jobs. The dissatisfiers were seldom mentioned as factors in positive satisfaction. Therefore Herzberg concluded that the extrinsic factors could, at best, eliminate bad feelings—not produce positively healthy feelings.

Herzberg had observed, though, that a few workers showed only extrinsic job motivations. He reasoned that such workers did not have the capacity for positive satisfaction or growth experiences on their jobs. Herzberg and Hamlin (1961, 1963) related the intrinsic and extrinsic factors to mental health and mental illness. People who are oriented toward intrinsic incentives (on a job or in other life situations) will achieve positive mental health if their intrinsic and extrinsic needs are met. Even if neither set of needs is satisfied, though, they will not be mentally ill—only unhappy and unfulfilled. However, those who are oriented only toward the extrinsic needs—toward just avoiding bad situations—can never be mentally healthy. If their extrinsic needs are not met, they may become mentally ill, but even if those needs are met, they will still be maladjusted (Herzberg, 1966, pp. 81–91).

Coping and Defending

Two other concepts deal with reactions to the psychological threats that we all experience. Psychoanalysts have long emphasized the "ego-defense mechanisms" (you remember them from introductory psychology—projection, repression, rationalization, etc.). Neo-Freudians or ego psychologists have, by contrast, emphasized coping mechanisms. Norma Haan makes the following distinction: "Coping behavior is distinguished from defensive behavior since the latter by definition is rigid, compelled, reality distorting, and undifferentiated, whereas the former is flexible, purposive, reality oriented, and differentiated" (1965, p. 374). The center of reference for ego-defense mechanisms is the ego or self; coping mechanisms focus on the demands of reality, of the threatening situation or task itself. This perspective suggests their relationship to Asch's ego-centered and task-centered orientations, as well as extrinsic and intrinsic motivations.

Research on Intrinsic and Extrinsic Motivations

Much of the research on intrinsic and extrinsic motivations is reviewed in two books with the title *Intrinsic Motivation* (Day, Berlyne, & Hunt, 1971; Deci, 1975). One early study provided evidence for the mental health implications of the two-factor theory of job motivation. Unimproved schizophrenic mental patients were more extrinsic and less intrinsic than were improved schizophrenic patients and college students (Hamlin & Nemo, 1962). Haywood and Dobbs (1964) studied the relation of intrinsic and extrinsic motivations to the S-R (for stimulus-response) Inventory of Anxiousness among high school boys. Intrinsic motivation was significantly related to tendencies to approach stimulating situations; extrinsic motivation was significantly related to the tendency to avoid such situations. In a similar study intrinsic and extrinsic scores on a Job Motivation Inventory (Kahoe, 1966) were related to items on the California Psychological Inventory for students at a church-related college (Kahoe & Polk, 1971). Box 20.1 shows sample items from the Job Motivation Inventory and representative personality items that were found to be related to intrinsic and extrinsic job motivations. As you can see, intrinsic motivation largely indicated willingness to engage in stimulating activities; extrinsic motivation was largely related to tendencies to feel insecure and to avoid threatening situations.

Jerome Bruner, an educational psychologist, studied coping and defending in normal schoolchildren and in those who had been referred to a clinic for "learning blocks." He discovered that the disturbed children differed from normal children in their approach to school subjects:

Box 20.1   **JOB AND PERSONALITY INVENTORY ITEMS RELATED TO INTRINSIC AND EXTRINSIC MOTIVATIONS**

Intrinsic motivation	Extrinsic motivation
Job Motivation Inventory	
To be placed in charge of a job and see that it is done right.	Working for an organization that is fair to its workers.
Chance to plan and construct things or procedures.	Freedom from danger or pain or injury.
Plenty of chances to develop my professional abilities.	Steady or regular employment.
California Psychological Inventory	
I sometimes feel that I do not deserve as good a life as I have.	The thought of being in an automobile accident is very frightening to me.
I enjoy planning things, and deciding what each person should do.	I don't like things to be uncertain and unpredictable.
I read at least ten books a year.	Sometimes I feel that I am about to go to pieces.

Source: Kahoe and Polk (1971).

> The learning activities of our disturbed children had certain distinctive features that had very little directly to do with the nature of effectiveness. . . . their efforts were to defend themselves from the activity of learning and its consequences [Bruner, 1966, p. 131].

The schoolwork set off conflicts, anxiety, and panic that called for self-defense, utterly displacing normal efforts to cope with the studies.

Other research looked at the relationship between extrinsic and intrinsic motivations. While it might seem that the two are opposites—that any person who is high in one of them would automatically be low in the other—this apparently is not the case. Both with regard to the intrinsic and extrinsic job factors (Kahoe, 1966) and with coping and defending, when we measure them as personality variables, they tend to be independent of one another. That is, they are not consistently related to one another in any way. In Haan's words, "the absence of pathology does not necessarily insure competence" (1965, p. 378).

INTRINSIC AND EXTRINSIC RELIGIOUS ORIENTATIONS

Allport's intrinsic and extrinsic religious orientations may not have been directly influenced by the constructs we have just reviewed. However, their roots do go deep into his own earlier works.

Origins of Intrinsic-Extrinsic Religion Concepts

In *Personality: A Psychological Interpretation* (1937) Allport introduced the concept of *functional autonomy* of motives. At that time most psychologists thought that virtually all human motivation, other than such physical needs as hunger and thirst, were learned. They thought needs for social contact, love, beauty, and religion developed by association with satisfaction of basic physical needs. They also assumed that the learned needs persisted because of their continued association with the physical needs. Allport proposed, however, that while the higher social and value needs may have originated from baser needs, those higher needs could become independent of the physical ones. That is, social contact or beauty could come to be valued in its own right, to supply its own motive forces—in Allport's term, to be "functionally autonomous" of the earlier needs. Now we may apply the term *intrinsic motivation* to drives that produce their own rewards, though we do not necessarily assume that they originate in more basic physical drives.

Allport's *The Individual and His Religion* (1950/1960) listed six characteristics of a mature religion. One was essentially the hallmark of intrinsic religion: the "derivative yet dynamic nature of the mature sentiment." By *sentiment* Allport meant "an organization of feeling and thought directed toward some definable object of value" (p. 63). So a mature religious sentiment, Allport said, becomes "largely independent of its origins, 'functionally autonomous' " (p. 72). Allport made this characteristic his chief criterion of a mature religion. Immature religion, far from being functionally autonomous, "is largely concerned with magical thinking, self-justification, and creature comfort. Thus it betrays its sustaining motives still to be the drives and desires of the body" (p. 72). This aspect of immature religion is, of course, basically the extrinsic orientation.

Allport again distinguished two kinds of religion in *The Nature of Prejudice* (1954). He called the two religious types "interiorized" and "institutionalized" and considered the latter form of religion to be related to ethnic prejudice. These concepts do not correspond precisely to the distinction made in *The Individual and His Religion,* but Allport incorporated them into the later concepts of intrinsic and extrinsic religion.

"The Religious Context of Prejudice" (Allport, 1966) acknowledged the sociologists of religion Herberg (1955) and Lenski (1961) for distinguishing "communal" and "associational" types of religious affiliation. Communal religious affiliation primarily meets sociocultural needs of people, providing a social identification that is as much secular as it is religious. By contrast, associational religious affiliation is primarily for the purposes of religious fellowship—for the sake of religion itself. It is easy to see how these terms reinforced and broadened Allport's extrinsic and intrinsic concepts.

Development of Intrinsic-Extrinsic Religious Concepts

The three major papers in which Allport developed the concepts of intrinsic and extrinsic religious orientations dealt with the relationship of prejudice to religion (1959; 1966; Allport & Ross, 1967). Hunt and King (1971) have traced the growth of the religious orientation concepts through these papers. We shall selectively review Allport's ideas as the intrinsic and extrinsic orientations developed. Box 20.2 cites Allport's formal definitions of the religious orientations from an introduction to his 1959 paper (Allport, 1960) and his last paper on the subject (Allport & Ross, 1967).

With regard to extrinsically religious persons, Allport noted that they frequently do have religious needs, but these needs are met by nominal church membership and irregular attendance. The 1967 definition indicates that extrinsic persons may use religion in a variety of instrumental ways. All of the needs in the definition (security and solace, etc.) might be involved, as well as more crass motives, such as making business contacts and gaining political power. While most extrinsic people are peripheral churchgoers, they may have a strong need to identify themselves with some church or creed. Allport described some as "ideological extremists" (1968, p. 231). They embrace some extreme religious position, along with attitudes of ethnic prejudice, as an attempt to escape from the complexities of modern life.

Allport reiterated the core concept of intrinsic motivation: "The intrinsic form of the religious sentiment regards faith as a supreme value in its own right" (1968, p. 232). That is, intrinsic religion is functionally autonomous, is sought for its own inherent rewards. Another characteristic of intrinsic religion was repeated: "Dogma is tempered with humility" (1959; 1968, p. 232). This phrase is relevant to the relation of intrinsic religion to dogmatism, which we shall note later. It also qualifies and limits the definitions of intrinsic religion in Box 20.2, which include, "interiorized the total creed . . . without reservation" and "Having embraced a creed the individual endeavors to internalize it and follow it fully."

Now we revive an earlier issue: Are the intrinsic and extrinsic religious ori-

---

Box 20.2   ALLPORT'S DEFINITIONS OF INTRINSIC AND EXTRINSIC RELIGIOUS ORIENTATIONS

"*Intrinsic* religion marks the life that has interiorized the total creed of [one's] faith without reservation, including the commandment to love one's neighbor. A person of this sort is more intent on serving . . . religion than on making it serve him [or her]."

"*Extrinsic* religion is a self-serving, utilitarian, self-protective form of religious outlook, which provides the believer with comfort and salvation at the expense of outgroups" (1960).

Intrinsic: "Persons with this orientation find their master motive in religion. Other needs, strong as they may be, are regarded as of less ultimate significance, and they are, insofar as possible, brought into harmony with the religious beliefs and prescriptions. Having embraced a creed the individual endeavors to internalize it and follow it fully. It is in this sense that [one] *lives* [one's] religion."

Extrinsic: "Persons with this orientation are disposed to use religion for their own ends. . . . Extrinsic values are always instrumental and utilitarian. Persons with this orientation may find religion useful in a variety of ways—to provide security and solace, sociability and distraction, status and self-justification. The embraced creed is lightly held or else selectively shaped to fit more primary needs. In theological terms the extrinsic type turns to God, but without turning away from self" (1967).

Source: Allport (1960, p. 257); Allport and Ross (1967, p. 434).

entations independent characteristics, or are they opposites of one another? All-port considered them polar opposites, and said that all religious people "fall upon a continuum between these two poles" (1968, p. 242). However the evidence, as reviewed by Hunt and King (1971), indicates otherwise. They cite correlations between measures of intrinsic and extrinsic religion that range from .37 to −.54. Subsequently reported correlations fall within this wide span, suggesting that in different populations the two orientations may range from modest positive to modest negative relationships. People who are not highly involved in religion tend indiscriminately to accept or reject any idea about religion—whether it be extrinsic or intrinsic. In such groups a positive relationship between the two holds. On the other hand, a study among seminary students (Batson, 1976b) produced one of the higher *negative* correlations between intrinsic and extrinsic religion (−.41), suggesting that people who are highly involved in religion make finer discriminations between intrinsic and extrinsic. Among them, then, the orientations appear more nearly to be polar opposites as Allport had asserted. We agree with Hunt and King (1971) that the two orientations should be measured separately in empirical research.

Measuring Intrinsic and Extrinsic Religion

Wilson (1960), with Allport's help, designed a 15-item psychological scale to measure extrinsic religious values. No specifically intrinsic items were written since that orientation was considered to be simply the opposite of extrinsicness. In one of Allport's seminars at Harvard, Feagin (1964) designed a 21-item "Intrinsic/Extrinsic Scale." A factor analysis (see Chapter 21) of Feagin's scale produced two separate intrinsic and extrinsic factors of six items each (see Box 20.3). These factoral scales are probably the most succinct and psychometrically the best measures of the two religious orientations—though unfortunately not the most frequently used.

Allport and Ross (1967) used 20 of Feagin's items—11 extrinsic and 9 intrinsic—in their research. Their scales were not as refined as Feagin's, and the identification and selection of items were not always consistent with Feagin's factors (Dittes, 1969; Hood, 1971; Hunt & King, 1971). Nonetheless this 20-item scale has been most often used in the research reported in this chapter. More recently Hoge (1972) elaborated the Wilson-Feagin-Allport-Ross item pool and evolved somewhat longer scales.

In Allport's and his students' questionnaires the religious orientation questions were asked with a four-choice response, such as: I definitely disagree; I tend to disagree; I tend to agree; or I definitely agree. Researchers have not reported reliability coefficients for this format (Allport, 1968, gave correlations of individual items with subscale scores). The same questions have also been used in a simpler true-false format, which produced reliabilities of .67 for extrinsic and .73 for intrinsic (Kahoe, 1974a). While these reliabilities are not as high as one might like, they are adequate for research purposes.

Hunt and King (1971) criticized measures of the intrinsic and extrinsic orientations on the grounds that they are not simple unitary traits. Their own re-

---

Box 20.3   FEAGIN'S FACTORAL INTRINSIC AND EXTRINSIC ITEMS

Intrinsic	Extrinsic
I try hard to carry my religion over into all my other dealings in life.	Religion helps to keep my life balanced and steady in exactly the same way as my citizenship, friendships, and other memberships do.
My religious beliefs are what really lie behind my whole approach to life.	
The prayers I say when I am alone carry as much meaning and personal emotion as those said by me during services.	One reason for my being a church member is that such membership helps to establish a person in the community.
It is important to me to spend periods of time in private religious thought and meditation.	The purpose of prayer is to secure a happy and peaceful life.
If not prevented by unavoidable circumstance, I attend church at least once a week or oftener[a] (or: two or three times a month, once every month or two, rarely).	The church is most important as a place to formulate good social relationships.
	What religion offers most is comfort when sorrow and misfortune strike.
I read literature about my faith (or church) frequently[a] (or: occasionally, rarely, never).	The primary purpose of prayer is to gain relief and protection.

[a]First choice is scored most strongly intrinsic.
Source: Feagin (1964).

---

search found that each orientation involved several different behavioral tendencies, which they preferred to measure instead of the more global orientations. We recognize that Allport's definitions of the two orientations were complex (recall all the different needs that might be served by the extrinsic religious orientation). We prefer, though, to evaluate the religious orientations by how they work. The rest of this chapter emphasizes the very fruitful results of more than a decade of research employing the intrinsic and extrinsic orientations in the psychology of religion.

Correlates of Intrinsic and Extrinsic Religion

One of the most certain things we have learned from the recent empirical study of religion is that religion generally should not be considered a single, unified variable. The intrinsic-extrinsic concepts have powerfully shown the different implications of religion, depending on one's religious motives.

Prejudice   As we mentioned, Allport studied ethnic prejudice (one of his long-time concerns) in all three papers that explicitly employed the intrinsic and extrinsic religion concepts. Wilson's (1960) early empirical study related his Extrinsic Religious Values Scale to anti-Semitism. In ten different groups relationships between the two measures were positive and statistically significant. Allport and Ross (1967) criticized Wilson's study on two counts. First was a "response set" problem. Wilson's scale items were all worded so that agreement indicated degree of extrinsicness, and the anti-Semitism items were also consistently worded to show anti-Semitism. Since some people tend generally to agree with or disagree with any statement, regardless of its content, this "response set" would tend to produce positive relationships between the variables—whether the two constructs being measured are really correlated or not. Also the anti-Semitism and extrinsic religion scales were both negatively related to educational level. So the relationship of extrinsic religion to anti-Semitism might be an artifact (a misleading result of the measures used), either of response set or of educational level, or of both. Feagin (1964) found that extrinsic religion but not intrinsic religion was related to prejudice against blacks. This finding seems to eliminate response set as an explanation, but does not discount the effects of education.

Allport and Ross (1967) did the most extensive study of the relationships of intrinsic and extrinsic religion to racial, ethnic, and other prejudices—using five different measures of prejudice, and 309 persons from six religious denominations in six states. Extrinsic religion was correlated with virtually all measures of prejudice, though not very highly (correlations ranged from .21 to .44). The combined extrinsic-intrinsic scale did not correlate with prejudice as highly as the extrinsic subscale alone. Allport and Ross divided their respondents into three groups: those who were more intrinsic than extrinsic, those who were more extrinsic than intrinsic, and the "indiscriminately proreligious" who agreed with both intrinsic and extrinsic items. With this distinction, the intrinsic were least prejudiced, and the "indiscriminate" were the most prejudiced. They concluded that the indiscriminately proreligious engaged in "undifferentiated thinking," showing strong "acquiescence" (going along with, agreeing) response set. Allport and Ross's findings can then be accounted for by two variables that are related to higher prejudice scores—extrinsic religion and acquiescence response set.

Subsequent research supports the basic findings of Feagin, Allport, and Ross, namely that extrinsic religion is positively related to prejudice, and intrinsic religion usually is not related to prejudice. This does not mean that an intrinsically religious person is not prejudiced—only that we cannot predict anything about a person's degree of prejudice from an intrinsic religion score. Some people who score high in intrinsic religion may be prejudiced; others may be highly tolerant. We return to these findings in Chapter 25.

Authoritarianism   Authoritarianism designates a type of personality that is presumably based on intense but repressed hostility toward one's parents and other authority figures. Outwardly the authoritarian person is very submissive to higher authority, but domineering and punitive toward subordinates. Authoritarian attitudes are highly conventional and stereotyped, and may be especially intolerant of deviations from conventional sexual standards. People who are high in authoritarianism tend to be prejudiced against all other racial and ethnic groups and support traditional sex roles that discriminate against women. Since extrinsic religion is related to prejudice, and authoritarianism is linked to prejudice, it is no surprise that the extrinsic religious orientation shows a consistent relationship to authoritarianism (Kahoe, 1974a; 1975a). This relationship is indicated in Table

20.1, which also includes findings for several other variables. One early study (Strickland & Shaffer, 1971) measured the religious orientation in Allport's original way (confounding intrinsic and extrinsic) and found no significant relationship to the California F scale (the most common measure of authoritarianism). The reason why became clear when it was found that intrinsic religion also has a correlation with the F scale, though a smaller and less consistent relationship than does extrinsic religion (see Chapter 25) (Kahoe, 1975a; 1977a). Strickland and Shaffer's way of measuring extrinsic religion apparently canceled out the relationship with authoritarianism.

Dogmatism   Social psychologist Milton Rokeach's (1960) concept of dogmatism indicates that personality rigidity includes both conventional or right wing authoritarianism and also radicals of the left. Rokeach found that conservative religious groups such as Catholics score high on his Dogmatism scale, and indeed that religious believers in general are more dogmatic than nonbelievers. Several studies, among Catholics and Protestants, students and adults, have consistently found the extrinsic religious orientation to correlate significantly with dogmatism (correlations ranging from .28 to .38). See Table 20.1 for one of these. Intrinsic religious orientation in the same studies has been just as consistently independent of dogmatism (r's ranging from .04 to .06), supporting Allport's claim that intrinsically religious persons temper dogma with humility. That is, they are not typically rigid about their beliefs.

Internal Control and Responsibility   Julian Rotter (1966) developed the concept of *internal locus of control of reinforcement* to characterize persons who feel they have a significant degree of control over the good and bad things that happen to them. This contrasts with a more fatalistic external control, or a passive attitude that whatever will be, will be. Persons higher in internal control are generally more effective in dealing with their world (see Chapter 15). Strickland and Shaffer's (1971) confounded measure of extrinsic-intrinsic religion was related to locus of control—the more extrinsic person was more external. Kahoe (see Table 20.1)

Table 20.1   **SOME CORRELATES OF INTRINSIC AND EXTRINSIC RELIGION**

Correlated variable	Religious orientation	
	Intrinsic	Extrinsic
Authoritarianism (F scale)	.03	.33[a]
Dogmatism scale	.04	.30[a]
Internal locus of control	.24[a]	−.25[a]
Responsibility	.29[a]	−.40[a]
Intrinsic motivation	.45[a]	−.25[a]
Extrinsic job motivation	−.01	.15[a]
Extrinsic personal motivation	−.04	.05
American College Test	.10	−.19[a]
Freshman grade point average	.25[a]	−.23[a]

[a] $p < .01$.
Source: Kahoe (1974a).

found that extrinsic religion was related to feelings of external control, and a separate measure of intrinsic religion was positively related to internal control. The religious orientations had similar relations with a measure of responsibility—a trait representing what is normally seen as someone being socially responsible, willing to act in a responsible manner, often without regard for oneself. Correlations with responsibility are shown in Table 20.1. Note that the *higher* the extrinsic orientation, the *lower* one's measured responsibility.

Education, Intelligence, and Achievement   Allport criticized Wilson's study because both anti-Semitism and extrinsic religion were related to lower levels of education. Allport himself found a correlation of $-.32$ between extrinsic religion and education (Allport, 1968, p. 244). Kahoe and Dunn (1975) found a higher $(-.56)$ correlation. Another study found a weaker but statistically significant tendency for extrinsic religion to go with lower scores on the American College Test—a standard college admissions aptitude test (see Table 20.1). While intrinsic religion does not seem to be related directly to intelligence or degree of education, among 186 freshmen at a church-related college the intrinsically religious students did better in their freshman year courses—with or without statistical controls for college aptitude (Kahoe, 1974a). The negative correlation between extrinsic religion and achievement in Table 20.1 apparently was due to the lower aptitude associated with extrinsic religion. When aptitude was statistically controlled, extrinsic religion and grade point were not significantly related.

Intrinsic and Extrinsic Motivations   The .45 correlation between intrinsic religion and intrinsic motivation, and the .15 correlation between extrinsic religion and extrinsic job motivation, in Table 20.1, show generality of the intrinsic and extrinsic orientations. This relationship was implied above in the theoretical elaboration of the religious orientations; the data suggest that the intrinsic orientation is more generalized than the extrinsic orientation. The measure of intrinsic motivation represented in Table 20.1 was based on the kinds of intrinsic items illustrated in Box 20.1. Extrinsic job motivation was based only on items taken from the Job Motivation Inventory, and extrinsic personal motivation was based on items from the California Psychological Inventory (Box 20.1).

CONCLUSION AND CRITICISM

Religious Orientations as Pervasive Motives

Dittes (1969) and Hunt and King (1971) characterized the intrinsic and extrinsic religious orientations as motivations for religion more than as characteristic ways of being religious. We have, of course, emphasized that the orientations are essentially motivational. The same critics also suggested that the religious orientations are not limited to religion, but might be pervasive personality variables. Our own research (Kahoe, 1974a, 1976a), partially presented in Table 20.1, supports this position, and we have shown that psychology recognizes a pervasive dichotomy, of which the intrinsic and extrinsic religious orientations are representative. This dichotomy of two contrasting dimensions has also been related to the separate and distinct natures of mental disorder and positive mental health (Kahoe, 1975a).

The disorder-health distinction is evident among the correlates of intrinsic and extrinsic religious orientations. In general the intrinsic orientation has been positively related to variables that psychologists have deemed to indicate positive personality attributes (internal control, responsibility, achievement). Similarly it has been either independent of or negatively related to most undesirable psychological traits (prejudice, dogmatism, extrinsic motivation). Likewise extrinsic religion tends to be related to such negative personality characteristics as authoritarianism, dogmatism, external control, and lower levels of education and academic aptitude. In short, many of the negative factors that have been related to religiousness or church attendance are correlates only of extrinsic religion and not of intrinsic religion.

Measurement and Research Problems

Our enthusiasm for the intrinsic and extrinsic dimensions should not blind us to shortcomings of either the concepts or the ways they have been measured. Allport criticized Wilson's anti-Semitism study for possible confounding of extrinsic religion and educational level. While the education-extrinsicness relation is notable in itself, it is possible that some of the other relationships between extrinsic religion and other variables may be partially due to the education factor. Educational level has not generally been controlled in studies of extrinsic religion.

Allport's other criticism of Wilson's research was the problem of acquiescence response set. Allport attempted to resolve that problem by including inventory items worded as intrinsic as well as extrinsic. However, we have seen that the two tend to be separate rather than bipolar, and subsequently both orientations have been measured by degree of agreement with items like those in Box 20.3. So the problem of acquiescence response set is still with us and typically has not been controlled in research. Its significance is signaled by the fact that intrinsic religion and authoritarianism had a negligible correlation (.03 in Table 20.1), but when respondents who showed strong response sets were eliminated, the correlation was higher and statistically significant (.18 in Kahoe, 1975a).

Another response set problem that has received less attention is social desirability. Some people answer self-report inventories, such as the intrinsic and extrinsic scales and other personality inventories, in such a way as to make themselves look good, with relatively little regard to how they really are. Some people probably find the intrinsic religious items more socially desirable than the extrinsic ones, which might affect relationships of the religious orientations with other self-report personality variables. This particular response set problem has been controlled in one intrinsic-extrinsic study that will be discussed in Chapter 22 (Batson, Naifeh, & Pate, 1978).

More critically, the conceptual and operational definitions of intrinsic religion have failed to confirm some attitudes or behaviors that might be expected to go along with a committed, internalized religious faith. For example, Batson (1976b) failed to find any significant relationship between intrinsic religiousness and willingness to help a person apparently in distress. At the same time he noted that people who score high in intrinsic religion tend also to be "true believers"—to endorse the traditional beliefs of their religious group perhaps too uncritically.

REVIEW OF KEY CONCEPTS

Introduction
   egocentric and growth functions
   objective and subjective worship and prayer
   D-needs and B-needs
General Intrinsic and Extrinsic Motivations
   task orientation and ego orientation
   intrinsic and extrinsic job motivations
   coping and defending
   schizophrenic patients and intrinsic-extrinsic motivations
   intrinsic as active approach tendency versus extrinsic as avoidance of threats
   coping and defending in school tasks
   intrinsic and extrinsic motives as independent, not opposites
Intrinsic and Extrinsic Religious Orientations
   functional autonomy
   derivative yet dynamic nature of mature religion
   interiorized and institutionalized religion
   communal and associational affiliation
   relation of intrinsic and extrinsic religion to prejudice
   Allport's definitions of intrinsic and extrinsic religion
   intrinsic and extrinsic religion—opposites or independent?
   measures of religious orientations: Allport and Ross, Feagin
   reliabilities of measures of intrinsic and extrinsic religion

Correlates of Intrinsic and Extrinsic Religion
   prejudice: Allport and Ross, Feagin, and others
   relationships with authoritarianism
   relationships found with dogmatism
   internal control and responsibility relationships
   education and intelligence with extrinsic religion
   academic achievement with intrinsic religion
   relations with intrinsic and extrinsic motivations
Conclusion and Criticism
   pervasiveness of intrinsic and extrinsic concepts
   disorder-health distinction
   measurement problems: confounding of educational level, acquiescence response set, social desirability
   intrinsic religion and helping behavior
   "true believers"

chapter *21*

Dimensions of Religiousness

We have looked at ways people are religious and studied the most common distinction in measuring religiousness. In this chapter, we survey a variety of ways scholars have measured religiousness. Three major approaches to this task are: (1) seeing religion as a single and distinct realm of human behavior; (2) measuring religion on bipolar dimensions (such as intrinsic-extrinsic); and (3) defining many dimensions that make up religiousness.

Dittes (1969) pointed out that when we look at religion from the outside, it seems to be one separate realm of life. But, when we look at it from the inside, we can distinguish many different aspects of religion and different ways of managing those aspects. Dittes argued for looking at religion in both ways.

UNIDIMENSIONAL MEASUREMENT APPROACHES

The earliest attempts to measure religiousness approached it as a single dimension. However, each scale that was developed focused on a narrow range of religious content, such as orthodoxy of belief or attitudes toward the church. Such scales were often used as a general measure of the person's religiousness.

Single-Dimension Scales

Sumner (1898) made one of the earliest recorded attempts to measure religion. He had people rank-order statements about religious belief according to how much they agreed with them. Which statements a person most agreed with determined how "religious" she or he was. Sumner thus defined religiousness by the belief items a person was willing to endorse. Thurstone (Thurstone & Chave, 1929) used a similar method to measure attitudes toward the church.

Several other unidimensional scales that emphasize belief items have been developed, such as those of Thouless (1935) and Poppleton and Pilkington (1963). The Allport-Vernon-Lindzey *Study of Values* test (Allport, Vernon, & Lindzey, 1931/1951) measures a person's religiousness, as a single dimension, along with five other values: theoretical, political, economic, aesthetic, and social.

Crude Unidimensional Measures

Some researchers do not use scale measures to assess religiousness, but simply count the frequency of such behaviors as attending church services, praying, and giving money to a church. They assume that the more people do such things, the more religious they are. Other researchers simply ask people to rate themselves on religiousness, compared to most people. Gorsuch and McFarland (1972) argued that such single-item measures tap intrinsic religiousness well, but that multiple-item scales are better to measure traditional Christian orthodoxy. They found two single-item measures particularly useful: (1) importance of religion to one's life and (2) degree of belief in Jesus as the Christ.

Argyle (1958) said that, although it has serious defects, the best single measure of religiousness is frequency of church attendance. Maslow disagreed: "Sheer behavioral going to church can mean practically anything, and therefore, for us, practically nothing" (Maslow, 1954, p. 25). Ross (1950) pointed out a vast discrepancy between the belief items that young people will agree with and their real convictions. He said that although 75% of college youth agree with orthodox belief statements, only about 16% are genuinely religious. More recently, others have argued that belief and churchgoing may underestimate religiousness. Many genuinely religious people are not traditional in the ways they practice religion.

Unidimensional Factor Analytic Studies

Factor analysis is a technique that determines, on the basis of correlations among different test items or measures, which ones appear to measure essentially the same thing. All items that vary together make up a separate factor, and each factor is taken to define one dimension (or aspect) of values, attitudes, or other characteristics of the people answering the test items. Some factor analytic studies identify religiousness as a single factor (dimension) of human experience. This means that a group of items measuring religion cluster together in factor analysis, and do not cluster with items measuring other content.

Attitude and Value Studies   Thurstone (1934) found that attitudes toward God and the church, religious conduct, and religious observances all clustered together and formed a single factor of religiousness. His findings were later replicated by Nelson (1956). Lurie (1937) and Brogden (1952) each factor analyzed the items on the *Study of Values* test and found a single religiousness factor. Hunt (1968) concluded that the factor defined by this religion scale primarily measures a person's active involvement in traditional religious forms to make life meaningful.

Ferguson (1939) wanted to identify people's primary social attitudes. He factor analyzed items measuring opinions about war, capital punishment, treatment of criminals, reality of God, evolution, and birth control. He found two factors, which he called "humanitarianism" and "religionism." In a similar later work, he reported three independent social attitudes factors: religionism, humanitarianism, and nationalism (Ferguson, 1944).

Personality Studies   Some researchers analyzed religious interests along with personality variables. In one such study, O'Neil and Levinson (1954) found an independent factor that they called "religious conventionalism."

Brown argues strongly that religion is a single factor among other personality variables. In two major studies (Brown, 1962, 1966b), he found a single religion factor. His measures included different combinations of Thouless (1935) religious belief items, Eysenck (1958, 1959) personality dimensions, authoritarianism items (Adorno, Frenkel-Brunswick, Levinson, & Sanford, 1950), an anxiety scale (Taylor, 1953), institutionalization-individualism items (Jeeves, 1959), frequency of religious practice items (Allport, Gillespie, & Young, 1948), rigidity items (Brengelmann, 1960), and some humanitarianism and aggression items. With many of these same items, some new religion items (Poppleton & Pilkington, 1963), and Rokeach's (1960) Dogmatism Scale, he again concluded that religion is a single factor (Wearing & Brown, 1972).

BIPOLAR DIMENSIONAL APPROACHES

Some researchers say that, although unidimensional measures help determine relationships between religious participation and certain environmental or demographic variables, they are of little value in understanding religious behavior. According to Maslow, in order to understand what religious behavior in a person means, "we must understand what religion means for him [or her] as an individual" (Maslow, 1954, p. 25).

Understanding Bipolar Dimensions

Theorists who use bipolar understandings of religion usually consider one pole "proper" religion and the other less desirable (as with intrinsic-extrinsic in the last chapter). Sometimes they use one dimension, with a "good" pole and a "bad" one; the more points a person gets toward one end, the farther that moves him or her from the other. Sometimes, however, they think in terms of two dimensions, and a person can get a high or low score on either dimension, regardless of what was scored on the other. (Recall the discussion in Chapter 20 about measuring intrinsic-extrinsic as one dimension or two.)

Box 21.1 summarizes several bipolar understandings discussed below. Also included are the important intrinsic-extrinsic distinction and several theorists' (Chapter 19) work that is similar, though not developed into scales to measure the ideas.

Arenas of Religiousness

Some thinkers questioned whether religion should be considered an explicit area *of* life—such as sports or school—or whether instead it represents underlying

---

Box 21.1 BIPOLAR APPROACHES TO MEASURING RELIGIOUSNESS

Theorist	Preferred religion	Nonpreferred religion
Allport	Intrinsic (for religious motives)	Extrinsic (for "fringe benefits")
Lenski	Associational (life-permeating commitment)	Communal (social-group focus)
Allen	Committed (internalized religious values)	Consensual (conformity to religious patterns)
Nock	Conversion (self-chosen commitment)	Adhesion ("inherited" social religion)
Dewey	Being religious (submission to a pervasive ideal)	Observing a religion (following the forms of a religion)
Clark	Primary religion (harmonizing life with one's vision)	Tertiary religion (habitual, conditioned religion)

Source: Allen (1965), Allport (1959, 1960), Clark (1958), Dewey (1934), Lenski (1961), Nock (1961).

attitudes *toward* life. As one area of life, it is concerned with specific socially identifiable behaviors such as creeds, beliefs, rituals, and churchgoing. This can be contrasted with viewing religion as a commitment that colors all of life—a "system of devotions, reverences, allegiances, and practices—whether avowed or implicit, conscious or unconscious" (Appel, 1959, p. 1777). Religion seems to function one way for some people, and the other for others. Thus, how religion is viewed depends on the attitudes of religious people, not on the nature of religion.

Communal and Associational Religion   Lenski believed that the way a person approaches religion is important for an understanding of that person's religiousness. He distinguished between communal religiousness (commitment to a group for primarily social reasons) and associational religiousness (commitment for religious reasons, and much more influential in the person's entire life) (Lenski, 1961).

Consensual and Committed Religion   Allen (1965) defined committed and consensual styles of religion, similar to Lenski's ideas.

> The committed style involves a personal and authentic commitment to religious values wherein the full creed with the attendant consequences are internalized and expressed in daily activities and behavior. . . . The consensual style involves a conformity or acquiescence to religious values wherein the full creed is not meaningfully internalized with respect to consequences for daily activities and behavior [Allen, 1965, p. 13].

In a later paper (Allen & Spilka, 1967), the committed and consensual styles were explained in more detail. You may recognize the similarity to the intrinsic-extrinsic concept. As theoretically explained, consensual and committed religion appear to mix the ideas of communal-associational and extrinsic-intrinsic religion. However, as measured by the *Religious Viewpoints Scale* (Raschke, 1973; Spilka, Read, Allen, & Dailey, 1968), communal and consensual religion contrast interiorized religious interest with a focus on public religious services.

THEORETICAL MULTIDIMENSIONAL MODELS

While some researchers used unidimensional or bipolar measures of religion, others wanted even more complex models. Their models look at religion from the inside, and ask how many different dimensions or aspects there are of a person's religiousness. We look first at some theoretical models, before examining some psychometric (measurement-based) ones.

Some Typical Theoretical Models

Thouless (1961) proposed several dimensions. (1) Sociological factors shape the element of tradition. (2) Three kinds of experience make up the experiential element: external nature of the world, moral conflict, and inner emotion. (3) Reason influences the intellectual element. (4) Thouless (1971) later added a fourth influence on religiousness: personal needs.

Kurts (1962) identified six categories common to many religions: God concepts, self-identity concepts, interpersonal attitudes, ethical concepts, security attitudes, and immortality concepts. Whiteman (1962) recommended viewing religion as four-dimensional: belief, commitment, participation, and feeling.

The Glock Model

Glock (1959, 1962) made the first major theoretical argument for the multidimensionality of religiousness, proposing five major dimensions derived from a study of world religions.

Glock's Dimensions   (1) The ideological dimension is concerned with belief and unbelief: scope and content of belief, saliency of beliefs, strength of personal beliefs, and style (traditional or nontraditional) of belief. (2) The ritualistic dimension covers public and private religious practices, and their meaning for the individual. (3) The experiential dimension is concerned with religious feeling, both positive and negative, and with intense religious experiences. (4) The intellectual dimension covers religious knowledge, attitudes toward it, and intellectual sophistication concerning one's tradition. (5) The consequential dimension focuses on the implications of one's religiousness for the general conduct of life. Box 21.2 compares Glock's dimensions with several other models.

Stark (1966) made subcategories of Glock's experiential dimension based on intensity of experience. (1) Confirming experience gives one a sense of the holy. (2) In the responsive experience God is felt to acknowledge the subject's presence. (3) In the ecstatic phase, some kind of intimate contact with God is experienced and, (4) in the relational state, the subject claims to be a chosen confidante and/or emissary of God.

Glock's dimensions do not necessarily describe anything unique to religion. For any venture in which people engage, we can ask what they think about it, how they go about doing it, what kinds of feelings and experiences are associated

---

**Box 21.2   SOME THEORETICAL MULTIDIMENSIONAL
             MODELS**

Glock	Whiteman	Thouless
Ideological	Belief	Intellectual
Ritualistic	Participation	Traditional
Experiential	Feeling	Experiential
Intellectual		Intellectual
Consequential	Commitment	
		Personal need

Source: Glock (1959, 1962), Thouless (1961, 1971), Whiteman (1962).

with it, how much they know about what they are doing, and what consequences it has for the rest of their lives.

Attempts to Scale Glock's Dimensions   Several researchers (Faulkner & De-Jong, 1966; Fukuyama, 1960, 1961; Salisbury, 1962) tried to develop scales to measure Glock's dimensions. However, the dimensions did not show up as separate factors in a factor analysis. Belief, participation, and emotional aspects were all highly intercorrelated, even when several different methods of scale development were used.

Clayton (1971) tried again, using a very large sample and what he considered to be improved methods. He again found a close correspondence among the ideological, experiential, intellectual, and ritualistic scales. The ideological one predominated; that is, from what people say about religious belief you can easily predict the rest of their scores. Clayton was concerned that such scales measure only endorsement of certain religious content, and not the importance of religiousness to a person. What a person says about religion may be held with widely different degrees of intensity.

MULTIDIMENSIONAL FACTOR ANALYTIC STUDIES

Some researchers have collected large numbers of items that cover many aspects of religious activity—beliefs, values, participation, etc. In addition, some also collect information about age, gender, and other characteristics of the people taking their test items. However, they do not add a lot of other personality items to their studies because they do not want to see if a single religion factor (dimension) will separate itself from other measures. Instead, they want to see how the many religion items will divide themselves up in the factor analysis. Then they can say—on the basis of these data—what different aspects or dimensions make up religion.

Some General Studies

Most factor analytic studies of religion were not later repeated on other subjects. This replication is usually considered a necessary step in scale development to see if the items will work the same in different groups of people. We outline some unreplicated studies to show the range of religion dimensions they suggest.

Allen and Hites (1961) produced the first major multidimensional factor analytic study of religion. They used religious attitude items, a Bible knowledge test, and participation measures on religiously involved young people from several churches. Table 21.1 shows the factors they got, along with those obtained in other studies. Comparable factors are shown on the same line, so that you can see which ones are most common across the studies.

Keene (1967b) used items measuring religious behavior and attitudes on a mixed group of Jews, Protestants, Catholics, and Baha'is. Two of his four factors were rather complex, with the first one emphasizing loyalty and commitment

Table 21.1 COMMON FACTORS OF RELIGIOUSNESS

Focus of factor	Allen & Hites (mixed group)	Keene (mixed group)	Research Nudelman (Catholics)	Nudelman (Protestants)	Nudelman (Christian Science)	Cline (Mormons)	Tapp (Unit.-Univ.)	Keene (Baha'is)	Strommen (Lutherans)
Organizational involvement		Loyalty/ participation	Involvement	Involvement	Organizational activities	Participation/ activity	Participation	Participation	
Worship/ prayer	God-relation		Devotion	Devotion	Devotion		Worship/ reflective	Meditation/ prayer	
Belief		Orthodoxy					Institutional Values	Belief	
Good behavior	Duty		Ethics		Social care	Compassionate Samaritan	Social and ethical	Religion in Daily life	"Gospel/ spiritual believers"
Doubt	Skepticism	Questioning							"Law-orientation"
Growth vs. security	Security need					Dogmatic authoritarian	Psychological growth		
Autonomy/ tradition	Tradition	Customs vs. autonomy							
Humanism	Humanism						Humanism	Religious autonomy	
Miscellaneous	Secularism					Tragedy and suffering	Friendship, religious education, knowledge		

Source: Allen & Hites (1961), Cline & Richards (1965), Keene (1967a, 1967b), Nudelman (1971), Strommen, Brekke, Underwager, & Johnson (1972), Tapp (1971).

to one's faith. The second factor appeared to contrast institutional with individual religiousness (a distinction discussed in Chapter 19).

Nudelman (1971) factor analyzed data from the Glock dimensions on Catholics, Protestants, and Christian Scientists. This replicated study found factors for both devotion and participation in all three groups. With a largely Mormon sample, Cline and Richards (1965) used interviews, questionnaires, and some personality tests. They obtained 12 factors for women and 14 for men. The four religiously relevant factors are in Table 21.1.

Studying Unitarian-Universalists, Tapp (1971) obtained many factors, all but the first two—theological/institutional values and social/ethical values—very small. Keene (1967a) found five equal-sized factors among Baha'is. Strommen, Brekke, Underwager, and Johnson (1972) factor analyzed items relevant to their faith on a nationwide sample of Lutherans. The first factor—"gospel" or spiritual believers—is similar to intrinsic religion. The second identified "law-orientation" Lutherans whose dogmatic, utilitarian, and authoritarian religiousness resembles both extrinsic religion and a strong institutional orientation (see Chapters 19 and 20).

The King-Hunt Inventory

King (1967) initiated the most highly developed factor analytic study of religion. Across the years, his item pool changed slightly. The final pool included items from many previous studies of religiousness. The frequency and knowledge measures were mainly from Glock and Stark. Also included were measures of intrinsic-extrinsic motivation and intolerance of ambiguity (Martin & Westie, 1959), and the *Purpose-In-Life Scale* (a measure of life satisfaction and meaningfulness) (Crumbaugh, 1968; Crumbaugh & Maholick, 1964).

With a group of urban Methodists, King (1967) found these dimensions: (1) creedal assent and personal commitment, (2) participation, (3) personal religious experiences, (4) friendships in the congregation, (5) intellectual search, (6) openness to religious growth, (7) dogmatism and extrinsic orientation, (8) financial behavior, (9) talking and reading about religion. King and Hunt (1969) revised the dimensions, dropping intellectual search, adding a religious knowledge scale, and changing item content of several other scales slightly.

King and Hunt (1972) replicated this study with slightly different items and with subjects from the Lutheran, Methodist, Disciples of Christ, and Presbyterian faiths. They produced a similar list of factors. Later, with a nationwide sample of 872 Presbyterians, they obtained nearly identical factors (King & Hunt, 1975). Box 21.3 lists some items from the scales of the replication and the national sample.

The consistency in findings allows the researchers to feel confident that their inventory will work similarly for a variety of people. Although it is the major contribution of its kind, much of the inventory is more relevant to sociology than psychology. (King is a sociologist.) The more psychological content in the dimensions comes from psychological measures previously in existence.

Box 21.3 KING AND HUNT SCALES WITH SAMPLE ITEMS

Scale name	Sample items and response range
Creedal Assent	I believe that Christ is a living reality.[a] I believe in eternal life.[a]
Devotionalism	How often do you pray privately in places other than at church?[b] How often do you ask God to forgive your sin?[b]
Church Attendance	If not prevented by unavoidable circumstances, I attend church.[b]
Organizational Activity	How would you rate your activity in this congregation? (Very Active to Inactive) I enjoy working in the activities of the church.[a]
Financial Support	Last year, approximately what percent of your total family income was contributed to the Church? (1% or less to 10% or more) In proportion to your income, do you consider that your contributions to the Church are: (Generous to Small)
Religious Despair	I often wish I had never been born.[a] Most of the time my life seems to be out of my control.[a]
Orientation to Growth/Striving	How often do you read the Bible?[b] I try hard to carry my religion over into all my other dealings in life.[a]
Salience: Behavior	How often do you talk about religion with your friends, neighbors, or fellow workers?[b] How often have you personally tried to convert someone to faith in God?[b]
Salience: Cognition	My religious beliefs are what really lie behind my whole approach to life.[a]
Ambiguity Intolerance	A person is either a 100% American or he isn't.[a] There are two kinds of people in the world; the weak and the strong.[a]
Purpose in Life	My life is full of joy and satisfaction.[a] I usually find life new and exciting.[a]

[a]Responses: strongly agree, agree, disagree, or strongly disagree.
[b]Responses: choices of frequency ranges.
Source: Adapted from King and Hunt (1975). Used with permission.

THEORY-BASED FACTOR ANALYTIC STUDIES

Early researchers were less sophisticated about factor analysis than contemporary ones. We now realize that factor analysis cannot identify the basic (or core) dimensions of any facet of human life or personality. Its results depend greatly on the items used; it can only tell which of these items cluster together. The computer adage "garbage in—garbage out" sums up this idea.

No pool of items can possibly cover all features of an area of human experience, and one could get quite different results using different items. Factor analysis works best when items are carefully chosen to test particular theoretical models. A researcher develops items to measure specific hypothesized dimensions. If the factor analysis clusters the items to form factors that match the researcher's dimensions, one can conclude that these dimensions are measurable aspects of, for example, religiousness. If the factor analysis fails to support any hypothesized dimension, it is not a unified, separate component of religiousness—at least not in the item pool used.

Broen's Study

Broen (1957) chose items that he thought would define five styles of religiousness that stress different features. The hypothesized emphases were: (1) sin, judgment, and negative commandments; (2) religious neediness that lacks a specific doctrine; (3) moral and ethical features; (4) worship and love of God; and (5) "spirit-filled"—seeking of intense religious behaviors and experiences. From a variety of churches he selected subjects that he thought would represent each of these types and also some "modal" Catholics and Lutherans.

Broen had his subjects sort 133 statements into different piles according to the degree of their agreement with them (a process called Q-sort). His factor analysis of the intercorrelations between Q-sorts gave him two significant factors. The first, nearness to God, described a feeling that God was real and accessible; it emphasized the loving presence of God. The second factor, fundamentalism-humanitarianism, contrasted a belief that humans are essentially sinful with one that people are good and have little need for divine help. Broen successfully cross-validated his factors (got the same results) on a different sample of religious people.

Maranell's Model

Maranell (1968) described eight dimensions of religious attitudes that he considered separate and distinct from each other. Factor analysis of replies of clergy from 11 denominations, to items measuring these dimensions, produced only two factors. The first grouped together three of his eight dimensions: fundamentalism, theism, and superstition. People scoring high on this factor would support such things as revival meetings, emotional conversions, faith healing, and orthodoxy trials. The second factor clustered the dimensions of altruism, idealism, church orientation, and mysticism. Maranell said it described a more sophisticated religiousness. Ritualism did not fall on either factor. Thus, Maranell's two factors divided between them content that he had expected to form seven independent dimensions.

A later study (Maranell & Rezak, 1970) used replies from university professors. These people produced a very large first factor, which added church orientation, ritualism, and mysticism to the clergy's first factor. Idealism and altruism defined the second factor. Maranell concluded that these religious nonprofessionals probably could not make distinctions in religious content as finely as the clergy, so all their highly correlated replies produced one very large factor.

Meadow's Inventory

Meadow (1976, 1977b) defined five broad areas of religious content. The first considers how people view deity. One set of items described seeing God as all-powerful, all-knowing, and "out there"; another described divinity as within ourselves and pervading all things. The second domain dealt with the free will question, with items defining both deterministic and free will positions. The third content area measured a distinction William James made. He said "healthy-minded" religious people are antimoralistic, unreflective, unrealistically optimistic, and see good in all things. The "sick soul" type are deeply sensitive to inner distress, highly conscious of personal failures, prone to guilt and sadness, and seldom feel pleasure (James, 1902). The fourth content domain described positions of cognitive rigidity and flexibility (see Chapter 13). The fifth area contrasted religious individualism with an institutional orientation (the distinction made in Chapter 19).

Cross-validated factors (factors that came out the same for different groups of subjects) closely matched many of the hypothesized dimensions. (Box 21.4 lists the Meadow scales with sample items from each. The numbers identify the factors in order of size.) The Christian God factor describes belief in a transcendent personal God who operates in human history. Sacred Monism depicts a mystical world view with divinity dwelling in all creation. Deterministic Fatalism consists mainly of determinism items, with a few free will items scored in the opposite direction. Other free will items clustered with some "healthy-minded" content to produce an unexpected factor that was given the descriptive name of Stoic Will.

Some healthy-minded items make up a Human Goodness factor, which describes a small part of James's idea of healthy-minded religion. The Religious Grief factor similarly matches only part of James's sick soul type. A very large factor, Truth-Seeker, described the cognitive flexibility dimension of open-mindedness to a variety of religious and philosophical positions. Church Traditionalism—also a large factor—defined encouragement of involvement in religious institutions.

The items written to describe the position of cognitive close-mindedness divided between two factors; this position characterizes people who score high on Church Traditionalism and low on Truth-Seeker. The items written to describe religious autonomy (individualism) split between Truth-Seeker and Human Goodness; religiously individualistic people would score high on both of these factors. Although Belief Rigidity and Religious Autonomy (Box 21.4) did not form their own separate factors, the items for each make up a homogeneous scale with high internal consistency.

CONCLUSIONS

Unidimensional and Bipolar Measures

Religiousness can validly be viewed and measured in different ways. As one set of specific observable behaviors, it describes an aspect of life that can be seen apart from other behaviors and can be studied in relation to values, personality, and

Box 21.4 MEADOW FACTOR SCALES WITH SAMPLE ITEMS

Scale name	Sample items (true-false response)
I. Christian God	God is the ruler of the universe.
	There must be a Supreme Being who made the laws of nature.
V. Sacred Monism	We find divinity in the world and people around us.
	The divine exists in even the most ordinary things.
IV. Deterministic Fatalism	Things outside of a person control most behavior.
	Good heredity and good luck account for most people's success in living.
VI. Stoic Will	In accounting for our actions, we should not be allowed to blame external circumstances and influences.
	We should forget our mistakes and begin fresh each day.
VIII. Human Goodness	Human nature is basically good.
	People are just naturally helpful and friendly.
IX. Religious Grief	Regular self-examination is necessary to keep from getting into sinful habits.
	We are only travelers through this life.
II. Truth-Seeker	Interpretations of my faith should and do change in every age.
	Differing religious views are good for society.
Belief Rigidity	There is no doubt about the truth of my religious beliefs.
	Scriptures are not subject to human error.
III. Church Traditionalism	The church is necessary to explain God's will.
	Organized religion is the most powerful developer of moral virtue.
Individual Autonomy	One can be a good person without reading scripture.
	Human reason and compassion are the best developers of love and concern for others.

Source: Meadow (1977b).

other psychological variables. The simplicity of unidimensional measures, however, limits their usefulness in understanding how religiousness functions in an individual's life and psyche.

Thinking in terms of such dimensions as intrinsic-extrinsic or committed-consensual advanced the assessment of religiousness considerably. Study of the intrapsychic aspects of religiousness began with such bipolar scales. Although bipolar dimensions are helpful for classifying people, they account for only a limited scope of an individual's religiousness.

Multidimensional Measures

Many multidimensional measures were based on factor analysis of a mixture of items drawn from various sources. Such studies demonstrated that religiousness can be seen as multidimensional. Except for the King and Hunt inventory, such studies have not been consistently replicated.

Three factor analytic studies based on theoretically developed item pools—Broen, Maranell, and Meadow—have been cross-validated. Although the first two studies each produced only two factors, Meadow's study proved it possible to cross-validate a larger number of psychologically meaningful factors.

Only multidimensional inventories are likely to be adequate for the fuller understanding of an individual's religiousness. The King and Hunt scales emphasize participation and sociometric aspects of religion. Meadow's more psychologically oriented inventory assesses religious concepts, values, stances, and attitudes. Each in its own way can provide a profile of the individual's religiousness, giving a person's standing relative to other people on different aspects of religiousness.

The Next Step

Global unidimensional scales or single-item measures may be useful for rough screening of religiousness. Bipolar models offer a few summary scales on which to assess religiousness. Multidimensional factor analytic studies provide scales that give a more complete picture of a particular person's religiousness. Each approach has its own utility.

When we want to understand religion in itself, however, each approach has drawbacks. The unidimensional and bipolar measures are too simplistic, and do not provide sufficiently fine distinctions. The multidimensional models tend to be complex and cumbersome to use. Nor do any of these approaches allow an understanding of the relationships among different dimensions of religiousness. In the next chapter, we suggest a solution to these problems.

REVIEW OF KEY CONCEPTS

Unidimensional Measurement Approaches
    looking at religion from the inside and the outside
    early methods of determining religiousness
    when single-item measures work best
    churchgoing as a measure of religiousness
    what factor analysis does
    primary social attitudes
    Brown's conclusions about religion and personality
Bipolar Dimensional Approaches
    "good" and "bad" religiousness

A Model of Personal Religiousness

The time has come to integrate the concepts and approaches we have outlined in the three previous chapters. Amid the variety and complexity of ways to look at personal religiousness, we see a model that we believe is both simple and relatively comprehensive.

BACKGROUND OF THE MODEL

Our model is based on many years' work by many different researchers in the psychology of religion. Still it is proposed as tentative, and subject to more elaboration, testing, and research.

Original Formulation

L. B. Brown (1964) originally applied the model to the religiousness of 319 Australian first-year psychology students. They were asked to complete several sentences, such as, "In my everyday life, religious beliefs. . . ." The students' sentence completions were intended to classify them as intrinsic or extrinsic (see Chapter 20). Judges soon realized that the simple dichotomy did not adequately identify the differences among the students. They eventually used seven categories, but these fit into a two-dimensional space defined by two bipolar dimensions, as sketched in Figure 22.1. That is, Brown identified all of the categories by a combination of their positions on the intrinsic-extrinsic dimension and an institutionalized-individualized dimension. The latter distinction was, of course, our frame of reference for Chapter 19.

Brown measured institutionalism and individualism with two four-item scales. Institutionalism—an "outer" orientation toward the church—is reflected in the item, "The church is necessary to establish and preserve concepts of right and wrong." Individualism was seen as an "inner" orientation toward the person,

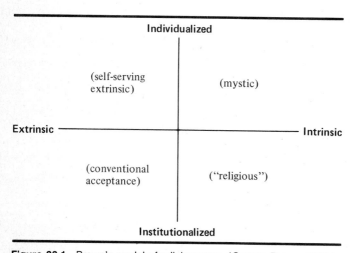

Figure 22.1 Brown's model of religiousness. (*Source:* Brown, 1964.)

self, or mind. One individualism item was: "A man ought to be guided by what his experience tells him is right rather than by what any institution such as the church tells him to do." The individual-institutional scales had relatively low correlations with the extrinsic-intrinsic dimension, and correlated negatively (though slightly) with one another. These findings, as well as the fit of the seven categories of sentence completions, were Brown's rationale for his two-dimensional model of personal religion.

Rediscovery and Elaboration

As Chapter 20 showed, the intrinsic and extrinsic dimensions have enjoyed considerable research popularity and usefulness. The institutional and individual dimensions did not immediately fare so well—perhaps in part because of low reliability of the scales Brown used. Nonetheless, the distinction has been found in factor analyses of religious attitudes, for example, studies by Keene (1967a) cited in Chapter 21. Other studies cited showed strong factors of institutional involvement, and of growth-security tensions.

Broen's Factor Analysis Although not widely recognized as such, Broen's (1957) factor analysis (described in Chapter 21) closely approximated three-fourths of Brown's model. The bipolar "fundamentalism-humanitarianism" factor is very much like an institutional-individual dimension, and "nearness to God" is closely allied to intrinsic religiousness. Broen's study did not include items that might be considered extrinsic (since it predated Allport's proposal of the concept), so the factor analysis could not identify an extrinsic factor.

Committed-Consensual Concepts As we observed in Chapter 21, Allen and Spilka's (1967) committed-consensual distinction had apparent similarities to the intrinsic-extrinsic dichotomy. Spilka (Minton & Spilka, 1975; Spilka and Minton, 1975) studied the relationships among the several concepts, suggesting that "extrinsic-intrinsic and committed-consensual religion are examining personal faith from two different vantage points, and are actually dealing with the same phenomena" (Spilka & Minton, 1975, p. 2). He found that indeed intrinsic and committed measures were highly correlated (average .85 in Spilka & Minton, 1975). However, extrinsic and consensual scales had an average correlation of only .14 in the same study.

Fleck's "Trichotomy" On the basis of Spilka's findings, just cited, Fleck (1976) suggested a "trichotomy" of personal religion. His intrinsic-committed dimension is essentially identical with Allport's intrinsic religion, and his extrinsic is similar to Allport's (see Chapter 20). His consensual dimension, adapted from Spilka and his colleagues, was characterized thus:

> Religious authority, beliefs, ceremony, membership, participation, practices, ritual, and the religious group itself are used as a personality support or haven

for personal comfort, relief and strength. Consensual religionists are characterized by a shallow and restrictive mode of thinking resulting in a simple conformist orientation to life including steady, routine, and regular participation in institutionalized religious beliefs and practices [Fleck, 1976, p. 198].

The consensual dimension, then, is clearly cast as an institutional orientation. With the intrinsic and extrinsic dimensions, it forms three-fourths of
Brown's model. Fleck considered committed religion to be mature religion, with
both consensual and extrinsic immature, though in different ways.

"Religion as Quest"   Batson (1976b) also developed a "three dimensional model
of religious orientation" that reflects three-fourths of Brown's model. Batson's
primary interest was to clarify "two different religious orientations confounded
in Allport's conceptualization of the intrinsically religious individual" (1976b,
p. 32). He developed an "interactional" scale that included items such as: "Questions are far more central to my religious experience than are answers," and "My
religious development has emerged out of my growing sense of personal identity."
A factor analysis of interactional religion and five other scales (including intrinsic
and extrinsic) produced three factors: Religion as Means (extrinsic), Religion as
End (primarily intrinsic), and Religion as Quest (interactional). The interactional
items show Religion as Quest to be an Individualism dimension, in the sense that
Brown originally defined it.

Batson (1976b) found that Religion as Quest was related to the way in
which people approached helping situations. "Questers" are more sensitive to the
other person's statement of his or her needs, rather than rigidly persistent in some
preconceived fashion. Later Religion as Quest was found to be more consistently
related to racial tolerance than was intrinsic religion (Batson, Naifeh, & Pate,
1978). When the tendency to respond to a questionnaire in a socially desirable
way (see Chapter 20) was controlled, or when racial tolerance was required in
an actual behavioral situation, the relationship with tolerance persisted for Religion as Quest but not for intrinsic religion.

Review   These models of religiousness have replicated three of the four poles
of Brown's (1964) model. Broen (1957) included all but extrinsic; Fleck (1976)
all but individual; and Batson (1976b) all but institutional. There seems to be
sufficient theoretical and empirical support to take Brown's total model seriously.
Knowledge of personality and religious psychology should make the model increasingly productive for studying, exploring, and explaining religion in individual lives.

THE DESCRIPTIVE MODEL

The Model

One of the content areas that contributed items for Meadow's (1977b) factor analysis was called Autonomy-Observance—essentially an individual versus institu-

tional dimension. We have adopted this terminology (along with Intrinsic-Extrinsic) in a contemporary version of Brown's model. Our model, along with other sources of the dimensions as outlined above, is shown in Figure 22.2.

Research Beginnings

We conducted a series of three factor analyses, using items from Meadow's scales for Church Traditionalism and Individual Autonomy (Box 21.4), and standard intrinsic-extrinsic scales. Our aim was to develop relatively short and "pure" measures of the four major elements of our model.

We gave several forms of our new scales to college and church groups and studied the religiousness of each sample in several ways. Included in the study were 45 students from a Baptist college and 108 students from a state university. As one might expect, the Baptist students were higher than the university students in Intrinsic and were lower than them in Autonomy. To a lesser extent they were also lower on the Extrinsic scale and higher on Observance. The patterns of relationships within the two groups were not identical. For example, Intrinsic and Observance correlated .48 for the university sample, but −.04 for the Baptist group. One might conclude that the four dimensions do not have any necessary relationships with one another (in a psychometric sense) but that they differ according to the particular religious styles and sensitivities of each group being studied (Kahoe & Meadow, 1977a).

We also measured how closely beliefs of the several groups agreed with be-

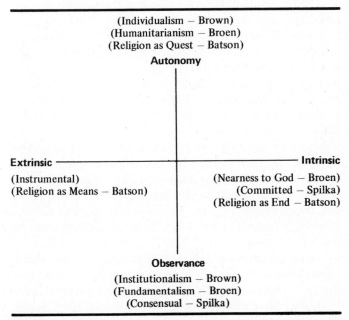

Figure 22.2 Integrated model of personal religiousness. (*Source:* Allen and Spilka, 1967; Batson, 1976b; Broen, 1957; Brown, 1964.)

liefs generally held by their own churches. The Intrinsic dimension was most consistently related to congruence with beliefs of their churches—supporting the "true believer" identification of the intrinsically religious noted in Chapter 20. Congruence was significantly related to low Autonomy in two-thirds of the cases, and it was significantly related to high Observance in half of the cases. These relationships tend to support the validity of the Autonomy and Observance scales. When we inspected data for individual respondents, though, we discovered that they differed widely in what scales were related to congruence. For some, agreement (or disagreement) with the standards of their church was related to the individual's Intrinsic religiosity; for others it was related to Observance, or one of the other dimensions. We might again conclude that the dimensions of our model are sensitive to differences among individuals. To understand personal religiousness, we cannot look solely at groups of religious persons. We must "get personal" and examine the religious perspectives of individuals (Kahoe & Meadow, 1977a).

THE DEVELOPMENTAL MODEL

The individual approach in psychology has been primarily identified with the developmental process. Can we relate our model, and this unit on psychometric approaches to religion, to the development of religiousness—the focus of Unit One? We believe this can be done.

Background Observations

We mentioned Fleck's (1976) view that committed (intrinsic) religion is mature, while extrinsic and consensual are immature. Implicit in Fleck's presentation was the idea that extrinsic religion is less mature than consensual. Few studies have compared the relative maturity of the extrinsic versus the consensual dimension. Allen and Spilka's (1967) study included a measure of extrinsic religious values, which failed to discriminate between prejudiced and unprejudiced persons (as Consensual did). However, they used Wilson's (1960) early and rather unsophisticated extrinsic scale. (Almost all other extrinsic religion measures have related to all kinds of prejudice in numerous studies.)

The relation of the other scales to positive psychological indicators is clear in the literature. Committed and intrinsic measures are related to less prejudice, in comparison with both consensual and extrinsic measures. Batson's studies (1976b; Batson, Naifeh, & Pate, 1978) indicate that autonomy (Religion as Quest) is even more "mature" than intrinsic religion. Autonomously religious persons were more flexible in helping situations and also were more consistently unprejudiced than the intrinsically religious.

From the above research, from theoretical views that we shall discuss shortly, and from direct observation of religious development in ourselves and other people, we have proposed the following model of religious development (Kahoe & Meadow, 1978, 1981). We believe that psychologically important religiousness in individuals typically begins near the extrinsic pole in our model (Figure 22.3). Development progresses in a counterclockwise fashion through observance religion, to intrinsic, and finally to the autonomous. As we shall see, not all religious persons travel the whole route, but this is the path we believe they tread.

The Developmental Sequence

Extrinsic Origins   We shall look briefly at the first part of Allport's characterization of the "derivative yet dynamic nature of the mature sentiment" (1950/1960, p. 71). Mature religion is derived from immature religion that "betrays its sustaining motives still to be the drives and desires of the body" (p. 72). Probably some of what passes for religion lacks the base motive forces of the lower nature; the person simply learns a religion as casually as she or he learns to use a knife and fork. Allport suggests that unless such persons come to invest their religion with physiological drives or energies (including anxiety and guilt), religion will be nothing more than empty habit. Nor is it likely to have the impetus for continued development such as we are describing.

To put the case more positively, psychologically significant religion has strong dynamic or motivational origins. Religious beliefs and practices may be motivated by numerous fears and anxieties: physical, social, psychological, and existential. Initially people seek religion primarily for security, as an ego defense. That is, it is extrinsically motivated. For some people religion remains on a self-serving, instrumental, extrinsic basis—this is the essence of "foxhole religion"—which produces no meaningful life changes after the immediate crisis is past.

We suggest that every person's mind has the capacity (call it the "collective unconscious" if you wish) spontaneously to produce religious responses under stress. Or a basic religious impulse may be activated in a mystical state. More commonly, though, some organized religious system serves as the mid-

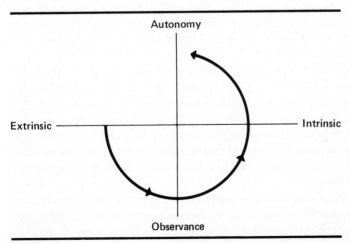

Figure 22.3 Developmental model of personal religiousness. (*Source:* Kahoe and Meadow, 1981.)

wife—sometimes deliberately creating guilt or other anxieties to evoke the birth pangs of a personal religious faith.

Observance Religiousness Religious persons typically identify with a religious system or institution, at least early in their religious development. There are several reasons for this, the most obvious being that such a system usually introduces the person to religious answers to life crises and anxieties. Few, if any, people have the creativity to develop their religious solutions on their own. There are also basic human needs to associate and identify with other people.

Under the influence of a religious system, religious persons move from a basically extrinsic orientation, toward an institutional or observance orientation—counterclockwise in our model (Figure 22.3). Religious institutions (as with any human organization) attempt to perpetuate themselves by inspiring observance in followers. This need applies to local congregations, denominational structures, and dogma or doctrinal systems. The shift toward an observance orientation requires the believer partially to turn away from purely self-serving extrinsic religion.

That shift is relative. Since most people maintain many of their extrinsic motives, religious institutions cultivate loyalty by directing attention and service to individuals' needs. An active church social group reduces a new convert's this-worldly loneliness, as it also forms an attachment to the church. Teachings about an afterlife of bliss soothe existential anxieties over the threat of nonexistence, and at the same time build support for the system that makes such a promise. The movement from extrinsic to observance is gradual, and a follower may be at any point on the lower-left quadrant of our model as this change occurs.

Observance refers to many religious items: "authority, beliefs, ceremony, membership, participation, practices, ritual, and the religious group itself," again to cite Fleck's (1976, p. 198) characterization of consensual religion. All of these elements are surely interrelated and frequently occur simultaneously, but some are likely to be emphasized before others. One of the first would seem to be the social factor—sheer belongingness. The social aspect is psychologically primitive, figuring strongly in operational definitions of the extrinsic orientation. It appears also to have little intrinsic potential.

Doctrinal systems are perhaps the latest developing aspect of observance religion. As we saw in Chapter 13, belief systems have extrinsic or ego-defensive functions. But they also have coping functions—providing "a cognitive framework to know and to understand" (Rokeach, 1960, p. 67). Surely many people's religious belief systems serve some extrinsic functions, but religious dogmas also have intrinsic implications. Allport said that intrinsically religious persons internalize and live by the belief system of their faith. Many of the intrinsically religious are "true believers."

Other aspects of observance religion—for example, ritual, participation, and ceremony—probably help mediate the change from merely identifying oneself socially with a religious group, to adopting their belief system. In this and other ways they also direct the believer's attention away from self—though such activities continue to meet various psychological needs.

Intrinsic Religiousness   The trend set by observance religion—increasingly to turn away from self—is continued by intrinsic religion. Virtually all of the higher religions advocate a self-giving devotion to religious causes and ideals. Intrinsic religion is self-actualizing in the paradoxical sense that growth requires one to turn away from self—to a task that is beyond and greater than self.

While intrinsic religion grows out of a religion of observance, many people fail to achieve any great degree of intrinsic faith. Some religious leaders or congregations fail to promote intrinsic religiousness as much as others, but individual differences also affect the development of the intrinsic religious orientation. The strong relationship between general intrinsic motivation and intrinsic religion cited in Chapter 20 suggests that the two are interdependent.

Among mainstream Christian groups most people who develop an intrinsic orientation seem also to keep a strong observance orientation. However, intrinsically religious "true believers" do not necessarily hold their religious doctrines in a rigid manner. Several studies have found the intrinsic religious orientation and Rokeach's Dogmatism scale to be uncorrelated (Kahoe, 1974a; Kahoe & Dunn, 1975; Thompson, 1974). Moreover, measures of intrinsic and observance orientations have produced diverse results—the correlations of .48 and $-.04$ for university and Baptist college samples, cited earlier (Kahoe & Meadow, 1977a).

Autonomous Religiousness   Progression toward autonomy or individualized religion is a step beyond an intrinsic faith. However, as not all religious persons reach the intrinsic level, so even fewer attain an autonomous orientation. Whereas the higher religions typically advocate intrinsic religion, seldom do they promote a thoroughly autonomous faith. Such independence of thought and practice is generally against the vested interests of organized religion. There are exceptional institutions, no doubt, that advocate a high degree of individual freedom in the follower's religious beliefs and participation. In most cases, though, a strong personal inclination leads the occasional person to religious autonomy despite institutional discouragement.

We must speculate as to what those personal factors might be. In an intrinsically oriented person an intense, personal (mystical) religious experience might be a most compelling motive. Probably general abstract intelligence, higher education, and training in reflective disciplines such as philosophy should be influential. However, many people tend to isolate religious experience from other areas of thinking (see Chapter 3), and such processes would work against autonomy, even in the above situations. Those who need social support from a traditional religious group, or the security of a rigid creed, are also likely to resist movement toward religious autonomy. Sometimes strong influences both toward and against autonomy create intense conflicts.

Theoretical Parallels

The developmental schema just sketched seems to possess an intuitive validity. This may occur because of relationships with a number of developmental stage theories, particularly some surveyed in Chapter 4.

Abraham Maslow   Although Maslow's (1943, 1971a) needs hierarchy is not a developmental sequence, it implies an order in which needs are expressed. It is consistent with our developmental model. Maslow's lowest level needs are the physiological and safety needs that motivate extrinsic religion. Next in the hierarchy are love and belongingness, which parallel the early, social phase of observance. Self-esteem, Maslow's next need, has two bases. The first and more primitive basis has social origins—others' positive evaluations of oneself—and is related to observance. The more advanced and stable basis of self-esteem is one's perceptions of his or her own responsible conduct, with strongly intrinsic implications.

The highest level in Maslow's early scheme—self-actualization—implies the more advanced levels of intrinsic religion, beyond sheer adoption of a given faith, reaching toward autonomy. Later Maslow proposed a higher level of needs that he called "meta-needs"—values that transcend actualization of any individual. The religion of autonomy is typically based on universal principles, which many religious systems reflect only imperfectly.

Box 22.1 summarizes the relationships of Maslow's and other theories to our model of personal religious development. These parallels should be considered tentative, and the alignments may shift up or down, depending on how one interprets or focuses on a given model.

Lawrence Kohlberg   Kohlberg's (1968) stages of moral judgment also parallel our model of religious development. Since his schema was discussed in Chapters 4 and 5, we shall refer you to Box 22.1 and the earlier chapters, and discuss the relations with our model only briefly. The reward and punishment emphases of Kohlberg's preconventional Stages 1 and 2 reflect the self-serving orientation of extrinsic religion. Stage 3—the "good boy/nice girl" orientation—reflects the social aspect that typically introduces observance religiousness. Similarly the Stage 4 focus on authority and fixed rules parallels the dogma aspect that develops later in the observance level. Kohlberg's Stage 5 stress on duty, obligation, and personal responsibility has strikingly intrinsic overtones. And finally, the Stage 6 orientation toward comprehensive ethical principles recalls both Maslow's meta-needs and the universal principles that support an autonomous or individualistic religious system.

Jane Loevinger   Loevinger's (1966, 1976) model of ego development (also described in Chapter 4) has similar relations to the developmental model of religion. The immediate pleasure-seeking and expedient "morality" of her impulsive and self-protective stages correspond to the extrinsic origins of religion. Loevinger's next stage (conformist) involves identification with the welfare of a group, and acceptance of the rules of the group; the parallel to our observance level is obvious.

The conscientious stage, in which one has an internalized morality, judges according to the consequences of behavior, and recognizes exceptions to rules, reflects the intrinsic orientation toward religion. Loevinger's highest stages (autonomous and integrated) are equivalent to religious autonomy. The person at

Box 22.1 SUMMARY OF RELATIONSHIPS OF OTHER MODELS TO RELIGIOUS DEVELOPMENT SCHEMA

Kahoe/Meadow	Maslow	Kohlberg	Fowler	Loevinger	Chakra
Autonomy	Meta-needs	Universal ethical principles	Universalizing faith	Integrated	Eyebrow
	Self-actualization		Paradoxical-consolidative faith	Autonomous	Throat
Intrinsic	Self-esteem (self)	Social contract, procedural rules	Individuative-reflexive faith	Conscientious	Heart
	Self-esteem (other)	Law and order, authority			
Observance		Interpersonal relations: "good boy / nice girl"	Synthetic-conventional faith	Conformist	Navel
	Love and belonging		Mythic-literal faith		
Extrinsic		Hedonistic	Intuitive-projective faith	Self-protective	Genital
	Physiological and safety needs	Punishment and obedience	Undifferentiated faith	Impulsive	Root

Source: Kahoe & Meadow (1981).

these levels tolerates ambiguity, values individual differences, and respects the autonomy of other people.

Fowler and Chakra Psychology   Box 22.1 also draws parallels between our model of religious development and James Fowler's stages of religious faith development, and the growth stages of yogic chakra psychology. You can refer to Chapter 4 to see how each level of those theories fits the corresponding level of our model.

OTHER CONSIDERATIONS

Generality

We believe our model has wide generality. We cite, not as proof, but as illustration, an unidentified yogic quotation:

> At first it is DISCIPLINE—you do it because someone you believe in tells you it is good for you, so you do it and try to experience that it is truly good for you and [she or] he was right. Next it is PRACTICE—you have experienced how good it feels and how good it is for you; you believe in it and want it to work for you, to improve you all over, so you do it willingly, of your own accord. Then it becomes WORSHIP. You no longer care about it as being good for you; you go beyond that, and it is done as a loving worship to the One who dwells within and makes it possible.

The sequence from discipline (extrinsic, self-serving acts—"it is good for you") to practice (habitual observance) to worship (an unselfish act of intrinsic religion) seems to depict three-fourths of our developmental model.

Description Versus Prescription

By suggesting a sequence of development, we imply that a later orientation is more mature than an earlier one. However, we hesitate to make value judgments about each orientation or to prescribe that everybody should try to attain each higher level. For one person in one situation, any given level might be the highest that she or he can expect to attain. We do not say this to discourage growth or development, but rather to accept and respect individual differences. We do not think that those who attain the higher levels should scorn those who linger in the valleys and on the plains of religious development. If we were pressed for a prescription, we might say that individuals should be encouraged toward the intrinsic semicircle of our model, but only those who are willing and able to pay the price should press toward the pole of autonomy.

Relations Among Levels

We have not called the levels of our schema "stages." We prefer to see religious development as a continuum—a pathway, with identifiable and characteristic milestones as we travel. Although our picture of the schema may imply that the different orientations are mixed only in the quadrants between two adjacent poles of the model, it would be more accurate to say that each new level incorporates all earlier steps. The idea of a spiral, upward and through our two-dimensional space, might be apt. The flat model implies, for example, that the move to autonomy leads back toward self-centered concerns. Autonomy probably is not so self-forgetful as intrinsic religiousness, but its self-reference is different from that of the extrinsic orientation. Jesus's disciples' plucking grain on the Sabbath (Mark 2 : 23–28) was only superficially extrinsic. Transformed and refined by the developmental process, it became an expression of religious autonomy.

Relations to Personality

The developmental levels of our model almost surely interact with a religious person's general personality development—especially in cognitive stages, moral judgment, ego development, motivational style, and socialization. The most regular development (within our model) might be observed in a child reared in a religious tradition or having a conversion experience prior to adolescence. Late adolescent or adult converts—with higher levels of moral judgment and ego development—presumably would experience the extrinsic and observance levels of religious growth in turn. But they would develop more rapidly toward orientations that were consistent with the rest of their personalities and cognitive styles.

Research Challenge

We believe our model has great potential for clarifying the development of personal religiousness. More importantly, it should challenge strenuous research on individual lives. Development within our model is not likely to be automatic any more than it is for Kohlberg, Fowler, and Loevinger. Religious development is one aspect of a total personality, but it also is influenced by the religious institutions with which the person identifies.

Study should be aided by the psychometrically identifiable dimensions on the developmental pathway, but group approaches would surely blur the peculiarities of individuals' religious life histories. Various longitudinal and retrospective designs (see Chapter 5), and the use of autobiographies, case histories, and similar psychohistorical methods and materials, should test the regularity and sequence of our religious dimensions. Possible exceptions to development within our model are suggested by increasing evidence of religious interests apart from institutional churches (Princeton Religion Research Center, 1979). Nonetheless, the pattern we have sketched could be the rule by which such exceptions are tested.

REVIEW OF KEY CONCEPTS

Background of the Model
> Brown's study and basic model: individualism and institutional scale items
> Broen's factor analysis and relation to Brown's model
> relationship of committed-consensual concepts to the model

Fleck's "trichotomy"—intrinsic, extrinsic, institutional
Batson's "Religion as Quest," and relations to the model

The Descriptive Model

the four dimensions: intrinsic, extrinsic, observance, autonomy
differences between church-related college and university students
congruence relationships to intrinsic, autonomy, observance
individual differences in congruence

The Developmental Model

relative maturity of the four dimensions, from prior research
extrinsic origins of religiousness
Allport, religion for security
role of religious institution in guilt-anxiety
observance religiousness—shift from self-centeredness
primitive social factors and later belief factors in observance
role of ritual and ceremony—the institution—in observance
intrinsic religiousness and paradoxical self-actualization
institutional and individual forces in intrinsicness
relationship of intrinsic religion and dogmatism
autonomous religiousness—its nature and occurrence
individual and institutional forces in autonomy
potential for conflict with autonomy religiousness
theoretical parallels: relationship to the model of Maslow, Kohlberg, Loev-
    inger, Fowler, and chakra psychology

Other Considerations

the generality of the model
prescriptions for religiousness—intrinsic, autonomy
relations among the levels—gradual change, incorporation of lower stages,
    transformations
relations to general personality structure
research prospects—merger of psychometric and developmental research
    traditions

chapter 23

Death Concerns and the Dimensionality of Religion

The gods . . . must reconcile one to the cruelty of fate, particularly as shown in death [Freud, 1927/1961, p. 24].

[Humans] alone of all creatures [are] aware of death, and it is a natural response in the face of insecurity to demand reassurance [DeYoung, 1977, p. 1].

The existential problem of individual death and the anxieties roused by the threat of corporal nonexistence are intimately involved with ultimate religious concerns [Kahoe & Dunn, 1975, p. 379].

Every religious system has dealt with the problem of death, celebrating its occurrence and hypothesizing about its meaning [Cerny & Carter, 1977, p. 1].

> Few realities are as central to the heart of religion as death. Some even claim the existence of death creates religious faith. Bergson suggested "religion is a defensive reaction of nature against the inevitability of death." Tillich is harsh in his condemnation of those who, in the name of religion, maintain life continues after death. He claims this popular view is not Christianity and refers to it in terms of "images, absurdities, self-deceptions" [Spilka, Stout, Minton, & Sizemore, 1977—minor deletions not indicated].

Empirical research on death and religion has only recently begun to match the extravagant and sometimes contradictory rhetoric that the subject generates. The relationship of death concerns and religion has been clarified so much by viewing religion as dimensional, that we devote this research chapter on religious dimensions entirely to death attitudes.

EARLY RESEARCH ON DEATH AND RELIGION

"Predimensional" Research

The earliest studies on religion and death concerns used impressionistic or unidimensional measures of religion, and narrow samples such as mental patients or the elderly. The findings were contradictory. Persons with religious beliefs sometimes had more fear of death than did the nonreligious (Feifel, 1959); sometimes no relationship between religiousness and death concerns appeared (Christ, 1961). In another study those with the greatest religious activity and more fundamental religious beliefs had less fear of death and looked forward to death more than did those who engaged in little religious activity (Swenson, 1961).

Perhaps the most illuminating was a study of terminally ill patients in England. The 10% who were most firm in their faith and attended religious services weekly were least afraid of dying, but those who held a loose religious faith were the most anxious. The nonreligious were intermediate in death anxiety (Hinton, 1972, p. 84). The two religious groups would seem to represent intrinsic and extrinsic types, respectively.

Broen's Religious Dimensions and Death

The intrinsic and extrinsic religious orientations were not generally popular in 1965 when Martin and Wrightsman did the first study of death concerns using a bidimensional measure of religion. They used Broen's (1957) two dimensions: Nearness to God and Fundamentalism versus Humanitarianism. Concerns about death were assessed by Sarnoff and Corwin's (1959) five-item fear-of-death scale, ten similar items that Martin and Wrightsman composed, and a seven-item sentence-completion task they also devised. The sentence-completion test was correlated rather modestly with the other fear-of-death measures (.46 and .34) and correlated significantly with none of the criterion measures in the study. Martin and Wrightsman's ten-item objective scale correlated only .46 with Sarnoff and Corwin's five-item scale—suggesting that the scales were low in reliability or not measuring quite the same attitudes. When the three fear-of-death scales were related to Broen's two dimensions for several groups, only one out of 24 correlations was significant at the .05 level. That is what one would expect by chance, so death concerns were not shown to be related to religious attitudes.

Later Stewart (1975) studied 117 college students, relating Broen's scales to Boyar's (1964) 18-item fear-of-death scale. High scores on both Nearness to God and Fundamentalism were related to low scores on fear of death. The .25 correlation with the former could occur by chance only once in 100 times, and the .16 with Fundamentalism only five times in 100.

Why did Stewart find relationships between death concerns and Broen's scales when Martin and Wrightsman did not? We can identify three probable reasons. As suggested above, Martin and Wrightsman's fear-of-death measures probably were not very stable or internally consistent, as shown by a reliability of about .45. On the other hand, Boyar (1964) reported reliabilities of .83 (on internal consistency) and .78 (by test-retest) for his fear-of-death scale.

Second, Stewart used twice as many subjects as Martin and Wrightsman, and opportunity to find a significant statistic increases with sample size. Finally, a group of college students is likely to be more varied in their religious attitudes and death concerns than active churchgoers—whom Martin and Wrightsman studied. This can account for their results, since greater variability increases the likelihood of finding larger and more significant correlation coefficients.

DEATH ANXIETY AND INTRINSIC-EXTRINSIC RELIGION

At least seven studies relating death anxiety to intrinsic and extrinsic religious orientations were published in the 1970s. One otherwise well designed study made the methodological error of measuring intrinsic-extrinsic as one scale and dividing subjects into two extremes—extrinsic and intrinsic. It found no significant differences between the two groups on either the Templer Death Anxiety Scale or the Collette-Lester Fear of Death Scale (Sullivan, 1977).

The Studies

The six other studies are summarized in Table 23.1. Procedures in the studies varied. Those done with students generally collected data in class; Spilka used 167 people (students and church members) who attended church at least twice a month and rated themselves at least seven on a nine-point scale of the importance of religion in their lives. The two studies that used churchgoers followed Martin and Wrightsman's (1965) procedure—passing out questionnaires at the end of church services and requesting mail returns (Kahoe & Dunn got 53% returns; Patrick 45%). DeYoung mailed questionnaires to all members of the church and received 30% returns.

Magni and Spilka used several other measures of uncertain value, not discussed here. Bolt also used seven "consequences of one's own death" statements (from Diggory & Rothman, 1961), which the students rank-ordered in terms of their own feelings. High intrinsic religion was related to low concern about "fate in life after death" ($r = -.38$) and high concern about "grief to relatives and

Table 23.1 STUDIES RELATING FEAR OF DEATH TO INTRINSIC AND EXTRINSIC RELIGIOUS ORIENTATIONS

Author	Samples and number of subjects	Fear-of-death measures	Correlations	
			IR	ER
Magni	Swedish student nurses (53)	Lester Attitudes toward Death Scale (.58[a])	−.38**	.37**
		Boyar Fear-of-Death Scale (.79,[a] .89[b])	−.09	.27*
Kahoe and Dunn	Kentucky churchgoers (70)	Improved Martin and Wrightsman Fear-of-Death Scale (.54[b])	−.28*	.10
Spilka et al.	Church-related college students and Methodist church members (167)	Lack of Fear of Death (.82[b])	−.09	−.18*
		Fear of the Dying Process (.66[b])	−.12	.19*
		Loss of Experience and Control in Death (.86[b])	−.09	.38*
Bolt	Church-related college students (62)	Templer Death Anxiety Scale (.83,[a] .76[b])	−.14	.29*
DeYoung	Presbyterian church members (375)	Avoidance of Death Scale	−.32**	.36**
		Boyar Fear-of-Death Scale (.78,[a] .83[b])	−.04	.10
Patrick	Buddhist churchgoers (35)	Templer Death Anxiety Scale (.83,[a] .76[b])	.12	.22
	Baptist churchgoers (40)		−.16	.31*
	Congregational churchgoers (16)		−.14	.72**
	Total sample (91)		−.02	.33*

*p < .05; **p < .01; ***p < .001.
[a]Test-retest reliability.
[b]Internal consistency reliability.
Source: Magni (1971); Kahoe and Dunn (1975); Spilka, Stout, Minton, and Sizemore (1976); Bolt (1977); DeYoung (1977); and Patrick (1979).

friends" ($r = .32$). High extrinsic religion was related to high concern about "fate in life after death" ($r = .48$). There were no other significant relationships among the 14 comparisons.

The Results

Ten of the 13 extrinsic correlations in Table 23.1 are statistically significant. All show increased fear of death when extrinsic motives are high (note that the first Spilka scale is scored for *lack* of fear). Three of the correlations with intrinsic religion are significant—showing less fear of death with high intrinsic motives.

The inconsistencies in Table 23.1 follow no apparent patterns with regard to subject populations or fear-of-death measures used. Four out of five of the extrinsic correlations below .27 are for groups of churchgoers. However, four other correlations with active churchgoers range from .31 to .72. The results do clarify the contradictory findings of "predimensional" research. Fear of death is usually related to religion insofar as the latter is extrinsically motivated. Fear of death is sometimes reduced by intrinsic religion—varying perhaps by the particular fear-of-death scale used. Perhaps the intrinsic dimension is simply weaker than the extrinsic, or is affected by other uncontrolled variables, and so usually is obscured. The intrinsic relationship with low death anxiety gets additional support from Bolt's (1977) research that showed a similar relationship with Broen's Nearness-to-God scale (which in Chapter 22 we suggested was related to intrinsic religion).

As Patrick (1979) pointed out, with particular relevance to his Buddhist sample, the relationships of death anxiety to intrinsic-extrinsic religion may vary among religious groups. (The content of intrinsic and extrinsic scales may make them not very relevant for some religious traditions.) The relationships may also vary, in part, with the diverse death concern scales used. Spilka's (Spilka, Stout, Minton, & Sizemore, 1976) five death anxiety measures were intended to help clarify the complex domain of death concerns. At the same time he broadened the scope of death attitudes beyond that of anxiety or fear. His work on "death perspectives" is reviewed next.

DEATH PERSPECTIVES AND RELIGIOUS DIMENSIONS

Scale Origins

Spilka and his associates (Hooper & Spilka, 1970; Minton & Spilka, 1976) followed the lead of Gardner Murphy (1959) in developing ten death perspective scales—views of death as Natural End, Pain, Loneliness, Unknown, Punishment, Forsaking Dependents, Failure, Afterlife-of-Reward, Courage, and Indifference. Because Spilka (Spilka, Stout, Minton, & Sizemore, 1976, 1977) found the scales too long and cumbersome, he and his collaborators conducted factor analyses that reduced the number to eight scales with four to six items each. Death as an Afterlife-of-Reward and Death as Courage reflect positive feelings; the rest are negative. Scale items for each scale are shown in Box 23.1; the total scales are in Spilka's published article (Spilka, 1977).

Research

Four known studies have used some or all of the death perspective scales. Table 23.2 illustrates the fairly consistent findings with selected death perspective scales as used in Spilka's (Spilka, Stout, Minton, & Sizemore, 1976, 1977) and Cerny's (Cerny & Carter, 1977) studies. The religious dimensions have been arranged to correspond to the developmental model set forth in Chapter 22 (with no distinction intended between intrinsic and committed). As Cerny and Carter point out, correlations for the consensual scale (equivalent to our observance) consistently fall between the extrinsic on the one hand and intrinsic-committed on the other. This finding supports the intermediate position of observance religion in psychological effects, if not in the developmental sequence.

Using public college students, with more varied religious attitudes than Spilka's active Christians, Cerny found many higher correlations than did Spilka. While his results parallel Spilka's, there are some minor differences. His committed and intrinsic correlations tend to be more consistent than Spilka's. The significant correlations for indifference and consensual are in opposite directions, but they still maintain the intermediate position between extrinsic and intrinsic-committed.

In general the death perspectives support and extend the conclusions from the previously reported intrinsic-extrinsic and fear-of-death research. Positive reactions to death (Afterlife-of-Reward; Courage) are associated with all orientations but extrinsic. Spilka noted that the relations between consensual and positive views of death may reflect "that exposure to this theme has resulted in some acceptance of it from church teachings" (Spilka, Stout, Minton, & Sizemore, 1977, p. 175). They also reinforce earlier research in which fundamentalism was related to less fear of death (Swenson, 1961; Stewart, 1975).

Negative reactions to death (including but not limited to the last three perspectives in Table 23.2) are consistently associated with the extrinsic orientation. Consensual religion produced mixed results: about half of the correlations are nonsignificant; some show the negative perspectives related to consensual (though less strongly than with extrinsic); and a few cases associate consensual with rejection of a negative death perspective. Generally, intrinsic and committed religion are associated with lower levels of the negative perspectives. Again we can note the continuum from extrinsic through consensual to intrinsic-committed.

In a third study (Patrick, 1979), three negative perspectives (Pain and Loneliness; Unknown; Indifference) clustered together and correlated positively with extrinsic religiosity ($r = .28, p < .05$), with a nonsignificant relation to intrinsic. Afterlife-of-Reward correlated .31 with intrinsic and $-.23$ with extrinsic ($p < .05$ for both).

In the fourth study, involving 235 American clergy, (Spilka, Spangler, & Rea, 1977), those from more conservative churches were least concerned with Forsaking Dependents and viewed death more as reward—like the more intrinsic subjects in studies reported above. Liberals were at the other extreme, with moderates in the middle. However, on Spilka's Lack of Fear of Death scale, the liberals were highest (showing least fear), with moderates and conservatives showing

Box 23.1 SAMPLE ITEMS FROM SPILKA'S DEATH PERSPECTIVES SCALES

Scale 1. Death is pictured as Pain and Loneliness:
   A last agonizing moment; the ultimate anguish and torment.

Scale 2. Death is seen as an Afterlife-of-Reward:
   Entrance to a place of ultimate satisfaction; union with God and eternal bliss.

Scale 3. Indifference toward Death:
   Of little consequence; something to be shrugged off and forgotten.

Scale 4. Death as Unknown:
   The biggest uncertainty of all; the end of the known and the beginning of the unknown.

Scale 5. Death as Forsaking Dependents plus Guilt:
   Leaving one's dependents vulnerable to life's trials; a reason for feeling guilty.

Scale 6. Death as Courage:
   A chance to show that one has stood for something during life; a great moment of truth for oneself.

Scale 7. Death as Failure:
   An event that prevents the realization of one's potentialities; the end to one's hopes.

Scale 8. Death as a Natural End:
   An experience that comes to each of us because of the normal passage of time; a natural aspect of life.

Source: Spilka, Stout, Minton, and Sizemore (1977).

Table 23.2 CORRELATIONS OF DEATH PERSPECTIVES WITH RELIGIOUS DIMENSIONS

Selected death perspective scales	Dimensions of personal religion			
	Extrinsic	Consensual	Intrinsic	Committed
Afterlife-of-Reward	−.07 [a]	.20 **	.37 **	.35 **
	.05 [b]	.51 ***	.72 ***	.77 ***
Courage	−.01	.14	.12	.20 *
	.10	.35 ***	.41 ***	.45 ***
Forsaking Dependents	.31 **	.14	−.13	−.11
	.31 ***	.12	−.13 *	−.07
Pain and Loneliness	.36 **	.13	−.26	−.08
	.41 ***	.18 **	−.21 ***	−.19 **
Indifference	.39 **	.18 *	−.25 **	−.09
	.14 *	−.14 *	−.38 ***	−.38 ***

$*p < .05; **p < .01; ***p < .001.$
[a] Main entries from Spilka, Stout, Minton, and Sizemore (1977).
[b] Italicized entries from Cerny and Carter (1977).

335

relatively more fear. Such perplexing findings show a need for still more research on the relationship of religion to death attitudes and death anxieties.

FUTURE RESEARCH DIRECTIONS

Death Perspectives Versus Anxieties

Spilka's death perspectives have made the complexity of death attitudes more explicit by replacing early scales (which mixed a number of reactions to death) with more focused scales. However, the shift has tended to emphasize beliefs at the expense of feelings. Yet what religion does to one's emotional reactions is probably more crucial than how it changes one's beliefs. Troublesome as the affective or emotional issues are, we feel they should be addressed more directly and expertly in future religion and death research.

Theoretical and Definitional Issues

Magni (1971) offered the most scholarly criticism of methods used in death research. Among other points, he noted the lack of theoretical bases for death concern scales. Potentially important distinctions have not been made among fear of death, death anxiety, and death phobia. Temporary *states* of anxiety are not distinguished from permanent *trait* anxiety (e.g., Spielberger, 1966b). Magni's study also directed attention to alternative personality (ego) defenses that might be triggered by death-related anxieties. Response to these issues in religion and death research could contribute to an improved general understanding of personality dynamics.

Theological Issues

Patrick's (1979) fear-of-death research with a Buddhist group contributed to a much-needed integration of death research with theology. In addition to the relatively well studied dimensions of personal religion, doctrinal and theological differences may shape the way one's religion affects feelings about death. For example, in a more detailed report of their study, Kahoe and Dunn (1975) noted a distinct pattern of relationships for Methodists. They suggested that the Methodist doctrine of "works" made religious activity relevant to the hope for external life. Explicit research on the effects of "unconditional grace" versus "salvation by works" might reveal distinctive relations between religiousness and death anxieties. Such an analysis could begin an empirical psychology of theology (psychotheology)—a largely ignored potential within the psychology of religion.

REVIEW OF KEY CONCEPTS

Early Research on Death and Religion
    English study of terminally ill patients
    Broen's dimensions and death fears

differences and probable reasons for them between findings of Martin and
    Wrightsman, and Stewart

Death Anxiety and Intrinsic-Extrinsic Religion
    three methods of collecting data
    Bolt's findings with "consequences of one's own death"
    summary of six studies: number and direction of correlations with intrinsic
        religion and extrinsic religion
    significance of Patrick's Buddhist sample

Death Perspectives and Religious Dimensions
    Spilka's eight perspectives
    relations of positive death perspectives to religious dimensions
    relations of negative death perspectives to religious dimensions
    relations among extrinsic, consensual, and intrinsic dimensions
    reason for Cerny and Carter's generally higher correlations
    findings for liberal, moderate, and conservative clergy

Future Research Directions
    distinction between perspectives and anxieties
    distinctions among anxiety, fear, and other constructs
    theological implications for death and religion research

chapter 24

Individual and Institutional Interactions

An American denomination split into separate black and white organizations after the Civil War. In 1966 the two bodies were reunited, leaving a Tennessee town with two congregations now in the same denominational structure: a prosperous downtown "First Church," and a struggling black church with a part-time lay minister. The pastor of the white First Church, a man in his early thirties, made a proposal to the church board. He suggested nothing earth-shaking, just that their church might send a letter to the black congregation expressing willingness to cooperate and share fellowship in any way that would be desired and helpful.

The pastor was surprised at the reaction of the church board. The one-fourth who agreed, "Why, of course, it's the least we can do as Christians," was not surprising. Neither was the one-fourth who heatedly responded, "Over our dead bodies will such a thing happen." He was surprised and disconcerted by the half remaining who said, "Yes, it's the only Christian thing to do, but if we did, it would tear this church apart. So we cannot agree to it." Soon thereafter the disillusioned pastor resigned to enter graduate school in psychology.

INSTITUTIONS AND INDIVIDUALS

Religious institutions have needs of their own—apart from the needs of the individuals who people them. The above incident, as told to us by the pastor, starkly illustrates such a need. However, it also shows different individuals' reactions within one congregation.

Institutional Importance

To ignore the corporate, institutional aspects of religious experience is to overlook important religious realities. Ashbrook (1966) studied 651 ministers and lay persons in 120 churches of six denominations. Ministers tended to be encouraged about their work when members were more interested in maintaining the church property than in one another and "in being part of the church." They were discouraged about their ministries when there was "intense interest in church life and little involvement in keeping property in good condition" (1966, p. 415). For the ministers at least, the institution seemed to be personally more significant than individual members' spiritual lives.

Psychological Interaction

Not only does most religious expression occur in an institutional context, but institutions themselves influence individuals' religiousness. And of course individuals make up and shape institutions. One review of psychology of religion posed the problem thus:

> Why have the attempts to relate personality variables and religiosity been unsuccessful? One reason is the complexity of variables and measurements we are dealing with. . . . Behavior is a function of both stable traits from the inside

and presses of the situation from outside, and these traits, needs and presses all change over time [Beit-Hallahmi, 1976, p. 6].

Need refers to individual forces that direct behavior; *press* refers to environmental forces that help shape the individual's behavior. Behavior, then, is determined jointly by needs and press, frequently in complex interactions (Murray, 1938). In this chapter we apply the concept of need and press interactions to the model of individual religiousness posed in Chapter 22.

RELIGIOUS TYPES AND LEVELS

Extrinsic Needs and Press

Although we have characterized extrinsic religion as immature and unhealthy, extrinsic needs are part of human life that churches should not ignore. (The word *church* in this chapter includes temples, synagogues, denominations, and all other general religious institutions.) A friend remarked, "I never would have started going to the Baptist church if I hadn't been invited to a dinner that followed a church service. As a Catholic, I thought going to another church was a sin, but I was reached through my stomach." As we noted in Chapter 2, all varieties of physical and psychological needs may be factors in religion.

Guilt and Anxiety Religions promise answers to feelings of guilt and anxiety over sin and the human condition. Yet religious press (the influence of the religious environment) occurs in deliberate efforts to rouse guilt and anxieties, creating conflicts that may be resolved by conversion or other religious solutions. Adolescents are particularly susceptible to such anxieties. There is no clear line between the creation of unnecessary and harmful guilt, which may aggravate neurotic tendencies, and an affirmation of the frailties and insecurities of the human condition. The latter may be a justifiable antidote to an overly optimistic view of the world (see Chapter 25).

Sorrow and Misfortune Religion almost everywhere attends to death, illness, and other conditions of human grief and misfortune. Persons are frequently drawn to the church by its ministries in those times. Even a committed, intrinsic, church member occasionally has extrinsic needs, and attention to them is a legitimate part of the church's ministry. A serious mistake, however, lies in the implication that that is all there is to the church. Another potential problem is that a particular religious interpretation of misfortune (e.g., "It's the will of God") may not provide comfort for a person's individual needs. One intrinsic way to help people resolve grief is to involve them in comforting others who encounter misfortune.

Social Privation Severe social privation, more than any other condition, may cause a church to develop a primarily extrinsic press. Cargo cults (see Chapter 2) are a most extreme example, but some lower-class and black churches also play this role. A black church, for example, may primarily offer emotional consolation and promise of escape from apparently inescapable social conditions. Such extrinsic press provides merely symbolic gratification, and should be distinguished from an activist church style that promotes civil rights and other means of improving people's objective conditions.

Social Needs and Press

Social needs for affiliating or associating with other people are considered one kind of extrinsic need, but they also lead into observance religion.

Loneliness and Other Social Needs   Most modern Western societies have lost traditional sources of social support, and many people feel lonely: a craving to belong, to feel wanted, to receive attention from other people (see Middlebrook, 1974, Chapter 5). We often expect the institutional church to fill such needs—and justifiably so, given the principle of love that most religions espouse. The quality of social relations available in a church may profoundly affect its ability to draw and retain members. After one former church staff member moved to a new town, he and his wife joined a church of a different denomination. When they had attended the church of their customary faith, very few people had spoken to them. The friendliness of the other church overcame doctrinal differences in their choice of church membership.

In a Gallup Poll 37% of the unchurched said that churches and synagogues were not warm and accepting of outsiders. Thirteen percent of the group said they would attend a church if they were invited by a member and liked the congregation (Proctor, 1979).

National Churches   In more traditional societies with strong national or ethnic churches, the social factors will be quite different from what we have been describing. For a Latin American Folk Catholic, an Israeli Orthodox Jew, or an Iranian Shi'ite Muslim, allegiance to the religious group is supported by a vast complex of cultural and social influences.

Social Press   Many Protestant churches and sects that have experienced the greatest growth in this century can be characterized by a strongly social, affiliation press, for example, warm interpersonal relations, visiting before and after worship services, and many social activities. Some people consider such social emphases an offense against such truly religious purposes as objective worship (see Chapter 12). Exclusive social concerns, like any extrinsic press, may justifiably be criticized. Yet a church might be equally remiss if it did not care for current and prospective members.

Extrinsic and Social Need-Press Interactions   People may become fixated on gratifying comfort and companionship needs, particularly if the religious press strongly affirms them. Some people need to be deliberately nurtured toward more mature religious expressions, while others will not make the transitions to higher levels anyway. On the other hand, the psychological makeup of some individuals with intrinsic religious needs leads them to transform or abandon a church that fails to go beyond the extrinsic and social levels. The institution and its members are interdependent, and each can influence the other for good or for bad.

Observance Needs and Press

Almost every conceivable religion devotes considerable attention to observance activities—rituals, prayers, worship, fasting, offerings of money or produce, study of religious texts, etc. As the keeper of such observances, the church is enhanced as followers practice them. Observance typically dominates religious press.

Observance Needs   Needs for observance are not so obvious as is the source of such press. However, rituals and routines give life stability, order, and meaning, and the lack of ritual connotes considerable insecurity. In residential "milieu therapies," particularly for children and adolescents, much of the treatment depends on establishing routines and habitual behavior.

Managing Observance Press   Churches differ widely in their forms of observance. Quakers or free-church Protestants may rebel against "high-church" ritual and liturgy, but they substitute relatively predictable routines of their own. A "low-church" congregation may be quite disoriented if the scripture is to be read in unison instead of responsively; or if two hymns, rather than one, precede the morning prayer; or if the offertory hymn is sung sitting rather than standing. Yet routine and habit have their limits (similarly to the mystery versus reality issue in worship, discussed in Chapter 12). "The way we've always done it" may become the wrong way, just because meaning is lost through repetition. As a rule may be proved by its exceptions, so the value of the routine may be enhanced by its carefully planned violation: a dramatic or dance routine instead of the sermon, or a night of family devotion and fellowship instead of an evening service.

Religious leaders need to appreciate the importance of observance practices of all kinds, both for the church and for the religious and ego development of followers. They should also realize that when special circumstances or advanced stages of religious development subvert established routines, the individual involved is not necessarily any less devout. The outward routines are only a means to an end: the individual's relationship and devotion to the Deity.

Belief Needs and Press

Some churches make orthodoxy of belief a crucial test of fellowship; others minimize belief or consider themselves noncreedal. Although almost every religion has developed a system of beliefs, dogma, symbols, and/or cosmology, evidence suggests that beliefs are a "secondary accretion" to religion. Casserly (1953) observed that the early church produced dogmatic formulas only when its integrity was threatened. Belief may be the most problematic area of religious life.

Belief Needs Within the Church   Belief serves both defensive and coping functions (see Chapters 2, 13, 22). Authoritarian dogmatists use rigid belief systems for security in a world they see as threatening. True believers commit themselves to a system of belief that gives meaning, purpose, and direction. It is said that Gordon Allport struggled to the end of his life with the quandary of how a person can make a complete commitment to a belief that must always be tentative.

Belief Press   No wonder that most religious groups take one of the easy routes: insisting on a strict adherence to a belief system, or easily accepting that "it doesn't really matter what you believe." Several years ago the religious education division of a major denomination proposed a new emphasis, labeled "Quest"—a search. The program was soundly defeated in the annual meeting; not ready for honest seeking, the denomination held that it already had the answers.

If Casserly's analysis is accurate, we might paraphrase scripture and say, "Belief was made for the church, and not the church for belief." Dogma may produce much abuse (see Chapter 26). Religious leaders have their own psychological needs and may impose their dogmatic defenses on their church members. The complexities of belief press can be illustrated by the 1980 church disciplining of Roman Catholic Hans Kung. Pope John Paul II defended stripping the Swiss theologian of his university teaching post because he denied the 110-year-old doctrine of papal infallibility. The pope claimed the doctrine as "the key itself for certainty in professing and proclaiming the faith, for the life and behavior of believers. . . . We profess the infallibility doctrine that is a gift from Christ to the church" (United Press International, 1980). Papal infallibility was considered necessary to give Catholic laity an absolute certainty of their belief. So theologian Kung was denied the relatively autonomous grounds of his own faith system.

If church leaders put religious beliefs in perspective (honoring the functions that belief serves for the institution and for individuals), valuable purposes might be met, while abuses are minimized. Firm belief is not to be disparaged; the true-believer stance has much to recommend it. However, intrinsic religion does not necessarily affirm dogma, and autonomy rejects personal dependence on it.

Intrinsic Needs and Press

Intrinsic motivation has been seen as an open, growing, coping, nondefensive, unselfish approach to life. Persons who accept a religious world view with such motivation tend to become intrinsically religious, even without strong religious press. On the other hand, some people probably are so dominated by extrinsic needs that they will resist all human efforts to nurture intrinsic religiousness within them. Most people, by personality and temperament, are at neither extreme, and the church with an appropriate press could impel them toward increasingly intrinsic religiousness. Although understandings of psychology and virtually all advanced theologies support the ideal of intrinsic religion, unfortunately some churches fail to promote it—perhaps they are overly occupied with extrinsic or observance concerns.

Intrinsic Needs   A Gallup Poll found that most people who rejected the church did so on intrinsically spiritual bases. Sixty percent of the unchurched agreed that "most churches and synagogues today have lost the real spiritual part of religion" (as did 52% of those who do attend church). The unchurched also felt that churches were more concerned with organization than with spiritual issues (56%), and that organized religion does not effectively help people to find meaning in life (49%) (Proctor, 1979). Many churches appear to neglect the intrinsic even more than extrinsic and observance needs.

Varieties of Intrinsic Religion   Meadow (1978a) describes two ways of achieving the self-giving spirituality of intrinsic religion. An "active" type symbolically takes up the cross daily, in the Christian idiom (e.g., Luke 9 : 23), while a "receptive" type surrenders, as a grain of wheat must die in order to yield a harvest (e.g., John 12 : 24). The active type is more likely to become a religious zealot or ascetic, whereas the receptive type inclines toward being a mystic or a "good neighbor" (see Chapter 19). Individuals are probably predisposed by personality to prefer one or the other form of spirituality. However, in their extremes both have pitfalls.

St. Paul's classic depiction of love (1 Corinthians 13 : 4–7—"love is patient and kind") weaves two themes: "Love makes one patient in enduring evil, active in conferring good" (Erdman, 1928, p. 118). The prime spiritual virtue includes control of one's own selfish interests (dying to self) and also a positive reaching out to others (giving of self). This involves accentuating the intrinsic drives and eliminating the extrinsic.

Autonomy Needs and Press

As we observed in Chapter 22, religious press for autonomy is rare and weak. Although a few churches defend and promote religious autonomy, they are seldom very influential and seem mainly to provide religious expression for persons who have matured within and beyond conventional faiths. One should not expect most faiths actively to advocate autonomy. Their main challenge is to deal with individuals who have reached that final level of religious development—other than with suppression and heresy trials.

Individuals and Autonomy Needs   A fundamentalist minister and leading university administrator made national news—in part from conflicts over his advancing level of religious development. He pleaded guilty to an offense that involved driving under the influence of alcohol. The minister had taken his first drink at 54, to relax after a mild heart attack. More health problems followed, and he began to doubt his religion, his church, and his role as a spiritual leader. He told the judge, "For years it had been increasingly difficult for me to accept the simplistic assumptions of the hell-fire and brimstone fundamentalism which most preachers in this church teach" (Footlick & Kasindorf, 1976, p. 49).

Another university chief executive, Pentecostal Holiness faith healer Oral Roberts, made a more successful transition. At age 50, in the prime of his career, he joined the United Methodist church. In defense of the change a Methodist bishop commented, "The church has men of various talents and interpretations" (Oral Roberts Joins the Methodists, 1968, p. 34). Having formed his own evangelistic, healing, and university organizations independently of any Pentecostal denomination, Roberts was able to move into a culturally, socially, and theologically more compatible group, without jeopardizing his ministry.

Churches and Autonomy Needs   Most churches, even the most orthodox, find ways to accommodate religiously autonomous individuals. When early Baptists were dissenting against established orthodoxies, they advocated the theological principle of the *priesthood of the believer*—that individuals before God could interpret the Bible according to their own consciences. Baptists have now developed their own orthodoxy, but the religiously autonomous can usually find defense in the still-accepted doctrine of the priesthood of the believer.

Recently Roman Catholics have apparently developed a different adaptive mechanism. In the 1960s Catholics who differed with the church on such issues as birth control felt compelled to leave the church. Now a Gallup Poll shows that most Catholics who had attended church at least once in the previous week think that divorced Catholics should be able to remarry in the church (67%), and that the church should allow birth control (72%). "Catholics are more inclined to disagree with the official position of the church, but less inclined to leave the church than in the past" (Proctor, 1979, pp. 62–63). Informal observation suggests that many dissident Catholics are quietly supported by sympathetic parish priests, who thus provide a buffer between them and the top levels of the church hierarchy.

CONCLUSION

The case of autonomy may be a suitable model for understanding the relationship of church press and individual needs in general. Each church is characterized by particular press (which may be related to the major dimensions of religion identified in this unit) because of its origins, traditions, socioeconomic and psychological context, theology, and other factors. Almost any religious tenet, pushed to its furthest extreme, may be rendered absurd and untenable, but the church has formal or informal ways of moderating its special emphases to adjust to individual differences and new situations. Otherwise, interdenominational mobility would be greater than it is now—from 13% for Jews to 45% for Disciples of Christ in one recent study (Kluegel, 1980). Any church might periodically evaluate the appropriateness of its press (in the light of theology and psychological needs) and make changes to enhance encounters of individuals with the Ultimate.

REVIEW OF KEY CONCEPTS

Institutions and Individuals
      evidence for institutional importance
      definitions of *need, press,* and *interaction*

Religious Types and Levels
 need and press in guilt and anxiety
 need and press in sorrow and misfortune
 extrinsic press in social privation
 role of loneliness in religion
 use and abuse of social press
 how need and press interact in extrinsic and social areas
 nature of observance press and needs
 how to manage observance press
 the purpose of ritual and routine
 needs met by belief within churches
 ways belief press can lead to abuse
 proper role of belief for the individual and for the institution
 patterns of developing intrinsic religiousness
 evidence for intrinsic religious needs
 active and receptive types of intrinsic religion
 rarity of autonomy press in churches
 conflict and resolution of autonomy needs
 how churches manage individuals' autonomy needs

Conclusion
 churches' need to reconcile their traditional press with individuals' needs

five

A CRITICAL EVALUATION OF RELIGION

chapter 25

The Church as Haven

We used to hear about a man who was afraid to go to a hospital: So many people died there! It is a bit ironic that hospitals—places of healing—harbor so much disease. But of course it is the diseased who need the cure.

The analogous religious condition may be reflected by that classic heretic's excuse: "The church is not for me; it's too full of hypocrites." If the accusation suggests that members of a religious group deliberately pretend to be something they are not, it probably deserves strong dissent. However, if the skeptic is pointing out a gap between the ideals of the faith and the spiritual lack of many adherents, there can be little defense. Empirical studies show consistent, striking psychological infirmities among those who identify with religious groups.

ADRIFT IN THE DOLDRUMS

In the days of yore, when men were iron and ships were wooden, those "iron" men quailed at thoughts of the doldrums—that equatorial belt of frequent calms, where sailing ships might lie for weeks beneath the searing sun. Many members of Western churches can be likened to such a becalmed ship, suffering from sundry deficits—no wind in their sails, or in more modern metaphor, too little steam in their boilers or fuel in their gas tanks. A major group in one fundamentalist church were the "comfort-seekers," insecure persons who were looking for security from death and hell, illness and old age (Monaghan, 1967).

Self-esteem

Low self-esteem is the most general condition of "personal inadequacy" among religious people (Dittes, 1969, 1971). Among 2842 graduate students in 25 universities, religious affiliation and church attendance were related to low scores on three measures of "self-esteem and confidence" (Dittes, 1971, p. 368; Stark, 1963). Scores on personality inventories similarly relate religiousness to low self-esteem. Among Protestants in one study, for example, high religious values on the Allport-Vernon inventory were associated with "low self-reliance" (Protho & Jensen, 1950).

Dittes, a Baptist minister as well as a psychologist, is not alarmed at such findings:

> Religious proponents and detractors alike can agree that religion functions to meet needs of those who feel frustrated, threatened, inadequate, deprived. The analyses of Freud and Marx ought not to be an insult to those whose highest religious celebrations commemorate a captivity or a crucifixion and whose scriptures find focus in such passages as the prophecy of the suffering servant in Isaiah or the Beatitudes of the gospels, or whose doctrine and practice enhance recognition of [humanity's] fallen state and fundamental helplessness [1971, p. 367].

Those who are most attracted to religion might be expected to show more personal deficiencies. Dittes quotes Jesus: "Those who are well have no need of a physician, but those who are sick; I came not to call the righteous but sinners" (Mark 2 : 17). Allport also observed the "tailored security" that religion offers those who are "tormented by self-doubt and insecurity" (1968, p. 225).

Loneliness

Since self-esteem depends partly on positive responses from other persons, it is not surprising that students who belonged to churches received fewer friendship choices than did non-church members, in a sociometric study (Bonney, 1949). Religious cults attract many people by offering friendship. This is especially true of cults that appeal to American young people, such as Sun Myung Moon's Unification church.

After a 3-year study of the appeal of Eastern cults, theologian Harvey Cox concluded, "Most of the members of these movements seem to be looking for simple human friendship" (1977b, p. 39; 1977a). The young people fail to find warmth and affection at work, school, church, or home, and when it is offered by members of a religious cult, many of them accept it. Interestingly, only new cult members admit the primary attraction of friendship. After a few weeks they tend to offer a "more theologically proper answer, such as . . . *It was my karma*" (1977b, p. 39). This observation supports our model of religious development (Chapter 22), which posits social affiliation (friendship ties) as an early step in observance religion, followed by a theological or belief emphasis.

Intelligence, Education, and Status

Another deficit that can contribute to low self-esteem is relatively low intelligence. At least five studies have shown negative relationships between religiousness and intelligence and/or education. Similarly, high status, as indicated by listing in *Who's Who,* has long been associated with religious skepticism and nonaffiliation (Dittes, 1969, 1971).

However, Kosa and Schommer (1961) found a *positive* relationship between intelligence and participation in college religious organizations. Similarly, national surveys show that higher social classes participate in more social and community activities, including church. Three such surveys in the late 1950s, with a total of over 5000 respondents, found higher education and occupational levels to be related to more frequent church attendance for Protestants and Catholics (for Jews, status and education were confounded with Orthodoxy). Table 25.1 summarizes some of these data. Interestingly, income was not reliably related to church attendance (Lazerwitz, 1961). Since education and occupational status *are* related to income, churches possibly include many people whose income is discrepant with their education and status—either with relatively low status and high income, or with higher status relative to income. Either case suggests self-esteem problems that may motivate church attendance.

Table 25.1   CHURCH ATTENDANCE BY YEARS OF SCHOOL COMPLETED

Group and education	Number	Percentages in groups	
		Regularly attend	Never attend
Protestants			
0–8 grades	1381	33	10
4 years college or more	374	52	4
Roman Catholics			
0–8 grades	436	63	7
4 years college or more	64	89	1

Source: Lazerwitz (1961, p. 306).

Boredom

No known study shows church members to be more bored than others, but some clearly indicate that boredom (or deficits of excitement) may cause people to seek certain kinds of religious experience. Cox found this motivation in studying Eastern cults' appeal. Although young people may sample a number of cults, they "do not seem to be looking for just another kick or 'trip' to add to their collection" (1977b, p. 39). Yet Cox summarized some of their motives this way:

> All I got at any church I ever went to were sermons or homilies *about* God, *about* "the peace that passes understanding." Words, words, words. It was all in the head. I never really *felt* it. It was all abstract, never direct, always somebody else's account of it. It was so dull and boring. . . . It was like reading the label instead of eating the contents [1977b, p. 39].

Some Eastern cults provide mystical experiences that help wean drug abusers from their dependence on psychedelic drugs—itself a response to craving for experience (Robbins, 1969). Similarly, in a study of Jim Jones's People's Temple, Lifton noted that "cults provide communal forms of ecstasy—psychic states so intense that time and death disappear" (1979, p. 28).*

Not only the routinization of traditional religions, but also our technological, materialistic society itself has been charged with a mind-deadening, dehumanizing sameness (G. Clark, 1979). When the search for stimulation turns toward religion, that deficit may produce a more genuinely religious response than resort to the church as a haven from ineptness and self-doubt.

Evaluation

Sick people go to a hospital not just as a haven, but to be healed; the psychologically deficient and infirm may similarly expect church to remedy their deficiencies and enrich their lives. As seen in Chapter 20, the more primitive extrinsic religious orientation is correlated with such psychological deficits, but intrinsic religion is not. Studies have reported correlations of $-.32$ and $-.56$ between educa-

*Copyright © 1979 by the New York Times Company. Reprinted by permission.

tional level and extrinsic religiousness; lower education goes with higher scores on extrinsic religion. Neither study found a notable correlation between education and intrinsic religion ($-.04$ in Kahoe & Dunn, 1975). At least six or seven other studies have shown various deficits only for the less mature (extrinsic and consensual) forms of religion (Dittes, 1969, 1971).

However, theological positions as varied as those of Martin Luther, Sören Kierkegaard, and Karl Barth do not expect the religious life to produce psychological healing. Such thinking stresses that religion is intended for worship, not a surrogate psychotherapy. In his discussion of Eastern mysticism as a way out of psychedelic drug use, Robbins (1969) implies that, once straightened out, former addicts often drop the religious world view and become secular. The religious purpose apparently gets lost in the therapeutic.

On the other hand, Father Eamonn O'Doherty (University College, Dublin) developed a concept of "multiple effect"—referring to

> the fact that any single act may have several consequences. . . . The action of a neurotic person that, from the point of view of a psychiatrist, may achieve a temporary relief from anxiety may, nevertheless, at the same time be an act of genuine worship [Bartemeier, 1965, p. 311; O'Doherty, 1964].

Coming to religion because of one's deficits reflects extrinsic religion. Not all such religion remains purely extrinsic; from egocentric origins, a self-giving religion may develop. However, when deficits are extreme, and no strong conflicts, anxieties, or incentives drive the person toward higher religious development, religion may remain a haven only, and leave one languishing still in the doldrums.

CIRCLE THE WAGONS

When the wagon train scout spotted a party of presumably hostile Native Americans (if one believes three generations of Saturday matinee movies and television westerns), the cry was passed to "circle the wagons." The "prairie schooners," the covered wagons, were drawn into a tight circle to defend against the anticipated onslaught. Some religious personalities reenact this pioneer vignette. Both the personality bases and the religious responses thus implied differ somewhat from those we have just discussed.

Defensive Authoritarianism

Many studies (e.g., Adorno et al., 1950; Rokeach, 1960) have shown relationships between highly "orthodox" or fundamentalistic religiousness and personality types noted for "desperate defenses": "The label of 'authoritarianism' has become the most popular general term to describe these characteristics, which seem to be primarily marked by an intolerance of ambiguity and a reliance on structure, either internal or external" (Dittes, 1971, p. 371).

Submission to an absolutely unquestionable set of religious dogmas and moral codes gives a great deal of security. The most common religious type in one fundamentalist church was the "authority-seeker," who displayed "a strong and consistent desire for a submissive relation toward authority" (Monaghan, 1967, p. 239). This source of authority may be a person, such as a cult leader or a minister, an orally transmitted dogma, or a written canon, such as the Bible or Qur'ān (Koran).

Resisting Change   Perceived threats to an established social order may motivate an insecure person toward an authoritarian organization—religious or secular (Photiadis & Schweiker, 1970). Lifton describes the "constricted style" of personality that characterizes some cults such as Jim Jones's ill-fated group:

> They are part of a worldwide impulse toward fundamentalism . . . —an illusory attempt to fend off currents of change through the construction of an airtight moral and social order, through restoring the perfect harmony of a past that never was, or projecting a similar future (as in the case of the People's Temple) based on imagery of a past golden age [1979, pp. 27–28].*

The preponderance of conversions to "authoritarian" denominations during economically bad times (Sales, 1972; see Chapter 7) strongly suggests a defensive use of authoritarian religion.

Controlling Impulses   People may adopt an authoritarian religion to help control their own hostile impulses. Such repressed hostility is considered a basic feature of the authoritarian personality. Many veterans of the 1960s antiwar and counterculture movements were later attracted to authoritarian religious cults: "They felt a need to inhibit their anarchistic questing with clear guidelines and firm structures, to purge themselves of the competitiveness, anxiety and anger that seemed to mar even their most selfless projects" (Gordon, 1979, p. 3).

Limits to Authoritarian Religion

Despite the conspicuous authoritarianism in some religion, and the crasser implications of the authoritarian personality, authoritarianism in religion usually finds limits. Several studies have failed to identify religion with the meaner aspects of authoritarianism—mental illness, extrapunitiveness (overt hostility toward others), and intrapunitiveness (hostility directed to oneself) (Dittes, 1969, 1971).

Clearer distinctions emerged in the relations of intrinsic and extrinsic religious orientations to authoritarianism (see Chapter 20). Generally extrinsic religion was positively correlated with authoritarianism; with a control for acquiescence response set, intrinsic religion was also related to authoritarianism, though less so than was extrinsic religion (Kahoe, 1974a).

Further studies (Kahoe, 1975b, 1977a) examined the relationships of intrinsic and extrinsic religion to individual items of the F scale—a measure of authoritarianism (Adorno et al., 1950). Extrinsic religion had a generalized relationship to this scale—with no items reliably different from the others in the relationship. Intrinsic religion, however, clearly was related to only certain aspects of authoritarianism. F scale items positively related to intrinsic religion included: "Science has its place, but there are many important things that can never possibly be understood by the human mind"; "Every person should have complete faith in some supernatural power whose decisions he obeys without question"; and "Young people sometimes get rebellious ideas, but as they grow up they ought to get over them and settle down." These items reflect things a committed but conventional Christian can be expected to believe. Thus specific religious beliefs—not a defensive personality—define "authoritarianism" in intrinsically religious persons.

Evaluation

People threatened by external change or internal impulses may be drawn to an authoritarian religion for structure and thus security. Both conventional fundamentalistic religions and unconventional authoritarian cults may serve such personal needs. However, no research indicates that *all* persons in such groups are motivated by their defenses or possess constricted personalities. Immature, extrinsically religious persons tend to show the whole scope of the authoritarian personality, but even intrinsically religious persons may adopt some authoritarian aspects. The "true believer" identity of the intrinsically religious suggests that some persons choose to live within a rigid, authoritarian structure as a matter of religious commitment. The person who most loudly declares the absolute authority of the Qur'ān or the Bible may be an intrinsic true believer, rather than one with a tightly drawn circle of defenses. Almost of necessity, though, the religious authoritarian will be locked into an observance form of religion (see model in Chapter 22) and never express the thoroughly intrinsic orientation, let alone the freedom of religious autonomy.

DON'T ROCK THE BOAT

Other timid souls find in religion another comfortable haven. Religion is one aspect among several attitudes and personality traits that form the fabric of a highly conventional "American way of life." Some people seem firmly committed to the status quo, or to keep our nautical metaphor limping along, follow the mottoes: "Make no waves," "Don't rock the boat."

Dependence and Suggestibility

Studies show religious persons, particularly the more orthodox ones, to be relatively more submissive, obedient, and dependent in interpersonal relations and more conforming in their social attitudes. "Most religious systems recommend humility and submissiveness. It is a good question whether such sanctions most likely produce, attract, or rationalize such personal characteristics" (Dittes, 1969, p. 638).

Social Desirability   Some research findings suggest that religious people respond to personality measures with a "social desirability set." They tend to score higher on measures of social desirability and on the Lie and K scales (used to measure test-taking attitudes) of the Minnesota Multiphasic Personality Inventory. The Lie scale has items like, "If I knew I wouldn't get caught, I would sneak into a movie house"—true for most people. The more subtle K scale measures the extent to which test takers tend to present themselves in a favorable light.

Highly religious persons' scores on such scales must be interpreted with caution. While they may see themselves as better than they really are, at the same time their religion probably has taught them to act in "proper" ways. Insofar as they have actually adopted conventional attitudes and behaviors, religious people may be completely honest and still score very high on a social desirability scale. However, they may have lost touch with unappealing aspects of their own feelings, behaviors, and motives. Some religious people are so scrupulously "correct" that they actually would not commit those little Lie scale misdemeanors that most people would. But this stance shows how very submissive and dependent they can be to parents and other religious figures. High Lie scale scorers are usually seen as rigid and psychologically naive people with strong needs to be seen as upright and virtuous.

Optimistic Denial   One long-standing religious tradition reflects "eternal optimism"—at the cost of denying substantial aspects of reality. In two of his classic Gifford lectures William James (1902) contrasted the "religion of healthy mindedness" with the "divided self" and the "sick soul." James equated "healthy mindedness" with "mind-cure" or "mind over matter." James documented the diverse roots and nature of "mind-cure":

> One of the doctrinal sources of Mind-cure is the four gospels; another is Emersonianism or New England Transcendentalism; another is Berkeleyan idealism; another is spiritism, with its messages of "law" and "progress" and "development"; another the optimistic popular science evolutionism . . .; and finally, Hinduism has contributed a strain. But the most characteristic feature of the mind-cure movement is an inspiration much more direct. The leaders in this faith have had an intuitive belief in the all-saving power of healthy-minded attitudes as such, in the conquering efficacy of courage, hope, and trust, and a correlative contempt for doubt, fear, worry, and all nervously precautionary states of mind [1902/1961, p. 90].

Denial has been considered an element of faith healing (see Chapter 11; Pattison et al., 1973). Similarly the Christian Science faith is largely based on systematically denying apparent realities that most people affirm as an inherent part of life—sickness, death, and evil. James clearly indicates the limitations of healthy-mindedness without denying that it is a genuine religious position with "dignity and importance," (1902/1961, p. 118):

> The only relief that healthy-mindedness can give is by saying "Stuff and non-sense, get out into the open air!" or "Cheer up, old fellow, you'll be all right

ere-long, if you will only drop your morbidness!" But in all seriousness, can such bald animal talk as that be treated as a rational answer? . . . Our troubles lie indeed too deep for *that* cure. The fact that we *can* die, that we *can* be ill at all, is what perplexes us; . . . Let sanguine healthy-mindedness do its best with its strange power of living in the moment and ignoring and forgetting, still the evil background is really there to be thought of, and the skull will grin in at the banquet [1902/1961, pp. 122–124].

Dittes (1969, 1971) also notes recent Christian advocacy of the "power of positive thinking" and "peace of mind" philosophies. Surely religion has consistently affirmed that "life and organization will win, that death and disorganization will lose" (Burhoe, 1975, p. 7). (Chapter 15 also stressed the role of religion in promoting hope.) Still, a one-sidedly optimistic religious faith connotes a rather naive suggestibility, predisposed to see religion as a haven by denying the harsher aspects of reality.

Racial Prejudice

Religionists have long been embarrassed by the relationship between racial prejudice and religious membership or participation (see Chapter 20). We now reexamine these data and place them in further perspective.

Empirical Research   Most early interpretations of the relationship of prejudice to religion assumed that personality weaknesses and defenses were involved. Allport concluded:

> A large number of people, by virtue of their psychological make-up, require for their economy of living both prejudice and religion. Some, for example, are tormented by self-doubt and insecurity. Prejudice enhances their self-esteem; religion provides them a tailored security. Others are guilt-ridden; prejudice provides a scapegoat, and religion relief [1968, p. 225].

The single most definitive review of "Christian faith and ethnic prejudice" was done by Gorsuch and Aleshire (1973), who examined all 72 of the relevant empirical studies published up to that time (1940–1972). Box 25.1 summarizes the review in their own words insofar as possible (minor deletions and alterations are not noted). The key empirical finding is number 7: Prejudice is associated with *marginal* church membership and participation. Nonreligious people and the most active, committed (intrinsic—number 5) church members are less prejudiced, and in the most careful studies the very active are less prejudiced than the nonreligious (number 8).

Interpretation   The results are interpreted to mean that "prejudiced people are conforming to 'the great American way of life,' a sentiment which includes strong elements of both white Anglo-Saxon supremacy and Christianity" (Gorsuch & Aleshire, 1973, p. 288). Lenski (1963, p. 192 ff.) is cited as finding that church members who were highly involved in the community but not in the church were

---

Box 25.1   RELATIONSHIPS BETWEEN CHRISTIAN FAITH AND ETHNIC PREJUDICE

---

1. Religion as a global construct is distinct from prejudice (284).
2. When church membership is the only measure of religious commitment, church members are more prejudiced than those who have never joined a church (283).
3. When fundamentalism is used as the criterion, the more religious people score higher on prejudice measures (284).
4. The extrinsically oriented person tends to be more prejudiced (284).
5. A person who is intrinsically committed to [a] religious position and is a member of a moderate denomination tends to be less prejudiced (284).
6. People who are extrinsic and accept stereotyped Christian beliefs are the most prejudiced subgroup (284).
7. The marginal church member manifested more prejudice than either the nonactive or the most active members (285).
8. Three of the four stratified or probability samples found the more actives to be less prejudiced than the nonreligious (286).
9. The general conclusions held regardless of when the studies were conducted, from whom the data came, the region where the data were collected, or the type of prejudice studied (281).
10. Additional personality characteristics were not needed to explain the relationship between religion and prejudice (281).

Source: Page numbers cited from Gorsuch and Aleshire (1973).

---

likely to be prejudiced. Such involvement in the larger community, then, is relevant to prejudice, and that "respectable" involvement includes both church membership and a little—but not too much—church activity. Lenski's church members who were highly involved in religious activities but not in the community were unlikely to be prejudiced; Gorsuch and Aleshire cite other evidence that both the "nuclear" church member and the nonreligious have stronger, independent values.

Gorsuch and Aleshire concluded that simple conformity to the conventional community explained the relationship between religion and prejudice. However, conformity and conventionality imply fundamentalist and stereotyped religious beliefs (Box 25.1, numbers 3 and 6). Adherence to such beliefs indicates consensual or observance religion (Chapter 22), which is relatively immature and long-related to prejudice (Allen & Spilka, 1967).

Sexism

Attitudes with regard to traditional sex roles, equivalent to prejudice in ethnic relations, have been labeled *sexism*. Sexism implies stereotyped sex roles that follow custom and do not recognize or respect differences among people of either gender. In recent practice, of course, it implies the denial of certain rights, roles, or prerogatives to women, just because they are of the female gender. Many empirical and conceptual studies indicate that religious people are more likely to hold sexist attitudes than are the nonreligious (e.g., Kahoe, 1974b; McClain, 1979; Meadow, 1977a, 1978c; Neal, 1979). The relationship parallels that for racial prejudice, especially since sexism, like prejudice, is related to authoritarianism (correlation .47 for both men and women in Kahoe, 1974b; .48 in Meadow, 1977a).

There are differences between sexism and racism as they relate to religion, as we shall see in Chapter 26. However, conventional, sexist people may find reinforcement and support for their sex-role stereotypes in churches that maintain traditional sex roles.

Conservatism

Prejudice and sexism are but two specific attitudes of general conservatism. Conservative attitudes are theoretically and empirically linked to authoritarianism and constricted personality defenses (e.g., Adorno et al., 1950; Wilson, 1973).

A previously cited (Chapter 5) study on the development of religious conservatism suggests that such attitudes come primarily from conventional socialization. Variables that imply defensive personalities—such as authoritarianism—are related primarily to racial conservatism (prejudice), but not to religious conservatism. The latter was related to intrinsic religion and responsibility—indices of conventional socialization (Kahoe, 1977b).

Nonconforming Orthodoxy

The attitudes reviewed above are "conventional" for American culture. When religion is not within the norm for a society, it might not at all be related to conformity. An officially nonreligious society like the Soviet Union might be a good test case, though formal empirical research would be difficult there. We do have access to some relevant observations.

For 40 years after the revolution and establishment of the Soviet regime, "the only religious people in Russia were uneducated and of simple faith" (Babris, 1978, p. 497). However, in recent decades religious interest has revived among the educated. Besides well-known individual dissidents like Aleksandr Solzhenitsyn, we are told that "the young intelligentsia of the mid-1960's were particularly open to conversion, and the trend continues to this day at an ever increasing rate" (Babris, 1978, p. 498). The renewal has occurred primarily among the Russian Orthodox.

> The most active section of Orthodox believers is composed of newly converted intellectuals and artists, aged between twenty-five and thirty-five. . . . the position of young Orthodox intellectuals can be summed up as being syncretic, abstract-Christian and "generally religious," and construed as a spiritual-intellectual reaction against the narrow sectarianism of official faiths [Babris, 1978, p. 498].

This portrait is clearly different from anything we see in the United States, and shows that religion can be a strongly *nonconformist* value. It reflects a position beyond the conventional faith (Chapter 4; Fowler, 1975) that distinguishes intrinsic or committed Christians in this country from the prejudiced, conventional majority in our churches.

Evaluation

We usually disparage people who are suggestible, conventional, and conforming. Persons in these religious categories are likely to be stuck in the observance semicircle of our model of religious development—almost as firmly as authority seekers. Some may become intrinsic "true believers," but rarely will they be transformed into autonomous religionists.

But is our idealization of autonomy, individuality, and self-sufficiency a universally valid value? In his American Psychological Association presidential address, "Perspectives on Selfhood," M. Brewster Smith reflected:

> I think of the chronic attrition of meaning, hope, and community—the basic supports of selfhood labeled by the Christian tradition as faith, hope and charity—that has generally accompanied technological modernity and the decline of mythic world views. . . . The individualistic version of selfhood that has characterized our Western tradition since the Renaissance, which we Americans have managed even to exaggerate, seems an increasingly poor fit to our requirements for survival in unavoidable interdependency [1978, p. 1062].

Perhaps with good reason, religion has been mostly conservative—"conserving" enduring values in a society. True, there have been the essential religious originals—the mystics, prophets, and other individualists—but in the long run they have constituted a small minority.

Clearly the majority of people must follow—some because of personal inadequacies, but others by choice. Paul Tillich (1952a) wrote of "the courage to be a part of" a group or movement. Active following requires trust as well as courage. To trust in another person, in a religious system, or in God requires and produces a degree of personality integrity. Choosing to "let go" seems prerequisite to certain religious experiences—conversion, glossolalia, and mysticism—which may, in turn, further integrate the personality.

CONCLUSION

The inept, the self-doubter, the insecure, the dependent, the suggestible, the authority seeker, the conformist—these are not a pretty array, but according to empirical studies, such persons constitute a substantial part of most American congregations. But, "Those who are well have no need of a physician" (Mark 2 : 17). Like a hospital, the church might better be judged not by whom it attracts, but by what it does for those who come. However, making psychological growth itself a major criterion would likely be self-defeating. The personal integration produced by religion comes at least partially as a by-product of the way one relates to and worships the Ultimate.

REVIEW OF KEY CONCEPTS

Adrift in the Doldrums
    identification of "comfort-seekers"
    relation of self-esteem to religiousness
    Dittes's explanation of personal deficiencies of religious people
    relation of need for friendship to self-esteem and religion
    relations of education, intelligence, and occupational level to religion
    implications of these relationships to church attendance
    effects of boredom on religious choices
    intrinsic-extrinsic relations to psychological deficits
    religious life and the healing and correction of deficits

Circle the Wagons
    characteristics of authoritarianism as a personality style
    authoritarianism and extrinsic and intrinsic religion
    religious authoritarians
    observance religion and true believers

Don't Rock the Boat
    religious orthodoxy, dependence, and submissiveness
    social desirability and religiousness
    "healthy mindedness" as denial
    faith healing and positive thinking
    Allport's interpretation of prejudice-religion relationship
    major conclusions of Gorsuch and Aleshire
    prejudice and marginal church members, nonreligious, and the most committed
    prejudice and conformity to the conventional community
    religiousness, sexism, and authoritarianism
    religious support for sex-role stereotypes
    conservatism: authoritarianism or socialization?
    nonconforming orthodoxy—religion as a nonconforming value
    conformists, observance religion, and true believers
    limitations to values of autonomy and individuality
    the "courage" to conform to religious values

Chapter 26

Religion as Negative Agent

A negative agent is one that works against what it is supposed to promote. Although some people report healing and integration from religion, others claim that religion has imposed unhelpful or even destructive perspectives on them. Outside observers also may see undesirable features in some religiousness. Clearly, religion sometimes produces unfavorable outcomes for some people.

> Religion has fostered unhealthy taboos against body and sex, premature altruism, provincialism and prejudice, legalisms and superstitions, excessive promotion of sin, excessive use of nonrational authority, and confusions among children and adolescents [Rosen, 1974, p. 289].

In this chapter we look at religion as a subtle negative agent in people's lives, and try to understand how this happens.

DISTURBED ATTITUDES TOWARD ONESELF

Negative attitudes such as self-doubt, anxiety, and depression may encourage one to seek religious comforts. However, religion may also foster some of these attitudes toward oneself.

Feelings of Worthlessness

Religions commonly emphasize human limitation and need. Some Christian songs describe the singer as a "worm" for whom the Savior bled or a "wretch" saved by grace. Although sophisticated adults can understand such teachings about human "sinfulness" without its destroying their sense of self-worth, such ideas may harm children or naive people. One needs a secure identity and good ego strength to withstand such references to one's personal value.

Authoritarian religion (Fromm, 1950) encourages people to see themselves as impotent and insignificant. When such people violate their consciences, their self-contempt deepens. They may deny their personal strengths and project their own good qualities onto the deity or some authority. (Recall *projection* from Chapter 2.) The more people exalt the deity or authority in this way, the more worthless they feel. As people are increasingly alienated from themselves, prayer becomes a begging for return of the good qualities originally projected onto the deity.

Self-constriction

A religion's repeated focus on sin leaves people needing to find something to which they can attach their feelings of guilt. Since the psyche guards against premature self-knowledge, which can be destructive, they may hit on one particular "sin" or flaw—often one that their religion describes as particularly evil—and concentrate on avoiding that sin. Baptists may feel safe by not drinking, or Catholics by avoiding nonmarital sexual behavior. Often people with such a style become very hostile toward others who engage in "forbidden" pleasures.

This obsession with a particular sin—or small group of sins—makes true self-knowledge more difficult to attain, and caricatures repentance and life-amendment. Seeking an "artificial" purity makes appropriate living difficult. "Purity . . . is *not* the one thing needful; and it is better that a life should contract many a dirt-mark, than forfeit usefulness in its efforts to remain unspotted" (James, 1902/1961, p. 281).

Dangerous Narcissism

Religion can also foster inflated self-concepts. "Malignant narcissism" is based on what one *has* rather than what one *does* (Fromm, 1964). Ideas of "a chosen people," election, or possession of a unique revelation can make one feel inappropriately superior to others.

Churches also may encourage people to construct an artificial sanctity. They identify goodness with particular practices of piety or virtue, and engaging in these practices makes one feel good. "So long as I tithe, attend church weekly, and bake cakes for the church dinners, then I am a good person." Such beliefs displace concern from social ills, public problems, and the particular needs of others. Indeed, people may resent these problems if they intrude upon their pietism. When people behave this way, we call them—with some injustice to Jewish history—Pharisees. Such people use "saintliness to serve . . . ego instead of putting . . . ego in the service of saintliness" (Kunkel, 1929, p. 278).

Vicarious Living

Some religious people are encouraged to live vicariously through a strong religious leader, a church, or a projected image of God. They measure their worth by the real or fantasized attitudes toward them of this "contact person," whom they require to make them complete human beings and justify their lives.

> The ego-ideal . . . is seen through another's eyes and becomes effective indirectly. . . . Someone sings a song, not because . . . joy urges [one] to do so, and also not because [one] believes [one]self a fine singer, but because [one] thinks the contact person might think so. As long as one has a contact person, one is fundamentally dependent [Kunkel, 1929, p. 128].

People who fear being found "empty" at the core of their being constantly need to be affirmed by another. They may use the idea of God for these needs, seeking to impress God with their value. They may interpret favorable life events as signs of God's pleasure with them, and unfortunate events as God's disfavor. Ultimately they end by seeking to be adored themselves, rather than offering true religious adoration. Religions often subtly encourage people to "perform" for the deity's "applause."

Giving up Personal Responsibility

Some people want others to assume responsibility for them, and may totally submit to anyone who promises the assurance of righteousness. Some are taught to believe that "one is certain of following the will of God in whatever one may do from obedience, but never certain in the same degree of anything which we may do of our own proper movement" (James, 1902/1961, p. 251). In the guise of surrendering to value, one may thus shirk responsibility for moral choices.

Established authoritarian religions often encourage dependence on a strong leader; this is also one of the least desirable features of many new cults. Recall (Chapter 25) that many participants enter cults when they are depressed or confused. "Cults supply ready-made friendships and ready-made decisions about careers, dating, sex, and marriage, and they outline a clear 'meaning of life.' In return, they may demand total obedience to cult commands" (Singer, 1979, p. 75). Once a person goes into any such system, his or her self-esteem increasingly depends upon surrender to the leader, who may foster and capitalize upon this dependence.

DISTORTED ATTITUDES TOWARD OTHER PEOPLE

Freud (1921) argued that both armies and religions protect themselves by demanding a group feeling from their members. Close group ties are maintained by externalizing all hostile or negative emotions. The stronger the in-group constraints become, the more outsiders must be scapegoated. When in-group conflicts cannot be expressed, prejudices and out-group hostility are inevitable.

Prejudice

However correct or incorrect Freud was, churchgoers have consistently been found more prejudiced than nonchurchgoers (see Chapter 20). Although psychologists have explained this with individual variables, Allport (1966) also noted some theological invitations to bigotry. Most religions promote universal love, but they often also endorse opinions that encourage prejudices. Although Christians now seldom call Jews "Jesus-killers" and Mormons have acknowledged the full personhood of blacks (Woodward & Goodman, 1978), subtle invitations to prejudice still exist.

Revelation   The doctrine of revelation leads a particular religion to claim exclusive possession of the truth and authority for interpreting it. Dissenting opinions may be considered a threat to the common good. Some believers consider intolerance of others' beliefs a service to God, and think that disbelievers of their "truth" deserve whatever treatment is needed to modify their "erroneous" opinions.

Election   *Election* holds that God has predestined certain people to salvation or has selected a chosen people. Such beliefs conveniently divide the "ins" from the "outs." If God has considered some people of special importance, humans should not be so bold as to disagree. The "outs" simply do not deserve the same status and privileges as the "ins"!

Theocracy   Theocracies believe civil government is divinely ordained and speaks for the will of God. They claim divine sanction for whatever restrictions or penalties they wish to impose. Since dissenters are considered in bad faith or out of divine favor, harsh penalization of them is God's will. Although the U.S. Constitution disallows theocracy, such ideas exist in other parts of the world. The Ayatollah Khomeini's Iran represents a theocracy. Some think that Sun Myong Moon's Unification church and Jerry Falwell's Moral Majority have theocratic goals.

Religion and Prejudice   Although some people deny that such doctrines as revelation and election lead to prejudice, their effects may be subtle. One may, without realizing it, enjoy considering oneself or one's group more important than others in God's plans. Individuals with poor self-esteem or other needs to feel superior are most likely to indulge in the satisfaction of being "special" to God (Allport, 1966).

Thus, while religion teaches altruism with its right hand, it may teach bigotry with its left one.

> We are taught to make definite distinctions between . . . believer and non-believer; and sometimes we are urged to act on the basis of these distinctions. . . . It is difficult psychologically to love infidels and heretics to the same extent that we love believers [Rokeach, 1968, p. 193].

Sexism

Religious Bases for Sexism   Although religions teach love of the stranger and the alien, some religious statements about women openly espouse sexist beliefs and standards. Many religious scriptures describe women as lower in the order of creation than men, more subject to the influence of evil, of greater moral weakness, of lesser intrinsic worth, and as designed to serve men. The patriarchal nature of most religions contributes to this sexism (Goldenberg, 1979). Such biases in the Jewish and Christian traditions are "swallowed with their milk" by many Western children; however, they are not limited to Western religion. The Hindu Code of Manu, for example, also contains such references.

However much religions may protest equal value of the genders, the arguments sound hollow when they reserve the positions of power and prestige for men. Women's seeking such positions in religion has been a quest fraught with hardships. Pope Paul VI declared: "If the role of Christ were not taken by a man . . . it would be difficult to see in the minister the image of Christ. For Christ himself was and remains a man" (Paul says no, 1977). Women in other traditions—such as the Episcopal (Woodward & Monroe, 1976; Montagno & Lisle, 1977) and Presbyterian (Woodward & Marbach, 1980)—also have difficulties. Furthermore, women who assert women's personhood and rights—such as the Catholic Sister Theresa Kane (Woodward & Lord, 1979) or the Mormon Sonia Johnson (1981; Weathers & Lord, 1979)—frequently suffer misunderstanding and persecution for their efforts.

Religious language and concepts play an important role in sexism. Most prayers in Western religions use masculine language—such as referring to all believers as brothers in Christ; this makes women "invisible." Each morning the orthodox Jewish man thanks God for having not created him a woman, while the Jewish woman blesses God for having created her according to "his" will.

Common understandings link God with the masculine gender since the deity is referred to by masculine pronouns, and male roles—such as king, father, or lord—are used to describe God. In Eastern religions, goddess concepts are important; however, in the West, the highest position accorded a woman is that of Mary, the mother of Jesus, and Christians deny her divine status. Young children grow up identifying deity with masculinity—a fact that implicitly endorses unequal value of the genders.

Implications of Sexist Religion   Women have often been denied equal opportunities, rights, and roles in society simply because they are women. Recall (Chapter 25) that religious people are more likely to hold sexist attitudes than are nonreligious ones. They are supported by scriptures, churches, and religious leaders in such unjust attitudes. General conventionalism and conformity may explain some of the relationship between religiousness and sexism since sexism, like racial and ethnic prejudice, is also strongly related to authoritarianism (see Chapter 25). However, evidence suggests that religious sexism is also fostered by personal neuroticism—fearful retreat from threat of change—in both genders, and by strong self-interest in men (Meadow, 1977a, 1978c). Religious leaders who teach sexism may be satisfying such needs in themselves, and playing into them in those whom they instruct.

Although prejudice is negatively related or unrelated to intrinsic religion in both genders, a traditional (sexist) attitude toward women is positively related to intrinsic religion for women (Kahoe, 1974b; McClain, 1979; Meadow, 1977a). The woman who internalizes her religious beliefs apparently also internalizes sexist religious attitudes. Traditional religious attitudes toward women and religion's endorsement of humility and service both likely contribute to this pattern. This relationship between intrinsic religion and sexism for women is declining in at least one denominational college in the South (Kahoe & Meadow, 1977b).

Sexist attitudes are associated with poor mental health (Kahoe & Meadow, 1977b), and work against the fullest development of those who hold them. Men seem most likely to use sexist religion to bolster failing self-esteem, while women accept such unhealthy attitudes toward themselves as an intrinsic aspect of religiousness (Meadow, 1979d). This leaves women with such unfortunate choices as holding negative attitudes about themselves, suffering the traumas of trying to reform the church, or reluctantly abandoning religion—at least in its traditional forms (Evans-Gardner, 1978).

Intolerance of Deviance

Like sexism, intolerance of deviance is a special kind of prejudice. It scapegoats those people who do not conform to one's ideas of what is moral or correct. Religious persons have censured many kinds of deviance. Unfortunately, churches and clergy often not only condone but actively encourage such behavior. In the 1960s the length of young men's hair took on such moral connotations that some were excluded from schools and churches until they submitted to a haircut!

Homosexuals and people with a prochoice stance on abortion are recent groups targeted for censure. The crusading efforts of Anita Bryant (Drake & Bru-baker, 1977) to restrict homosexuals' rights because of their "sinfulness" are well known. (Bryant has since changed her mind somewhat.) Such crusaders commonly say that they hate the sin, but love the sinner. However, they require homosexuals to declare themselves sinners, refrain from sexual expression, and try to change their sexual orientation. Those who refuse are considered willfully immoral (Evans, 1975).

Those who campaign against the deviance of others—be it their sexual behavior, drinking, length of hair, political opinions, etc.—typically support their own positions with many scriptural passages (often taken out of context) and traditional values. Their strong need to condemn others suggests that they are engaging in reaction formation; that is, they feel righteous by condemning "evils" to which they themselves are attracted—perhaps unconsciously.

In spite of scriptures urging religious people not to judge others and to attend first to their own faults, churches and religious leaders are often in the forefront of such attacks on nonconformers—thus encouraging intolerance of deviance in their followers. Yet, "from the standpoint of monotheism carried through to its logical consequences . . . no [one] can presume to have any knowledge of God which permits [one] to criticize or condemn [others]" (Fromm, 1950, p. 113).

REALITY TESTING AND ATTITUDES TOWARD THE WORLD

"Religious beliefs are teachings and assertions about facts . . . of . . . reality which tell one something one has not discovered for oneself and which lay claim to one's belief" (Freud, 1927/1961, p. 37). Religious ideas are not scientifically verifiable, yet sometimes state facts about science's domain—the material world. A church's confusion of scientific and religious discourse may encourage faulty reality testing in its members. Since beliefs often serve as emotional defenses—"to ward off threatening aspects of reality" (Rokeach, 1960, p. 67)—they may distort reality to relieve emotional distress. Religious people who are vulnerable because of insecurity, limited intelligence and/or education, or fear of deviating from a church's prescriptions may become unable to distinguish religious claims from scientific ones.

Concretism and Conceptual Confusion

Many people interpret religious beliefs literally because they lack the cognitive complexity to think abstractly. Some religions, however, encourage

> a radically literal interpretation of scriptures, which refuse to admit any change whatsoever, or which depict specific and almost tangible Antichrists in popes, taverns, or sex. [Extreme concretism shows] an inability to come to grips with mere possibilities, . . . assumptions, or speculations. The world has shrunk to visible and tangible realities [Pruyser, 1968, p. 92].

With this concrete style of thinking, the person cannot deal with symbolism or ambiguities. Changes in belief statements, rituals, or religious interpretations produce panic. Alternate ways of understanding religious realities are simply not acceptable. In extreme cases, threat of such change may "produce irrational fantasies of persecution, revenge, and world catastrophe" (Pruyser, 1968, p. 94).

Institutional Dogmatism

As concretism insists on simple, unchanging literal-mindedness, dogmatism insists upon certainty. From Chapters 4 and 13, you recall that increasing personal maturity brings tolerance for ambiguity and uncertainty; dogmatism tends to be associated with general personal immaturity. Also, "threats or assaults on a person's self-esteem can propel [one] to greater impulsiveness in seeking out certainty of meaning and cognitive clarity" (Dittes, 1959/1973, p. 264). Institutions work much as individuals in this regard. They encourage dogmatism when it is needed to ensure the survival of the institution and the belief systems it teaches.

> The church only resorted to dogmatic formulation when . . . confronted with some heresy which threatened to overthrow the very foundations of the characteristically Christian way of life and worship. The true purpose of the dogmatic formula is . . . to deny and decisively reject some preferred but inadequate solution. . . . Dogma is not made for dogma's sake. Where there is no great heresy, there is no dogma [Casserly, 1953, p. 57].

James (1902) described a historical pattern that religious institutions follow. First, some prophet with intense religious experience attracts enough followers that the movement is called a heresy by the existing orthodoxy. If it survives the persecution that follows, it becomes a new orthodoxy itself. It is passed on to followers who, in turn, stone new prophets.

Syncretism

"Syncretism is a fumbling overinclusiveness which combines discordant things under flimsy constructs, with a formula which is usually too trite to be false and too meaningless to be correct" (Pruyser, 1968, p. 95). Syncretism is usually based on strong wishes; people believe what they want to be true, even if they must overlook sloppy inconsistencies to do it. When God, seen as the loving parent of humankind, becomes someone highly invested in having "our" team win the football game, or "our" candidate the beauty contest, the wish-fulfilling distortion is obvious. Some religious hymns are guilty of syncretism. In the hymn "In the Garden," Jesus is depicted as a romantic lover sharing intimate joys with the believer in a beautiful garden—ideas that harmonize poorly with each other and with a biblical view of Jesus.

We are rational because we "arrive at decisions which other rational creatures would regard as a fair estimation of the evidence . . . and because we are honest about the deficiencies of our position" (Pojman, 1979, p. 167). Religions sometimes have trouble admitting their limitations when faced with difficult problems. To keep people's loyalty and to avoid admitting uncertainty, they may encourage syncretistic judgments that, on close examination, reveal peculiar inconsistencies. Global explanations—such as "Whatever happens is God's will"—are too general to judge by the rules of careful thought. One who insists "God's in . . . heaven, and all's well with the world" avoids acknowledging unsatisfying or unfortunate realities.

Superstition

Just as dogmatism may be a desperate attempt to avoid cognitive dissonance, some superstitious interpretation may be attribution run wild. Such explanations as "God made me sick to slow me down" discount alternate understandings or rational objections to such conclusions. Commonly, religions tend to approve of practices in their own traditions that they would discount in others. For example, they may urge members to reject astrological or occult interpretations, but let them believe that God is punishing the sinfulness of another person (or group or nation) who undergoes hardships.

Some psychologists tell the story of a dog who happened to be lifting its leg to urinate when someone threw a bone into its yard. Thereafter, whenever the dog wanted a bone, it lifted its leg. This situation describes superstitious interpretation followed by superstitious action—seeing a causal relationship between two events that happen to occur together, and acting on that "knowledge."

When religion fosters a utilitarian attitude toward religious acts—what one "gets out of it"—superstitious behavior is encouraged. "A $2 bill·. . . had been tucked under a candlestick on the altar of a college chapel. . . . An engineering student, worried about a girl, thought that bribery of the Deity might help" (Davies, 1978, p. 23).

Popular religious opinion sanctions many such forms of superstition. Yet behavior analogous to one's own—but in another tradition—is likely to be considered magical manipulation. A Native American rain dance is seen as very different from a Christian prayer meeting for rain. Consulting the *I Ching* is "superstition," but "setting out the fleece" (Judges 6 : 37–40)—asking the Judeo-Christian God for a sign—is not. Drawing the line between faith and superstition is difficult. However, "reverence for authority which excludes free investigation turns religion itself into a superstition" (Radhakrishnan, 1955, p. 70). Myers (1978) offers an excellent longer treatment of superstition.

ATTITUDES TOWARD GOD AND RELIGIOUS ENDEAVOR

Religions can distort not only attitudes toward self, others, and world, but also religion's own objects: God and itself.

Unworthy Conceptions of Deity

Phillips argued that if many people "are not strenuously defending an outgrown conception of God, then they are cherishing a hothouse God who could only exist between the pages of the Bible or inside the four walls of a Church" (Phillips, 1961, pp. 7–8). Inadequate images of God come from projections of one's own personal traits onto God, the teachings of a particular church, or the influences of one's culture.

Some inadequate views depict God as an old man, a meek and mild pushover, a colorless killjoy, or a reflection of one's parent. For some God is either the source of all comfort or one who always lets them down. Others make God into absolute perfection, managing director, or a projected conscience. Deeply ingrained "small" conceptions of God prevent adequate formulations (Phillips, 1961). Churches and religious people are often afraid to examine the adequacy of their God concepts.

Intellectualization

Sometimes religions reduce faith to a cognitive exercise—intellectual assent to the stories written to support religious ideas. They may ask people to assert either the historical and/or scientific accuracy of religious story. However,

> one confronts a problem; one lives a mystery. A problem is an impersonal concern; a mystery involves us personally. A problem permits a number of solutions; a mystery permits only some form of acceptance . . . and stirs us to commitment [Gleason, 1964, p. 14].

Religions may encourage reduction of the living mystery of faith to mental activity. When they teach that salvation or justification rests on belief, people often interpret this as meaning that one must feel cognitive certainty about an idea. Some people become overly concerned about the strength of their belief, and struggle to make their thinking fit acceptable modes. Such intellectualization produces distorted understandings of faith, and may distract people from genuinely living a life of faith. Carl Jung (1965) wrote angrily about his clergy father's desperate struggle for belief orthodoxy, and concluded that this compulsion made his father incapable of genuine religiousness.

Compartmentalization of Faith

Compartmentalization—the making of tight distinctions between sacred and secular—is similar to intellectualization, but reduces religion to certain behaviors instead of to thought. Although religions seldom approve of isolating devotion from life, they may inadvertently reinforce it by emphasizing particular holy times and places. Maslow complained of those who define religion just as going to a particular building on Sunday and hearing a particular kind of formula repeated . . . in terms of the supernatural, or ceremonies, or rituals, or dogmas [Maslow, 1965, p. 62].

Such people may be "Sunday Christians" and live the rest of their lives divorced from religious concern.

Other-Worldliness

Many people who go to convents, monasteries, ashrams, and religious communes do so to express religious values, and they retain broad concern with social issues. Others are fleeing from involvement in the real problems of everyday life. James identified an "imaginative absorption in the love of God to the exclusion of all practical human interests" as "theopathic," and considered it most likely "where devoutness is intense and the intellect feeble" (James, 1902/1961, p. 273). Although retreating to other-worldliness is less common today than in earlier centuries, some religions still offer this option to ego-defensive individuals who are not growth motivated.

Fanaticism

The appeal of Christianity to many people in the anxiety-ridden Roman Empire may have been that "it lifted the burden of freedom from the shoulders of the individual: one choice, one irrevocable choice, and the road to salvation was clear" (Dodds, 1963, p. 133). People who strongly need simplistic solutions are easy prey for totalitarian movements. Events such as the mass suicide of the People's Temple in Jonestown (full reports in *Newsweek,* December 4, 1978; *Time,* December 4, 1978) focused attention on religious groups that go to extreme forms of expression.

Fanaticism is "loyalty carried to a convulsive extreme [by] an intensely loyal and narrow mind [that] idealizes the devotion itself" (James, 1902/1961, p. 271). Unsettled social conditions that do not meet people's needs for structure, meaning, and stability support fanaticism. Fearful individuals with strong needs for meaning, conceptual simplicity, and relief from anxiety are most prone to fanaticism. Concrete religious formulations may narrow mental perspectives and leave a person susceptible to fanatic persuasion.

Control over fearful and anxious followers is enhanced by keeping communications within a closed environment, creating and manipulating guilt feelings, and leading followers to believe that their worth rests upon being God's chosen members of that group. Giving oneself to such a situation can produce intensely ecstatic states that further bond a follower to a charismatic leader. This relationship and the controlled environment of a fanatic group produce strong influence on the minds and behavior of followers (Lifton, 1979). These understandings make global concepts such as brainwashing unnecessary in explaining how such religious movements work (Robbins & Anthony, 1980).

Fanatics often behave in ways that distress other people. They may try to proselytize unwilling others or follow practices that others consider dangerous or destructive. Apocalyptic groups focus on world calamities, natural catastrophes, and "moral deterioration" to "warn" the nation and humankind of impending holocausts (see Woodward, Gram, & Lisle, 1977).

Although affiliation with a fanatic group may have very negative consequences, many characteristics of such groups are very similar to the early history of such established faiths as Judaism and Christianity (see Meadow, 1978a; and Chapter 19). Many traditionally religious people express "admiration for the days when people *really* believed, when they cared enough to persecute or form inquisitions or go on crusades. Real belief, in such terms, must be absolutist" (Marty, 1979, p. 213). Moreover, membership in such groups is often relatively short-lived. After several years, many people find themselves changing so that the needs the group served become less important. Most eventually abandon such groups if they are not pressured to do so, but can find sufficient social support to alleviate feelings of alienation on their return.

SUMMARY

We have looked at many ways in which religion may foster immaturity and poor mental health. We next turn our attention to the relationships between religion and more serious psychopathology.

REVIEW OF KEY CONCEPTS

Disturbed Attitudes Toward Oneself
 concept of negative agent
 projecting one's good onto the deity
 artificial purity
 malignant narcissism
 contact person and vicarious living
 the security of obedience

Distorted Attitudes Toward Other People
 revelation as invitation to prejudice
 election and the creation of an in-group
 how a theocracy works
 sexist religious views of women
 the deity as male
 women's sexism and intrinsic religiousness
 intolerance of deviance as reaction formation

Reality Testing and Attitudes Toward the World
 scientific versus religious discourse
 concretism and reactions to religious change
 bases for institutional dogmatism
 syncretism and wish fulfillment

bases for superstitious interpretation and behavior
religion itself as superstition

Attitudes Toward God and Religious Endeavor
a "hothouse God"
some inadequate concepts of God
belief orthodoxy and the intellectualization of religion
similarities between intellectualization and compartmentalization
"theopathy"
James's understanding of fanaticism
techniques of totalitarian religious control

chapter 27

Religion and Psychopathology

We have seen how personal immaturity and insecurity motivate some people's religiousness, and also how religion may encourage immaturity and poor mental health. In this chapter, we discuss more serious psychopathology in relation to religion. Many seriously disturbed people use religious language to describe their delusions (irrational beliefs) and hallucinations (perceptions that occur without an external stimulus—i.e., seeing or hearing something that is not there). Because of this, some people assume that religion causes psychopathology or is just another form of such pathology.

RELIGIOUS LANGUAGE AND COSMIC ISSUES

Attribution to Spiritual Causes

Attribution theory (see Chapter 13) says that when things happen to us, we look for causes. From early history people have believed that unusual behavior is caused by spirits, and people's earliest healers were their religious leaders. Atypical behavior called for religious management (Loschen, 1974). Some contemporary people still frequently use such explanations. (For an example, see Gavira & Wintrob, 1976.)

Sometimes atypical behavior was considered a valuable visitation by the gods. To qualify as a religious leader or shaman in many cultures, one had to behave in ways we might consider schizophrenic. Many Native American youths sought a vision to signify receiving spirit protection. Today's closest analogy is glossolalia (see Chapter 9). Although other people might think it crazy behavior, some religious groups consider speaking in tongues a sign of divine visitation.

O'Dea's Puerto Rican immigrants who had intense Pentecostal conversions attributed them to supernatural causes. Their reported feelings of "sinfulness" related to their personal and social disorganization when they first arrived in New York. The conversion experience itself came when they identified with a group whose values they adopted. Finally, the security and sustenance they continued to get from their new religious group was called "regeneration." Thus their being "saved" from their disorientation, and integrated into a supportive social group, was explained (and experienced) in the religious idiom of sinfulness-conversion-regeneration. This language—with ideas of "lostness," "being saved," and "being rebuilt"—described the transition from immigrant to citizen status more adequately than any other available language (O'Dea, 1966, pp. 59–65).

Religion as Metaphor for Emotional Distress

Why do seriously disturbed people often speak of religious ideas? "A schizophrenic may weave into the system of . . . paranoid delusions any psychological material—sexual, social, philosophical or religious" (Zilboorg, 1962, p. 46). Whatever experiences we have, we try to communicate. We have many different styles of communication: rational and logical, poetic and symbolic, or empirical and descriptive. Different experiences call for different language.

Disturbed people often use religious language and ritual in fragmented, magical, and distorted ways. Psychotic (crazy) people are dealing with issues of cosmic importance to them. Religious language also deals with cosmic issues, and so may be the best language available to describe the magnitude and intensity of what they are experiencing. "Any experience that involves the possible shattering of one's being is religious" (Switzer, 1976, p. 325) in that it is "ultimate," although it may not fit the orthodoxy of any particular religious system. A psychotic patient also may justify or rationalize behavior and experiences by religious delusions (Field & Wilkerson, 1973).

Defining Problems Religiously

The following examples illustrate some ways in which particular psychological conflicts may be expressed in religious language. Although one could describe these experiences in other words, religious ones are particularly appropriate.

Frustration and Futility   In extreme frustration, when all seems ultimately futile and psychological survival cannot be maintained, people may well talk of "the end of the world." Their own "world" has come to an end as they have nothing to look forward to. They may hope against hope if they have some notion of a "second coming" that might produce a better world for them. When this expectation is frustrated, their experience of "hell" or the work of demons may become delusional.

Unmanageable Impulses   In a 1980 Minnesota trial, a woman accused of murdering her infant insisted that she had to kill the child to save its soul since it was possessed by the devil, and that she was also under control of the devil. This woman, a Catholic, had conceived the child while taking birth control pills. Even after "damning" herself by using contraceptives, she still became pregnant and had to care for this unwanted child. Her outward behavior was of a model mother until her delusions revealed how much she resented the pregnancy and wished to be free of the child. How easy it was to see herself as property of the devil and to see the child as the "devil's spawn"—for surely it must have seemed so to her. (The woman was acquitted on grounds of insanity.)

Intense Anxiety   People suffering intense anxiety live with constant feelings of impending doom. They often find highly fascinating such religious literature as the *Book of Revelation* with its images of chaos and disaster. Cataclysmic and eschatological (about things to come) language may be very apt to describe their experience—as may feeling as if God or the devil is closely watching and threatening them. One intensely anxious patient believed that every psychologist trying to interview him was a judging agent of God. Although such thinking is clearly delusional, it dramatically describes the young man's feelings.

Self-contempt and Guilt   Although some religion seems to encourage feelings of guilt and self-contempt, some nonreligious people also have such feelings. Some intensely "guilty" people "invent" a God who wants a "pound of flesh" in payment for human frailty. It is "apparent that the rigid and revengeful attitude that they attribute to God is nothing else but a projection of their own aggressivity and . . . rigidity" (Mora, 1962, p. 23). God, seen as the ultimate, demanding punisher, describes their own brutal consciences.

Sometimes such people feel they must "buy off" the devil, the "cause" of their guilt-producing behavior. In the novel *Lord of the Flies* (Golding, 1959), one of the stranded boys decided about the "beast" on the mountain: "When we kill we'll leave some of the kill for it. Then it won't bother us, maybe" (p. 123). A more insightful boy fantasized the beast as saying, "Fancy thinking the Beast was something you could hunt and kill. . . . You knew, didn't you? I'm part of you. Close, close, close!" (p. 133).

Interpersonal Conflicts   Oates (1955) concluded that patterns of family relationships and the God concept are closely interwoven. Mentally disturbed people often project onto God a distorted parent-child relationship. Other disturbed relationships may also produce peculiar God concepts. Freud's patient Schreber (1955), who had problems of psychosexual identity, delusionally believed that God was transforming him into a woman.

Boisen's (1936) religious image of a "Family of Four" described his views about the worth of different people whom he placed in four categories. This, in turn, reflected his relationship concerns over a woman whom he idealized and wished to marry, but of whom he felt unworthy (Bregman, 1979a). After his schizophrenic experiences, he concluded that God symbolizes whatever we consider supreme in interpersonal relationships. Thus, when a person is lonely, God is seen as a good friend. A shattering emotional experience may be described as God's entering one's life.

Mortality Concerns   Much anxiety and depression comes from unwillingness to accept that one will someday die. This basically religious problem is thus often seen as a psychological one. Some people have genuine cosmic issues in their lives, and psychiatric treatment is not appropriate therapy for them (Howland, 1971). Unfortunately, many clergy send such people to mental health professionals. Also unfortunately, therapists seldom refer people to the clergy, although some recognize distinctive tasks for clergy and psychotherapists (Schofield, 1979).

POSITIVE ASPECTS OF DISTORTED RELIGIOUSNESS

Although religion may be used to express psychological conflicts, some people carry religious expression itself to pathological extremes. Yet some psychologists see value even in distorted religiousness.

Survival Value of Distorted Religion

Personal Psychological Survival   The ordinary routines of religion, such as ritual and fellowship, help people express and meet ordinary human needs. Many religious practices have obvious significance for coping but carry a potential for distortion. "Religious behavior becomes symptomatic when these practices are carried to . . . imbalance and self-defeating exaggeration. To pray all night, to starve oneself can scarcely be described as pure piety" (Menninger, Mayman, & Pruyser, 1963, pp. 143–144). Atonement may be excessively self-punitive, and trying to control one's aggression by magic or ritual is a problem when such practices become ends in themselves.

In defining religion as the opiate of the people, Karl Marx suggested that it can help individuals continue to function, though at a cost to their integrity. Lloyd (1973) considers all religion a coping device, and says that people with faltering coping skills are inclined to seek irrational and emotionally expressive sects where their personal excesses will be supported and protected. Some research supports the idea that prepsychotic people are indeed drawn to such religious groups (Spencer, 1975). Extreme religious practices are expensive ways to preserve oneself psychologically, but may be the best or only means available to a person.

Social Survival   We have previously seen how religion controls some social pathology and may curb deviant behavior. Although at a severe cost to the disturbed individual, even a pathological religiousness may prevent some antisocial behavior. One who believes herself or himself regularly visited by tempting demons at least keeps on fighting the demons!

For many important religious figures—for example, Boisen, George Fox, or Francis of Assisi—periods of psychopathology apparently preceded their concern with social service. Some such people offer society much; their charity is "a genuinely creative social force. . . . The saints are authors . . . of goodness" (James, 1902/1961, p. 283).

Personal Growth in Religious Suffering

Unsatisfied Religious Needs   Religious ideas in psychological disturbances may indicate that the person has unfulfilled religious needs. Indeed, some psychologists hold that all, or almost all, psychological disturbances reflect religious problems. Jung most clearly expressed this viewpoint:

> All my patients in the second half of life . . . fell ill because [they] had lost that which the living religions of every age have given to their followers, and none of them has been really healed who did not regain [a] religious outlook. This of course has nothing whatever to do with a particular creed or membership of a church [Jung, 1933, p. 229].

Some suffering may reflect a need to change or develop one's religious perspectives. Jung (1965) himself reported psychotic-like experiences that transformed his own spiritual outlooks. The psychotic Hennell (1967) had visions of a charismatic, shining, and joyful being quite different from the somber religious figures with which he had been reared; this vision may have been "an attempt to correct [his] normative religiousness with something else more immediate, numinous, and to him more profound" (Bregman, 1979b, p. 66).

Impetus to Needed Self-healing   Of his own psychosis Boisen wrote: "The anxiety, the distress of mind (guilt), even when carried to the point of psychosis, was, as I see it, nature's way of seeking to effect needed changes" (Boisen, 1960, p. 198). His experiences spurred him to originate the pastoral ministries to patients in mental hospitals. He argued convincingly that even very bizarre religiousness can be used constructively when we understand the psychological needs that spurred it (Boisen, 1936).

In seeing growth potential in psychosis, Boisen did not glamorize it and recognized that for some people it might have no such potential. Highly romantic views of psychosis are not justified. Although religious symptoms in psychopathology may encourage personal growth, often they are simply the language used to describe regressive tendencies, immaturity, or other conflicts.

Spiritual Growth and Emotional Sensitivity

Many religious "geniuses" appear to have suffered psychological disturbances. Does this mean that one must go through neurosis to develop spiritually? Fromm argues that "the vast majority of people in our culture are well adjusted because they have given up the battle for independence sooner and more radically than the neurotic person" (Fromm, 1950, p. 80). By adjusting themselves to the expectations of society and others, they avoided the pain necessary to develop full humanness.

Mowrer (1961) believed that a person who engages in immoral behavior must go through neurosis to reach normal human functioning. He disagreed with Freud's opinion that neurotic people have overly severe consciences, and said that neurotics deserve their suffering. They have dulled their consciences sufficiently to engage in immoral actions, so must accept the neurotic suffering associated with their guilt, which is real guilt.

Some theorists see the capacity for neurosis as a valuable human asset. "Perhaps the most significant sign of a healthy religion is precisely the result of this basic neurotic capacity, which constitutes [human] superiority over the brutes" (Miller, 1965, p. 296). "If there were such a thing as inspiration from a higher realm, it might well be that the neurotic temperament would furnish the chief condition of the requisite receptivity" (James, 1902/1961, p. 38). These theorists do not mean that one must be a diagnosed neurotic to be religious, but that a sufficient sensitivity to values and inner discord makes one capable of both deep religiousness and neurotic suffering.

DISTINGUISHING RELIGIOUSNESS FROM PSYCHOPATHOLOGY

When people are given written accounts of what happened in psychotic and intense religious experiences, they usually cannot tell which is which. However, Margolis and Elifson (1979) reported some success in training people to make such distinctions. We now discuss some selected religious phenomena and suggest ways to distinguish them from similar psychopathological experiences.

Conversion and Delusions

People sometimes change their minds about what they believe. When such changes involve religious content, we call it conversion (see Chapter 7). Religious people usually consider conversion to their own beliefs good, and abandonment of those beliefs bad. However, some research suggests that people who convert to a faith other than that in which they were reared have better mental health than average (Srole, Langner, Michael, Opler, & Rennie, 1962).

Kiev urges us to evaluate a person's religious beliefs against those of peers to determine their healthiness. Distortion of the beliefs of one's religious community should be considered pathological (Kiev, 1969). However, this criterion would rule out the religious insights of such supraorthodox (see Chapter 19) individuals as the Buddha, and would consider all new religious ideas the work of unstable individuals. Bregman (1977) argued for the religious value in idiosyncratic religious formulations.

Examining the effects of a person's belief change is a better way to evaluate. A pathological conversion may be "characterized by a greater likelihood of . . . backsliding and includes intolerance, compulsive proselytizing, and an exaggerated irrationality and intensity of beliefs" (Johnson, 1977, p. 104). Salzman (1965) considers the following pathological: (1) irrational intensity of belief; (2) more concern with doctrine than with ethical principles; (3) contempt and hatred for one's former beliefs; (4) intolerance of deviates; (5) an alienating need to proselytize; and (6) a masochistic need for martyrdom to prove one's devotion. The line between some conversions and delusion may be thin!

Ritual and Compulsion

Freud (1907) noted the close resemblance between religious ritual and compulsions (irrational actions that obsessional people use to reduce anxiety). These people feel they must go through personal rituals in a set manner—such as preparing for sleep in precisely the same way each night—and become very upset if prevented. Both these and religious rituals are carried out in conscientious detail, are isolated from other life activities, and produce guilt when neglected. Fromm held that religious ritual can be either rational or irrational. When it is rational, failure to perform it or deviations in performance do not cause anxiety. "One can always recognize the irrational ritual by the degree of fear produced by its violation in any manner" (Fromm, 1950, p. 103).

People may use religious confession compulsively. After confessing in precise detail every aspect of their wrongdoing, they still fear that they may not have confessed correctly. Relief from anxiety lasts only a short time, so they feel compelled to confess repeatedly. Their confession is not an act of religion, but a "magic" guarantee of security. They typically also feel need to carry out penances in precisely defined ways. In churches that do not practice confession, repeated conversions or presentations of oneself at revivals can serve the same function.

Asceticism and Masochism

The human impulse to self-denial for the sake of value has produced many virtuous and fruitful lives. However, some people become unable to be comfortable unless they are "cramping" themselves. If it hurts, you must be in grace; if it feels good, it is probably sinful. Such an attitude is humorously summed up in the graffiti: "Everything I like is illegal, immoral, or fattening." The relationships between religion and suffering are complex (Bakan, 1968; Brena, 1972, 1973).

James described pathological asceticism. Some people feel need to suffer so they will not fear future punishment. Even more disturbed is a need to suffer to have any peace of mind at all. Finally, some people seem to have perverted senses, and pain is actually experienced as pleasure. In pathological asceticism, "we have morbid melancholy and fear, and the sacrifices made are to purge out sin, and to buy safety" (James, 1902/1961, p. 242).

Excessively self-punishing people are actually very self-centered. "One takes pride in the battle fought against the self. One falls into an obsessive dread of the good, so that all the good things that do come to one are self-righteously taxed by guilt" (Ulanov & Ulanov, 1975, p. 181). Such sufferers try to impress an audience. "Even for the solitary monks . . . who subjected themselves to the most terrible flagellations, there was the one and all-important witness: God" (Reik, 1949, pp. 241–242). Masochistic religion morbidly links "the ideas of being loved and of being punished" (Reik, 1949, p. 242), with suffering considered a sign of God's special favor.

Self-abandonment and Depression

All deeply religious people report some religious sadness and loneliness. Some even say that "faith presupposes the resignation of all finite goods and the dissociation from all wish-fulfillments" (Meissner, 1969, p. 51). How does one distinguish such a religious condition from depression, which is commonly characterized by sadness, loneliness, and apathy?

Andreasen (1972) suggests some distinctions. (1) Religious depression should be brief and self-limited. (2) It should be balanced by an ability to see joy in life. (3) The depression should be used as a source for growth. (4) One's capacity to function in ordinary duties should not be impaired very long. (5) One should not lose contact with reality or show disproportionate despair.

Although this list is helpful, many religious mystics have at times failed on some of these criteria. In such extreme cases, we would suggest that at least the sense of loss and loneliness should reflect a felt absence of God rather than other pleasures. Also, the religiously depressed should not be excessively preoccupied with a personal ego-centered guilt, but should sorrow over human foibles in general. They should still try to meet their obligations to work and other people. Their resignation should not be a helpless passivity, but rather a religious submission that embraces all conditions of their lives. Finally, they should not excessively focus on their own suffering.

The Problems of Diagnosis

Although we have suggested some guidelines, distinguishing religiousness from psychopathology is not always easy.

> Much of what goes for Judaic or Christian religion is psychological distortion or full-blown pathology. . . . Much of what goes for theological and ethical truth is not the consequence of the insight of grace but of the pathology of the psyche [Ellens, 1975, p. 17].

Judging particular cases is difficult.

Spiritual practices that have been honored in religious traditions can become distorted to pathological proportions. Attempts to overcome personal faults may turn into excessive self-constriction; preservation and promotion of the values of one's group may become an overzealous fanaticism; devotional enjoyment of God may become excessive withdrawal from life; and neighborly service may become officious do-gooding (Meadow, 1978a). Some personal dispositions may be mistaken for religiousness. Docility may be confused with obedience, insecurity and self-effacement with humility, and need to please others with charity (Bartemeier, 1965).

RELATIONSHIPS BETWEEN RELIGIOUSNESS AND PSYCHOPATHOLOGY

Religious Interest as a Sign of Psychopathology

Freud (1913) considered religion itself a neurotic attempt to remain a dependent child with God as a "superparent" to whom one could appeal for help with life's problems. He called religion the "universal obsessional neurosis," and said that adopting this universal neurosis may save some people from personal neurosis (1927). Another psychoanalyst, Fenichel (1946), considered religious ideation an attempt to control schizophrenic thoughts by verbalizing them.

Not everyone agrees with such opinions. Jung (1938) considered unconscious processes genuinely religious, and called religion a valid submission to powers higher than one's ego. Stark argued that "pathological conditions logically cannot account for the predominant behavior of stable social groups" (Stark, 1971, p. 166). That is, it is absurd to consider pathological such a common human behavior as religion. No one has adequate grounds for seeing religious behavior as pathological in itself.

Religiousness as a Cause of Psychopathology

Religious Background   If we cannot equate religion with psychopathology, does religiousness predispose one to psychopathology? Freud (1913) considered mental illness to be caused by severe conscience, which inhibits impulse expression. Repressed impulses may break through as symptoms or inappropriate behaviors. Since religion is a major shaper of conscience, Freud held religious training responsible for much neurotic misery. Lorand (1962) similarly believed neurotic conflicts can result from early family situations in which strong religious influences lead one to deny expression of biological urges.

Though some patients blame their psychiatric problems on religion, Switzer (1976) does not consider religion the original source of their psychopathology. Repressive and constrictive religious teachings can be interpreted in alternative ways. Parents who use repressive interpretations are usually marginally adjusted and may use religion to control their own impulses. A generally repressive style of parenting becomes associated with religion, and anger against the parents is projected onto God. Switzer admits that a patient's religious content often creates problems; however, these difficulties result from inadequate parenting, which produced both low self-esteem and distorted religiousness.

Religiousness of Psychiatric Patients   Many psychiatric patients have no religious concern or preoccupation with religion. Different studies found no religious concerns in 43% of 173 schizophrenics (Boisen, 1952), over half of 68 schizophrenics (Oates, 1954), and two-thirds of 170 patients (Southard, 1956). Walters (1964) found 18.8% of schizophrenics had religious concerns compared to 7.7% of mental patients in general.

Psychiatric patients, however, are "more likely to hold a promordial, personalized, and concretized religious outlook" than normals (Burns & Daniels, 1969, p. 165). Some religiously preoccupied psychiatric patients showed certain religious similarities (Rosen & Farnell, 1962). All were authoritarian (see Chapter 20) and interpreted the Bible literally. Some engaged in grandiose, wish-fulfilling religious ideas, and others used religion to control their strong hostility. Their beliefs described a demanding, punitive God.

Studies find conflicting relationships between religiousness and psychopathology. Lindenthal, Meyers, Pepper, and Stern found that "as psychological impairment increases participation in organized religious activity decreases" (1970, p. 149), though such people pray more than before. Psychiatric patients are less likely to attend church than normals (Burns & Daniels, 1969), and negative relationships exist between religious commitment and mental illness, neurotic distrust, and psychic inadequacy (Stark, 1971).

Interpretive Cautions Since most studies that relate religiousness and mental health are correlational, they prove nothing concerning causes. Peculiar religious language or practices may simply be disturbed explanatory or coping devices. Repressive religion may produce psychopathology in some people. Disturbed people may participate less in religion either because they lack the capacity to do so, or out of angry rejection of it. Lowe (1953) believed that religious concerns of the mentally disturbed simply reflect their severe personality disorders, and are not related to real religiousness. Failure to adopt a broadly religious philosophy may itself produce psychopathology in some people (Jung, 1933). However, after extensive literature reviews, Argyle (1958; Argyle & Beit-Hallahmi, 1975) concluded that little evidence exists to support religion's being either a cause or prevention of emotional disorders. We need much more research before we can draw any valid conclusions about any possible relationships.

NEUROSIS AND SIN

Some psychologists believe that having something in your life that you are afraid to admit to yourself or others produces the fear, guilt, and suffering of mental disorder (see Chapter 18). Isolation and estrangement are the real evils, not any conflicts between desire and conscience.

Neurosis as an Outcome of Deception

Mowrer proposed a daring alternative to Freud's understanding of neurosis: "Anxiety comes not from acts which the individual would commit but dares not, but from acts which [one] has committed but wishes that [one] had not" (1961, p. 26). Thus, conflicts imposed by an overly severe conscience are not the problem; disturbance comes from engaging in behavior that a more fully developed conscience would inhibit. If secrecy and deception follow, one will develop neurosis. Psychiatric symptoms are evidence of unacknowledged guilt. The greater the person's deception and deceit, the worse the symptoms. Mere wrongdoing will not make one neurotic if she or he is honest about mistakes and atones for them; only when deceit is added does the risk of neurosis occur (Mowrer, 1961, 1964).

Mowrer further suggested redefining neurosis as sin. Sin is theologically defined as behavior that puts one in danger of hell. Psychiatric disturbance is a hell on earth. Thus, sin and neurotic (deceitful) behavior are essentially the same thing (Mowrer, 1961, 1964). Menninger (1973) later agreed that, if guilt is still around, sin must be also, although people no longer like to use that term. Sadly, he concluded that some people "no longer consider themselves or anyone else to be answerable for any evil—or any good" (Menninger, 1973, p. 17).

Mental Illness as Myth

Psychiatrist Thomas Szasz (1974) does not want mental and emotional disturbance considered an illness. The illness model leads people to believe that such disturbances simply happen to them. Szasz argues strongly that people bring these conditions upon themselves—although without full conscious awareness. To call them illness relieves neurotics of their responsibility for both the situation they helped create and their other obligations, since we do not expect sick people to be productive members of society.

Szasz has said that all mental patients fall into three categories: those who want others to be responsible for them (most "neurotics"), those who do not want to obey society's ordinary rules (character-disordered people), and those who are desperately seeking some way to be unique (psychotic people). His views on psychiatric patients' need for responsibility are similar to those of Glasser (Chapter 18).

Neurosis and Hidden Motives

Fingarette (1962) said just because neurotic people deceive themselves and other people does not relieve them of responsibility for motives outside their awareness. They feel guilty because they *are* genuinely guilty; they conspire to satisfy impulses against their values without admitting it. They refuse to recognize the real motives behind their symptoms. Fingarette notes that all the world's major religious traditions believe that guilt rests in interior motives; for example, one who lusts in the heart has already committed adultery. Religions also add that translating the wish into an action compounds the wrongdoing. Neurotics refuse to acknowledge their inner motives and symbolically act them out in their symptoms. Their guilt is less than that of overt wrongdoers, but exists in spite of their self-deceptive evasion of awareness and responsibility.

Fringe Benefits of Neurosis

Some psychiatric symptoms seem to have effects that support ideas like those of Mowrer, Szasz, and Fingarette. Depressed and suicidal people usually do get others to take care of them. Some people literally get away with murder by being declared psychotic. The bizarre behavior of some psychotic patients makes them unique indeed. Some phobias (irrational fears) get people out of situations for which they want a face-saving excuse. Compulsive people—generally considered spitefully angry by mental health professionals—tax the patience of those who must live with them. Getting a headache or bellyache gives some people an excuse for getting out of unwanted obligations. The list of possible fringe benefits of emotionally based symptoms is long. The way such symptoms often function in the lives of patients provides some basis for equating neurosis and sin. Although "neurotic" people may well be advised toward greater self-knowledge, these considerations do not warrant punitive treatment of them.

Implications of Equating Sin and Neurosis

Writing from a Jewish perspective, Spero points out that sin and neurosis produce many similar psychological symptoms. We usually put moral connotations on sin, but see neurosis as a natural occurrence, and expect different treatments for these disorders. However, viewed existentially, both sin and neurosis "signify rebellion, self-worship, and the inability to integrate and unify the sacred/infinite with the temporal" (Spero, 1978, p. 284). Neurosis thus has moral implications. The basic disorder in both sin and neurosis is the failure to regard one's ultimate meaning. This suggests a religious cure, and encourages the sufferer to search for and adopt transcendent values.

DRAWING CONCLUSIONS

Interaction of Religion and Psychopathology

"The religious structure is so often and so easily perverted" (Miller, 1965, p. 299) since it chooses its symbols and images out of an "infinite diversity." All faith systems and rules of discipline can be pushed to the point of distortion. Fromm (1950) pointed out that religion can either have a positive creative function or simply still anxiety and stultify growth toward psychological wholeness. Ellis (1977) strongly objects to the use of religion to instill hope and meaning in people's lives. According to him, that solution glosses over problems and encourages further neurosis.

Religion may also indirectly precipitate serious disturbance. People who lose contact with reality may use religious explanations for their unusual feelings and behavior, in a desperate attempt to avoid personality fragmentation. Such rationalizing behavior, however, not only supports the person, but can also provide content for additional psychopathology—such as delusions of omniscience or grandiose identification with the deity.

Religious thinking and feeling can also operate on many levels of personal involvement (Nussbaum, 1974). In "inspiration" one has well-preserved contact with reality. In "ecstasy" reality control is at least temporarily lost. In the extreme, one may be flooded with uncontrollable religious imagery. It would be audacious to dictate what would or would not be an appropriate or pathological religious experience (Wilber & Meadow, 1979).

Argyle and Beit-Hallahmi (1975) summarize the possible relationships between religion and mental health: (1) religion contributes to well-being; (2) religion contributes to psychopathology or is psychopathological; (3) religion is used by disturbed people for help with their problems. Switzer (1976) urges clinicians to carefully examine distorted religiousness, to better understand a patient's experience. He believes faith may be a focus for the organization of healthy aspects of personality during a psychiatric crisis.

The Meeting of Religion and Psychiatry

Many theorists who argue for the essential unity of religion and psychology point out that they share the same roots. Though this understanding has not prevailed, some people agree that for both psychology and religion the aims "are the same. Both seek abundant life for the individual and ideal social life for the group" (Barbour, 1931, p. 26). Becker is even more explicit: "Psychiatric experience and religious experience cannot be separated either subjectively in the person's own eyes or objectively in the theory of character development" (1973, p. 67).

Others point out problems with such opinions. Psychiatric science "seeks concrete answers to abstract questions, while religion supplies abstract answers to undefinable questions" (Loschen, 1974, p. 141). Each may be better suited for only its task. Tournier holds that "every illness calls for two diagnoses: one scientific . . . and causal, and the other spiritual, a diagnosis of its meaning and purpose" (1960, p. 13).

Whether psychological and spiritual health and disease can or cannot ultimately be equated with each other, models of personal growth often describe similar results. (Recall the summary table in Chapter 22.) With this conclusion, we now turn our attention to mature religiousness.

REVIEW OF KEY CONCEPTS

Religious Language and Cosmic Issues
   similarities between glossolalia and Native American vision quests
   conversion as metaphor for social integration
   religious language as best in life-shattering situations
   frustration and "the end of the world"
   anxiety and cataclysmic religious imagery
   God as a projection of harsh conscience
   God as symbol of what is supreme in relationships
   religious versus psychological problems

Positive Aspects of Distorted Religiousness
   self-defeating exaggeration in religious practice
   religion for psychological survival
   Jung's views of the needs of older patients
   suffering as signaling need for religious growth
   Fromm's views on neurosis and "adjustment"
   sensitivity, neurosis, and religiousness

Distinguishing Religiousness from Psychopathology
   evaluation of conversion: Kiev, Johnson, and Salzman
   relations between religious ritual and compulsions
   James on pathological asceticism
   religious sadness contrasted with clinical depression
   psychopathology masquerading as religiousness
   personal dispositions confused with religiousness

chapter 28

Mature Religiousness

In most areas of life, our own developing skills and pressures from the external environment impel us toward more effective functioning. Religion works rather differently. Religiousness may remain "private" because we often are uncomfortable revealing our religious needs and aspirations, and because we usually consider other people's religion too personal to intrude upon or comment about.

"Hence, in probably no region of personality do we find so many residues of child-hood as in the religious attitudes of adults" (Allport, 1950/1960, p. 59).

Although Chapter 22 sketched a framework of religious development that implies maturing, religious maturity may be looked at in other ways. In this chapter, we focus on some specific ways in which mature religiousness is expressed, on signs that signal a mature religious sentiment.

MATURE RELIGIOUS VISION

Since religion is concerned with the ultimate environment and cosmic issues, the world view underlying other expressions of religion is very important. Immaturity in the individual's approach to and concepts of reality makes maturity in other aspects of religiousness highly problematical.

Comprehensive Unifying Philosophy of Life

In his criteria for mature personality, Allport (1937) said one needs a unifying philosophy of life. This need not be a religious view, but should be sufficiently broad to integrate and give meaning to the person's total existence. Though not all religious philosophies would meet this test of maturity, religions can offer the most comprehensive philosophies of life. Some forms of narrow zeal may indeed unify a life, but a comprehensive and mature religious sentiment "seems never satisfied unless it is dealing with matters central to all existence" (Allport, 1950/1960, p. 78).

For Strunk (1965), mature religious belief involves conviction that something greater than oneself exists—some being or symbol that transcends the individual. Mature religious belief must be quite comprehensive, since a mature person cannot be satisfied with "small" religion. Feinsilver (1960) also insisted that religious vision should involve intense awareness of a larger design into which one fits, and thus meet a test of "relatedness." Mature faith involves transcendental meaning, found in a relationship with something greater than oneself (Anderson, 1970).

A unifying philosophy of life thus gives direction to life. It covers "everything within experience and everything beyond experience . . . under a unifying conception of the nature of all existence" (Allport, 1964, p. 16).

Critical Evaluation of Faith

Mature belief will have been refined and purged of childish immaturities by critical thought (Strunk, 1965). Introspection and critical reflection get one past seeing religion as a set of learned beliefs and rules, to an intellectual and spiritual awareness of the essence of one's faith. Such religion is able to integrate faith with the arts and sciences. Feinsilver's (1960) "test of reason" asks if religious belief has become integrated with other branches of knowledge to form a comprehensible pattern. Both he and Oates (1973) note that unexamined faith may deteriorate into faddism, sentimentalism, fantasy, and magic.

Allport specified that one must critically look at belief so that the mature faith will be differentiated and integral.

> But differentiation implies more than criticism; it implies an articulation and ordering of parts [and knowing one's] attitude toward the chief phases of theoretical doctrine and the principal issues in the moral sphere, while at the same time maintaining a genuine sense of wholeness into which the articulated parts fit [Allport, 1950/1960, pp. 68–69].

To be integral, faith must deal with and work through many religious issues such as determinism and the problem of evil, which Allport considered among the most difficult. Some people simply keep scientific and religious frameworks separate, but the mature believer must work on the difficult task of assimilating scientific frameworks within an expanded religious one—a task at which one can seldom succeed completely. "Faith is . . . an ongoing process, and the presence of the Spirit is not caught once and for all, but again and again" (Kao, 1981, p. 285).

Heuristic Nature of Mature Belief

"An heuristic belief is one that is held tentatively until it can be confirmed or until it helps us discover a more valid belief. . . . Faith is [a] working hypothesis . . . a risk" (Allport, 1950/1960, p. 81). Religiously mature believers affirm particular beliefs to help them toward better and fuller answers to religious questions. They believe so that they can understand, and then successively refine beliefs as deeper understandings emerge. One who cannot hold religious propositions with less than full certainty lacks the ability to tolerate ambiguity and paradox—an ability mature faith requires (Oates, 1973).

Strunk (1965) believes that a critical tentativeness saves a faith commitment from bigotry and fanaticism. One criterion for the maturity of religious beliefs is whether one embraces this tentativeness and can avoid an absolutist stance. Healthy faith recognizes that it is not science, but rather a symbolism that offers "a structure of imaginative unity, a picture of the whole, without in the least diminishing the inner tensions and obvious contradictions" (Miller, 1965, p. 298).

A mature believer realizes that considering one's own beliefs superior to others' beliefs is simply one more belief. Since each person's life and experience captures only one small part of the meaning and value of life, other people are also invested in their own values and truths. "The religion of maturity makes the affirmation 'God is,' but only the religion of immaturity will insist, 'God is precisely what I say' " (Allport, 1950/1960, p. 78).

Unitive Consciousness

Maslow defined unitive consciousness as:

> the simultaneous perception of the sacred and the ordinary, or the miraculous and the ordinary, or the miraculous and the rather constant or

easy-without-effort sort of thing . . . a constantly high level in the sense of illumination or awakening. . . . It is to take rather casually the poignancy and the pre-
ciousness and the beauty of things, but not to make a big deal out of it because
it's happening every hour [Krippner, 1972b, pp. 113–114].

Strunk (1965) also holds that mature religiousness will involve profound experiences of mystical oneness.

This "perception of the miraculous" (Ouspensky, 1949) freshens one's vision with a sense of majesty and mystery. It typically leaves an undercurrent of
serenity and bliss in life—even under conscious pain or anxiety. One feels totally
open and present to experience, and free and resilient in putting life events in
perspective (Stark & Washburn, 1977). "The mystical state expresses the ideal
of the human soul in search of unity and harmony with the universe . . . and
the Ultimate" (Kao, 1981, p. 252). Such is one fruit of Zen enlightenment, yogic
samādhi, and Christian, Jewish, or Islamic mysticism.

MATURE RELIGIOUS STRIVING

Several developmental models (see Chapters 4 and 22) consider that as individuals mature their motives move through such goals as security, pleasure, power,
duty, self-esteem, and self-transcendence. The striving of religiously mature individuals should thus have its own distinctive character.

Extension of Ego Boundaries

Another of Allport's (1937) criteria for personal maturity is the extension of concern beyond one's own biological and psychological interests and desires. This
movement from narcissism to wider perspectives should also characterize mature
religiousness. Movement progresses from purely physiological desires, through
valuing integrity of one's own self and personhood in general, to "developing finally to embrace both an ethics and a theology . . . eager that no value should
perish" (Allport, 1950/1960, pp. 16–17). Religiously mature people have concerned involvement in their environments (Strunk, 1965).

The fostering of values beyond immediate personal concerns necessarily requires self-discipline. Two of James's (1902) characteristics of sanctity relate to
this issue: purity and asceticism. Purity involves enhanced sensitivity to spiritual
discord and things incompatible with the religious life. Deeply religious people
feel the need to purge such elements from life, and often wage relentless battles
with themselves to discard habits and inclinations they consider inappropriate.
However, "the act of endurance of pain, poverty, or discomfort has no moral
value in and of itself, unless it is borne out of a moral conscience for some altruistic purpose" (Kao, 1981, p. 317).

Asceticism may operate on several levels. It may simply reflect disgust with
too much ease in life, or may be a by-product of the search for purity. For some,
asceticism involves sacrifices made for the love of God. Just as purity may be
carried to extremes, so also asceticism can become pathological when it derives

from a negative self-concept (James, 1902; see also Chapter 27). Most religions either impose on devotees some ascetic practices to foster purity and self-discipline, or at least recommend them strongly. Be it abstaining from flesh meat or intoxicating drink, depriving oneself of unnecessary bodily or psychological comforts, attacking particular habits, or engaging in communal ascetic practices, some discipline of body and mind is prescribed.

Former American Psychological Association president Leona Tyler pointed out some psychological values that religious asceticism may offer: "Depth, solidity, and individuality depend upon self-limitation" (Tyler, 1961, p. 296). Although excessive discipline becomes an unhealthy focus of attention, religiously mature individuals use appropriate discipline to free their energies for service to ideals beyond themselves.

Autonomous and Effective Motivation

Allport argued that, although religious striving may begin with self-centered motives, a mature religious concern supplies its own motivational power. The religious sentiment becomes functionally autonomous and behaves as a master motive in its own right (see intrinsic religion, Chapter 20). "No longer goaded and steered exclusively by impulse, fear, wish, it tends rather to control and to direct those motives toward a goal that is no longer determined by mere self-interest" (Allport, 1950/1960, p. 72).

The religious personality is aware of self-determination and makes a gift of self in this freedom (Van Kaam, 1968). "In self-surrender, we find true autonomy" (Kao, 1981, p. 197). "Whoever not only says, but *feels*, 'God's will be done,' is mailed against every weakness" (James, 1902/1961, p. 230). Such strength of soul shows the power of autonomous religious motivation. Fears, weaknesses, inhibitions, and personal motives pale into insignificance as the individual is captivated by this one master motive.

Intentions that never become carried out give no integrity and consistency to personality; they are the kind with which the road to hell is paved. The religious motive must also be effective and produce a consistent morality. An effective religious intention will "close the gap that exists between the actual state of one's values and the possibility of their fuller realization" (Allport, 1950/1960, p. 149). Such intentionality gives meaning to one's existence and is the basis for realistic hope. Magic hope is

> the mere wishful expectation and anticipation that somehow things will change for the better, while realistic hope is based on the attempt to . . . engage in such efforts of thoughtful action as might be expected to bring about the hoped-for change [Menninger, Mayman, & Pruyser, 1963, pp. 385–386].

Living with Insecurity

"To flee from insecurity is to miss the point of being human" (Bertocci, 1958, p. 14). The title of Alan Watts's book *The Wisdom of Insecurity* (1951) shows how he valued action committed without the comforting security of certainty.

"It is a characteristic of the mature mind that it can act wholeheartedly even without absolute certainty. It can be sure without being cocksure" (Allport, 1950/1960, p. 81). Writers from many faiths make this same point, which is a common theme in Eastern thought. The Catholic Cardinal Newman concluded that faith and love make "it reasonable to take probability as sufficient for internal conviction" (1912, p. 43) strong enough to guide one's life.

In his imprisonment, theologican Bonhoeffer claimed that maturity demands living in the world without the comfort of religious certainty: The religiously mature person need not rely on the security of believing that God will right all wrongs. "The God who makes us live in this world without using [God] as a working hypothesis is the God before whom we are ever standing. Before God and with [God] we live without God" (Bonhoeffer, 1953, p. 122). This paradoxical statement says that mature people must not use ideas of God to satisfy dependency needs and calm anxiety. A strong faith seeks personal integrity and committed involvement without such distracting comforts.

Altruistic Service to Others

Allport (1937) considered the capacity to respect the dignity of others and be compassionate toward them as a general characteristic of maturity. Religious love is commonly considered the crown of religious endeavor, and most descriptions of mature religiousness mention it. "When a person becomes unselfish . . . , he or she is capable of releasing . . . the power of love, which is redemptive and has the capacity to heal" (Kao, 1981, p. 321).

Spiritual motivation usually brings an:

> increase of charity, tenderness for fellow-creatures. The ordinary motives to antipathy, which usually set such close bounds to tenderness among human beings, are inhibited. The saint loves . . . enemies and treats loathsome beggars as [family] [James, 1902/1961, p. 222].

In saints, the joy of religious commitment spills over into a "prophetic" charity toward others.

> Treating those whom they met, in spite of the past, in spite of all appearances, as worthy, they have stimulated them to *be* worthy, miraculously transformed them by their radiant example and by the challenge of their expectation [James, 1902/1961, p. 283].

In such fashion, a saint "is an effective ferment of goodness, a slow transmuter of the earthly into a more heavenly order" (James, 1902/1961, p. 285).

MATURE RELIGIOUS ATTITUDES

Self-objectivity

The capacity for self-objectivity, for seeing yourself as others see you, is another of Allport's (1937) general criteria for maturity. This cosmic perspective on oneself is manifest in the ability to laugh at one's own foibles, pretensions, and self-inflations. Mature people understand themselves in the present, as influenced by the past, and neither underestimate nor overestimate themselves and their abilities. Such self-knowledge is important in Maslow's (1954) self-actualized person and in Van Kaam's (1968) authentic religious personality.

Both Feinsilver (1960) and Jourard (1964) hold that one really knows oneself only in meaningful interaction with a significant other person. Relationships involving honest self-revelation establish one's sense of selfhood, expose defenses, and build solidarity with other people. One's self-understanding is strengthened when one shares it in a way that another person can understand. Encounter and sensitivity groups follow this principle; unfortunately, they may encourage self-revelation in carefully selected "safe" environments without teaching participants to have self-revealing relationships with the salient people in their lives. They also tend to lack a spiritual focus.

Although confession can be misused (see Chapters 18 and 27), this time-honored religious practice is endorsed by many spiritually advanced people as a good means of self-objectivity. James was frankly enthusiastic: One "who confesses . . . lives at least on a basis of veracity. . . . One would think that in more [people] the shell of secrecy would have had to open" (James, 1902/1961, p. 360). Allport (1950) extolls confession as a therapeutic means of housecleaning, but thinks its effectiveness is seriously limited by the usual lack of further consultation with the confessor. Mowrer (1961) echoed this concern.

Acceptance of Human Foibles

Personality results from a long process of self-integration. *Becoming* is viewing oneself and others as an ongoing process of assimilating complementary characteristics—not as finished products (Allport, 1955). The poster that proclaims "Please be patient—God is not finished with me yet" catches the essence of these ideas. The purpose of this personal formation is to relate oneself to all of human life and reality. Allport considered it an essentially religious task to view oneself as a process rather than a product. Many personality psychologists have expressed similar opinions, but without religious overtones.

"Acceptance means that the self or other selves are approved as persons or personalities apart from however many imperfections exist" (Carter, 1973, p. 90). Accepting oneself and others as processes increases tolerance for human imperfections and the ability to see beyond another's surface faults. "Now we may at last learn to fully love one another as and for what we truly are with all our faults and imperfections" (Trevett, 1963, p. 176). Mature people relate to others in ways that respect their inner dignity—with universal compassion and patience with human limitations. Such universality does not stop with valuing and appreciating people like ourselves—in race, ethnicity, citizenship, religion, etc.—but extends caring to humanity as a whole.

Finally, the religiously mature person is able to forgive—both self and others. Self-forgiveness is often the hardest forgiveness to win, for people concerned with implementing values in their lives often feel they must somehow earn or deserve forgiveness. Yet those who cannot forgive themselves lack the capacity to forgive or love others; if we cannot be objects of our own loving forgiveness, then we do not love maturely (Fromm, 1956). A contemporary novelist captured some important insights:

> We are looking around for someone to forgive us, but there's nobody. Perhaps there never will be, until we learn to forgive ourselves. . . . I am changed because I know that I cannot change what I was or what I did. . . . I have paid everything by accepting that I can pay nothing [West, 1965, pp. 229, 275].

Mature Conscience and Values

Many existentially oriented psychologists say that maturity requires a strong ethical sense, with the ability to resist cultural pressures, a concern for ultimate good, and the courage to choose and live for higher values. This orientation is incompatible with immature conscience formation. Mature conscience is far more than

> a troublesome baggage of parental injunctions. . . . My discomfort when I violate my sense of "ought" is a discomfort wholly apart from my fear of physical sanctions I incur if I violate nature's or society's laws [Allport, 1950/1960, p. 100].

What characterizes mature conscience? (1) Moral choices must be truly personal, proceeding from one's own moral convictions. This means not acting from "extrinsic motives, or under the domination of extrinsic sources, such as fear, desire of reward, conformity to social pressures or even to authority and law as merely external norms" (Clarke, 1969, p. 359). (2) Mature conscience is based on what works best for the common good—beyond the limits of oneself, family, and community (religious or national) to humanity and the cosmos as a whole. (3) Mature conscience is based on practical, prudent judgment of what behavior is most appropriate at any given time, place, and circumstance. Prudent judgment requires knowledge of the situation, consideration of consequences of possible choices, respectful consideration of established moral wisdom (though one does not follow it slavishly), courage to break rules that do not apply, and willingness to live with the choice made without anxiety and endless rehashing of the problem (Clarke, 1969, pp. 357–368).

Avoiding Idolatries

The essence of idolatry is "the deification of things, of partial aspects of the world, and . . . submission to such things, in contrast to an attitude in which . . . life is devoted to the realization of the highest principles of life" (Fromm, 1950, p. 114). Contemporary people have many possible idols: pleasure, power, success, the state, science, public opinion, political groups, words, machines, money—or the view of God one's religious group holds. "The religious intolerance so characteristic of Western religions . . . has led to a new form of idolatry" (Fromm, 1950,

p. 111). Fromm argues for making nothing—not even our own necessarily limited religious views—absolute.

Science is another contemporary idolatry. The common purpose in science and religion is "to reach out toward the unmanifest. . . . This impulse presupposes that the manifest is but the barest hint of reality, that beyond the manifest there exist the major portions of reality" (Bakan, 1966, p. 5). Religion and science conflict when either abandons this quest—becomes "idolatrous"—by "worshiping" its own understandings as the whole of reality.

People who have achieved full "ego integrity" (Erikson, 1963) avoid even the subtle idolatries; they transcend the limits of their own cultural and religious understandings to recognize differing mature persons. Surely the great saints, those achieving what Fowler (Chapter 4) calls "universalizing faith," avoid these pitfalls of idolatry.

PSYCHOLOGICAL VERSUS SPIRITUAL MATURITY

Are psychological and spiritual maturity the same thing? Unfortunately, this question has no easy answer.

Self-actualization and the Ultimate Goal

Psychology has been accused of deifying the individual and of encouraging people in narcissistic self-absorption (see Vitz, 1977). Clearly, such an emphasis can be detected in some psychology. Tension between the individual and the larger society will probably always exist. People need a basically healthy society to develop and maximize their potential. To be healthy, a society must have harmony among its members, and individual needs and wishes must sometimes be subordinated to social need. However, a healthy society must also be concerned with individual growth needs.

In Maslow's (1954) first statement of his need hierarchy, he posited self-actualization as the highest need. When lower needs were met, the need to be fully oneself would emerge. However, in his later writings (Maslow, 1971a), he spoke increasingly of the need to transcend the limits of self, to experience and actualize values beyond the individual ego. Although some contemporary psychologists do not concern themselves with transcendence, many consider it important.

Religiously mature people seem able to meet their own growth needs—even those that oppose society's common rules—yet also enhance the well-being of others. Their self-concern respects personal needs that work for both self-completion and self-transcendence. Without proper ego development, one cannot transcend ego. Without self-actualization, one has a lesser self to give. Sins against the self may stunt necessary self-development; errors in favor of the self may result in self-worship—the greatest idolatry of all. Clearly, knowing when to choose for self and when to subordinate self is a task probably mastered only by the most mature.

Points of Convergence and Divergence

Chapters 4 and 22 compared several models of religious development with models of psychological development. Religious and psychological models clearly contain many points of convergence in their views of human ripening. Some models appear to describe a spiritual interpretation of growth phenomena that are presented in a secular fashion in other models. The correspondence seems closest in the earlier stages of development. At the higher stages, religious models either use concepts beyond the realm of psychology or rest on value judgments that not all psychologies would endorse.

Giffin (1964) compared the value judgments of psychiatry and religion. Both endorse four cardinal points: (1) the importance of dialogue and self-disclosure; (2) a recognition that conscious awareness does not comprise all of human psychological functioning; (3) the value in continuing self-observation and evaluation of life events; and (4) the value of a theoretical framework for making value judgments.

Drapela (1969) compared psychological adjustment and religious growth. The concept of freedom is the same in both; the concepts of self-enhancement, acceptance, transcendence, and creative work differ in motivation and range, but not in basic content. Similarities in the processes are striking, although "personality adjustment precedes religious growth at least logically if not chronologically" (Drapela, 1969, p. 96). Neither arena can replace the other since their goals differ.

Toward Synthesis

Some synthesis of psychology and religion was attempted in Chapters 4 and 22. Your authors agree with other scholars in both disciplines, however, that religion and psychology cannot replace each other, though they may enrich each other. Both approaches describe similar observable changes in growth; however, at some point many secular interpretations of development falter. Although these psychologies stop short of considering the individual in a context larger than personal ego, others recognize dimensions of life important to religion. "Human existence is not authentic unless it is lived in terms of self-transcendence. Self-actualization is an unintentional effect of the intentionality of life. Self-transcendence is the essence of existence" (Frankl, 1966, p. 104). This perspective sounds very similar—if not identical—to the religious task.

Must self-development and self-transcendence ever be at odds? The concept of synergy suggests at least a theoretical way out of the dilemma. Synergy describes:

> social-institutional conditions which fuse selfishness and unselfishness, by arranging it so that when I pursue "selfish" gratifications, I automatically help others, and when I try to be altruistic, I automatically reward and gratify myself also [Maslow, 1971a, p. 138].

The saying "All things work to the good for those who love God" suggests synergy. Unfortunately, much of society does not operate synergistically. The person who chooses religious maturity often must make costly decisions against personal gains, and this goodness is likely to be unappreciated or even abused.

CONCLUSIONS

Psychologically mature individuals endorse many different modes of religious expression; some do not embrace any single religion. Also, the characteristics of mature religiousness are not unique to any particular faith. All faiths have produced saints or religious geniuses, as all also embrace many who fall short even of healthy religion. No predetermined set of specific religious beliefs or behaviors establishes the criteria of mature religiousness. Probably some—because of obvious immaturity or pathological features—can be ruled out. One's manner or style of being religious—not particular contents or behaviors of religion—determines one's degree of religious maturity. Although there are some grounds for considering psychological and spiritual maturity interrelated, it is heuristically best to keep the two conceptually distinct.

REVIEW OF KEY CONCEPTS

Mature Religious Vision
>function of a unifying philosophy of life
>Feinsilver's "test of reason"
>tasks of an integral faith
>heuristic use of belief
>critical tentativeness
>definition of unitive consciousness
>"perception of the miraculous"

Mature Religious Striving
>extending ego boundaries
>purity and asceticism
>psychological values of asceticism
>functional autonomy of motives
>magic hope versus realistic hope
>Bonhoeffer's "living without God"
>"prophetic" charity

Mature Religious Attitudes
>role of relationship in self-objectivity
>"becoming" and seeing selves as processes
>need for self-forgiveness
>mature conscience and parental injunctions
>Clarke's description of mature conscience
>contemporary forms of idolatry
>Bakan on why science and religion clash

Psychological Versus Spiritual Maturity
    deification of the individual
    self-transcendence as a basic need
    religious versus secular models of development
    value judgments psychiatry and religion both accept
    synergy and how it works

Conclusions
    basis for determining maturity of one's religiousness
    psychological versus spiritual maturity

chapter 29

Religion, the Quality of Life, and Spiritual Well-Being

INTRODUCTION

Countless empirical studies bear on the issues of religion's relationship to mental health and mental illness. No simple generalizations appear in this work. Just as religion is multidimensional (see Unit Four), so there are no simple unidimensional measures of psychological adjustment. The complexities of religion and mental health relationships have been emphasized in the last two units. Rather than present further data in the same vein, we turn in this research chapter to a relatively global view of psychological health that emerged in the 1970s.

Quality of Life and Well-Being

In the late 1960s the *social indicators movement* led in the development of statistical surveys "monitoring change in such areas of life as education, health, employment, crime victimization, political participation, and population growth and movement" (Campbell, 1976, p. 118). The goal of such work was to assess the *quality of life* of any community of people. The subjective or psychological view of quality of life has been called *well-being*. Although often neglected as social indicators, religion and religious institutions typically have peace and well-being of believers among their goals (Moberg & Brusek, 1978).

Religion and well-being were further drawn together in the 1971 White House Conference on Aging (Moberg, 1971b), with its emphasis on spiritual well-being among the elderly. After the conference Moberg and other sociologists did a great deal of conceptual and empirical work on spiritual well-being (Moberg, 1979b). In an American Psychological Association symposium the subject was posed as a challenge to psychologists (Perkins, 1977). This chapter reviews and briefly evaluates selected empirical research by workers in both disciplines.

SOCIOLOGICAL RESEARCH

Religion and the Quality of Life

In one major quality-of-life study religion produced the most diverse response of all social indicators; people tended to rate it either highly important or quite unimportant for their well-being (Campbell, Converse, & Rodgers, 1976, p. 83). The study concluded that religion was negatively related both to personal competence and to overall well-being. Several reinterpretations of the same data by other sociologists led, however, to quite different conclusions.

The data were based on interviews with a representative sample of 2164 persons 18 years and older, conducted by the Survey Research Center (SRC) at the University of Michigan in the summer of 1971. Hadaway (1978) found that when statistical errors in the data were corrected, religious-mindedness was positively related to both competence and well-being.

Faith and Well-Being In an extensive analysis of the same SRC data, Hadaway and Roof (1978) found "importance of religious faith" to be related to an index of the "worthwhileness of life" more strongly than number of friends, marital status, age, education, health, income, or race—social status variables that tend to relate highly to well-being. The percentages of high (1), medium (2–4), and low (5) ratings of "worthwhileness" by "importance of faith" categories are shown in Table 29.1.

The main difference is at the highest level of faith importance—an extreme checked by 38% of the sample, on a 5-point scale. Similarly, frequency of church attendance made the most difference at the high extreme. Of the 13% who went to church more than once a week, 62.7% rated the worthwhileness of life as "high," compared to 39.1% of those who did not go to church at all. The relationship recalls the lower prejudice among *very* frequent church attenders (Struening,

Table 29.1 WORTHWHILENESS OF LIFE BY IMPORTANCE OF FAITH

Worthwhileness	Importance of faith		
	Extremely	Moderate	Not at all
High	58.9	35.9	34.6
Medium	35.3	57.8	54.3
Low	5.8	6.3	11.1

Source: Hadaway and Roof (1978, Table 1, page 300).

1963; see also Chapters 20 and 25). Hadaway and Roof found that importance of faith related to worthwhileness more strongly than did frequency of church attendance and concluded that with regard to well-being "psychological variables are better predictors than social and belonging types of correlates" (1978, p. 303).

Religion and Life Satisfactions McNamara and St. George (1979) also reanalyzed part of the complex set of SRC data, with the aim of determining whether religious-mindedness and childhood religious instruction (used by Campbell, Converse, & Rodgers, 1976) were the best religious predictors of quality of life. They found a number of relationships among the data, indicating rather specific influences of various religious variables on life satisfaction and competence. Overall life satisfaction was best predicted by frequency of church attendance ($r = .18$); satisfaction with marriage, satisfaction with family life, and general affect (feeling state) were best predicted by satisfaction from religion (r's .15, .27, and .24, respectively), and overall personal competence by church group membership ($r = .10$).

Religion and Well-Being in the Elderly Steinitz (1980) studied religiosity and well-being among 1492 elderly respondents to national surveys taken in 1972–1977. She measured religion by (1) frequency of church attendance, (2) whether considered strong or not so strong in their particular faith, (3) belief in life after death, and (4) degree of confidence in organized religion. Well-being was measured by self-reports of happiness, health, excitement in and satisfaction with one's city or other locale, family life, and health. For the total sample and subsamples of men and women, whites and blacks, 19 of 30 relationships between church attendance and well-being were statistically significant. However, church attendance was not related to well-being among the physically healthy; it did not appear to mean much to them. Among the relatively infirm, though, having a faith strong enough to overcome physical limitations was associated with psychological well-being. From another perspective, it seems that something is valued only when it is costly.

In Steinitz's study four out of the five highest correlations were with the religious variable "belief in life after death," especially for the well-being variable "Is life exciting?" As we observed in Chapter 5, belief in immortality is especially salient for the elderly. Steinitz recommends it as perhaps a more accurate index of religiosity than church attendance, at least in well-being studies with the elderly (1980, p. 64)—despite the implied bias against religions that do not emphasize the afterlife.

Some limitations of survey data are suggested by the above studies. Single items have low reliability, so correlation coefficients based on them tend to be quite small. Composite measures—for example, of satisfaction and competence—composed of three to six individual items, have little internal consistency and so low reliability also. Nonetheless the huge numbers of respondents allow one to identify relationships that can be further studied with more reliable indices.

Correlates of Spiritual Well-Being

Moberg (1979a) surveyed 121 students in three private midwestern colleges. Sixty-five percent considered they personally "had spiritual well-being," with 26% unsure and only 9% saying no. Some beliefs about spiritual well-being were generally accepted by the three groups, for example: It is possible for a person to know whether he or she has spiritual well-being (SWB) (92–99%), or whether *someone else* has SWB (67–70%); everybody *can* have SWB (64–82%), but only a few people actually do have SWB (45–55%); and SWB is a process of growth and development (83–96%). Moberg asked whether several indicators were essential, present, absent, or not related with SWB. Table 29.2 shows the most common responses to each indicator, for the groups who felt they personally did or did not have SWB.

Those who did and did not consider themselves to have spiritual well-being differed somewhat in their interpretation of the state. Those who said they had SWB put less emphasis on conventional success and physical health and more on helping others. Given the Christian identity of most respondents, they tended to value faith in Christ somewhat more, but good morals were valued somewhat less.

Sociologist Fichter (1979) studied correlates of relative spirituality among recovering alcoholic clergy. He contrasted those who professed "very much" pos-

Table 29.2 BELIEFS ABOUT INDICATORS OF SPIRITUAL WELL-BEING

Indicator and status	Respondents have SWB?	
	Yes (78)	No (12)
Peace with God: Essential	73	67
Inner peace: Essential	67	67
Faith in Christ: Essential	53	42
Good morals: Present	55	64
Helping others: Present	62	42
Good physical health:		
Present	36	42
Not related	49	17
Being successful:		
Essential	3	25
Present	32	33
Not related	57	33

Source: Moberg (1979a, Table 2, page 8).

itive change in (1) dependence on God's grace, (2) better and frequent prayer, and (3) a deeper sense of humility (i.e., "supersaints") with "minisaints" who responded "very much" on none of the three criteria. Spirituality was not related to continued abstinence from alcohol, but the most spiritual were much more likely to rate themselves on the highest level on a scale of serenity (45% versus 23% for the minisaints). Further, they had better relations with other people, with ministries to other alcoholics, and with the institutional church, as shown in Table 29.3. Some of these relations are supported by more promotions, since treatment, for the supersaints than for the minisaints.

Sociological Measures of Spiritual Well-Being

The sociological research suffers from inconsistent measures of spiritual well-being. Besides the operational definitions used by Moberg (1979a) and Fichter (1979), three factor analytic studies in sociology have tried to identify consistent measures of spiritual well-being. Factor analyses of 57 religious belief and attitude statements among three groups of current and former Roman Catholic sisters produced clusters of items related to spiritual well-being (Marcum, 1979). Two items clustered together in all three groups: "Spiritual well-being is a strong awareness of God," and "It is a good sense of reality which is grounded in prayer." This devotional focus is probably more relevant to religious sisters than to most other people. Further, the analysis of so many items with relatively few subjects violates customary standards for the factor analytic method.

Hynson (1979) factor analyzed six interview items he considered related to spiritual well-being. Four of the six items loaded substantially on the first factor (which he then used as a composite index of spiritual well-being): "Man has a soul that does not die after the death of the body," "The value of any religion can best be assessed according to its usefulness for life's everyday problems," "Without religion, life does not make any sense," and "God exists." Few of Hynson's items have content obviously relevant to spiritual well-being.

More recently Moberg (1981) developed a total of ten indices of spiritual well-being from an 82-item questionnaire. The preliminary instrument was given

**Table 29.3   SELF-RATINGS OF RECOVERING ALCOHOLIC
CLERGY**

Rating	Supersaints % ($N = 229$)	Minisaints % ($N = 101$)
More compassion for people in trouble	90	36
More available to the people served	82	24
Improved quality of ministry	82	26
Do Twelfth-Step work (in AA)	66	41
Act as sponsor for alcoholic in AA	50	27
Stronger in theological beliefs	73	5
Greater loyalty to church tradition	69	4
Closer ties with fellow clergy	43	4

Source: Fichter (1979, Tables 2, 3, 4; pp. 259–262).

to 761 Americans in 17 different groups and 320 Swedes in 15 groups in Sweden. Factor analysis identified seven indices from 45 of the questionnaire items; they included 13 items in a Christian faith factor, 9 items in Self-Satisfaction, 6 in Personal Piety, 5 in Subjective Well-Being, 4 in Optimism, 3 in Religious Cynicism, and 3 in Elitism. Three other indices measured involvement in political, religious, and charitable activities. These indices were not intended to be either comprehensive or pure measures, or even "scales" in a psychometric sense. Nonetheless they do represent an advance in sociological research—both in the breadth of conception of "spiritual well-being" and in measurement methodology.

PSYCHOLOGICAL RESEARCH ON SPIRITUAL WELL-BEING

After the concept of spiritual well-being was introduced to psychologists in an American Psychological Association symposium (Perkins, 1977), Ellison and Paloutzian (1978) presented a paper on efforts to develop measures of spiritual well-being. A symposium the next year (Paloutzian, 1979) reported refinements of the measurements and studies that used the measures.

Factor Analyses

Spiritual well-being came to be defined through a series of three factor analyses, using a total of 22 questionnaire items and 389 respondents (Ellison & Paloutzian, 1978; Paloutzian & Ellison, 1979). The final study produced three factors that were used as bases for two scales—Religious Well-Being and Existential Well-Being—plus a composite Spiritual Well-Being measure. Existential Well-Being was based on two factors that might have been used as separate scales (Malony, 1979). The factors, the items, and their loadings on the respective factors are shown in Box 29.1. Items that are scored negatively (i.e., highest for disagreement) are indicated by (N).

Religious items alternate with existential items in the Spiritual Well-Being Scale. Respondents indicate agreement/disagreement on a 6-point scale from Strongly Agree through Strongly Disagree, with scores from 1 to 6 on each item. Test-retest and internal consistency reliabilities for the scales are shown in Table 29.4. Retest was after one week; internal consistencies are for the first testing.

Construct Validity

Several exploratory studies related the well-being scales to variables that might yield some *construct validity*. That is, the relationships tend to show that the scales are measuring what they are intended to measure. Three studies contrasted Christians who professed to have "received Christ as personal Savior and Lord" with those who "attempted to follow the moral and ethical teachings of Christ." The "born agains" were much higher than the "ethicals" on Religious Well-Being in all three studies. On Existential Well-Being the "born agains" were also higher, but much less so, and still significant at the .001 level in two of the studies (nonsignificant in the other) (Camprise, Ellison, & Kinsman, 1979; Ellison & Paloutzian,

---

Box 29.1   SPIRITUAL WELL-BEING FACTORS AND SCALES

Factor 1. Religious Well-Being

I don't find much satisfaction in private prayer with God. .68 (N)[a]
I believe that God loves me and cares about me. .77
I believe that God is impersonal and not interested in my daily situations. .62 (N)
I have a personally meaningful relationship with God. .81
I don't get much personal strength and support from God. .70 (N)
I believe that God is concerned about my problems. .77
I don't have a personally satisfying relationship with God. .77 (N)
My relationship with God helps me not to feel lonely. .79
I feel most fulfilled when I'm in close communion with God. .86
My relation with God contributes to my sense of well-being. .90

Factor 2. Life Satisfaction (Existential Well-Being)

I feel that life is a positive experience. .65
I don't enjoy much about life. .55 (N)
I feel that life is full of conflict and unhappiness. .42 (N)
Life doesn't have much meaning. .68 (N)
I believe there is some real purpose for my life. .61

Factor 3. Life Direction (Existential Well-Being)

I don't know who I am, where I came from, or where I'm going. .31 (N)
I feel unsettled about my future. .49 (N)
I feel very fulfilled and satisfied with my life. .38
I feel a sense of well-being about the direction my life is headed in. .85
I feel good about my future. .76

---

[a](N) indicates scoring for negative response.
Source: Paloutzian and Ellison (1979, pp. 4–5).

1979). Correlational relationships are shown in Table 29.5. Religious and Existential Well-Being scales correlated .32 and .20 in two of the studies (Camprise et al., 1979).

To some extent these studies share the bias of most of this chapter, namely a predominantly Christian orientation of the subject samples. However, the separate well-being scales, one worded in terms of conventional religion, and one independent of such language, allows some discrimination. High self-esteem and purpose in life and low loneliness are more strongly associated with Existential Well-Being, whereas high intrinsic religion and low individualism and personal freedom are associated with well-being in traditional Christian language.

Table 29.4   RELIABILITIES FOR WELL-BEING SCALES

Well-being scale	Test-retest	Consistency
Spiritual Well-Being	.93	.88
Religious Well-Being	.96	.87
Existential Well-Being	.86	.75

Source: Paloutzian and Ellison (1979, p. 6).

Table 29.5   CORRELATIONS WITH SPIRITUAL WELL-BEING
              SCALES

Variable and study	Well-being scale	
	Religious	Existential
Self-esteem		
(CEK #1)	.07	.49***
(CEK #2)	—	.31***
Perceived quality of parent-child relationships		
(CEK #1)	.28**	—
(CEK #2)	—	.28***
Family togetherness		
(CEK #1)	.30**	.17*
(CEK #2)	—	.25***
Social skills (CEK #2)	.29***	.37***
Individualistic values (CEK #1)	−.53***	−.34***
Success orientation (CEK #1)	−.33***	−.36***
Importance of personal freedom		
(CEK #1)	−.45***	−.18*
Loneliness		
(UCLA scale) (EP)	−.31**	−.55***
(ABLS scale) (EP)	−.19*	−.66***
Intrinsic religion (EP)	.80***	.29**
Purpose in life (EP)	.29***	.73***

*$p > .05$; ** $p > .01$; *** $p > .001$.
Source: Camprise, Ellison, and Kinsman (1979) (CEK); and Ellison and Paloutzian (1979) (EP).

EVALUATION

The sociological and psychological research on spiritual well-being has been primarily correlational. We can only guess whether well-being affects or is affected by other variables—or if both are influenced by some third factor. Further, almost all of the relationships are based on self-report measures. Social desirability, halo effects, or other biases may account for many of the statistical relationships.

Further studies need to establish cause-effect relationships, with spiritual well-being both as dependent and as independent variables. For example, would the relationship between spiritual well-being and quality of childhood relations with one's parents (Camprise et al., 1979) hold true if someone else made relatively objective measurements of the respondents' early relationships with their parents?

As an independent variable, spiritual well-being should relate to helping others, based on Moberg's (1979a) and Fichter's (1979) findings (see Tables 29.2 and 29.3). Social psychology experiments have shown that people are more likely to help others when they are made to feel good—by events so trivial as unexpectedly being given a cookie or finding a dime in a pay telephone (Isen & Levin, 1972). Similar experiments might determine whether people who are high in spiritual well-being have such a perennial good mood that they actually engage in more helping behavior. If so, can the feeling of well-being be manipulated, and result in greater altruism? Or does the altruistic, helping behavior produce the feelings of well-being?

In all of these explorations reliable and valid measures of spiritual well-being are essential. The scales developed by Ellison and Paloutzian are at least a good beginning in that direction. The two subfactors included in their Existential Well-Being scale should be used separately, at least on an exploratory basis. Moberg (1979b) suggests that different measures of spiritual well-being may have to be constructed for each religious tradition, with different ideas of well-being. Then any overlap among the diverse definitions could lead to a general measure of spiritual well-being. Regardless, we judge the psychological approach of first constructing suitable operational definitions of spiritual well-being to be more productive in the long run than the ad hoc and often ill-conceived measures in sociological studies. Nonetheless, the earlier studies yield fruitful hypotheses, such as the one about helping behavior suggested above.

REVIEW OF KEY CONCEPTS

Introduction
  social indicators
  definition of quality of life and well-being
  spiritual well-being: sociological and psychological origins

Sociological Research
  conclusions of Survey Research Center study
  Hadaway's reinterpretations—effects at *high* levels of faith importance and
    church attendance
  relative predictability of psychological and social factors
  church attendance and well-being among healthy and infirm elderly persons
  salience of belief in immortality for the elderly
  limitations and usefulness of massive survey data
  differences of beliefs about spiritual well-being according to personal spiri-
    tual well-being
  well-being and functioning of supersaints and minisaints
  general status of sociological measures of spiritual well-being
  nature of Moberg's indices

Psychological Research on Spiritual Well-Being
  factor analyses and measures of well-being
  reliability of well-being measures
  validity: "born agains" versus "ethicals"
  religious well-being and individualism, freedom, and intrinsic religion
  existential well-being and self-esteem, loneliness, and purpose
  well-being and family and parent-child variables and social skills

Evaluation
  limitations of present research on spiritual well-being
  cause-effect relationships
  relationship of sociological findings to psychological research

chapter *30*

Religion and Psychology Working Together

Some people consider psychology and religion necessarily at odds with each other. Psychology may appear to urge a self-concern incompatible with many religious perspectives. In this chapter we explore ways in which psychology and religion may fruitfully interact.

PSYCHOLOGY AND RELIGION IN POSSIBLE CONFLICT

The word *psyche* means soul. As psychology abandoned study of people's presumed interior lives and focused on measurable variables, such as behavior or reported attitudes, some psychologists charged that "psychology thus became a science lacking its main subject matter, the soul" (Fromm, 1950, p. 6).

Rival Recruiting Agencies

The observation that "some of the conflict of science and religion is a competition of rival recruiting agencies" (Cattell, 1938) touches a major root of tension between psychology and religion. Maslow (1954) agreed that many psychologists now attempt to do for people what organized religion tried to accomplish. Freud (1933) considered the rivalry unavoidable because, in satisfying human desire for knowledge, religious belief is doing the same thing science tries to do by its own methods.

Religious Fears   The antagonism comes in part from the fears each camp has concerning the other. Some religious people see as psychology's goal a caricature of Skinnerian society in which a master planner controls all human behavior. More widely feared is a reductionism that considers religion fully explained when certain typical conditions of its appearance and ways of its operation are discovered.

Logical positivism assumes that the ultimate basis of knowledge is empirical verification—a stance that renders faith positions meaningless. Psychologists are usually methodologically conscientious, and identify with positivistic reductionism. Some religionists think that such empirical study—which seeks only statistical norms and ignores personal elements—keeps people from accepting anything that is not empirically demonstrated.

Some psychologists recognize that "determinism and its (seeming) implications constitute for the psychologist both a scientific . . . and a moral stumbling block" (Meehl, 1958, p. 174). James (1902) protested against a "nothing but" approach to religion; he insisted that religion can be judged only by the criteria of "philosophical reasonableness" and "moral helpfulness." R. B. Cattell (1938) noted the possibility of interpreting life and events by more than one system of thought, and said that religious institutions must not be crushed by the superficial logic of immature scientific approaches.

Psychology's Complaints   Psychologists have countercomplaints against some religious people. Since they seek adequate explanations of behavior, psychologists dislike the tendency to classify any apparently religious response—no matter how maladaptive or deviant—as purely religious and untouchable by psychology.

Expanding knowledge makes it increasingly difficult to deny that variations in religious behavior are related in part to cultural background, social roles, and differences in personal experience. Psychologists feel frustrated when such findings are ignored, and religious persons differ in their acceptance of at least some determinism in religious behaviors.

Rules for the Study of Religion

Dittes (1969) outlined four possible ways to discuss religious behavior. The most parsimonious and reductionistic sees the same psychological variables and relationships operating in religion as in other events. A second position considers certain patterns particularly discernible in religious behavior, so that the study of religion is the best way to understand them. Still another position holds that there are variables unique to religion, which interact with basic psychological variables. A final position considers religious behavior made up of basically unique variables "beyond" psychological study.

Argyle (1958) said psychology's proper task in studying religion is to discover empirical generalizations or laws governing religious beliefs, behavior, and experiences, and to formulate theories or mechanisms to explain these laws. Its role is not to attack, defend, or establish the truth of religious phenomena. Later, he (Argyle & Beit-Hallahmi, 1975) focused on the antecedents and correlates of religious belief and behavior.

Others hold that psychology must neither abandon scientific method nor believe it defines all knowledge. "Recognize the limitations of the scientific method, derive from it all the information possible, but under no circumstances limit the subject of knowledge to its methodology" (Finch, 1964, p. 14). Recall Bakan's (1966) opinion that science and religion clash when one or the other absolutizes its own vision, engages in the idolatry of worshiping partial understandings.

Interpretation of psychological data has caused tensions with religion. This results mainly from the carrying over of either religious or scientific attitudes from the setting where each belongs into the other setting (Strommen, 1965). Psychologists must be cautious not to draw unwarranted conclusions or apply simplistic labels to religiousness. They must recognize that patterns of causation in religious behavior may be very complex, and different processes may operate for different people.

ALTERNATE UNDERSTANDINGS OF BASIC CONCEPTS

Religion and psychology use some of the same words—such as guilt, belief, and conscience. The different connotations they attach to these words are sources of possible confusion and antagonism.

Constructs to Explain Religious Events

A construct is an idea used to explain observed events or processes. A psychologist sees people acting in intelligent ways, and uses the construct of *intelligence* to explain this. Such words as *imagination, ego, memory, conscience,* and many other psychological ideas are used similarly. Constructs are particularly useful for discussing religious behavior. When we speak of *conscience* or *altruism* we are not referring to "things" that exist inside the person, but to a complex of behaviors, feelings, and attitudes relevant to religious concerns.

The Jungian idea of archetypes (see Chapter 2) is another such example. Jung cautiously pointed out that a psychologist can study only psychological contents, and can say nothing about the metaphysical status of the ideas themselves. "The real facts do not change, whatever names we give them. Only we ourselves are affected. If . . . we speak of 'God' as an 'archetype,' we are saying nothing about [God's] real nature" (Jung, 1965, p. 457).

The Unconscious as Construct

The idea of *the unconscious* is also used to discuss religion. This is not a "part" of a person, but refers to psychological processes outside conscious awareness. Some authors speak of uncovering the unconscious to describe getting in touch with important memories or feelings outside awareness. Rather than reducing or explaining away religion, these explanations simply say that individuals can be influenced by personal processes outside of awareness and choice.

William James called unconscious functioning "the subliminal region" and said, "If the grace of God miraculously operates, it probably operates through the subliminal door" (1902/1961, p. 219). He believed that "in persons deep in the religious life, . . . the door into this region seems unusually wide open" (p. 376). He concluded: "Whatever it may be on its *farther* side, the 'more' with which in religious experience we feel ourselves connected is on its *hither* side the subconscious continuation of our conscious life" (p. 396). In other words, if God comes to us, it is through aspects of our mental life beyond full conscious awareness.

Lovekin and Malony found "the experience of speaking in tongues . . . one . . . of trust and surrender" (1977, p. 392). If one thinks of glossolalia as unconscious automatic behavior (Chapter 9), this surrender to the "unknown" supports both James's contention that experience attributed to God comes through unconscious mentation, and the Jungian idea that experiencing the unconscious is essentially a religious act.

The Example of Guilt

Different ways of viewing the alienating experience of guilt lead to different ways of labeling people (Belgum, 1963). Theology calls one a penitent, the law a prisoner, and medicine a patient. Theology concerns itself with alienation from God, and stresses the human need for salvation. The law is concerned with social alienation, with bad conduct toward other people, and focuses on the need for community. Medicine concerns itself with one's alienation from oneself, and with its effects on personal health and well-being.

We saw (Chapter 14) that Arnold, Narramore, and yoga distinguish the emotion of guilt from an objective judgment made about one's own conduct. This self-judging faculty may occur along with the emotion of guilt, but these two different experiences—both called guilt—may occur separately. Many people equate *feeling* guilty with *being* guilty. Such failure to distinguish psychological from religious use of words creates confusion and causes difficulty between the two disciplines.

THE DEFEAT OF THE RELIGIOUS INTENTION

Recognizing Mistaken Religiousness

Although religious people may fear that psychology inappropriately understands religious behavior, and may draw unwarranted conclusions about its merits, an informed psychology can help religion achieve many of its goals. One help it offers is a "negative" one; the social science study of religion at least "can and does relate the drama of *the defeat of the religious intention*" (Salomen, 1949, p. 595) (emphasis in the original). Psychology can adequately explain many distortions of religiousness, and can define some criteria for mature and healthy religiousness.

Religion can be the highest task in which one involves oneself, or it can be used to meet gross neurotic needs. The individual's religiousness may be a conscientious commitment, an unthinking habit, or a perversion of religion's core values. People who take religion seriously can profit from psychology's help in indicating where the religious intent itself needs purifying.

> Spiritual persons who are aware of their own limitations as creatures and desire to grow in love of God and . . . human beings will not hesitate to seek awareness of their own personal immaturities and endeavor to rid themselves of infantilisms and self-seeking in their religious response [Meadow, 1978a, p. 68].

Religious Infantilism and Personal Needs

Many people's religiousness lags behind development in other areas. Infantilism is "the persistence of responses in the adult that indicate a manner of coping . . . that corresponds to the psychological modality of childhood" (Oraison, 1963, p. 133). Freud's (1927) opinion that the average person looks to God as a "super-parent" to supply needs may be an exaggeration. However, many people seek religion more for comfort than for growth. The pull to security is one of the major obstacles to personal growth (Maslow, 1968). Awareness of one's comfort-seeking in religion may lead to deepened religious commitment. An unknown French spiritual writer commented that people who are into religion for comfort only clutter up the doorstep!

Our understanding of deity is shaped by background, education, life experience, and emotionality. We all, to some extent, create God in our own image and likeness. Psychology can offer corrective information on how personal needs color religious understanding; this can help refine understanding of and relationship with God or Ultimate Reality.

Psychological Defenses

One of Maslow's (1971a) rules for self-actualization is recognizing and stripping oneself of psychological defenses. This also assists religious growth. "Defense" implies being dishonest with oneself about motives and behavior. To strip away defenses, one can refuse the easy answer when suspicious of oneself, and use the occasion to uncover true reasons for behavior.

We tend to see our own faults in other people; others' sins that especially distress us may reflect our own innate tendencies—likely unrecognized. Psychology teaches us to be suspicious when we feel compelled to protest against the vices of others. Desire to be a good or holy person may simply be disguised perfectionism—ways we convince ourselves that we are worthwhile. Performing good deeds or personal sacrifices may be "showing off" for God or others. Sometimes focusing attention on a trivial flaw prevents one's having to look at deeper or more important faults.

The defense of rationalization involves convincing ourselves that we acted for acceptable motives, when these were not the real ones. We may say, "She really needed to know what others think of her," after saying cruel things to another. Or we may call insistence on meddling in others' affairs "helpfulness." Prejudices can be called "standing up for the faith," and harsh punitiveness "appropriate discipline." Many motives one would be ashamed to acknowledge can be disguised as religious ones. Psychology helps religious people uncover such pathology of religion, the defeat of the religious intention.

The Tibetan Precepts of the Gurus lists ten major ways of mistaking other motives for religious ones. These include: (1) mistaking desire for faith, (2) mistaking attachment for compassionate love, (3) seeing those who profess, but do not practice, religion as true devotees, (4) mistaking deceptive actions for prudence, (5) seeing self-seeking behavior as altruistic, and (6) mistaking charlatans for wise people. Many other faiths show similar psychological astuteness.

PSYCHOTHERAPY: RELIGIOUS AND SECULAR

Religion and psychology necessarily meet each other in psychotherapy, or "soul-healing." Each has a strong interest in the outcomes of this activity.

Similarities and Differences in Approach

Process Similarities   Are religious and secular therapists doing the same thing? Fromm (1950) considered the relationships between religion and psychotherapy so complex that one cannot simply posit either identity or opposition of interests. Jung (1933) detailed the steps in successful therapy, and noted their similarity to religious practices. One first confesses human fallibility. Next comes understanding the reasons behind the mistakes. For some sensitive individuals these are sufficient, but most need to be educated to translate insights into appropriate action. Finally, changes in one's life become apparent. Jung cautioned against considering oneself a "finished product" at this point; one has only corrected some things that had gone wrong.

Angyal (1952) sees similar relationships between repentance and psychotherapy. In both one recognizes that certain features of one's life are unsound, and desires to change them. One then assumes responsibility for making those changes and paying the costs of so doing. Finally, one strongly regrets the unhealthiness of past behavior. Moss (1979) argues strongly that many pastors and therapists serve identical functions and are "of one blood." Although psychohistorians and anthropologists have studied the helpfulness of religious healers, "the wisdom of priestly counsel has not received much close attention" (Moss, 1979, p. 182).

Distinctions Noted   Religion and therapy deal with the same problems of "salvation" and "abundant life." Religion emphasizes factors outside human control, while therapy stresses those within control (Parsons, 1953). Bonnell (1969) agreed on many common goals, styles, and stances for therapist and pastoral counselor, but believed that they work on different levels and in different areas of life. For example, a therapist removes neurotic guilt, while a pastor builds creative self-acceptance. Box 30.1 contrasts a number of the differences.

Psychology of religion focuses on personal integration and transformation, so pastoral care should consider "transformation of personal motivational structure" (Capps, 1978, p. 199) a basic aim that can be realized. Although pastors might hope this leads to increased personal integration, such results are not certain and lie beyond human control. This reference to divine purpose is echoed in a comparison of yoga and therapy:

Box 30.1   CONFESSION AND PSYCHOTHERAPY COMPARED

Aspect	Confession	Psychotherapy
Aim	Restoration to community and God	Improved individual functioning
Format	Universal similar procedure	Idiosyncratic procedures
Viewpoint	Bad behavior causes unhappiness	Bad behavior results involuntarily
Concern	Evils of human freedom	Results of human compulsion
Deals with	Willful misdeeds and thoughts	Dynamics of unconscious motivation
Judgment of	Subjective morality of acts	Causes of the problem
Purpose	Forgiveness	Cure
Cause	Conscious intention	Inability to cope effectively

Source: Worthen (1974, pp. 279–280). Used with permission.

The most significant aspect of yoga, and the one which distinguishes it from ordinary physio-psychotherapy, is the transcendence of its aims. . . . The psychic healing of yoga has its centre above the psyche; here the wholeness aspired for is that of holiness [Ravindra, 1978, p. 396].

Pastoral Competencies

Collins (1975) holds that mainstream pastoral counseling borrows uncritically from secular humanistic psychologies, and often fails to take conservative theology seriously enough. It emphasizes personal experience rather than the consensus of a faith community. Other pastoral approaches suffer from such problems as psychological naiveté, theological naiveté, difficulty to understand, and overly simplistic popularization. Ad hoc borrowing from contemporary psychological therapies confuses pastoral work, which may become remote from the flux of history and culture (Capps, 1978).

Mowrer, who strongly endorsed the therapeutic value of confession, found serious weaknesses in the Catholic handling of it (see Chapter 18). He considered Protestant pastoral counseling a disguised form of confession, and saw even more serious flaws in it. Its sporadic and voluntary nature makes it devoid of deterrent value. It does not take sin seriously when based on the premises of secular therapy, and emphasizes insight and self-acceptance. Such "confession" without expiation can leave one overwhelmed by guilt not adequately managed (Mowrer, 1961).

Many pastoral counseling training programs now exist, and they have become more common since World War II. Although they take different approaches, most attempt to deal with the competency issues discussed. Training programs in spiritual direction are also becoming more common.

TOWARD A THERAPEUTIC PARTNERSHIP

Directions for Working Together

Most who hope for happy relations between religion and psychology encourage more specialization of functions. Mowrer (1961) bluntly said that pastoral counselors who try to be psychologists should return to the business of saving lost sheep and take guilt seriously.

Call for Traditional Roles   "Appropriate" pastoral techniques are too often abandoned for insight therapy and self-awareness training in which pastoral counselors are typically inadequate to function. Appropriate counseling may "allay anxiety . . . in meeting life challenges, or it may bolster controls by setting firm limits. . . . Such responses may serve to diminish the level of conflict within the personality and thus enhance the parishoner's sense of wholeness" (Clemens, Corradi, & Wasman, 1978, p. 229). Pastoral counseling should aim to be religious, with effective training, and a focus on preventive psychology (Collins, 1975).

The pastoral counseling movement seems to have gone astray in:

training programs for pastoral counseling which have too much psychiatry, too much psychology, and too little that is pastoral counseling . . . dealing with particular problems arising out of the *loss* or *failure* of faith. Too much of pastoral counseling is simply orthodox psychotherapy of common neurotic problems [Schofield, 1979, p. 199]

Pastoral counselors should not identify with psychology since that could "further confuse their identification and encourage them to perceive themselves as and to try to behave like psychologists—which they are not" (Schofield, 1979, p. 200). Schofield fears clients may be harmed when they are sent to pastoral experts who are indoctrinated in the orthodox psychotherapies and forget they are pastors.

Need for Varied Approaches   Mental health professionals are often uneasy dealing with patients' existential or spiritual problems, although such issues are common. Pastoral counselors, who should be best equipped to manage such issues, need their own technology for treating their area of human problems—not the techniques of another discipline. "The pastoral counselor should not underrate . . . religious inspiration, resources, and knowledge of human illness in order to gain acceptance by the scientific community" (Mollica, 1979, p. 108).

Some individuals' "yearnings and hopes of the soul are adequately expressed—as for instance in some living religion" (Jung, 1933, p. 210). People whose inner life has gone in other directions may need the help of psychology to deal with things the church cannot handle. "The various forms of religion no longer appear to modern [people] to come from within—to be expressions of [one's] own psychic life" (Jung, 1933, p. 206). Accepting one religion—experienced as external—would not be authentic for people who may need to work outside institutional religious frameworks to reclaim their own spirituality. Unfortunately, there are few psychologists who could be of help to them, either.

Clients are harmed by the neglect of world view factors in therapy, according to Strunk. Although pastoral counselors should deal with such issues, unfortunately their own vision is often restricted. "A greater consideration of referral and consultative courses—including the possible utilization of philosophers, theologians, spiritual directors" (Strunk, 1979, pp. 195–196) should occur.

Complementarity of Functions   To break from egocentrism, people need confession, amendment, and repentance (Belgum, 1963). Psychotherapy can free people from inner compulsions and prepare them for further religious steps. "These separate functions of psychotherapy and confession can work on a progression toward the goal of being oneself in truth . . . wholly integrated" (Worthen, 1974, p. 283). Allport (1950) saw a similar progression. Such alien factors in a life as restricting and stagnating patterns of thought are more adequately handled by a therapist; the clergy may then better help a person establish values and purposes. Each discipline has its own specialization, and should be aware of its inability to be solely responsible for mental health. Therapist plows, and clergy then plants (Allport, 1950/1960, p. 85).

> Pastoral counseling should be a legitimate field of specialized clinical practice
> . . . of individuals who have received specialized education and training for the
> management and relief of suffering arising from doubts or conflicts in the philo-
> sophical-spiritual domain [Schofield, 1979, p. 201]

Psychotherapists should be aware of this specialty, and should be able to refer
to its practitioners, confident that they have received this training and can do
this work.

Values Issues in Religious and Secular Therapy

Adjustment Versus Cure of Soul   Either secular or religious therapy might attempt to cure existential crises by simply removing symptoms. While symptomatic treatment often effects psychological cures of certain specific problems, it is
not helpful for more complex disturbances. A blessing, absolution, or reassur-
ances of God's care might help some religious problems, but the answer here,
too, must often be more sophisticated. Both disciplines sometimes err by being
overly simplistic.

One who considers adjustment paramount tries to get clients to act like
most other people in the culture or in a group. This may violate an individual's
integrity, since many "adjusted" people are simply conforming. One who aims
for cure of soul seeks full realization of each client's individuality; this is a religious task. "Adjustment therapy' can have no religious functions, provided that
by religious we refer to the attitude common to the original teachings of humanistic religions" (Fromm, 1950, p. 73).

Many problems arise in people who have "no love, but only sexuality; no
faith, because . . . afraid to grope in the dark; no hope, because . . . disillusioned
. . . ; and no understanding, because [they have] failed to read the meaning of
[their] own existence" (Jung, 1933, pp. 225–226). Frankl's work—logotherapy—which "offers techniques of search for meaning and hope of finding it
. . . aims at correcting the human condition of meaninglessness" (Crumbaugh,
1979, p. 189). Other existential therapies—bridging secular and religious perspectives—seek similar ends.

Choosing a Helper   Many people today choose a psychologist instead of clergy
counsel, hoping to avoid responsibility for their own troubles (Allport, 1950;
Jung, 1933). They expect psychotherapists to look for causes outside themselves,
while the clergy might impose on them guilt, superstition, or prejudice. Many
people who recognize the spiritual roots of their problems also avoid the clergy,
believing they lack truly spiritual perspectives or cannot help (Jung, 1933). Psychology's scientific prestige draws some people to it (Allport, 1950). Clergy are
an underused resource.

If one needs help, how should one choose? A beginning is to ask what the
problem is: Is one alienated from self or from God? This is sometimes easy to
determine. One seeks a psychotherapist to deal with definite habit problems or

adjustment to ordinary life situations. One seeks the clergy for sacraments, theological understanding, and religious judgment.

In many cases, however, the issues are more complex. Some cases calling for "soul cure" are not clearly the domain of either specialist. The healer's characteristics may be more important than the discipline. Insensitive or incompetent helpers—and also excellent ones—work in both professions. One can ask others with satisfactory healing experiences for names of useful helpers. One can also interview helpers to learn of their values and procedures before agreeing to work with them. It is best to avoid legalistic or dogmatic helpers, or those who put all their faith in simplistic techniques. Finally, one might consult one's own inner wisdom regarding desirable directions, and choose a helper accordingly.

Conclusions   In conclusion, we need to recognize the essential unity of the individual person. Functioning in one aspect of being affects other aspects. Physicians and psychologists have long recognized that psychological and physical health affect each other. People are becoming increasingly aware that one's spiritual health also affects other functioning (Ford, 1971). An important factor in human well-being is religion in individual lives.

REVIEW OF KEY CONCEPTS

Psychology and Religion in Possible Conflict
 psychology without a soul
 religion and psychology trying to serve the same functions
 logical positivism and its implications
 four ways to look at religious behavior
 psychology's proper task in studying religion

Alternate Understandings of Basic Concepts
 the use of constructs
 the "subliminal region" in religious persons
 glossolalia as an example of the unconscious in religion
 Belgum's three views of guilt
 equating feeling guilty with being guilty

The Defeat of the Religious Intention
 some ways of mistaken religiousness
 creating God in one's own image
 how psychological defenses work
 rationalization
 Tibetan Precepts of the Gurus

Psychotherapy: Religious and Secular
 Jung's steps of successful therapy
 some distinctions between confession and psychotherapy
 divine purpose in religious healing
 criticisms of mainstream pastoral counseling
 problems of confession without expiation

Toward a Therapeutic Partnership
>   Schofield's views of pastoral counselor's role
>   appropriate techniques for pastoral counseling
>   world view factors in psychotherapy
>   complementary roles of psychotherapy and pastoral counseling
>   problems of symptomatic treatments
>   "adjustment therapy" versus "cure of soul"
>   motives for choosing a psychotherapist or pastoral counselor
>   implications of the essential unity of the person

Bibliography

Abrahamson, L. Y.; Seligman, Martin E. P.; & Teasdale, J. D. Learned helplessness in humans: Critique and reformulation. *Journal of Abnormal Psychology,* 1978, **87,** 49–74.

Abramson, H. A. (Ed.). *The use of LSD in psychotherapy.* New York: Josiah Macy, Jr. Foundation, 1960.

Abramson, H. A. (Ed.). *The use of LSD in psychotherapy and alcoholism.* Indianapolis: Bobbs-Merrill, 1967.

Abramson, Paul R.; Mosher, Donald L.; Abramson, Linda M.; & Woychowski, Bernard. Personality correlates of the Mosher Guilt Scales. *Journal of Personality Assessment,* 1977, **41,** 375–382.

Aden, LeRoy. Faith and the developmental cycle. *Pastoral Psychology,* 1976, **24,** 215–230.

Aden, LeRoy. Counseling and the development of responsibility. *Pastoral Psychology,* 1979, **27,** 164–170.

Adler, Alfred. *The practice and theory of individual psychology.* New York: Humanities Press, 1955. (Originally published, 1927.)

Adler, Alfred. *Social interest: A challenge to mankind* (Trans. J. Linton & R. Vaughan). London: Faber & Faber, 1938.

Adler, Alfred. *Superiority and social interest* (2nd ed.) (Ed. H. L. Ansbacher & R. R. Ansbacher). Evanston IL: Northwestern University Press, 1970.

Adorno, T. W.; Frenkel-Brunswik, E.; Levinson, D. J.; & Sanford, R. N. *The authoritarian personality.* New York: Harper & Row, 1950.

Alland, Alexander, Jr. "Possession" in a revivalistic Negro church. *Journal for the Scientific Study of Religion,* 1962, **1,** 204–213. In Benjamin Beit-Hallahmi (Ed.), *Research in religious behavior: Selected readings.* Monterey CA: Brooks/Cole, 1973. Pp. 256–275.

Allen, E. E.; & Hites, R. W. Factors in religious attitudes of older adolescents. *Journal of Social Psychology,* 1961, **55,** 265–273.

Allen, G. W. *William James.* New York: Viking Press, 1967.

Allen, Robert M.; Haupt, Thomas D.; & Jones, R. Wayne. Analysis of peak experiences reported by college students. *Journal of Clinical Psychology,* 1964, **20,** 207–212.

Allen, R. O. *Religion and prejudice: An attempt to clarify the patterns of relationship.* Unpublished doctoral dissertation, Univ. of Denver, 1965.

Allen, R. O.; & Spilka, Bernard. Committed and consensual religion: A specification of religion-prejudice relationships. *Journal for the Scientific Study of Religion,* 1967, **6,** 191–206.

Allinsmith, W. The learning of moral standards. In D. R. Miller & G. E. Swanson (Eds.), *Inner conflict and defense.* New York: Holt, Rinehart and Winston, 1960. Pp. 141–176.

Allport, Gordon W. *Personality: A psychological interpretation.* New York: Holt, Rinehart and Winston, 1937.

Allport, Gordon W. *The individual and his religion.* New York: Macmillan, 1950. Cited from Macmillan paper, 1960. [All selections reprinted with permission of Macmillan Publishing Co., Inc. Copyright 1950 by Macmillan Publishing Co., Inc., renewed 1978 by Robert B. Allport.]

Allport, Gordon W. *The nature of prejudice.* Reading MA: Addison-Wesley, 1954.

Allport, Gordon W. *Becoming.* New Haven CT: Yale University Press, 1955.

Allport, Gordon W. Religion and prejudice. *The Crane Review,* 1959, **2,** 1–10.

Allport, Gordon W. *Personality and social encounter.* Boston: Beacon Press, 1960.

Allport, Gordon W. *Pattern and growth in personality.* New York: Holt, Rinehart and Winston, 1961.

Allport, Gordon W. Mental health: A generic attitude. *Journal of Religion and Health,* 1964, **4,** 7–21.

Allport, Gordon W. The religious context of prejudice. *Journal for the Scientific Study of Religion,* 1966, **5,** 447–457.

Allport, Gordon W. Gordon W. Allport. In Edwin G. Boring & Gardner Lindzey (Eds.), *A history of psychology in autobiography* (Vol. 5). Englewood Cliffs NJ: Prentice-Hall, 1967. Pp. 1–25.

Allport, Gordon W. *The person in psychology.* Boston: Beacon Press, 1968.

Allport, Gordon W.; Gillespie, J. M.; & Young, J. The religion of the post-war college student. *Journal of Psychology,* 1948, **25,** 3–33.

Allport, Gordon W.; & Kramer, Bernard M. Some roots of prejudice. *Journal of Psychology,* 1946, **22,** 9–39.

Allport, Gordon W.; & Ross, J. Michael. Personal religious orientation and prejudice. *Journal of Personality and Social Psychology,* 1967, **5,** 432–443.

Allport, Gordon W.; & Vernon, Philip E. *A study of values.* Boston: Houghton Mifflin, 1931. (Rev. ed. with Gardner Lindzey, 1951)

Alpert, Hollis. The possession of Linda Blair: The making of "The Exorcist." *World,* February 13, 1973, **2**(4), 60–62.

Altman, I.; & Taylor, D. A. *Social penetration: The development of interpersonal relationships.* New York: Holt, Rinehart and Winston, 1973.

Anderson, G. *Your religion: Neurotic or healthy.* Garden City NY: Doubleday, 1970.

Andreasen, N. J. C. The role of religion in depression. *Journal of Religion and Health,* 1972, **11,** 153–166.

Angyal, A. The convergence of psychotherapy and religion. *Journal of Pastoral Care,* 1952, **5,** 9–12.

Annis, L. V. Emergency helping and religious behavior. *Psychological Reports,* 1976, **39,** 151–158.

Anthony, Dick; & Robbins, Thomas. Religious movements and the "brainwashing" issue. Paper presented for The American Psychological Association, New York, September, 1979.

Appel, K. E. Religion. In Silvano Arieti (Ed.), *Handbook of psychiatry* (Vol. 2). New York: Basic Books, 1959. Pp. 1777–1782.

Argyle, Michael. *Religious behavior.* Boston: Routledge & Kegan Paul, 1958; & New York: Free Press, 1958.

Argyle, Michael. Seven psychological roots of religion. *Theology,* 1964, **67,** 1–7. Also in L. B. Brown (Ed.), *Psychology and religion.* Baltimore: Penguin Books, 1973. Pp. 23–30.

Argyle, Michael; & Beit-Hallahmi, Benjamin. *The social psychology of religion.* Boston: Routledge & Kegan Paul, 1975.

Arieti, Silvano (Ed.). *Handbook of psychiatry* (Vol. 2). New York: Basic Books, 1959.

Arieti, Silvano. *The will to be human.* New York: Quadrangle, 1972.

Arieti, Silvano; & Arieti, J. *Love can be found.* New York: Harcourt Brace Jovanovich, 1977.

Arintero, John G. *The mystical evolution* (2 vols.) (Trans. Jordan Aumann). St. Louis: B. Herder, 1949–1951.

Arnold, Magda B. *Emotion and personality* (2 vols.). New York: Columbia University Press, 1960.

Arnold, Magda B.; & Gasson, J. A. *The human person: An integral approach to personality.* New York: Ronald Press, 1954.

Arnold, William J.; & Levine, David (Eds.). *Nebraska symposium on motivation* (Vol. 17). Lincoln NE: University of Nebraska Press, 1969.

Aronson, Elliott. *The social animal.* San Francisco: Freeman, 1972.

Arya, Usharbudh. Personal communication, June 1976.

Asch, Solomon E. *Social psychology.* Englewood Cliffs NJ: Prentice-Hall, 1952.

Asch, Solomon E. Studies of independence and conformity: A minority of one against a unanimous majority. *Psychological Monographs,* 1956, **70**(9, Whole No. 416).

Ashbrook, James B. The relation of church members to church organization. *Journal for the Scientific Study of Religion,* 1966, **5,** 397–419.

Asimov, Isaac. *Asimov's guide to science* (Rev. ed.). New York: Basic Books, 1972.

Assagioli, Roberto. *The act of will.* New York: Viking Press, 1973. Cited from Penguin Books, 1974.

Atkins, Susan (with Slosser, Bob). *Child of Satan, child of God.* Plainfield NJ: Logos International, 1977.

Austin, R. L. Empirical adequacy of Lofland's conversion model. *Review of Religious Research,* 1977, **18,** 282–287.

Ausubel, D. P. Relationships between shame and guilt in the socializing process. *Psychological Review,* 1955, **62,** 378–390.

Babris, Peter J. *Silent churches.* Arlington Heights IL: Research Publishers, 1978.

Bach, Paul J. Demon possession and psychopathology: A theological relationship. *Journal of Psychology and Theology,* 1979, **7,** 22–26.

Bacovcin, Helen (Trans.). *The way of a pilgrim.* Garden City NY: Doubleday, 1978.

Baer, Hans A. A field perspective of religious conversion: The Levites of Utah. *Review of Religious Research,* 1978, **19,** 279–294.

Bagwell, H. Roberts. The abrupt religious conversion experience. *Journal of Religion and Health,* 1969, **8,** 163–178.

Bahr, H. Aging and religious disaffiliation. *Social Forces,* 1970, **49,** 59–71.

Baird, Robert D. (Ed.). *Methodological issues in religious studies.* Chico CA: New Horizons Press, 1975a.

Baird, Robert D. Postscript: Methodology, theory and explanation in the study of religion. In Robert D. Baird (Ed.), *Methodological issues in religious studies.* Chico CA: New Horizons Press, 1975b. Pp. 111–122.

Baird, R. M. The creative role of doubt in religion. *Journal of Religion and Health,* 1980, **19,** 172–179.

Bakan, David. *The duality of human existence.* Boston: Beacon Press, 1966.

Bakan, David. *Disease, pain and sacrifice.* Chicago: University of Chicago Press, 1968.

Baker, G. W.; & Chapman, D. W. (Eds.). *Man and society in disaster.* New York: Basic Books, 1962.

Balswick, J. *Why I can't say I love you.* Waco TX: Word Books, 1978.

Balswick, J. O.; & Balkwell, J. W. Religious orthodoxy and emotionality. *Review of Religious Research,* 1978, **19,** 308–319.

Baltes, P. B.; & Schaie, K. W. (Eds.). *Life-span developmental psychology: Personality and socialization.* New York: Academic Press, 1973.

Bandura, Albert. Self-efficacy: Toward a unifying theory of behavioral change. *Psychological Review,* 1977, **84,** 191–215.

Bandura, Albert; & Huston, A. C. Identification as a process of incidental learning. *Journal of Abnormal and Social Psychology,* 1961, **63,** 311–318.

Bandura, Albert; & Kupers, C. J. Transmission of patterns of self-reward through modeling. *Journal of Abnormal and Social Psychology,* 1964, **69,** 1–9.

Bandura, Albert; & Mischel, Walter. Modification of self-imposed delay of reward through exposure to live and symbolic models. *Journal of Personality and Social Psychology,* 1965, **2,** 698–705.

Bandura, Albert; & Walters, R. H. *Social learning and personality development.* New York: Holt, Rinehart and Winston, 1963.

Barber, Theodore X. *Hypnosis: A scientific approach.* New York: Van Nostrand Reinhold, 1969.

Barbour, C. E. *Sin and the new psychology.* London: George Allen & Unwin, 1931.

Barlow, David H.; Abel, Gene G.; & Blanchard, Edward B. Gender identity change in a transsexual: An exorcism. *Archives of Sexual Behavior,* 1977, **6,** 387–395.

Baron, A. R. Behavioral effects of interpersonal attraction: Compliance with requests from liked and disliked others. *Psychonomic Science,* 1971, **25,** 325–326.

Barron, Milton Leon. *The aging American: An introduction to social gerontology and geriatrics.* New York: Crowell, 1961.

Bartemeier, L. H. Healthy and unhealthy patterns of religious behavior. *Journal of Religion and Health,* 1965, **4,** 309–314.

Batson, C. Daniel. Creative religious growth and pre-formal religious education. *Religious Education,* 1974, **69,** 302–315.

Batson, C. Daniel. Rational processing or rationalization? The effects of disconfirming information on stated religious beliefs. *Journal of Personality and Social Psychology,* 1975, **32,** 178–184.

Batson, C. Daniel. Moon madness: Greed or creed? *American Psychological Association Monitor,* June 1976a, **7,** 1,32.

Batson, C. Daniel. Religion as prosocial: Agent or double agent? *Journal for the Scientific Study of Religion,* 1976b, **15,** 29–45.

Batson, C. Daniel. Religion and biological bases for human altruism: A mixed blessing. Paper presented for The American Psychological Association, Toronto, August, 1978.

Batson, C. Daniel; Naifeh, Stephen J.; & Pate, Suzanne. Social desirability, religious orientation, and racial prejudice. *Journal for the Scientific Study of Religion,* 1978, **17,** 31–41.

Becker, Ernest. *The denial of death.* New York: Free Press, 1973.

Beit-Hallahmi, Benjamin (Ed.). *Research in religious behavior: Selected readings.* Monterey CA: Brooks/Cole, 1973.

Beit-Hallahmi, Benjamin. Psychology of religion—What do we know? Paper presented for The American Psychological Association, Washington D.C., September, 1976.

Belgum, David. *Guilt: Where psychology and religion meet.* Englewood Cliffs NJ: Prentice-Hall, 1963.

Bellah, Robert N. Civil religion in America. In William G. McLoughlin & Robert N. Bellah (Eds.), *Religion in America.* Boston: Beacon Press, 1968.

Benassi, V. A.; Singer, B.; & Reynolds, Craig B. Occult belief: Seeing is believing. *Journal for the Scientific Study of Religion,* 1980, **19,** 337–349.

Bender, Irving E. Changes in religious interest: A retest after fifteen years. *Journal of Abnormal and Social Psychology,* 1958, **57,** 41–46.

Benedict, Ruth. *The chrysanthemum and the sword.* Boston: Houghton Mifflin, 1946.

Benson, Peter; & Spilka, Bernard. God image as a function of self-esteem and locus of control. *Journal for the Scientific Study of Religion,* 1973, **12,** 297–310.

Berkowitz, Leonard (Ed.). *Advances in experimental social psychology* (Vol. 7). New York: Academic Press, 1974.

Berkowitz, Leonard (Ed.). *Advances in experimental social psychology* (Vol. 10). New York: Academic Press, 1977.

Berkowitz, Leonard; & Connor, W. H. Success, failure, and social responsibility. *Journal of Personality and Social Psychology,* 1966, **4,** 664–669.

Berkowitz, Leonard; & Daniels, L. R. Affecting the salience of the social responsibility norm: Effects of past help on the response to dependency relationships. *Journal of Abnormal and Social Psychology,* 1964, **68,** 275–281.

Berman, A. L.; & Hays, J. E. Relation between death anxiety, belief in afterlife, and locus of control. *Journal of Consulting and Clinical Psychology,* 1973, **41,** 318.

Berryman, Jerome W. Being in parables with children. *Religious Education,* 1979, **74,** 271–285.

Bertocci, Peter A. *Religion as creative insecurity.* New York: Association Press, 1958.

Bharati, Agehananda. *The light at the center.* Santa Barbara CA: Ross-Erikson, 1976.

Bickman, L. The effect of another bystander's ability to help on bystander intervention in an emergency. *Journal of Experimental Social Psychology,* 1971, **7,** 367–380.

Bier, William C. (Ed.). *Conscience: Its freedom and limitations.* New York: Institute of Pastoral Psychology, Fordham Univ., 1969.

Black, M. S.; & London, Perry. The dimensions of guilt, religion, and personal ethics. *The Journal of Social Psychology,* 1966, **69,** 39–54.

Blakney, Raymond B. (Trans.). *Meister Eckhart: A modern translation.* New York: Harper & Row, 1941.

Blatty, W. P. *The exorcist.* New York: Harper & Row, 1971.

Bohr, Ronald H. Dogmatism and age of vocational choice in two religious orders. *Journal for the Scientific Study of Religion,* 1968, **7,** 282–283.

Boisen, Anton. *The exploration of the inner world.* Philadelphia: University of Pennsylvania Press, 1971. (Originally published, 1936.)

Boisen, Anton. The genesis and significance of mystical identification in cases of mental disorder. *Psychiatry,* 1952, **15,** 287–296.

Boisen, Anton. *Out of the depths: An autobiographical study of mental disorder and religious experience.* New York: Harper & Row, 1960.

Bolles, R. C. Psychological determinism and the problem of morality. *Journal for the Scientific Study of Religion,* 1963, **2**, 182–189.

Bolt, Martin. Religious orientation and death fears. *Review of Religious Research,* 1977, **19**, 73–76.

Bonhoeffer, Dietrich. *Letters and papers from prison.* London: S. C. M. Press, 1953.

Bonnell, G. C. Salvation and psychotherapy. *Journal of Religion and Health,* 1969, **8**, 382–398.

Bonner, H. *On being mindful of man.* Boston: Houghton Mifflin, 1965.

Bonney, M. E. A study of friendship choices in college in relation to church affiliation, in-church preferences, family size, and length of enrollment in college. *Journal of Social Psychology,* 1949, **29**, 153–166.

Bourguignon, Erika. *Possession.* San Francisco: Chandler & Sharp, 1976.

Bowlby, J. *Attachment and loss* (Vol. 1: *Attachment*). New York: Basic Books, 1969.

Bowles, Norma; & Hynds, Fran. *Psi search.* New York: Harper & Row, 1978.

Boyar, J. I. *The construction and partial validation of a scale for the measurement of the fear of death.* Unpublished dissertation, Univ. of Rochester, 1964.

Braaten, C. E. Toward a theology of hope. *Theology Today,* 1967, **24**, 208–226.

Brandon, O. *Battle for the soul: Aspects of religious conversion.* London: Hodder & Stroughton, 1960.

Brandt, Priscilla. *Two-way prayer.* Waco TX: Word Books, 1979.

Bregman, Lucy. Religion and madness: Schreber's *Memoirs* as personal myth. *Journal of Religion and Health,* 1977, **16**, 119–135.

Bregman, Lucy. Anton Boisen revisited. *Journal of Religion and Health,* 1979a, **18**, 213–229.

Bregman, Lucy. Spiritual dimensions to psychotic experience? *The Journal of Transpersonal Psychology,* 1979b, **11**, 65–66.

Brena, Steven F. *Pain and religion.* Springfield IL: Thomas, 1972.

Brena, Steven F. *Yoga and medicine.* New York: The Julian Press, 1972; & Baltimore: Penguin Books, 1973.

Brengelmann, J. C. Extreme response set, drive level, and abnormality in questionnaire rigidity. *Journal of Mental Science,* 1960, **106**, 171–186.

Brentano, Franz. *Psychologie vom empirischen standpunkt* (2 vols.). Leipzig: Verlag Felix Meiner, 1924. (Originally published, 1874.)

Bretall, Robert (Ed.). *A Kierkegaard anthology.* New York: Random House, 1946.

Bridges, Dorothy C. *Your child's self-esteem.* Garden City NY: Doubleday, 1970.

Brink, T. L. A psychotherapeutic model for religious education. *Religious Education,* 1977, **72**, 409–413.

Brock, Timothy C. Implications of conversion and magnitude of cognitive dissonance. *Journal for the Scientific Study of Religion,* 1962, **1**, 198–203.

Brock, Timothy C. Implications of cognitive dissonance theory for selected religious phenomena. Paper presented for The American Psychological Association, New York, September, 1979.

Broen, W. E., Jr. A factor-analytic study of religious attitudes. *Journal of Abnormal and Social Psychology,* 1957, **54**, 176–179.

Brogden, H. E. The primary personal values measured by the Allport-Vernon test, "A Study of Values." *Psychological Monographs,* 1952, **66**(16, Whole No. 348).

Brown, George A.; Spilka, Bernard; & Cassidy, Stephen. The structure of mystical experience and pre- and post–experience lifestyle correlates. Paper presented for The Society for The Scientific Study of Religion, Hartford CT, October, 1978.

Brown, L. B. A study of religious belief. *British Journal of Psychology,* 1962, **53,** 259–272. Also in L. B. Brown (Ed.), *Psychology and religion: Selected readings.* Baltimore: Penguin Books, 1973. Pp. 33–53.

Brown, L. B. Classifications of religious orientation. *Journal for the Scientific Study of Religion,* 1964, **4,** 91–99.

Brown, L. B. Egocentric thought in petitionary prayer: A cross-cultural study. *The Journal of Social Psychology,* 1966a, **68,** 197–210.

Brown, L. B. The structure of religious belief. *Journal for the Scientific Study of Religion,* 1966b, **5,** 259–272.

Brown, L. B. (Ed.). *Psychology and religion: Selected readings.* Baltimore: Penguin Books, 1973.

Bruner, Jerome S. *Toward a theory of instruction.* Cambridge MA: Harvard University Press (Belknap Press), 1966.

Bruno de Jesus-Marie, P. *Love and violence.* New York: Sheed & Ward, 1954.

Bucke, Richard M. *Cosmic consciousness.* Secaucus NJ: Citadel Press, 1977. (Originally published, 1923.)

Burhoe, Ralph W. Genetic, neurophysiological, and other determinants of religious ritual and belief. Paper presented for The Society for the Scientific Study of Religion, Milwaukee, October, 1975.

Burhoe, Ralph W. Religion's role in human evolution. Paper presented for The Society for the Scientific Study of Religion, Chicago, October, 1977.

Burhoe, Ralph W. Religion's role in human evolution: The missing link between ape-man's selfish genes and civilized altruism. Paper presented for The American Psychological Association, Toronto, August, 1978.

Burns, R. Hugh; & Daniels, Aubrey. Religious attitudes among psychiatric patients and normals. *Journal for the Scientific Study of Religion,* 1969, **8,** 165.

Burton, R. V.; Maccoby, Eleanor E.; & Allinsmith, W. Antecedents of resistance to temptation in four-year-old children. *Child Development,* 1961, **32,** 689–710.

Buscaglia, Leo. *Love.* Greenwich CT: Fawcett Books, 1972.

Byrne, Donn. *The attraction paradigm.* New York: Academic Press, 1971.

Byrne, Donn. *An introduction to personality.* Englewood Cliffs NJ: Prentice-Hall, 1974.

Campbell, Angus. Subjective measures of well-being. *American Psychologist,* 1976, **31,** 117–124.

Campbell, Angus; Converse, Philip E.; & Rodgers, Willard L. *The quality of American life.* New York: Russell Sage Foundation, 1976.

Campbell, Donald T. On the conflicts between biological and social evolution and between psychology and moral tradition. *American Psychologist,* 1975, **30,** 1103–1126.

Campbell, Joseph. *Myths to live by.* New York: Viking Press, 1972.

Campbell, Joseph. *The mythic image.* Princeton NJ: Princeton University Press, 1974.

Campbell, Joseph. Schizophrenia—The inward journey. In Daniel Goleman & Richard J. Davidson (Eds.), *Consciousness: Brain, states of awareness, and mysticism.* New York: Harper & Row, 1979. Pp. 195–203.

Campbell, Thomas C.; & Fukuyama, Yoshio. *The fragmented layman.* Philadelphia: Pilgrim, 1970.

Camprise, Rick; Ellison, C. W.; & Kinsman, Rita. Spiritual well-being: Some exploratory relationships. In Raymond F. Paloutzian (Chair), Spiritual well-being, loneliness, and perceived quality of life. Symposium presented for The American Psychological Association, New York, September, 1979.

Capps, Donald. Pastoral care and psychology of religion: Towards a new alliance. *Pastoral Psychology,* 1978, **26**, 187–200.

Capps, Walter H.; & Wright, Wendy M. *Silent fire.* New York: Harper Forum Books, 1978.

Carrigan, R. L. Where has hope gone? Toward an understanding of hope in pastoral care. *Pastoral Psychology,* 1976, **25**, 39–53.

Carter, John D. Maturity: Psychological and biblical. *Journal of Psychology and Theology,* 1973, **2**, 89–96.

Casserly, J. V. L. *The retreat from Christianity in the modern world.* New York: McKay, 1953.

Cattell, Raymond B. *Psychology and the religious quest.* London: Thomas Nelson & Sons, 1938.

Cavan, R. S.; Burgess, E. W.; Havighurst, R. J.; & Goldhammer, H. *Personal adjustment in old age.* Chicago: Science Research Associates, 1949.

Cerny, Leonard J., II. *Death perspectives and religious orientation as a function of Christian faith with specific reference to being "born again."* Unpublished dissertation, Rosemead Graduate School of Psychology, 1977.

Cerny, Leonard J., II; & Carter, John. Death perspectives and religious orientation as a function of Christian faith. Paper presented for The Society for the Scientific Study of Religion, Chicago, October, 1977.

Chaudhuri, Haridas. Yoga psychology. In Charles T. Tart (Ed.), *Transpersonal psychologies.* New York: Harper & Row, 1975. Pp. 231–280.

Chesen, E. *Religion may be hazardous to your health.* New York: Collier, 1972.

Christ, Adolph E. Attitudes toward death among a group of acute geriatric psychiatric patients. *Journal of Gerontology,* 1961, **16**, 56–59.

Christensen, Carl W. Religious conversion. *Archives of General Psychiatry,* 1963, **9**, 207–216.

Christopher, Milbourne. *ESP, seers, and psychics.* New York: Crowell, 1970.

Cialdini, R. B.; & Kenrick, D. T. Altruism and hedonism: A social development perspective on the relationship of negative mood state and helping. *Journal of Personality and Social Psychology,* 1976, **34**, 907–914.

Clark, Elmer T. *The psychology of religious awakening.* New York: Macmillan, 1929.

Clark, Grahame. Archaeology and human diversity. *Annual Review of Anthropology,* 1979, **8**, 1–20.

Clark, H. R. The dynamics of creation. *Journal of Religion and Health,* 1979, **18**, 139–143.

Clark, R. D. III; & Word, L. E. Where is the apathetic bystander? Situational characteristics of the emergency. *Journal of Personality and Social Psychology,* 1974, **29**, 279–287.

Clark, Walter H. *The psychology of religion.* New York: Macmillan, 1958.

Clark, Walter H. The mystical consciousness and world understanding. *Journal for the Scientific Study of Religion,* 1965, **4**, 152–161.

Clark, Walter H. The relationship between drugs and religious experience. *The Catholic Psychological Record,* 1968, **6**, 146–155.

Clark, Walter H. *Chemical ecstasy: Psychedelic drugs and religion.* New York: Sheed & Ward, 1969.

Clark, Walter H. The phenomena of religious experience. In Walter H. Clark; H. Newton Malony; James Doane; & Alan R. Tippett, *Religious experience: Its nature and function in the human psyche.* Springfield IL: Thomas, 1973. Pp. 21–40.

Clark, Walter H. Art and psychotherapy in Mexico. *Art Psychotherapy,* 1977, **4**, 41–44.

Clark, Walter H. Fear and terror in religious experience: A theoretical commentary. Paper presented for The Society for the Scientific Study of Religion, San Antonio, October, 1979a.

Clark, Walter H. Personal communication, December, 1979b.

Clark, Walter H.; Malony, H. Newton; Doane, James; & Tippett, Alan R. *Religious experience: Its nature and function in the human psyche.* Springfield IL: Thomas, 1973.

Clarke, G. The need for new myths. *Time,* January 17, 1972, 50–51.

Clarke, W. Norris. The mature conscience in philosophical perspective. In William C. Bier (Ed.), *Conscience: Its freedom and limitations.* New York: Institute of Pastoral Psychology, Fordham Univ., 1969. Pp. 357–368.

Clayton, R. R. 5–D or 1? *Journal for the Scientific Study of Religion,* 1971, **10**, 37–40.

Clemens, N. A.; Corradi, R. B., & Wasman, M. The parish clergy as a mental health resource. *Journal of Religion and Health,* 1978, **17**, 227–232.

Cline, V. B.; & Richards, J. M., Jr. A factor-analytic study of religious belief and behavior. *Journal of Personality and Social Psychology,* 1965, **1**, 569–578.

Clouse, Bonnidell. The teachings of Jesus and Piaget's concept of mature moral judgment. *Journal of Psychology and Theology,* 1978, **6**, 175–182.

Coe, George A. *The spiritual life.* New York: Eaton & Mains, 1900.

Coleridge, Samuel T. *Biographia Literaria,* 1817.

Collins, Gary R. *Search for reality.* Santa Anna CA: Vision House, 1969.

Collins, Gary R. The pulpit and the couch. *Christianity Today,* August 29, 1975, 5–9.

Conrad, William. A magnetic Pope tugs at opposing Latin forces. *Christianity Today,* 1979, **23**, 623–626.

Conze, Edward (Ed.). *Buddhist wisdom books.* New York: Harper Torchbooks, 1958.

Coulson, J. E.; & Johnson, R. W. Glossolalia and internal-external locus of control. *Journal of Psychology and Theology,* 1977, **5**, 312–317.

Counts, W. M. The nature of man and the Christian's self-esteem. *Journal of Psychology and Theology,* 1973, **1**, 38–44.

Cox, Harvey. Eastern cults and Western culture: Why young Americans are buying Oriental religions. *Psychology Today,* July 1977a, **11**, 36–42.

Cox, Harvey. *Turning east.* New York: Simon & Schuster, 1977b.

Cranston, Ruth. *The miracle of Lourdes.* New York: Popular Library, 1957.

Crumbaugh, James C. Cross-validation of Purpose-in Life test based on Frankl's concepts. *Journal of Individual Psychology,* 1968, **24**, 74–81.

Crumbaugh, James C. Logotherapy as a bridge between religion and psychotherapy. *Journal of Religion and Health,* 1979, **18**, 188–191.

Crumbaugh, James C.; & Maholick, L. T. An experimental study in existentialism. *Journal of Clinical Psychology,* 1964, **20**, 200–207.

Cult of death. *Time,* December 4, 1978.

Cumont, F. *Oriental religions in Roman paganism.* New York: Dover, 1956.

Custance, John. *Wisdom, madness, and folly.* London: Victor Gollancz, 1951.

Cutten, George B. *Speaking with tongues.* New Haven: Yale University Press, 1927.

Dahms, A. *Thriving: Beyond adjustment.* Monterey CA: Brooks/Cole, 1980.

Darley, John M.; & Batson, C. Daniel. "From Jerusalem to Jericho": A study of situational and dispositional variables in helping behavior. *Journal of Personality and Social Psychology,* 1973, **27**, 100–108.

Darley, John M.; & Latane, Bibb. Bystander intervention in emergencies: Diffusion of responsibility. *Journal of Personality and Social Psychology,* 1968, **10**, 202–214.

Dass, Ram. *The only dance there is.* Garden City NY: Doubleday, 1974.

Davies, Robertson. A few kind words for superstition. *Newsweek,* November 20, 1978, 23.

Davis, W. L.; & Phares E. Jerry. Internal-external control as a determinant of information-seeking in a social influence situation. *Journal of Personality,* 1967, **35,** 547–561.

Dawkins, R. *The selfish gene.* New York: Oxford University Press, 1976.

Day, H. I.; Berlyne, D. E.; & Hunt, D. E. (Eds.). *Intrinsic motivation: A new direction in education.* New York: Holt, Rinehart and Winston, 1971.

Deci, E. L. *Intrinsic motivation.* New York: Plenum, 1975.

Deikman, Arthur J. Experimental meditation. *Journal of Nervous and Mental Diseases,* 1963, **136,** 329–343.

Deikman, Arthur J. Deautomatization and the mystic experience. *Psychiatry,* 1966, **29,** 324–338.

Deikman, Arthur J. Bimodal consciousness. *Archives of General Psychiatry,* 1971, **25,** 481–489.

Deikman, Arthur J. Comments on the GAP Report on mysticism. In Daniel Goleman & Richard J. Davidson (Eds.), *Consciousness: Brain, states of awareness, and mysticism.* New York: Harper & Row, 1979. Pp. 191–194.

Denis, Margaret. Religious education among North American Indian peoples. *Religious Education,* 1974, **69,** 343–354.

De Vore, I.; & Morris, S. The new science of genetic self-interest. *Psychology Today,* February 1977, 42–51, 84–88.

Dewey, John. Religious education as conditioned by modern psychology and pedagogy. *Proceedings of the First Annual Convention of the Religious Education Association,* February 10–12, 1903, 60–66. In *Religious Education,* 1974, **69,** 6–11.

Dewey, John. *A common faith.* New Haven: Yale University Press, 1934.

De Young, Robert N. Religious variables and death attitudes. Paper presented for The Society for the Scientific Study of Religion, Chicago, October, 1977.

DiCaprio, N. S. *The good life.* Englewood Cliffs NJ: Prentice-Hall, 1976.

Diggory, J. C.; & Rothman, D. Z. Values destroyed by death. *Journal of Abnormal and Social Psychology,* 1961, **63,** 205–210.

DiRenzo, G. J. Professional politicians and personality structures. *American Journal of Sociology,* 1967, **73,** 217–225.

Dittes, James E. Justification by faith and the experimental psychologist. *Religion in Life,* 1959, **58,** 567–576. In L. B. Brown (Ed.), *Psychology and religion.* Baltimore: Penguin Books, 1973. Pp. 255–264.

Dittes, James E. Psychology of religion. In Gardner Lindzey & E. Aronson (Eds.), *The handbook of social psychology* (Vol. 5) (2nd ed.). Reading MA: Addison-Wesley, 1969. Pp. 602–659.

Dittes, James E. Religion, prejudice, and personality. In Merton P. Strommen (Ed.), *Research on religious development.* New York: Hawthorn Books, 1971. Pp. 355–390.

Dodds, E. R. *The Greeks and the irrational.* Boston: Beacon Press, 1957.

Dodds, E. R. *Pagan and Christian in an age of anxiety.* New York: Norton, 1963.

Donahue, Michael J. Religious conversion: A review and integration. Paper presented for The American Psychological Association, New York, September, 1979.

Donaldson, William J. (Ed.). *Research in mental health and religious behavior.* Atlanta: Psychological Studies Institute, 1976.

Drake, S.; & Brubaker, B. A cooler crusader. *Newsweek,* October 3, 1977, 11.

Drakeford, John W. *Psychology in search of a soul.* Nashville: Broadman, 1964.

Drakeford, John W. *Integrity therapy.* Nashville: Broadman, 1967.

Drapela, V. J. Personality adjustment and religious growth. *Journal of Religion and Health,* 1969, **8,** 87–97.

Dunlap, K. *Religion: Its function in human life.* New York: McGraw-Hill, 1946.

Durkheim, Emile. *The elementary forms of the religious life* (Trans. J. W. Swain). New York: Free Press, 1915.

Easterbrook, Joseph A. *The determinants of free will.* New York: Academic Press, 1978.

Efran, J. *Some personality determinants of memory for success and failure.* Unpublished doctoral dissertation, Ohio State University, 1963.

Eisenberg-Berg, N.; & Geisheker, E. Content of preachings and power of the model/preacher: The effect on children's generosity. *Developmental Psychology,* 1979, **15,** 168–175.

Elias, John L. B. F. Skinner and religious education. *Religious Education,* 1974, **69,** 558–567.

Elkind, David. The child's conception of his religious identity. *Lumen Vitae,* 1964a, **19,** 635–646.

Elkind, David. Piaget's semi-clinical interview and the study of spontaneous religion. *Journal for the Scientific Study of Religion,* 1964, **4,** 40–47. In L. B. Brown (Ed.), *Psychology and religion.* Baltimore: Penguin Books, 1973b. Pp. 130–141.

Elkins, D. P. To learn, to do, to fulfill: Humanistic education for Jewish life. *Religious Education,* 1976, **71,** 187–201.

Ellens, J. H. Anxiety and the rise of religious experience. *Journal of Psychology and Theology,* 1975, **3,** 11–18.

Ellis, Albert. Religious beliefs in the United States today. *Humanist,* 1977, **37,** 38–40.

Ellis, Albert; & Harper, Robert A. *A new guide to rational living.* Hollywood: Wilshire, 1976.

Ellison, Craig W.; & Paloutzian, Raymond F. Assessing quality of life: Spiritual well-being and loneliness. Paper presented for The American Psychological Association, Toronto, August, 1978.

Ellison, Craig W.; & Paloutzian, Raymond F. Religious experience and quality of life. In Raymond F. Paloutzian (Chair), Spiritual well-being, loneliness, and perceived quality of life. Symposium presented for The American Psychological Association, New York, September, 1979.

Ellwood, Robert S., Jr. *Mysticism and religion.* Englewood Cliffs NJ: Prentice-Hall, 1980.

Erdman, Charles R. *The first epistle of Paul to the Corinthians.* Philadelphia: Westminster, 1928.

Erikson, Erik H. *Young man Luther.* New York: Norton, 1958.

Erikson, Erik H. Identity and the life cycle. *Psychological Issues,* 1959, **1,** 1–171. Also *Identity and the life cycle.* New York: International Universities Press, 1959.

Erikson, Erik H. *Childhood and society* (2nd ed.). New York: Norton, 1963.

Erikson, Erik H. *Identity: Youth and crisis.* New York: Norton, 1968.

Erikson, Erik H. *Dimensions of a new identity.* New York: Norton, 1974.

Erikson, Erik H. *Toys and reasons: Stages in the ritualization of experience.* New York: Norton, 1977.

Evans, T. D. Homosexuality: Christian ethics and psychological research. *Journal of Psychology and Theology,* 1975, **3,** 94–98.

Evans-Gardner, JoAnn. Varieties of discontent: Female response to religious mysogyny. *Journal Supplement Abstract Service Catalog of Selected Documents in Psychology,* 1978, **8,** 27 (Ms. No. 1667). Also in *Resources in Women's Educational Equity* (WE 006 433).

Evans-Pritchard, E. E. *Theories of primitive religion.* New York: Oxford University Press, 1965.

Everson, T. C. Spontaneous regression of cancer. *Connecticut Medical Journal,* 1958, **22,** 637–643.

Eysenck, Hans J. A short questionnaire for the measurement of two dimensions of personality. *Journal of Applied Psychology,* 1958, **42,** 14–17.

Eysenck, Hans J. *The Maudsley Personality Inventory.* London: University of London Press, 1959.

Eysenck, Hans J. *Crime and personality.* London: Paladin, 1970.

Eysenck, Hans J. The biology of morality. In Thomas Lickona (Ed.), *Moral development and behavior.* New York: Holt, Rinehart and Winston, 1976. Pp. 108–123.

Fagan, Joe; & Breed, George. A good, short measure of religious dogmatism. *Psychological Reports,* 1970, **26,** 533–534.

Fairchild, Louis. ". . . as Thyself." *Journal of Religion and Health,* 1978, **17,** 210–214.

Faulkner, J.; & De Jong, G. Religiosity in 5–D: An empirical analysis. *Social Forces,* 1966, **45,** 246–254.

Feagin, J. R. Prejudice and religious types: A focused study of southern fundamentalists. *Journal for the Scientific Study of Religion,* 1964, **4,** 3–13.

Feather, N. T. Acceptance and rejection of arguments in relation to attitude strength, critical ability and intolerance of inconsistency. *Journal of Abnormal and Social Psychology,* 1964, **69,** 127–136. In L. B. Brown (Ed.), *Psychology and religion.* Baltimore: Penguin Books, 1973. Pp. 233–248.

Feifel, Herman (Ed.). *The meaning of death.* New York: McGraw-Hill, 1959a.

Feifel, Herman. Attitudes toward death in some normal and mentally ill populations. In Herman Feifel (Ed.), *The meaning of death.* New York: McGraw-Hill, 1959b. Pp. 114–130.

Feinsilver, A. *In search of religious maturity.* Yellow Springs OH: Antioch, 1960.

Fenichel, Otto. *The psychoanalytic theory of neurosis.* Boston: Routledge & Kegan Paul, 1946.

Ferguson, L. W. Primary social attitudes. *Journal of Social Psychology,* 1939, **8,** 217–223.

Ferguson, L. W. A revision of the Primary Social Attitudes scales. *Journal of Psychology,* 1944, **17,** 229–242.

Ferguson, Marilyn. Karl Pribram's changing reality. *Re-Vision,* 1978, **1,** 8–13.

Ferm, R. C. *The psychology of Christian conversion.* Old Tappen NJ: Fleming H. Revell, 1959.

Feshbach, S. The catharsis hypothesis and some consequences of interaction with aggressive and neutral play objects. *Journal of Personality,* 1956, **24,** 449–462.

Festinger, Leon. *A theory of cognitive dissonance.* Stanford CA: Stanford University Press, 1957.

Festinger, Leon; Riecken, Henry W.; & Schachter, Stanley. *When prophecy fails.* New York: Harper Torchbooks, 1956.

Fichter, Joseph H. Supersaints and minisaints: Being a comparison of the most spiritual and the least spiritual among recovering alcoholic clergy. In David O. Moberg (Ed.), *Spiritual well-being: Sociological perspectives.* Washington D.C.: University Press of America, 1979. Pp. 255–263.

Field, W. E., Jr.; & Wilkerson, S. Religiosity as a psychiatric symptom. *Perspectives in Psychiatric Care,* 1973, **11,** 99–105.

Finch, J. Toward a religious psychology and psychotherapy. *Insight,* 1964, **3,** 10–16.

Fingarette, Herbert. On the relation between moral guilt and guilt in neurosis. *Journal of Humanistic Psychology,* 1962, **2,** 96–100.

Fischer, Roland. A cartography of the ecstatic and meditative states. *Science,* 1971, **174,** 897–904.

Fischer, Roland. Cartography of conscious states: Integration of east and west. In A. Arthur Sugerman & Ralph E. Tarter (Eds.), *Expanding dimensions of consciousness.* New York: Springer-Verlag, 1978. Pp. 24–57.

Fisher, Seymour. Acquiescence and religiosity. *Psychological Reports,* 1964, **15,** 784.

Flavell, John H. *The developmental psychology of Jean Piaget.* New York: Van Nostrand Reinhold, 1963.

Fleck, J. Roland. Dimensions of personal religion: A dichotomy or trichotomy? In William J. Donaldson, Jr. (Ed.), *Research in mental health and religious behavior.* Atlanta: Psychological Studies Institute, 1976. Pp. 191–201.

Fletcher, Joseph. *Situation ethics.* Philadelphia: Westminster, 1966.

Footlick, Jerrold K.; & Kasindorf, Martin. A double standard? *Newsweek,* February 23, 1976, 44, 49.

Ford, Peter S. *The healing trinity.* New York: Harper & Row, 1971.

Forgus, R. & Shulman, B. *Personality: A cognitive view.* Englewood Cliffs NJ: Prentice-Hall, 1979.

Fowler, James W. Some uses and limits of the structural developmental perspective in psycho-historical study. Paper presented for The Society for the Scientific Study of Religion, Milwaukee, October, 1975.

Fowler, James W. Stages in faith: The structural developmental perspective. In T. Hennessy (Ed.), *Values and moral development.* New York: Paulist, 1976. Pp. 173–211.

Fowler, James W. Faith and the structuring of meaning. Paper presented for The American Psychological Association, San Francisco, August, 1977.

Fowler, James W. *Stages of faith: The psychology of human development and the quest for meaning.* New York: Harper & Row, 1981.

Fowler, James; & Keen, Sam. *Life maps: Conversations on the journey of faith* (Jerome Berryman, Ed.). Minneapolis: Winston, 1978; & Waco TX: Word Books, 1978.

Francesco, E. A pervasive value: Conventional religiosity. *The Journal of Social Psychology,* 1962, **57,** 467–470.

Frank, Jerome D. *Persuasion and healing.* Baltimore: Johns Hopkins, 1961.

Frankl, Viktor. *Man's search for meaning.* Boston: Beacon Press, 1962a. Cited from Pocket Book edition, 1975.

Frankl, Viktor. Psychiatry and man's quest for meaning. *Journal of Religion and Health,* 1962b, **1,** 93–103.

Frankl, Viktor. *The doctor and the soul: From psychotherapy to logotherapy* (2nd ed.). New York: Knopf, 1965.

Frankl, Viktor. Self-transcendence as a human phenomenon. *Journal of Humanistic Psychology,* 1966, **6,** 97–106.

Franklin, J. C.; Schiele, B. C.; Brozek, J.; & Keys, Ancel. Observations on human behavior in experimental semistarvation and rehabilitation. *Journal of Clinical Psychology,* 1948, **4,** 28–45.

Frazer, James G. *The Golden Bough* (Abridged ed.). New York: Macmillan, 1925.

Freud, Anna; Hartmann, Heinz; & Kris, E. (Eds.). *The psychoanalytic study of the child* (Vol. 2). New York: International Universities Press, 1946.

Freud, Sigmund. Obsessive actions and religious practices (1907). In James Strachey (Ed. & Trans.), *The standard edition of the complete psychological works of Sigmund Freud* (Vol. 9). London: Hogarth, 1959. Pp. 117–127.

Freud, Sigmund. Leonardo da Vinci and a memory of his childhood (1910). In James Strachey (Ed. & Trans.), *The standard edition of the complete psychological works of Sigmund Freud* (Vol. 11). London: Hogarth, 1957. Pp. 63–137.

Freud, Sigmund. Totem and taboo (1913). In James Strachey (Ed. & Trans.), *The standard edition of the complete psychological works of Sigmund Freud* (Vol. 13). London: Hogarth, 1953. Pp. 1–162. Also New York: Random House (Vintage Books), 1946.

Freud, Sigmund. Group psychology and the analysis of the ego (1921). In James Strachey (Ed. & Trans.), *The standard edition of the complete psychological works of Sigmund Freud* (Vol. 18). London: Hogarth, 1955. Pp. 69–143. Also in R. M. Hutchins (Ed.), *Great books of the Western world* Vol. 54: *Freud.* Chicago: Encyclopedia Britannica, 1952. Pp. 664–696.

Freud, Sigmund. Inhibitions, symptoms, and anxiety (1926). In James Strachey (Ed. & Trans.), *The standard edition of the complete psychological works of Sigmund Freud* (Vol. 20). London: Hogarth, 1959. Pp. 87–172.

Freud, Sigmund. The future of an illusion (1927). In James Strachey (Ed. & Trans.), *The standard edition of the complete psychological works of Sigmund Freud* (Vol. 21). London: Hogarth, 1961. Pp. 5–56. Cited from W. D. Robson-Scott (Trans.). Garden City NY: Doubleday Anchor, 1961.

Freud, Sigmund. A religious experience (1928). In James Strachey (Ed. & Trans.), *The standard edition of the complete psychological works of Sigmund Freud* (Vol. 21). London: Hogarth, 1961. Pp. 169–172. Also in *Character and culture.* New York: Collier, 1963.

Freud, Sigmund. Civilization and its discontents (1930). In James Strachey (Ed. & Trans.), *The standard edition of the complete psychological works of Sigmund Freud* (Vol. 21). London: Hogarth, 1961. Pp. 64–145. Also in R. M. Hutchins (Ed.), *Great books of the Western world* Vol. 54: *Freud* (Trans. J. Riviere). Chicago: Encyclopedia Britannica, 1952. Pp. 767–806. Cited from New York: Norton, 1961.

Freud, Sigmund. New introductory lectures on psychoanalysis (1933). In James Strachey (Ed. & Trans.), *The standard edition of the complete psychological works of Sigmund Freud* (Vol. 22). London: Hogarth, 1964. Pp. 5–182.

Freud, Sigmund. Moses and monotheism (1939). In James Strachey (Ed. & Trans.), *The standard edition of the complete psychological works of Sigmund Freud* (Vol. 23). London: Hogarth, 1964. Pp. 7–137.

Friedrich, L. K.; & Stein, A. Prosocial television and young children: The effects of verbal labeling and role playing on learning and behavior. *Child Development,* 1975, **46,** 27–38.

Fromm, Erich. *Escape from freedom.* New York: Holt, Rinehart and Winston, 1941.

Fromm, Erich. *Man for himself: An inquiry into the psychology of ethics.* New York: Holt, Rinehart and Winston, 1947.

Fromm, Erich. *Psychoanalysis and religion.* New Haven: Yale University Press, 1950. Cited from Bantam edition, 1967.

Fromm, Erich. *The sane society.* New York: Holt, Rinehart and Winston, 1955.

Fromm, Erich. *The art of loving.* New York: Harper & Row, 1956. Cited from Harper Colophon, 1962.

Fromm, Erich. *The heart of man.* New York: Harper & Row, 1964. Cited from Perennial Library, 1971.

Fromm, Erich. *The dogma of Christ.* Boston: Routledge & Kegan Paul, 1970a.

Fromm, Erich. *The revolution of hope.* New York: Harper Colophon, 1970b.

Fromm, Erich. *The anatomy of human destructiveness.* New York: Holt, Rinehart and Winston, 1973.

Fukuyama, Y. *The major dimensions of church membership.* Unpublished doctoral dissertation, Univ. of Chicago, 1960.

Fukuyama, Y. The major dimensions of church membership. *Review of Religious Research,* 1961, **2,** 154–161.

Furse, Margaret L. *Mysticism: Window on a world view.* Nashville: Abingdon, 1977.

Gaede, Stan. Religious participation, socioeconomic status, and belief-orthodoxy. *Journal for the Scientific Study of Religion,* 1977, **16,** 245–253.

Galton, Francis. *Inquiries into human faculty and development.* New York: Macmillan, 1883.

Garrigou-LaGrange, Reginald. *The three ages of the interior life* (2 vols.) (Trans. M. Timothea Doyle). St. Louis: B. Herder, 1947–1948.

Garvin, Paul (Trans.). *The life and sayings of Saint Catherine of Genoa.* Staten Island NY: Alba House, 1964.

Gavira, M.; & Wintrob, R. M. Supernatural influence in psychopathology. *Canadian Psychiatric Association Journal,* 1976, **21,** 361–369.

Gay, Volney P. Public rituals versus private treatment: Psychodynamics of prayer. *Journal of Religion and Health,* 1978, **17,** 244–260.

Gaylin, W. *Caring.* New York: Knopf, 1976. Cited from Avon Books, 1979.

Gergen, K. J.; Gergen, M. M.; & Meter, K. Individual orientation to prosocial behavior. *Journal of Social Issues,* 1972, **28,** 105–130.

Gerrard, Nathan L.; & Gerrard, Louise B. *Scrabble Creek folk: Mental health, Part II.* Charleston WV: Dept. of Sociology, Morris Harvey College, 1966.

Gibbons, Don; & DeJanrette, James. Hypnotic susceptibility and religious experience. *Journal for the Scientific Study of Religion,* 1972, **11,** 152–156.

Giffin, M. Value judgments in psychiatry and religion. *Journal of Religion and Health,* 1964, **4,** 180–187.

Gilbert, Albin R. Pseudo-mind expansion through psychedelics and brain wave programming versus true mind expansion through life conditioning to the Absolute. *Psychologia,* 1971, **14,** 187–192.

Gill, M. M.; & Brenman, M. *Hypnosis and related states.* New York: International Universities Press, 1959.

Gillin, J. Magical fright. *Psychiatry,* 1948, **11,** 387–400.

Gilmore, S. K. Personality differences between high and low dogmatism groups of Pentecostal believers. *Journal for the Scientific Study of Religion,* 1969, **8,** 161–166.

Glasser, William. *Reality therapy: A new approach to psychiatry.* New York: Harper & Row, 1965.

Glazier, Stephen D. *Bibliography: Spirit mediumship and possession to 1975.* Storrs CT: Author, 1975.

Gleason, R. W. *The search for god.* New York: Sheed & Ward, 1964.

Globus, G. Maxwell; & Savodnick, I. (Eds.). *Consciousness and the brain.* New York: Plenum, 1976.

Glock, Charles Y. The religious revival in America. In Jane Zahn (Ed.), *Religion and the face of America.* Berkeley CA: University Extension, Univ. of California, 1959. In Charles Y. Glock & Rodney Stark, *Religion and society in tension.* Skokie IL: Rand McNally, 1965. Chapter 4.

Glock, Charles Y. On the study of religious commitment. *Research Supplement to Religious Education,* July-August, 1962, 98–110. In Charles Y. Glock & Rodney Stark, *Religion and society in tension.* Skokie IL: Rand McNally, 1965. Chapter 2.

Glock, Charles Y.; & Stark, Rodney. Is there an American Protestantism? *Transaction,* 1965a, **3,** 8–14.

Glock, Charles Y.; & Stark, Rodney. *Religion and society in tension.* Skokie IL: Rand McNally, 1965b.

Gnaneswarananda, S. *Yoga for beginners.* Chicago: Vivekananda Vedanta Society, 1975.

Godin, Andre. Some developmental tasks in Christian education. In Merton P. Strommen (Ed.), *Research on religious development: A comprehensive handbook.* New York: Hawthorn, 1971. Pp. 109–154.

Golden, M.; Montare, A.; & Bridger, W. Verbal control of delay behavior in two-year-old boys as a function of social class. *Child Development,* 1977, **48,** 1107–1111.

Goldenberg, Naomi. *The changing of the gods.* New York: Harper & Row, 1979.

Goldfarb, W. Infant rearing and problem solving. *American Journal of Orthopsychiatry,* 1943, **13,** 249–266.

Goldfarb, W. Emotional and intellectual consequences of psychological deprivation in infancy: A revaluation. In P. Hoch & J. Zubin (Eds.), *Psychopathology of childhood.* New York: Grune & Stratton, 1955. Pp. 105–119.

Golding, William. *Lord of the flies.* New York: Capricorn, 1959.

Goldman, Ronald J. *Religious thinking from childhood to adolescence.* New York: Seabury, 1964a.

Goldman, Ronald J. Researches in religious thinking. *Educational Research,* 1964, **6,** 139–155. In L. B. Brown (Ed.), *Psychology and religion.* Baltimore: Penguin Books, 1973b. Pp. 165–185.

Goldman, Ronald J. *Readiness for religion.* New York: Seabury, 1965.

Goldstein, Jeffrey. Religion in the autobiographies of three psychotics. Paper presented for The American Academy of Religion, New York, November, 1979.

Goldstein, Kurt. *The organism.* New York: American, 1939.

Goldstein, Kurt. *Human nature.* New York: Schocken Books, 1940.

Goleman, Daniel. *The varieties of the meditative experience.* New York: Dutton, 1977.

Goleman, Daniel; & Davidson, Richard J. (Eds.). *Consciousness: Brain, states of awareness, and mysticism.* New York: Harper & Row, 1979.

Goodenough, Erwin R. *The psychology of religious experience.* New York: Basic Books, 1965.

Goodnick, B. Mental health from the Jewish standpoint. *Journal of Religion and Health,* 1977, **16,** 110–115.

Gordon, James S. Jim Jones and his people. *The New York Times Book Review,* January 7, 1979, 3 ff.

Gore, P. M.; & Rotter, Julian B. A personality correlate of social action. *Journal of Personality,* 1963, **31,** 58–64.

Gorsuch, Richard L. Religion as a significant predictor of important human behavior. In William J. Donaldson, Jr. (Ed.), *Research in mental health and religious behavior.* Atlanta: Psychological Studies Institute, 1976. Pp. 206–221.

Gorsuch, Richard L.; & Aleshire, Daniel. Christian faith and ethnic prejudice: A review and interpretation of research. *Journal for the Scientific Study of Religion,* 1973, **12,** 281–307.

Gorsuch, Richard L.; & McFarland, Sam G. Single versus multiple-item scales for measuring religious values. *Journal for the Scientific Study of Religion,* 1972, **11,** 53–64.

Goslin, D. A. (Ed.). *Handbook of socialization theory and research.* Skokie, IL: Rand McNally, 1969.

Gough, Harrison. *California Psychological Inventory Manual* (Rev. ed.). Palo Alto CA: Consulting Psychologists Press, 1964. (Originally published, 1957.)

Gould, S. J. Biological potential versus biological determinism. *Natural History,* 1976, **85,** 12–20.

Greeley, Andrew M. *Ecstasy: A way of knowing.* Englewood Cliffs NJ: Prentice-Hall, 1974.

Greeley, Andrew M. *The sociology of the paranormal, a reconnaissance.* Beverly Hills: Sage, 1975.

Greeley, Andrew M.; & McCready, W. C. Are we a nation of mystics? *New York Times Magazine,* January 26, 1975, 12–25.

Greenwald, A. G. Does the good Samaritan parable increase helping? A comment on Darley and Batson's no-effect conclusion. *Journal of Personality and Social Psychology,* 1975, **32,** 578–583.

Grof, Stanislav. Varieties of transpersonal experiences: Observations from LSD psychotherapy. *Journal of Transpersonal Psychology,* 1972, **4,** 45–80.

Grof, Stanislav. Theoretical and empirical basis of transpersonal psychology and psychotherapy: Observations from LSD research. *Journal of Transpersonal Psychology,* 1973, **5,** 15–53.

Grof, Stanislav. *Realms of the human unconscious: Observations from LSD research.* New York: Dutton, 1976.

Gruder, C. L.; & Cook, T. D. Sex, dependency, and helping. *Journal of Personality and Social Psychology,* 1971, **19,** 290–294.

Haan, Norma. Coping and defense mechanisms related to personality inventories. *Journal of Consulting Psychology,* 1965, **29,** 373–378.

Hadaway, Christopher K. Life satisfaction and religion: A reanalysis. *Social Forces,* 1978, **57,** 636–643.

Hadaway, Christopher K.; & Roof, Wade Clark. Religious commitment and the quality of life in American society. *Review of Religious Research,* 1978, **19,** 295–307.

Hadden, Jeff K. *The gathering storm in the churches.* Garden City NY: Doubleday, 1969.

Hall, Calvin S.; & Lindzey, Gardner. *Theories of personality* (2nd ed.). New York: Wiley, 1970.

Hall, Calvin S.; & Lindzey, Gardner. *Theories of personality* (3rd ed.). New York: Wiley, 1978.

Hall, G. Stanley. *Adolescence: Its psychology and its relations to physiology, anthropology, sociology, sex, crime, religion, and education* (Vol. 2). Englewood Cliffs NJ: Prentice-Hall, 1904.

Hall, G. Stanley. *Jesus, the Christ, in the light of psychology.* Englewood Cliffs NJ: Prentice-Hall, 1917.

Hamburgh, M. Is the holocaust relevant to sociobiology? *Journal of Religion and Health,* 1980, **19,** 320–325.

Hamlin, Ray M.; & Nemo, R. S. Self-actualization in choice scores of improved schizophrenics. *Journal of Clinical Psychology,* 1962, **18,** 51–54.

Hammond, Sally. *We are all healers.* New York: Harper & Row, 1973.

Hankins, N.; & Bailey, R. *Psychology of effective living.* Monterey CA: Brooks/Cole, 1980.

Hansel, C. E. M. *ESP: A scientific evaluation.* New York: Scribner, 1966.

Hardyck, A. J.; & Braden, M. Prophecy fails again: A report on a failure to replicate. *Journal of Abnormal and Social Psychology,* 1962, **62,** 131–141.

Hare, R. D. Acquisition and generalization of a conditioned-fear response in psychopathic and non-psychopathic criminals. *Journal of Psychology,* 1965, **59,** 367–370.

Haring, Bernard. *Hope is the remedy.* Garden City NY: Doubleday, 1973.

Harlow, Harry F. *Learning to love.* New York: Aronson, 1974.

Harms, Ernest. Ethical and psychological implications of religious conversion. *Review of Religious Research,* 1962, **3,** 122–131.

Harner, Michael J. *Hallucinogens and Shamanism.* New York: Oxford University Press, 1973.

Harris, Marvin. *Cows, pigs, wars, and witches: The riddles of culture.* New York: Random House, 1974.

Hartup, W. W. (Ed.). *The young child: Reviews of research* (Vol. 2). Washington D.C.: National Assn. for the Education of Young Children, 1972.

Hauck, P. A. *How to do what you want to do.* Philadelphia: Westminster, 1976.

Havens, Joseph. Memo on the religious implications of the consciousness-changing drugs. *Journal for the Scientific Study of Religion,* 1964, **3,** 216–226.

Havighurst, Robert J. *Developmental tasks and education* (2nd ed.). New York: McKay, 1952.

Hay, David. Religious experience amongst a group of postgraduate students—a qualitative study. *Journal for the Scientific Study of Religion,* 1979, **18,** 164–182.

Hay, David; & Morisy, Ann. Reports of ecstatic, paranormal, or religious experience in Great Britain and the United States—a comparison of trends. *Journal for the Scientific Study of Religion,* 1978, **17,** 255–268.

Haywood, H. Carl; & Dobbs, Virginia. Motivation and anxiety in high school boys. *Journal of Personality,* 1964, **32,** 371–379.

Hazard, David M. Meet Ben! *Christian Herald,* October, 1979, 32–35, 69–72.

Heenam, E. Sociology of religion and the aged: The empirical lacunae. *Journal for the Scientific Study of Religion,* 1972, **12,** 171–176.

Heiler, Friedrich. *Prayer* (Trans. S. McComb & J. E. Park). New York: Oxford University Press, 1932.

Hennell, Thomas. *The witnesses.* New Hyde Park NY: University Books, 1967.

Hennessy, Thomas C. (Ed.). *Values and moral development.* New York: Paulist, 1976.

Herberg, Will. *Protestant, Catholic, Jew.* Garden City NY: Doubleday, 1955.

Herzberg, Frederick. *Work and the nature of man.* Cleveland: World, 1966.

Herzberg, Frederick; & Hamlin, Roy M. A motivation-hygiene concept of mental health. *Mental Hygiene,* 1961, **45,** 394–401.

Herzberg, Frederick; & Hamlin, Roy M. The motivation-hygiene concept and psychotherapy. *Mental Hygiene,* 1963, **47,** 384–397.

Herzberg, Frederick; Mausner, B.; & Snyderman, B. *The motivation to work* (2nd ed.). New York: Wiley, 1959.

Hilgard, Ernest R. Christianity and contemporary psychology. In George F. Thomas, *The vitality of the Christian tradition.* New York: Harper & Row, 1944. Pp. 286–301.

Hilgard, Ernest R. Altered states of awareness. *The Journal of Nervous and Mental Disease,* 1969, **149,** 68–79.

Hiltner, Seward; & Rogers, William R. Research on religion and personality dynamics. *Research Supplement to Religious Education,* July–August, 1962. Pp. S128–S140.

Hine, Virginia H. Pentecostal glossolalia: Toward a functional interpretation. *Journal for the Scientific Study of Religion,* 1969, **8,** 211–226. In Benjamin Beit-Hallahmi (Ed.), *Research in religious behavior: Selected readings.* Monterey CA: Brooks/Cole, 1973. Pp. 276–307.

Hinton, John. *Dying* (2nd ed.). Baltimore: Penguin Books, 1972.

Hoch, P.; & Zubin, J. (Eds.). *Psychopathology of childhood.* New York: Grune & Stratton, 1955.

Hocking, William E. *The meaning of God in human experience.* New Haven CT: Yale University Press, 1922.

Hocking, William E. *Types of philosophy.* New York: Scribner, 1929.

Hodge, M. *Your fear of love.* Garden City, NY: Doubleday, 1967.

Höffding, Harald. *The philosophy of religion* (Trans. B. E. Meyer). New York: Macmillan, 1906.

Hoffman, Martin L. Development of internal moral standards in children. In Merton P. Strommen (Ed.), *Research on religious development: A comprehensive handbook.* New York: Hawthorn, 1971. Pp. 211–263.

Hoge, Dean R. A validated intrinsic religious motivation scale. *Journal for the Scientific Study of Religion,* 1972, **11**, 369–376.

Hoge, Dean R.; & Petrillo, Gregory H. Determinants of church participation and attitudes among high school youth. *Journal for the Scientific Study of Religion,* 1978, **17**, 359–379.

Holzer, Hans. The truth about ESP. *Grit,* December 8, 1974, 15–16, 30.

Hood, Ralph W., Jr. Religious orientation and the report of religious experience. *Journal for the Scientific Study of Religion,* 1970, **9**, 285–291.

Hood, Ralph W., Jr. A comparison of the Allport and Feagin scoring procedures for intrinsic-extrinsic religious orientation. *Journal for the Scientific Study of Religion,* 1971, **10**, 370–374.

Hood, Ralph W., Jr. Hypnotic susceptibility and reported religious experience. *Psychological Reports,* 1973, **33**, 549–550.

Hood, Ralph W., Jr. The construction and preliminary validation of a measure of reported mystical experience. *Journal for the Scientific Study of Religion,* 1975a, **14**, 29–41.

Hood, Ralph W., Jr. Intense religious experience and church participation. Paper presented for The Society for the Scientific Study of Religion, Milwaukee, October, 1975b.

Hood, Ralph W., Jr. Eliciting mystical states of consciousness with semistructured nature experiences. *Journal for the Scientific Study of Religion,* 1977, **16**, 155–163.

Hood, Ralph W., Jr. Anticipatory set and setting: Stress incongruities as elicitors of mystical experience in solitary nature situations. *Journal for the Scientific Study of Religion,* 1978, **17**, 279–287.

Hooker, Douglas. *The healthy personality and the Christian life.* North Quincy MA: Christopher, 1977.

Hooper, T.; & Spilka, Bernard. Some meanings and correlates of future time and death among college students. *Omega,* 1970, **1**, 49–56.

Hornstein, H. A. *Cruelty and kindness: A new look at aggression and altruism.* Englewood Cliffs NJ: Prentice-Hall, 1976.

Howland, E. S. A psychiatrist looks at religion. *Journal of Religion and Health,* 1971, **10**, 111–120.

Hunt, Richard A. The interpretation of the religious scale on the Allport-Vernon-Lindzey Study of Values. *Journal for the Scientific Study of Religion,* 1968, **7**, 65–77.

Hunt, Richard A. Mythological-symbolic religious commitment: The LAM scales. *Journal for the Scientific Study of Religion,* 1972, **11**, 42–52.

Hunt, Richard A.; & King, Morton. The intrinsic-extrinsic concept: A review and evaluation. *Journal for the Scientific Study of Religion,* 1971, **10**, 339–356.

Hutchins, R. M. (Ed.). *Great books of the Western world.* Vol. 53: *William James.* Chicago: Encyclopedia Britannica, 1952a.

Hutchins, R. M. (Ed.). *Great books of the Western world.* Vol. 54: *Freud.* Chicago: Encyclopedia Britannica, 1952b.

Hynson, Larry M., Jr. Spiritual well-being and integration in Taiwan. In David O. Moberg (Ed.), *Spiritual well-being: Sociological perspectives.* Washington D.C.: University Press of America, 1979. Pp. 281–289.

Isen, Alice M. Success, failure, attention and reaction to others: The warm glow of success. *Journal of Personality and Social Psychology,* 1970, **15**, 294–301.

Isen, Alice M.; Clark, M.; & Schwartz, M. Duration of the effect of good mood on helping: "Footprints in the sands of time." *Journal of Personality and Social Psychology,* 1976, **34**, 385–393.

Isen, Alice M.; Horn, N.; & Rosehan, D. R. *Effects of success and failure on children's generosity.* Unpublished manuscript, Franklin and Marshall College, 1971.

Isen, Alice M.; & Levin, Paula F. Effect of feeling good on helping: Cookies and kindness. *Journal of Personality and Social Psychology,* 1972, **21,** 384–388.

Isen, Alice M.; Shalker, T. E.; Clark, M.; & Karp, L. Affect, accessibility of material in memory and behavior: A cognitive loop. *Journal of Personality and Social Psychology,* 1978, **36,** 1–12.

Izard, C. E. *Human emotions.* New York: Plenum, 1977. Chapter 16: Guilt, Conscience and Morality. Pp. 421–452.

Jahoda, G. Supernatural beliefs and changing cognitive structures among Ghanaian university students. *Journal of Cross-Cultural Psychology,* 1970, **1,** 115–130.

James, William. *The principles of psychology* (2 vols.). New York: Holt, Rinehart and Winston, 1890. Cited from R. M. Hutchins, (Ed.), *Great books of the Western world.* Chicago: Encyclopedia Britannica, 1952. Volume 53: *William James.* Also New York: Dover, 1950.

James, William. *Psychology, briefer course.* New York: Holt, Rinehart and Winston, 1892. Cited from Harper Torchbook, New York, 1961.

James, William. The dilemma of determinism. In *The will to believe and other essays in popular philosophy.* New York: McKay, 1897a. Cited from J. K. Roth (Ed.), *The moral philosophy of William James.* New York: Crowell, 1969. Pp. 103–131.

James, William. The moral philosopher and the moral life. In William James, *The will to believe and other essays in popular philosophy.* New York: McKay, 1897b. Cited from John K. Roth (Ed.), *The moral philosophy of William James.* New York: Crowell, 1969. Pp. 169–191.

James, William. The will to believe. In William James, *The will to believe and other essays in popular philosophy.* New York: McKay, 1897c. Cited from John K. Roth (Ed.), *The moral philosophy of William James.* New York: Crowell, 1969. Pp. 192–213.

James, William. *The will to believe and other essays in popular philosophy.* New York: McKay, 1897d.

James, William. *Human immortality: Two supposed objections to the doctrine.* Boston: Houghton Mifflin, 1898.

James, William. *The varieties of religious experience.* New York: McKay, 1902. Cited from Collier Books, New York, 1961.

James, William. A suggestion about mysticism (1910). In *Collected essays and reviews.* New York: McKay, 1920. Also New York: Russell & Russell, 1969. Pp. 500–513.

James, William. *The letters of William James.* New York: McKay, 1926. Pages 212–215 in L. B. Brown (Ed.), *Psychology and religion.* Baltimore: Penguin Books, 1973. Pp. 123–125.

Janis, Irving L. Psychological effects of warnings. In G. W. Baker & D. W. Chapman (Eds.), *Man and society in disaster.* New York: Basic Books, 1962. Pp. 55–92.

Jarymowicz, M. Modification of self-worth and increment of prosocial sensitivity. *Polish Psychological Bulletin,* 1977, **8,** 45–53.

Jastrow, Morris. *The study of religion.* New York: Scribner, 1902.

Javillonor, G. *Toward a social psychological model of sectarianism.* Unpublished doctoral dissertation, Univ. of Nebraska, 1971.

Jaynes, Julian. *The origin of consciousness in the breakdown of the bicameral mind.* Boston: Houghton Mifflin, 1976.

Jeeves, M. A. Contributions on prejudice and religion (Symposium on Problems of Religious Psychology). *Proceedings of the 15th International Congress of Psychology.* Brussels: North Holland, 1959. Pp. 508–509.

Jenkins, Peter. *A walk across America.* New York: Morrow, 1979.

Johnson, C. B. Process of change: Sacred and secular. *Journal of Psychology and Theology,* 1977, **5,** 103–109.

Johnson, Harry M. (Ed.). *Religious change and continuity.* San Francisco: Jossey-Bass, 1979.

Johnson, Paul E. *Psychology of religion* (2nd ed.). Nashville: Abingdon, 1956.

Johnson, Raynor C. *The imprisoned splendour.* Wheaton IL: The Theosophical Pub. House, 1971. (Originally published, 1953.)

Johnson, Sonia. *From housewife to heretic.* Garden City NY: Doubleday, 1981.

Jones, E.; & Gerard, H. B. *Foundations of social psychology.* New York: Wiley, 1967.

Jones, Marshall R. (Ed.). *Nebraska symposium on motivation* (Vol. 12). Lincoln: University of Nebraska Press, 1964.

Jones, Rufus M. Why I enroll with the mystics. In Vergilius Fern (Ed.), *Contemporary American theology: Theological autobiography.* New York: Round Table, 1932. Pp. 196–197.

Jones, W. Lawson. *A psychological study of religious conversion.* London: Epworth, 1937.

Jourard, Sidney M. *The transparent self.* New York: Van Nostrand Reinhold, 1964.

Jourard, Sidney M. *Healthy personality.* New York: Macmillan, 1974.

Jung, Carl G. *Modern man in search of a soul.* New York: Harcourt Brace Jovanovich, 1933.

Jung, Carl G. *Psychology and religion.* New Haven CT: Yale University Press, 1938.

Jung, Carl G. *Psyche and symbol.* Garden City NY: Doubleday (Anchor Books), 1958.

Jung, Carl Gustav. The archetypes and the collective unconscious. *Collected works* (Trans. R. F. C. Hull). New York: Pantheon Books, 1959. Volume 9, Part 1.

Jung, Carl G. *Man and his symbols.* London: Aldus, 1964.

Jung, Carl G. *Memories, dreams, reflections.* New York: Random House (Vintage Books), 1965.

Kahoe, Richard D. *Development of an objective factorial motivation-hygiene inventory.* Doctoral dissertation, George Peabody College for Teachers, 1966. (University Microfilms No. 67-3615.)

Kahoe, Richard D. Personality and achievement correlates of intrinsic and extrinsic religious orientations. *Journal of Personality and Social Psychology,* 1974a, **29,** 812–818.

Kahoe, Richard D. The psychology and theology of sexism. *Journal of Psychology and Theology,* 1974b, **2,** 284–290.

Kahoe, Richard D. Authoritarianism and religion: Relationships of F scale items to intrinsic and extrinsic religious orientations. *Journal Supplement Abstract Service Catalog of Selected Documents in Psychology,* 1975a, **5,** 284–285. (Ms. No. 1020.)

Kahoe, Richard D. A search for mental health. *Journal of Psychology and Theology,* 1975b, **3,** 235–242.

Kahoe, Richard D. The intrinsic and extrinsic dimensions: A value base for evaluating religious behavior? In William J. Donaldson, Jr. (Ed.), *Research in mental health and religious behavior.* Atlanta: Psychological Studies Institute, 1976a. Pp. 178–190.

Kahoe, Richard D. Longitudinal and retrospective studies in the psychology of religion. In C. Nelson (Chair), Methodological challenges in psychology of religion research. Symposium presented for The American Psychological Association, Washington D.C., September, 1976b.

Kahoe, Richard D. Intrinsic religion and authoritarianism: A differentiated relationship. *Journal for the Scientific Study of Religion,* 1977a, **16,** 179–182.

Kahoe, Richard D. Religious conservatism in a quasi-longitudinal perspective. *Journal of Psychology and Theology,* 1977b, **5,** 40–47.

Kahoe, Richard D. Toward a task-centered Christianity. *Pastoral Psychology,* 1977c, **25,** 197–207.

Kahoe, Richard D. Hope. Paper presented for The American Psychological Association, Montreal, September, 1980.

Kahoe, Richard D.; & Dunn, Rebecca F. The fear of death and religious attitudes and behavior. *Journal for the Scientific Study of Religion,* 1975, **14,** 379–382.

Kahoe, Richard D.; & Meadow, Mary Jo. Religious orientation dimensions: Individual and institutional interrelations. Paper presented for The Society for the Scientific Study of Religion, Chicago, October, 1977a.

Kahoe, Richard D.; & Meadow, Mary Jo. Three dimensions of sexist attitudes: Differential relationships with personality variables. Paper presented for The American Psychological Association, San Francisco, August, 1977b. (ERIC Document Reproduction Service No. ED 151 619.) (Resources in Women's Educational Equity No. WE 004 022.)

Kahoe, Richard D.; & Meadow, Mary Jo. A developmental perspective on religious orientation dimensions. Paper presented for The Society for the Scientific Study of Religion, Hartford CT, October, 1978.

Kahoe, Richard D.; & Meadow, Mary Jo. A developmental perspective on religious orientation dimensions. *Journal of Religion and Health,* 1981, **20,** 8–17.

Kahoe, Richard D.; & Polk, John D., Jr. Personality scales assessing intrinsic and extrinsic motivational variables. *Faculty Studies Bulletin,* Southwest Baptist College, 1971, **2,** 38–42.

Kane, Steven M. Holiness fire handling in Southern Appalachia: A psychophysiological analysis. In John D. Photiadis (Ed.), *Religion in Appalachia.* Morgantown WV: West Virginia University, 1978. Pp. 113–124.

Kanfer, F. H. Personal control, social control, and altruism. *American Psychologist,* 1979, **34,** 231–239.

Kao, Charles C. L. *Search for maturity.* Philadelphia: Westminster Press, 1975.

Kao, Charles C. L. *Psychological and religious development: Maturity and maturation.* Washington D.C.: University Press of America, 1981.

Kaplan, Pascal M. Toward a theology of consciousness. *Re-Vision,* 1978, **1,** 34–41.

Kaplan, Pascal M. A conversation with Murshida Ivy O. Duce. *Re-Vision,* 1979, **2,** 30–38.

Kaufmann, H. *Aggression and altruism.* New York: Holt, Rinehart and Winston, 1970.

Kavanaugh, Kieran; & Rodriguez, Otilio (Trans.). *Teresa of Avila: The interior castle.* New York: Paulist, 1979.

Keene, J. J. Baha'i world faith: Redefinition of religion. *Journal for the Scientific Study of Religion,* 1967a, **6,** 221–235.

Keene, J. J. Religious behavior and neuroticism, spontaneity, and world-mindedness. *Sociometry,* 1967b, **30,** 137–157.

Keerdoja, Eileen. Rescuing cultists. *Newsweek,* February 12, 1979, 17.

Keerdoja, Eileen; & Sciolino, Elaine. The town that faith built. *Newsweek,* July 23, 1979, 12.

Kellenberger, J. Mysticism and drugs. *Religious Studies,* 1978, **14,** 175–191.

Kelman, H. C. Compliance, identification, and internalization: Three processes of attitude change. *Journal of Conflict Resolution,* 1958, **2,** 51–60.

Kelman, H. C. Processes of opinion change. *Public Opinion Quarterly,* 1961, **25,** 57–78.

Kennell, J.; Jerauld, R.; Wolfe, H.; Chesler, D.; Kreger, N.; McAlpine, W.; Steffa, M.; & Klaus, M. Maternal behavior one year after early and extended postpartum contact. *Developmental Medicine and Child Neurology,* 1975, **16,** 172–179.

Kenrick, D. T.; & Cialdini, R. B. Romantic attraction: Misattributions versus reinforcement explanations. *Journal of Personality and Social Psychology,* 1977, **35,** 380–391.

Keyes, Ken. *Handbook to higher consciousness.* Berkeley CA: Living Love Center, 1974.

Khan, S. R.; & Hassan, Q. Locus of control among Hindus and Muslims. *Indian Psychological Review,* 1977, **15,** 19–24.

Kiev, A. Primitive religious rites and behavior: Clinical considerations. In E. Mansell Pattison (Ed.), *Clinical psychiatry and religion.* Boston: Little, Brown, 1969. Pp. 119–131.

Kildahl, John P. The personalities of sudden religious converts. *Pastoral Psychology,* 1965, **16,** 37–44.

Kildahl, John P. *The psychology of speaking in tongues.* New York: Harper & Row, 1972.

Kilpatrick, D. G.; Sutker, L. W.; & Sutker, P. B. Dogmatism, religion, and religiosity: A review and re-evaluation. *Psychological Reports,* 1970, **26,** 15–22.

King, Morton B. Measuring the religious variable: Nine proposed dimensions. *Journal for the Scientific Study of Religion,* 1967, **6,** 173–190.

King, Morton B.; & Hunt, Richard A. Measuring the religious variable: Amended findings. *Journal for the Scientific Study of Religion,* 1969, **8,** 321–323.

King, Morton B.; & Hunt, Richard A. Measuring the religious variable: Replication. *Journal for the Scientific Study of Religion,* 1972, **11,** 240–251.

King, Morton B.; & Hunt, Richard A. Measuring the religious variable: National replication. *Journal for the Scientific Study of Religion,* 1975, **14,** 13–22.

King, Winston L. *Introduction to religion* (2nd ed.). New York: Harper & Row, 1968.

Klingberg, G. A. A study of religious experience in children from nine to thirteen years of age. *Religious Education,* 1959, **54,** 211–216.

Klink, Thomas W. Ecumenical sensitivity: A dimension of institutional worship. *Pastoral Psychology,* 1967, **18,** 17–22.

Kluegel, James R. Denominational mobility: Current patterns and recent trends. *Journal for the Scientific Study of Religion,* 1980, **19,** 26–39.

Knight, John R.; & Clark, Walter H. Variations in self-reported intensity of subjective effects of altered states of consciousness as a function of participation in selected activities. Paper presented for The Society for the Scientific Study of Religion, Milwaukee, October, 1975.

Knight, John R.; & Clark, Walter H. Traditional religious, mysterium tremendum, and aesthetic factors in modern American self-transcendence. Paper presented for The Society for the Scientific Study of Religion, Philadelphia, October, 1976.

Knox, Ian. Religion and the expectations of modern society towards the adolescent. *Religious Education,* 1975, **70,** 649–660.

Koch, S. (Ed.). *Psychology, the study of a science Vol. 3: Formulations of the person and the social context.* New York: McGraw-Hill, 1959.

Koepp, E. F. Authoritarianism and social workers: A psychological study. *Social Work,* 1963, **8,** 37–43.

Kohlberg, Lawrence. *The development of modes of moral thinking and choice in the years ten to sixteen.* Unpublished doctoral dissertation, Univ. of Chicago, 1958.

Kohlberg, Lawrence. Moral development and identification. In Harold W. Stevenson (Ed.). *Child psychology.* Chicago: University of Chicago Press, 1963.

Kohlberg, Lawrence. The child as a moral philosopher. *Psychology Today,* September, 1968, **2**(4), 25–30.

Kohlberg, Lawrence. Stage and sequence: The cognitive-developmental approach to socialization. In David A. Goslin (Ed.), *Handbook of socialization theory and research.* Skokie, IL: Rand McNally, 1969. Pp. 347–480.

Kohlberg, Lawrence. Continuities in childhood and adult moral development revisited. In P. B. Baltes & K. W. Schaie (Eds.), *Life-span developmental psychology: Personality and socialization.* New York: Academic Press, 1973.

Kohlberg, Lawrence. Moral stages and moralization: The cognitive-developmental approach. In Thomas Lickona (Ed.), *Moral development and behavior.* New York: Holt, Rinehart and Winston, 1976. Pp. 31–53.

Kohlberg, Lawrence. Implications of moral stages for adult education. *Religious Education,* 1977, **72,** 18.–201.

Kohlberg, Lawrence. *Moral development, moral education, and Kohlberg: Basic issues in philosophy, psychology, religion and education* (Ed. Brenda Munsey). Birmingham AL: Religious Education Press, 1980.

Kopp, Sheldon. If you meet the Buddha on the road, kill him. In R. S. Spitzer (Ed.), *Tidings of comfort and joy.* Palo Alto CA: Science and Behavior Books, 1975.

Koppe, William A. A developmental theory of character education. *Review of Religious Research,* 1965, **6,** 23–28.

Kosa, J.; & Schommer, C. O. Religious participation, religious knowledge, and scholastic aptitude: An empirical study. *Journal for the Scientific Study of Religion,* 1961, **1,** 88–97.

Krebs, D. L. Altruism: An examination of the concept and a review of the literature. *Psychological Bulletin,* 1970, **73,** 258–302.

Krieger, Dolores. Therapeutic touch: The imprimatur of nursing. *American Journal of Nursing,* 1975, **75,** 784–787.

Krieger, Dolores. Healing by the "laying-on" of hands as a facilitator of bioenergetic change: The response of in-vivo human hemoglobin. *Psychoenergetics Systems,* 1976, **1,** 121–129.

Krippner, Stanley. Religious implications of paranormal events occurring during chemically-induced "psychedelic" experiences. *Pastoral Psychology,* 1970, **20,** 27–34.

Krippner, Stanley. Altered states of consciousness. In John White (Ed.), *The highest state of consciousness.* Garden City NY: Doubleday, 1972a. Pp. 1–5.

Krippner, Stanley. The plateau experience: A. H. Maslow and others. *Journal of Transpersonal Psychology,* 1972b, **4,** 107–120.

Krishnamurti, J. *Truth and actuality.* New York: Harper & Row, 1978.

Kunkel, Fritz. *Let's be normal.* New York: Ives Washburn, 1929.

Kurts, P. S. An inventory for the measurement of religious attitudes. In *Research plans in the fields of religion, values, and morality.* New York: The Religious Education Association, 1962.

Laing, R. D. Transcendental experience. In Daniel Goleman & Richard J. Davidson (Eds.), *Consciousness: Brain, states of awareness, and mysticism.* New York: Harper & Row, 1979. Pp. 184–186.

Langer, E. J.; Janis, Irving L.; & Wolfer, J. A. Reduction of psychological stress in surgical patients. *Journal of Experimental Social Psychology,* 1975, **11,** 155–165.

Langer, E. J.; & Rodin, J. The effects of choice and enhanced personal responsibility for the aged: A field experiment in an institutional setting. *Journal of Personality and Social Psychology,* 1976, **34,** 191–198.

Lanternari, Vittorio. *The religions of the oppressed.* New York: Knopf, 1963.

Lapsley, J. N. (Ed.). *The concept of willing.* Nashville: Abingdon, 1967a.

Lapsley, J. N. Willing and selfhood. In J. N. Lapsley (Ed.), *The concept of willing.* Nashville: Abingdon, 1967. Pp. 177–213b.

Larsen, Stephen. *The shaman's doorway.* New York: Harper Colophon, 1976.

Laski, Marghanita. *Ecstasy.* Bloomington: University of Indiana Press, 1961.

Latane, Bibb. Field studies of altruistic compliance. *Representative Research in Social Psychology,* 1970, **1,** 49–61.

Latane, Bibb; & Darley, John M. *The unresponsive bystander: Why doesn't he help?* Englewood Cliffs NJ: Prentice-Hall, 1970.

Latane, Bibb; & Rodin, J. A lady in distress: Inhibiting effects of friends and strangers on bystander intervention. *Journal of Experimental Social Psychology,* 1969, **5,** 189–202.

Lazerwitz, Bernard. Some factors associated with variations in church attendance. *Social Forces,* 1961, **39,** 301–309.

Leary, Timothy; & Clark, Walter H. Religious implications of consciousness expanding substances. *Religious Education,* 1963, **58,** 251–256.

Lee, John A. *The colors of love.* New York: Bantam Books, 1976.

Lee, R. R. I found God on a walk across America: An interview with Peter Jenkins. *Christian Herald,* September, 1979, **102,** 36–41, 55, 58–61.

Leeds, R. Altruism and the norm of giving. *Merrill-Palmer Quarterly,* 1963, **9,** 229–240.

Lefcourt, H. M. The function of the illusions of control and freedom. *American Psychologist,* 1973, **28,** 417–425.

Lenski, Gerhard. *The religious factor.* Garden City NY: Doubleday, 1961.

Lenski, Gerhard. *The religious factor* (2nd ed.). Garden City NY: Doubleday, 1963.

Lepp, Ignace. *The psychology of loving.* Baltimore: Helicon, 1963.

Lepp, Ignace. *The ways of friendship.* New York: Macmillan, 1966.

LeShan, Lawrence. *How to meditate.* Boston: Ethel Brown, 1974.

LeShan, Lawrence. *Alternate realities.* New York: Ballantine Books, 1976.

Leuba, James H. *A psychological study of religion.* New York: Macmillan, 1912.

Leuba, James H. *The psychology of religious mysticism.* New York: Harcourt Brace Jovanovich, 1925.

Levin, Paula F.; & Isen, Alice M. Further studies on the effect of feeling good on helping. *Sociometry,* 1975, **38,** 141–147.

Levine, M. E.; Villena, J.; Altman, D.; & Nadien, M. Trust of the stranger: An urban/small town comparison. *Journal of Psychology,* 1976, **92,** 113–116.

Lévi-Strauss, Claude. *Structural anthropology.* New York: Basic Books, 1963. (Originally published in French, 1958.)

Lévi-Strauss, Claude. *The savage mind.* Chicago: University of Chicago Press, 1966. (Originally published in French, 1962.)

Lévy-Bruhl, L. *Primitive mentality* (Trans. L. A. Clare). London: George Allen & Unwin, 1923.

Lewinsohn, R. *Science, prophecy, and prediction.* New York: Harper & Row, 1961.

Lewis, C. S. *Miracles.* New York: Macmillan, 1947.

Lewis, C. S. *The four loves.* New York: Harcourt Brace Jovanovich, 1960.

Lewis, David (Trans.). *Life and works of St. John of the Cross* (2 vols.). London: Thomas Baker, 1889–1891.

Lickona, Thomas (Ed.). *Moral development and behavior.* New York: Holt, Rinehart and Winston, 1976.

Liebert, R. M.; Neale, J. M.; & Davidson, E. S. *The early window: Effects of television on children and youth.* Elmsford NY: Pergamon Press, 1973.

Lifton, R. J. The appeal of the death trip. *New York Times Magazine,* January 7, 1979, 26 ff.

Ligon, Ernest M. *Dimensions of character.* New York: Macmillan, 1956.

Lilly, John C. *The center of the cyclone.* New York: Julian, 1972.

Lindenthal, Jacob J.; Meyers, Jerome K.; Pepper, Max P.; & Stern, Maxine S. Mental status and religious behavior. *Journal for the Scientific Study of Religion,* 1970, **9,** 143–149.

Lindzey, Gardner; & Aronson, Elliott (Eds.). *The handbook of social psychology* (Vol. 5) (2nd ed.). Reading MA: Addison-Wesley, 1969.

Lipp, L.; Kolstoe, R.; James, W.; & Randall, H. Denial of disability and internal control of reinforcement: A study using a perceptual defense paradigm. *Journal of Consulting and Clinical Psychology,* 1968, **32,** 72–75.

Lloyd, J. H. Religion and insanity. *Australian and New Zealand Journal of Psychiatry,* 1973, **7,** 193–199.

Lloyd, R. G. Social and personal adjustment of retired persons. *Sociology and Social Research,* 1955, **39,** 312–316.

Loevinger, Jane. The meaning and measurement of ego development. *American Psychologist,* 1966, **21,** 195–206.

Loevinger, Jane. *Ego development.* San Francisco: Jossey-Bass, 1976.

Lofland, J. *Doomsday cult.* Englewood Cliffs NJ: Prentice-Hall, 1966.

London, Perry; Schulman, R. E.; & Black, M. S. Religion, guilt, and ethical standards. *The Journal of Social Psychology,* 1964, **63,** 145–159.

Long, D.; Elkind, David; & Spilka, Bernard. The child's conception of prayer. *Journal for the Scientific Study of Religion,* 1967, **6,** 101–109.

Lorand, S. Psychoanalytic therapy of religious devotees. *International Journal of Psychoanalysis,* 1962, **43,** 50–56.

Loschen, E. L. Psychiatry and religion: A variable history. *Journal of Religion and Health,* 1974, **13,** 137–141.

Lovekin, Adams; & Malony, H. Newton. Religious glossolalia: A longitudinal study of personality changes. *Journal for the Scientific Study of Religion,* 1977, **16,** 383–393.

Lowe, Walter L. Psychodynamics in religious delusion and hallucination. *American Journal of Psychotherapy,* 1953, **7,** 454–464.

Lurie, W. A. A study of Spranger's value-types by the method of factor analysis. *Journal of Social Psychology,* 1937, **8,** 17–37.

Lykken, David T. *A study of anxiety in the psychopathic personality.* Unpublished doctoral dissertation, Univ. of Minnesota, 1955.

Lynch, W. F. *Images of hope: Imagination as healer of the hopeless.* Baltimore: Helicon, 1965.

Machalek, Richard; & Martin, Michael. "Invisible" religions: Some preliminary evidence. *Journal for the Scientific Study of Religion,* 1976, **15,** 311–321.

Magni, K. G. The fear of death: Studies of its character and concomitants. Death and presence, *Lumen Vitae,* 1971, **5,** 129–142. In L. B. Brown (Ed.), *Psychology and religion.* Baltimore: Penguin Books, 1973. Pp. 329–342.

Maher, Brendan A. (Ed.). *Progress in experimental personality research* (Vol. 3). New York: Academic Press, 1966.

Malinowski, Bronislaw. Magic, science and religion. In James Needham (Ed.), *Science, religion, and reality.* New York: Macmillan, 1925. Also in Bronislaw Malinowski, *Magic, science, and religion and other essays.* New York: Free Press, 1948; & Garden City NY: Doubleday (Anchor Books), 1948. Pp. 17–92.

Malinowski, Bronislaw. *Magic, science, and religion and other essays.* New York: Free Press, 1948.

Mallick, S. K.; & McCandless, B. R. A study of catharsis of aggression. *Journal of Personality and Social Psychology,* 1966, **4,** 591–596.

Malony, H. Newton (Ed.). *Psychology and faith.* Washington D.C.: University Press of America, 1978.

Malony, H. Newton. Discussant's remarks. In Raymond F. Paloutzian (Chair), Spiritual well-being, loneliness, and perceived quality of life. Symposium presented for The American Psychological Association, New York, September, 1979.

Maltz, Maxwell. *Psychocybernetics.* New York: Warner, 1975.

Maranell, G. M. A factor analytic study of some selected dimensions of religious attitude. *Sociology and Social Research,* 1968, **52,** 430–437.

Maranell, G. M.; & Rezak, W. N. A comparative study of the factor structure among professors and clergymen. *Journal for the Scientific Study of Religion,* 1970, **9,** 137–141.

Marcum, Regina. Religious women's communities and spiritual well-being. In David O. Moberg (Ed.), *Spiritual well-being: Sociological perspectives.* Washington D.C.: University Press of America, 1979. Pp. 266–279.

Marett, R. R. *The threshold of religion.* London: Methuen, 1914.

Margolis, R. D.; & Elifson, K. W. A typology of religious experience. *Journal for the Scientific Study of Religion,* 1979, **18,** 61–67.

Martin, David; & Wrightsman, Lawrence S., Jr. The relationship between religious behavior and concern about death. *Journal of Social Psychology,* 1965, **65,** 317–323.

Martin, J. G.; & Westie, F. R. The tolerant personality. *American Sociological Review,* 1959, **24,** 521–528.

Martin, Malachi. *Hostage to the Devil.* New York: Reader's Digest Press, Crowell, 1976.

Martin, R. A.; & Poland, E. Y. *Learning to change.* New York: McGraw-Hill, 1980.

Marty, Martin E. Religious cause, religious cure. *The Christian Century,* February 28, 1979, 210–215.

Maslow, Abraham H. A theory of human motivation. *Psychological Review,* 1943, **50,** 370–396.

Maslow, Abraham H. *Motivation and personality.* New York: Harper & Row, 1954. (Reissued, 1970.)

Maslow, Abraham H. *Religions, values, and peak experiences.* Columbus: Ohio State University Press, 1964.

Maslow, Abraham H. *Eupsychian management.* Homewood IL: Irwin & Dorsey Press, 1965.

Maslow, Abraham H. *Toward a psychology of being* (2nd ed.). New York: Van Nostrand Reinhold, 1968.

Maslow, Abraham H. Religions, values, and peak-experiences. *Religious Humanism,* 1970, **4,** 100–103.

Maslow, Abraham H. *The farther reaches of human nature.* New York: Viking, 1971a.

Maslow, Abraham H. (Ed.). *New knowledge in human values.* Chicago: Regnery, 1971b.

Matheson, George. Hypnotic aspect of religious experiences. *Journal of Psychology and Theology,* 1979, **7,** 13–21.

Mathews, K. E.; & Canon, L. K. Environmental noise level as a determinant of helping behavior. *Journal of Personality and Social Psychology,* 1975, **32,** 571–577.

Maven, Alexander. The mystic union: A suggested biological interpretation. In John White (Ed.), *The highest state of consciousness.* Garden City NY: Doubleday, 1972. Pp. 429–435.

Maves, P. B. Aging, religion and the church. In C. Tibbitts (Ed.), *Handbook of social gerontology: The social aspects of aging.* Chicago: University of Chicago Press, 1960. Pp. 698–749.

May, L. Carlyle. A study of glossolalia and related phenomena in non-Christian religions. *American Anthropologist,* 1956, **58,** 75–96.

May, Rollo. The healing power of symbols. *Pastoral Psychology,* 1960, **11,** 37–39.

May, Rollo. *Psychology and the human dilemma.* New York: Van Nostrand Reinhold, 1967.

May, Rollo. *Love and will.* New York: Norton, 1969.

May, Rollo. *The meaning of anxiety* (Rev. ed.). New York: Norton, 1977.

Mayeroff, M. *On caring.* New York: Harper & Row Perennial Library, 1971.

Mayo, S. C. Social participation among the older population in rural areas of Wake County, North Carolina. *Social Forces,* 1951, **30**, 53–59.

McClain, Edwin W. Religious orientation: The key to psychodynamic differences between feminists and nonfeminists. *Journal for the Scientific Study of Religion,* 1979, **18**, 40–45.

McEwen, Richard C.; & Aseltine, Herschel E. Prayer in primitive religion. *Religious Studies,* 1979, **15**, 99–106.

McGuire, Meredith B. Toward a sociological interpretation of the "Catholic Pentecostal" movement. *Review of Religious Research,* 1975, **16**, 94–104.

McLoughlin, W. G.; & Bellah, Robert N. (Eds.). *Religion in America.* Boston: Beacon Press, 1968.

McNamara, Patrick H.; & St. George, Arthur. Measures of religiosity and the quality of life. In David O. Moberg (Ed.), *Spiritual well-being: Sociological perspectives.* Washington D.C.: University Press of America, 1979. Pp. 229–236.

Mead, Margaret. Some anthropological considerations concerning guilt. In Martin L. Reymert (Ed.), *Feelings and emotions.* New York: McGraw-Hill, 1950. Pp. 362–373.

Meadow, Mary Jo. Philosophical-religious attitudes inventory: Factor analytically derived scales. Paper presented for The Society for the Scientific Study of Religion, Philadelphia, October, 1976.

Meadow, Mary Jo. Need, value, and motivational correlates of religious attitudes toward women. Paper presented for The Society for the Scientific Study of Religion, Chicago, October, 1977a.

Meadow, Mary Jo. The structure of religious attitudes: A factor-analytic study. *Dissertation Abstracts International,* 1977b, **37**, 6339B. (University Microfilms No. 77-12, 767.)

Meadow, Mary Jo. The cross and the seed: Active and receptive spiritualities. *Journal of Religion and Health,* 1978a, **17**, 57–69.

Meadow, Mary Jo. Personal growth: An Eastern yogic and a Western ego approach. Paper presented at The American Academy of Religion, New Orleans, November, 1978b.

Meadow, Mary Jo. Personality characteristics related to religious attitudes toward women. Paper presented for The Society for the Scientific Study of Religion, Hartford CT, October, 1978c.

Meadow, Mary Jo. A tardy pilgrim. In H. Newton Malony (Ed.), *Psychology and faith.* Washington D.C.: University Press of America, 1978d.

Meadow, Mary Jo. Women and religion: Customs, crisis, and conclusions. *Journal Supplement Abstract Service Catalog of Selected Documents in Psychology,* 1978e, **8**, 27. (Ms. No. 1667.) (Resources in Women's Educational Equity No. WE 006 433.)

Meadow, Mary Jo. The dark side of mysticism: Depression and "the dark night." Paper presented for Mysticism in Everyday Life, Minneapolis, MN, May, 1979a.

Meadow, Mary Jo. Introduction: Dealing with religious issues in counseling and psychotherapy: A symposium. *Journal of Religion and Health,* 1979b, **18**, 176–178.

Meadow, Mary Jo. Mysticism, masochism, and narcissism. Paper presented for The Association for Transpersonal Psychology, Monterey CA, July, 1979c.

Meadow, Mary Jo. Personal development and women's religious sex role attitudes. Paper presented for The American Psychological Association, New York, August, 1979d.

Meadow, Mary Jo. The psychology of religion course as a personal growth experience. In Albert S. Rossi; Mary Jo Meadow; H. Newton Malony; Gary R. Collins; & W. Mack Goldsmith, Teaching the psychology of values and religion. *Journal Supplement Abstract Service Catalog of Selected Documents in Psychology,* 1979e, **9**, 21–22. (Ms. No. 1829.)

Meadow, Mary Jo. The spiritual and/versus the transpersonal. *Journal Supplement Abstract Service Catalog of Selected Documents in Psychology,* 1979f, **9,** 77–78. (Ms. No. 1960.)

Meadow, Mary Jo. Psychological consequences and correlates of sexist religion. Paper presented for The Society for the Scientific Study of Religion, Cincinnati, October, 1980a.

Meadow, Mary Jo. Mysticism, dependency, and oral imagery. *Journal of Religion and Psychical Research,* 1980b, **3,** 122–126.

Meadow, Mary Jo. Wifely submission: Psychological/spiritual growth perspectives. *Journal of Religion and Health,* 1980c, **19,** 103–120.

Meadow, Mary Jo. Facts, fantasies, fiction, and faith. In E. Mark Stern (Ed.), *The other side of the couch: What therapists believe.* New York: Pilgrim, 1981. Pp. 215–225.

Meadow, Mary Jo. "True womanhood" and women's victimization. *Counseling and Values,* 1982a, **26,** 93–101.

Meadow, Mary Jo. Comments on papers delivered in the symposium: Spiritual practice and psychotherapy. In Albert S. Rossi (Chair), Spiritual practice and psychotherapy. *Journal Supplement Abstract Service Catalog of Selected Documents in Psychology,* May, 1982b. (Ms. No. 2449.)

Meadow, Mary Jo; Ajaya, Swami; Bregman, Lucy; Clark, Walter H.; Greene, Gordon; Krippner, Stanley; Rambo, Lewis R.; Ring, Kenneth; Tart, Charles T.; & Wilber, Ken. Spiritual and transpersonal aspects of altered states of consciousness: A symposium report. *The Journal of Transpersonal Psychology,* 1979, **11,** 59–74.

Meehl, Paul. *Symposium: What then is man?* St. Louis: Concordia, 1958.

Meissner, W. W. Notes on the psychology of faith. *Journal of Religion and Health,* 1969, **8,** 47–75.

Meissner, W. W. Notes on the psychology of hope. *Journal of Religion and Health,* 1973, **12,** 7–29, 120–139.

Menninger, Karl. *Love against hate.* New York: Harcourt Brace Jovanovich, 1942.

Menninger, Karl. *Whatever became of sin?* New York: Hawthorn, 1973.

Menninger, Karl; Mayman, M.; & Pruyser, Paul. *The vital balance.* New York: Viking Press, 1963. Also New York: Penguin Books, 1977.

Mes, G. M. *Faith healing and religion.* New York: Philosophical Library, 1975.

Meserve, Harry C. The therapeutic age. *Journal of Religion and Health,* 1977, **16,** 77–80.

Messick, D. M. Genetic basis of behavior. *American Psychologist,* 1976, **31,** 366–369.

Meyer, Stephen G. Neuropsychology and worship. *Journal of Psychology and Theology,* 1975, **3,** 281–289.

Middlebrook, Patricia N. *Social psychology and modern life.* New York: Knopf, 1974.

Midlarsky, E.; & Midlarsky, M. Some determinants of aiding under experimentally induced stress. *Journal of Personality,* 1973, **41,** 305–327.

Miller, D. R.; & Swanson, G. E. (Eds.). *Inner conflict and defense.* New York: Holt, Rinehart and Winston, 1960.

Miller, J. G. *Eyeblink conditioning of primary and neurotic psychopaths.* Unpublished doctoral dissertation, University of Missouri, 1964.

Miller, S. H. Religion: Healthy and unhealthy. *Journal of Religion and Health* (Human Sciences Press, publisher), 1965, **4,** 295–301.

Mills, Liston O. *Conversion experiences in a revival of the First Southern Baptist Church of Clarksville, Indiana.* Unpublished doctoral dissertation, Southern Baptist Theological Seminary, 1963.

Mills, R. An anatomy of hope. *Journal of Religion and Health,* 1979, **18,** 49–52.

Mindel, Charles H.; & Vaughan, C. Edwin. A multidimensional approach to religiosity and disengagement. *Journal of Gerontology,* 1978, **33,** 103–108.

Minton, Barbara A.; & Spilka, Bernard. Perspectives on death in relation to powerlessness and form of personal religion. Paper presented for The Rocky Mountain Psychological Association, Salt Lake City, May, 1975.

Minton, Barbara; & Spilka, Bernard. Perspectives on death in relation to powerlessness and form of personal religion. *Omega,* 1976, **7,** 261–267.

Mischel, Walter. Theory and research on the antecedents of self-imposed delay of reward. In Brendan A. Maher (Ed.), *Progress in experimental personality research* (Vol. 3). New York: Academic Press, 1966. Pp. 85–132.

Mischel, Walter. *Personality and assessment.* New York: Wiley, 1968.

Mischel, Walter; & Ebbesen, E. B. Attention in delay of gratification. *Journal of Personality and Social Psychology,* 1970, **16,** 329–337.

Mischel, Walter; Ebbesen, E. B.; & Zeiss, A. R. Cognitive and attentional mechanisms in delay of gratification. *Journal of Personality and Social Psychology,* 1972, **21,** 204–218.

Mischel, Walter; & Mischel, Harriet N. A cognitive social-learning approach to morality and self-regulation. In Thomas Lickona (Ed.), *Moral development and behavior.* New York: Holt, Rinehart and Winston, 1976. Pp. 84–107.

Mischel, Walter; & Staub, E. Effects of expectancy on working and waiting for larger rewards. *Journal of Personality and Social Psychology,* 1965, **2,** 625–633.

Moberg, David O. Religiosity and old age. *Gerontologist,* 1965, **5,** 78–87.

Moberg, David O. Religious practices. In Merton P. Strommen (Ed.), *Research on religious development.* New York: Hawthorn, 1971a. Pp. 551–598.

Moberg, David O. *Spiritual well-being: Background and issues.* Washington D.C.: White House Conference on Aging, 1971b.

Moberg, David O. The development of social indicators of spiritual well-being for quality of life research. In David O. Moberg (Ed.), *Spiritual well-being: Sociological perspectives.* Washington D.C.: University Press of America, 1979a. Pp. 1–13.

Moberg, David O. (Ed.). *Spiritual well-being: Sociological perspectives.* Washington D.C.: University Press of America, 1979b.

Moberg, David O. Subjective measures of spiritual well-being. Paper presented for The Society for the Scientific Study of Religion, Baltimore, October, 1981.

Moberg, David O.; & Brusek, Patricia M. Spiritual well-being: A neglected subject in quality of life research. *Social Indicators Research,* 1978, **5,** 303–323.

Mollica, R. F. On the technology of pastoral counseling. *Pastoral Psychology,* 1979, **28,** 97–109.

Monaghan, Robert R. Three faces of the true believer: Motivations for attending a fundamentalist church. *Journal for the Scientific Study of Religion,* 1967, **6,** 236–245.

Montagno, M. Is deprogramming legal? *Newsweek,* February 21, 1977, 44.

Montagno, M.; & Lisle, L. Women ordained. *Newsweek,* January 17, 1977, 85.

Montgomery, John W. Exorcism: Is it for real? *Christianity Today,* 1974, **18,** 1183–1186.

Moody, Raymond A., Jr. *Life after life.* Atlanta: Mockingbird Books, 1975.

Moore, Evelyn G. *Try the spirits: Christianity and psychical research.* New York: Oxford University Press, 1977.

Mora, George. Interpersonal dynamics between priest and penitent. *Insight,* 1962, **1,** 21–28.

Morgan, C. H. Attitudes and adjustments of old age recipients in state and metropolitan New York. *Archives of Psychology,* 1937, **214,** 1–131.

Morlan, G. K. An experiment on the recall of religious material. *Religion in Life,* 1950, **19,** 589–594. In L. B. Brown (Ed.), *Psychology and religion.* Baltimore: Penguin Books, 1973. Pp. 249–254.

Morris, Charles W. *Paths of life: Preface to a world religion.* Chicago: University of Chicago Press, 1973. (Originally published, 1942.)

Mosher, Donald L. The development and multitrait-multimethod matrix analysis of three measures of three aspects of guilt. *Journal of Counseling Psychology,* 1966, **30,** 25–29.

Moss, David M. Priestcraft and psychoanalytic psychotherapy: Contradiction or concordance? *Journal of Religion and Health,* 1979, **18,** 181–188.

Moustakas, C. E. *Loneliness.* Englewood Cliffs NJ: Prentice-Hall, 1961.

Mowrer, O. Hobart. *Learning theory and behavior.* New York: Wiley, 1960.

Mowrer, O. Hobart. *The crisis in psychiatry and religion.* New York: Van Nostrand Reinhold, 1961.

Mowrer, O. Hobart. *The new group therapy.* New York: Van Nostrand Reinhold, 1964.

Müller, Friedrich Max. *Lectures on the origin and growth of religion.* New York: McKay, 1968. (Originally published, 1878.)

Müller, Friedrich Max. *Introduction to the science of religion.* New York: McKay, 1893.

Muller, S. Our youth should serve. *Newsweek,* July 10, 1978, 15.

Murphy, Gardner. Discussion. In Herman Feifel (Ed.), *The meaning of death.* New York: McGraw-Hill, 1959. Pp. 317–340.

Murray, Henry A. *Explorations in personality.* New York: Oxford University Press, 1938.

Mussen, P. H. (Ed.). *Carmichael's manual of child psychology* (Vol. 1) (3rd ed.). New York: Wiley, 1970.

Mussen, P.; & Eisenberg-Berg, N. *Roots of caring, sharing, and helping.* San Francisco: Freeman, 1977.

Mussen, P.; Rutherford, E.; Harris, S.; & Keasey, C. B. Honesty and altruism among preadolescents. *Developmental Psychology,* 1970, **3,** 169–194.

Myers, David G. *The human puzzle: Psychological research and Christian belief.* New York: Harper & Row, 1978.

Naranjo, Claudio. *The one quest.* New York: Ballantine Books, 1972.

Naranjo, Claudio; & Ornstein, Robert E. *On the psychology of meditation.* New York: Viking Press, 1971.

Narramore, Bruce. Guilt: Its universal hidden presence. *Journal of Psychology and Theology,* 1974, **2,** 104–115, 182–189.

Neal, Marie A. Civil religion and the development of peoples. *Religious Education,* 1976, **71,** 244–260.

Neal, Marie A. Women in religious symbolism and organization. In Harry M. Johnson (Ed.), *Religious change and continuity.* San Francisco: Jossey-Bass, 1979.

Needham, J. (Ed.). *Science, religion, and reality.* New York: Macmillan, 1925.

Nelson, E. N. P. Patterns of religious attitude shifts from college to fourteen years later. *Psychological Monographs,* 1956, **70** (17, Whole No. 424).

Nelson, L. D.; & Dynes, R. R. The impact of devotionalism and attendance on ordinary and emergency helping behavior. *Journal for the Scientific Study of Religion,* 1976, **15,** 47–59.

Nelson, M. W.; & Jones, E. M. An application of the Q-technique to the study of religious concepts. *Psychological Reports,* 1957, **3,** 293–297.

Newcomb, T. M. Autistic hostility and social reality. *Human Relations,* 1947, **1,** 69–86.

Newman, John Henry. *Apologia pro vita sua.* New York: Dutton, 1912.

Newman, M.; & Berkowitz, B. *How to be your own best friend.* New York: Ballantine Books, 1971.

Nicholson, H. Curtis; & Edwards, Keith J. A comparison of four statistical methods for assessing similarity of God concept to parental images. Paper presented for The Society for the Scientific Study of Religion, San Antonio, October, 1979.

Nicholson, R. A. *Rumi, poet and mystic.* London: George Allen & Unwin, 1964.

Nock, A. D. *Conversion.* New York: Oxford University Press, 1961.

Norton, H.; & Slosser, B. *The miracle of Jimmy Carter.* Plainfield NJ: Logos International, 1976.

Nudelman, A. E. Dimensions of religiosity: A factor-analytic view of Protestants, Catholics, and Christian Scientists. *Review of Religious Research,* 1971, **13**, 42–56.

Nussbaum, K. Abnormal mental phenomena in the prophets. *Journal of Religion and Health,* 1974, **13**, 194–200.

Oates, Joyce Carol. *Son of the morning.* New York: Fawcett Crest, 1978.

Oates, Wayne E. *The role of religion in human behavior.* New York: Association Press, 1954.

Oates, Wayne E. *Religious factors in mental illness.* New York: Association Press, 1955.

Oates, Wayne E. *On becoming children of God.* Philadelphia: Westminster, 1969.

Oates, Wayne. *The psychology of religion.* Waco TX: Word Books, 1973.

O'Dea, Thomas F. *The sociology of religion.* Englewood Cliffs NJ: Prentice-Hall, 1966.

O'Doherty, Eamonn F. *Religion and personality problems.* New York: Alba House, 1964.

O'Donoghue, Noel. *Heaven in ordinaire.* Edinburgh: Clarke, 1979.

O'Neil, W. M.; & Levinson, D. J. A factorial exploration of authoritarianism and some of its ideological correlates. *Journal of Personality,* 1954, **22**, 449–463.

Oraison, Marc. *Love or constraint?* New York: Paulist, 1961.

Oraison, Marc. *Illusion and anxiety.* New York: Macmillan, 1963.

Oral Roberts joins the Methodists. *Christianity Today,* April 12, 1968, **12**, 34.

Orbach, H. L. Aging and religion: Church attendance in the Detroit metropolitan area. *Geriatrics,* 1961, **16**, 530–540.

Ornstein, Robert E. *The psychology of consciousness* (2nd ed.). New York: Harcourt Brace Jovanovich, 1977.

Osgood, Charles E.; & Tannenbaum, P. H. The principle of congruity in the predictions of attitude change. *Psychological Review,* 1955, **62**, 42–55.

Otto, Rudolph. *The idea of the holy* (Trans. J. W. Harvey). London: Humphrey Milford & Oxford University Press, 1926.

Our father in heaven. *Catholic Digest,* 1953, **17**(6), April, 86–91.

Ouspensky, P. D. *In search of the miraculous.* New York: Harcourt Brace Jovanovich, 1949.

Pahnke, Walter N.; & Richards, William A. Implications of LSD and experimental mysticism. *Journal of Religion and Health,* 1966, **5**, 175–208.

Palmberg, L.; & Scandrette, O. Self-disclosure in biblical perspective. *Journal of Psychology and Theology,* 1977, **5**, 209–219.

Paloutzian, Raymond F. Purpose-in-life and value changes following conversion. Paper presented for The American Psychological Association, Washington D.C., September, 1976.

Paloutzian, Raymond F. (Chair) Spiritual well-being, loneliness, and perceived quality of life. Symposium presented for The American Psychological Association, New York, September, 1979.

Paloutzian, Raymond F.; & Ellison, Craig W. Developing a measure of spiritual well-being. In Raymond F. Paloutzian (Chair), Spiritual well-being, loneliness, and perceived quality of life. Symposium presented for The American Psychological Association, New York, September, 1979.

Paloutzian, Raymond F.; Jackson, S.L.; & Crandall, J. E. Conversion experience, belief system, and personal and ethical attitudes. *Journal of Psychology and Theology,* 1978, **6,** 266–275.

Parrinder, Geoffrey. *Mysticism in the world's religions.* New York: Oxford University Press, 1976.

Parsons, H. L. Theology and therapy. *Journal of Pastoral Care,* 1953, **7,** 215–223.

Pascal, Blaise. *Thoughts of Blaise Pascal* (Trans. C. Kegan Paul). London: George Bell & Sons, 1889. (Originally published, 1670.)

Patrick, John W. Personal faith and the fear of death among divergent religious populations. *Journal for the Scientific Study of Religion,* 1979, **18,** 298–305.

Pattison, E. Mansell. Speaking in tongues and about tongues. *Christian Standard,* February 15, 1964, 1–2.

Pattison, E. Mansell. Behavioral science research on the nature of glossolalia. *Journal of the American Scientific Affiliation,* 1968, **20,** 73–86.

Pattison, E. Mansell (Ed.). *Clinical psychiatry and religion.* Boston: Little, Brown, 1969.

Pattison, E. Mansell; Lapins, Nikolajs A.; & Doerr, Hans A. Faith healing: A study of personality and function. *The Journal of Nervous and Mental Disease,* 1973, **157,** 397–409.

Paul says no. *Newsweek,* February 7, 1977, 77.

Peers, E. Allison (Trans. & Ed.). *The life of Teresa of Jesus.* Garden City NY: Doubleday Image, 1960.

Pelletier, Kenneth R.; & Garfield, Charles. *Consciousness East and West.* New York: Harper Colophon, 1976.

Pempel, Alice M. Demonic encounters in altered states of consciousness. Paper presented for The American Academy of Religion, San Francisco, December, 1977.

Perkins, Mark L. Spiritual well-being: A mission in aging. Symposium presented for The American Psychological Association, San Francisco, August, 1977.

Perry, R. B. *The thought and character of William James* (briefer version). Cambridge: Harvard University Press, 1948.

Phares, E. Jerry. Differential utilization of information as a function of internal-external control. *Journal of Personality,* 1968, **36,** 649–662.

Phares, E. Jerry; Ritchie, D. E.; & Davis, W. L. Internal-external control and reaction to threat. *Journal of Personality and Social Psychology,* 1968, **10,** 402–405.

Phillips, J. B. *Your god is too small.* New York: Macmillan, 1961.

Photiadis, John D. (Ed.). *Religion in Appalachia.* Morgantown WV: West Virginia University, 1978.

Photiadis, John D.; & Schweiker, William. Attitudes toward joining authoritarian organizations and sectarian churches. *Journal for the Scientific Study of Religion,* 1970, **9,** 227–234.

Piaget, Jean. *The child's conception of the world.* Totowa NJ: Littlefield, Adams, 1965a. (Originally published 1929.)

Piaget, Jean. *The moral judgment of the child.* New York: Free Press, 1965b. (Originally published, 1932.)

Piaget, Jean. Piaget's theory. In Paul H. Mussen (Ed.), *Charmichael's manual of child psychology* (Vol. 1) (3rd ed.). New York: Wiley, 1970. Pp. 703–732.

Piers, G.; & Singer, M. B. *Shame and guilt: A psychoanalytic and a cultural study.* Springfield IL: Thomas, 1953.

Piliavin, Irving M.; Rodin, J.; & Piliavin, Jane A. Good Samaritanism: An underground phenomenon. *Journal of Personality and Social Psychology,* 1969, **13,** 289–299.

Piliavin, Jane A.; & Piliavin, Irving M. Effect of blood on reactions to a victim. *Journal of Personality and Social Psychology,* 1972, **23,** 353–362.

Pixley, E.; & Beekman, E. The faith of youth as shown by a survey in public schools of Los Angeles. *Religious Education,* 1949, **44,** 336–342.

Poggie, John J., Jr.; & Gersuny, Carl. Risk and ritual: An interpretation of fisherman's folklore in a New England community. *Journal of American Folklore,* 1972, **85,** 66–72.

Poggie, John J., Jr.; Pollnac, Richard B.; & Gersuny, Carl. Risk as a basis for taboos among fishermen in southern New England. *Journal for the Scientific Study of Religion,* 1976, **15,** 257–262.

Pojman, Louis. Rationality and religious belief. *Religious Studies,* 1979, **15,** 159–172.

Poppleton, P. K.; & Pilkington, G. W. The measurement of religious attitudes in a university population. *British Journal of Social and Clinical Psychology,* 1963, **2,** 20–36.

Porteous, Alvin C. Hymns and heresy. *Pastoral Psychology,* 1966, **17,** 46–48.

Potvin, Raymond H. Adolescent God images. *Review of Religious Research,* 1977, **19,** 43–53.

Power to the Laity. *Newsweek,* March 6, 1978, 91, 95 ff.

Poythress, Norman G. A study of multiple religious orientations. *Journal for the Scientific Study of Religion,* 1975, **14,** 271–284.

Prather, L. Paul. Does God still perform miracles? *Western Recorder,* April 1, 1976, 8.

Pratt, J. B. *The religious consciousness.* New York: Macmillan, 1920.

Prescott, D. A. *The child in the educative process.* New York: McGraw-Hill, 1957.

Pribram, Karl. *Languages of the brain.* Englewood Cliffs NJ: Prentice-Hall, 1971.

Pribram, Karl. Problems concerning the structure of consciousness. In G. Maxwell Globus & I. Savodnick (Eds.), *Consciousness and the brain.* New York: Plenum, 1976. Pp. 295–313.

Prince, Morton. *The dissociation of a personality.* New York: McKay, 1913.

Prince, Raymond; & Savage, Charles. Mystical states and the concept of regression. In John White (Ed.), *The highest state of consciousness.* Garden City NY: Doubleday, 1972. Pp. 114–133.

Princeton Religion Research Center. *Religion in America 1979–1980.* Princeton NJ: Author, 1979.

Proctor, William. The gospel according to Gallup. *Christian Herald,* October, 1979, **102,** 58–65.

Propst, L. Rebecca. A comparison of the cognitive restructuring psychotherapy paradigm and several spiritual approaches to mental health. *Journal of Psychology and Theology,* 1980, **8,** 107–114.

Protho, E. T.; & Jensen, J. A. Inter-relations of religious and ethnic attitudes in selected southern populations. *Journal of Social Psychology,* 1950, **32,** 45–49.

Proudfoot, Wayne; & Shaver, Phillip. Attribution theory and the psychology of religion. *Journal for the Scientific Study of Religion,* 1975, **14,** 317–330.

Pruyser, Paul W. Phenomenology and dynamics of hoping. *Journal for the Scientific Study of Religion,* 1963, **3,** 86–96.

Pruyser, Paul W. Problems of will and willing. In J. N. Lapsley (Ed.), *The concept of willing.* Nashville: Abingdon, 1967. Pp. 23–50.

Pruyser, Paul W. *A dynamic psychology of religion.* New York: Harper & Row, 1968.

Pruyser, Paul W. A psychological view of religion in the 1970's. *Bulletin of the Menninger Clinic,* 1971, **35,** 77–97.

Pruyser, Paul W. *Between belief and unbelief.* New York: Harper & Row, 1974.

Pruyser, Paul W. Psychological roots and branches of belief. *Pastoral Psychology,* 1979, **28,** 8–20.

Radha, Swami Sivananda. *Kundalini yoga for the West.* Spokane: Timeless Books, 1978.

Radhakrishnan, Sarvepalli. *Recovery of faith.* New York: Harper & Row, 1955.

Radin, Paul. *Primitive religion: Its nature and origin.* New York: Viking Press, 1937.

Rama, Swami; Ballentine, Rudolph; & Ajaya, Swami. *Yoga and psychotherapy.* Glenview IL: Himalayan Institute, 1976.

Raschke, V. Dogmatism and committed and consensual religion. *Journal for the Scientific Study of Religion,* 1973, **12**, 339–344.

Ravindra, R. Is religion psychotherapy? An Indian view. *Religious Studies,* 1978, **14**, 389–397.

Rehder, H. Wunderheilungen, ein experiment. *Hippokrates,* 1955, **26**, 577–580.

Reik, Theodor. Masochism in modern man. In *Of love and lust,* New York: Farrar, Straus & Giroux, 1949.

Religious Education Association. *Research plans in the fields of religion, values, and morality.* New York: Author, 1962.

Remmers, Hermann H. (Ed.). *Anti-democratic attitudes in American schools.* Evanston IL: Northwestern University Press, 1963.

Reymert, M. L. (Ed.). *Feelings and emotions.* New York: McGraw-Hill, 1950.

Ribble, M. *The rights of infants.* New York: Columbia University Press, 1943.

Richards, William A. Mystical and archetypal experiences of terminal patients in DPT-assisted psychotherapy. *Journal of Religion and Health,* 1978, **17**, 117–126.

Richardson, James T. Psychological interpretations of glossolalia: A reexamination of research. *Journal for the Scientific Study of Religion,* 1973, **12**, 199–207.

Riesman, David. *The lonely crowd.* New Haven CT: Yale University Press, 1961.

Ring, Kenneth A. A transpersonal view of consciousness: A mapping of farther regions of inner space. *Journal of Transpersonal Psychology,* 1974, **6**, 125–155.

Ring, Kenneth A. Mapping the regions of consciousness: A conceptual reformulation. *Journal of Transpersonal Psychology,* 1976, **8**, 77–88.

Ring, Kenneth A. (Chair). Near death research: Religious aspects and clinical implications. Symposium presented for The American Psychological Association, New York: September, 1979a.

Ring, Kenneth A. Religiousness and near-death experiences: An empirical study. Paper presented for The American Psychological Association, New York, September, 1979b.

Ring, Kenneth. *Life at death: A scientific investigation of the near-death experience.* New York: Coward, McCann & Geoghegan, 1980.

Ritzema, Robert J. Attribution to supernatural causation: An important component of religious commitment? *Journal of Psychology and Theology,* 1979, **7**, 286–293.

Rizzuto, Ana-Maria. *The birth of the living god: A psychoanalytic study.* Chicago: University of Chicago Press, 1979.

Robbins, Thomas. Eastern mysticism and the resocialization of drug users: The Meher Baba cult. *Journal for the Scientific Study of Religion,* 1969, **8**, 308–317.

Robbins, Thomas; & Anthony, Dick. Brainwashing and the persecution of "cults." *Journal of Religion and Health,* 1980, **19**, 66–69.

Roberts, F. J. Some psychological factors in religious conversion. *British Journal of Social and Clinical Psychology,* 1965, **4**, 185–187.

Rogers, Carl R. *Client-centered therapy: Its current practice, implication and theory.* Boston: Houghton Mifflin, 1951.

Rogers, Carl R. A theory of therapy, personality, and interpersonal relationships, as developed in the client-centered framework. In S. Koch (Ed.), *Psychology, the study of a science,* Vol. 3: *Formulations of the person and the social context.* New York: McGraw-Hill, 1959. Pp. 184–256.

Rogers, Tommy. Manifestations of religiosity and the aging process. *Religious Education,* 1976, **71**, 405–415.

Rokeach, Milton. *The open and closed mind.* New York: Basic Books, 1960.

Rokeach, Milton. *Beliefs, attitudes, and values.* San Francisco: Jossey-Bass, 1968.

Rosen, I. M. Some contributions of religion to mental and physical health. *Journal of Religion and Health,* 1974, **13,** 189–294.

Rosen, I. M.; & Farnell, K. Religion and the chronic psychotic. *Journal of Pastoral Care,* 1962, **16,** 165–167.

Rosenhan, D. Prosocial behavior of children. In W. W. Hartup (Ed.), *The young child: Reviews of Research* (Vol. 2). Washington D.C.: National Assn. for the Education of Young Children, 1972. Pp. 340–359.

Rosenhan, D.; & White, G. M. Observation and rehearsal as determinants of prosocial behavior. *Journal of Personality and Social Psychology,* 1967, **5,** 424–431.

Rosenzweig, Linda W. Toward universal justice: Some implications of Lawrence Kohlberg's research for Jewish education. *Religious Education,* 1977, **72,** 606–615.

Rosner, Fred. The efficacy of prayer: Scientific vs. religious evidence. *Journal of Religion and Health,* 1975, **14,** 294–298.

Ross, A. S. The effect of increased responsibility on bystander intervention: The presence of children. *Journal of Personality and Social Psychology,* 1971, **19,** 306–310.

Ross, M. G. *Religious beliefs of youth.* New York: Association Press, 1950.

Rossi, Albert S. (Chair). Spiritual practice and psychotherapy. *Journal Supplement Abstract Service Catalog of Selected Documents in Psychology,* May, 1982. (Ms. No. 2449.)

Rossi, Albert S.; Meadow, Mary Jo; Malony, H. Newton; Collins, Gary R.; & Goldsmith, W. Mack. Teaching the psychology of values and religion. *Journal Supplement Abstract Service Catalog of Selected Documents in Psychology,* 1979, **9,** 21–22. (Ms. No. 1829.)

Roth, John K. (Ed.). *The moral philosophy of William James.* New York: Crowell, 1969.

Rotter, Julian B. Generalized expectancies for internal vs. external control of reinforcement. *Psychological Monographs,* 1966, **80**(1, Whole No. 609).

Rotter, Julian B. External control and internal control. *Psychology Today,* June, 1971, 37–42, 58–59.

Rotter, Julian B.; Chance, J. E.; & Phares, E. Jerry. *Applications of a social learning theory of personality.* New York: Holt, Rinehart and Winston, 1972.

Royce, J. R. The present situation in theoretical psychology. In Benjamin B. Wolman (Ed.), *Handbook of general psychology.* Englewood Cliffs NJ: Prentice-Hall, 1973. Pp. 8–21.

Rubin, Z. *Liking and loving: An invitation to social psychology.* New York: Holt, Rinehart and Winston, 1973.

Rudestam, K. E. *Methods of self-change.* Monterey CA: Brooks/Cole, 1980.

Rumke, H. D. *The psychology of unbelief.* New York: Sheed & Ward, 1962. (Originally published, 1949.)

Rushton, J. P.; & Wiener, J. Altruism and cognitive development in children. *British Journal of Social and Clinical Psychology,* 1975, **14,** 341–349.

Rychlak, Joseph F. *The psychology of rigorous humanism.* New York: Wiley, 1977.

Sales, Stephen M. Economic threat as a determinant of conversion rates in authoritarian and nonauthoritarian churches. *Journal of Personality and Social Psychology,* 1972, **23,** 420–428.

Salisbury, W. S. Religiosity, regional subculture, and social behavior. *Journal for the Scientific Study of Religion,* 1962, **2,** 94–101.

Sall, Millard J. Demon possession or psychopathology: A clinical differentiation. *Journal of Psychology and Theology,* 1976, **4,** 286–290.

Sall, Millard J. A response to "Demon possession and psychopathology: A theological relationship." *Journal of Psychology and Theology,* 1979, **7,** 27–30.

Salomen, A. Prophets, priests, and social scientists. *Commentary,* June, 1949, 594–600.

Salzman, Leon. The psychology of religious and ideological conversion. *Psychiatry,* 1953, **16,** 177–187.

Salzman, Leon. Healthy and unhealthy patterns of religion. *Journal of Religion and Health,* 1965, **4,** 322–327.

Samarin, William J. The linguisticality of glossolalia. *Hartford Quarterly,* 1968, **8,** 49–75.

Samarin, William J. Glossolalia as learned behavior. *Canadian Journal of Theology,* 1969, **15,** 60–64. In L. B. Brown (Ed.), *Psychology and religion.* Baltimore: Penguin Books, 1973. Pp. 376–382.

Samarin, William J. Glossolalia. *Psychology Today,* August, 1972, **6**(3), 48–50, 78–79.

Sanua, Victor. Religion, mental health, and personality: A review of empirical studies. *American Journal of Psychiatry,* 1969, **125,** 1203–1213.

Sargant, William. *Battle for the mind.* Garden City NY: Doubleday, 1957.

Sargant, William. The physiology of faith. *British Journal of Psychiatry,* 1969, **115,** 505–518.

Sarnoff, I.; & Corwin, S. Castration anxiety and the fear of death. *Journal of Personality,* 1959, **27,** 374–385.

Schachter, Stanley; & Latane, Bibb. Crime, cognition and the autonomic nervous system. In Marsha R. Jones (Ed.), *Nebraska symposium on motivation* (Vol. 12). Lincoln: University of Nebraska Press, 1964. Pp. 221–275.

Scheibe, Karl E. *Beliefs and values.* New York: Holt, Rinehart and Winston, 1970.

Scheidt, R. J. Belief in supernatural phenomena and locus of control. *Psychological Reports,* 1973, **32,** 1159–1162.

Schleiermacher, Friedrich. *On religion* (Trans. J. Oman). London: Kegan Paul, Trench, Trübner, 1893.

Schmauk, F. A. *A study of the relationships between kinds of punishment, autonomic arousal, subjective anxiety and avoidance learning in the primary sociopath.* Unpublished doctoral dissertation, Temple University, 1968.

Schnaper, Nathan,; & Schnaper, H. William. A few kind words for the devil. *Journal of Religion and Health,* 1969, **8,** 107–122.

Schneiderman, Leo. Psychological notes on the nature of mystical experience. *Journal for the Scientific Study of Religion,* 1967, **6,** 91–100.

Schoenherr, J. C. *Avoidance of noxious stimulation in psychopathic personality.* Unpublished doctoral dissertation, University of California, 1964.

Schofield, William. Discussion: Psychology, inspiration, and faith. *Journal of Religion and Health,* 1979, **18,** 197–202.

Schreber, Daniel P. *Memoirs of my nervous illness* (Trans. Ida Macalpine & Richard Hunter). London: William Dawson & Sons, Ltd., 1955.

Schreiber, F. R. *Sybil.* Chicago: Henry Regnery, 1973.

Schwartz, S. H. Normative influences on altruism. In Leonard Berkowitz (Ed.), *Advances in experimental social psychology* (Vol. 10). New York: Academic Press, 1977.

Scobie, Geoffrey E. W. Types of Christian conversion. *Journal of Behavioral Science,* 1973, **1,** 265–271.

Scobie, Geoffrey E. W. *Psychology of religion.* New York: Wiley, 1975.

Scroggs, James R.; & Douglas, William G. T. Issues in the psychology of religious conversion. *Journal of Religion and Health,* 1967, **6,** 204–216.

Sears, Robert R.; Maccoby, Eleanor E.; & Levin, H. *Patterns of child rearing.* Evanston IL: Row, Peterson, 1957.

Seeman, M. Alienation and social learning in a reformatory. *American Journal of Sociology,* 1963, **69,** 270–284.

Segal, Julius; & Yahraes, Herbert. *A child's journey.* New York: McGraw-Hill, 1978.

Seggar, J.; & Kunz, P. Conversion: Evaluation of a steplike process for problem-solving. *Review of Religious Research,* 1972, **13,** 178–184.

Selig, Sidney; & Teller, Gerald. The moral development of children in three different school settings. *Religious Education,* 1975, **70,** 406–415.

Seligman, Martin E. P. *Helplessness: On depression, development, and death.* San Francisco: Freeman, 1975.

Selman, R. L. Social-cognitive understanding. In Thomas Lickona (Ed.), *Moral development and behavior: Theory, research, and social issues.* New York: Holt, Rinehart and Winston, 1976. Pp. 299–316.

Shaffer, L. F. Fear and courage in aerial combat. *Journal of Consulting Psychology,* 1947, **11,** 137–143.

Shah, Idries. *Tales of the dervishes.* New York: Dutton, 1970.

Shah, Idries. *The exploits of the incomparable Mulla Nasrudin.* New York: Dutton, 1972.

Shaver, Kelly G. *An introduction to attribution processes.* Cambridge MA: Winthrop, 1975.

Shaver, Kelly G. Attribution theory and the explanation of religious experience. Paper presented for The American Psychological Association, New York, September, 1979.

Shrauger, J. S.; & Silverman, R. E. The relationship of religious background and participation to locus of control. *Journal for the Scientific Study of Religion,* 1971, **10,** 11–16.

Silverman, Hirsch L. *Relationships of personality factors of religious background among students.* Unpublished doctoral dissertation, Yeshiva Univ., 1954.

Silvestri, P. J. Locus of control and God-dependence. *Psychological Reports,* 1979, **45,** 89–90.

Singer, M. T. Coming out of the cults. *Psychology Today,* January, 1979, 72–83 passim.

Skinner, B. F. *Science and human behavior.* New York: Knopf, 1953.

Skinner, B. F. *Beyond freedom and dignity.* New York: Knopf, 1971.

Smith, Huston. *The religions of man.* New York: Harper & Row, 1958.

Smith, Huston. *Forgotten truth: The primordial tradition.* New York: Harper Colophon, 1977.

Smith, M. Brewster. Perspectives on selfhood. *American Psychologist,* 1978, **33,** 1053–1063.

Smith, Margaret. *An introduction to mysticism.* New York: Oxford University Press, 1977.

Smoke, Jim. *Growing through divorce.* Irvine CA: Harvest House, 1976.

Sorokin, P. A. The powers of creative unselfish love. In A. H. Maslow (Ed.), *New knowledge in human values.* Chicago: Regnery, 1971. Pp. 3–12.

Southard, S. A. *Communism, civil liberties, and conformity.* Garden City NY: Doubleday, 1956.

Special report: The cult of death. *Newsweek,* December 4, 1978.

Spencer, J. The mental health of Jehovah's witnesses. *British Journal of Psychiatry,* 1975, **126,** 556–559.

Spero, M. H. Sin as neurosis—neurosis as sin: Further implications of a Halachic metapsychology. *Journal of Religion and Health,* 1978, **17,** 274–287.

Spielberger, Charles D. (Ed.). *Anxiety and behavior.* New York: Academic Press, 1966a.

Spielberger, Charles D. Theory and research on anxiety. In Charles D. Spielberger (Ed.), *Anxiety and behavior.* New York: Academic Press, 1966b.

Spilka, Bernard; Addison, James; & Rosensohn, Marguerite. Parents, self, and God: A test of competing theories of individual-religion relationships. *Review of Religious Research,* 1975, **16,** 154–165.

Spilka, Bernard; & Minton, Barbara. Defining personal religion: Psychometric, cognitive, and instrumental dimensions. Paper presented for The Society for the Scientific Study of Religion, Milwaukee, October, 1975.

Spilka, Bernard; Read, S.; Allen, R. O.; & Dailey, K. Specificity vs. generality: The criterion problem in religious measurement. Paper presented for The American Association for the Advancement of Science, Dallas, December, 1968.

Spilka, Bernard; Spangler, John D.; & Rea, M. Priscilla. Religion and death: The clerical perspective. Paper presented for The Society for the Scientific Study of Religion, Chicago, October, 1977.

Spilka, Bernard; Stout, Larry; Minton, Barbara; & Sizemore, Douglas. Death perspectives, death anxiety, and form of personal religion. Paper presented for The Society for the Scientific Study of Religion, Philadelphia, October, 1976.

Spilka, Bernard; Stout, L.; Minton, Barbara; & Sizemore, Douglas. Death and personal faith: A psychometric investigation. *Journal for the Scientific Study of Religion,* 1977, **16**, 169–178.

Spitz, Rene A. Hospitalization: A follow-up report on investigations described in Volume 1, 1945. In Anna Freud; H. Hartmann; & E. Kris (Eds.), *The psychoanalytic study of the child* (Vol. 2). New York: International Universities Press, 1946. Pp. 113–117.

Spitzer, R. S. (Ed.). *Tidings of comfort and joy.* Palo Alto CA: Science and Behavior Books, 1975.

Spivak, C. D. Hebrew prayers for the sick. *Annals of Medical History,* 1917, **1**, 83–85.

Srole, L.; Langner, T.; Michael, S. T.; Opler, M. K.; & Rennie, T. A. C. *Mental health in the metropolis* (Vol. 1). New York: McGraw-Hill, 1962.

Stace, Walter T. *Mysticism and philosophy.* Philadelphia: Lippincott, 1960a.

Stace, Walter T. *The teachings of the mystics.* New York: New American Library, 1960b.

Stanley, Gordon. Personality and attitude characteristics of fundamentalist university students. *Australian Journal of Psychology,* 1953, **15**, 199–200.

Stanley, Gordon. Personality and attitude characteristics of fundamentalist theological students. *Australian Journal of Psychology,* 1963, **15**, 121–123.

Stanley, Gordon. Personality and attitude correlates of religious conversion. *Journal for the Scientific Study of Religion,* 1965, **4**, 60–63.

Starbuck, Edwin D. *The psychology of religion.* New York: Scribner, 1903.

Starbuck, Edwin D. *The psychology of religion* (3rd ed.). New York: Walter Scott, 1911.

Stark, M. J.; & Washburn, M. C. Beyond the norm: A speculative model of self-realization. *Journal of Religion and Health,* 1977, **16**, 56–68.

Stark, Rodney. On the compatibility of religion and science: A survey of American graduate students. *Journal for the Scientific Study of Religion,* 1963, **3**, 3–20.

Stark, Rodney. A taxonomy of religious experience. *Journal for the Scientific Study of Religion,* 1966, **5**, 97–116.

Stark, Rodney. Age and faith: A changing outlook or an old process? *Sociological Analysis,* 1968, **29**, 1–10.

Stark, Rodney. Psychopathology and religious commitment. *Review of Religious Research,* 1971, **12**, 165–176.

Stark, Rodney; & Glock, Charles Y. *American piety: The nature of religious commitment.* Berkeley: University of California Press, 1970.

Staub, Ervin. A child in distress: The influence of nurturance and modeling on children's attempts to help. *Developmental Psychology,* 1971a, **5**, 124–132.

Staub, Ervin. Helping a person in distress: The influence of implicit and explicit "rules" of conduct on children and adults. *Journal of Personality and Social Psychology,* 1971b, **17**, 137–144.

Staub, Ervin. Use of role playing and induction in training for prosocial behavior. *Child Development,* 1971c, **42,** 805–816.

Staub, Ervin. Helping a distressed person: Social, personality, and stimulus determinants. In Leonard Berkowitz (Ed.), *Advances in experimental social psychology* (Vol. 7). New York: Academic Press, 1974.

Staub, Ervin. *Positive social behavior and morality,* Vol. 1: *Social and personal influences.* New York: Academic Press, 1978.

Steininger, M. P.; Durso, B. E.; & Pasquariello, C. Dogmatism and attitudes. *Psychological Reports,* 1972, **30,** 151–157.

Steinitz, Lucy Y. Religiosity, well-being, and Weltanschauung among the elderly. *Journal for the Scientific Study of Religion,* 1980, **19,** 60–67.

Stern, E. Mark (Ed.). *The other side of the couch: What therapists believe.* New York: Pilgrim, 1981.

Stevenson, H. (Ed.). *Child psychology.* Chicago: University of Chicago Press, 1963.

Stewart, David W. Religious correlates of the fear of death. *Journal of Thanatology,* 1975, **3,** 161–164.

Strachey, James (Trans.). *The standard edition of the complete psychological works of Sigmund Freud.* London: Hogarth, 1953–1966.

Strickland, Bonnie R.; & Shaffer, Scott. I-E, I-E, & F. *Journal for the Scientific Study of Religion,* 1971, **10,** 366–369.

Strommen, Merton P. The relation of Christian theology to psychological research. *Religious Education,* 1965, **60,** 199–208.

Strommen, Merton P. (Ed.). *Research on religious development: A comprehensive handbook.* New York: Hawthorn, 1971.

Strommen, Merton P.; Brekke, Milo L.; Underwager, R. C.; & Johnson, Arthur L. *A study of generations.* Minneapolis: Augsburg, 1972.

Struening, Elmer L. Anti-democratic attitudes in a midwest university. In Hermann H. Remmers (Ed.), *Anti-democratic attitudes in American schools.* Evanston IL: Northwestern University Press, 1963. Pp. 210–258.

Strunk, Orlo, Jr. *Mature religion: A psychological study.* New York: Abingdon, 1965.

Strunk, Orlo, Jr. The world view factor in psychotherapy. *Journal of Religion and Health,* 1979, **18,** 192–197.

Sugerman, A. Arthur; & Tarter, Ralph E. (Eds.). *Expanding dimensions of consciousness.* New York: Springer-Verlag, 1978.

Sullivan, Harry S. *The interpersonal theory of psychiatry.* New York: Norton, 1953.

Sullivan, Walter J. Effect of religious orientation, purpose in life, and locus of control on the death anxiety of college students. *Dissertation Abstracts International,* 1977. (University Microfilms No. 77-14, 912.)

Sumner, R. B. A statistical study of belief. *Psychological Review,* 1898, **5,** 616–631.

Sunday School Board of the Southern Baptist Convention. *Study of opinion and practices concerning the reception and orientation of new members in Southern Baptist churches.* Nashville: Author, 1965.

Swanson, Guy E. Trance and possession: Studies of charismatic influence. *Review of Religious Research,* 1978, **19,** 253–278.

Swenson, Wendell M. Attitudes toward death in an aged population. *Journal of Gerontology,* 1961, **16,** 49–52.

Swindell, D. H. & L'Abate, L. Religiosity, dogmatism, and repression-sensitization. *Journal for the Scientific Study of Religion,* 1970, **9,** 249–251.

Switzer, D. K. Considerations of the religious dimensions of emotional disorder. *Pastoral Psychology,* 1976, **24,** 317–328.

Szasz, Thomas. *The myth of mental illness* (2nd ed.). New York: Harper & Row, 1974.

Tagore, Rabindranath. *Gitanjali.* New York: Macmillan, 1971. (Originally published, 1913.)

Tanenbaum, Marc H. Civil religion: Unifying force or idolatry? *Religious Education,* 1975, **70,** 469–473.

Tanner, I. J. *Loneliness: The fear of love.* New York: Harper & Row Perennial Library, 1973.

Tapp, Robert B. Dimensions of religiosity in a posttraditional group. *Journal for the Scientific Study of Religion,* 1971, **10,** 41–47.

Tart, Charles (Ed.). *Transpersonal psychologies.* New York: Harper & Row, 1975.

Taylor, Janet A. A personality scale of manifest anxiety. *Journal of Abnormal and Social Psychology,* 1953, **48,** 285–290.

Taylor, R. S. *The disciplined life.* Minneapolis: Bethany, 1962.

Teilhard de Chardin, Pierre. *The phenomenon of man.* New York: Harper & Row, 1959. Cited from Harper, 1961.

Tellegen, Auke. Personal communication on absorption and psychopathology, 1978.

Tellegen, Auke. *Manual for the differential personality questionnaire.* Unpublished manuscript, University of Minnesota, 1979.

Tellegen, Auke; & Atkinson, Gilbert. Openness to absorbing and self-altering experiences ("absorption"), a trait related to hypnotic susceptibility. *Journal of Abnormal Psychology,* 1974, **83,** 268–277.

Templer, D. I. The construction and validation of a death anxiety scale. *Journal of General Psychology,* 1970, **82,** 165–177.

Thankful for miracle. *Minneapolis Tribune,* September 10, 1979, 2A.

Thayer, Nelson S. T. Perspectives on contemporary mysticism. *Journal of Religion and Health,* 1979, **18,** 230–240.

Thibaut, J. W.; & Kelley, H. H. *The social psychology of groups.* New York: Wiley, 1959.

Thigpen, C. H.; & Cleckley, H. M. *The three faces of Eve.* New York: McGraw-Hill, 1957.

Thomas, Alexander; Chess, Stella; & Birch, Herbert G. *Temperament and behavior disorders in children.* New York: New York University Press, 1968.

Thomas, George F. *The vitality of the Christian tradition.* New York: Harper & Row, 1944.

Thomas, L. Eugene; & Cooper, Pamela E. Measurement and incidence of mystical experiences: An exploratory study. *Journal for the Scientific Study of Religion,* 1978, **17,** 433–437.

Thompson, Andrew D. Open-mindedness and indiscriminate antireligious orientation. *Journal for the Scientific Study of Religion,* 1974, **13,** 471–477.

Thouless, Robert H. The tendency to certainty in religious belief. *British Journal of Psychology,* 1935, **26,** 16–31.

Thouless, Robert H. *The psychology of religion* (2nd ed.). London: Cambridge University Press, 1961.

Thouless, Robert H. *An introduction to the psychology of religion* (3rd ed). London: Cambridge University Press, 1971.

Thurstone, L. L. The vectors of mind. *Psychological Review,* 1934, **41,** 1–32.

Thurstone, L. L.; & Chave, E. J. *The measurement of attitude: A psychophysical method and some experiments with a scale for measuring attitude toward the church.* Chicago: University of Chicago Press, 1929.

Tibbitts, C. (Ed.). *Handbook of social gerontology: The social aspects of aging.* Chicago: University of Chicago Press, 1960.

Tilker, H. A. Socially responsive behavior as a function of observer responsibility and victim feedback. *Journal of Personality and Social Psychology,* 1970, **14,** 95–100.

Tillich, Paul. *The courage to be.* New York: Yale University Press, 1952a.

Tillich, Paul. *Systematic theology.* Chicago: University of Chicago Press, 1952b.

Tournier, Paul. *A doctor's casebook in the light of the Bible.* New York: Harper & Row, 1960.

Tremmel, William C. *Religion: What is it?* New York: Holt, Rinehart and Winston, 1976.

Trevett, Reginald. *The tree of life.* New York: P. Kenedy & Sons, 1963.

Trieschman, Albert E.; Whittaker, James K.; & Brendtro, Larry K. *The other 23 hours.* Chicago: Aldine, 1969.

Trimakas, K. A.; & Nicolay, R. C. Self concept and altruism in old age. *Journal of Gerontology,* 1974, **29,** 434–439.

Trueblood, D. E. *The logic of belief.* New York: Harper & Row, 1942.

Turiel, Elliot. An experimental test of the sequentiality of developmental stages in the child's moral judgments. *Journal of Personality and Social Psychology,* 1966, **3,** 611–618.

Turner, P. R. Religious conversion and community development. *Journal for the Scientific Study of Religion,* 1979, **18,** 252–260.

Tyler, Leona. *The work of a counselor.* Englewood Cliffs NJ: Prentice-Hall, 1961.

Tylor, E. E. *Primitive culture* (2 vols.). London: Murray, 1903.

Ulanov, Ann; & Ulanov, Barry. *Religion and the unconscious.* Philadelphia: Westminster, 1975.

Underhill, Evelyn. *Mysticism.* New York: New American Library, 1974. (Originally published, 1911.)

Underwood, B.; Berenson, J. F.; Berenson, R. J.; Cheng, K. K.; Wilson, D.; Kulik, J.; Moore, B, S.; & Wenzel, G. Attention, negative affect, and altruism: An ecological validation. *Personality and Social Psychology Bulletin,* 1977, **3,** 54–58.

United Press International. Pope says infallibility is gift from Christ. May 23, 1980.

Valeriani, Richard. *Travels with Henry.* Boston: Houghton Mifflin, 1979.

Vanauken, Sheldon. *A severe mercy.* New York: Harper & Row, 1977.

Van Kaam, Adrian. *Religion and personality,* Garden City NY: Doubleday Image, 1968. (Rev. ed.) Denville NJ: Dimension, 1980.

Vietze, P. M.; O'Connor, S.; Falsey, S.; & Altemeier, W. A. Effects of rooming in on maternal behavior directed toward infants. Paper presented for The American Psychological Association, Toronto, August, 1978.

Virkler, Henry A.; & Virkler, Mary B. Demonic involvement in human life and illness. *Journal of Psychology and Theology,* 1977, **5,** 95–102.

Vitz, Paul C. *Psychology as religion: The cult of self-worship.* Grand Rapids, MI: Eerdmans, 1977.

Vivier, Lincoln M. Van Eetvelt. *Glossolalia.* Unpublished thesis, Univ. of Witwatersrand, 1960. (Microfilm at University of Chicago and Union Theological Seminary.)

Waddington, C. H. *The ethical animal.* London: Allen & Unwin, 1960.

Wahking, Harold L. Why people go to church and why they do not go to church. *Pastoral Psychology,* 1966, **17,** 52–54.

Walters, Annette; & Bradley, Ritamary. Motivation and religious behavior. In Merton P. Strommen (Ed.), *Research on religious development: A comprehensive handbook.* New York: Hawthorn, 1971. Pp. 599–651.

Walters, O. S. Religion and psychopathology. *Comprehensive Psychiatry,* 1964, **101,** 24–35.

Wambach, Helen. *Life before life.* New York: Bantam Books, 1979.

Wapnick, Kenneth. Mysticism and schizophrenia. *Journal of Transpersonal Psychology,* 1969, **1,** 49–67.

Warren, A. B.; & Grant, D. A. The relations of conditioned discrimination to MMPI and personality variables. *Journal of Experimental Psychology,* 1955, **49,** 23–27.

Warren, R. L. Old age in rural township. In *Old age is no barrier.* Albany NY: New York State Joint Legislative Committee on Problems of Aging, 1952.

Wasson, R. G.; Hofmann, A.; & Ruck, C. A. P. *The road to Eleusis.* New York: Harcourt Brace Jovanovich, 1978.

Watson, D. L.; & Tharp, R. G. *Self-directed behavior* (2nd ed.). Monterey CA: Brooks/Cole, 1977.

Watts, Alan. *The wisdom of insecurity.* New York: Pantheon Books, 1951. Cited from 1968 edition.

Wearing, A. J.; & Brown, L. B. The dimensionality of religion. *British Journal of Social and Clinical Psychology,* 1972, **11,** 143–148.

Weatherhead, Leslie D. *Psychology, religion, and healing.* New York: Abingdon-Cokesbury, 1951.

Weathers, D.; & Lord, M. Can a Mormon support the ERA? *Newsweek,* December 3, 1979, 88.

Weber, Max. *The sociology of religion.* Boston: Beacon Press, 1922.

Weil, Andrew. *The natural mind.* Boston: Houghton Mifflin, 1972a.

Weil, Andrew. The natural mind. *Psychology Today,* October 1972b, 51–97 passim.

Weil, Simone. *Waiting for God* (Trans. Emma Craufurd). New York: Harper & Row, 1973. (Originally published, 1951.)

Weisz, J. R. Choosing problem-solving rewards and Halloween prizes: Delay of gratification and preference for symbolic reward as a function of development, motivation, and personal investment. *Developmental Psychology,* 1978, **14,** 66–78.

Welford, A. T. Is religious behavior dependent upon affect or frustration? *Journal of Abnormal and Social Psychology,* 1947, **42,** 310–319.

Wentz, R. E. Revolutionary hope. *Encounter,* 1969, **30,** 25–31.

Wesley, John. *The journal of John Wesley.* London: Epworth, 1938.

West, Morris. *The ambassador.* New York: Morrow, 1965.

Westerhoff, John. *Values for tomorrow's children.* Philadelphia: Pilgrim, 1970.

White, G. M. Immediate and deferred effects of model observation and guided and unguided rehearsal on donating and stealing. *Journal of Personality and Social Psychology,* 1972, **37,** 139–148.

White, John (Ed.). *The highest state of consciousness.* Garden City NY: Doubleday, 1972.

White, Robert W. Motivation reconsidered: The concept of competence. *Psychological Review,* 1959, **66,** 297–333.

Whiteman, P. H. Formulation of an index of individual religious involvement: A measure of religiosity irrespective of religious group membership. In *Research plans in the fields of religion, values, and morality.* New York: The Religious Education Assn., 1962.

Wiesel, Elie. *Souls on fire: Portraits and legends of Hasidic masters.* New York: Random House, 1972.

Wilber, Ken. *The spectrum of consciousness.* Wheaton IL: Theosophical Quest Book, 1977.

Wilber, Ken. Spectrum psychology, Part IV. *Re-Vision,* 1979, **2,** 65–72.

Wilber, Ken. *The atman project.* Wheaton IL: Theosophical Quest, 1980.

Wilber, Ken; & Meadow, Mary Jo. Discussion of symposium presentations: Spiritual and transpersonal aspects of altered states of consciousness. *Journal of Transpersonal Psychology,* 1979, **11,** 68–71.

Wilkerson, David. *The cross and the switchblade.* New York: Pyramid, 1962.

Williams, D. D. *The spirit and the forms of love.* New York: Harper & Row, 1968.

Williams, R. L.; & Long, J. D. *Toward a self-managed life style* (2nd ed.). Boston: Houghton Mifflin, 1979.

Wilson, E. O. *Sociobiology: The new synthesis.* Cambridge MA: Harvard University Press, 1975.

Wilson, G. D. *The psychology of conservatism.* New York: Academic Press, 1973.

Wilson, R. Ward. *A social-psychological study of religious experience with special emphasis on Christian conversion.* Doctoral dissertation, University of Florida, 1976a. (Ann Arbor: University Microfilms, 1976.)

Wilson, R. Ward. Some characteristics of Christian conversion experience. Paper presented for The Society for the Scientific Study of Religion, Philadelphia, October, 1976b.

Wilson, W. C. Extrinsic religious values and prejudice. *Journal of Abnormal and Social Psychology,* 1960, **60,** 286–288.

Wilson, William P. Mental health benefits of religious salvation. *Diseases of the Nervous System,* 1972, **33,** 382–386.

Windemiller, D. A. *The psychodynamics of change in religious conversion and community brainwashing.* Unpublished doctoral dissertation, Boston University, 1960.

Wispe, L.; & Freshley, H. Race, sex, and sympathetic helping behavior: The broken bag caper. *Journal of Personality and Social Psychology,* 1971, **17,** 59–65.

Wolman, Benjamin B. (Ed.). *Handbook of general psychology.* Englewood Cliffs NJ: Prentice-Hall, 1973.

Woodroffe, John. *The serpent power.* Madras, India: Ganesh, 1973.

Woodruff, C. R. Toward a theology of maturity in pastoral care. *Pastoral Psychology,* 1978, **27,** 26–38.

Woodward, Kenneth L.; & Goodman, J. Race revelations. *Newsweek,* June 19, 1978, 67.

Woodward, Kenneth L.; Gram, D.; & Lisle, L. The boom in doom. *Newsweek,* January 10, 1977, 49, 51.

Woodward, Kenneth L.; & Lord, M. A sister speaks up. *Newsweek,* October 22, 1979, 125.

Woodward, Kenneth L.; Manning, Richard; Whitmore, Jane; Copeland, Jeff B.; & Mark, Rachel. The Pope of promise. *Newsweek,* October 8, 1979, 36–47.

Woodward, Kenneth L.; & Marbach, W. D. Testing time for Presbyterians. *Newsweek,* June 16, 1980, 55.

Woodward, Kenneth L.; & Monroe, S. Women priests at last. *Newsweek,* September 27, 1976, 62.

Worthen, Valerie. Psychotherapy and Catholic confession. *Journal of Religion and Health* (Human Sciences Press, publisher), 1974, **13,** 275–284.

Wrightsman, Lawrence S. (Ed.). *Contemporary issues in social psychology.* Monterey CA: Brooks/Cole, 1968.

Wuthnow, Robert. Astrology and marginality. *Journal for the Scientific Study of Religion,* 1976, **15,** 157–168.

Wuthnow, Robert; & Glock, Charles Y. The shifting focus of faith: A survey report, God in the gut. *Psychology Today,* 1974, **8,** 131–136.

Yakimovich, D.; & Saltz, E. Helping behavior: The cry for help. *Psychonomic Science,* 1971, **23,** 427–428.

Yancey, Philip. The ironies and impact of PTL. *Christianity Today,* 1979, **23,** 1249–1254. (#22, September 21, 28–33.)

Zaehner, R. C. *Mysticism sacred and profane.* New York: Oxford University Press (Clarendon Press), 1957.

Zahn, Jane (Ed.). *Religion and the face of America.* Berkeley CA: University Extension, University of California, 1959.

Zales, Michael R. Mysticism: Psychodynamics and relationship to psychopathology. In A. A. Sugerman & Ralph E. Tarter (Eds.), *Expanding dimensions of consciousness.* New York: Springer-Verlag, 1978. Pp. 253–272.

Zilboorg, Gregory. *Psychoanalysis and religion.* New York: Farrar, Straus & Giroux, 1962.

Zimbardo, Philip G. The human choice: Individuation, reason, and order versus de-individuation, impulse, and chaos. In William J. Arnold & David Levine (Eds.), *Nebraska symposium on motivation* (Vol. 17). Lincoln: University of Nebraska Press, 1969. Pp. 237–307.

Zimbardo, Philip G. *Shyness: What it is, what to do about it.* Reading MA: Addison-Wesley, 1977.

Zimmerman, Carle C. Family influence upon religion. *Journal of Comparative Family Studies,* 1974, **5,** 1–16.

Name Index

Subject Index